T0189640

They Create Worlds

They Create Worlds
The Story of the People and Companies That Shaped the Video Game Industry

Volume I: 1971–1982

Alexander Smith

CRC Press
Taylor & Francis Group
Boca Raton London New York

CRC Press is an imprint of the
Taylor & Francis Group, an **informa** business

CRC Press
Taylor & Francis Group
6000 Broken Sound Parkway NW, Suite 300
Boca Raton, FL 33487-2742

© 2020 by Alexander Smith
CRC Press is an imprint of Taylor & Francis Group, an Informa business

No claim to original U.S. Government works

Printed on acid-free paper

International Standard Book Number-13: 978-1-138-38992-2 (Hardback)
International Standard Book Number-13: 978-1-138-38990-8 (Paperback)

Visit the Taylor & Francis Web site at
http://www.taylorandfrancis.com

and the CRC Press Web site at
http://www.crcpress.com

Contents

Acknowledgments

Seeing this book in print is the culmination of over a decade of research and writing during which countless people helped along the way. My thanks to Sean Connelly, Jessica Vega, and the crew at CRC Press for giving this project a home and being patient as I wrangled a final draft together. A special thanks also to Simon Careless, who helped arrange first contact with the publisher. I would also like to express my gratitude to Jon-Paul Dyson, Jeremy Saucier, Beth Lathrop, Julia Novakovic, and everyone else at the International Center for the History of Electronic Games and the Brian Sutton-Smith Library and Archives at the Strong Museum in Rochester, New York, for making me feel welcome during two research trips to take deep dives into their collections (and for the cup full of arcade tokens to use in the museum!).

There are a wonderful array of independent scholars working to preserve video game history today, and they have been an invaluable resource while putting this book together both in terms of helping track down obscure materials and being excellent partners with which to bounce around ideas. So shout-outs to Leonard Herman of *Phoenix* fame; Marty Goldberg from the Atari Museum and many other endeavors; Ken Horowitz of Sega-16; Devin Monnens, Frank Cifaldi, and the good folks at the Video Game History Foundation; and Dustin Hubbard's colorful international crew over at Gaming Alexandria. And a special shout-out to Keith Smith of the Golden Age Arcade Historian blog, who not only shared his impressive collection of old trade publications, but also graced me with an advance copy of his wonderful *All in Color for A Quarter* tome, an exhaustive look at the early coin-operated video game industry. At least a quarter (har!) of the material in this book would not be possible without him. My thanks as well to coin-op historians Nic Costa and Freddy Bailey and the collectors at pennymachines. co.uk, who provided some important perspective on pre-video coin-operated game developments.

Of all the people striving to preserve the history of this great industry, few match the passion of Ethan Johnson, who has made it his mission to connect as many independent scholars and professional enthusiasts together as he possibly can and pool their resources for the betterment of all our work. I have spent many an hour on the Internet marveling over new discoveries and venting frustrations with Ethan, and he has also been generous in sharing his materials, including rare Japanese monographs and audio recordings of interviews with some fascinating industry figures that have otherwise had no outlet to tell their stories. This book would not be the same without his input.

Until recently, it had been nearly impossible to discover much information on the Japanese industry without knowing Japanese, but Alex Hightower of Shmuplations has changed that by creating professional translations of interviews with Japanese developers and executives. My thanks for these translations as well as several I commissioned from him myself.

Special thanks as well to Jeff Daum, my best friend nearly as long as I have been alive and my co-host on the *They Create Worlds* podcast for putting up with my incessant rambling about video game history and then kindly suggesting that we buy some sound equipment and share these stories with the rest of the world. Thanks as well to our listeners and subscribers who make it all worthwhile.

In the course of this project, I have interviewed over 100 industry figures, of which roughly 50 contributed recollections and insights pertinent to this first volume. Everyone has been exceptionally generous with their time and candid in their answers, which has enriched this book immeasurably. A full list of subjects that contributed to this volume may be found before the References and Bibliography

This work aims to build a new foundation off which future scholars can craft their own analyses of the industry, but I too stand on the shoulders of those who came before. I owe a debt of gratitude to Steven Kent, David Sheff, Russel DeMaria, Tristan Donovan, and the aforementioned Leonard Herman for writing some of the earliest monographs examining the industry and inspiring my own efforts to do the same. Without their work, this book would not exist.

Finally, I must thank my parents and my girlfriend for being supportive through this entire process, and my father in particular for lending his own writing expertise and providing another pair of eyes during the editing process. If he had not assured me that my work was good enough to seek a publisher, you would probably not be holding this book in your hands now.

Author

Alexander Smith is a reference librarian with a background in history, research, and law who has been delving into the history of the video game industry for over ten years. He has played a crucial role in the preservation of certain documents and artifacts in early video game history and has conducted over 100 oral history interviews with key executives in the evolution of the industry. Currently, he co-hosts a bi-monthly podcast dedicated to the history of the industry (also called "They Create Worlds") and serves as a researcher and consultant for the Video Game Pioneers Archive oral history project of the Smithsonian Institution.

Introduction

In 2005, Erkki Huhtamo lamented that video game scholarship was stuck in what he called the "chronicle era," in which authors were more concerned with amassing data than analyzing it.[1] More than a decade on, the situation is much improved, but there is still a fundamental problem with much of the fine analytical work being done today: it is based on a faulty chronicle. Journal articles and monographs are still largely drawing from the same narrative sources developed 10–20 years ago, which can largely be divided into two categories: works of journalists who approach their monographs in much the same way as they might an in-depth magazine cover story and works of enthusiasts who are passionate about their area of focus but not necessarily trained in researching it. The result has been a body of well-meaning and often commendable literature that nevertheless often falls down on accuracy through lack of research and context.

This volume and the two projected to follow aim to fix this deficiency through careful examination of the available contemporaneous sources. As the video game industry is still young and most of its key pioneers are still alive, there are not yet many archival collections of corporate documents or personal papers available for study, but there is a wealth of secondary source material penned in close proximity to the events in question that has never been fully evaluated. Trade publications like *RePlay*, *Play Meter*, *Playthings*, *Merchandising*, and *Weekly Television Digest with Consumer Electronics* documented the emerging video game medium in the 1970s and 1980s week by week and month by month, while several pioneers provided accounts of their endeavors under oath in depositions and trial testimony recorded just a few years after the fact. These sources have often been ignored in favor of

---

[1] Erkki Huhtamo, "Slots of Fun, Slots of Trouble: An Archaeology of Arcade Gaming," in *Handbook of Computer Game Studies*, ed. Joost Raessens and Jeffrey Goldstein (Cambridge, MA: The MIT Press, 2005), 1–21.

participant recollections imparted decades after the fact. In some cases, this has distorted our view of history.

They Create Worlds is a comprehensive examination of early video game development in all its major commercial facets. This book gives equal attention to significant milestones in the coin-operated amusement industry, the home console industry, and the home computer industry from their inception until the initial high-water mark of the medium in early 1982, right before the collapse of the North American console market. It strives for a global scope by covering events not just in the United States, but also in Japan, the United Kingdom, and Continental Europe. It does not, however, strive to be a complete account of how every individual market reacted to the emergence of the video game: the thrust of this book is examining the forces that shaped the global industry, and it therefore only covers those developments that are significant in that context.

As the work is the first of a projected three volumes covering the history of interactive entertainment through 2005, not all the narrative threads end in exactly the same place. Though the subtitle speaks of progressing through 1982, in truth only the coverage of the home console industries touches upon that date, and then only slightly. The coin-operated amusement narrative ends in 1981, which is when video games in the arcade reached their own apex before sales ground to a halt in the middle of 1982 and the industry experienced a crash separate from that which the console and cartridge companies would feel just a few months later. The home computer narrative ends earliest of all: progressing only to the beginning of 1979. This is largely for practical reasons, for if this book were to progress further, it would need to introduce another dozen software makers and a good 150 pages would be added to its already prodigious length.

Even these timelines are not hard and fast. Readers may notice a favored game (*Star Castle*, *Donkey Kong*) or a favored subject (early Japanese consoles, the beginning of the British microcomputer industry) mysteriously absent. Rest assured, all these topics and more will be coming in volume two. They are only omitted here either because their inclusion did not fit thematically into any chapter or would open a new avenue of exploration that fits better within the context of events occurring deeper into the 1980s.

This book and its successors chart the coalescence and expansion of the video game industry. As such, the focus is on technological and business development rather than on cultural or social history or impact. While these areas are not completely ignored, exploring the full ramifications of video gaming in these spheres must be left to others. The goal is to provide a foundational work upon which future scholars may construct their own arguments and to help ensure they will no longer be constrained by an incomplete or inaccurate recounting of events.

While much of the work unfolds in a narrative style, it does not function solely as a chronicle, as it does put events into some context and examines "whys" and "hows" alongside "whats" and "whos." However, it is less interested in advancing a focused thesis than in setting the record straight. If one were to ascribe a common theme to the chapters of this book, it might be that the "video game industry" did not really exist as such in the 1970s and early 1980s (and indeed probably not until the mid 1990s, but that is a subject for another volume). Instead, there emerged a repeating pattern of a group of individuals discovering new technology, experimenting with it for their own edification, and then forcing their way into an existing manufacturing/publishing/distribution infrastructure to bring a product to market. Sometimes this was the coin-operated amusement industry, other times the toy or consumer electronics industries, and yet other times even more wide-ranging fields such as sporting goods, book publishing, or the record industry. Invariably, the video game would prove a disruptive new force in the established industry and proceed through a series of rapid boom-bust cycles driven largely by improving technology and cheaper products before ultimately burning out in spectacular fashion in a burst of oversaturation. It is a testament to the pull of interactive entertainment that new programmers and entrepreneurs continued to rush into the void left by the collapse of those that came before.

A Note on Sales Figures

Unlike in the movie and music industries, there is not and has never been comprehensive retail tracking in the video game industry. Except in those rare cases that companies have reported their own sales figures (and not exaggerated them) or internal company documents have surfaced that reveal unit sales, every sales figure that has been reported in secondary sources is based on estimates of varying quality. This book gives unit and dollar sales figures for individual games and market segments wherever possible, but as these are generally estimates from tracking groups and market research companies, they may not be accurate in all cases and might even conflict with each other from time to time. At the very least, these figures are useful for identifying general trends and relative performance.

One special note on the coin-op industry. Starting in the late 1970s, the principal trade publications for coin-operated amusements, *RePlay* and *Play Meter*, began running operator polls in which they asked subscribers to reveal the top earning games at their locations. The magazines published the results of these polls on a monthly basis. These rankings are not based on hard and fast figures, sophisticated formulas, or even necessarily on broad canvassing of all types of locations that housed coin-operated games. Instead, they reflect the opinions of the respondents as to which games they felt were earning particularly well. As such, they do not necessarily reflect a precise ranking of which games were bringing in the most money, and the polls in the two publications often ranked games differently from each other. This book uses these charts to gauge the relative performance of various coin-operated games on a monthly basis. Wherever the popularity of a coin-operated game is indicated without a specific citation, it is safe to assume the information was derived from these charts.

Prologue: Genesis

On August 31, 1966, an electrical engineer serving as a division head for a large New Hampshire defense contractor called Sanders Associates sat on a cement step outside a New York City bus terminal waiting for a colleague to arrive so they could meet a client together. A television engineer in earlier days, he considered this appliance – now present in over 90% of American homes – almost completely useless. Sure, the typical family loved its TV set, gathering around it in the evening to watch Walter Cronkite deliver the news or catch the latest happenings in Mayberry on the *Andy Griffith Show*, but with only three networks on the air, programming lacked variety, and the engineer considered these meager offerings to be a passive and dull form of entertainment. His own television sat unused in his living room much of the time, and he figured he was not alone. Certainly, he thought, the television must be able to offer something more.

In 1951, the engineer had almost done something about it. Tasked with building the "best television set ever" by his employer, the Loral Corporation, the engineer would sometimes fool around with test equipment that placed lines and color bars on the screen and allowed the user to move them around to adjust the set. Before long, he came to believe that moving objects around on a television might just be a fun way for a person to pass a few spare moments. Inspired, the engineer suggested incorporating some type of game into his new ultimate television, but the project was already behind schedule, and his boss would not hear of it.

Now, on this warm summer's day in 1966 the concept came to the engineer again, rising unbidden out of his subconscious mind as he idly watched traffic passing by. Pulling out his notebook, he began scribbling furiously. Upon returning to his office the next day, the engineer turned this disorganized jumble into a four-page disclosure document for a "TV Gaming Display" in which a "low cost data entry device" could generate a video signal conveyed directly to the television through its antenna terminals. Conflicted

at proposing such a frivolous project to a defense contractor, the engineer
couched the opening sentences of his document in generic technical language
before finally gaining confidence and christening the channel on which the
device would broadcast "Channel LP," which stood for "Let's Play."[2]

The engineer in our story was not the first person to dream of controlling an object rendered on a screen in order to play a game. Indeed, college
students across the United States had already been hunting each other in
the cold vacuum of computer-generated space for nearly half a decade when
Ralph Henry Baer signed his name at the top of each page of his proposal
on that fateful Thursday in September, while an eminent physicist with the
Dickensian name Willy Higinbotham had wowed visitors to the Brookhaven
National Laboratory in New York with a primitive tennis game displayed on
an oscilloscope even earlier than that. But Baer was the first person to suggest
creating an interactive entertainment experience by conveying game data to
a display through the use of a video signal, so even though he never used the
term in any of his subsequent documentation or patents, he is nevertheless
the progenitor of what we now call the video game.

Narrowly speaking, there is no video game without that video signal, the
key conceptual breakthrough that Baer introduced in his pioneering Brown
Box. Practically speaking, the term "video game" now encompasses so much
more. Virtually any program run by hardware containing electronic logic
circuits in which the user directly manipulates objects rendered on a display
for entertainment purposes now falls under the definition of the term, which
long ago shed its purely technical roots. Under this broader definition, video
games have been deployed on practically any device with a screen, from televisions and computers to phones, calculators, and watches. One enterpris-
ing hacker even modified the LCD on a Canon printer to run the classic
first-person shooter *DOOM*. As smart media devices continue to pervade
all corners of our culture in the Information Age, the definition of the video
game will no doubt continue to evolve to cover an ever-expanding array of
entertainment platforms.

Just as the term has widened in common usage, so too has the player base.
Once merely considered a simple past time for children, the video game has
evolved into a visual feast as exciting as any summer blockbuster, a storytelling device as sophisticated as the novel, and a competition of skill to rival
any professional sport. And in a landmark decision in 2011 the U.S. Supreme
Court recognized that a video game could be a work of art communicating

[2] Ralph Baer, *Videogames: In the Beginning* (Springfield, NJ: Rolenta Press, 2005), 18–27.

"ideas – and even social messages – through many familiar literary devices ... and through features distinctive to the medium."[3]

Over 1 billion people around the world now play video games, indulging in products ranging from simple match three puzzle games to sophisticated first-person shooters and story-driven role-playing games. In the United States, until recently the largest market for video games, the average player age is now 34, and the percentages are almost evenly split between children, adults aged 18–35, and older adults.[4] Once almost exclusively the province of the young male, new genres and platforms have opened gaming to women in larger numbers, and they now make up 45% of the U.S. gaming population.[5] Many would argue that the video game industry still has a long way to go to become fully inclusive, but the player base is still more diverse than it has ever been.

Despite ever-increasing popularity and mainstream acceptance, however, the video game is still in its infancy. The commercial industry is just shy of 50 years old. By comparison, the motion picture industry had only been producing talkies for about a decade at that point in its own history and had yet to truly separate itself from Vaudeville and the theater in its conventions and techniques. Indeed, while the video game has become ubiquitous in the developed world, it has not come close to realizing its full potential. The industry arguably still awaits its *Citizen Kane* moment, in which an auteur with a singular vision breaks from the conventions of previous media in daring ways to tell a story or evoke an emotional response by taking advantage of the unique characteristics of the medium to challenge and transform our ideas on the power of interactive entertainment. The video game may theoretically be capable of telling a story as sophisticated as any great work of literature, but individual games rarely approach those heights. In 1983, Electronic Arts asked in a famous ad whether a computer can make you cry. So far, the answer has largely been no.

Of course, the question remains as to whether a video game should even try to reach the same heights as Shakespeare or Hollywood. If a game, whether played with cards, balls, boards, or controllers, is primarily a test of skill or a battle of wits against other human beings, does storytelling interfere with the pure gaming experience? And even if narrative holds value in a game

---

[3] Brown v. Entertainment Merchants Association, 564 U.S. 786 (2011)

[4] "Essential Facts about the Computer and Video Game Industry: 2018 Sales, Demographic, and Usage Data," Entertainment Software Association, accessed May 27, 2019, http://www.theesa.com/wp-content/uploads/2018/05/EF2018_FINAL.pdf.

[5] Ibid.

world, should the story be dictated by the designer through a canned plot, or should the player merely be placed inside a virtual world with a coherent set of rules but little to no structure to discover his or her own narrative through interactions with the people around them? These are just some of the challenges that the video game industry faces as it approaches its 50th birthday.

These questions were of little consequence to Ralph Baer in 1966–1967 as he and a small group of technicians struggled just to display two or three dots on a television screen at the same time. That in such a brief span of time the medium has progressed from barely recognizable representations of simple objects to photo-realistic landscapes encompassing hundreds of square miles of virtual real estate is a testament to both the brilliant technical and creative minds that have birthed so many enthralling virtual worlds and the shrewd businessmen who have disseminated these visions to the masses. Here then are their stories and the story of what stands to become the most important entertainment medium of the twenty-first century: the video game.

1

Searching for Bobby Fischer

The definition of the term "video game" remains unsettled as digital entertainment continues to evolve. Broadly speaking, the term encompasses any entertainment experience powered by electronic logic circuits that requires a player to manipulate an input device to interact with objects presented on a display. By this definition, the development of the first video games coincided with the rise of digital computing in the latter half of the twentieth century. While computers had existed for well over a century by that point, their function had been markedly different and unsuited to playing a game. In the eighteenth and early nineteenth centuries, a computer was merely a person doing basic addition and subtraction to complete mathematical tables.[1] In the late nineteenth century, human computers were augmented by analog devices like Lord Kelvin's tide predictor that physically simulated specific phenomena through the aid of mechanical devices like levers, pulleys, and gears. In the early twentieth century, the analog computer largely become the domain of the electrical engineer, who used room-sized machines full of resistors, capacitors, and inducers to simulate the operation of power grids as the developed world rapidly electrified. Analog computing reached its high-water mark in 1931 when MIT professor and electrical engineer Vannevar Bush completed his differential analyzer, which could solve a wide array of differential equations, but remained limited to a relatively small set of problems.[2]

As the first digital computers entered development in the late 1930s, the goal of their creators remained solving specific equations, making them little more than complicated and expensive calculating machines. A computer

[1] Martin Campbell-Kelly, William Aspray, Nathan Ensmenger, and Jeffrey R. Yost, *Computer: A History of the Information Machine*, 3rd ed. (Boulder, CO: Westview Press, 2014), 3–4.
[2] Ibid, 50–54.

created under this philosophy merely replaced human computers – laborers undertaking arithmetic tasks that required little independent thought. By the conclusion of World War II, which saw the construction of the first electronic digital computers, there was a small group of engineers, mathematicians, and logicians who felt it should be possible to create a computer that could think for itself. When it came time to prove to the rest of the world this dream was possible, these thinkers felt the most effective way to do so was to craft a computer program able to match a human opponent in a strategy game.

Over the next decade and a half, multiple individuals undertook the challenge of creating an artificial intelligence (AI) that could play a convincing game of checkers or chess, all in aid of a larger goal of creating a computer program that could learn and think for itself. By the early 1950s, these pioneers had determined the basic obstacles they would need to overcome to achieve this goal and had developed shortcuts like decision trees and alpha-beta pruning derived from the nascent field of game theory to overcome these difficulties. Applying these methods to fashion a credible intelligence took longer, with engineers hampered primarily by the capability of the hardware architectures and programming languages with which they were forced to work. These engineers were not striving to create entertainment products, but their research represents some of the earliest instances of developing a computer program to play a game on a computer against an artificial opponent.

***

In early 1935, a recent mathematics graduate of King's College, Cambridge, named Alan Mathison Turing attended a course taught by King's College fellow Max Newman regarding certain foundational principles of mathematics and logic while awaiting word on his own application to become a fellow at the college. One topic Newman discussed was systematic procedures that can be accomplished step-by-step by following instructions without any real understanding of how the procedures work. According to Newman, these tasks required so little knowledge or insight that even a machine could undertake them successfully.[3]

Unlike many of his mathematical peers, Turing was not content to confine his studies to purely philosophical constructs. Possessed of both a love of invention and a desire to explore abstract concepts through the material world, Turing found his imagination fired by Newman's concept of a

---

[3] B. Jack Copeland, *Turing: Pioneer of the Information Age* (Oxford: Oxford University Press, 2012), kindle, chap. 2.

machine performing calculations based on instructions. For the next year, he attacked the *Entscheidungsproblem* originally posed by David Hilbert in 1928 through the lens of a theorized mathematical device inspired by Newman's lecture.

Hilbert, the dean of the international mathematics community, had long believed that no problem in mathematics was unsolvable, and his *Entscheidungsproblem* posited that any mathematical formula could be proven through formal logic to be universally valid. To examine this assertion, Turing envisioned a universal machine consisting of a scanner reading an endless roll of paper tape. The tape would be divided into individual squares that could either be blank or contain a symbol. By reading these symbols based on a simple set of hardwired instructions and following any coded instructions conveyed by the symbols themselves, the machine would be able to carry out any calculation possible by a specialized machine, output the results, and even incorporate those results into a new set of calculations. In April 1936, Turing completed his paper, entitled "On Computable Numbers, with an Application to the *Entscheidungsproblem*" and demonstrated that his universal machine proved Hilbert incorrect. While merely a hypothetical device employed to serve a theoretical purpose, Turing's universal machine defined the basic attributes of the general-purpose digital computer.[4]

With the onset of World War II, Turing joined His Majesty's Code and Cypher School at Bletchley Park to decipher high-level German military codes and took part in the construction of increasingly elaborate cryptographic machines – called bombes for the ticking noises they emitted while decrypting – to crack the German military's Enigma code. With what had once been a hobbyist interest in cryptology now transformed into his primary vocation, Turing increasingly turned to math and logic problems to unwind in what little leisure time his work afforded him. In particular, he began pondering whether there might be a machine method to play a "perfect" game of chess.[5]

Game theory was still in its infancy in the 1940s, but the concept of "minimaxing," the idea that in any contest where both participants possess complete information regarding the state of play there exists a pair of strategies that allow each player to minimize and maximize his losses, had already been articulated in 1928 by one of the founders of the discipline, John von Neumann. In 1941, Turing began discussing with fellow mathematician Jack

[4]Ibid.

[5]Andrew Hodges, *Alan Turing: The Enigma* (London: Vintage, 2014), 266.

Good on how a device akin to his universal machine might employ mini-maxing theory to play a game of chess. Turing and Good went so far as constructing a basic decision tree for chess and determining that the number of moves the computer would have to "look ahead" needed to be variable so that the computer could accurately identify potential capture moves, but then set the problem aside.[6]

In early 1943, Turing traveled to Washington, DC to share information with the cryptographers employed by the U.S. Navy. While abroad, he called on Bell Labs, where he discussed his universal machine with Claude Shannon. An electrical engineer with a master's degree from MIT, Shannon combined a passion for logic with practical experience working with Bush's differential analyzer to conceptualize a calculating device incorporating Boolean logic to not just solve mathematical problems but also to carry out symbolic logic tasks as well. Shannon's work paved the way for machines that could not just perform a rote operation, but actually decide how to tackle problems on its own, for almost any decision, no matter how complex, can be broken down into a basic series of yes or no, on or off, 1 or 0 proposi-tions. Published in his master's thesis in 1937, Shannon's framework for the binary digital circuit proved instrumental to transforming Turing's idea of a universal machine into reality. Turing and Shannon held several discussions during their time together at Bell, which helped crystallize both their desires to build machines that could go beyond the computing devices of the day and actually reason.[7]

Shortly after returning to Bletchley, Turing struck up a friendship with newly arrived Oxford student Donald Michie, who had begun his course of study in the classics, but ended up at Bletchley Park when he took a cryptol-ogy course in the hopes of making himself useful to the war effort and dis-covered a heretofore unknown aptitude for code breaking. In Michie, Turing discovered a kindred soul interested in chess and probability and teaching machines to think.[8] By now, the Bletchley cryptologists had turned to break-ing more complicated German ciphers than Enigma for which even the elab-orate bombe machines proved insufficient. In a new section headed by Max Newman, electrical engineers were now building more complicated elec-tronic code-breaking equipment, culminating in the revolutionary Colossus completed by Tommy Flowers in 1944, the world's first fully functional

[6] Ibid, 267–270.
[7] Ibid, 312–316.
[8] Ibid, 332–334.

electronic digital computer.[9] Electronic machines were now fully integrated into the daily lives of the Bletchley cryptographers, so talk naturally turned toward what should be done with the technology after the war. From his discussions with Good, Shannon, and Michie, Turing decided the only logical course was to construct a machine that could think for itself.

***

The earliest electronic computers like Colossus were wholly unsuited to serve as the basis for a thinking machine, for they were built for highly specific tasks, and their function was entirely governed by their hardware, so they could only be reprogrammed for a new task by physically rewiring the machine.[10] This bottleneck could be eliminated if computer programs dictating the operation of the computer could also be stored in memory alongside the numbers they were manipulating. In theory, the binary circuits envisioned by Shannon could represent these instructions via symbolic logic, but in practice the vacuum tubes found in early computers could only house around 200 characters in memory, which was fine for storing a few five- or ten-digit numbers for calculations, but not for instruction sets that required thousands of characters. In the late 1940s, engineers began developing more expansive memory options to create the first stored-program computers.

One of the first people to whom Turing gave a copy of his landmark 1936 paper was its principle inspiration, Max Newman. Upon reading it, Newman became interested in building a Universal Turing Machine himself. He tried to interest Tommy Flowers in the paper while he was building his Colossi for the Newmanry at Bletchley Park, but Flowers was an engineer, not a mathematician or logician, and by his own admission did not really understand Turing's theories. As early as 1944, Newman began expressing enthusiasm for applying wartime electronic advances to a project to build a Universal Turing Machine at the war's conclusion.[11]

In September 1945, Newman took the Fielden Chair of Mathematics at Manchester University and soon after applied for a grant from the Royal Society to establish the Computing Machine Laboratory at the university. After the grant was approved in May 1946, Newman arranged for portions

---

[9] The first known electronic digital computer project was started at Iowa State College in 1937. Retroactively named the ABC after its designers, John Atanasoff and Clifford Berry, the computer remained incomplete when abandoned in 1942 due to the demands of World War II.

[10] Earlier electromechanical computers had been reprogrammable by feeding in new instructions using paper tape, but this process was too slow for machines running at electronic speeds.

[11] B. Jack Copeland and Diane Proudfoot. "Alan Turing: Father of the Modern Computer," *Rutherford Journal*, accessed May 27, 2019, http://www.rutherfordjournal.org/article040101.html.

of the dismantled Colossi to be shipped to Manchester for reference and assembled a team to tackle a stored-program computer project. Perhaps the most important members of the team were electrical engineers Freddie Williams and Tom Kilburn.[12]

While working on radar during the war, Williams and Kilburn developed a method through which a cathode ray tube (CRT) could "remember" a piece of information by virtue of firing an electron "dot" onto the surface of the tube to create a persistent charge well. By placing a metal plate against the surface of the tube, this data could be "read" via a voltage pulse transferred to the plate whenever a charge well was created or eliminated by drawing or erasing a dot. Originally developed to eliminate stationary background objects from a radar display, a Williams tube could also serve as computer memory and store 1,024 characters. As any dot on the tube could be read at any given time, it functioned as an early form of random access memory (RAM).[13]

In June 1948, Williams and Kilburn completed the Manchester Small Scale Experimental Machine (SSEM) to test the viability of the Williams Tube as a computer memory device. While this computer contained only 550 tubes and was therefore not practical for computing projects, the SSEM was the first device in the world with all the characteristics of a stored-program computer. Building on this work, the team completed the Manchester Mark 1 in October 1949.

Meanwhile, Turing took up residence at the National Physical Laboratory (NPL) after the war to commence his own attempt at building a universal machine, a stored-program computer he named the Automatic Computing Engine (ACE). He remained convinced that chess represented one of the best avenues for pursuing machine learning, so in the summer of 1948 he and economist David Champernowne began developing a chess program in their spare time that could run on the computer. Meanwhile, Michie returned to Oxford to continue his studies, but did not forget his discussions with Turing at Bletchley regarding a computer capable of playing chess. Along with colleague Shaun Wylie, he outlined on paper a basic chess-playing program christened *Machiavelli*. When Turing learned of Michie's work in September 1948, he quickly applied the finishing touches to his own program, dubbed *Turochamp* after its creators, with the intention of pitting the two systems against one another.[14]

By the time he completed *Turochamp*, Turing had departed NPL to join Newman at the University of Manchester after becoming increasingly

[12] Ibid.

[13] Campbell-Kelly et al., 2014, 88.

[14] Hodges, 2014, 488–489.

frustrated by bureaucratic obstacles placed in the path of his overly ambitious design for the ACE computer. Therefore, the Manchester Mark I served as the new target platform for *Turochamp* and *Machiavelli*. Unfortunately, the programs proved too complicated for the computer, and Turing never succeeded in making either one operational before his untimely death in 1954. Nevertheless, these two programs represent the earliest known attempt to harness a digital computer to play a game.

***

Alan Turing may have left NPL in 1947, but his quest to build a universal machine continued in scaled-down fashion in the form of the Pilot ACE computer, completed in 1950 by a team that included Donald Davies. A follower of Turing, Davies also held a fascination for the possibility of playing games on a computer and authored a paper that appeared in the June 1950 edition of *Penguin Science News* entitled "A Theory of Chess and Noughts and Crosses."[15] This article exerted a profound impact on the first generation of computer programmers in Britain, including a scientist named Christopher Strachey.

Born in 1916, Strachey descended from a distinguished family of artists and puzzle solvers. His father, Oliver, became a cryptographer during World War I and was named a Commander of the Order of the British Empire (CBE) for helping establish the Canadian cryptographic operation during World War II, while his Uncle Lytton was a member of the celebrated Bloomsbury Group of writers and intellectuals. Christopher received a fine secondary education and matriculated to Cambridge in 1935, where he socialized with Turing but was most likely not introduced to his theories. An indifferent student, Strachey failed to achieve sufficient marks to earn a desired research position at the college and took a low-paying job as a physicist with Standard Telephones and Cables (STC). After doing radar and radio research for STC during the war, he took a position as a school master at St. Edmunds in 1945 before moving to the more prestigious Harrow School in 1949.[16]

A lover of puzzles and games, Strachey became interested in the nascent research into automatic computing devices before the war, but he never had an opportunity to engage in the field himself. In January 1951, he gained an introduction to a member of the Pilot ACE team named Mike Woodger through a mutual friend and spent a day learning the inner workings of the machine.

---

[15] D.W. Davies, "A Theory of Chess and Nought and Crosses," *Science News*, no. 16 (1950): 40–64.

[16] Martin Campbell-Kelly, "Christopher Strachey, 1916–1975: A Biographical Note," *Annals of the History of Computing* 7, no. 1 (1985): 20–23.

Inspired by Davies's article and his own love of games, Strachey resolved to gain a greater understanding of the machine by programming it to play draughts.[17] That May, Strachey returned to NPL with what he thought was a complete draughts program, but it failed to run due to programming errors. By the time he corrected the defects a month or so later, the Pilot ACE had undergone a hardware upgrade that would have forced a major redesign of the program. By then, Strachey had learned of the Ferranti Mark 1 at the University of Manchester, a commercial update of the original Manchester Mark 1 that included greater storage capacity. In July 1951, he traveled to Manchester to see the computer and consult with Turing, who had recently completed the programmer's handbook for the machine. Turing encouraged Strachey to switch his programming efforts to the Mark 1, though he also convinced Strachey to put his draughts program aside in favor of other programming pursuits. In November 1951, Strachey accepted a job with the National Research and Development Corporation (NRDC) and returned to his draughts program. He completed it over the next year, with most of the programming occurring in June and July 1952.[18]

Strachey's draughts program represents an important milestone in computer programming. The match was played between a human player, who flicked toggle switches on the computer to identify the piece he wanted to move and the space to which he wanted to move it, and the computer itself, which displayed its moves via a teletype. The computer opponent incorporated a heuristic algorithm that looked ahead several moves to determine the best course of action, making it perhaps the first software program capable of thinking for itself. Strachey also manipulated the Mark 1's CRT storage tubes 3 and 5 so that one would constantly display the current state of the board, while the other could be used to preview moves.[19] This is most likely the first graphical display used by a computer program.[20]

The United Kingdom, so central to the development of computer technology in the 1940s through computers like the Colossus, the Manchester

---

[17] Ibid, 24. Checkers to an American audience.

[18] Ibid, 24–25 and David Link, "Programming ENTER: Christopher Strachey's Draughts Program," *Resurrection*, no. 60 (2012–2013): 23.

[19] Ibid, 24–25.

[20] In 1952, a graduate student at Cambridge University named Alexander Douglas created a tic-tac-toe program on a computer called EDSAC that displayed the board via the tube memory in a similar manner to Strachey's chess game. Many sources identify this game, later dubbed OXO by historians, as the first computer game to make use of a display, but it is likely that Strachey's program came first. It was certainly publicized first, as Strachey presented it at a conference in September 1952, while Douglas did not promulgate his program before including it in his dissertation in 1954.

Mark 1, and the Pilot ACE, fell increasingly behind as the 1950s progressed. Conservative British businesses refused to embrace computer technology, while Continental Europe was still recovering from the devastation of the war.[21] Consequently, the market for British computers remained limited, allowing domination of the international market by firms in the United States.

***

In America, the major axis for early electronic computer research ran on a line between two Ivy League institutions, the University of Pennsylvania and Princeton. At Pennsylvania, John Mauchly and J. Prepser Eckert built the first widely known and influential electronic computer, ENIAC, between 1943 and 1945 to calculate ballistic tables for the U.S. Army. Subsequently, the duo collaborated with Princeton mathematician John von Neumann to tackle the stored-program concept.[22] In his "First Draft of a Report on the EDVAC,"[23] distributed in June 1945, von Neuman articulated the first logic design for a stored-program computer and defined its basic building blocks as the input, the output, the control unit, the arithmetic unit, and the memory. This so-called "von Neumann architecture," largely defined by Eckert and Mauchly despite the name, remained the basic architecture of the digital computer for over 50 years.[24]

After collaborating on the early stages of the EDVAC project, von Neumann began development on his own computer at the Institute for Advanced Study (IAS) at Princeton. Although not completed until 1952, the specifications for von Neumann's IAS Machine were widely disseminated in the late 1940s, so when the U.S. government began investing heavily in computer technology as defense spending skyrocketed with the onset of the Korean War, over a dozen universities, research laboratories, and government think tanks adopted the IAS Machine architecture as the basis for their own stored-program computers, including the University of Illinois (ILLIAC I, 1952), the Los Alamos National Laboratory (MANIAC I, 1952), and the RAND Corporation (JOHNNIAC, 1953). As in Britain, it would not take

---

[21] Campbell-Kelly et al., 2014, 98.

[22] Colossus predated ENIAC but remained classified until the 1970s. ENIAC was unveiled publicly in February 1946 and served as the inspiration for a wide variety of computer projects.

[23] EDVAC was the successor to the ENIAC and the first stored-program computer to be conceptualized, though project delays meant that other computers like the Manchester Mark 1 were completed first.

[24] Paul Ceruzzi, *A History of Modern Computing*, 2nd ed. (Cambridge, MA: The MIT Press, 2003), chap. 1, Kindle.

long for engineers and mathematicians interested in thinking machines to co-opt these computers for their own research, which often involved programming games.

As Turing set the tone for early research into thinking machines in Britain, his friend at Bell Labs, Claude Shannon, did the same in the United States. Like Turing, Shannon attacked the problem of playing chess on a computer through the lens of game theory. Unlike Turing, who worked on his program only informally and did not publish any of his work until 1953, Shannon built an electromechanical machine called Caissac in 1949 to test some of his theories and released his findings in 1950 in two articles: "A Chess-Playing Machine" in the February edition of *Scientific American* and "Programming a Computer for Playing Chess" in the March issue of *Philosophical Magazine*.[25]

In his *Philosophical Magazine* article, Shannon articulated both why chess was the perfect game around which to build a thinking machine and how best to craft a program with a reasonable chance of defeating a human opponent. Shannon presents a game of chess as a complex decision tree in which each node represents a specific board layout and each branch outlines a possible move. Theoretically, a computer could play a perfect game of chess by working backwards through the decision tree for any given board state. Unlike in simpler games like tic-tac-toe in which such a "brute force" approach is relatively simple, a game of chess can unfold in upwards of 10^{120} variations, meaning that a computer running 1 million variations per second would need over 10^{90} years just to calculate the first move of the game. This was far beyond the capabilities of the computers of the day, so the only way for one to play a game of chess in a reasonable period of time was to react and adapt to a human player through a basic understanding of the value of particular pieces and strategies.

Shannon solved this problem by having the computer only track moves to a certain depth on the tree – in his case, two moves – and then choose the best move under the circumstances. This would be determined by evaluating a series of static factors such as the value and mobility of pieces – weighted based on their importance in the decision-making process of expert chess players – and combining these values with a minimaxing procedure. Although this plausible move method would ultimately be discarded as computers became more sophisticated and could analyze many potential

[25] Claude E. Shannon, "A Chess-Playing Machine," *Scientific American*, February 1950, 48–51 and Claude E. Shannon, "Programming a Computer for Playing Chess," *Philosophical Magazine* 41, no. 314 (1950): 256–275.

moves in a small amount of time, Shannon's approach defined the parameters of computer chess research for the next two decades.

The first person to apply Shannon's ideas to a working program did so not through chess, but through checkers. Electrical engineer Arthur Samuel became an expert on vacuum tubes after joining Bell Labs in 1928 and worked to improve radar displays during World War II. After the war, he took a teaching position at the University of Illinois and became involved with the nascent ILLIAC computer project. In 1947, when it seemed no one was willing to fund additional work on the machine, Samuel and his colleagues toyed with building a stripped-down version that could perform a few headline-grabbing feats to acquire additional funding. At the time, Shannon was traveling the country delivering lectures on developing a chess-playing computer, and Samuel figured that if Shannon were closing in on solving the chess problem (which he actually was not), then it should be a snap to create a checkers program capable of defeating a human opponent. Coincidentally, a world championship checkers match would be held the next spring in the nearby town of Kankakee, so Samuel decided to throw together a program capable of defeating a champion player to generate headlines at the event and secure crucial funding.[26]

Building a competent checkers program proved more difficult than Samuel expected, and his design remained unfinished when he left Illinois for International Business Machines (IBM) in 1949. After some delay, the tabulating machine and office equipment giant was preparing to embrace the electronic computer revolution, and Samuel contributed important breakthroughs in CRT storage that allowed the company's debut 701 computer, yet another offshoot of von Neumann's IAS Machine, to incorporate memory that was both higher capacity and more reliable than that found in earlier machines. Needing a program to test the new machine's instruction set, Samuel returned to his checkers program and had it working by the end of 1952.[27]

Samuel continued refining his program over the next decade, mostly working on his own time because IBM frowned on its engineers engaging in frivolous activities like teaching a computer to play checkers. He earned

---

[26]Jonathan Schaeffer, *One Jump Ahead: Computer Perfection at Checkers*, Rev. ed. (New York: Springer, 2009), 87–88.

[27]Ibid, 88–89. Samuel may have been inspired to return to his checkers program by a presentation Christopher Strachey gave on his draughts program in 1952. Jack Copeland, "What is Artificial Intelligence?" AlanTuring.net, May 2000, http://www.alanturing.net/turing_archive/pages/Reference%20Articles/what_is_AI/What%20is%20AI04.html.

a small measure of respect in 1955, however, after the program gained the ability to apply past experience to future games, making it the first known program that could learn and improve over time. Like Shannon's proposed chess program, Samuel's checkers game evaluated the board by searching a decision tree to a certain depth and made a move decision based on static factors and minimaxing, but it also maintained a record of each board position previously encountered and the value of previous moves made from that position, allowing it to favor more effective moves over time. IBM management was so impressed by this breakthrough that it demonstrated the program on national television on February 24, 1956.[28]

In 1962, Samuel challenged a champion checkers player named Robert Nealey to a match against his program, which emerged victorious.[29] At first glance, this feat stands as proof that a thinking computer had mastered its first game, but the truth of the matter is different. Nealey was merely the self-proclaimed "world blind checkers champion," a title he claimed by default when no other players showed up for a tournament held in Peoria, Illinois.[30] Furthermore, analysis of the match between man and machine demonstrates that Nealey executed several poor moves that a true grand master would never make, so the program won more through luck than skill. Indeed, a rematch was arranged the next year that Nealey won handily, and when Samuel took his checkers program to a championship tournament in 1966, it went 0-8 against two actual grand masters. Therefore, while Samuel's program is noteworthy as the first capable of self-learning, it never achieved its author's original goal of defeating a true champion player.[31]

***

While Turing and Shannon were among the first to ponder the ramifications of a thinking machine, a professor named John McCarthy gave it a name and an academic discipline. Born in 1927 to communist parents, McCarthy became interested in science at an early age when he read a Soviet technology book called *100,000 Whys*. A precocious student, he studied college-level calculus on his own time while a junior at Belmont High School in Los Angeles, California, and skipped 2 years of math courses when he matriculated to the

---

[28] Schaeffer, 2009, 90.

[29] Ibid, 91.

[30] Romaine Kosharsky, "Robert Nealey, World Blind Checker Champ," *St. Petersburg Times*, February 26, 1980.

[31] Schaeffer, 2009, 91–94. The first accomplished checkers AI was the PAASLOW program developed by Eric Jensen and Tom Truscott at Duke University in the late 1970s. In 1977, it defeated the Samuel program in a two-game match.

California Institute of Technology (Caltech) in 1944. Upon graduating with a B.S. in mathematics in 1948, McCarthy did a year of graduate work at Caltech and attended the university's Hixon Symposium on Cerebral Mechanisms in Behavior in September 1948. During the conference, several eminent psychologists gave lectures on the workings of the human brain, but the highlight of the show for McCarthy was a lecture by game theory and computer pioneer John von Neumann on self-replicating automata – machines capable of creating copies of themselves. While no lectures were delivered regarding thinking machines, von Neumann's lecture sparked McCarthy's interest in trying to create an automaton that could model human intelligence.[32]

In 1949, McCarthy moved to Princeton to continue his studies, where he earned his PhD in mathematics in 1951 and subsequently became an instructor. The next year, one of his graduate students suggested McCarthy collect papers on machine intelligence. McCarthy contacted Shannon, and together they published a book of papers called *Automata Studies*. Few of the papers related to machine intelligence, however, which disappointed McCarthy.[33] After a brief foray to Stanford, McCarthy established himself at Dartmouth in 1955 and attempted to attract interest in machine intelligence again. Inspired by Defense Department workshops, he decided to stage a gathering of eminent thinkers in the field to work on projects and solve problems together.[34] Remembering the confusion engendered by the term "automata studies" in 1952, he decided to name the event the Summer Research Project on Artificial Intelligence.

With funding from the Rockefeller foundation, McCarthy successfully hosted his AI workshop in the summer of 1956 with the aid of Shannon, Harvard professor Marvin Minsky, and Nathaniel Rochester of IBM. While it failed to achieve all its lofty goals, the workshop established AI research as a distinct discipline within computer science. It also exposed McCarthy to the work of Carnegie Institute of Technology (later Carnegie-Mellon University) professors Allan Newell and Herbert Simon.[35]

At the time of the conference, Newell and Simon were working with RAND employee Cliff Shaw to develop a high-level programming language called Information Processing Language (IPL) on RAND's JOHNNIAC computer to serve as the heart of a program called the Logic Theory Machine

---

[32] Nils J. Nilsson, *John McCarthy, 1927–2011*, National Academy of Arts and Sciences, 2012, 1–3.

[33] Ibid, 5.

[34] John McCarthy, interview by Nils Nilsson, September 12, 2007, Computer History Museum, https://archive.computerhistory.org/resources/access/text/2012/10/102658149-05-01-acc.pdf.

[35] Nilsson, 2012, 7–8.

that could complete elementary logic proofs. Unlike other programming languages, IPL was created not to instruct a computer to perform calculations, but to serve as the basis for an AI. Therefore, the language incorporated concepts like dynamic memory allocation and recursion and was the first language built around list processing. McCarthy loved the idea of list processing, but preferred working in FORTRAN, the pioneering high-level language developed by John Backus at IBM in 1956. FORTRAN could not perform recursion, however, which was essential to AI programming, so McCarthy developed his own programming language combining the best features of FORTRAN and IPL called List Processing Language, or LISP.[36]

Later in 1956, McCarthy moved to MIT and reunited with Minsky, who had been doing research into neural networks at Harvard. They convinced the electrical engineering department at MIT to establish an AI Lab to further their research with a staff initially consisting of a secretary, two programmers, and six graduate students. In spring 1959, McCarthy decided to offer the first computer course at the university open to freshman, one of whom was gifted electrical engineering student named Alan Kotok.[37]

Raised in the New Jersey suburbs of Philadelphia, Kotok began wiring lamps on his own at the tender age of six. In high school, he participated in a field trip to a SOCONY-Mobile research facility in Paulsboro, New Jersey, where he not only saw his first computer, but had the opportunity to run through a simple programming exercise on the machine. From that day forward, Kotok knew his destiny lay with computers, so he enrolled at MIT and leapt at the chance to take McCarthy's freshman programming course. The class only increased Kotok's desire to program on the department's IBM 704 computer, so at its conclusion he and friends Elwyn Berlekamp, Michael Lieberman, Charles Niessen, and Robert Wagner approached McCarthy and begged for the chance to do a project for him. McCarthy had just barely started implementing a chess program on the 704, so he turned the project over to the students.[38]

By 1959, chess programs had made great strides after over half a decade of frustration, but no program had emerged that could play the game competently. In 1956, James Kister, Paul Stein, Stanisław Ulam, William Walden, and Mark Wells completed the first chess program that adhered to Shannon's

---

[36] McCarthy, 2007.

[37] Ibid.

[38] Alan Kotok, interview by Gardner Hendrie, November 15, 2004, Computer History Museum, https://archive.computerhistory.org/resources/access/text/2013/05/102657916-05-01-acc.pdf.

methods on the MANIAC I at Los Alamos,[39] but only by reducing the size of the board from 8 × 8 squares to 6 × 6 and eliminating bishops. The next year, IBM employees Alex Bernstein, Michael de V. Roberts, Timothy Arbuckle, and Martin Belsky implemented a complete chess program on an IBM 704 by reducing the number of moves examined by the computer through a series of "plausible move generators," so the computer only considered 2,500 of over 800,000 possible permutations. AI pioneers Newell, Simon, and Shaw took their own crack at the problem in 1958 by developing the NSS chess program on the JOHNNIAC.[40] Programmed in the IPL language, the NSS program used a more sophisticated move evaluation routine than Bernstein and managed to defeat a human opponent – a novice taught the rules of the game right before the match – but it was still a weak player.[41]

After 3 years of work, Kotok and company unveiled a chess program on an IBM 7090 – the successor to the 704 at MIT – that for the first time could play the game on the level of a passable amateur. The advance allowing the program to play a better game of chess than its predecessors was a technique called alpha-beta pruning in which the computer assigns a value to each move and only considers moves that fall within a certain range of values. By employing this procedure, Kotok's program became smarter over time as it experienced and assigned values to board positions and could soon consider fewer moves than earlier programs while largely ignoring only poor choices.[42] Kotok published an undergraduate thesis describing the program in 1962 before he and his friends set it aside.[43]

In 1965, an MIT student named Richard Greenblatt learned about the Kotok group's work and built his own program incorporating his own vast chess knowledge through a series of 50 heuristics to create what he called MacHack, which played a better game of chess than any program to come before it. In 1967, Greenblatt took MacHack VI to a chess tournament to challenge human opponents. It defeated a player with a rating around 1,400,

---

[39] In November 1951, Ferranti employee Dietrich Prinz created a chess program that simulated the "mate in two problem," that is, it identified the best move to make when two moves away from checkmate. This would technically be the first known chess program, but it merely ran through every last possible move to determine its next course of action and was therefore not a thinking program in the vein of Shannon's work.

[40] The NSS program was named after the initials of its three creators.

[41] Allen Newell, J.C. Shaw, and H.A. Simon, "Chess-Playing Programs and the Problem of Complexity," in *Computers and Thought*, ed. Edward A. Feigenbaum and Julian Feldman (New York: McGraw-Hill, 1963), 46–50.

[42] The NSS chess program employed a "branch-and-bounds" method that was essentially a primitive form of alpha-beta pruning, while Samuel's checkers program also used a similar method.

[43] Kotok, 2004.

roughly the level of an average tournament player, though it also lost several matches.[44] Although AI research still had a long way to go, the dream of Turing and Shannon that a machine could exhibit sufficient intelligence to play a complex strategy game with some degree of skill had been realized.

In the 1950s and 1960s, programming a computer to play checkers or chess was simply an academic exercise intended to improve the state of AI research and to pave the way for true intelligent machines. These programs were played almost exclusively by a small circle of academics and rarely packaged in a manner suitable for public consumption. Truly, they were not "games" at all, as they just replaced one of the players in a two-player contest. Nevertheless, AI research represented one of the two primary avenues for computer game creation in the 1950s. The other was the military-industrial complex, which created increasingly sophisticated simulations as the decade progressed.

[44]Richard Greenblatt, interview by Gardner Hendrie, January 12, 2005, Computer History Museum, https://archive.computerhistory.org/resources/access/text/2012/12/102657935-05-01-acc.pdf.

2

Shall We Play a (War) Game?

Between February 4 and June 8, 1952, the RAND Corporation administered a training exercise codenamed "Casey" involving 28 students from the
University of California, Los Angeles (UCLA). The exercise served as the first
test for an initiative called "Project Simulator" designed to teach the staff of
Air Defense Direction Centers (ADCCs) how to identify enemy aircraft on
radar displays and scramble interceptor jets to shoot them down. In many
ways, Project Simulator differed little from exercises conducted by militaries
for more than a century save for one important distinction: the scenario was
driven by an IBM 701 computer that simulated the flight paths of the aircraft
trainees were required to identify, pinpoint, and interdict. As the computer
charted the paths of the planes over the course of two hours, an IBM 407
printer constantly produced new paper readouts that approximated an actual
radar display.[1]

Project Simulator was developed by a RAND group established in May
1951 called the Systems Research Laboratory (SRL) staffed by a mix of psychologists and mathematicians studying the impact of new technologies on
the battlefield by focusing on the "human factors" present in man–machine
interaction. SRL gravitated toward early warning systems due to growing
paranoia regarding Soviet nuclear strikes using long-range bombers. Casey
proved successful, so in early 1953 SRL conducted a second round of tri-
als with Project Simulator codenamed "Cowboy," this time with active-duty
military personnel.[2]

---

[1] Willis Ware, *RAND and the Information Revolution: A History in Essays and Vignettes* (Santa
Monica, CA: RAND Corporation, 2008), 94–98.
[2] F.N. Marzocco, "The Story of SDD," SD-1094, October 1, 1956, 1–2.

The U.S. Air Force was so pleased with the results of Casey and Cowboy that it deployed Project Simulator across the service and funded upgrades like a high-resolution camera and a CRT display to replace the printer readouts of the original system.[3] In September 1955, work on the renamed "System Training Project" (STP) moved to a new division, the System Development Division (SDD), which by May 1956 had installed the STP at seven air divisions.[4] In December 1957, RAND spun off SDD as its own company, System Development Corporation, which became a major defense contractor in its own right. While the STP was not a fully automated exercise and required a human team to administer the scenario and interpret the results, it represented the first training simulation constructed around a computer.

***

Like the AI researchers located primarily at major universities, the U.S. Armed Forces were quick to realize that computerized games could be a boon to their work, in this case determining effective strategies to thwart the Soviet military if the Cold War turned hot. The computer arrived at the perfect time in the evolution of military strategy, as over the course of World War II the nature of war gaming, which for two centuries had largely focused on tactical encounters between opposing armies and decision-making by field commanders, fundamentally shifted. The new buzzword in the think tanks of the emergent military-industrial complex was "operations research" (OR), a discipline focused on a commander making decisions to overcome an implacable simulation model rather than a fellow military leader. Once the earliest computers started coming online in the 1940s, the OR crowd quickly embraced the technology to run its simulations.

In the late 1950s, top business leaders, particularly those working for defense contractors, took notice of the complex decision-making models the military had developed and realized that they could model business markets and corporate organizations the same way. Thus, computer simulations migrated from the war room to the classroom, and America's business students became some of the first laymen to challenge each other in computer-mediated competition. As with the chess programs, these military and business simulations were not entertainment products, but the individuals being trained through these programs were among the first in the world to compete through a computer game.

---

[3] Ware, 2008, 97.
[4] Marzocco, 1956, 8.

Abstract depictions of warfare are nearly as old as civilization. One of the most celebrated of these games is chess, which developed in Medieval Europe on the model of an earlier Indian game called *chaturanga* that dates back to at least the 700s. While chess and its many variants became popular across Europe, they took on particular significance in the Holy Roman Empire, where in 1616 Duke Augustus the Younger of Braunschweig-Lüneburg wrote a treatise under the pseudonym Gustavus Selenus entitled *Das Schach-oder König-Spiel* positing chess as not just a game, but as a tool for instruction in war and statecraft.[5] Over a century of conflict in Germany reinforced the need to train the princes of the empire how to wage war effectively, and chess variants proliferated throughout the period.[6]

In 1780, Johann Christian Ludwig Hellwig, Master of Pages for the city of Braunschweig, published the rules for a game intended to educate his young charges in the prosecution of war that adopted the basic configuration of chess, but evolved the game in a new direction. Instead of an abstract board, Hellwig's playfield consisted of squares representing different terrain types with their own rules. He maintained the traditional chess pieces but divided them among the contemporary military branches of infantry, cavalry, and artillery alongside several new pieces. In 1803, Hellwig published a revised version of his game that eliminated traditional chess pieces altogether in favor of contemporary military formations under the name *Das Kriegsspiel*, which literally translates as "The War Game."[7]

Unlike chess and similar abstract strategy games, *Das Kriegsspiel* attempted to simulate real battlefield conditions by taking into account terrain, the facing of units, the varying capabilities of military formations, and other elements of warfare. The game spread slowly, but steadily after its initial publication, and eventually new games based on the same principles appeared as the kriegspiel concept gained adherents across Europe. Its most important convert was one of its first, a minor Prussian noble and civil servant named Georg Leopold von Reiswitz.

The son of a military veteran who settled in Silesia after the War of Austrian Succession, Reiswitz was instructed in both chess and warfare as a youth, but was forced to forego military service after suffering a serious arm injury. He adored military tactics, however, and was introduced to Hellwig's game by his friend the prince of Anhalt-Pless. Hellwig's game was

---

[5] Translated into English, the title of the work is *The Game of Chess or Kings*.

[6] Jon Peterson, *Playing at the World: A History of Simulating Wars, People and Fantastic Adventures From Chess to Role-Playing Games* (San Diego, CA: Unreason Press, 2012), chap. 3.1.1, Kindle.

[7] Ibid, chap. 3.1.2.

so expensive that only members of the upper nobility could afford to own a set, but Reiswitz grew so enamored with it that when he left Silesia to attend university at Halle, he introduced his friends to the rules and worked with them to construct a variant from cheaper materials.

In 1809, Reiswitz read a critique of Hellwig-style kriegspiel decrying the use of chess-like squares, which inhibited the realism of military maneuvers within these games. Inspired, Reiswitz reunited with one of his university friends the next year to create a new kriegspiel that eliminated a grid in favor of a sand table upon which terrain could be accurately modeled in three dimensions. Reiswitz demonstrated this game to the sons of Prussian King Friedrich Wilhelm III in 1811, who were so taken with it that a demonstration for the king himself followed in 1812, by which time the sand table had been replaced by modular terrain blocks.[8]

Although Reiswitz was initially motivated to create his game due to the expense of the Hellwig game, after its adoption by the Prussian monarchy, his game became more elaborate and far costlier. Therefore, Reiswitz never attempted to prepare a version for commercial distribution and never finished codifying the rules. After the Napoleonic Wars, Reiswitz's son, a decorated Prussian artillery officer named Georg Heinrich Rudolf Johann, began further developing the ruleset with an eye toward increased battlefield realism. Completed in 1824, the younger Reiswitz's kriegspiel introduced two important elements that continued to define war games in subsequent centuries: the application of probabilities in resolving combat and the appointment of one player as a "referee" to develop scenarios and arbitrate rule disputes.[9] Reiswitz demonstrated his new game for General Karl Freiherr von Müffling, chief of the Prussian general staff, who adopted it as a training tool for the Prussian Army.

The popularity of kriegspiel waned in the middle of the nineteenth century as Europe experienced a prolonged period of relative peace, but after the accession of Wilhelm I and the appointment of his ambitious chancellor Otto von Bismarck, warfare became a central policy tool in their push to unify the German states under Prussian rule. Kriegspiel experienced a resurgence as the Prussian military conducted extensive war games while planning the campaigns against Austria and France that resulted in a unified German Empire.[10] The swift and overwhelming success of these campaigns led other nations in the developed world to model many aspects of their own

---

[8] Ibid, chap. 3.1.3.
[9] Ibid.
[10] Ibid, chap. 3.1.4.

militaries along the Prussian model and spurred adoption of kriegspiel on a large scale.

Battlefield war games remained a popular planning and training tool through the end of World War II, but afterwards experienced a decline. Just as the association of war games with the Prussian kriegsspiel drove their adoption in the aftermath of German reunification in the 1870s, the central villainous role of the Third Reich in World War II discredited the war game amid accusations that war gamers were also warmongers. Additionally, some thought the dawn of the nuclear age rendered these exercises obsolete, as any major conflict that devolved into the use of nuclear weapons would wreak devastation over a larger area than any war -gaming table could capture.[11]

Perhaps the leading cause in the decline of the traditional war game was the rise of OR in military planning during World War II. Unlike kriegspiel, which attempt to predict future success based on past decision-making, OR simulations rely on mathematical models to determine the most efficient strategies or tactics in a given situation. Rather than pitting two commanders against each other, OR games work from the premise that a commander encounters a fixed problem that must be overcome, is constrained in his decision-making by the rules of the game, and must run these decisions through a precise mathematical framework to determine success or failure.[12] The advent of the earliest computers only reinforced the military strategy community's fascination with OR simulations, as these mainframes were ideal for running the mathematical models crucial to these games. Although OR as a discipline evolved out of radar research conducted by the British in the late 1930s, the rise of the United States as the central hub for computer research after World War II positioned that country as the hotbed for this new style of war gaming in the 1950s.

***

The emergence of the United States as the primary war-gaming innovator of the late twentieth century is somewhat surprising, as the U.S. military had previously paid little attention to the discipline. Before World War II, several American authors dabbled in war games, but none of them exerted much influence outside the United States. The first such games were introduced to the U.S. military in 1867 and were based on existing German kriegspiel.[13]

---

[11] Ibid, chap. 3.1.7.
[12] Francis J. McHugh. *U.S. Navy Fundamentals of War Gaming* (New York: Skyhorse Publishing, 2013), chap. 2, Kindle.
[13] Ibid.

The earliest American treatise on war gaming, *American Kriegsspiel* by Major William Livermore first circulated in 1879 and divided war gaming into five disciplines with detailed rules for tactical encounters arbitrated by an umpire.[14]

In 1880, army officer Charles Totten published an influential American war gaming system called *Strategos*. Feeling that European kriegspiel were overly complicated and time-consuming for a U.S. military staffed by only a small core of professionals spread across a vast frontier, Totten fashioned his game into a series of escalating encounters designed to gradually acclimate players to the command of an entire army. Totten adhered closer to chess than many of his contemporaries, but in 1908 Captain Farrand Sayre published an influential tome called *Map Maneuvers and Tactical Rides* that replaced chess-like squares with maps. He also extolled the use of one-sided war games, in which the referee controls the opposing forces in addition to enforcing the rules, a forerunner of the OR approach that would gain popularity half a century later.[15]

Before World War II, the U.S. military primarily employed war gaming for training at staff colleges rather than for planning, and war games were especially valued by the U.S. Navy.[16] Indeed, the Navy proposed the first computerized war game in 1945, the Navy Electronic Warfare Simulator (NEWS). The need for an electronic system arose from the evolving nature of naval warfare during World War II, in which carrier battle groups were displacing battleships at the heart of naval engagements. Constantly updating game boards to account for the latest changes in tactics proved difficult, so when staff at the Naval War College learned of a combat information center trainer being developed at the University of California, they petitioned the Chief of Naval Operations in June 1945 to develop a training program around it.[17]

The Navy Electronics Laboratory was inaugurated in San Diego, California, in November 1945 to begin work on NEWS. Initially, the Navy envisioned an electromechanical system that would speed up the process of moving ships and adjudicating enemy contact but would not perform any calculations. The NEWS team soon realized that adding a computer to the system would allow it to process complicated damage calculations but would require an extended period of research and construction. Consequently, while NEWS was the first computer-assisted war game conceived, it was not

---

[14] Ibid. These disciplines were the tactical game, the grand tactical game, the strategic game, the fortification game, and the naval game. Livermore spent most of the book detailing the first two games and did not include rules for naval gaming at all.

[15] Ibid.

[16] Ibid.

[17] Ibid.

the first one to be completed and did not enter service at the Naval War College until 1957.[18]

The Navy also conducted the first OR war game in the United States at its Naval Ordnance Laboratory in 1942 under the auspices of Dr. Ellis Johnson, chief of the countermeasures section of the laboratory.[19] The other military branches subsequently formed their own OR groups, which fostered a high degree of cooperation between the military, academia, and industry in the research and application of new technology. The effectiveness of these programs in developing new strategies encouraged the military to continue OR activities after the war's conclusion via "think tanks" staffed by a mixture of civilian and military personnel.

Dr. Johnson established one of the earliest post-war think tanks in 1948, the Operations Research Office (ORO), which primarily served the U.S. Army and worked in conjunction with Johns Hopkins University.[20] From its inception, ORO desired to run simulations, though these were generally computer-assisted rather than fully automated programs due to the slow speed of analog and digital computers at the time. ORO began developing models for computer simulations as early as 1948, but complete programs did not emerge for several more years.

One of the earliest finished programs was a theater-level war game called *HUTSPIEL* first played in 1955 on an analog computer developed by the Goodyear Aircraft Corporation called the Goodyear Electronic Differential Analyzer (GEDA). Intended to study the use of tactical nuclear weapons and conventional air support in Western Europe in the event of a Soviet invasion, the game places one player in control of NATO forces in France, Belgium, and West Germany, while the other directs a Soviet force attempting to penetrate the region across a frontage of roughly 150 miles.[21] At the start of the game, each player allocates his forces across the sectors he controls and chooses targets for his planes and nukes, which can consist of enemy troops, airfields, supply depots, and transportation facilities. GEDA then determines the results. In the original version of the game, the simulation would continue without human intervention until a player paused to issue new orders, but in subsequent versions play was divided into turns of fixed time increments.

---

[18] Ibid.

[19] Alfred H. Hausrath, *Venture Simulation in War, Business, and Politics* (New York: McGraw-Hill, 1971), 39.

[20] Ibid, 64

[21] Joseph O. Harrison, Jr., "Computer-Aided Information Systems for Gaming," RAC-TP-133, September 1964, 19–20.

In 1957, ORO completed a second computer-assisted game to model air defense called *ZIGSPIEL*. In 1961, the Army terminated the ORO and replaced it with a new organization dubbed the Research Analysis Corporation (RAC) that continued the work of ORO in computer-assisted war gaming and military simulation. In the early 1960s, RAC promulgated two additional computer-assisted war games along the model of *HUTSPIEL* called *TACSPIEL* and *THEATERSPIEL*. *TACSPIEL* evolved out of an ORO game called *INDIGO I* first played in 1958 and models ground warfare at the division level and lower over a time frame of roughly eight hours. The state of the battlefield is conveyed by maps covered with pieces of various shapes, sizes, and colors representing individual units, while the computer calculates the results of individual encounters. *THEATERSPIEL* also focuses on ground combat, but as a theater-level simulation it incorporates air operations and logistics into its computer modeling to simulate a complete contained ground war.[22]

ORO also deployed what is likely the first military simulation designed to run unassisted on a digital computer. This game evolved out of work performed by Dr. George Gamow, a physicist at George Washington University and participant in the Manhattan Project at Los Alamos who began working with Monte Carlo simulations, so-called because they contain a considerable element of random chance as in a casino game, during his work on the atomic bomb. After he became a consultant for ORO in 1950, he began applying these same methods to warfare and developed a simple manual game called *Tin Soldier* in which two players assumed the role of commanders of opposing tank formations depicted on a contour map.[23]

A fellow Los Alamos alum at ORO, Richard Zimmerman, began working on a computerized version of *Tin Solider* around 1953, which became operational on an ERA 1101 scientific computer around 1954 as the *Maximum Complexity Computer Battle*.[24] The next year, ORO installed an ERA 1103 computer, and Zimmerman began adapting his test program into a complete simulation. This game became fully operational in 1959 as *CARMONETTE*, which stood for "Computerized Monte Carlo Simulation."

The first version of *CARMONETTE* pitted two opposing tank companies designated Red and Blue against each other in a simulated encounter replayed upwards of 50 times to develop a casualty distribution for both sides. By tweaking the characteristics of the tanks between runs and

---

[22] Hausrath, 1971, 172–187.

[23] Ibid, 64–67.

[24] Ibid, 67–68.

comparing results, military planners could optimize tank designs to minimize losses on the battlefield. The game became more complex as time went on, with *CARMONETTE II* adding infantry in 1960, *CARMONETTE III* incorporating helicopter support in 1966, and *CARMONETTE IV* adding communications and night vision into the mix in 1969. *CARMONETTE V* and *CARMONETTE VI* followed in 1970 and 1972, respectively. As the Army continued updating the game, it also moved to more powerful computers, first an IBM 7040 in 1965 and then a CDC 6400 in 1969.[25] While deemed a useful tool for military research, *CARMONETTE* demonstrated the limits of early computers, as it could only simulate reasonable approximations of combat conditions and needed to be supplemented by extensive field testing.

***

Like the Army and Navy, the U.S. Air Force embraced military simulations in the 1950s, which were initially run largely through its own think tank, the RAND Corporation. Originally established as Project RAND in December 1945, the organization – whose name is short for "Research & Development" – started as a collaboration between the Douglas Aircraft Company and the United States Army Air Forces (USAAF) and evolved out of advanced weapons research conducted during World War II. In 1948, Douglas ended its involvement with the project, and RAND spun out as its own corporation.[26]

From its inception, RAND's goal was to bring together researchers across disciplines to tackle problems related to national security. Perhaps the most famous policy to come out of this research was the mutual assured destruction approach to nuclear deterrence that defined the Cold War. It also played a critical role in the space race with the Soviet Union. To develop its many doctrines and strategies, the organization relied heavily on OR simulations.

RAND's earliest war game, a strategic-level manual game called SAW, was conducted in 1948. A less complex version called STRAW followed in 1953, and its successor, SWAP, became a regular part of the U.S. Air Force Academy curriculum after its introduction in 1959. War gaming became so integral to the RAND mission that in 1954 the organization constructed a war gaming facility called Project SIERRA dedicated to exploring Air Force

---

[25]"Carmonette Volume I: General Description," CAA-D-74-11, prepared for General Research Corporation, November 1974, 69–71.

[26]Ware, 2008, 5–9.

strategy in a limited war. Within a decade, over 50 war games had been conducted at the facility.[27]

RAND placed itself at the forefront of computer simulation as well, beginning with its pioneering Project Simulator in 1952. The most complex computer game developed by the Corporation in the 1950s was the Air Battle Model I (ABM), which simulated a nuclear war by modeling the deployment of missiles, bombers, and refueling tankers and assessing their effectiveness against ground targets. First tested in 1955 at the Air War College, the program was completed by a civilian contractor, Technical Operations Research, Inc., in 1957.[28]

RAND also focused on supply issues through its Logistic Simulation Laboratory, which developed a series of computer-assisted games beginning with *Laboratory Problem 1 (LP-1)* in 1957 that trained personnel in the management of aspects of the Air Force Supply system.[29] The lab also developed several manual logistics simulations, and the most celebrated of these, *MONOPOLOGS*, helped spur the expansion of simulation games out of the military and into the realms of business and academia.

First played in 1955, *MONOPLOGS* evolved out of a RAND study to model the entire Air Force supply system mathematically and placed the player in the role of a spare-parts inventory manager. While ostensibly tailored to the Air Force system, the game had general utility for any organization that needed to determine the best way to move goods quickly through a distribution network at low cost and attracted the attention of the American Management Association (AMA). The AMA invited members of the Logistic Simulation Laboratory to join a team it assembled in 1956 to create a computer game derived from the decision-making models present in military simulations to train top executives.[30]

Working alongside business consultants and IBM programmers, the RAND staff helped develop a business management simulation called *The Top Management Decision Simulation*. Programmed on an IBM 650 and delivered in May 1957, the game challenges five teams of three to five players to run single-product firms in direct competition with each other. The game plays out in turns representing a quarter of a year, during which each team

---

[27] Sharon Ghamari-Tabrizi, "U.S. Wargaming Grows Up: A Short History of the Diffusion of Wargaming in the Armed Forces and Industry in the Postwar Period up to 1964," StrategyWorld.com, accessed May 27, 2019, https://www.strategypage.com/articles/default.asp?target=wgappen.htm.

[28] Ibid.

[29] R. M. Rauner, "Laboratory Evaluation of Supply and Procurement Policies: The First Experiment of the Logistics Systems Laboratory," *R-323*, July 1958, 1–5.

[30] Ghamari-Tabrizi, "U.S. Wargaming Grows Up."

decides how much to spend on marketing and R&D, determines a rate of production for its product, chooses whether or not to increase manufacturing capacity, and considers whether or not to purchase marketing research on competitors. The computer then calculates the market share of each company at the end of the quarter based on these decisions.[31]

The AMA incorporated a version of *The Top Management Decision Simulation* into its Management Development Seminar and its Executive Decision Making Program, and by March 1958 it had already been played by 350 corporate executives and 50 scientists and business school professors.[32] The positive reception of the AMA game led to the adoption of similar games by both corporations and university business schools. The first known business simulation used in a university classroom was the *Top Management Decision Game* created at the University of Washington in 1957, which was a direct adaptation of the AMA game. UCLA also adapted the game as the *UCLA Executive Decision Game No. 2* and added the wrinkle of allowing companies to borrow money.[33] This game was further revised as the *UCLA Executive Game No. 3*, in which companies could sell up to three different products.[34]

Business games reached a new level of complexity in 1958 with the development of *The Management Game* by Kalman Cohen, Richard Cyert, and William Dill at the Carnegie Institute of Technology in Pittsburgh – renamed Carnegie Mellon University in 1967 after a merger with the Mellon Institute of Industrial Research. Still used by the university to this day after a major overhaul in 1986, the game runs over the course of two semesters as the player takes control of one of three competing detergent companies and makes as many as 100-300 decisions a month over a 3-year period regarding everything from R&D to marketing. As the complexity and utility of computer business simulations continued to increase, they were widely adopted across both the business and academic worlds.[35] By 1961, over 100 business games had been created, and over 30,000 executives had played them.[36]

---

[31] Kalman J. Cohen and Eric Rhenman, "The Role of Management Games in Education and Research," *Management Science* 7, no. 2 (1961): 135–136.

[32] Ghamari-Tabrizi, "U.S. Wargaming Grows Up."

[33] As the title implies, this game obsoleted a short-lived *UCLA Executive Decision Game No. 1*.

[34] Hugh J. Watson, *Computer Simulation in Business* (New York: John Wiley & Sons, 1981), 238.

[35] "Management Game: More Difficult than Chess, and More Fun to Watch," Carnegie Mellon University, 2007, http://cmu.edu/corporate/news/2007/features/mgmt game.shtml.

[36] A.J. Faria and Ray Nulsen, "Business Simulation Games: Current Usage Levels, A Ten Year Update," *Developments in Business Simulation & Experiential Exercises* 23 (1996): 22.

Like the AI research projects undertaken by select universities and corporations, the simulations developed by the military-industrial complex were not intended as entertainment programs and were played only by small groups of students, military recruits, and executives. Furthermore, many of these programs were limited merely to calculating the results of player action and required manual administering and/or scoring alongside additional play aides such as maps or markers. As such, these programs exerted virtually no impact on the subsequent expansion of computer gaming to the world at large. At the same time these simulations were being conducted, however, computer games were slowly being introduced to the general public through a variety of fairs, trade shows, and open houses.

3

The Priesthood at Play

In the 1940s, the electronic digital computer was a new, largely unproven machine developed in response to specific needs like the code-breaking requirements of Bletchley Park or the ballistics calculations required by the Aberdeen Proving Grounds. Once these early computers proved their worth, projects like the Manchester Mark 1 and the EDVAC implemented a stored-program capability allowing digital computers to become useful for a variety of scientific and business tasks. In the early 1950s, several for-profit corporations built on this work by offering mass-produced computers to businesses, universities, and government organizations around the world.

ENIAC creators Eckert and Mauchly established the first commercial computer company in 1946 and sold it to office equipment giant Remington Rand in 1950 after several years of financial difficulty. Early the next year, the company released its first computer, the UNIVAC I.[1] This computer delivered one of the more effective demonstrations of the coming revolution in 1952 when it successfully predicted Dwight Eisenhower's landslide victory over Adlai Stevenson in the U.S. presidential election despite traditional polling that called for a close race. These results were aired on national television by CBS and turned UNIVAC into a household name.[2]

For the general public, a computer was a device straight out of science fiction, and to some, it was terrifying. Science fiction stories from Kurt Vonnegut's *Player Piano* (1952) to Harlan Ellison's *I Have No Mouth and I Must Scream* (1967) depicted dystopian futures in which self-aware computers made human

---

[1] Campbell-Kelly et al., 2014, 109-110. The UNIVAC I was the first commercially available computer in the United States but was predated by the Ferranti Mark 1 in Britain by about a month. Technically, Eckert and Mauchly built the first commercially sold computer, BINAC, in 1949, but it was a one-off design.

[2] Ceruzzi, 2003, Chap. 1.

endeavor obsolete, or worse, wiped out humanity in a fiery apocalypse. Therefore, companies like Remington Rand faced a daunting task in preparing society to accept these contraptions that would soon catapult humanity into the Information Age. One way to help the public feel more comfortable around computers was to allow people to see, touch, or interact with the new machines. To provide these opportunities, computer companies began giving demonstrations of their products at trade shows, exhibitions, and fairs.

A 1950s-era computer was not an exciting machine to watch in action, for it carried out tasks through batch processing, in which a stack of punched cards or a reel of tape would load a program and/or some data into memory, execute the requested operations, and spit out a result via a printer or teletype. Aside from a few blinking lights or whirring reels of tape, there were no indications that the computer was actually doing anything. Consequently, when a computer was demonstrated to the general public, it was usually either custom-built or specially programmed to perform some feat of logic, display something visually interesting, or play a game against a human opponent.

***

The first known public exhibition of a game-playing electronic computer occurred in 1950. The instigator was Josef Kates, an Austrian Jew who fled the annexation of Austria into Germany in 1938 and spent the latter part of World War II earning mathematics and physics degrees at the University of Toronto while working on radar for the Rogers Vacuum Tube Company. Kates had recently invented a new type of vacuum tube called the additron that was smaller and less power hungry than the tubes currently in use. Rogers was eager to sell the device, but the company had trouble patenting it in the United States and was unable to bring it to market until 1955, by which time it was already obsolete. In the meantime, Rogers wanted to show off the invention and asked Kates to build a custom machine incorporating additron tubes for the 1950 Canadian National Exhibition. Kates and his colleagues had already programmed a prototype computer at the University of Toronto called UTEC to play a few games, so he decided that to hold the interest of the general public, he should build a computer that could play a game of tic-tac-toe.[3]

---

[3] Matt Blitz, "Bertie the Brain Still Lives: The Story of the World's First Arcade Game," Popular Mechanics, November 2, 2016, https://www.popularmechanics.com/technology/gadgets/a23660/bertie-the-brain.

Dubbed "Bertie the Brain: The Electronic Wonder" by Rogers, Kates's four-meter-tall creation was exhibited from August 25 to September 9, 1950, alongside the latest Rogers radio and television sets. A player entered his move at a large panel in front of the computer with buttons in the configuration of a tic-tac-toe board, and the moves were displayed on a lighted panel on the computer itself. Kates programmed the machine to be unbeatable, but he also included variable difficulty levels and would adjust them for children, so they had a chance to win. While merely intended as a curiosity, the computer game proved more popular than anyone at Rogers had anticipated, and a constant throng of people flocked around Bertie throughout the show. Nevertheless, Bertie largely avoided attracting wider coverage save for one unpublished *Life Magazine* photo spread chronicling comedian Danny Kaye's quest to defeat the computer – finally accomplished only after Kates had greatly adjusted the difficulty downward.[4] The next year, a second demo computer garnered international attention.

As the 1950s began, Great Britain was in sorry shape. The empire that once covered 25% of the globe was being dismantled, the great city of London was largely in ruins, and food was still being rationed as it had been throughout World War II. In this atmosphere of hardship and uncertainty, the British government decided to encourage its people to look not at the state of their lives at present, but at how their lives could only improve in the future. A Festival of Britain was organized for 1951, both to commemorate the centenary of the famous Great Exhibition and to demonstrate how British contributions to the arts, science, and technology were helping to build a better world out of the ashes of the recent war. Individual displays were organized all over the country, but the centerpiece of the festival was the South Bank Exhibition in the Waterloo District of London, where British contributions to science, technology, and industrial design were displayed.

For Ferranti, just putting the finishing touches on its Mark 1 computer, the festival represented an important advertising and public relations event, so the firm signed on to display at South Bank. Soon after pledging its support, the company realized it could not build a computer in time for display at the exhibition. Enter John Bennett, an Australian electrical engineer who helped build the EDSAC computer at Cambridge University. Bennett proposed constructing a custom machine that would play the mathematical game of Nim against a human player and incorporate a special display to illustrate

---

[4] Ibid.

how the computer operated as a means of introducing basic algorithms and programming principles.[5]

Built by engineer Raymond Stuart-Williams between December 1950 and April 1951, Bennett's computer, designated Nimrod, premiered at the festival on May 4, 1951.[6] It remained on display until the exhibition closed in October, after which it was displayed for three more weeks at the Berlin Industrial Show before being dismantled. Like Bertie, Nimrod consisted of a computer with a light bulb display with a panel of buttons situated in front of it on which the player would enter his moves. The lights not only displayed the state of the game but also blinked in patterns that corresponded to the operations being performed by the computer to demonstrate how the program worked.[7]

Nimrod was not intended for entertainment: the goal was to introduce the public to basic programming principles. Indeed, the official guidebook for the machine – available to festival goers for one shilling and sixpence – betrayed Ferranti's embarrassment at presenting a game in the first place, quick as it was to point out that creating a machine to play games is not just a waste of time, but rather illustrates how a computer can approach complex problems such as modeling world economies. The guidebook also described in detail how the computer approached playing a game of Nim and offered advice on how to defeat it in the hopes that members of the public would take the opportunity to educate themselves on the ins and outs of computer programming.[8]

Few people took any interest in how Nimrod worked, but throngs of people did stop to gawk at the computer, and the press covered it extensively in Britain and Germany.[9] As the decade progressed, Nim variants emerged as standard demonstration programs for computer projects, appearing on the first Norwegian computer, NUSSE (1954),[10] the early Swedish computer SMIL (1956),[11] the first Australian computer, SILLIAC (1956),[12] the Polish

---

[5]John M. Bennett, "Early Computer Days in Britain and Australia: Some Autobiographical Snippets," *Annals of the History of Computing* 12, no. 4 (1990): 281–285.

[6]R. Stuart-Williams, "Nimrod: A Small Automatic Computer," *Electronic Engineering* 23, no. 283 (1951): 344.

[7]Bennett, 1990, 281–285.

[8]*Faster Than Thought: The Ferranti Nimrod Digital Computer* (Hollinwood: Ferranti, 1951).

[9]Tirstan Donovan, *Replay: The History of Video Games* (Lewes: Yellow Ant, 2010), kindle, chap. 1.

[10]Lars Konzack, "Scandinavia," in *Video Games around the World*, ed. Mark J.P. Wolf (Cambridge, MA: The MIT Press, 2015), iTunes.

[11]Ibid.

[12]Thomas H. Apperley and Daniel Golding, "Australia," in *Video Games around the World*, ed. Mark J.P. Wolf (Cambridge, MA: The MIT Press, 2015), iTunes.

Odra 1003 computer (1962),[13] the custom-built Dutch computer Nimbi (1963),[14] and the French computer Antinéa (1963).[15] This fascination with Nim as a demonstration program predated digital computers and was most likely inspired by an analog computer called the Nimatron developed by Westinghouse for the 1940 World's Fair in New York City.[16]

***

By 1955, computers were well on their way in becoming fixtures at government agencies, defense contractors, academic institutions, and large corporations, but their function remained limited to a small number of activities revolving around data processing and scientific calculation through batch processing. For companies like IBM and Remington Rand that had produced electromechanical tabulating equipment for decades, this was a logical extension of their preexisting business, and there was little impetus for them to discover novel applications. The enduring image of this period, as codified in the seminal 1974 work *Computer Lib* by Ted Nelson, is of a "priesthood" (the operators) that interceded between a fickle god (the computer) and those wretched souls beseeching it to manifest its divine powers.[17]

In some circles, however, there was a belief that computers could move beyond data processing and be used to control complex systems. This would require a completely new paradigm in computer design based around interacting with the computer in real time – i.e., giving the computer a command and receiving feedback nearly instantaneously. The quest for real-time computing not only expanded the capabilities of the computer, but also led to important technological breakthroughs instrumental in lowering the cost of computing and opening computer access to a greater swath of the population. Therefore, the development of real-time computers served as the crucial final step in transforming the computer into a device capable of delivering credible interactive entertainment.

The path to the first real-time computer began with a project that was never supposed to incorporate digital computing in the first place. In 1943, the U.S. Bureau of Aeronautics began to explore creating a universal flight

---

[13] Bartłomiej Kluska and Mariusz Rozwadowski, *Bajty Polskie* (Łódź: Samizdat Orka, 2011), 6. While the Odra 1003 was commercially available, the Nim game, called Marienbad, was not publicly released.

[14] Christelvan Grinsven and Joost Raessens, "The Netherlands," in *Video Games around the World*, ed. Mark J.P. Wolf (Cambridge, MA: The MIT Press, 2015), iTunes.

[15] Alexis Blanchet, "France," in *Video Games around the World*, ed. Mark J.P. Wolf (Cambridge, MA: The MIT Press, 2015), iTunes.

[16] Donovan, 2010, chap. 1.

[17] Theodore H. Nelson, *Computer Lib/Dream Machines* (Chicago, IL: Hugo's Book Service, 1974), 46.

simulator for military training. While flight simulators had been in wide-spread use since Edwin Link introduced a system based around pneumatic bellows and valves called the Link Trainer in 1929, these trainers could only simulate a single airplane model and could not be tailored to specific flight conditions. The Bureau envisioned using an analog computer to simulate the handling characteristics of any extant aircraft to provide a significant cost savings over existing training systems and turned to MIT to transform this vision into reality.[18]

At the time, MIT was already the foremost center in the United States for developing control systems thanks to the establishment of the Servomechanisms Laboratory in 1941, which worked closely with the military to develop electromechanical equipment for fire control, bomb sights, aircraft stabilizers, and similar projects. The Bureau of Aeronautics established Project Whirlwind within the Servomechanisms Laboratory in 1944 to create its flight trainer.[19] Leadership of the Whirlwind project fell to an assistant director of the Servomechanisms Laboratory named Jay Forrester, an engineering genius who had been building electrical systems since constructing a 12-volt electrical system out of old car parts as a teenager to provide his family's ranch with electricity After graduating from the University of Nebraska, Forrester came to MIT as a graduate student in 1939 and joined the Servomechanisms Laboratory at its inception.[20] By 1944, Forrester was getting restless and considering establishing his own company, so he was given his choice of projects to oversee to prevent his defection. Forrester chose Whirlwind.[21]

In early 1945, Forrester drew up the specifications for a trainer consisting of a mock cockpit connected to an analog computer that would control a hydraulic transmission system to provide feedback to the cockpit. As work on Whirlwind began, the mechanical elements of the design came together quickly, but the computing element remained out of reach. To create an accurate simulator, Forrester required a computer that updated dozens of variables constantly and reacted to user input instantaneously. Bush's Differential Analyzer, perhaps the most powerful analog computer of the time, was far too slow to handle these tasks, and Forrester's team could not figure out how to produce a more powerful machine solely through analog components.[22]

[18] Campbell-Kelly et al., 2014, 143–144.

[19] Ibid, 144.

[20] Peter Dizikes, "The Many Careers of Jay Forrester," *MIT Technology Review*, June 23, 2015, https://www.technologyreview.com/s/538561/the-many-careers-of-jay-forrester.

[21] Jay Forrester, interview by Renee Garrelick, December 6, 1994, Concord Free Public Library, https://concordlibrary.org/special-collections/oral-history/Forrester.

[22] Campbell-Kelly et al., 2014, 144–145.

In summer 1945, the flight simulator project gained a new lease on life when a fellow MIT graduate student named Perry Crawford who had written a master's thesis in 1942 on using a digital device as a control system alerted Forrester to the breakthroughs being made in digital computing at the University of Pennsylvania. In October, Forrester and Crawford attended a Conference on Advanced Computational Techniques hosted by MIT and learned about the ENIAC and EDVAC. By early 1946, Forrester was convinced that the only way forward for Project Whirlwind was the construction of a digital computer that could operate in real time.[23]

The shift from an analog computer to a digital computer for the Whirlwind project created an incredible technical challenge. In a period when the most advanced computers under development were struggling to achieve 10,000 operations a second, Whirlwind would require the capability of performing closer to 100,000 operations per second for seamless real-time operation. Furthermore, the first stored-program computers were still 3 years away, so Forrester's team also faced the prospect of integrating cutting-edge memory technologies that were still under development. By 1946, the size of the Whirlwind team had grown to over a 100 staff members spread across ten groups each concentrating on an aspect of the system to meet these challenges. All other aspects of the flight simulator were placed on hold as the group focused its attention on creating a working real-time computer.[24]

By 1949, Forrester's team had succeeded in designing an architecture fast enough to support real-time operation, but the computer could not operate reliably for extended periods. With costs escalating and no end to development in sight, continued funding for the project was placed in jeopardy. It was saved on August 29, 1949, when the Soviet Union detonated its first atomic bomb. With the threat of a nuclear attack on the United States suddenly a very real prospect, the military required a new early warning system to blanket the country, and such a system required a real-time computer at its heart that could decipher radar signals, track moving objects, and continuously update a display so that operators could identify threats and scramble aircraft to intercept long-range Soviet bombers. In 1951, Whirlwind moved to a new home at the Lincoln Laboratory – a joint MIT–U.S. Air Force facility – and formed the heart of Project SAGE, an ambitious attempt to create such a command and control computer system.[25]

---

[23] Ibid, 145–146.
[24] Ibid, 146.
[25] Ibid, 148–150.

By April 1951, the Whirlwind I computer was operational, but rarely worked properly due to faulty memory technology. The only memory theoretically fast enough to support real-time operation was CRT memory, but tube technology failed at regular intervals and was therefore unsuitable for incorporation into a real-time computer. Forrester and his team developed a new form of memory based around magnetic cores made of ferrite, a material that can be magnetized or demagnetized by passing a large enough electric current through it.[26] The Whirlwind's core memory array came online in August 1953, finally providing a fast and reliable enough memory for a viable real-time computer. Within 5 years, core memory would replace all other forms of memory in mainframe computers.[27]

With Whirlwind I finally operating effectively, the Lincoln Laboratory turned its attention to transforming the computer into a command-and-control system suitable for installation in the U.S. Air Force's air defense system. This undertaking was beyond the scope of the lab because it would require fabrication of multiple components on a large scale. Lincoln Labs evaluated three companies for this task, defense contractor Raytheon, Remington Rand, and IBM. At the time, Remington Rand was still the powerhouse in the new commercial computer business, while IBM was only just preparing to bring its first products to market. Nonetheless, Forrester and his team were impressed with IBM's manufacturing facilities, service force, integration, and experience deploying electronic products in the field and chose the new kid on the block over its more established competitor to build a command and control system that would become known as the Semi-Automatic Ground Environment, or SAGE.[28]

As the first deployed real-time computer system, SAGE inaugurated a number of firsts in commercial computing such as the ability to generate text and vector graphics on a display screen, the ability to directly enter commands via a typewriter-style keyboard, and the ability to select or draw items directly on the display using a light pen, a technology developed specifically for Whirlwind in 1955. To remain in constant contact with other segments of the air defense system, the computer was also the first outfitted with a new technology called a modem developed by Bell Labs in 1956 that allowed

---

[26] In a core memory array, two wires are threaded through the center of each core, and only when currents are run through both wires in the same direction will the magnetization change, allowing it to serve as a switching unit. A third wire is threaded through all the cores to allow any portion of the memory to be read at any time.

[27] Ibid, 150.

[28] Ceruzzi, 2003, chap. 2.

data to be transmitted over a telephone line. The expertise IBM developed through building and deploying the SAGE computers proved definitive in vaulting the company past early market leader Remington Rand and its UNIVAC machines to establish a total dominance of the computer industry unchallenged for 30 years.

***

The emergence of real-time computing represented a significant milestone in computer design, and institutions working on such machines turned to demonstration programs to illustrate all the new features a real-time environment offered. Oliver Aberth created the first real-time demo on the Whirlwind I in February 1951, a simple bouncing ball represented by a single dot that would appear at the top of the computer's CRT screen, fall to the bottom of the display, and then bounce accompanied by a sound from the computer's speaker.[29] While exceedingly simple, the effect proved stunning in a time when no other computer could update a CRT display in real time. Later that year, Adams and Gilmore modified the program so that a user could turn a knob to adjust the frequency of the bounces and added a hole at the bottom through which the ball could disappear. Afterwards, the members of the lab treated this interactive demo as a game by challenging themselves to set the frequency perfectly to hit the small hole in the floor.[30] It did not take a great leap to transform a ball and some rudimentary physics calculations into a more complex interactive demonstration, which is exactly what a group of programmers did at the University of Michigan's Willow Run research facility.

Established by the Ford Motor Company in 1941, Willow Run initially built aircraft components before producing roughly half of the B-24 Liberator bombers that flew in World War II. After the war, an airfield within the complex passed to civilian control, and the University of Michigan established a research facility there. This lab undertook defense projects ranging from air traffic control systems to the BOMARC (Boeing-Michigan Air Research Center) guided missile. Between 1951 and 1953, a team of engineers led by John DeTurk built two computers at Willow Run to aid in this research, the Michigan Digital Automatic Computer (MIDAC) and the Michigan Digital

---

[29] "Bi-Weekly Report, Project 6673, February 2, 1951," Memorandum M-2084, prepared by the Electronic Computer Division of the Servomechanisms Laboratory of the Massachusetts Institute of Technology, February 2, 1951, 5.

[30] Hurst, Jan, Michael Mahoney, Norman Taylor, Douglas Ross, and Robert Fano, "Retrospectives: The Early Years in Computer Graphics at MIT, Lincoln Lab and Harvard," in *ACM SIGGRAPH 89 Panel Proceedings Boston, July 31–August 4 1989* (New York: ACM, 1989), 21. Note that Taylor gives the year as 1949 in this talk, but other sources show that his dates are off.

Special Automatic Computer (MIDSAC). Both were based on the design of the SEAC computer, an EDVAC derivative built by the National Bureau of Standards in 1950.[31] While MIDAC was unremarkable compared to its contemporaries, MIDSAC was intended as a control system and therefore processed information in real time.[32]

In early 1954, the Willow Run staff decided to stage a public demonstration of its computers that June for members of the Association of Computing Machinery, who would be meeting in nearby Detroit. In order to hold the interest of their audience, the engineers programmed both computers to play games. MIDAC was programmed to play tic-tac-toe and craps against a human opponent entering commands via a teletype, while MIDSAC hosted a pool game incorporating a CRT monitor that updated the state of the table in real time.[33]

MIDSAC pool was initially programmed by Ted Lewis and later refined by William Brown, two avid pool players who felt the game was perfect for highlighting the intended purpose of MIDSAC since it would require updating the positions of 16 objects rapidly enough to give the illusion of seamless movement. Unlike Whirlwind, MIDSAC did not incorporate a display, but it did possess a digital-to-analog converter, so attaching a CRT to the computer proved a relatively simple exercise. A 13-inch point-plotting display was duly sourced, and an engineer working on mapping projects in another department cobbled together a sine-wave generator that could draw circles on the display to represent the balls. Brown and Lewis then wrote a program that accurately modeled the physics of the game so that the balls realistically bounced off each other and the sides of the table. The entire process took about 6 months.[34]

The resulting program displayed 16 balls, represented by circles, and a cue stick, represented by a line, on the CRT. While the positions of the pockets were calculated by the game, the table itself could not be displayed electronically and was drawn on the CRT with a grease pencil. Controls consisted of one joystick to move the cue stick around the screen, one joystick to rotate

[31] Norman R. Scott, *Computing at the University of Michigan: The Early Years Through the 1960s* (Ann Arbor: University of Michigan, 2008), 4–7.

[32] Although MIDSAC was slower than Whirlwind, it incorporated a hybrid serial-parallel design that made it much faster than many of its contemporaries. The computer never worked well because it incorporated unreliable tube memory rather than the core memory that helped make Whirlwind a success, and it was ultimately dismantled.

[33] Gibbons, Roy, "Meet Midac and Midsac: Dice, Pool Shooting Fools," *Chicago Tribune*, June 27, 1954.

[34] William G. Brown, Deposition, Magnavox Co. v. Bally Manufacturing Corp., No. 74-1030 (N.D. Ill), June 25, 1976, 40–100.

the angle of the stick, and a button to shoot. Two additional buttons were required to rack the balls to begin the game and make the cue ball reappear in the event of a scratch. At the start of the game, one player would perform the break, which happened in slow motion due to the number of objects moving on the screen at once, and then play proceeded at regular speed until all the balls were knocked into the holes, which would cause them to disappear from the screen. There was no way to identify individual balls due to the primitive graphics save for the cue ball, which was rendered brighter than the rest.[35]

The MIDSAC pool game was demonstrated to a group of roughly 25–50 people, who were given a rundown of the basic operation of the computer and the controls for the game and then invited to play it themselves. The response to the program was enthusiastic, but the system was dismantled soon after. The only point of the game was to demonstrate how the computer could track multiple objects at the same time, and once it had served that purpose, it was no longer needed. Nevertheless, MIDSAC pool is the first known publicly demonstrated computer game to incorporate graphics that updated in real time.

***

Like the AI research programs and military simulations, the demonstration programs of the 1950s were not intended primarily to entertain: they were developed to introduce the general public to the capabilities of modern computing technology through an interactive experience designed to hold their interest. The first known computer game to break with that convention and be presented largely with pure entertainment in mind was a demonstration program that historians have retroactively labeled as *Tennis for Two* developed by Willy Higinbotham.

The son of a Presbyterian minister, William Alfred Higinbotham was born in Bridgeport, Connecticut, in 1910 and grew up in western New York. His interest in electronics blossomed at the age of 14 after he began building and modifying his own radios to pick up early commercial stations. Higinbotham studied physics at Williams College in Massachusetts and entered the graduate program at Cornell University. Although forced to abandon doctoral studies during the Great Depression for financial reasons, in 1940 he nevertheless parlayed his experience working with electronics and CRT displays into a posting at the MIT Radiation Laboratory, where

---

[35] Ibid.

scientists were engaged in groundbreaking work on the new technology of radar.[36] From there, it was off to Los Alamos in 1943 to head the electronics division and develop the timing circuits necessary to properly detonate an atomic bomb.[37] Like so many involved with the Manhattan Project, the specter of nuclear annihilation haunted Higinbotham to the end of his days. A founding member of the Federation of American Scientists, an organization committed to the peaceful spread of nuclear energy and the non-proliferation of nuclear weapons, Higinbotham dedicated the rest of his life to the eradication of the powerful bombs and warheads he helped make possible.[38]

But Willy Higinbotham also understood there is more to life than work. He called square dances, played the accordion, and entertained the public at the head of a Dixieland band called the Isotope Stompers. In the kitchen, he exhibited creative flair as he mixed and matched ingredients with wild abandon so his family never knew what he might serve them next. He also understood how to make technology fun: when cutting grass astride his power mower, he would often pull two wagons behind him so his three children could ride along.[39] As a man who knew how to effortlessly blend serious work and fun in his own life, who recognized that any practical technology could provide entertainment under the right circumstances, and who was fond of surprising people in creative ways, Higinbotham possessed the perfect temperament to create the world's first true computer entertainment product.

After World War II, Higinbotham spent nearly two years in Washington, DC, promoting nuclear non-proliferation on behalf of the American Federation of Scientists before taking employment at the newly established Brookhaven National Laboratory in 1947, which was dedicated to discovering peaceful uses for atomic energy. Every fall, Brookhaven held a series of three open houses – one each for high school students, college students, and the general public – to showcase the work being done at the facility. Visitors were bused around the buildings of the Brookhaven campus to view such fascinating sites as the high-energy proton-accelerator and the nuclear research reactor before winding up in the gymnasium to view a series of static displays discussing the work of each department at the lab. After several years of this routine, Higinbotham sensed that these displays were not captivating their audience and thought perhaps he could liven up the experience and

[36] William Higinbotham, testimony, Magnavox Co. v. Activision, Inc., No. 82-5270 (N.D. Cal), August 12, 1985, 89–90.

[37] Robert P. Goldman, "Wonderful Willie from Brookhaven," *Parade*, May 18, 1958, 15–18.

[38] Higinbotham, 1985, 89–90.

[39] Goldman, 1958, 15–18.

demonstrate the practical relevance of Brookhaven's technology in everyday life by allowing visitors to play some sort of game.[40]

Brookhaven possessed an electronic analog computer called the Donner Model 30. The manual for the computer described how it could be hooked up to an oscilloscope and employ resistors, capacitors, and relays to display curves useful for modeling a missile trajectory or a bouncing ball, complete with an accurate simulation of gravity and wind resistance. The bouncing ball reminded Higinbotham of tennis, so he sketched out a system to interface an oscilloscope with the computer and then gave the diagram to technician Robert Dvorak to implement. Laying out the initial design only took Higinbotham a couple of hours, after which he spent a couple of days putting together a final specification based on the components available in the lab. Dvorak then built the system over three weeks and spent a day or two debugging it with Higinbotham. The game was largely driven by the vacuum tubes and relays that had defined electronics for decades, but to render graphics on the oscilloscope, which required rapidly switching between several different elements, Higinbotham and Dvorak incorporated transistors, which were just beginning to transform the electronics industry.[41]

The graphics of *Tennis for Two* consisted of a side-view image of a tennis court – rendered as a long horizontal line to represent the court itself and a small vertical line to represent the net – and a ball represented by a trajectory arc displayed on the oscilloscope. Each player used a controller consisting of a knob and a button. To start a volley, one player would use the knob to select an angle to hit the ball and then press the button. At that point, the ball could hit the net, hit the other side of the court, or sail out of bounds. Once the ball made it over the net, the other player could either hit the ball on the fly or the bounce by selecting his own angle and pressing the button to return it.[42] Like MIDSAC pool, the entire game played out in real time.[43]

Introduced during Brookhaven's visitor days in October 1958, *Tennis for Two* proved a great success, with long lines of eager players forming to play the game. Based on this positive reception, Higinbotham brought the game back in 1959 on a larger monitor and developed variants that simulated the low gravity of the Moon and the high-gravity environment of Jupiter. After the second round of visitor days, the game was dismantled so its components

---

[40] William A. Higinbotham, "The Brookhaven TV-Tennis Game" (unpublished notes, c. 1983), 1–2.

[41] Ibid.

[42] Originally, the velocity of the ball could be chosen by the player as well, but Higinbotham decided that three controls would make the game too complicated and therefore left the velocity fixed.

[43] Ibid.

could be put to other uses. Higinbotham never patented the device because he felt that he was just adapting the bouncing ball program already discussed in the manual and had created no real breakthrough. While he appears to have been proud of creating the game, he stated in his own notes that he considered it a "minor achievement" at best and wanted to be remembered as a scientist who fought the spread of nuclear weapons rather than as the inventor of a computer game.[44]

Higinbotham's attitude toward his own invention was typical of the scientists, engineers, and programmers who built and operated the first generation of computers, few of whom could discern any long-term value in a computer dedicated solely to entertainment. This attitude was perfectly understandable under the circumstances, for in the 1950s a computer represented a multi-million-dollar investment, and there was simply no way to justify wasting computer time on frivolous pursuits or to create a viable entertainment platform for use by the general public. While serious academics saw no benefit to creating games, their students and research assistants often did. When a group of these budding young computer enthusiasts at MIT were finally able to secure direct access to the computers at their university in the late 1950s, they created the first widespread and highly influential computer game: *Spacewar!*

---

[44]Ibid.

4

One, Two, Three, Four
I Declare a Space War

On December 23, 1947, electrical engineer John Bardeen and physicist Walter Brattain demonstrated their newly invented solid-state amplification and switching device, the transistor, to their superiors at Bell Labs. Since the development of the first triodes, invented by Lee De Forest in 1906 but not perfected and put to general use until around 1912, electrical amplification had been achieved through use of the vacuum tube, in which a current is passed through a vacuum-sealed glass cylinder containing a coil from a negatively charged anode to a positively charged cathode.[1] In 1918, British physicists William Eccles and F.W. Jordan created the first electronic flip-flop using vacuum tube triodes, which could transmit information in the binary language of 1's and 0's as the current in individual tubes switched on and off. In 1932, another British physicist named Charles Wynn-Williams developed an electronic counter using vacuum tubes. Similar switching and counting devices carried instructions and facilitated mathematical calculations for computers from Colossus to Whirlwind.

While this method produced perfectly functional computers, vacuum tubes came with a host of problems. First and foremost, they generated a lot of heat, which led to increased power consumption and a tendency to burn out over long periods of use. They could also not be miniaturized passed a

---

[1] The first vacuum tube diode was developed by John Fleming in 1904 for use as a rectifier to boost a wireless signal for transatlantic communication. Lee De Forest was the first person to add a grid to a tube to create a triode that could serve as an amplifier, but he believed that a small amount of gas needed to be present in the tube, which hindered its function. Harold Arnold at AT&T corrected this flaw in 1912 so the company could use De Forest's invention to amplify signals for long-distance telephone calls.

certain point and had to be spaced relatively far apart from each other due to their thermal output, so a computer built with tubes would always be large and bulky, and the more powerful the computer, the larger and bulkier it would be. The only way to create powerful computers of reasonable size, power consumption, and durability would be to manipulate the flow of electrons at the subatomic level instead.

As early as the 1820s, scientists had observed that certain elements like germanium acted as conductors in some situations and insulators in others, but they did not possess the requisite knowledge of atomic structure to explain the behavior of these so-called "semiconductors." By the 1930s, the related fields of quantum mechanics and solid-state physics had advanced sufficiently to tackle the problem. At Bell Labs, a team led by physicist William Shockley began studying semiconductors in 1936 as part of an effort to replace the relays and vacuum tubes employed in AT&T's nationwide telephone switching system, but World War II interrupted their research. After the war, Shockley's team returned to work, leading to Bardeen and Brattain's breakthrough in 1947.[2]

Years of refinement followed before the germanium transistor could be mass produced reliably, but by the early 1950s it had reached an appropriate level of sophistication to begin replacing vacuum tubes in electronic products. Incorporating transistors into highly sensitive defense projects like guided missiles proved difficult, however, due to the low melting point and considerable electron leakage of germanium. A different element, silicon, promised both a better semiconducting capability and a higher temperature tolerance, but initially proved impossible to dope with the necessary impurities to transform it into a transistor. The solution to this problem came not from Bell Labs, but from a relative newcomer to the electronics field called Texas Instruments (TI).

Established by Clarence Karcher and Eugene McDermott in 1930 in New Jersey before moving to Dallas four years later, the company that morphed into TI originated as an oil exploration company called Geophysical Services, Inc. (GSI). After a failed attempt to expand into oil production, the founders sold the company to Stanolind Oil and Gas, but McDermott joined with R&D head J. Erik Jonsson, field exploration head Cecil Green, and crew chief H. Bates Peacock to purchase the oil exploration business on December 6, 1941, the day before the United States was dragged into

---

[2] Jeffrey Young, *Forbes Greatest Technology Stories: Inspiring Tales of the Entrepreneurs and Inventors Who Revolutionized Modern Business* (New York: John Wiley & Sons, 1998), 54–71.

World War II. The war put a halt to GSI's extensive international oil exploration efforts, but Jonsson realized that the same technology used to locate oil deposits beneath the surface of the earth could be used to locate airplanes above it, and GSI became a major defense contractor by the end of the war.[3]

With the war's conclusion, GSI established a new Laboratory and Manufacturing Division to expand its wartime electronics work in both the military and private sectors and tapped a former Navy procurement officer named Patrick Haggerty to run it. By 1950, Haggerty had grown the division's annual sales to nearly $10 million a year. With manufacturing now a far more important part of the business than oil exploration, company executives realized the name GSI no longer fit the firm. They decided to change the name to General Instruments, which conjured up visions of the great electronics concerns of the East like General Electric. Unfortunately, there was already a defense contractor by that name, so the Pentagon asked them to pick something else. They chose Texas Instruments.[4]

As Haggerty explored avenues to expand the newly renamed company's burgeoning electronics business, he quickly settled upon the transistor. Due to anti-trust problems with the federal government, Bell Labs parent AT&T decided not to keep the transistor to itself to avoid further government scrutiny and instead licensed the technology relatively cheaply to any firm willing to research the application of transistors in hearing aids, which had been a personal passion of company founder Alexander Graham Bell. TI took a license in 1952, but the company was far smaller than fellow licensees like Raytheon, Zenith, and RCA and proved unable to compete for clients. Haggerty decided the only way TI could remain competitive was to seize the technological lead, so he resolved to bring the first silicon transistor to market. To accomplish this goal, Haggerty hired the Bell Labs chemist instrumental in developing the doping process for the first germanium transistors, Gordon Teal. Teal created the world's first silicon transistor in 1954, which propelled TI to the top of the transistor industry.[5]

***

The emergence of fast, reliable silicon transistors paved the way for semiconductors to replace vacuum tubes in computers. A new revolution in electronics was at hand, and Ken Olsen and Wes Clark wanted Lincoln Labs

---

[3] T.R. Reid, "The Texas Edison," *Texas Monthly*, July 1982, 104.
[4] Ibid.
[5] Young, 1998, 72–77.

to be at its forefront. Born in Bridgeport, Connecticut, Olsen tinkered with radios as a teenager and received his first formal electronics training through an 11-week Navy course at the tail end of World War II. Matriculating to MIT in 1947, Olsen graduated three years later and pursued a master's degree from the institution, during which time he joined the Whirlwind team.[6]

One of Olsen's jobs at Whirlwind was to construct a smaller version of the computer called the Memory Test Computer (MTC) in order to experiment with core memory configurations. In this project, he was aided by Clark, a physicist who had recently joined the Whirlwind team after a stint at the Hanford nuclear site in Washington State. Through their work on the MTC, Olsen and Clark became proponents of efficiently designed real-time computer architectures geared toward individual use by scientists and researchers in a lab environment, a new approach to computing different from the giant batch-processing mainframes controlled by a group of trained operators or even the real-time systems like SAGE dedicated to controlling larger systems. The emergence of the transistor, with its potential to be smaller, cheaper, and more reliable than the vacuum tube, appeared poised to transform this vision into reality.[7]

In 1954, Olsen and Clark mapped out the design for a machine they called the TX-1, one of the most ambitious computers conceived to that point in history. Fully transistorized, the TX-1 would have far outperformed the Whirlwind and its progeny at SAGE but would also have taken up nearly half an acre of space and required the largest core memory array ever built. Consequently, Forrester turned the project down as overly ambitious. Olsen and Clark returned to the drawing board and created a simpler design in 1955 to prove the merits of a fully transistorized computer. As this felt like a precursor to their TX-1, they dubbed it the TX-0. Olsen and Clark completed the TX-0 in 1956 and turned their attention back to adapting the technology on a larger scale, resulting in the completion of the TX-2 in 1958.[8] Having served its purpose, the TX-0 was placed on permanent loan to the MIT electrical engineering department, where it attracted the attention of a newly minted professor named Jack Dennis.

***

An electrical engineer with bachelor's, master's, and doctor's degrees from MIT, Jack Dennis was first exposed to computing in 1954 through a graduate

---

[6] Ken Olsen, interview by David Allison, September 28–29, 1988, National Museum of American History, https://americanhistory.si.edu/comphist/olsen.html.

[7] Young, 1998, 97–99.

[8] Ibid, 98–100.

course taught by Charlie Adams, the bouncing ball demo programmer helping Jay Forrester build the Whirlwind. Dennis enjoyed programming on the Whirlwind and soon learned that if he came in at night he could bypass the operators and work directly with the computer himself. Dennis's experiences with Whirlwind instilled within him a belief that student programming experiments could be just as valuable as official programming tasks and that greater student access to computing should be encouraged.[9]

In the fall of 1958, Dennis joined the MIT electrical engineering faculty and settled into his new office in Building 26. Uninterested in continuing his dissertation research, Dennis was briefly at a loss for what to do next. He found new purpose when he discovered the recently donated TX-0 being installed just down the hall in the Research Laboratory for Electronics (RLE). Dennis dedicated himself to improving both the computer's hardware and software, most importantly by creating an assembler for the machine and developing a debugger called FLIT.[10] He also sensed an opportunity to advance his philosophy of providing opportunities for unofficial student experimentation and resolved to recruit interested undergraduates to program on the TX-0.[11] Dennis knew just where to go to find students who would welcome a chance to have direct access to a computer, for as a freshman in 1949 he had joined a student organization full of electrical tinkerers called the Tech Model Railroad Club (TMRC).

Established in 1946 by 26 members of the MIT student body with interests in electrical engineering, model making, and scenery construction, TMRC maintained an elaborate HO gauge model railroad network in Building 20 on campus, a ramshackle structure built during World War II as temporary quarters for the MIT Radiation Laboratory. While most of its membership concentrated on constructing train cars, erecting buildings, and sculpting scenery, a small group of students called the Signals & Power (S&P) subcommittee developed and maintained the complex maze of wires, switches, and relays running the length and breadth of the railroad that controlled the entire setup.[12]

The members of the S&P subcommittee of TMRC all shared one trait in common: an insatiable desire to understand the inner workings of electrical and electronic technology so they could harness it for their own purposes.

---

[9] "The TX-0: Its Past and Present," *The Computer Museum Report*, Spring 1984, 9.

[10] Flit was a popular brand of pesticide in the 1950s, so the name was a pun on the concept of debugging. A version of the debugger was later ported to the PDP-1 as DDT.

[11] "The TX-0," 9.

[12] Steven Levy, *Hackers* (Sebastopol, CA: O'Reilly Media, 2010), 8–9.

For many of them, this was their real reason for being at MIT, far more important than their coursework or their degree programs. As its members bonded under the tables of Building 20, they developed their own culture and their own language. Garbage, for example, was referred to as "cruft," while an individual more interested in studying or following the rules than exploration and discovery was labeled a "tool." When a member made a particularly profound discovery or accomplished an especially clever feat of engineering – especially if he had done so just for the hell of it – then his endeavor was designated a "hack." For the members of S&P, there was no higher calling than that of the "hacker."[13]

In late 1958, Jack Dennis approached several members of TMRC and offered to show them how to sign up for time on and program the TX-0 in the RLE. These students included future computer chess pioneers Alan Kotok and Bob Wagner; a freshman named Peter Samson, who had once tried to build his own computer from the relays he pried from discarded pinball machines after seeing a documentary on computers on Boston public television; and junior Bob Saunders, the current president of the S&P sub-committee. Many of these students had come to MIT specifically due to an interest in computers but had grown disappointed with their lack of access to the MIT Computation Center, guarded as it was by its white-coated IBM priests.

Jack Dennis arranged for these students to have unfettered access to the TX-0 during any period no one had signed up to do actual work, which usually meant overnight or on weekends. A half dozen or so TMRC members leapt at this chance and could soon be found slaving away over a flexowriter in furious all-night coding sessions, foregoing their studies and all semblance of a social life to play with their new toy.[14] The language of TMRC naturally transferred over to their programming exploits, so they referred to the programs they wrote as hacks and to themselves as computer hackers.

The TMRC members developed several interesting, though largely frivolous, programs for the TX-0. Peter Samson programmed an Arabic to Roman numeral converter and a simple music program using the TX-0's speaker. Alan Kotok interfaced an FM radio receiver with the computer's analog-to-digital converter to create what he called the "Expensive Tape Recorder," while Robert Wagner built a program he called "Expensive Desk Calculator." They were also introduced to the computer's capacity as a game machine

---

[13] Ibid, 9–10.
[14] Ibid, 14–16.

through a program developed for public demonstrations of the TX-0 by faculty members Doug Ross and John Ward. Called *MOUSE* and deployed in January 1959, the demo allowed the player to use a light pen to draw a maze on the display and to place three pieces of cheese that a computer-controlled mouse attempts to collect before running out of energy.[15] TMRC's fascination with the TX-0 lasted until late 1961, when a new computer moved into the room next door, a groundbreaking machine called the PDP-1.

***

When Ken Olsen completed the TX-0 at Lincoln Labs in 1956, he felt he had proven a new era of computing was at hand, but the rest of the world disagreed. It was one thing, people said, to deploy a prototype real-time system in a controlled academic environment, but quite another to mass produce such a system for use in a real laboratory setting. To prove these naysayers wrong, Olsen left MIT in 1957 with fellow Whirlwind staff member Harlan Anderson to form a new company dedicated to bringing small, interactive real-time computers to market. They planned to call their company the Digital Computer Corporation but were unable to secure financing from investors leery of backing two academics attempting to challenge IBM. Pioneering venture capitalist George Doriot finally agreed to sign on, but only after Olsen and Anderson agreed to limit themselves to building test equipment and components like power supplies. Therefore, they named the company the Digital Equipment Corporation (DEC) instead.[16]

As core memory began supplanting CRT memory in the late 1950s, DEC experienced a surge in demand for its memory testing equipment and quickly exceeded its profit forecasts. Consequently, Doriot agreed to let the founders return to their computer plans. Designed primarily by Ben Gurley and first unveiled at the Eastern Joint Computer Conference in December 1959, the Programmed Data Processor-1 – more commonly referred to as the PDP-1 – was essentially a more powerful version of the TX-0 that could be equipped with an optional point-plotting display. While not nearly as capable as the latest computers from IBM and its competitors in the mainframe space, the PDP-1 only cost $120,000, a stunningly low price in an era when buying a computer would typically set an organization back a million dollars or more. Although sales only reached roughly 53 units, its arrival presaged a new era

[15] John E. Ward, "MOUSE Preliminary Instructions" (memorandum MIT Servomechanisms Laboratory, January 16, 1959).

[16] Glenn Rifkin and George Harrar, *The Ultimate Entrepreneur: The Story of Ken Olsen and Digital Equipment Corporation* (Chicago, IL: Contemporary Books, 1988), 9–15.

in which improving technology coupled with falling prices would lead to improved computer access.[17]

In September 1961, DEC donated one of the first PDP-1 computers to MIT, which it placed next door to the TX-0. Although not installed until the fall, news of its impending arrival swept through the programming community that summer and attracted the attention of a university employee named Martin Graetz. An Omaha, Nebraska, native, Martin Jerrold Graetz, who preferred the moniker J. Martin and was known to his friends as "Shag" after once offering to tell a shaggy dog story as a freshman, originally came to MIT in 1953 to study chemistry, but ultimately failed to graduate.[18] While he was not a particularly adept chemist, he found a new calling in computer programming thanks to his good friend, Wayne Wiitanen.

Raised in the suburbs of Detroit, Wiitanen originally planned to attend the Michigan College of Mines, but stellar grades and a slew of science awards gained him a scholarship to MIT. Wiitanen and Graetz first met as freshman through the MIT Outing Club and bonded over shared interests, spending hours together rock climbing, mountaineering, playing piano duets, and singing in the MIT-Wellesley madrigal group. Like Graetz, Wiitanen failed to graduate from MIT, but he became an experienced computer programmer through several part-time and work-study jobs starting in 1955. Therefore, Wiitanen secured employment in the MIT Meteorology Department in the summer of 1957 programming an IBM 704 computer for weather prediction. That fall, he and Graetz decided to room together and moved into a men's cooperative called Old Joe Clark's.[19]

In the late 1950s, the military draft was still in full force in the United States, and being of an age, both Wiitanen and Graetz learned in spring 1958 that they could expect to be drafted within 30 days. To forestall active military duty, both men joined an artillery unit as reservists and trained together for six months at Fort Dix, New Jersey, and Fort Sill, Oklahoma. With this training complete, Wiitanen took a new programming job with the MIT Electronic Systems Laboratory, where he worked under Doug Ross on the APT project on the IBM 704 and (later) IBM 709 computers. In 1959, Wiitanen moved on to the Littauer Statistical Laboratory at Harvard, where he worked as a systems programmer on yet another 704 system. By this time, Wiitanen and Graetz had left Old Joe Clark's for an upstairs apartment at a

---

[17] Ibid, 16–49.

[18] Martin Graetz, interview with the author, December 3, 2015.

[19] Wayne Wiitanen, email message to author, May 16, 2015.

rundown tenement located at 8 Hingham Street in Cambridge. A friend and fellow MIT alum named Dave Freeman rented the downstairs apartment, and the three decided to give the building the tongue-in-cheek name "The Hingham Institute," a play on the nickname of their alma mater.[20]

While Wiitanen worked with computers, Graetz struggled to find work as a chemistry lab technician. After brief stints at Massachusetts General Hospital and MIT, Graetz found himself out of work for several months, so Wiitanen helped secure him a job at Littauer as a junior operator helping feed cards into the computer and retyping any that were mangled by the system. At the same time, Graetz immersed himself in the inner workings of the 704 and learned how to program in both assembly language and FORTRAN. In early 1961, Graetz was dismissed from Littauer, so to find new employment he called on Jack Dennis, whom he knew through their time together in the MIT science fiction club, and secured a job working on a diagnostic program for a new magnetic tape unit for the TX-0.[21]

Graetz learned about the imminent arrival of the PDP-1 while working for Dennis on the TX-0. Eager to put the new computer through its paces, he convened the Hingham Institute, consisting now of himself, Wiitanen, and fellow Harvard programmer Steve "Slug" Russell, to formulate a plan of action for creating a demo program on the PDP-1. Over tea one afternoon at 8 Hingham Street, the trio discussed the attributes of a truly great demo and determined that it must tax the target computer to its limits, never play out the exact same way twice, and engage the user in a pleasurable activity. Building on these basic concepts, Wiitanen further articulated the need for skilled user input and giving the player direct control over some object displayed on the CRT – perhaps a spaceship – and engaging in a thrilling activity such as exploring, racing, or fighting. All three were science fiction aficionados – Graetz had even been published in a pulp magazine once – and particularly enjoyed the space operas of E.E. Smith, intergalactic tales of war and romance full of melodramatic dialogue, sudden plot twists, and clichéd battles pitting good against evil.[22] Therefore, Graetz and Russell honed in on the idea of a conflict between spaceships, and the concept for *Spacewar!* was born.[23]

Despite playing a critical role in conceptualizing *Spacewar!*, Wayne Wiitanen provided no further development input for the game. As tensions

---

[20] Ibid.

[21] Graetz, 2015.

[22] E.E. Smith (1890–1965) was a chemist who wrote science fiction stories on the side. He is best known for his *Skylark* and *Lensman* cycles, written in the 1920s and 1930s, respectively.

[23] J.M. Graetz, "The Origin of Spacewar," *Creative Computing*, August 1981, 60–61.

between the United States and the Soviet Union over the future of Germany culminated in the Berlin Wall crisis of October 1961, President John F. Kennedy deployed additional military units to Western Europe and then called up several reserve units to fill their slots back in the United States. On August 10th, Wiitanen was ordered to report to Fort Bragg, North Carolina, on October 31, 1961, to fill a slot as a surveyor for an artillery unit, ending his involvement with the Hingham Institute.[24] His friend Graetz remained involved with the game, but he passed on handling programming duties because since finishing his tape drive diagnostic for Jack Dennis over summer 1961, he had been working at the MIT Electronic Systems Laboratory in a different building from the PDP-1. Therefore, the task of turning the plans of the "Hingham Institute Study Group on Space Warfare" into reality fell on its third member, Steve Russell.

Steven Rundlet Russell, known since high school as "Slug" for reasons never explained to him, was born in Hartford, Connecticut, but spent his high school years in Washington State after his father, a mechanical engineer, was laid off and turned to farming. Fascinated with trains from an early age, Russell immersed himself in electronics so that he could build more elaborate model railroads. Russell received his introduction to computing on a trip back east to visit his uncle, Harvard professor George Pierce, who took him on a tour of Howard Aiken's electromechanical Harvard Mark I computer.[25] Pierce believed in the importance of a college education and later paid Russell's tuition so he could attend Dartmouth, where he eventually fell in with AI pioneer John McCarthy.[26]

McCarthy and Russell barely interacted while McCarthy was at Dartmouth, but after the professor moved to MIT, he contacted his former employer to restore an early electronic AI machine developed by Marvin Minsky called SNARC that had been loaned to some Dartmouth students and subsequently disassembled.[27] Russell became involved in the project, impressed McCarthy with his mechanical skill, and not only secured employment as a research assistant at the MIT AI Lab in the summer between his

[24] Wiitanen, 2015.

[25] One of the first digital computers ever built, the Automatic Sequence Controlled Calculator, informally known as the Harvard Mark I, was a joint project between Aiken, who articulated the basic design of the computer, and IBM that built it. Constructed between 1937 and 1944, the computer used relays as switching units rather than the vacuum tubes found in Colossus and ENIAC.

[26] Steve Russell, interview by Al Kossow, August 9, 2008, Computer History Museum, https://archive.computerhistory.org/resources/access/text/2012/08/102746453-05-01-acc.pdf.

[27] Developed in 1951, the Stochastic Neural Analog Reinforcement Calculator, or SNARC, was a neural net simulator designed to approximate a mouse learning the correct path through a maze.

junior and senior years, but also the promise of a permanent position at the lab upon graduation. Russell failed to complete a required senior thesis and therefore did not graduate, but McCarthy still brought him on staff in 1958 to help implement the LISP programming language.[28]

In his first two years at MIT, Russell was so focused on LISP that he did not pay attention to the hacking scene emerging on the TX-0. After work on the first version of LISP was largely complete, however, Russell befriended Alan Kotok and other student programmers from TMRC, which he joined in 1960. By 1961, Russell had burned out on LISP and left MIT for Harvard, where he became a programming consultant at Littauer and worked with Graetz and Wiitanen, whom he had previously met while living at Old Joe Clark's.

Despite no longer being an MIT employee, Russell remained close to his former companions in TMRC and at the AI Lab and continued to frequent Building 26 to watch the hacking scene unfold on the PDP-1. During this period, he began discussing the *Spacewar!* concept with his TMRC friends and insisted that someone should implement it. Russell's friends agreed the program was a great idea but argued that as the person who brought the idea to their attention, he should be the one to implement it. Russell did not want to put in the work, so he began making excuses for why he was not up to the task. The TMRC hackers continued to press Russell until he offered what became his final excuse: he did not possess the sine and cosines routines he would need to place and move the spaceships around the screen. An exasperated Alan Kotok responded by driving to DEC headquarters in nearby Maynard, locating the routines himself, and plopping them down in front of Russell. Realizing he had run out of excuses, Russell soon began coding.[29]

On December 29, 1961, the point-plotting display for MIT's PDP-1 was installed, finally allowing the computer to run graphical programs.[30] Coding on *Spacewar!* commenced in January 1962, and before the end of the month Russell was able to place and move dots around the screen. The transition from dots to fully rendered spaceships appeared impossible at first due to hardware limitations until Russell realized that because the points comprising the spaceship would always remain in the same relative position to each other, he only needed to calculate the angle once per frame and then implement code that rotated the entire grid as necessary. Two spaceships were duly

---

[28] Ibid.

[29] Ibid.

[30] John McKenzie, Deposition, Magnavox Co. v. Bally Manufacturing Corp., No. 74-1030 (N.D. Ill), October 28, 1975, 87.

designed that resembled the curvy spaceship of the *Buck Rodgers* serials, and the long and slender Redstone rocket. They gained the nicknames "Wedge" and "Needle," respectively. Before the end of February, Russell finished the basic program, in which the two ships could accelerate, rotate clockwise, or rotate counterclockwise when the player flipped the appropriate toggle switch on the PDP-1. Flipping another toggle switch allowed the player to fire torpedoes that destroyed the opposing ship on contact.[31]

With the basic functions in place, programmers from both the TMRC hacker community and the AI Lab began to play the game regularly and offered suggestions for improvements. Peter Samson disliked the random placement of stars on the monitor and incorporated an accurate star chart he labeled "Expensive Planetarium," while AI Lab graduate student and TMRC member Dan Edwards felt the game lacked sufficient strategy and introduced a star in the middle of the playfield that exerted a gravitational field affecting the movement of the ships.[32] These features were in place by March 25, 1962. The final major addition came from Graetz, who toiled away on his own in the Electronic Systems Laboratory to create a hyperspace function for the game. Conceived during the original brainstorming sessions between Wiitanen, Graetz, and Russell and inspired by E.E. Smith's stories, hyperspace served as a "panic button" that could be used a limited number of times during a match to take the ship instantly out of danger, but would deposit the player in a random, and potentially even more dangerous, position on the screen. Hyperspace was added in May, as was a scoring mechanic designed to limit individual playing sessions.[33]

After roughly four months in development, *Spacewar!* made its public debut at the annual MIT open house in May 1962, where the PDP-1 was hooked up to a second, larger monitor to facilitate spectator viewing of matches. While the game had originally been played by flicking toggle switches, it now sported custom-made control boxes installed on March 19, 1962[34] that featured two levers – one for controlling left and right rotation and the other controlling thrust and hyperspace – and a button for firing torpedoes. These were crafted by Bob Saunders, who scoured the TMRC stores in Building 20 for the necessary components to build the boxes in order to

---

[31] Graetz, 1981, 62.

[32] Due to runtime limitations, the torpedoes fired by the players' craft were not affected by the star's gravity well. Russell and friends decided these projectiles were "photon torpedoes" unaffected by gravity to explain this physics defect.

[33] Ibid, 62–66.

[34] McKenzie, 1975, 147–148.

combat the "Space War Elbow" caused by hunching in front of the PDP-1 for hours at a time. *Spacewar!* proved a sizable hit at that open house and at many that followed as the decade progressed, with throngs of children forming long lines to take turns playing the game.

***

While a handful of games were programmed in the 1950s and early 1960s, few of them achieved notoriety outside of the institution where they were created due to a lack of distribution capability. At the time, there were no widespread network infrastructures across which these games could travel and no easy way to port programs to new hardware systems, as they were generally written in the machine or assembly language unique to their computer of origin rather than in a high-level language like FORTRAN. *Spacewar!* overcame these difficulties to find a home in computer labs across the United States.

Three interrelated factors aided the initial spread of *Spacewar!*. First, due to Ken Olsen and Harlan Anderson's ties to MIT, DEC practically served as a branch of the school, with MIT students coming and going constantly as they took internships, found employment after graduation, or just dropped by to hang out with the DEC staff. With its close ties to MIT, DEC learned about *Spacewar!* soon after its creation, and by 1963 the company had created an official brochure highlighting the computing power required to run *Spacewar!* while also providing demonstrations of the game to entice potential buyers of the PDP-1.[35]

Second, *Spacewar!* was one of the most technically impressive programs yet created for the PDP-1 and used nearly every last instruction and every last ounce of processing power the machine could muster, so it garnered attention as a showcase for the PDP-1 beyond those interested in playing the game. Furthermore, as *Spacewar!* used virtually the entire PDP-1 instruction set, it proved a great final diagnostic program to ensure the computer was in working order and would therefore ship to new buyers already resident in memory.[36]

Third, DEC followed a hardware-first approach and created little software of its own, so PDP-1 users were always on the lookout for new programs and formed networks to trade software. This led to the creation of

---

[35] "PDP-1 Computer and Spacewar" (brochure, Digital Equipment Corporation, c. 1963).

[36] The story of *Spacewar!* being used as a diagnostic program has been widely reported in the secondary literature and claimed by both Steve Russell and Martin Graetz in interviews. However, there has yet to be confirmation of this practice from DEC primary sources, and it may well be apocryphal.

the Digital Equipment Computer Users' Society (DECUS) to support organizations that owned a DEC computer by staging conferences and publishing a monthly newsletter called DECUSCOPE featuring program libraries
for DEC computers. Graetz presented a paper entitled "SPACEWAR! Real-
Time Capability of the PDP-1" in May 1962 at the inaugural meeting of
DECUS and encouraged interested parties to contact Steve Russell for a copy
of the game.[37]

While the efforts of both DEC and DECUS played a role in publicizing
Spacewar!, in truth they were not primary factors in the game's emerging
popularity across the United States. Fewer than half of the 53 PDP-1 computers sold were equipped with a display, and not all those computers were as
readily accessible as the computer at MIT. Furthermore, the mere availability
of a computer with the game installed did not automatically equate to excitement for playing it. At the University of Michigan, the sole PDP-1 was housed
in the basement of a physics building, and only a handful of programmers
were even aware the game existed. Likewise, the PDP-1 at Harvard was used
in conjunction with an electron accelerator in constant operation and was
therefore rarely available to play the game. Still other PDP-1 systems were
installed in secure government facilities, where security protocols would have
prevented anyone playing the game even if they wanted to.[38] Ultimately, it
was a small group of evangelists from the MIT hacker community itself that
took the lead in establishing the game at computer labs around the country.

One of the first *Spacewar!* hotspots outside of MIT was defense contractor Bolt, Beranek, & Newman (BBN), where it was evangelized by multiple
MIT alumni. The game proved so popular at the defense contractor that
staff were forced to create custom control boxes because they were constantly
breaking the switches on the PDP-1 during playing sessions.[39] Another
hotspot was the University of Minnesota, where a 1963 MIT graduate
named Albert Kuhfeld adapted the game. While Minnesota did not possess
a PDP-1, Kuhfeld missed his *Spacewar!* playing days so much that he recre-
ated the game on a CDC 3100 in 1967–1968. While his version was largely
faithful to the original, Kuhfeld added a few features of his own, including
limited ammunition and a cloaking device that would temporarily render the

[37] J.M. Graetz, "Spacewar!: Real-Time Capability of the PDP-1," *DECUS Proceedings 1962: Papers and Presentations of the Digital Equipment Computer Users Society*, 1962, 37–39.

[38] Devin Monnens and Martin Goldberg, "Space Odyssey: The Long Journey of Spacewar! from MIT to Computer Labs Around the World," *Kinephanos*, Cultural History of Video Games Special Issue, June 2015, https://www.kinephanos.ca/Revue_files/2015_Monnens_Goldberg.pdf.

[39] Ibid.

ship invisible, though both its thrust and torpedoes could still give away its position.[40] Kuhfeld submitted an article to science fiction magazine *Analog* describing his game, which was published in 1971 and represented one of the first instances of national exposure for *Spacewar!*.[41] While Kuhfeld's article brought the game some attention, however, the most important *Spacewar!* hub of all, even more prominent than MIT itself, was the Stanford Artificial Intelligence Laboratory (SAIL).

***

As John McCarthy pondered the creation of an intelligent machine at MIT in 1957, he realized that interacting with an intelligent program would leave the user with a great deal of idle time, as the basic idea was to run the program, review its operation, and then make improvements so it could reason more effectively. During the long periods when the programmer would be dissecting the performance of the AI, the computer could theoretically be performing tasks for other people, but practically speaking this was not possible because a computer could only handle one user and one task at a time. Out of these ruminations, McCarthy developed the basic idea for time-sharing, in which multiple users, each equipped with a personal terminal, could feed problems to the computer concurrently.[42] Since none of the users would actually be exercising the processor continuously, McCarthy reasoned, it should be possible to allocate processing time to give each user the illusion that the computer is working on his task the entire time when the processor is actually rapidly switching between dozens, if not hundreds, of users. Though this would cause some inevitable slowdowns due to the need to juggle so many different processes at once, the greater efficiency of allowing multiple simultaneous users would more than make up for this deficiency.[43]

In January 1959, McCarthy drafted a memo outlining his idea for time-sharing, which served as the basis for a feasibility prototype, the Compatible Time-Sharing System (CTSS), built by Fernando Corbató and operational on the IBM 709 in the Computation Center before the end of 1961. Based on the success of this experiment, a committee formed to discuss upgrades

---

[40]Albert W. Kuhfeld, "Spacewar," *Analog Science Fiction Science Fact Magazine*, July 1971, 67–79.

[41]The first known national coverage of *Spacewar!* occurred on January 26, 1969 when Walter Cronkite played the game at the Air Force Cambridge Research Laboratory for an episode of a program called *21st Century* (Monnens and Goldberg, 2015).

[42]McCarthy, 2007.

[43]McCarthy was not the first computer scientist to publicly propose a time-sharing scheme, that was Bob Bemer at IBM, but McCarthy can take credit for being the earliest theorist on the subject to contribute to a working system.

to MIT's computing capability chaired by McCarthy recommended the Institute's next computer be a time-shared system, but the university proved reluctant based on the cost of the project and ordered a feasibility study. Annoyed at the university's recalcitrance, McCarthy opted in September 1962 to accept the offer of a full professorship from Stanford University, where he established SAIL.[44] Meanwhile, Steve Russell, who lost his draft deferment when he left the AI Lab for Harvard, spent six months in the Army Reserve in 1962 and returned to Littauer only to discover it had come under new management. Unimpressed with his new boss and ready for a change, Russell accepted an offer from McCarthy to join him at Stanford, and he brought *Spacewar!* with him.[45]

Once he arrived at Stanford, McCarthy wasted no time in securing a grant from the Advanced Research Projects Agency (ARPA) to implement a time-shared PDP-1 system to form the heart of his new AI lab. Thanks to Russell, *Spacewar!* was one of the first programs up and running on this system, and by the end of 1963 the game was so popular with the programmers at SAIL that an edict had to be issued banning play during regular business hours.[46] In 1966, the lab moved to the D.C. Power Laboratory in the rolling hills above Stanford and upgraded to a PDP-6, so *Spacewar!* was adapted to run on the new machine as well. The next year, the SAIL programmers created a special time-sharing setup called "Spacewar Mode" that optimized the operation of the PDP-6 so it devoted just enough processing power for *Spacewar!* to run smoothly without disrupting any research being conducted on the computer concurrently.[47]

In 1971, a graduate student at SAIL named Ralph Gorin began modifying *Spacewar!*, now running on a combined PDP-6/PDP-10 setup, so that five players could play at the same time. He also added new features like mines and the ability for ships to survive multiple hits.[48] This version attracted the attention of noted counterculture figure and computer evangelist Stewart Brand, then working on a feature story on the potential of computing for *Rolling Stone* magazine. Brand convinced SAIL to hold a competition on October 19, 1972, called the "Intergalactic Spacewar Olympics" using the Gorin version of the game, most likely the first organized video game tournament. Brand published an account of the proceedings in the

---

[44] Ibid.

[45] Russell, 2008.

[46] Edward K. Yasaki, "Computing at Stanford," *Datamation*, November 1963, 43–45.

[47] Monnens and Goldberg, 2015.

[48] Ralph Gorin, interview with the author, September 19, 2017.

December 7, 1972, issue of *Rolling Stone*, bringing computer gaming into the cultural zeitgeist for the first time.[49]

***

When Steve Russell and the TMRC hackers first created *Spacewar!* in 1962, they did it purely for the challenge and thrill of taxing the PDP-1 to its limits, but once the game proved popular, they were not blind to the potential commercial implications of their hack. For a heartbeat, they considered how they might profit from the game, but quickly realized there was no way to turn a program that ran on a $120,000 computer into a consumer product. For almost a decade, the game remained trapped in the computer labs of MIT, BBN, Minnesota, and a host of other institutions until in 1970, it was discovered at SAIL by a recent electrical engineering graduate named Nolan Bushnell.

---

[49] Stewart Brand, "Spacewar: Fanatic Life and Symbolic Death among the Computer Bums," *Rolling Stone*, December 7, 1972.

5

The Stars Are Right

In late 1967, electrical engineer Ed de Castro stood before the DEC Operations Committee, the company's main decision-making body, and attempted to sell its members on a radical new product idea. At the time, DEC found itself in a delicate period of transition. In 1964, the company had launched its first high-end computer system, the PDP-6, a $300,000 machine optimized for time-sharing. Designed by Gordon Bell and championed by company co-founder Harlan Anderson, the machine proved too ambitious for the small company and became an expensive flop due to a faulty architecture.[1]

In response, CEO Ken Olsen reorganized DEC around product lines, with the manager of each company product completely responsible for its development and market positioning and forced to bid for resources from the functional units like sales and manufacturing that comprised the Operations Committee that now had final say over which products would be built. In effect, each project manager became an entrepreneur, and the functional managers became investors allocating their resources based on which projects the Operations Committee felt deserved the strongest backing.[2]

Harlan Anderson resisted the new structure, particularly after Olsen put him in charge of the PDP-6 that was now clearly destined to be a failure. This conflict drove Anderson out of the company in 1966. Meanwhile, Olsen turned his back on large computers and poured resources into another computer designed by Bell called the PDP-5. Conceived at the request of a client as a front-end for another failed large computer, the PDP-4, Bell chose to make it a general-purpose computer instead, albeit one with limited functionality due to its minimalist design. DEC initially projected sales of only

---

[1] Rifkin and Harrar, 1988, 55–56.
[2] Ibid, 57–58.

ten units, but at $27,000 the PDP-5 was the cheapest core-memory computer on the market by far and consequently sold roughly 1,000 units.[3]

The PDP-5 was one of the earliest products in a new category called the minicomputer.[4] Unlike the hulking mainframes of IBM and its competitors – by now contemptuously referred to as the "seven dwarfs" in recognition of IBM's total market dominance[5] – a minicomputer was a relatively small and cheap computer that compensated for a lack of raw processing power or expansive memory through efficient design and clever tricks in order to perform most routine operations just as well as its larger cousins. Faced with the success of the PDP-5 and the failure of the PDP-6, Ken Olsen decided the minicomputer was the future of DEC.

In 1965, DEC released a follow-up to the PDP-5 designed by Ed de Castro called the PDP-8. Despite a smaller memory capacity than a full-sized mainframe, the PDP-8 was cleverly designed to perform virtually any operation a larger computer could, albeit sometimes much slower. While complex calculations might take a long time, however, many simpler operations could be performed just as quickly on a PDP-8 as on a much larger and more expensive computer.[6] The PDP-8 was also incredibly small, as de Castro employed an especially efficient board design that allowed the entire computer to fit into a case that occupied only eight cubic feet of volume, meaning it was small enough to place on top of a standard workbench. DEC priced the computer at just $18,000 and sold 1,400 of them by 1968 to cement the minicomputer as an important new product category.[7]

Despite the success of the PDP-8, DEC found itself already behind the curve by the time it was released. In April 1964, IBM announced its System 360 series of mainframe computers, a revolutionary concept that unified the company's entire product line from the extreme low end all the way up to its most powerful supercomputers. Previously, an expanding company that

---

[3] Ibid, 59.

[4] Ibid. The PDP-5 helped popularized the minicomputer concept, but it was not the first one designed. Earlier prototypical minicomputers included the LINC from TX-0 designer Wes Clark and the CDC 160 from brilliant computer designer Seymour Cray.

[5] These companies, which never controlled more than 20%–30% of the mainframe market between them, were General Electric, RCA, Control Data Corporation (CDC), Burroughs, National Cash Register (NCR), Honeywell, and Sperry Rand – formed when UNIVAC maker Remington Rand merged with Sperry Gyroscope in 1955.

[6] Ceruzzi, 2003, chap. 4.

[7] Lamont Wood, *Datapoint: The Lost Story of the Texans Who Invented the Personal Computer Revolution* (Austin: Hugo House Publishers, 2012), kindle, chap. 5. By the time it was discontinued in 1990, the PDP-8 reached sales of 50,000 units. Rifkin, 1988, 71.

required additional computing power would not only need to acquire a new mainframe, but also need to buy new peripherals like printers and storage devices and commission new software. With the scalable 360 architecture, however, a company could upgrade to a more powerful member of the 360 family while leaving its devices and programs intact. By 1970, IBM had achieved an install base of over 35,000 System 360 computers and cemented an ironclad grip on between 70% and 80% of the mainframe computer market.[8]

In addition to introducing widespread compatibility, the System 360 adopted a memory word length based on multiples of eight bits rather than the previous standard of six. With IBM's commanding lead in the marketplace, the 8-bit byte became the standard building block of computer memory — as it remains in the present day — so the PDP-8, built around a 12-bit architecture, appeared primitive by comparison. De Castro knew that his computer would soon be obsolete as the fledging minicomputer industry turned to 16-bit designs, and he looked to IBM for inspiration in crafting its successor.[9]

Now after months of work with colleagues Henry Burkhardt and Dick Sogge, de Castro proudly unveiled his minicomputer of the future to the Operations Committee, the PDP-X, which like the 360 would be based on the 8-bit byte and feature scalability across 16- and 32-bit computer architectures while retaining software compatibility. De Castro felt the PDP-X line would secure DEC's place in the minicomputer market for decades to come, but the project proved too ambitious for Ken Olsen. The company founder was still smarting from the failure of the PDP-6 mainframe in 1964, so he was nonplussed when de Castro indicated the PDP-X project could be even more complicated and expensive. Furthermore, the managers in charge of DEC's existing computer lines did not appreciate the thought of their products being rendered obsolete instantly, while the sales and marketing departments were wary of cannibalizing sales of the existing product line. In the end, the Operations Committee turned de Castro's proposal down.[10]

Furious at what he saw as a complete lack of vision, de Castro left DEC and in conjunction with Burkhardt, Sogge, and a Fairchild Semiconductor

---

[8] Ceruzzi, 2003, chap. 5.
[9] Rifkin and Harrar, 1988, 90–91.
[10] Ibid, 87–93.

salesman named Herb Richman established a new computer company called Data General in early 1968. Deciding that a computer family in the vein of the PDP-X would be too ambitious for a young startup, de Castro resolved instead to bring a low-cost 16-bit computer to market. The result was the Nova, a particularly small minicomputer that fit comfortably on a desktop and sold for a mere $3,950.[11]

The technological advance that paved the way for the development of a small, relatively cheap computer like the Nova was the integrated circuit (IC), in which all the components of a circuit – transistors, resistors, capacitors, etc. – are etched on a single sliver of material, commonly referred to as a "chip," and are therefore smaller, cheaper, and more durable than discrete components connected by wires. The development of the IC was spurred by the needs of the Pentagon's Minuteman guided missile program and the exceptionally small and durable electronic components it required. Jack Kilby at transistor market leader Texas Instruments developed the first IC in late 1958, but his design could not be mass-produced because even though he succeeded in placing all the components on a single chip he failed to eliminate wires entirely.[12]

The company that perfected the IC was one of TI's main rivals in transistors, Fairchild Semiconductor. Founded on September 19, 1957, Fairchild was formed by eight scientists and engineers originally recruited by transistor co-inventor William Shockley for his Palo Alto-based Shockley Semiconductor, which he established in 1955 after leaving Bell Labs.[13] The eight men had grown tired of Shockley's jealous and controlling behavior and resolved to resign en masse and convince a company to form a research group around them so they could continue to work together. Their plans changed after they wrote to a New York investment bank, where bankers Bud Coyle and Arthur Rock advised them to think bigger and find a business willing to form an entire semiconductor company around them instead. After several companies rejected the idea, Coyle convinced inventor Sherman Fairchild that his Fairchild Camera and Instrument should

---

[11] This was just the price of the basic computer. A standard configuration with 4K of memory and a teletype cost a still very reasonable $7,950. Dag Spicer, "The Data General Nova," *Core*, March 2001, 2–3.

[12] Young, 1998, 123.

[13] The eight men were chemist Gordon Moore, mechanical engineers Eugene Kleiner and Julius Blank, metallurgist Sheldon Roberts, and physicists Jay Last, Jean Hoerni, Vic Grinich, and Robert Noyce.

put forth the capital, leading to the creation of Fairchild Semiconductor.[14] The new company quickly established itself by developing a new transistor fabrication method dubbed the planar process that rendered all previous methods of transistor creation obsolete.[15]

Early in 1959, Fairchild Semiconductor co-founder Robert Noyce designed an IC that could be manufactured using the planar process, thus paving the way for mass production. In 1962, the engineers at MIT building the computer for use in the Apollo moon-landing program chose to use ICs in their architecture, and by 1964, the Apollo program's high-volume purchases helped drive the cost of ICs down far enough that they could be used in other applications. Early ICs only integrated between one and ten transistors on a single chip, but the Nova was an early adopter of medium-scale integration (MSI) circuits, which could integrate up to 500 transistors and allowed Data General to undercut all its competitors in the minicomputer space on price and smash through the $10,000 barrier.

In December 1968, Data General unveiled the Nova at the Fall Joint Computer Conference in San Francisco in advance of its commercial release in early 1969. For this occasion, the engineers at the company hooked up a 4K Nova to a display and showcased the capabilities of the system through a version of what by now had become one of the principle programs for demonstrating the power of a small computer: *Spacewar!*.[16] While the Nova was still too expensive to classify as a consumer electronic device, it was potentially cheap enough to incorporate into a commercial entertainment product exhibited in a public venue like a bar or bowling alley. Doing so, however, would require a visionary entrepreneur who was both comfortable with computer technology and understood the dynamics of the existing commercial amusement industry. One man who fit this profile perfectly was Nolan Bushnell.

***

Nolan Kay Bushnell was born on February 5, 1943, in Ogden, Utah, and grew up in nearby Clearfield, the home of his parents Clarence, a cement

[14] Sherman Fairchild established his first company, the Fairchild Aerial Camera Corporation, in 1920 after inventing an aerial photography camera for the U.S. Army during World War I. After founding several more companies, he consolidated his businesses under the holding company Fairchild Aviation in 1927, which he renamed Fairchild Camera and Instrument in 1944 after spinning back out his aviation business.

[15] Michael S. Malone, The Intel Trinity: How Robert Noyce, Gordon Moore, and Andy Grove Built the World's Most Important Company (New York: Harper Business, 2014), 7–16.

[16] Monnens and Goldberg, 2015.

contractor, and Delma, a teacher and librarian. He discovered his true calling in the third grade when his teacher assigned him to teach a unit on
electricity. Fascinated by the batteries and magnets at the school, he soon
began looking for other outlets to feed his insatiable curiosity. While neither
of his parents were particularly tech savvy, one of their neighbors ran an
electronics surplus store and was also a HAM radio operator. The neighbor
became young Nolan's mentor, leading him to become one of the youngest HAM radio operators in the state at the tender age of 11. From there it
was a small step to raiding local area junkyards for discarded components
from the military bases in the Clearfield area and cultivating an interest in
model rocketry.[17] By the time he was a teenager, Bushnell began subsidiz-
ing his electronics habit through a job with a local firm owned by a second
cousin called Barlow Electronics as a deliveryman and appliance and TV
repairman.[18]

In high school, Nolan's love of electronics cooled off a bit. He traded his
HAM radio in for skis, joined the basketball and debate teams, and started
reading philosophy as a hobby.[19] In the summer of 1958, the Bushnell family
received a shock when patriarch Clarence suffered a heart attack on the job
and died. Raised in the Mormon faith – though he ultimately left it behind –
Nolan had been steeped in the importance of family and hard work all his
life, so at just 15 years of age he finished his father's outstanding contracts
himself. For Nolan, this feat stood as proof that with a little hard work and
determination, he could accomplish anything.[20]

In 1961, Nolan matriculated to Utah State University to study engineering, but he quickly found that the major did not agree with him. As a member of the Pi Kappa Alpha fraternity, he enjoyed partying with his fraternity
brothers more than spending hours doing homework, and he soon switched
his major to business.[21] To help pay his way, he continued to work at Barlow
for a time and also took several other jobs over the next few years including
assembler and test tech at Litton Guidance and Control Systems, draftsman
for a faculty member in the industrial engineering department of Utah State
planning irrigation systems, salesman for a company called Hadley Clothing,

---

[17] Nolan Bushnell, interview with the author, January 21, 2015.

[18] Nolan Bushnell, Deposition, Magnavox Co. v. Bally Manufacturing Corp., No. 74-1030 (N.D. Ill),
January 13–14, 1976, 13–14.

[19] Robert Slater, *Portraits in Silicon*, rev. ed. (Cambridge, MA: MIT Press, 1989), 298–299.

[20] Steven Kent, The Ultimate History of Video Games: From Pong to Pokémon and Beyond – The
Story Behind the Craze That Touched Our Lives and Changed the World (New York: Three Rivers
Press, 2001), 28.

[21] Bushnell, 2015.

and vendor for *Encyclopedia Americana*.[22] His most successful venture was an advertising business he established called the Campus Company that produced a blotter three times a year containing a calendar of events for the school surrounded by advertising.[23] Worried he would fritter away his earnings through his partying lifestyle if he had nothing to occupy his evenings, Nolan accepted a new job in 1963 with the Lagoon Amusement Park in Farmington, Utah.[24]

Lagoon proved the perfect match for Nolan's boundless energy and enthusiasm, and he soon gained a reputation as a fantastic barker and showman. Starting on the midway running a bottle toss booth, Nolan rotated through a series of carnival games over the next two years before being placed in charge of the amusement park arcade, for which he shared full profit and loss responsibility in conjunction with another employee.[25] This job introduced Nolan to the world of coin-operated amusements, electromechanical contraptions like pinball and shooting galleries in which playtime is regulated by inserting a coin into a slot mounted on the machine. Throughout his life, Nolan had bounced between multiple activities, academic disciplines, and vocations in his unquenchable thirst for knowledge and new experiences, but in coin-operated games, he finally found a field that satisfied his creative, technical, and entrepreneurial drives equally.

The increased time commitment of his new job rendered the hour plus commute from Utah State to Lagoon unpalatable, so in early 1965 Nolan transferred to the University of Utah to major in economics.[26] After marrying Paula Nielson in 1966, however, he developed a new sense of responsibility, swore of partying, and switched his major back to engineering. The same year that Nolan arrived at Utah, the school established a computer science department under the auspices of noted alumnus David Evans, who had spent the early part of the decade doing pioneering work in time-sharing and computer graphics at the University of California at Berkeley. Nolan found himself drawn to the new Utah Computer Center, and when he switched his major back to electrical engineering, he chose a focus in computer design.[27] He also took introductory programming courses in FORTRAN

---

[22] Bushnell, January 1976, 5–8.

[23] Slater, 1989, 299.

[24] Bushnell, January 1976, 8.

[25] Ibid, 9–14.

[26] Bushnell, 2015.

[27] Nolan Bushnell, Deposition, Magnavox Co. v. Bally Manufacturing Corp., No. 74-1030 (N.D. Ill), July 3, 1974.

and Algol,[28] but his focus was on hardware rather than software.[29] Anxious to leave Utah, Nolan travelled to Northern California shortly before graduating in December 1968 to look for work among the high concentration of technology companies in a region that would soon be christened "Silicon Valley" due to the large number of semiconductor manufacturers in the area.

Bushnell placed his resume in the hands of as many Bay Area tech companies as he could during his brief visit to the region and attracted his most enthusiastic response from the Ampex Corporation,[30] one of the world's foremost purveyors of magnetic tape recording technology.[31] Ampex hired him into its division developing a digital replacement for vertical filing called the Videofile Information System in which individual documents were filmed on videotape and indexed electronically for quick recall at remote readers connected to the central database by microwave links. Bushnell joined the project in early 1969 as an associate engineer to work on developing error correction solutions to increase the accuracy of the recording process.[32]

Growing up, Nolan was an avid player of games, and at the University of Utah, he played number two board on the chess club. One day, Nolan opined to the number one board, a Korean, that chess was surely the most complicated game ever created. His friend disagreed and introduced Nolan to the ancient Chinese game of *Go*.[33] Nolan developed an obsession for the game, so when he relocated to California he began frequenting several *Go* clubs in the area, including one that met on the campus of Stanford University. At the Stanford club, Nolan became friendly with a man named Jim Stein who worked at the Stanford AI Lab. One night, Jim offered to take Nolan over to the lab to show him the cool programs they had running on their

---

[28] Bushnell, January 1976.

[29] Reports that he actually programmed games at the University of Utah appear to be apocryphal, as in his deposition in the Magnavox case Bushnell explicitly stated that he was not aware of any games at the institution other than *Spacewar!*. Nolan Bushnell, Deposition, Magnavox Co. v. Bally Manufacturing Corp., No. 74-1030 (N.D. Ill), March 4, 1976, 323.

[30] Bushnell, 2015.

[31] Established as a motor manufacturer by Alexander Poniatoff in 1944, Ampex pivoted to recording technology after World War II, releasing the first magnetic tape recorder available in the United States in 1948 and the world's first videotape recorder in 1956.

[32] Morgan Ramsey, *Gamers at Work: Stories Behind the Games People Play* (New York: Apress, 2012), Kindle, chap. 2.

[33] Bushnell, 2015.

computer,[34] thus introducing Nolan to one of the favorite pastimes of the AI Lab students and employees: *Spacewar!*[35]

From the moment Nolan arrived at Ampex, he had been plotting his departure. Restless and fiercely independent, he was only truly happy when he was operating on his own dreaming up the next big thing in technology and/or entertainment. Indeed, the place he had really hoped to work was the Walt Disney Company, which employed a group of engineers dubbed the Imagineers to develop new attractions for its theme parks, but the company did not hire fresh graduates.[36] After becoming enthralled by *Spacewar!*, Nolan felt he should commercialize the game, but like so many players before him he could not initially figure out how to do so. That changed in spring 1970 when he happened upon a sales flyer for the Nova minicomputer. With his arcade background, Bushnell realized that at $4,000 a Nova cost the same as roughly a half dozen standard electromechanical arcade games. Therefore, if he could figure out a way to time-share the computer so that six users could play simultaneously and scrounge up some cheap displays, he just might have a viable commercial product.

***

Nolan Bushnell was creative, energetic, even visionary, but he was not a particularly accomplished engineer. Although he remained an eager learner and read up constantly at Ampex, too many years of partying, running side businesses, and periodically switching majors left him without sufficient background to handle an ambitious project like a commercial computer game by himself. Fortunately, he shared his office with an older and more experienced engineer who possessed many of the skills he lacked named

---

[34] Ramsay, 2012, chap. 2.

[35] Mr Bushnell has, of course, claimed for decades that he first saw and played *Spacewar!* as a student at the University of Utah in the mid-1960s. The earliest known instance of this claim dates from a November 1973 article in *Systems Engineering Today*, and Bushnell testified to the same while under oath during multiple depositions in the mid-1970s. There are serious reasons to doubt this claim due to a lack of corroborating evidence that *Spacewar!* was present at Utah before the early 1970s. In-depth research in university records of the computer equipment available at Utah in the 1960s by Marty Goldberg indicated no machines capable of playing the game were present, other students affiliated with the computer center at the time do not remember the game (Randall Willie, interview with the author, May 25, 2017), and the university newspaper makes no mention of it, unlike at MIT and Stanford where it was covered soon after appearing. Furthermore, in the earliest known interview with Bushnell, conducted for a documentary called *Games Computers Play* filmed in early 1973, Nolan explicitly states he was inspired to create a commercial video game due to his experience playing games at Stanford and does not mention Utah at all. The narrator of the documentary then states that Bushnell first saw *Spacewar!* at Stanford.

[36] Slater, 1989, 303.

Ted Dabney. Born in 1937 in San Francisco, California, Samuel Frederick "Ted" Dabney was the complete opposite of Bushnell. Whereas Bushnell was creative, Dabney was stodgy. Whereas Bushnell was a dreamer, Dabney remained focused on day-to-day practicalities. And whereas Bushnell was ambitious, driven, and entrepreneurial, Dabney was perfectly content working for a large company on whatever projects came his way.

As a youth, Dabney had been aimless and barely completed high school, though he did display an aptitude for mathematics. His geometry skills earned him employment as a surveyor, but work proved hard to come by in this seasonal profession. With college out of the question, Dabney enlisted in the U.S. Marine Corps and received a thorough grounding in electronics through a 16-week course at Naval Station Treasure Island in San Francisco supplemented by a radio relay course at the Marine Corps Communication Electronics School in San Diego. After leaving the Corps in 1959, Dabney worked briefly for Bank of America and Hewlett-Packard before joining the Military Products Division of Ampex. One of his primary projects there was creating video amplifiers and gamma correctors for an electron beam scanning system intended to digitally convert U-2 spy plane footage, so when the Videofile project commenced in 1966, Dabney was one of the first engineers brought on board. For Videofile, Dabney's primary duties were adapting a vidicon camera for use with the system, evaluating monitors and building the circuitry to allow them to interface with the system, and designing additional components such as power supplies. Much of the circuit design Dabney contributed to the project was virtually identical to the work he did in military products except that he used transistors rather than vacuum tubes.[37]

When Bushnell joined the Videofile team three years later, he and Dabney bonded over their similar family lives – despite their age differences, they both had daughters roughly the same age – and a shared love of engineering. Bushnell taught Dabney to play *Go* and spent many a lunch hour engaged in matches with the older man. After deciding to transform *Spacewar!* into a commercial product, Bushnell took Dabney up to Stanford to see the game for himself in an effort to enlist his aid in building a commercial version of the game. When Bushnell described his plan for a time-shared coin-op system, Dabney was not quite sure what to make of it, but he was perfectly happy to give it a try.[38]

---

[37] Samuel F. (Ted) Dabney, interview by Chris Garcia, July 16, 2012, Computer History Museum, https://archive.computerhistory.org/resources/access/text/2012/10/102746459-05-01-acc.pdf.

[38] Marty Goldberg and Curt Vendel, *Atari, Inc.: Business is Fun* (Carmel, NY: Syzygy Company Press, 2012), kindle, chap. 1.

Between them, Bushnell and Dabney possessed all the analog, digital, and video engineering skills required to build interfaces between a Nova computer and a display, but to develop the necessary time-sharing routines to run multiple instances of *Spacewar!* they required a programmer. For this task, Bushnell turned to another friend in the Videofile division with whom he often played chess and *Go* at lunch and socialized with outside of work named Larry Bryan. A mathematician from Florida, Bryan entered the programmer's trade strictly by accident after answering an ad from UNIVAC in 1963 while waiting to take a teaching job that fall. Bryan took to his new profession quickly and bounced around several companies working on defense projects before coming to Ampex in 1967 as the first programmer in the Videofile division. Like Dabney, Bryan proved content to go along with Bushnell's scheme, and a three-way partnership was born.[39]

In the summer of 1970, Bushnell, Dabney, and Bryan held several meetings to finalize their plans and agreed that Bushnell would handle the electronic engineering for the game, Dabney would do the video engineering, and Bryan would program the software.[40] They also chose a name for their venture. Bushnell and Dabney originally wanted something incorporating their initials such as D&B Enterprises, but decided D&B could be confused with Dunn and Bradstreet, while B&D might be mistaken for Black & Decker.[41] They were at an impasse until Bryan suggested another name, Syzygy, because they were forming a partnership of three people and he remembered that the term had something to do with the confluence of three things. The trio proceeded to look up the word in the dictionary and discovered that it referred to a straight-line configuration of three celestial bodies in a gravitational system.[42] Satisfied with this definition, the trio adopted the name for what at this point was an informal partnership.

Around August 1970, Larry Bryan commenced work on the game and spent roughly two weeks tinkering with a program for the Nova. The results were not promising. The Nova was capable of running *Spacewar!* – witness the Joint Computer Conference demonstration in 1968 – but it had nowhere near enough power to run four to six versions of the game at once, which was the only way to make the entire enterprise economical. Despite his best

---

[39] Larry Bryan, unpublished interview by Martin Goldberg, March 2015.
[40] Ibid.
[41] Goldberg and Vendel, 2012, chap. 1.
[42] Bryan, 2015.

efforts, Bryan could simply not see how to make the concept work, so after delivering the preliminary results to Bushnell, he left the partnership.[43]

Although Bryan declared a cost-effective *Spacewar!* coin-operated game impossible, Bushnell continued to work on the problem over the next several months. Realizing the whole game could not be executed in software, he decided to move as many functions as he could into specialized hardware instead, which would reduce the strain on the computer.[44] An informal lab was established in the bedroom of Ted Dabney's daughter, where the hardware slowly came together.[45] To fund the project, Bushnell and Dabney each contributed $100, which proved more than sufficient to buy components that generally cost only $0.15–$0.25 each, especially since they could procure many of the items they needed from Ampex, which encouraged employees to take small amounts of inventory for their own projects.[46] The most expensive parts of the system were a used television purchased from Goodwill Industries and a power supply, neither of which cost more than $30.[47] As a stand-in for the computer, Bushnell and Dabney built an "exerciser," a simple piece of hardware that emulated some of the capabilities of the Nova and allowed them to generate and move a dot around the screen to make sure the rest of the equipment was working properly.[48]

Once he was satisfied with the basic hardware, Bushnell opened a dialogue with Data General in January 1971 about ordering a few Nova 1200 computers, a cheaper model of the computer introduced at the end of 1970.[49] With their venture finally ready to begin in earnest, Bushnell and Dabney also took steps that same month to formalize their business relationship by officially organizing Syzygy, Co. as a partnership. As part of this process, both partners invested another $250 into the venture, bringing their total contributions to $700.[50] On January 26, 1971, Bushnell drafted a letter to a

---

[43] Ibid.

[44] Bushnell, January 1976, 40–41.

[45] For decades, Mr Bushnell claimed that the prototype unit was built in his own daughter's bedroom, which is the version of events reported in most secondary media. In 2009, Ted Dabney emerged after almost 40 years of silence to tell his side of the story and claimed that it was built in his daughter's bedroom. Since then, Bushnell has acknowledged that some of the work took place at Dabney's house, but continues to claim work proceeded at his house as well. Based on the recollections of both Dabney and Dabney's daughter combined with Bushnell's partial admission, I believe Dabney's story to be more plausible.

[46] Kent, 2001, 31.

[47] Ramsay, 2012, chap. 2.

[48] Bushnell, January 1976, 59–60.

[49] Ibid, 50–55.

[50] "Statement of Owner's Equity: Year Ended December 31, 1971 (Unaudited)," Syzygy Company, c. 1972.

salesman at Data General ordering "six of everything" so that he and Dabney could build their first games.[51] He never sent it.

At some point in late January or early February 1971, Bushnell reserved some time on a local area Nova to make sure his program would run properly on the actual computer. One of the staff at the computer facility looked over the program and called Bushnell's attention to some errors in his calculations. Due to these problems, it turned out that what Bushnell and Dabney were now calling *Cosmic Combat* would not run smoothly on the Nova even after moving much of the functionality to specialized hardware.[52] For a day or two, Bushnell was despondent, but then he realized that between the specialized hardware they had constructed and the exerciser that replicated some of the Nova's functionality, he and Dabney had practically created the entire game in hardware already, and it would be relatively simple to increase the complexity of the exerciser and do away with the computer altogether.

By spring 1971, Nolan and Ted had completed a rough prototype of *Cosmic Combat*. With their hardware plans now entering their final stage, the duo turned their attention to securing the financial backing necessary to produce the game. They first tried to interest Ampex in the project through their boss, Ed De Benedetti, but he turned them down. Next, Dabney turned to one of his mentors, a former engineer in the Ampex Military Products Division named Irving Roth, but he turned them down as well. Unsure where to turn next, Bushnell made a fortuitous connection through his dentist. During a routine dental appointment, Bushnell began describing the game he was working on and learned that a fellow patient named Dave Ralstin served as the sales manager of a local firm called Nutting Associates, one of a very few companies involved in the manufacture of coin-operated games not located in the industry hub of Chicago. Bushnell contacted Ralstin, and two days later delivered his pitch to create a video arcade game for the company.[53] By April 1971, Bushnell had resigned from Ampex and joined Nutting as chief engineer,[54] where he prepared to unleash the first commercial video game through the coin-operated amusement industry, which had played host to a wide variety of novelty entertainment concepts over the past century, none more significant than the game of pinball.

---

[51] Bushnell, January 1976, 50–51.
[52] Ibid, 56–57.
[53] Goldberg and Vendel, 2012, chap. 1.
[54] Bushnell, January 1976, 72.

6

Pinball Wizards

Shortly before Christmas 1930, a Youngstown, Ohio, carpenter named Arthur Paulin was cleaning out his barn when he chanced upon a board with several holes carved out of it and about 30 nails stuck in it. The board reminded Paulin of the game of bagatelle, a countertop game derived from a billiard variant first played in eighteenth-century France that requires the players to shoot the cue ball up the side of a sloped table to land it in one of several scoring holes guarded by nests of pins. In 1871, an English inventor living in Cincinnati, Ohio, named Montague Redgrave created a countertop version of the game with a spring-loaded plunger replacing the cue stick, and variations on this design achieved modest popularity in subsequent decades.[1] The recent onset of the Great Depression wreaked havoc upon the steel mills that drove the Youngstown economy, and with his own financial situation precarious, Paulin decided to fashion the board into a bagatelle game as a Christmas present for his daughter. The game proved a hit with the neighborhood children, who formed lines around the house to play the game.[2]

With his game board proving popular, Paulin thought he might have a salable product on his hands, so he brought it to his friend Myrl Park, operator of a local drug store. Park felt the game lacked appeal as a consumer product, but he also knew that coin-operated countertop games had recently come into vogue and thought they might be able to market it as a commercial product. Therefore, Paulin took the board to another friend, electrical salesman Earl Froom, who helped him design a coin slot, a ball return, and

---

[1] Redgrave's game was not coin-controlled. The first bagatelle game with coin control and a glass enclosure was a "Coin Game Board" patented by Charles Young in 1892.

[2] Richard M. Bueschel, *Pinball 1: Illustrated Historical Guide to Pinball Machines* (Wheat Ridge, CO: Hoflin Publishing, 1988), 13.

a glass enclosure. Completed around the middle of January 1931, the final game, dubbed *Whiffle*, consisted of a sloped playfield encased in glass sporting a series of scoring holes surrounded by pins. For a nickel, the player received ten balls launched via a spring-loaded plunger that would subsequently deflect off the pins into the holes, each of which carried a specific point value.[3]

Paulin and Froom tested the game in Park's drug store, where it took in $2.60 worth of nickels in just one hour. The three subsequently formed a partnership called Automatic Industries on January 28, 1931, to sell their new game all over the country. Before long, they were booking orders for over 2,000 *Whiffle* games per month, but could not manufacture boards fast enough to meet demand. The pinball boom had begun.

***

Pinball was the latest entrant into a coin-operated machine industry that first emerged in the late nineteenth century. The earliest coin-operated amusements began appearing in the United Kingdom in the 1870s and were primarily displayed at fairs and other travelling shows. The first widely exhibited amusement was a figure of a chimney sweep developed by Henry Davidson in 1871 that came to life and performed a series of actions upon the insertion of a coin. The chimney sweep was one of the first examples of a "working model," a category of coin-operated amusements that achieved significant popularity in the late nineteenth century.[4]

The first recorded individual able to make a living entirely through the manufacture of coin-operated machines was a Leeds mechanic named John Dennison. In May 1875, Dennison displayed his first working models, demonstrations of a drilling machine and a hand lathe, at the Yorkshire Exhibition, where they were well received by the public. He soon began building both mechanical fortune teller machines and working model dioramas for installation at exhibitions, fairs, and bazaars. In the early 1890s, Dennison struck a deal with the Blackpool Tower Company – formed to build a replica of the Eiffel Tower in the English coastal resort town of Blackpool – to supply his working models to the tower exclusively from its opening in 1894. This arrangement afforded Dennison a steady income for the rest of his life and continued long after his death in 1924 until his daughters finally sold their

---

[3] Ibid, 14.

[4] Richard M. Bueschel and Steve Gronowski, *Arcade 1: Illustrated Historical Guide to Arcade Machines* (Wheat Ridge, CO: Hoflin Publishing, 1993), 15.

interest in the venture to Blackpool Tower in 1944.[5] The tower continued to operate the original machines until 1963.

While Dennison was successful, he was not an entrepreneur and contented himself with building a small number of custom installations. The man who birthed a full-fledged coin-operated industry was British inventor and entrepreneur Percival Everitt. In 1883, Everitt introduced the first successful vending machine, a penny postcard vendor of his own design, and in 1884, he debuted one of the first popular coin-operated amusements, a penny-activated weighing machine. Between 1885 and 1887, Everitt established the Post Card and Stamped Envelope Company, the Weighing Machine Company, and the Sweetmeat Automatic Delivery Company to place coin-operated scales and machines vending everything from chocolate to chewing gum to cigarettes in thousands of locations across the United Kingdom and Continental Europe.[6]

Frustrated by scarce capital in Europe, Everitt leaned on family connections to set up shop in the United States, thus playing a critical role in introducing coin-operated machines across the Atlantic as well. The first known American coin-operated amusement machine was a working model of a steam locomotive developed by William Smith of Providence, Rhode Island, in 1885 and displayed in several East Coast railroad stations. Everitt was not far behind with both scales, which he launched through the Vermont-based E. & T. Fairbanks Company in 1885,[7] and vending machines, debuted in 1886 through his own New York-based Automatic Delivery Company.

In the wake of his success with coin-operated scales, Everitt also led a host of British inventors who turned their attention to the attractions found in bars and saloons. These locations often featured devices such as grip, punch, and lung testers that patrons could use to settle arguments about who was stronger, but did little to increase revenue for bar owners aside from a small amount of custom from the losers buying drinks for the winners. Sensing an opportunity, Everitt and others began designing coin-activated testers that allowed owners to monetize these contests. These were joined by coin-operated machines designed to deliver an electric shock, as electricity was thought to provide significant health benefits.[8]

[5] Kitty Ross, "The Dennisons of Leeds: Pioneers of Penny Slot Machines," Secret Lives of Objects (blog), Leeds Museums and Galleries, August 31, 2016, https://secretlivesofobjects.blog/2016/08/31/the-dennisons-of-leeds-pioneers-of-penny-slot-machines.

[6] Nicholas Costa, *Automatic Pleasures: The History of the Coin Machine* (Cincinnati, OH: Seven Hills Books, 1988), 12–16.

[7] Bueschel and Gronowski, 1993, 30–31.

[8] Ibid, 16–27.

While scales, testers, and shock machines proved popular, the lynchpin of the rapidly developing coin-operated amusement industry as it entered the 1890s was the phonograph. Although invented by Thomas Edison in 1877, the phonograph remained little more than a curiosity until the underlying technology improved in the late 1880s. In 1888, a businessman named Jesse Lippincott successfully commercialized the phonograph by purchasing companies established by both Edison and his main rival in sound technology, Alexander Graham Bell, to unite all the important patents under his own North American Phonograph Company. Lippincott proceeded to divide the United States into regional sales territories and assigned franchises to entrepreneurs willing to peddle the new invention.[9] The phonograph attracted attention as a modern marvel and novelty attraction, but it proved prohibitively expensive for ordinary citizens. Therefore, Lippincott's franchisees began exhibiting machines publicly at venues like bars, saloons, and train stations and emulated the testers appearing in the same locations by regulating their play through coin control.

The first coin-operated phonograph installed in the United States was placed in San Francisco's Palais Royal Saloon by Louis Glass of the Pacific Phonograph Company in 1889,[10] but it soon became apparent that bars were not a good venue for phonographs because the patrons were rough on the machines and the establishments were not frequented by the women and children constituting the prime demographic for this new form of entertainment. The solution to this problem came from James Andem, a Civil War veteran, former stenographer, and proprietor of the Ohio Phonograph Company. Andem opened storefront locations in Cincinnati and Cleveland in which a dozen phonographs were grouped together so an attendant could keep them in working order and easily change out cylinders to provide new experiences. The Cincinnati location opened in a building called the Emery Arcade, which may have played a role in the adoption of the term "arcade" to identify an establishment offering coin-operated entertainment.[11]

In 1892, the Edison workshop struck again with the first motion picture player, the Kinetoscope. Invented by William Dickson, the device allows a viewer to peer into a wooden box containing a roll of film displaying a short

[9] Raymond Wile, "The North American Phonograph Company: Part 1," *ARSC Journal* 35, no. 1 (2004): 1–36.

[10] In Britain, an American engineer named Charles Adam Randall patented a coin-operated phonograph in 1888 called the Automatic Parlophone, but it did not appear to have any influence on developments in the United States.

[11] "The Penny Arcade," *Billboard Magazine*, March 15, 1947, 124.

scene. The first Kinetoscope parlors opened two years later, but the establishments quickly merged with the existing phonograph parlors. In 1898, Dickson, who had since broken with Edison, co-founded the American Mutoscope Company to introduce an improved moving picture viewer called the Mutoscope. Rather than a filmstrip, the Mutoscope displays a series of pictures attached to a wheel similar to a rolodex in rapid succession when a patron turns a crank, giving the illusion of movement. The Mutoscope displaced the phonograph and the Kinetoscope to form the heart of the rapidly expanding arcade industry.[12]

The arcades of the late nineteenth and early twentieth centuries were not centers for playing games as they would be in later years. Instead, they were positioned as mechanical Vaudeville shows in which rows of phonographs, Kinetoscopes, and Mutoscopes provided a variety of music, recorded messages, and short films to entertain the public. These would be supplemented by strength and lung testers, coin-operated weighing machines, electric shock machines, card vendors dispensing fortunes, jokes, love letters, and other messages, and machines vending small items like perfume and scented handkerchiefs.[13]

These early coin-operated machines were typically priced at a nickel per play until a Buffalo, New York, entrepreneur named Mitchell Mark discovered during the 1901 Pan American Exposition that an arcade located in an area that experienced high-volume foot traffic could achieve greater profits by lowering the cost for using a machine to a penny. In 1904, Mark partnered with two furriers named Morris Kohn and Adolph Zukor to open a new arcade on Union Square in an upscale New York City shopping district under the banner of the Automatic One Cent Vaudeville Company,[14] which established a template for subsequent arcades and began a shift toward penny play.[15] At the height of their success, the penny arcades represented perhaps the most popular form of public entertainment for the working class in the big cities of the United States and attracted waves of immigrants who could not afford to frequent the theater or similar attractions.

---

[12] Bueschel and Gronowski, 1993, 71–101.

[13] "The Penny Arcade," 1947, 125.

[14] Stephen Birmingham, *The Rest of Us: The Rise of America's Eastern European Jews* (New York: Open Road Media, 2015), Google Books.

[15] Mark was also a pioneer in movie theaters credited with installing the first theater organ in 1907 and establishing one of the first so-called "movie palaces" designed exclusively for the viewing of motion pictures, The Strand, in 1914. His partner at Automatic Vaudeville, Adolph Zukor, later co-founded Paramount Pictures, while a fourth partner brought in later, Marcus Loew, became an early movie theater magnate.

In the latter half of the first decade of the twentieth century, the American arcade industry fell apart. The introduction of cheap spring motors finally brought phonograph ownership within the reach of the working class, while the rise of the Nickelodeon transformed the motion picture industry, which reinvented itself around public viewing of projected feature films. With the emerging popularity of the cinema, arcades no longer attracted the high-volume traffic required to maintain themselves in high-rent locations. Consequently, they relocated to dark, cramped, poorly ventilated facilities on side streets and were mostly frequented by men looking to view one of the racier film shorts not welcomed in the more respectable movie houses. By the end of World War I, the arcade had become a relic of an earlier age.

***

As the arcade lay dying, coin-operated entertainment evolved in a different direction. Starting in the late 1880s, a variety of countertop devices called "trade stimulators" were developed in which a patron could insert a coin to spin a wheel, shoot at a target with a mechanical toy gun, or navigate nests of pins like those found in a drop case carnival game for a chance at winning a prize.[16] In the 1890s, these devices evolved into the first slot machines, culminating in the introduction of the first three-reel slot machine with automatic payout by Charles Fey of San Francisco sometime between 1898 and 1905. Fey only produced small quantities of his *Liberty Bell* for the local market, but after the 1906 San Francisco Earthquake destroyed his shop, Fey's design was either licensed or stolen (depending on whom you ask) by the largest coin-operated machine manufacturer in the country, the Mills Novelty Company. Mills began mass production of its three-reel *Mills Bell* slot machine in 1907, which attained nationwide popularity.[17] The rapid spread of slots was slowly curtailed by government regulation, but during Prohibition, the cash-only nature of the machines drew elements of organized crime, and they could soon be found in all manner of illegal speakeasies and private clubs.

Early slot machines, like the penny arcade machines that preceded them, were large floor models unsuited for mass distribution. Outside larger cities

---

[16] The earliest known trade stimulator is a device called the "Guessing Bank" developed by New Yorker Edward McLoughlin in 1876, in which inserting a coin would cause a dial to spin and stop on a random number, but trade stimulators did not achieve wide distribution and popularity until the next decade.

[17] Tony Wohlers and Eric Schmaltz, "Charles August Fey," in *Immigrant Entrepreneurship: German-American Business Biographies, 1720 to the Present*, vol. 3, ed. Giles R. Hoyt. German Historical Institute, last modified March 25, 2014, http://www.immigrantentrepreneurship.org/entry.php?rec=51.

they could only be found in select establishments. As the United States rapidly motorized in the 1920s, a new breed of coin-operated machine operator emerged who maintained truck delivery routes to place and service machines at retail and restaurant locations across small-town America.[18] This phenomenon led to a new emphasis on countertop games, which could be shipped more easily and find a place in even the smallest establishments. As slot machines faced increasing legal challenges and confiscations during the decade, however, coin-operated machine manufacturers began injecting a degree of skill into their countertop games of chance.

In 1926, a company called A.B.T. Manufacturing deployed a countertop pistol game called *Target Skill* that became an industry sensation, selling over 300,000 units and remaining in production into the 1960s.[19] That same year, a company called Norwat Amusement Devices deployed a machine called *Steam Shovel* in which the player controlled a miniature replica of a steam shovel and attempted to pick up candy and nuts strewn about the base of the cabinet.[20] The machine proved so popular that the "digger machine," the ancestor of the modern crane unit, became a staple not just at amusement parks, boardwalks, traveling carnivals, and the few surviving penny arcades, but also in hotel lobbies and department stores. Even the Mutoscope briefly came back into vogue. As the industry expanded on the back of these products, it gained its own trade publication – *Automatic Age* – and annual trade show before the end of the decade.

The coin-operated amusement business of the 1920s was largely a countertop and carnival trade as penny arcades continued to experience a protracted slump that changed in 1930 when the Chester-Pollard Amusement Company developed a new arcade concept. Brothers Frank, Charles, and Ernest Chester – Pollard was their mother's maiden name – first entered the coin-op business with a fortune telling machine in the early 1920s, but experienced their first real success in 1926 when they acquired the rights to a British manikin soccer game called *Play Football*. In this game, housed in a large wooden freestanding cabinet, two players control the sides of a soccer match by pressing a lever to cause all the players to kick their legs at once. For a nickel, the players receive a single ball and must time their kicks to score a goal on their opponent. The Chester brothers changed the theme of the game to American football and had a hit on their hands.[21] Golf and horse

---

[18] Bueschel, 1988, 72.
[19] Ben Knauf, "Pa, Ma, and Kids Are Totin' Shootin' Irons," *Billboard*, November 20, 1954, 1.
[20] Bueschel and Gronowski, 2003, 244.
[21] Bueschel and Gronowski, 1993, 250.

racing games followed, and Chester-Pollard cabinets could soon be found in thousands of hotels, clubs, and railway depots.[22]

With nickel sports games proving so popular, the Chesters developed a new arcade paradigm called the Sportland. In this setup, a variety of coin-operated machines like strength testers, target shooting games, diggers, sports games, and pinball machines would be placed at the front of the venue, while the majority of the space consisted of a fenced area occupied by large table games with themes like baseball, table tennis, hockey, and bagatelle. The table games would not be coin-operated; patrons would buy 30 minutes of time in the table area for a quarter. The first Sportland opened in an outlying district of Brooklyn, New York, in 1930 and proved profitable despite its less-than-ideal location.[23] By 1933, there were 52 Sportlands in the New York City area alone, which served as models for entrepreneurs across the nation.[24] Consequently, the arcade completed its transition from a novelty attraction to a venue for games of skill, taking on the basic form it would maintain for the next 60 years.

The success of the Sportland arcade – and indeed of the entire coin-operated game industry – can largely be attributed to the Great Depression. With worsening economic conditions severely restricting the amount of money most Americans could afford to spend on leisure activities, arcade machines that could be played for a nickel, or even a penny, were some of the few affordable means of entertainment in the country. In 1930, over 250 companies manufactured 250,000 units of over 400 different games,[25] and by 1934, these manufacturers were taking in over $10 million annually.[26] Meanwhile, many arcades were soon raking in over $800 worth of pennies and nickels a week, while venues in prime locations could pull in as much as $1,200 a week despite an ever-worsening economy.[27]

***

Pinball first hit the coin-operated amusement industry in early 1931 through both the Automatic Amusement *Whiffle* and a game called *Whoopee* independently developed in Chicago by a Belgian immigrant

---

[22] Robert Cantwell, "The Fun Machines," *Sports Illustrated*, July 4, 1977, 29.

[23] William Gersh, "'Sportlands' Seen as Evolution of the Penny Arcade," *Automatic Age*, April 1932, 28–31.

[24] "Sport in the Nickel Age," *Business Week*, March 29, 1933, 14.

[25] Ibid.

[26] "Business & Finance: Pin Game," *Time*, December 24, 1934.

[27] "Sport in the Nickel Age," 1933, 14.

named George Deprez.[28] While both games experienced immediate popularity, the tables were relatively expensive and set to nickel play, and were thus unsuitable for the new economic realities brought on by the Depression. Subsequent tables quickly appeared that were both cheaper to purchase – around $16.50 rather than $100 – and capable of accepting pennies, but most of these machines were shoddily constructed, and the manufacturers could not keep up with burgeoning demand. The man who finally struck the proper balance between availability, quality, and affordability was Dave Gottlieb.

Born in May 1900 in Milwaukee to Russian Jewish immigrants, David Gottlieb served in World War I and then spent two years at the University of Minnesota. Gottlieb left school in 1920 to work as a movie theater booker and traveling salesman based in Minneapolis before relocating to Dallas, Texas, two years later. Gottlieb rode the rails across Texas to sell punchboards, pressed paper boards full of holes each containing a slip of paper that listed a cash or merchandise prize, to workers at isolated oilfields.[29]

Quickly growing tired of lugging around suitcases full of coins and sleeping with a gun under his pillow, Gottlieb turned to the motion picture business. Procuring a Ford Model T automobile, he carted a film projector around Texas to show films in towns too small to have their own cinemas while also pedaling slot machines and countertop games. When Texas cracked down on slot machines, Gottlieb acquired the rights to produce a countertop grip tester and relocated to Chicago, already the manufacturing center of the coin-operated machine industry due to the success of Mills and several other early slot machine manufacturers, to establish D. Gottlieb and Company in 1927.[30]

In September 1931, Gottlieb obtained exclusive rights to manufacture a pinball game called *Bingo* from its designers, Nate Robin and Al Rest, who had been unsuccessful selling it themselves due to quality issues. Gottlieb redesigned the game and began manufacturing units, only to have Robin and Rest break their exclusivity agreement. Gottlieb responded by designing a new game called *Baffle Ball*. Unlike previous pinball manufacturing efforts, Gottlieb developed an assembly line to churn out his new game, the first to achieve true high-volume production. Producing 400 machines a day at his height, Gottlieb sold an astounding 50,000 units of *Baffle Ball* after its November 1931 release. While this represented far greater sales than any

---

[28] Bueschel, 1988, 14–16.
[29] Roger C. Sharpe, "Gottlieb Changes Name but Legacy Endures," *Play Meter*, February 1, 1984, 64–65.
[30] Ibid.

coin-operated game to come before it, Gottlieb still fell short of demand by a good 25,000 units.[31]

Why did pinball suddenly take the United States by storm in 1931? Once again, the Depression was the main culprit. Unlike the big Chester-Pollard sports games, early pinball cabinets like *Baffle Ball* cost less than $20.00, so even at the height of the economic crisis, it was possible for someone to scrape together enough money to buy a few machines and experience a sizable return on investment in coin drop. Indeed, while a significant number of entrepreneurs lost their businesses in the early years of the Depression, they did not necessarily forfeit their entire savings, and many of them invested in pinball machines and other countertop games to make a living.[32] This led to a surge in operators and jobbers and the subsequent rise of a new middleman, the regional distributor. Distributors essentially served as sales representatives for the manufacturing companies by marketing and selling their products to operators within a geographic sales territory. The operators would then place the games on location, keep them in working order, and split the proceeds with the venue owner.

Early pinball machines were also small, contained few moving parts, and were relatively easy to maintain, making them suitable for a wide variety of retail venues more than willing to try anything to attract customers into their stores. As a result, pinball quickly spread from arcades, boardwalks, and amusement parks to roadside stands, bus and rail depots, gas stations, cafés, drug stores, tobacco stores, barber shops, and the bars and taverns that were once again legal with the repeal of Prohibition in 1933. By 1941, when the industry peaked, an estimated 250,000 pinball machines were on location in the United States.[33]

***

In 1931, when *Whiffle* and *Bingo* started spreading around the country, no pinball games were shown at the annual coin machine trade show. In 1932, with *Baffle Ball* a national sensation, roughly 60 games crowded the show floor, and over 100 pinball games were introduced over the course of the next year.[34] Despite the competition, one machine stood head and shoulders above the rest: the *Ballyhoo* table introduced by Ray Moloney.

---

[31] Richard M. Bueschel, *Encyclopedia of Pinball Volume 1: Whiffle to Rocket 1930–1933* (LaGrangeville, NY: Silverball Amusements, 1996), 19–20.

[32] Walter W. Hurd, "A History of Pinball," *Billboard*, May 29, 1943, 91.

[33] "The Coin Machine Industry," *Billboard*, February 26, 1944, 66.

[34] Russ Jensen, Pinball Expo '96, summary of talk given by pinball historian Richard Bueschel, http://www.scholzroland.de/VPStuff/EXPO96.htm.

Born in November 1899 in Cleveland, Ohio, Raymond Thomas Moloney, Sr. spent his early adult life wandering the country while tackling a variety of jobs. After trying his luck in the oil fields of Texas and Oklahoma, harvesting crops in California, and working in sugar refineries in the South, he returned to his birth city to work in a steel mill where his father served as the foreman. After losing that job, Moloney relocated to Chicago in 1921, and his brother-in-law secured his employment in a print shop that produced punchboards like those Dave Gottlieb was selling in Texas.[35]

At the print shop, Moloney became close friends with a co-worker named Joe Linehan. When Joe and a partner named Charlie Weldt bought out the firm to create the Joseph P. Linehan Printing Company in 1922, they placed Moloney in charge of its punchboard operation. The trio named the punch-board subsidiary the Lion Manufacturing Company after deciding to make use of stationary ordered from Linehan Printing bearing that name that had never been picked up. In 1925, the trio bought out one of the suppliers of prizes for its punchboards to establish the Midwest Novelty Company as a subsidiary of Lion and began distributing coin-operated products such as slot machines and trade stimulators via mail order. Moloney served as president of both Lion and Midwest Novelty, while his partners remained focused on the printing business.[36]

When *Baffle Ball* became a hit, Moloney could see that pin games were going to be the next great fad in the industry and signed on as a distributor. When Gottlieb could not fill his orders in a timely manner, Moloney decided to manufacture his own game instead. Both his partners balked at entering the manufacturing business, but Moloney convinced them that pin games would be hot over the next year, and they would be foolish not to dive in. Linehan and Weldt agreed to a limited investment in a new manufacturing subsidiary on the condition that they pull out as soon as they recouped their costs. All three partners figured they were catching a passing fad and planned to end production once they cleared $100,000.[37]

With funding in place, Moloney began working his industry contacts for a game idea, which lead to a royalty deal with designers Oliver Van Tyl and Oscar Bloom for their new pin game. While Moloney liked how it played, he felt the design lacked the pizzazz necessary to stand out in what looked to become a crowded field. To make the table more eye-catching, he designed a

---

[35] Christian Marfels, *Bally: The World's Game Maker*, 2nd ed. (Enterprise, NV: Bally Technologies, 2007), 1–2.

[36] Ibid, 2–3.

[37] Bueschel, 1996, 23.

colorful playfield based on the cover of the December 1931 edition of satiri-
cal magazine *Ballyhoo*. Consequently, Moloney named the pintable *Ballyhoo*
and dubbed the new manufacturing subsidiary he officially organized on
January 10, 1932, the Bally Manufacturing Company. The game quickly
caught fire, selling 50,000 units in just seven months to rocket Bally to the
top of the industry.[38]

Over the next two years, the hits kept coming as what could have easily
just been a fad turned into a thriving business. In August 1932, Gottlieb
and Bally each released a follow-up to their original hit products, *Five Star
Final* and *Goofy*, respectively, thus proving neither company was a one-hit
wonder. That same year, the Mills Novelty Company, the leader in coin-
operated amusements and gambling machines, debuted a machine dubbed
"the Official," providing a certain legitimacy to the pin table industry. The
Mills Official was also the first table advertised under the name "pinball."[39]
Each of these games altered the standard pin game formula in small ways,
but the most important innovations of the period came from a West Coast
designer named Harry Williams.

Born in New York City in June 1906, Harry Edward Williams moved
with his family to Los Angeles when he was 15 years old. Although he graduated from Stanford with an engineering degree, Williams took employment
as an artist in the advertising industry. Out of work with the advent of the
Depression in 1929, Williams supported himself by turning to carpentry, set
design, and the occasional bit part in Hollywood films, but had great difficulty making ends meet.[40]

Desperate for a better source of income, Williams attended a sales convention for a coin-operated game called *Jai Alai* and spent his entire savings
purchasing five machines at $100 each. He proved unable to secure prime
locations for the games, however, and his new business failed. The owner of
one of his locations then told him about the latest coin-op game sweeping the
region, Geroge Miner's *All-American Automatic Baseball*, which was similar
to the Chester-Pollard sports output but was the first game to adapt that formula to the National Pastime. Williams purchased ten machines on credit
and later bought the rights to the game from Miner when it proved successful, but the rise of pinball ended the brief hegemony of the sports games in

---

[38]Ibid, 23–29.

[39]Ibid, 55–56.

[40]Richard M. Bueschel, *Encyclopedia of Pinball Volume 2: Contact to Bumper 1934–1936*
(Poughkeepsie, NY: Silverball Amusements, 1997), 3–5.

the coin-op world. Williams once again found himself stuck with a game that could not earn any money.[41]

Williams beheld his first pinball game at a lunch counter across from Universal Studios in Hollywood and took note of its popularity. As pinball continued to spread in the Los Angeles area, Williams decided he had finally found the game he was looking for. In early 1933, he bought out the owner of a local company called Automatic Amusements to begin manufacturing pinball games himself. He started by creating new playfields for existing machines before entering full production on new product in August 1933.

Williams was likely one of the first actual engineers to create pinball games, and he pushed the design of pinball in directions no one had thought to before. His first major innovation came in his second pingame, *Advance*, released in October 1933. Frustrated with patrons cheating at pinball by banging on the tables or even lifting them off the floor, Williams developed an early tilt mechanism, which would cause the game to end if the table was jostled too much.[42] His next machine proved even more significant. In *Contact*, Williams introduced more action to the game through a battery-powered kicker that launched the ball back onto the table after it entered a scoring hole to give the player the opportunity to score more points. Released by carburetor manufacturer Fred McClellan through a new firm called the Pacific Amusement Manufacturing Company in November 1933, the game became a nationwide sensation after Pacific opened a Chicago plant in spring 1934 and ultimately sold somewhere between 28,000 and 33,000 units.[43] Williams subsequently relocated to Chicago, where he played a key role in the continuing innovation of pinball over the next several decades.

After *Contact*, electricity, playfield action, sound effects – the game featured a bell that would ding when a ball was kicked out of a hole – and the tilt mechanism all became standard components of pinball, and an arms race commenced to add new features to the game. Bally struck the next major blow in 1936 when it eliminated pins and holes from the playfield entirely and replaced them with long, thin rods attached to coil springs it

---

[41] Ibid, 5–7.

[42] In his own lifetime, Williams claimed to have invented the tilt, but this is not true. The earliest known mechanism dates back to a trade stimulator in 1931. Several pinball tables from Gottlieb and others introduced the tilt to pinball earlier in 1933, though it is certainly possible he had not seen them yet when he developed the idea.

[43] Russ E. Jensen, "A Visit with Harry Williams," accessed May 28, 2019, http://www.pinballcollectorsresource.com/russ_files/harryvisit.html.

dubbed bumpers.[44] Now instead of scoring points when a ball fell into a hole, the player scored points whenever the ball made contact with one of the bumpers, while a display on the backglass would keep a running tally of the player's total points. Introduced by Bally in 1936 in a game called, appropriately enough, *Bumper*, the bumper completed the transition of pinball from a variant of bagatelle into a new game. Just as the industry was entering the height of its success, however, a product appeared that signaled the beginning of the end of pinball's first golden age.

**

In February 1933, Bally released a pintable called *Airway* to which a New York distributor named Herman Seiden added a dry cell battery to power a payout slot that transformed the table into a game of chance that delivered a cash prize if the ball landed in the proper hole. Seiden shared this innovation with the engineers at Bally, who adapted it into a new table called *Rocket*. Released in October 1933, *Rocket* became an immediate sensation and took in enough money that Moloney was able to take full control of Lion Manufacturing and its Bally subsidiary by buying out Linehan and Weldt.[45]

In 1935, Moloney moved Bally into a 75,000 square foot facility on Belmont Avenue in Chicago that remained the company's home for half a century and capitalized on the success of *Rocket* by instigating development of the company's first pure gambling machines. He introduced a dice machine called *Reliance* at the annual industry trade show in January 1936 and followed it with a miniature countertop slot machine called *Bally Baby* later that year. Though never a leader in the field, Bally remained a major player in slot machines for just over a decade.[46] This placed Bally in a prime financial position, but came at a cost for the larger pinball industry as it faced difficulties in the late 1930s due to its increasing ties to gambling.

The success of *Rocket* created a schism in the industry regarding the desirability of payout games. David Gottlieb ultimately refused to manufacture them after a brief flirtation because he figured they would draw unnecessary attention from crusaders against gambling. Harry Williams went a step further by pioneering the concept of awarding an extra play for achieving a certain score on his 1935 machine *Flash* in an attempt to provide the player

---

[44]Bally borrowed the flipper from a bowling-themed game called *Bolo* released by a New York company called Pacent Manufacturing. Pacent only had limited manufacturing capability, so Bally popularized the bumper. Bueschel, 1997, 110–113.

[45]Marfels, 2007, 13–14.

[46]Ibid, 15–30.

an alternative reward to a cash prize. Ray Moloney, however, continued to strengthen his company's position in the payout pinball and slot machine businesses, and many smaller companies followed suit.

Even without payouts, pinball had already been attacked in many circles as a game that incited juvenile delinquency and petty crime and corrupted the youth. Now with the gambling connection as well, it drew attention from crusaders against organized crime. Since the start of Prohibition, slot machines had served as a money-laundering outlet for bootleggers, but by the late 1930s, they had been pushed to the fringes of society by law enforcement efforts to wipe out the industry. Now that pinball could provide a payout, politicians believed that the machines were an attempt by organized crime to circumvent laws against slot machine operation.

Chicago, the center of the coin-op industry, outlawed pinball in the mid-1930s.[47] In 1939, Los Angeles followed suit through a narrowly passed ballot initiative.[48] In New York City, Mayor Fiorella La Guardia launched a spirited campaign against pinball machines as part of his larger assault on organized crime and scored a major victory in 1942 when New York Supreme Court Justice Aaron Levy upheld an earlier ruling from a magistrate that pinball machines were gambling devices and therefore properly subject to seizure.[49] The ruling effectively criminalized the operation of pinball machines in New York City, although they were not formally banned by the city council until 1948.[50] These bans, alongside many in smaller communities, assured that pinball manufacturers and operators would be linked with organized crime in the public mind and forced them to wage constant battles over the legality of the game for more than 30 years.

While the long-term effects of pinball being linked to organized crime were devastating, the entry of the United States into World War II in December 1941 provided a more immediate threat to the industry. With raw materials and parts needed for military production, the government effectively banned the manufacturing of new pinball machines by deeming the amusement industry non-essential to the war effort, so the major pinball manufacturers turned to war-related work for the duration.

---

[47] The exact date appears to be lost to history, at least without a deep dive into city council records, but a group lost an appeal against the ban in 1938. Ryan Smith, "Chicago once waged a 40-year war on pinball," Chicago Reader, May 5, 2018, https://www.chicagoreader.com/Bleader/archives/2018/05/05/chicago-once-waged-a-40-year-war-on-pinball.

[48] Scott Harrison, "From the Archives: Pinball games banned in Los Angeles," Los Angeles Times, November 19, 2018.

[49] "City Wins Twice in its Pinball Ban," New York Times, February 12, 1942.

[50] "Beame Signs Bill, Pinball Machines Are Legal Again," New York Times, June 2, 1976.

To fill this void, a small number of designers began creating refurbished games by recycling old cabinets and parts and combining them with new playfield designs. One of the leaders in this field was consistent pinball innovator Harry Williams. While working for pinball and jukebox manufacturer Rockola in 1935, Williams met a young engineer named Lyndon Durant who impressed him with his innovative engineering designs.[51] The duo continued to work together at several manufacturers for the rest of the decade, but with the start of the war, they went into business for themselves by establishing the United Manufacturing Company in 1942 both to refurbish old games and to seek out lucrative war contracts.[52] In 1943, Williams sold his share in United to Durant and established the Williams Manufacturing Company, which refurbished old games and built radar components for the remainder of the war.[53]

***

The leading pinball manufacturers of the 1930s and 1940s were small, family-run companies founded by individuals who had generally started as distributors or operators of coin-operated equipment and found their entrée into manufacturing when pinball grew so popular so fast that it was impossible for existing firms to keep up with demand. Over 200 companies would go on to release at least one pinball machine in the 1930s as demand continued unabated until the production halt brought on by World War II.

Immediately after the war, it appeared the coin-operated machine industry was poised to enter another boom period as manufacturers entered the post-war era with both better equipment and larger manufacturing capacity due to wartime innovations and operators needed to replace roughly 90% of the estimated 5,000,000 coin-operated machines in operation at the start of the war.[54] Instead, the arcade industry experienced a decline as small-town locations established to serve military training camps folded due to insufficient custom. The number of arcades in the United States fell by nearly half, and amusement manufacturers curtailed the introduction of new units and raised prices to compensate for the drop off in locations.[55]

---

[51] Bueschel, 1997.

[52] "United Mfg. Co. Enters Games Field," *Billboard*, August 22, 1942, 76.

[53] The founding year of Williams Manufacturing fluctuates frequently in the sources, but an examination of the trades shows conclusively that it was 1943, as Williams was still noted as being at United early in the year, and the first mentions of Williams Electronics come later in the year.

[54] "New Markets Seen for Coin Machines," *New York Times*, April 22, 1946.

[55] "Holiday Play Sparks New Year Outlook for Arcade Operators," *Billboard*, January 10, 1948.

Amusements were further hurt by continued attacks on pinball as a gambling device controlled by organized crime that led either to complete bans or heavy per-unit licensing fees around the country. Manufacturers attempted to compensate with a new type of game called a rolldown that operated similar to a standard pinball machine minus the plunger and with no possibility of winning a free game. Rolldowns surged in popularity in 1947, but skeptical lawmakers ultimately decided they could easily be modified into gambling machines and banned them alongside the regular pinballs.[56]

With pinball no longer able to form the heart of the industry in many parts of the United States, a succession of new novelty products arose to replace it that would each spend two or three years in the spotlight before giving way to the next big thing. First came shuffleboard, a centuries-old game that suddenly became a popular coin-operated amusement in 1948. Next, United Manufacturing introduced a shuffleboard variant called the shuffle alley in 1949, in which the player slides a small metal-cased object similar to a hockey puck down an eight-foot lane to trigger switches on the playing field that cause suspended bowling pins to retract. Then came the kiddie rides in 1951 – mostly mechanical horses, but also cars, boats, and spaceships.[57] Bumper pool followed in 1955, in which players attempt to shoot a ball into a single hole surrounded by bumpers on one end of a pool table. Finally, in late 1956 coin-operated standard six-pocket billiards tables began to proliferate, which helped spur a new pool table boom at the beginning of the 1960s. Pool became a second pillar in the amusement industry just as crucial to its continued success as pinball.

These novelty games were introduced into a rapidly transforming industry in which the decline of the inner city and the rise of suburbia coupled with the onset of the Baby Boomer generation signaled a shift in coin-op venues once again. While the big inner city arcades did not disappear entirely, in the late 1950s coin-operated amusements began dispersing across fun spots like bowling alleys and skating rinks and shopping venues like department stores and discount houses. These locations generally housed fewer games and were interested largely in children's entertainment rather than pinballs and shuffle alleys. As demand for many types of games declined, the industry began to consolidate until by 1965 what had been over a dozen major manufacturers at the end of World War II were whittled down to just five.

---

[56] Horowitz, Iz, "Rolldowns' Future Puzzles Industry," January 24, 1948, 82.

[57] The first coin-operated horse was created by a Sikeston, Missouri man named Otto Hahs in 1931, but they suddenly surged in popularity in late 1951.

Of the remaining players in the industry, Gottlieb remained most closely wedded to pinball and became the leading manufacturer before the end of the 1950s. While an individual pinball table in this period might sell only 1,000–2,000 units – down from tens of thousands in the early 1930s – Gottlieb maintained an aggressive release schedule of between ten and twenty tables a year to establish its dominance. The company also introduced the two most important pinball innovations of the period, flippers and multi-player tables. The flipper, first introduced on the *Humpty Dumpty* table in 1947, may well have saved pinball, as it injected a degree of skill into the game by allowing the player to press a button at the right moment to bat the ball back up the playfield and score more points.[58] Multi-player tables, meanwhile, introduced the concept of two players taking turns on the same machine and competing for the best score and played a leading role in raising the price per play of coin-operated amusements from a nickel to a dime.[59]

The number two company in pinball during the period was the recently established Williams Manufacturing Company, which also played a significant role in modernizing the game in 1948 through the introduction of the pop bumper on its *Saratoga* machine. Unlike traditional bumpers, a pop bumper violently kicks the ball in a new direction when it makes contact, providing considerably more action on the playfield. In conjunction with the flipper, the pop bumper completely changed the way pinball played as the ball ricocheted around the table at high speeds and the player did his best to keep the game going with a well-placed flipper shot.

In 1948, Harry Williams sold 49% of his company to a distributor named Sam Stern. While working as a foreman in a coat factory in 1931, Stern received a tip from a Philadelphia police officer that people were making big money in coin-operated amusements, so he decided to put a few machines on location.[60] He became a major player after buying up a number of routes and then becoming a Rockola jukebox distributor in the city in 1939.[61] Eager to

---

[58] Roger C. Sharpe and James Hamilton, *Pinball!* (New York: E.P. Dutton, 1977), 54–55. *Humpty Dumpty* sported three sets of flippers that faced outward. In early 1948, a competitor called Genco released a table called *Triple Action* featuring just a single pair of flippers facing outwards at the bottom of the playfield. In 1950, Gottlieb released a table called *Just 21* with two flippers facing inward, establishing the standard configuration that exists to the present day.

[59] Shuffle alleys were set to dime play from the start. Two-player pins and coin-operated pool tables were important in the migration of the entire industry to dime play, as two players justified double the cost. Gottlieb first attempted multi-player pinball in 1954 with a four-player game called *Super Jumbo*, but when it proved unsuccessful, they released a two-player game called *Duette* in 1955 that established the popularity of multi-player pinball. Bueshcel, 1988, 217.

[60] Keith Smith, *All in Color for a Quarter* (unpublished manuscript, 2016), 486.

[61] "Sam and Gary on Stern's," *RePlay*, December 1977, 33.

move further up the chain, Stern walked into Williams's office in 1947, put his feet up on the desk, and asked Williams to give him just under half the company. Williams had never been fond of managing the firm that bore his name, far preferring to focus on designing new games, so after some thought, he agreed to the deal.

Stern became a vice president at Williams in January 1948 and held the post for the next 11 years before orchestrating a buy-out of Williams in 1959 by Consolidated Sun Ray, a New York retail conglomerate that operated a variety of businesses from drug stores to discount houses. Both owners were offered cash or stock in the deal. Williams opted for cash and left the company, while Stern took stock and replaced Williams as president of the renamed Williams Electronic Manufacturing Corporation.[62] The merger with Sun Ray did not work out, and Williams became independent again in 1961.[63]

Under Stern's leadership, Williams retooled its manufacturing line and deployed a series of pinball tables in the early 1960s that introduced new features like moving targets that could change position as the game progressed,[64] drop targets that would fall beneath the table when hit,[65] and a multi-ball function that allowed multiple balls to bounce around the table at once if the player hit the proper targets.[66] These innovations transformed pinball once more by turning it into a game of structure and sequence with a primary objective of hitting a group of targets in a specific order or targeting a specific part of the playfield at a specific time to gain added benefits and bonus points.

Although Williams never dethroned Gottlieb in the 1960s, the transformation of the company under Stern attracted the attention of jukebox powerhouse Seeburg Corporation, itself undertaking an aggressive expansion program aimed at transforming the company into the largest coin-operated machine manufacturer in the world. The architects of this expansion were Herbert Siegel and Delbert Coleman, who in the early 1950s went into business together as turnaround artists. In 1956, they bought a troubled Pittsburgh brewing company called Fort Pitt and merged it with two coat companies owned by Siegel's family. Next, they marshaled the combined

---

[62] Ken Knauf, "Williams Mfg. Purchased by Consolidated Sun Ray, Inc.," *Billboard*, July 27, 1959, 94.

[63] "Williams Deal with Sun Ray Is Called Off," *Billboard*, June 26, 1961, 50.

[64] First introduced in *Magic Clock* in 1960.

[65] First introduced in *Vagabond* in 1962.

[66] First introduced in *Beat the Clock* in 1963.

financial resources of the conglomerate to purchase Seeburg from the son of founder Justus Seeburg in November 1956.[67]

After consolidating the Seeburg purchase, Siegel and Coleman led a board coup in March 1957 to oust the president of Fort Pitt and have themselves appointed chairman and president of the company, respectively. They subsequently sold off the brewing business in November, and renamed Fort Pitt to Seeburg Corporation in April 1958.[68] A series of vending machine company purchases followed, before they purchased game manufacturers Williams and United Manufacturing in June and September 1964, respectively.[69] Stern stayed on to run the amusement business, continued under the Williams name but at the United factory, which remained the number two company in pinball as well as the leader in shuffle alleys and baseball games.

***

Once the leading manufacturer in the 1930s, Bally fell to third in traditional pinball after the war, but remained one of the leading producers of shuffle alleys and the newly emerging field of coin-operated kiddie rides. Nevertheless, Ray Moloney remained fixated on the games of chance he felt were more profitable. In 1951, however, the U.S. Congress struck the death knell of the traditional slot machine industry through the passage of the Johnson Act, which made it a federal offense to transport gambling devices to states where they were illegal, which at the time meant every state save Idaho and Nevada.[70] Two years later, Illinois outlawed the manufacture of slot machines in the state.

With sentiment once again turning against gambling machines, Bally exited the slot machine business in 1949, but Moloney found another way to stay in the gaming business. In 1951, the company released a table called *Bright Lights* that fell into a new category of pinball called the

---

[67]"Corporations: Money in the Box," *Time Magazine*, October 27, 1958. Seeburg was originally established to manufacture player pianos in 1902. It entered the jukebox business in the 1920s and became the leading company in the field after releasing the first 100-selection unit in 1948.

[68]"Seeburg Elects Siegel, Coleman," *Billboard*, April 28, 1958, 73.

[69]"Seeburg Acquires Williams," *Billboard*, June 13, 1964, 42.

[70]Marfels, 2007, 23. At the time the bill was passed, Idaho was in the middle of a brief flirtation with legal slot machines that proved so troublesome that they were banned again soon after, leaving Nevada as the only state where slots were legal. Certain states like Maryland left the decision on whether to ban slots to local government authorities, however, so there were a few isolated counties that allowed slot machines as well.

bingo machine.[71] Unlike the newly emerging flipper games, a bingo machine required the player to launch his balls onto a playfield featuring holes in a standard bingo card configuration in the hopes of completing a bingo to win a prize.[72] These machines were initially legal under the Johnson Act, which focused on slot, roulette, and crane machines. In 1957, however, the U.S. Supreme Court ruled that pinball machines designed to deliver a cash payout were, in fact, gambling devices and could therefore properly fall under the Act.[73] As a result, when the U.S. House of Representatives looked to expand the definition of gambling devices found in the Johnson Act in 1962, the body proposed outlawing the transport of pinball entirely.[74] This outcome was averted after the bill passed to the Senate, where a compromise was reached only to restrict the transport of payout pinball machines.[75] With bingo machines discredited and subsequently banned by many states, Bally shifted its focus back to the manufacture of traditional pinball machines.

On February 26, 1958, Ray Moloney died suddenly of a heart attack at just 58 years old. His death threw Bally into turmoil. His entire estate, including Lion Manufacturing and its Bally subsidiary, was placed in a trust administered by the Chicago-based American National Bank and Trust Company. A new board of directors was elected that appointed long-time Bally executive Joseph Flesch as president, who subsequently ceded control of the company to Moloney's sons, Ray Jr. and Donald, two years later. By that time, the decline in sales of bingo machines brought on by the 1957 Supreme Court decision had significantly impacted Bally's bottom line, and the company was losing money. Ray and Donald proposed bringing Bally back into the slot machine business to turn the company around, but American National had no interest in entering a business that it assumed would have deep connections to organized crime and wanted to liquidate the company instead to pay off its debts.[76] Bally ultimately survived through the intervention of Bill O'Donnell.

Born in 1922, William Thomas O'Donnell was educated at Loyola Academy and Sullivan High School, but was forced to drop out in 1939 at the age of 17 to support his family after the death of his father. O'Donnell

---

[71] *Bright Lights* was not quite the first bingo machine, as it was beaten by a month by United Manufacturing's *ABC*. *Bright Lights* was the more popular unit, however, and deserves credit for inaugurating the product category.

[72] Marfels, 2007, 24.

[73] "Pinball Machines Lose in Supreme Court Tilt," *New York Times*, June 18, 1957.

[74] "House Passes Bill to Curb Gaming Device Shipments," *New York Times*, June 30, 1962.

[75] "Compromise Crime Bill Is Passed in Senate," *New York Times*, September 29, 1962.

[76] Marfels, 2007, 26–28.

went to work for the Underground Construction Company as a laborer helping to build the Chicago subway system before enlisting in the Marines in
1941 and serving in the Pacific theater during World War II. Discharged in
fall 1945, O'Donnell briefly served as a postal worker before a cousin who
served as Ray Moloney's bookmaker suggested he seek employment with
Bally. O'Donnell joined the firm in 1946 to work in the purchasing department and caught the eye of Moloney, who named him assistant sales manager
six months later. In 1951, Moloney promoted O'Donnell to sales manager,
and upon Moloney's death American National named him to Lion's board
of directors.[77]

O'Donnell worked hard to secure a management buyout of Bally to save
the company, but he could not secure financing due to the company's alleged
connections to organized crime. Therefore, he turned to the company's distributors for help. Runyon Sales, a powerful New Jersey distributor fronted
by Abe Green and Barnett Sugarman, proved amenable and brought in two
additional investors of their own, a Brooklyn pool table manufacturer named
Irving Kaye and a well-connected former vending executive named Sam
Klein. Klein, in turn, brought in a concessions magnate named Lou Jacobs to
finance a portion of the deal. Together, this motley group of investors – many
of whom had ties to underworld figures – formed K.O.S. Enterprises and
bought certain assets of Lion Manufacturing and the Bally corporate name
on June 17, 1963, for $2.85 million. K.O.S. subsequently changed its name
to the Lion Manufacturing Corporation with Bill O'Donnell as president
and largest shareholder Sam Klein as executive vice president.[78]

In 1963, Illinois repealed its decade-long ban on slot machine manufacture, and O'Donnell prepared to lead the new Bally back into the gaming
business. Because the Johnson Act and the Illinois ban had been passed
so soon after the complete halt in slot machine production brought on by
World War II, the majority of slot machines in service still relied on decades
old mechanical technology, so the industry was ripe for modernization. In
1964, Bally introduced the first electromechanical slot machine, *Money
Honey*, and revolutionized the industry. Capable of more flexible payout
schemes than traditional machines and incorporating a coin-hopper that
allowed the payout of large sums without the need to stop playing and find
an attendant, *Money Honey* increased casino profits by as much as 400% and
created intense demand for modern slot machines. With little competition

---

[77] Ibid, 29.
[78] Sal Recchi, "Gaming Giant has Checkered Past, Local Ties," *Boca Raton News*, July 15, 1979.

in the field, Bally cornered 94% of the Nevada market by 1968. Buoyed by this success, O'Donnell incorporated Lion as the Bally Manufacturing Corporation with the intent of taking the company public. A long Securities & Exchange Commission investigation followed to insure the company was not a front for organized crime, after which Bally became the first publicly traded coin-op manufacturer on March 13, 1969.[79]

***

Rounding out the big five coin-op manufacturers were two smaller companies that largely avoided pinball to focus on novelty products: Chicago Coin and Midway Manufacturing. Chicago Coin founder Samuel Harry Gensburg was born in Brest, Russia, in 1893, but the family immigrated to the United States not long after he was born and settled in Pittsburgh. A natural businessman, Gensburg helped out in his father's grocery store for a time until opening his own store at 16. Before long, his store was outperforming his father's, and he opened a second store the next year followed by a nickelodeon cinema the year after that when he was just 18. At around age 20, Gensburg left Pittsburgh to seek new opportunities in California, but those plans ended in Chicago when he stopped to visit relatives only to meet and fall in love with Dora Wolberg. He decided to stay in the city and worked as an order filler for Sears Roebuck before marrying Dora in 1919 and moving to Manchester, Iowa, to run a grocery store.[80]

Eight years later, Sam learned about a company in Milwaukee that had installed a coin-operated machine that vended Hershey bars and decided to install one in his store. When it proved successful, he bought 100 of the machines and relocated to Chicago to place them in bars and taverns in partnership with his brother, Dave. Around 1929 or 1930, Sam and Dave were introduced to a countertop game called *Little Whirlwind* developed by coin-op innovator Howard Peo.[81] Dave started placing the game on location until another brother, a manufacturer of prizes for Cracker Jack boxes named Louis, developed a knockoff of the game called *Hearts* that Dave could sell for a cheaper price. When Peo threatened legal action, the duo brought in a cousin who had previously invented an electric pencil sharpener and a bicycle

---

[79] Marfels, 2007, 31–33.

[80] Roger C. Sharpe, "A Final Farewell to Sam Gensburg," *Play Meter*, May 15, 1985, 50–51.

[81] Like the early pinball games, *Little Whirlwind* was a countertop unit in which the player launched steel balls onto a playfield and hoped they landed in scoring holes, but it had a vertical orientation rather than a horizontal one and featured spiral lanes rather than pins, taking inspiration from the allwin gambling games currently popular in Europe.

coaster brake to build a new version that did not run afoul of Peo's patents. With this new game in hand, Louis, David, and a fourth Gensburg brother named Meyer established the Genco Manufacturing Company and became big players in the early pinball industry by pursuing a strategy of taking concepts developed by other companies and building higher quality versions of their own.[82]

As his brothers entered the manufacturing business, Sam Gensburg joined with his brother-in-law Sam Wolberg in 1931 to establish a trade-in business for used coin-op equipment dubbed the Chicago Coin Machine Exchange. Before long, Sam concluded he could make better pinball tables than his brothers and established Chicago Dynamic Industries as a manufacturer of games marketed under the Chicago Coin name.[83] The company started by making replacement boards for popular existing games like *Ballyhoo* before deploying its first original pin table in 1933.

Like Genco, Chicago Coin prided itself on improving on the ideas of others rather than pursuing technological innovation, so the company rarely had a leading game in the market. It released a constant flow of games across multiple genres, however, to remain an important player in the industry. In fact, although he entered the business after his brothers, Sam Gensburg ultimately surpassed them. In the early 1950s, Genco began to experience difficulties in part due to the owners' attempts to break into the casino business in Nevada, so Sam bought his brothers' company in 1952 and operated it as a separate subsidiary of Chicago Dynamic Industries under the direction of his son Avron until shutting it down in 1959.

While Chicago Coin dabbled in pinball even as it focused its main efforts on novelty products, the final important amusement manufacturer of the post-war period avoided the business almost entirely. Mechanical engineer Marcine Wolverton, who went by "Iggy" because many people considered Marcine a girl's name, designed aircraft ordnance during World War II and then entered the coin-op industry after the war's conclusion. He briefly worked at jukebox maker Wurlitzer before landing at the United Manufacturing Company. In 1947, he was joined at United by electrical engineer Hank Ross, who had previously worked for the amusement manufacturer Exhibit Supply. When United encountered financial difficulties in the late 1950s, Wolverton and Ross, regarded as two of the company's top designers, decided to strike out on their own. Scraping together $5,000, they

---

[82] Ibid, 51.
[83] Ibid, 52.

formed an equal partnership in October 1958 based in the Chicago suburb of Franklin Park, Illinois, called the Midway Manufacturing Company.[84]

Wolverton and Ross planned to survive as a small company in the highly competitive coin-op industry through a low-overhead factory operation that would allow them to undercut competitors on price. To that end, they leased a modest 5,000 square foot manufacturing facility and fabricated most of their factory installations and game parts themselves.[85] Working long hours at the plant during the day, both men also attended night school to brush up on business. In January 1959, the duo began production of their first game, a shuffleboard with a rebound feature called *Bumper Shuffle*, followed in May by a unique game called *Red Ball* in which the player presses buttons to launch balls onto a bingo-style playfield in the hopes of arranging them in various configurations to score points. In 1960, Midway scored its first major hit with a pellet shooting game called *Shooting Gallery* and thereafter focused largely on gun games and pitch-and-bat baseball games. It also added a shuffle alley line in 1966 shortly before moving to a larger facility in nearby Schiller Park. Although the smallest and newest manufacturer among the big five, Midway proved itself one of the most innovative.

***

By the mid-1960s, the coin-operated amusement industry was running out of steam. In 1954, the U.S. Census Bureau estimated the average revenue generated by amusement machines on location in the United States was $722 per machine.[86] By 1963, the average revenue per machine had fallen to $639 despite nearly ten years of inflation and the widespread adoption of dime play.[87] No major new product categories had emerged since the spread of shuffle alleys, bumper pool, and two-player pinball in the mid-1950s, while the combination of dwindling markets and consolidation had whittled down the number of manufacturers in Chicago to just five. With returns declining and so little competition in the marketplace, stagnation set in as manufacturers cut back on research and development. New game designs became stale and predictable, often merely incorporating small gameplay tweaks or cosmetic changes into existing concepts to differentiate them from the models released the year before. An increasing interest in pinball

---

[84]Smith, 2016, 162.

[85]"Midway in Groundwork on Three New Games," *Billboard*, November 24, 1958, 102.

[86]"U.S. Releases 1954 Juke, Game Totals," *Billboard*, July 15, 1957, 124.

[87]"1963 Industry Figures In," *Billboard*, December 31, 1966, 45. The magazine reported the average for pinball and other amusements separately. I have taken a combined average.

in Europe – particularly after France opened its market to imports and Italy partially lifted a pinball ban in 1961 – helped sustain sales for the surviving manufacturers, but without new game concepts, the long-term future of the industry looked grim. Just as coin-operated amusements appeared ready to enter an irreversible decline, a savior appeared in the form of a new type of arcade machine from Japan.

7

Rising Sun

When Nate Robin and Al Rest broke their exclusivity agreement with David Gottlieb to sell *Bingo* in late 1931 and thus set in motion the series of events that led Gottlieb to release *Baffle Ball*, they did so at the behest of a Chicago tool and die maker named Leo Berman. At the time, pinball remained a Midwestern phenomenon, but Berman harbored ambitions to take the game nationwide. Doing so required cracking the competitive New York City market with its thriving Sportland arcades, and doing that required a man with solid connections throughout the five boroughs. Berman turned to an acquaintance named Irving Bromberg.[1]

The son of Russian Jewish immigrants like so many of the early pinball magnates, Irving Bromberg was born in June 1899 and grew up in Brooklyn, New York. After marrying as a teenager, Bromberg secured a job selling glassware before joining with two other men in 1922 to establish the Greenpoint Motor Car Corporation, for which he served as president.[2] In 1930, Bromberg became a salesman again, this time in the penny candy trade that operated on an honor system in which a patron was supposed to leave a penny when taking a candy from a store display. Bromberg was not selling games when Berman contacted him and did not even have his own showroom, but he borrowed some space from a friend in the gum vending business and put the machines on display.[3] After some initial difficulty generating interest in the product, Bromberg attracted the attention of Bill

---

[1] Bueschel, 1988, 106–107.

[2] U.S. Congress, Senate, Committee on Government Operations, *Fraud and Corruption in Management of Military Club Systems*, Report No. 92-418, 92nd Cong., 1st Sess., 1971, 5. Note the report gets the founding year of the Greenpoint Motor Company wrong per "New Boro Corporations," *Brooklyn Daily Eagle*, June 2, 1922.

[3] Bueschel, 1988, 107.

Shorck, one of the last great penny arcade moguls from their heyday at the turn of the century,[4] and sales took off.[5] Before the end of 1931, Bromberg established the Irving Bromberg Company as a distributor of coin-operated amusements. The next year, he began selling Bally tables, and his business expanded rapidly until he was one of the largest distributors on the East Coast with his primary office in Brooklyn and branch offices in Manhattan, Boston, and Washington, DC.

In early 1933, Bromberg moved to Los Angeles to become the only Bally distributor on the west coast and sold off his east coast distributorships a few months later. When Harry Williams and Fred McClellan required help selling *Contact* nationwide, however, Bromberg established the Pacific Amusement Distributing Company to ship units into the New York area, once again playing a crucial role in the spread of an influential machine.[6] Bromberg remained a major force on the west coast into the late 1940s, but his most important legacy was a series of new businesses in Hawaii that grew into a global empire and transformed Japan into one of the most important centers of the coin-operated game industry in the world.

∗∗∗

Coin-operated amusements first entered Japan during the Meiji period of rapid industrialization and modernization. As in the West, peep shows were some of the first machines to arrive in the late nineteenth century, but it appears they never achieved the same level of success as they did in the United States and Great Britain.[7] Instead, it was bagatelle, introduced around 1924, that first interested the Japanese public in coin-operated amusements.[8] The game was initially seen as a children's pastime and became common in candy stores, where it gained the name "pachi-pachi," the Japanese onomatopoeia for the clicking sounds made by the metal balls. Before long, the game spread to market stalls, where it morphed into a gambling game in which adult players could win prizes like soap or cigarettes.

---

[4] Ben Smith, "The Phenomenal Sportlands," *Automatic Age*, January 1935, 109.

[5] Shorck entered the penny arcade business in 1904 as an employee of the influential Automatic One Cent Vaudeville Company. He started his own penny arcade operation called Shorck and Schaffer with partner Max Schaffer in 1916, which managed to weather the fallow period between the end of the penny arcade boom and the rise of the sportland.

[6] "Carload of Machines from West Coast," *Automatic Age*, May 1034, 173.

[7] Eric Eickhorst, "Game Centers: A Historical and Cultural Analysis of Japan's Video Amusement Establishments" (Master's thesis, University of Kansas, 2002), 13.

[8] In Japan, bagatelle is known as the "Corinth Game," because tables in the style called "Corinthian Bagatelle" were among the first imported into the country.

Because space was at a premium in the crowded markets and narrow streets of Japan's major cities, the Japanese transformed their bagatelle games into something new by mounting them vertically rather than horizontally and borrowing elements from the European coin-operated gambling device called the allwin such as a lever in place of a plunger and circular tracks to supplement the traditional bagatelle pins. This new game gained the name *pachinko*, a combination of the aforementioned "pachi" and "ko," the Japanese word for ball. As the game's popularity grew, Japan's first dedicated *pachinko* parlor opened in Nagoya in 1930.[9]

Meanwhile, a man named Yoshikazu "Kaichi" Endo began laying the groundwork for a broader Japanese amusement industry. Born in 1899, Endo opened a medical supplies company in Osaka in 1922 and designed his own vending machine the next year.[10] After the Great Kanto earthquake devastated a wide swath of Japan around the cities of Tokyo and Yokohama in 1923, Endo's business grew rapidly due to increased demand for vending machines and automatic signs to replace those destroyed in the calamity.[11] After developing a fortune telling machine for the Takarazuka Family Land amusement park, Endo renamed his company the Japan Automatic Machine Recreational Equipment Manufacturing Company, Ltd. and refocused on amusement machines, which he handcrafted in limited quantities.[12]

In 1931, Endo approached the Matsuya Department Store in Asakusa, Tokyo, to open an amusement venue on its roof. Dubbed "Sports Land," Endo's attraction combined activities like roller skating, archery, and cycling with equipment like rocking horses, coin-operated testers, and peep shows.[13] Other department stores soon began emulating Sports Land, but just as both novelty amusements and *pachinko* machines were poised to enter a major growth phase, the Japanese government halted the production of coin-operated machines in 1937 due to the need for resources to support its war against China. As the conflict intensified, the government came to view leisure activities and luxury items as a dangerous distraction from the war effort, so in 1938 it ordered the closure of all the *pachinko*

---

[9] Eric Sedensky, *Winning Pachinko: The Game of Japanese Pinball* (Tokyo: Charles E. Tuttle Press, 1991), ebook.

[10] "Arcade Game History," Amusement Press, accessed May 29, 2019, http://www.ampress.co.jp/archive.htm.

[11] Eickhorst, 2002, 16.

[12] "Arcade Game History," Amusement Press.

[13] Eickhorst, 2002, 16.

parlors in the nation. Japan's *pachinko* halls and rooftop amusement spaces subsequently vanished in the fires of World War II.[14]

In 1946, *pachinko* returned to Nagoya and began spreading across the country once more. Over the next four years, the game gained increasing popularity through the work of designer Shoichi Masamura. In 1948, Masamura debuted a new layout called the "Positive Gauge Forest" that added spinners and additional pins to increase playfield action and scoring opportunities. In 1949 and 1950, he introduced machines that ejected ten and fifteen balls, respectively, whenever one of the player's balls entered a scoring hole. Any balls remaining at the end of a play session could be exchanged for prizes. Playing *pachinko* now provided a person the opportunity to win everything from soap to vegetables to cigarettes, all of which were in incredibly short supply after World War II. Therefore, the number of *pachinko* parlors in the country expanded rapidly to a peak of 70,000 in 1953 housing over 2 million machines.[15] These parlors were taking in over $42 million per month, more than all the department stores in Japan combined.[16] After the government began regulating the industry more closely in 1954, the number of parlors dropped rapidly to a low of 8,000 housing half a million machines in 1956. The introduction of lighting and electrically powered "tulip" scoring pockets around 1960 helped revive interest in the game again, which continued to grow steadily in popularity over the next two decades.[17]

While *pachinko* proved popular in the early 1950s, the widespread adoption of the game by the Japanese public did not spearhead the return of other coin-operated amusements to Japan. Still reeling from the devastation caused by World War II, Japanese citizens were working six and a half days a week for meager compensation that barely covered heavily rationed necessities and had little time or money for frivolous pursuits. The outbreak of the Korean War changed everything. As the United States stepped up aid and investment in the country so as to have a strong ally in the region to forestall the spread of communism in Asia, the economy began to improve rapidly, setting the stage for the country's "economic miracle." Furthermore, the war brought with it a rapid influx of American servicemen to bases leased from the Japanese government. While it would still be several years before the Japanese people would have the time and disposable income to engage in recreational pursuits, American soldiers required entertainment during their

[14] Sedensky, 1991.

[15] Ibid.

[16] "Jap Pinballs Out-Grossing Dept. Stores," *Billboard*, October 9, 1954.

[17] Sedensky, 1991.

downtime, so American military bases became the first point of entry for coin-operated amusements into post-war Japan.

***

As Japan was finding its feet again during the Korean War, so were Irving Bromberg and his son, Marty. Born in 1919, Martin Jerome Bromberg – who later changed his last name to Bromley – grew up surrounded by coin-operated machines and even maintained his own route in Los Angeles while in high school after earning his driver's license at the age of 13. Marty entered his father's business full time upon graduation and relocated to Hawaii, where he joined with his father and two friends named Glen Hensen and James Humpert to establish a new company on January 9, 1940, called Standard Games to operate slot machines and coin-operated amusements in the territory.[18] The outbreak of World War II soon after only increased the fortunes of the nascent company. Though inducted into the Navy, Bromley took work in a local shipyard so that he could be placed on the inactive duty list and continue to run his business in his off hours.[19]

Over the next few years, Bromley and Humpert established a network of companies with various partners both inside and outside the coin-op industry. These included Jimmy and Ray Music Service with Ray Cheong and Jimmy Sugiyama and Pacific Tobacco Company with Curtis Suber.[20] In August 1945, the Brombergs dissolved Standard Games,[21] but continued operating amusement equipment in Hawaii through California Games, established in May 1945.[22] This company was wound up as well the next year and superseded by a new partnership established by both Brombergs and Humpert on September 1, 1946, called Service Games.[23]

In 1951, Service Games faced a serious threat to its business activities with the passage of the Johnson Act, which not only limited the transport of coin-operated gambling devices, but also banned their operation on military bases within the United States. Left with a stock of suddenly worthless slot machines, Bromberg and Bromley sent a company salesman named Richard Stewart and a company mechanic named Raymond Lemaire to Japan to establish a new firm that would buy the equipment from Service Games and

[18] "Legal Notice," *Honolulu Star-Bulletin*, January 12, 1940.
[19] U.S. Congress, *Fraud and Corruption*, 5.
[20] Bromley v. Commissioner, 23 T.C.M. 1936 (1964).
[21] "Notice of Dissolution of Co-Partnership," *Honolulu Star-Advertiser*, September 17, 1945.
[22] "Notice of Co-Partnership," *Honolulu Star-Advertiser*, June 20, 1945.
[23] Most sources state that Service Games was established in 1945, but the *Honolulu Star-Advertiser* gives the correct date. "Notice of Co-Partnership," *Honolulu Star-Advertiser*, December 28, 1946.

operate it at American military bases in the country, which were not subject to the ban. The duo established a partnership called Lemaire & Stewart for this purpose in May 1952.[24]

With the Japanese company proving a success, Stewart, Lemaire, Bromley, Bromberg, and Humpert formed a new Service Games company in September 1953 as a Panamanian Corporation with Irving Bromberg as president and Dick Stewart as general manager. The sole purpose of the company was to purchase coin-operated equipment from Chicago firms like Gottlieb, Bally, and United and ship it to Lemaire and Stewart's partnership, incorporated in 1953 as Japan Service Games, so they could operate the machines in the officers' clubs and open messes of U.S. military bases not just in Japan, but also in Korea, the Philippines, and Guam.[25] The original Service Games in Hawaii continued to operate as a subsidiary of the new Panamanian company as well until Bromley sold it in 1961.[26]

Once Service Games opened the Far Eastern military market, other companies followed. The company's biggest competitor in its early days was an entrepreneur named Kenneth Cole. A former navy pilot, Cole established the Cosdel Amusement Machine Company in 1953 to operate coin-operated amusements and jukeboxes across Japan, Okinawa, Hong Kong, and Taiwan,[27] though within a decade he had left coin-operated amusements to focus on the record business. As Service Games and Cosdel brought an increasing amount of coin-operated equipment into Asia, a new Japanese coin-operated industry began to take hold as machines originally intended for U.S. military bases migrated into the local economy through the work of entrepreneurs like Russian businessman Mike Kogan.

Born into a Jewish family in Odessa, Ukraine, in 1920, Michael Kalman Kogan fled with the rest of his family to Harbin, Manchuria, in 1929 to escape persecution in the Soviet Union.[28] When Japan occupied the region in 1931, Kogan and other Jewish refugees endured anti-Semitism from Japanese soldiers, but they were also afforded unique opportunities after a small group of military leaders led by Norihiro Yasue bought into anti-Semitic conspiracy literature describing Jewish control of world finance and media and believed they should harness the expertise of Jewish refugees in Manchuria to further

---

[24] Bromley v. Commissioner, 23 T.C.M. 1936 (1964).

[25] Ibid.

[26] "Mynah Matters," *Honolulu Star-Advertiser*, July 21, 1961.

[27] "Cosdel Hdqr's in Tokyo, Offices Cover Okinawa, Korea, Hong Kong," *Billboard*, June 16, 1956.

[28] Masumi Akagi, *It Started from Pong* (Nishinomiya: Amusement Press, 2005), 44.

develop Japan.[29] While Yasue never realized his so-called Fugu Plan, the brief pro-Jewish sentiment his ideas generated gave Kogan the opportunity to study economics at the prestigious Waseda University beginning in 1939.

While studying at Waseda, Kogan roomed with Russian literature scholar Masao Yonekawa and helped him translate the works of Dostoevsky into Japanese. With the outbreak of World War II, Japan mobilized its college students for the war effort, so Kogan ended up working in a factory.[30] In 1944, he left the country to join his father in Shanghai and founded a trading company that operated under the name Taitung – which translates to "Taito" in Japanese[31] – specializing in floor coverings, hog bristles, and natural hair wigs.[32] After the Communist takeover of China, Kogan liquidated his business and relocated to Tokyo to establish a new import business called Taito Yoko in 1950 that handled clothing and other products.

Taito Yoko struggled mightily because careless employees regularly lost goods and/or failed to collect full payment. In August 1953, Kogan wound up the company and started a new firm called the Taito Trading Company. At the new business, he was joined by a lawyer and retired newspaper man named Akio Nakatani, whom Kogan met at a karate dojo he attended where Nakatani served as an instructor.[33] Nakatani became Kogan's right hand man as the new Taito began a vodka distilling business while also importing and distributing a popular line of peanut vending machines and a less successful line of perfume machines.[34]

Taito left the vodka business in 1955 due to increased competition, but the success of the vending machines led Kogan to enter the jukebox business in 1954. Unable to secure a license to import machines from the United States because they were classified as luxury items by the Ministry of Industry and Trade (MITI), Kogan turned to U.S. military bases to purchase broken-down machines so his employees could salvage parts from three or four of them at a time to cobble together working units. As the Japanese economy improved, Taito secured a deal to become the official Japanese distributor of AMI jukeboxes in 1958, ending its reliance on refurbished machines. The jukebox business was not lucrative at first, but once Taito began mixing in

---

[29] Elaine Markoutsas, "Japan's Secret Plan for 'Israel' in Asia," *Chicago Tribune*, July 10, 1979.

[30] Akagi, 2005, 44.

[31] The name appears to be a combination of the Japanese terms for the Pacific Ocean (*Taiheiyou*) and the Far East (*Kyokutou*).

[32] Michael L. Millenson, "Firm Seeks Right Button for a 2d 'Space Invaders,'" *Chicago Tribune*, November 29, 1981.

[33] Akagi, 2005, 45.

[34] Taito, series of history tweets on Taito's Twitter Account, 2010.

traditional Japanese records with American popular music sales began to climb until there were over 1,500 jukeboxes on location in Japan by 1960. As the jukebox market continued to expand, a deal with industry leader Seeburg to become the exclusive Japanese agent for the company in 1962 further solidified Taito's position as one of the top jukebox companies in the nation.[35]

***

At the same time Taito began exposing Japan to the jukebox, an American named David Rosen began laying the groundwork for a company that would finally bring a full-fledged coin-operated amusement industry to the country. A native of Brooklyn born in January 1930, Rosen attended Columbia University after high school, but cut his education short to volunteer for the U.S. Air Force, in which he served from 1949 to 1952. Rosen's assignment as a script writer and program producer for the Armed Forces Radio Service saw him posted to a string of Far Eastern locations from Shanghai to Okinawa before and during the Korean War, but he spent the majority of his time in Japan and fell in love with the country. After witnessing a Japanese painter earning a living through portraiture, he established a side business called Rosen Enterprises in 1951 that arranged for American photos to be sent to Japan to be turned into portraits by local artists.[36]

Upon leaving the Air Force, Rosen returned home to New York with the intention of finishing his degree while furthering the interests of his portrait business in his native country. The venture proved unsuccessful, however, so Rosen dropped out of school once again and returned to Japan in April 1954 to transform Rosen Enterprises into a trading company that exported products like paintings, sculptures, and woodcrafts and manufactured small items like cigarette lighters and money clips for the domestic market festooned with advertising for American companies.[37]

Before long, Rosen chose to pursue a new business opportunity. With heavy rationing still in place following World War II, the most important possession of any citizen was his or her photo ID, required for everything

[35] Ibid.

[36] Steven L. Kent, "Entertainment Empire of the Rising Sun: A Conversation with Sega Founder David Rosen," Sad Sam's Palace, 2006, http://www.sadsamspalace.com/VideoGames/4-Rosen-Sega-story.html.

[37] "Great Achievers: David Rosen," RePlay, July 1982, 40. There is some confusion as to whether the earlier portrait business and the trading company were one and the same. Most sources date the founding of Rosen Enterprises to 1954, but in some interviews, Rosen seems to imply that his earlier company was also Rosen Enterprises.

from buying rice to acquiring a railway pass to registering for work or school. As part of applying for an ID, a Japanese citizen was required to have a photo taken, which cost around 250 yen and took 2–3 days to develop. In the United States, however, there had recently been a surge in popularity for photomat booths, which could not only provide a picture at a cheaper price but could develop the film nearly instantaneously. Rosen decided to import photomats into Japan, but he soon discovered a problem: as the photos were intended as novelty souvenirs, they would actually fade within 2 years due to inadequate temperature controls in the booths rendering them useless for official IDs. After some thought, Rosen modified the booths so they were manned by an attendant who could regulate the temperature, allowing for the creation of pictures that could last up to five years. Rosen soon had a massive hit on his hands as people proved willing to wait in line for over an hour to have a picture taken for just 150 yen that would be developed within two minutes.[38]

In short order, Rosen had placed over 100 booths around the country under the Photorama brand name. This success came at a cost when the owners of traditional photo studios began staging protests over unfair American business practices. Rosen established a franchise system for local photographers, but licensing his technology opened the market to unsanctioned competition that cut deeply into his profits. Rosen kept his Photorama business going into the early 1960s, but he also looked for new avenues to expand.[39]

By 1957, the Japanese economic revival was well underway, and for the first time since the war Japanese citizens were beginning to have both leisure time and disposable income. Therefore, Rosen decided to enter the business of what the Japanese Ministry of International Trade and Industry designated "luxury goods," which required an import license that until recently had been nearly impossible to acquire. Rejecting the currently popular entertainments of *pachinko*, dance studios, bars, and cabarets, Rosen focused on coin-operated games. He negotiated a license to bring in $100,000 worth of merchandise and acquired older games at a relatively cheap price from distributors in the United States that had accepted the games as trade-ins for newer product and then just piled them in warehouses with no idea what to do with them.[40]

---

[38] Kent, 2001, 334–335.
[39] Ibid, 335–336.
[40] Kent, 2006.

Rather than concentrate on pinball, which presumably would have faced stiff competition from *pachinko*, Rosen largely imported target shooting games, a coin-operated amusement that had enjoyed intermittent popularity for over 50 years. The earliest such games had been developed in the United Kingdom in the late nineteenth century in the form of electric rifle games in which the gun was connected to a target by wires and registered a hit through the use of wipers and contacts. In 1934, a Tulsa, Oklahoma, company called the Rayolite Rifle Range Company introduced a new target shooting system based around the recently invented light gun, in which pressing the trigger focuses a narrow beam of light that can be detected by a photosensitive vacuum tube in order to register a hit.[41] The company incorporated this technology into a new game called the *Rayolite Rifle Range* that featured a duck as the target. In 1935, Seeburg Corporation took over the manufacturing of the game. When it proved popular, the company released several additional light gun games over the next two decades including *Chicken Sam* (1939), *Shoot the Bear* (1947), and *Coon Hunt* (1952).

Light gun games and elaborate electric rifle games enjoyed their peak popularity in the early 1940s as the United States prepared to enter World War II. After the war, a more compact version of the old electric rifle game developed by a man named Eldon Dale predominated in which the gun is anchored to a swivel stand attached to a metal rod that extends under a truncated playfield given the illusion of greater depth through the use of strategically placed mirrors. If the rod is in contact with a target when the player pulls the trigger, a circuit completes and the game registers a hit. Dale-style gun games entered arcades in 1949,[42] achieved peak popularity in 1954,[43] and remained an arcade staple over the next decade.

In Japan, gun games became the premier coin-op amusement through the efforts of David Rosen. Through his photo booth business, he had established good relations with two prominent Japanese movie theater chains, Toho and Shochiku, so it proved relatively simple to reach agreements with both to place "gun corners" in the lobbies of their theaters.[44] With Japan's strict gun control laws, these locations proved incredibly popular with target shooting enthusiasts and paved the way for rapid growth in the new industry. In June 1960, Rosen opened Japan's first large arcade, the Hibiya

---

[41] The first known patent for a light gun was filed by Englishman W.G. Patterson in 1920, but the Rayolite Rifle Range is the first known game featuring the technology.

[42] "Exhibit Rushes Production on Dale Gun Game," *Billboard*, February 5, 1949, 109.

[43] Knauf, 1954, 1.

[44] Kent, 2006.

Gun Corner, in Tokyo.[45] In July 1960, Taito joined Rosen in the amusement business by opening its own large gun corner near Ureoku Station in Osaka stocked with over 40 shooting games and pinball tables.[46] In April 1961, Rosen countered by opening his own large Osaka location, the Umeda Gun Corner.[47] Coin-operated amusements were now a major pastime in Japan for children and adults alike.

In 1963, Taito expanded its amusement operation by becoming the official Japanese distributor for pinball manufacturer Gottlieb.[48] Rosen, meanwhile, looked for new avenues to expand outside of traditional coin-op. With space at a premium in Japanese cities, he purchased an indoor computer golf game he felt certain would become a hit, but it failed because the Japanese proved interested in playing golf only outdoors. Next he turned to slot cars, but only succeeded in creating a passing fad. Finally, in 1962 he decided to open a bowling alley. At the time, bowling had been popular in the United States since the development of the first automatic pin-setters roughly a decade before but had yet to penetrate Japan save for one Tokyo alley that strictly catered to American servicemen. To ensure his alley would be a success, Rosen located it in the Shinjuku district of Tokyo, a popular entertainment area that would guarantee high turnover. He secured space for 14 lanes by approaching the president of one of the movie theater chains that housed his gun corners and reaching an agreement to place the alley over one of his theaters. Rosen's alley ultimately set business records as the Japanese embraced bowling as a pastime.[49]

After Rosen proved there was a viable market for bowling in Japan, the two largest U.S. bowling equipment firms, AMF and Brunswick, partnered with Japanese companies C. Itoh and Mitsui, respectively, in 1961 and ultimately captured two-thirds of the domestic bowling business between them. Consequently, bowling alley operation never became an important component of the Rosen Enterprises business. Bowling alleys did, however, become a prime venue for coin-operated games, so as the number of locations in the country grew into the hundreds and then into the thousands, coin-operated amusements became ubiquitous across the nation.

As demand for coin-operated games increased to new heights, Taito expanded its operations in 1963 by establishing a subsidiary called Pacific

---

[45] Akagi, 2005, 40.
[46] Taito, 2010.
[47] Akagi, 2005, 40.
[48] Taito, 2010.
[49] Kent, 2001, 338–339.

Amusements Limited to develop and manufacture original coin-operated amusement products.[50] At the time, the Japanese industry was experiencing a fad centered around crane machines after a model imported from Italy proved popular, so in 1965 Pacific developed the first domestically produced crane, the Crown 602, and helped cement the place of a product category that has been popular in Japanese game centers ever since. Before Taito established Pacific, most amusement machines in the Japanese market were imported, but after the success of the Crown 602, dozens of small companies followed Taito's lead by setting up their own manufacturing operations.

***

While Taito and Rosen Enterprises focused on the Japanese market, Marty Bromley and Irving Bromberg took steps to turn the country's other large coin-operated amusement provider, Service Games, into an international coin-op empire. Since 1953, the father and son duo had been funneling amusement equipment into U.S. military bases in the Far East from Panama-based Service Games to Service Games Japan. Now, they prepared to reverse this process by bringing equipment produced in Japan to the rest of the world.

In 1956, Bromley and Bromberg organized a new wholly owned subsidiary of Service Games in Panama called Club Specialty Overseas, Inc. (CSOI) to serve as a financial clearing house for the global operation and act as the middle man between Service Games manufacturing and distribution operations.[51] Then, in 1957, they incorporated Service Games Nevada to give the company a presence in the U.S. market and function as a final assembly point for slot machines to circumvent a law requiring equipment purchased by the government to be American made.[52] The same year, the company bought a never-before-used Mills slot machine tooling set from Bell-O-Matic Corporation – for which Service Games already served as a distributor in the Far East – and began manufacturing replacement parts and modified Mills designs in Japan.[53] These machines were then funneled through CSOI to

---

[50] Taito, 2010.

[51] U.S. Congress, Senate, Committee on Government Operations, *Hearings before the Permanent Subcommittee on Investigations of the Committee on Government Operations*, 91st Cong., 1st and 2nd Sess., 1970–1971, 1767.

[52] Ibid, 1768.

[53] Bell-O-Matic Corporation was the former slot machine arm of the Mills Novelty Company, which had introduced the first mass-produced three-reel slot machine in 1907 and continued to dominate the field until Bally introduced electromechanical slot machines in the early 1960s. Bell-O-Matic was originally established as a subsidiary of Mills in 1946 and became an independent company in 1954.

Service Games Japan and Service Games Korea in the Far East and another Bromley distributor called Firm Westlee in West Germany for distribution to American military bases.[54] Service Games marketed both its Mills-produced slots and the machines it manufactured itself under the brand name Sega, a contraction of the company name.

As the Service Games complex expanded its operations, it attracted intense scrutiny from both the U.S. and Japanese governments. Starting in 1954, the company continually faced accusations of smuggling, fraud, bribery, tax evasion, coercion, and intimidation in its quest to become the largest supplier of coin-operated equipment to the U.S. Armed Forces around the world. The charges rarely stuck, but there were consequences. In 1959, the U.S. Navy banned Service Games from all its bases in Japan, followed by a complete ban in the Philippines the next year.[55] In 1961, the U.S. Civil Administration of Okinawa fined Service Games for smuggling, fraud, bribery, and tax evasion.[56] In 1963, the Fifth Air Force banned Service Games from all its bases worldwide.[57]

Perhaps due to so many government investigations tarnishing the Service Games name, Bromley reorganized his web of businesses in the early 1960s. First, on May 31, 1960, Service Games Japan was terminated and two new companies were formed to replace it.[58] Nihon Goraku Bussan KK, literally Japanese Amusement Products Company, Inc., which also did business as Utamatic Inc., was led by Dick Stewart and managed the Service Games operating business in Japan. Nihon Kikai Seizo KK, literally Japanese Machine Manufacturing Company, Inc., which also did business as Sega, Inc., continued the Service Games manufacturing operation under the leadership of Ray Lemaire. That same year, Firm Westlee changed its name to Standard Equipment & Service, while Service Games Korea became Establishment Garlan.[59] Finally, in 1962 Service Games Panama was dissolved and superseded by CSOI,[60] which became the new heart of the Service Games complex and expanded aggressively into Southeast Asia and England to complement its business in Japan, Korea, Taiwan, and West Germany. Controversy continued to plague the company, however, culminating in a U.S. Congressional investigation in 1971 focused on activities in South Vietnam, where Service

---

[54] Ibid, 1767–1768.
[55] U.S. Congress, *Fraud and Corruption*, 6–7.
[56] Ibid, 7.
[57] U.S. Congress, 1970–1971, 1779.
[58] Ibid, 1802.
[59] Ibid, 1766.
[60] Ibid.

Games had cornered the coin-operated machine market in the late 1960s through an intermediary company called Sarl Electronics owned by William Crum, who allegedly owed his success to widespread bribery of military personnel.[61]

In Japan, Nihon Goraku Bussan and Nihon Kikai Seizo played a key role in the growth of the local coin-op industry. Like Taito, Nihon Goraku Bussan became a major supplier of machines for the domestic market, with a particular focus on jukeboxes. Though it did not run its own arcades, the company imported Rockola jukeboxes and amusements manufactured by Bally and Williams.[62] In 1960, Nihon Goraku Bussan developed the first Japanese-designed jukebox to enter production, the Sega 1000.[63] The jukebox was manufactured by Nihon Kikai Seizo, which also offered a diverse line of slot machines – though only for international markets since they were illegal in Japan. As both companies continued to flourish, they became one again in June 1964 when Nihon Goraku Bussan absorbed Nihon Kikai Seizo.[64] By 1965, Nihon Goraku Bussan had placed over 3,000 jukeboxes on location and opened branch offices across Japan.

As Nihon Goraku Bussan and Taito grew in size and scope, a wave of new companies entered the market, and rival firms captured the new bowling business, Dave Rosen watched his prime position in the Japanese arcade industry began to dissipate. His rivalry with Japan's other two significant coin-op enterprises remained friendly, however, so in 1964 he proposed a merger between Nihon Goraku Bussan and Rosen Enterprises to form a company large enough to stay on top of the increasingly competitive Japanese industry. On July 1, 1965, Nihon Goraku Bussan acquired Rosen Enterprises and changed its name to Sega Enterprises, Ltd.[65] Rosen became CEO and managing director of the company, while Dick Stewart became president, and Ray Lemaire took the title director of production and planning. Under Rosen, the combined company began phasing out slot machine production and equipment sales and leasing to military bases so that it could focus on a new primary objective: becoming the top coin-operated amusement company in Japan to facilitate becoming a publicly traded corporation.

---

[61] "Crum Paid Off U.S. General, Solons Told," *San Antonio Express*, February 23, 1971.

[62] "Sega and Utamatic Purchase Assets of Service Games," *Billboard*, September 5, 1960, 71.

[63] In 1956, Taito developed the first jukebox designed and built entirely in Japan, but abandoned manufacturing plans when Kogan realized purchasing American machines remained more economical due to the small size of the domestic market. Taito, 2010.

[64] *Moody's International Manual, Volume 3* (New York: The Service, 1998), 5574.

[65] U.S. Congress, 1970–1971, 1802.

By the time Sega Enterprises formed, Rosen had long since moved from importing used games to brand new products, but he soon grew disenchanted with the games coming out of Chicago. While game development costs were rising in the 1960s, operators had found it nearly impossible to move beyond nickel and dime play on their machines, so coin drop remained stagnant. Consequently, manufacturers were forced to sell new games at prices too low to completely recoup their costs and began cutting back heavily on R&D and slimming down to just their most popular lines. The result was a relatively static industry in which the manufacturers only invested in small cosmetic changes on existing equipment in order to keep costs down.[66] Feeling he could do better, in April 1966 Rosen established a new sales division under Shunichi Shiina and prepared to develop his own products.[67]

With U.S. manufacturers refocusing on a narrower product line, Rosen also saw an opening for Sega Enterprises to develop an international audience. Leveraging the company's large factory operation and the global reach of its worldwide agent, CSOI, Rosen planned to develop a line of low-cost novelty games for export to complement the pinball, baseball, shuffle alley, and target shooting games dominating the output of the big five manufacturers in the United States. In September 1967, Sega became the first company outside of North America to join the Music Operators of America (MOA), the principle trade organization of the U.S. coin-operated amusement industry,[68] and in October the company secured a deal with Williams to bring its line to the United States.[69] Sega also began eyeing the European markets, where the company already had a formidable distribution presence, and in 1967 it introduced a large, expensive game there based on a concept originally developed by a competitor called the Nakamura Manufacturing Company.

Born in 1925 in the Kanda district of Tokyo, Masaya Nakamura was the son of a manufacturer of handcrafted shotguns named Yutarou, whose business was destroyed during World War II. At the war's conclusion, Yutarou Nakamura salvaged what he could from the rubble and established a gun repair shop in the Matsuya department store in Asakusa, Tokyo. Masaya had always been drawn to the sea and harbored dreams of becoming a sailor, but weak eyesight put an end to those ambitions. Instead, he chose to study shipbuilding at Yokohama State University. Masaya graduated in 1948, but

---

[66]"Sega Introducing Low-Cost Amusement Equipment Line," *Billboard*, May 27, 1967, 83.

[67]Akagi, 2005, 42.

[68]"MOA Signs First Foreign Firm," *Billboard*, 78.

[69]"Sega, Seeburg in Games Agreement," *Billboard*, November 11, 1967, 64.

proved unable to find a job in the depressed post-war economy.[70] He joined his father in the family business and performed all manner of odd jobs from sweeping floors to managing the books to designing and hanging advertising posters around the city.[71]

Over time, the Nakamuras transitioned from repairing old rifles to selling brand new air guns, but increasing restrictions on gun ownership and shooting threatened the business. Masaya started modifying the air guns for sale as harmless toys and began pondering how the company could expand into other forms of children's entertainment. In the 1930s, Yutarou Nakamura had manufactured cork guns for Kaichi Endo, who since the end of World War II had been leading the way in reestablishing department store amusement spaces through his Japan Recreational Equipment Company, Ltd.[72] Masaya felt he and his father should capture a portion of this business as well, but Yutarou was opposed to the idea. Therefore, Masaya broke with his father to establish the Nakamura Manufacturing Company in June 1955 with just two employees and roughly $1,200 in capital to operate rooftop amusements.[73]

Nakamura's first installation consisted of two pre-war horse rides that he refurbished and placed on the roof of the Matsuya store in Yokohama. Over the next decade, Masaya added two or three more small locations to his route, but received his first big break in 1963 when he secured a contract to build a rooftop amusement park for the flagship location of Japan's premiere department store chain, Mitsukoshi, located in the Nihonbashi District of Tokyo.[74] In addition to horse rides, Nakamura added a 3D sound and picture viewing machine, a pond out of which children could scoop goldfish, and an elaborate amusement machine called the "Roadway Ride." Based on the success of this venue, Mitsukoshi decided to add rooftop amusement parks to all its locations, and Nakamura was soon operating ten facilities across Japan.[75] The Mitsukoshi deal made Nakamura Manufacturing one of the larger department store amusement operators in Japan, which in turn allowed the company to buy in bulk from coin-op manufacturers at

---

[70] Akagi, 2005, 50.

[71] Rupert Steiner, "Pac-Man Creator Bites into County Hall," *The Sunday Times*, August 31, 1997.

[72] Endo renamed his Japan Automatic Machine Recreational Equipment Manufacturing Company to Japan Recreational Equipment Company in 1947.

[73] Akagi, 2010, 40.

[74] Ibid.

[75] Steiner, 1997.

a discount. Consequently, Masaya Nakamura decided to expand into coin-op distribution by supplying smaller operators with equipment as well.[76]

With the Japanese industry expanding rapidly in the late 1960s, Nakamura Manufacturing had trouble securing the equipment it needed for its roof-top spaces because manufacturers proved unable to keep up with increasing demand. Worse, larger companies like Taito and Sega that served as both operators and manufacturers began invading Nakamura's traditional strong-hold of department store play areas.[77] Nakamura responded by opening his own factory in the Ota-ku district of Tokyo in February 1966 and securing a license from the Walt Disney Company to use its characters on his products. The factory largely produced kiddie rides modeled primarily on popular anime and Walt Disney characters, but Nakamura also turned his attention to more elaborate coin-operated amusements beginning with a game called *Periscope*.

A target shooting game, *Periscope* broke new ground in the genre with a gigantic cabinet featuring a plexiglass ocean and plastic ships on a motorized carriage, great electronic sound effects, and an innovative control scheme in which up to three players peered through actual periscopes to target and destroy the ships with torpedoes represented by points of light that trav-eled across the fake waters.[78] While more expensive than the typical coin-operated machine of the day, *Periscope* became a hit when arcade operators realized that it could bring in sustained earnings far in excess of most coin-operated games.

As Nakamura manufacturing remained focused on the domestic market, Sega saw an opportunity to bring the popular concept overseas. In 1966, Sega engineer Ochi Shikanosuke created his own version of the game that debuted at the ATE trade show in London that November.[79] After placing a small number of units on location in Europe in 1967, David Rosen real-ized that it was too large and expensive to export practically and ordered his engineers to develop a smaller single-player unit. Released internationally in March 1968,[80] the single-player version of *Periscope* remained too large

---

[76] "Projection Racing: Conversation with Masaya Nakamura, Inventor of F-1," *Play Meter*, January 1977, 12.

[77] Ibid.

[78] In 1946, Bally produced a target shooting game called *Undersea Raider* that operated in a similar manner to *Periscope*, but with a far smaller cabinet and play area. The game proved popular and most likely served as an inspiration for the Namco game.

[79] The direct link between the Namco and Sega *Periscope* games cannot be determine from available sources, but it is clear that the games are nearly identical. Sources identify the Nakamura game as a 1965 product and the Sega game as a 1966 product.

[80] "Modified 'Periscope' Unit Released by Sega Ent.," *Cash Box*, March 23, 1968, 99.

for typical street locations, but found a home in retail establishments like department stores and shopping malls that would never typically host coin-operated amusements.[81] It remained expensive, costing roughly $1,295 when the typical arcade piece would sell for half that amount, and distributors continued to complain that no one would be able to make money on the game. Rosen responded in late 1968 by reconfiguring the game for quarter play and heavily lobbying distributors and operators to accept 25 cents as a new standard price point.[82]

With revenues increasing at Sega thanks to *Periscope* and the continued growth of the jukebox business – in which Sega had captured just under half of the Japanese market with 5,000 machines on location by 1967 – Rosen's dream of going public now appeared feasible. The company retained an underwriter to begin work on an initial public offering, but ultimately decided the hurdles would be too great. Not only would Sega have been the first American company to go public in Japan since World War II, but it would have also been the first coin-operated amusement company to ever go public in the nation. Therefore, Rosen and his partners began a search for a publicly-traded American company they could purchase so as to turn Sega into a subsidiary. This effort also failed, so the group sold out to Gulf & Western in 1969, where CEO Charles Bludhorn was on a massive acquisition spree that created one of the largest conglomerates in the world.[83] Between June 1969 and January 1970, Gulf & Western purchased 80% of the stock of Sega Enterprises – the entire company save Ray Lemaire's 20% stake – for a total price of $9,977,043.[84] Bromley and Stewart ended their direct involvement with the company at that point, while Rosen remained as chairman and CEO.

***

With *Periscope* proving a hit despite its technical complexity and high price per play, the game spearheaded a revival of the moribund novelty game manufacturing business through a new category labeled "realistic" or "audio-visual" games by the trade press that incorporated advanced special effects to provide a closer simulation of the real world than previous arcade pieces. The most important of these realistic games were a new wave of driving games pioneered by a Japanese firm called Kasco.

---

[81] Earl Paige, "Realistic Games Sound Out Extra Dollars for 'Centers,'" August 22, 1970, 1.
[82] "Take up 25¢-Play, See Prototypes at Sega Meet," *V/T Music & Games*, April 1969, 14.
[83] Kent, 2006.
[84] U.S. Congress, *Fraud and Corruption*, 7–8.

Established in 1955 by engineer Kenzou Furukawa under the name Kansei Seiki Seisakusho and incorporated three years later, Kasco's first product was a magic lantern device called the "Stereo Talkie" intended to help guide shoppers around the stores of the Hankyu Department chain. As rooftop amusement spaces regained popularity in post-war Japan, Furukawa repurposed the Stereo Talkie as a picture viewer amusement device called the "Viewbox" that displayed images from Japanese folktales and small comic strips, often accompanied by music. Like Nakamura Manufacturing, Kasco began installing and maintaining kiddie rides in rooftop gardens and transitioned into importing, operating, and manufacturing other types of coin-operated amusements.[85]

Furukawa created his first driving game, *Mini Drive*, in 1958 after seeing an International Mutoscope machine. Established in New York by Ukrainian immigrant William Rabkin in 1920, International Mutoscope first made a name for itself by reintroducing the peep shows that had long since fallen out of favor, but the trained machinist Rabkin soon expanded into other coin-operated products, most notably the burgeoning market for crane machines that flourished in the 1920s and 1930s.[86] In 1941, he introduced a game called *Drive-Mobile* derived from several British games released in the 1930s in which the player uses an actual steering wheel to control a model car set atop a metal drum and keep it centered on a road painted on the drum that constantly shifts to the left and right as it rotates.[87] *Mini Drive* followed a similar format, though in a longer cabinet that allowed for a bigger road.

Ten years later, Kasco introduced an elaborate new driving game called *Indy 500* featuring a circular racetrack and cars painted on individual rotating discs illuminated by a lamp, providing striking, colorful graphics and allowing the game to detect collisions between the vehicles. The player not only has to keep his car on the track, but he also has to dodge the other cars to avoid a crash that brings his vehicle to a halt. Electronic sound provides both the steady hum of the car engines and the sounds of impact. More realistic and exhilarating than any driving game released before, it became a smash hit in Japan with sales of over 2,000 units.[88]

---

[85] "Kasco and the Electro-Mechanical Golden Age," Shmuplations, accessed May 30, 2019, http://shmuplations.com/kasco.

[86] Robert Rice, "Penny Arcade Philanthropist," *The New Yorker*, October 16, 1948, 36–38.

[87] International Mutoscope continued to release a wide array of coin-operated novelties until William Rabkin died in a fall from the window of his sixth floor apartment in 1956, perhaps after suffering a dizzy spell brought on by high blood pressure. International Mutoscope exited the manufacturing business to focus on distribution soon after.

[88] Kasco, Shmuplations, 2019.

With *Indy 500* proving so successful, Kasco exported the game to the United States and Europe, where it captured the attention of Sam Gensburg of Chicago Coin. Gensburg ordered his engineers to create their own version, which saw release as *Speedway* in 1969 and became the biggest smash hit the industry had seen in years with sales of 7,500 units.[89] The game also played a critical role in the growth of quarter play: Chicago Coin wanted to set the machine to one game for a quarter just like Sega's *Periscope*, but operators initially balked and asked for two plays per quarter. Chicago Coin responded by testing the game both ways and discovered both models received roughly equal play, meaning the quarter play machine took in twice the money since a single coin bought half the playtime.[90] *Speedway* consequently shipped with one play per quarter and helped cement a new price point that would persist for over 20 years.[91]

In 1969, Sega scored another major hit in the U.S. with *Missile*. Continuing to push state of the art graphical effects, the game features a rotating film-strip displaying silhouettes of jet planes projected onto the back of the cabinet to create the illusion that waves of bombers are flying toward the player. As the planes move across the cabinet, a wiper blade travels along a circuit board containing a series of contacts. The player must shoot down the planes by aiming his missile using two buttons to rotate it left or right, then firing by pressing a button on top of a joystick. The missile is attached to its own wiper that passes over a series of contacts, and if both the player's missile and the wiper tied to bombers are touching the same contact when the player presses the button, a circuit completes to register a hit, while a solenoid pulls a different slide in front of the projector displaying a red explosion graphic.

By 1970, a slew of manufactures both old and new were rushing to emulate the cartoon-like graphics and realistic sound effects of *Speedway* and *Missile*, setting off a technological arms race to provide new games incorporating experiences unlike any the public had witnessed in an arcade before. As a result, the early 1970s were perhaps the best opportunity since the Great Depression for a clever inventor with a slick new product to break into the industry despite having little working capital and/or no previous track record with coin-operated amusements. In short, there would probably never be a better time for Nolan Bushnell and Ted Dabney to introduce the first coin-operated video game.

---

[89] "FAMA Hears Industry Views," *Billboard*, May 23, 1970, 43.

[90] "Chicago Coin Shipping 'Motorcycle,'" *Billboard*, August 15, 1970, 49.

[91] Pinball remained either ten cents per play or two plays for a quarter for several more years, but most novelty games, including the video games that would soon hit the arcade, adopted the higher price of *Periscope* and *Speedway*.

8

A Nutty Idea

October 14, 1964, marked the opening of the 15th annual Music Operators of America Convention and Trade Show at the Sherman House Hotel in Chicago, Illinois, which had been hosting coin-op industry events since the 1930s. Forged in 1948 from a loose collection of state and local jukebox operators' associations by George Miller of Oakland, California, and Al Denver of New York City, the Music Operators of America (MOA) was originally formed to combat efforts to eliminate the traditional music royalty exemption afforded to jukeboxes in the United States, but had since morphed into something greater.

The first jukebox, a device allowing a user to select among several records to play a song upon inserting a coin, entered the market in 1927; three years after Western Electric pioneered electrical recording techniques allowing for both improved sound quality and amplification.[1] Jukeboxes became popular in bars and taverns in the 1930s and emerged as one of the backbones of the coin-op industry, but total sales were eclipsed by games.[2] In the 1950s, the jukebox experienced a surge in popularity on the back of the 45 RPM record and rock and roll music, while coin-operated games entered a period of decline as the U.S. population dispersed and left the inner city arcades behind. As a result, the jukebox jobbers took over the majority of the operating business of music and games alike, and the MOA show became the principle convention

---

[1] The first jukebox, the National Automatic Selection Phonograph, was introduced by a company called the Automatic Musical Instrument Company (AMI), which itself was formed in 1925 out of the merger of two companies both founded in 1909, the National Piano Manufacturing Company, which built coin-operated musical instruments, and the National Automatic Music Company, which operated them. AMI was purchased by Rowe AC in 1962.

[2] While there were an estimated 400,000 jukeboxes in operation by 1941, there were thought to be 1.2 million coin-operated games. "The Coin Machine Industry," *Billboard*, February 26, 1944, 66.

of the entire amusement trade.[3] By 1964, the primacy of the jukebox and the decline of the arcade had largely relegated coin-operated amusements to bars, taverns, and restaurants, which were typically only interested in operating a jukebox, a pool table, a cigarette vending machine, and one or two pinball tables or shuffle alleys.[4] A man named Bill Nutting came to the Sherman Hotel that year feeling there was room for something more.

***

Born May 3, 1926, William Gilbert Nutting was the son and grandson of executives of the Marshall Field's Department Store and grew up in the affluent Chicago suburb of River Forest, Illinois. A lifelong airplane enthusiast, he joined his high school's aviation club and entered Army Air Corps cadet training after graduating in the middle of World War II. After the war, Nutting attended Colgate University for two years before transferring to Colorado University, where his high school sweetheart Claire Ullmann also attended school. In 1948, Bill and Claire were married, and two years later Bill graduated with a degree in business administration.[5]

Neither Bill nor Claire were interested in returning to Chicago society with its rituals and obligations, so they moved west to San Francisco.[6] Bill briefly worked for the National Motor Bearing Company before moving on to Rheem Manufacturing in 1951, where he started as a production line foreman before cycling through inventory control, purchasing, and sales. Bill took a sales and office management position in Rheem's Chicago office in 1956 to be closer to family again, but the Nuttings ultimately returned to California in 1959.[7] Bill decided to follow in his father's footsteps by becoming a buyer for the San Francisco luxury department store Raphael Weill & Company, known as the White House for its impressive beaux-arts façade.[8]

For his entire professional life, Bill found himself torn between following a retail path like his father or a manufacturing path like his father-in-law, Herbert Ullmann, who was a highly placed executive at Revere Ware, but his

---

[3] Before the formation of the MOA, the principle coin-op trade organization was the Coin Machine Institute (CMI), established in 1931 as the National Association of Coin Operated Machine Manufacturers, which was a manufacturers association rather than an operator's association. CMI fell apart in the late 1940s in a dispute between Dave Gottlieb and Bally's Ray Moloney over the prevalence of payout games and held its last trade show in 1952.

[4] Smith, 2016, 74–75.

[5] Norm Petersen, "Bill and Claire Nutting's Waco SRE," *Vintage Airplane*, March 1992, 12.

[6] Claire Nutting, interview with the author, April 14, 2017.

[7] "Profile On: William G. Nutting – Heading Up the Computer Generation," *Cash Box*, February 17, 1968, 74.

[8] Goldberg and Vendel, 2012, chap. 1.

ultimate dream was to own his own business. He took his first step in that direction when his father-in-law informed him that his acquaintance Eugene Kleiner, one of the founders of Fairchild Semiconductor, needed investors for a startup called Edex Teaching Systems.[9] Bill became a partner in the new firm in 1962, which marketed a teaching machine in which thousands of multiple-choice questions were stored on a filmstrip and projected onto a screen for students to answer by pushing the button located next to the correct answer. In 1963, a former Lockheed engineer named Thomas Nisbet adapted the Edex technology into a coin-operated entertainment system called the *Knowledge Computer* that featured questions in four categories – entertainment, travel, sports, and general knowledge.[10] Nutting led the marketing of the product in 1964, which was tested in bowling alleys, student unions on college campuses, and transportation depots.[11] He then exhibited the game at the 1964 MOA show through a new Edex division called Scientific Amusements.[12]

Edex was sold to Raytheon in 1965, which had no interest in pursuing coin-operated amusements further, so Nutting acquired the rights to the *Knowledge Computer* and started selling it through a company he called the Nutting Corporation. By the end of 1965, Nutting had placed roughly two dozen *Knowledge Computer* machines in the San Francisco area,[13] but by then it was clear to Bill that the machine was both too expensive and too difficult to service in the field. Therefore, he began exploring a complete redesign of the system in partnership with his younger brother Dave.

Born December 26, 1930, David Judd Nutting was a tinkerer from an early age. After taking apart the family toaster when he was eight years old and putting it back in working order before his parents found out, he graduated to increasingly complex machinery until he finally disassembled the outboard motor of his father's boat and failed to reassemble it. Like older brother Bill, Dave was fond of airplanes, but he preferred building the model variety

---

[9] Claire Nutting, 2017. Edex was short for "Educational Excellence."

[10] Thomas Nisbet, Instructional Apparatus, U.S. Patent 3,300,875A filed January 7, 1964, and issued January 31, 1967. The *Knowledge Computer* was not the first coin-operated quiz game. In 1946, a Detroit engineer named Richard Sisson adapted a training system that he had developed for the U.S. Navy similar to the Edex design into a coin-operated game called *Telequiz*. This game caused a brief sensation in the industry in the late 1940s. What influence it may have exerted over the *Knowledge Computer* is not known. "Detroit Free Press Tells Story of 'Telequiz,'" *Cash Box*, August 26, 1946, 51.

[11] "Knowledge at the Drop of a Coin," *Cash Box*, August 22, 1964, 52.

[12] "Convention Clippings," *Billboard*, October 24, 1964, 66.

[13] "Coinmen in the News," *Billboard*, October 23, 1965, 58.

to flying them. After assembling every kit he could find, Dave transitioned to designing his own.[14]

Dave's father wanted him to continue the family tradition at Marshall Field's, but with his love of creating things, he was only interested in the relatively new field of industrial design. After two years at Denison University, Nutting enrolled in the Pratt Institute School of Industrial Design in New York City. After graduating in 1955, he served in the U.S. Army and then took employment with Brooks Stevens Design Associates in Milwaukee in 1957[15] There he designed a wide array of products ranging from aluminum pots and pans to outboard motors to tractors to helicopters. Perhaps his most impressive design was the Jeep Grand Wagoneer, considered the first SUV, of which 500,000 were built in 29 years of continuous production.[16]

Eager to work with his brother, Dave contacted a good friend who worked for electrical engineering firm Cutler Hammer named Harold Montgomery to propose partnering on a redesign of the *Knowledge Computer*.[17] Meanwhile, Bill contacted a Michigan-based distributor and former schoolteacher named Gene Wagner, whom he had first met at the MOA show in 1964, to harness his coin-op experience for the venture. Bill gave Wagner the rights to market the quiz game east of the Mississippi River, while Wagner advised Bill, Dave, and Harold on how best to rebuild the quiz game.[18] Dave and Harold subsequently took a first pass at a redesign, with Dave handling the cabinet design and rebuilding the projector and Harold developing circuit boards that accepted plug-in relays in order to make the whole system more reliable and easier to repair.[19] They subsequently visited Bill in California to work out a deal, but after two or three days of meetings, he ultimately turned their proposal down.[20]

With his brother out of the picture, Bill established a new company, Nutting Associates, in January 1966 and turned to a local company called Marketing Services for help redesigning his quiz game, which assigned an

---

[14] David Judd Nutting, *Secrets to a Creative Mind: Become the Master of Your Mind* (Denver: Outskirts Press, 2012), 20–21.

[15] David Nutting. Testimony, Bally Manufacturing v. Williams Electronics, No. 78-2246 (N.D. Ill), January 6, 1983, 559.

[16] David Nutting, 2012, 32–33.

[17] David Nutting, interview with the author, November 13, 2017.

[18] Gene Wagner, interview with Ethan Johnson, July 16, 2016.

[19] Harold Montgomery, interview with Ethan Johnson, August 16, 2016.

[20] According to a letter Bill wrote to his son Craig in 2002, Bill and Dave Nutting had a complicated relationship going back to their childhood, and Bill always felt that Dave was jealous and resentful of him. Therefore, he distrusted his brother's motives and was uneasy about going into business with him. For his part, Dave apparently believed Bill was willing to work with him until Claire talked him out of it.

industrial designer named Richard Ball to the project. Ball started by placing a *Knowledge Computer* unit on test at the College of San Mateo and was amazed when he emptied the machine five days later and discovered it filled to the brim with dimes. Sensing a hit, Ball subsequently redesigned the game for easier manufacturing. The *Knowledge Computer* relied on copper relays for its operation, which created extreme service headaches, so Ball approached a company called Applied Technology to design a circuit board that would accept plug-in relays. He also rebuilt the projector from scratch.[21]

In late 1966, Nutting Associates commenced manufacturing and marketing Ball's redesigned game, now called *Computer Quiz*. Over the next year, Nutting Associates placed between 300 and 400 units on location through a franchise system,[22] including several on or around the Stanford University campus that were operated by a Vietnam veteran and Stanford MBA student named G. Ransom White. In summer 1967, White came on board as director of marketing and prepared for the game's official coming out at the MOA show in the fall, when the company would begin selling the game to traditional coin-op distributors. Dave Nutting, meanwhile, stuck with parts for around 100 machines when his brother called off their deal, formed his own company with Harold Montgomery and Gene Wagner called Nutting Industries and debuted his version of the *Knowledge Computer*, now dubbed *I.Q. Computer*, at the same show.

Computer Quiz and *I.Q. Computer* ignited a coin-op trivia fad. Arriving at a time when the industry was battling for legitimacy and when operators felt they had basically saturated all available locations, quiz games possessed an important quality that a pinball machine or pool table lacked: a perceived educational value. Consequently, the game was welcome at college campuses, department stores, large apartment complexes, and other locations that would never think of placing coin-operated amusements on the premises. Once an operator established himself in a location with a quiz game and the money started rolling in, location owners who had grown used to having a coin-operated game around would often start accepting other pieces as well, particularly after the new audio-visual games like *Periscope* and *Speedway* began hitting the market. In a time when most coin-operated games would sell no more than 1,500 units and 3,000 units constituted a

---

[21] Richard Ball, interview with the author, May 23, 2014.
[22] "A Look at Your Future with Nutting Associates," *Employee Handbook*, Nutting Associates, 1968, 2.

major hit, Nutting Associates sold 4,200 units of *Computer Quiz*, while Nutting Industries supplied 3,600 units of *I.Q. Computer*.[23]

Over the next two years, both Nutting brothers offered new variations on the quiz game concept. Nutting Associates developed a horoscope machine called *Astro Computer*, a sports trivia game called *Sports World*, and a blinking light guessing game called *ESP*, while Nutting Industries developed a golf trivia game called *Golf IQ* and a bowling instruction machine called *Sensorama*.[24] Both companies also continued to refine their original trivia games by releasing two-player versions, designing updated film packs with new questions, and improving the underlying technology. The concept reached its most advanced form in the summer of 1968 when Richard Ball worked with Applied Technology to eliminate the plug-in relays in *Computer Quiz* to create what was most likely the first solid-state product in the coin-op industry upon its release that October.[25] Technology improvements and expansion packs could only carry coin-operated trivia games so far, however, and by 1970, it was clear that the market was largely played out.

Dave Nutting responded to the end of the trivia game craze by moving more heavily into the education market through a new subsidiary called MODEC that developed filmstrip-training equipment for businesses. He also adapted the underlying filmstrip technology in *IQ Computer* to create a coin-operated target shooting game called *Red Baron*. Bill Nutting could not adapt so easily. In late 1968, Richard Ball and recently promoted general manager Ransom White fell out with their boss over his use of company funds to purchase two airplanes and left to form their own coin-operated amusement manufacturer named Cointronics.[26] Nutting refreshed his executive staff by hiring Rod Geiman away from pen manufacturer Micropoint International to serve as his new executive vice president in late 1968 and Dave Ralstin as his marketing director roughly a year later, but he lacked competent designers or engineers to develop new equipment. Consequently,

---

[23] Donovan, 2010, chap. 2.

[24] Nutting Industries had particularly targeted bowling alleys with its original *I.Q. Computer* because Harold Montgomery had a friend highly placed in the American Bowling Congress, so the *Sensorama* was an attempt to further capitalize on that market. Montgomery, 2016.

[25] In 1961, a company called the Victor Electronics Corporation debuted a coin-operated golf game called *Golf-It* at a trade show in which a player swung at a golf ball affixed to a tee and then the path of the ball was calculated electronically. This may have been the industry's first solid-state game, but it appears to have only received a limited test release and faded quickly. *Computer Quiz* was probably the first solid-state game to attain a wide release. "New Coin Golf Game Measures Player's Drive Electronically," *Billboard*, November 27, 1961, 37.

[26] Ball, 2014. Cointronics only released a handful of unremarkable games before going out of business in 1970.

when Nolan Bushnell called Ralstin on the advice of his dentist in early 1971, Nutting wasted no time in hiring him to finish developing his video game.

***

Nolan Bushnell knew he needed a company like Nutting to back the creation of his hardware, but he was not about to hand his future over to someone else. Perhaps sensing Nutting's desperation for new product, he negotiated a deal allowing him to retain the rights to his video game technology. He also stipulated that he would work on projects for Nutting during regular business hours while confining his work on the video game to evenings and weekends so Nutting would not acquire shop rights to his work. In return, Nutting would manufacture the finished product and pay Syzygy a royalty on each unit sold.[27]

When Bushnell joined Nutting, he had a basic hardware system that could move dots around the screen and a desire to create a product like *Spacewar!*, but he did not yet have a fully formed game concept due to the continuing difficulties he and Dabney faced in developing cost-effective hardware. In fact, at one point they toyed with moving to a simpler concept by just designing a piloting game in which the player controlled a spaceship and dodged asteroids.[28] In the end, the partners decided to press on with the *Cosmic Combat* shooting game. The limitations of the hardware necessitated some changes from *Spacewar!*, however. Gone was the sun and its gravity, the hyperspace function, and two-player combat. Instead, Bushnell crafted a game in which the player controls a rocket ship and attempts to shoot down two flying saucers that also shoot back at him. Both the player and the saucers score a point each time they destroy one another. If the player has more points than the saucers at the end of a 90-second round, he gets another 90 seconds of play; otherwise the game ends.

Over the next several months, Bushnell spent his days hunched over a drafting table just outside his office door at Nutting plotting out the circuitry that would tell the spot generator where to place dots on the screen and how they should interact with the player's controls. He also created the graphics for the game by rendering the player's ship and the flying saucers as a series of dots and creating routines allowing them to rotate smoothly. In one of his cleverer feats of engineering, Bushnell employed mirroring techniques

---

[27] Benj Edwards, "Computer Space and the Dawn of the Arcade Video Game," Technologizer, December 11, 2011, https://www.technologizer.com/2011/12/11/computer-space-and-the-dawn-of-the-arcade-video-game.

[28] Bushnell, deposition, January 1976.

so that he would only have to store four different ship positions in memory rather than the 16 needed to cover every possible facing. He also chose to lay out the diode matrix in which the graphics were stored – core and semi-conductor memory being far too expensive at the time – in the shapes of the ships themselves to allow operators to easily figure out which diode needed to be replaced in case of malfunction. Finally, Bushnell crafted the AI of the hardware-controlled opponents by dividing the playfield into quadrants and giving the saucers the ability to detect which quadrant the player's ship currently inhabited, so they would fire in that direction.[29]

Dabney, meanwhile, remained at Ampex but joined Bushnell in the evenings to design many of the features required to turn their prototype into an actual arcade system such as the cabinet, coin slot, control panel, and power supply. He also developed a primitive sound system by taking a voltage regulating diode that generated pink noise and attaching an amplifier and integrator in order to provide the sound of the rocket's engines.[30] By the middle of summer, Dabney had become so impressed with Bushnell's progress on the game that he joined Nutting full time.

By August 1971, Bushnell and Dabney's game, now named *Computer Space* to line up with the hit *Computer Quiz*, was far enough along that Nutting decided to do a location test, an important step in the coin-op industry in which a prototype game is placed on location and the coin-drop is measured to see if the game is shaping up to be a hit.[31] Shortly after coming to Nutting Associates, Rod Geiman had established a company called ACEM Incorporated to operate a route of roughly 50 machines,[32] so he placed the game in a bar on the route frequented by students of Stanford University called the Dutch Goose. Packing the prototype unit into Dabney's Datsun pickup truck, Bushnell and Dabney brought the game to the bar and watched as players flocked to the machine. It looked like the duo had a hit, but a second test at a pizza place did not go nearly so well. Like *Spacewar!*, *Computer Space* used a multi-button control scheme and realistically depicted the physics of movement in a zero-g environment – in which an object continues to move in the same direction until a force is exerted in the opposite direction. The Stanford engineering students at the Goose, some of whom

---

[29] Edwards, 2011.
[30] Paul Drury, "The Making of Computer Space," *Retro Gamer* no. 93, 2011, 28–29.
[31] Goldberg and Vendel, 2012, chap. 1.
[32] Rodney Geiman, interview with Ethan Johnson, August 30, 2016.

were probably *Spacewar!* veterans, caught on right away. The working-class patrons at the pizza place did not.[33]

Around the same time that *Computer Space* went out on test, the duo learned they were not the only people pursuing a coin-operated version of *Spacewar!* Through mutual contacts, Bushnell learned that a young man named Bill Pitts was in the process of recreating *Spacewar!* on a minicomputer. Worried that Pitts had found some revolutionary new way to create a fully functioning port of the game on a cost-effective coin-op system, Bushnell called Pitts to setup an information sharing session. The duo met for coffee at Stanford, after which Nolan invited Pitts back to Nutting Associates to show off his *Computer Space* work. By the time the meeting was over, Bushnell was relieved to learn that while Pitts's system was technically impressive, there was no way it would ever prove economically viable.

***

As Bill Nutting prepared to unveil the Edex *Knowledge Computer* in the fall of 1964, Palo Alto native Bill Pitts was just beginning his first semester at Stanford University. Interested in chemistry and physics in high school, Pitts was assigned an academic advisor in the electrical engineering department. Noting the new student's interests, the advisor arranged for him to push back Stanford's required "History of Western Civilization" course so he could take the newly offered "Introduction to Computer Science" course instead. Pitts was immediately hooked.[34] At the time, the university did not offer an undergraduate computer science degree, so Pitts chose to major in statistics, a relatively unpopular field that allowed its students to take graduate-level courses to attract greater enrollment, so he could take additional computer courses.[35]

Alongside his interest in computers, Pitts also held a fondness for exploring the complex array of steam tunnels running under the campus and breaking into restricted areas of university buildings. One night in 1966, Pitts left the heart of campus bound for Rossotti's, a popular student hangout west of the university. By now, Pitts had already broken into every building on the main campus, but this night he noticed a sign for an unfamiliar building set in the rolling hills outside the university. Returning later that night to practice his craft, Pitts was disappointed to discover the building was unlocked. What

[33] Goldberg and Vendel, 2012, chap. 1.
[34] Greta Lorge and Mike Antonucci, "Bill Pitts, '68," *Stanford Magazine*, April 30, 2012, https://stanfordmag.org/contents/bill-pitts-68.
[35] Smith, 2016, 55.

did not disappoint him was the PDP-6 time-sharing system sitting in the heart of the building. Pitts had just discovered John McCarthy's Artificial Intelligence Laboratory.[36]

Through his coursework, Pitts had worked with the systems available in the computer science department in Polya Hall, but nothing there compared to SAIL's PDP-6. Although this computer was technically restricted to the staff and students working for SAIL, Pitts pleaded with McCarthy's right-hand man, Lester Earnest, to allow him to program on the computer. Earnest decided that since Pitts was a Stanford student, he could have access to the machine when no official projects were in operation. For the next two years, Pitts began sleeping during the day and staying up all night programming at SAIL, skipping class so he could spend as much time with the computer as possible. His persistence eventually paid off, as he secured a position as a research assistant at SAIL in 1967. The next year, he aided Arthur Samuel, who came to SAIL after leaving IBM in 1966, in further developing his pioneering checkers program.[37]

Pitts had played *Spacewar!* in Polya Hall before discovering SAIL,[38] so he was quickly sucked into the AI Lab's obsession with the game. On several occasions, he even brought his high school friend Hugh Tuck to play the game when he was in town. A mechanical engineering student at California Polytechnic in San Luis Obispo, Tuck had never been one for playing pinball or other coin-operated amusements, but he was so blown away by *Spacewar!* that he told Pitts if they could just attach a coin slot to the machine, they could become rich.[39] A PDP-6 cost well north of $100,000, however, and the other computers available circa 1968 were no better. Therefore, Tuck's ambition was cast aside unrealized.

After graduating from Stanford in 1968, Pitts did a brief stint in the Navy and continued to work on the checkers program at SAIL, which was ported to the PDP-10 in 1969. He subsequently parlayed his work at SAIL into a position at Lockheed as a PDP-10 programmer. Lockheed did not actually own a PDP-10 yet when he was hired, however, so in late 1970 as he waited for that job to begin he had ample free time to take stock of the current state of the computer world. By now, minicomputers had come down drastically in price in the wake of the release of the Data General Nova, and DEC was

---

[36] Donovan, 2010, chap. 2.
[37] "Mini-Computer Applications Business Plan," c. 1972.
[38] Smith, 2016, 56.
[39] Hugh Tuck, interview with the author, April 6, 2016.

preparing to launch a product that would become a new industry standard, the PDP-11.

***

The departure of Ed de Castro and friends to form Data General in 1968 had gutted DEC's engineering talent at just the moment the company desperately needed a new 16-bit computer to remain relevant in the minicomputer industry it had created. Therefore, to bring a computer to market quickly would require going outside the company. DEC hired Andrew Knowles from RCA to serve as the product manager for the new 16-bit computer and then poached Roger Cady from Honeywell and Julius Marcus from General Electric to head up engineering and marketing, respectively. After a year of work, however, all the trio had managed to produce was an incredibly flawed prototype design.

Enter Gordon Bell, one of DEC's first engineers and the originator of the company's minicomputer line with the PDP-5 back in 1964. After the debacle of the PDP-6, Bell had taken an extended sabbatical from DEC to teach at Carnegie Mellon University. With their computer design going nowhere, Knowles, Cady, and Marcus traveled to Carnegie Mellon to consult with Bell, who over the course of a long weekend oversaw the design of a completely new architecture developed by one of his graduate students. This effort culminated in the release of the PDP-11 minicomputer in late 1970, which not only offered superior performance to the Nova at only a slightly higher price – $10,800 – but was designed to be scalable like the abandoned PDP-X.[40] By 1972, DEC had recaptured the lead in the minicomputer market from Data General on its way to selling over 600,000 PDP-11 units by the time it was discontinued in the 1990s.

When Pitts took note of the PDP-11 during his downtime at Lockheed, he thought back to Tuck's ambition to transform *Spacewar!* into an arcade game and contacted him to say this project now appeared possible. Tuck remained on the fence for several months, but after the duo surveyed both the coin-op and minicomputer markets, he ultimately decided to go ahead. Pitts and Tuck established a company called Mini-Computer Applications in May 1971 to transform *Spacewar!* into a coin-operated game.[41]

Pitts and Tuck designed the initial version of their game between July and November 1971. As the computer expert, Pitts took primary responsibility

---

[40] Rifkin and Harrar, 1988, 100–104.
[41] Mini-Computers Business Plan, 1972.

for programming the game and interfacing the computer with a monitor, while the mechanical engineer Tuck designed the cabinet and other components. Tuck also served as the company's main financing connection, as his father owned one of the Bay-area's largest HVAC firms, the Atlas Heating and Ventilating Company. Although never comfortable around computers himself, the elder Tuck became the largest investor in Mini-Computer Applications, while Hugh also put in some of his own money alongside contributions from a sister and a couple of cousins. In all, building the initial prototype of the game cost $20,000.[42]

Completed in late November 1971, Pitts and Tuck's game, which they called *Galaxy Game* rather than *Spacewar!* due to the anti-war sentiment prevalent on university campuses at the time,[43] consisted of a PDP-11/20 with 8K of memory, a Hewlett Packard 1300A Electrostatic Display, and a point-plotting display interface designed by a man named Ted Panofsky. The coin box for the game was donated by jukebox company Rowe International, while the joysticks used to control the spaceships were military surplus out of a B-52 bomber purchased by Pitts from J&H Outlet in San Carlos. The massive walnut cabinet that Tuck designed to house the game was built by an engineering firm in Palo Alto and incorporated a seat to encourage long playing sessions. The duo set a price of ten cents per game or twenty-five cents for three games and reached an agreement with the manager of the Tresidder Union on the Stanford campus to place the game in a music listening room on the second floor.[44]

For the first few days it was on location, *Galaxy Game* was barely touched despite an advertisement placed in the *Stanford Daily* newspaper. Then, interest suddenly blossomed until it was not uncommon for 20–30 people to be clustered around the machine at once waiting for the chance to play a match. In December, the game was moved to the more accommodating coffee house on the first floor of the union, and players were soon forming long lines and waiting an hour or more for their shot on the machine.[45] For a time, there was even a second monitor installed above the cabinet to facilitate easier spectator viewing of matches.[46]

---

[42]Tuck, 2016.

[43]Hugh Tuck believes his sister suggested the name change, though he is not certain. She was attending UC Berkeley at the time, which was one of the centers of the student protest movement. Tuck, 2016.

[44]Smith, 2016, 58.

[45]Mini-Computer Applications Business Plan, 1972.

[46]Bill Pitts, email to Marty Goldberg, 2015.

With the prototype proving a hit, Pitts and Tuck began work on a production model suitable for commercial release. Pitts built a new display interface capable of driving four monitors at once to make the whole system cost effective. These monitors could each run separate games, or they could be linked to allow more than two players to play in the same game. The duo also designed a striking blue fiberglass cabinet to increase the system's aesthetic appeal. In June 1972, this version replaced the original in the coffee house in the Tresidder Union, though it had to be cut down to only two monitors to fit into the space allotted by the university.[47] Once version two went live at Stanford, Pitts carted version one to other locations around town, but it never did as well as the installation on campus. Building the new system ran the cost of the project to $60,000.[48]

Pitts and Tuck realized their game was too expensive for the traditional coin-op market, but they thought they could market it to college campuses, which required entertainment in student unions and large dorms, but were often hesitant to purchase traditional coin-operated equipment like pinball machines. The duo envisioned owning and servicing all the machines through their company, thereby requiring no commitment from the university other than space. After a three-month trial period, the university would enter a three-year lease in which the institution would keep 12% of the gross coin drop in the first year, 16% in the second, and 20% in the third. This was a far different arrangement from that found in the traditional coin-op industry, in which operators and location owners would generally split the take 50-50 but was necessary if Pitts and Tuck were ever going to recoup their costs. To further increase the appeal of their system, they also planned to design several more games.[49]

In early 1972, Pitts and Tuck drew up a business plan in hopes of attracting investors to get their venture off the ground, but they found no takers. While the duo had developed an extremely faithful recreation of *Spacewar!* with immense play appeal, it was simply too expensive for any reasonable business model to work. Therefore, while the second prototype continued to run at Stanford until the display malfunctioned in 1979, and Pitts was able to harness the profits from that machine to pay back all the original investors, *Galaxy Game* never achieved a wider release and remains a footnote in the early history of video games. Instead, it would be Bushnell and Dabney's

---

[47] Bill Pitts, "The Galaxy Game," Stanford Infolab, October 29, 1997, http://infolab.stanford.edu/pub/voy/museum/galaxy.html.

[48] Smith, 2016, 47-48.

[49] Mini-Computer Applications Business Plan, 1972.

more compromised, but also far cheaper, *Computer Space* that would become the first coin-operated video game to enter mass production.

***

Roughly a month before *Galaxy Game* debuted at the Tresidder Union, the Nutting Associates team flew to Chicago to attend the MOA show, held that year from October 15–17 at the Conrad Hilton Hotel, to reveal *Computer Space* to the world. The original prototype debuted at the Dutch Goose was housed in a simple wooden cabinet built by Dabney, but by the MOA, the game sported a futuristic-looking fiberglass cabinet designed by Bushnell using modeling clay and built by a seamless swimming pool manufacturer named John Hebbler located by Dabney. The controls were placed on a lighted panel jutting out from the cabinet and consisted of four buttons – two for left and right rotation, one for thrust, and one for firing.[50] The panel bore the Nutting Associates name and logo, but in a nod to the game's creators, it also included the phrase "Syzygy engineered."

Nutting brought four cabinets to the MOA show to give the appearance the game was already in production, though in truth these were the only four copies of the game in existence. Each game was housed in a different color cabinet – yellow, red, white, and blue. Disaster nearly struck when the team discovered the monitors had all broken loose from their cabinets during shipping, but Bushnell was able to repair three of the units. The fourth was left open as a display of the internal components of the system, a clever ploy to mask the accident from distributors.[51] Kept completely secret in advance of its debut, the game was met with a mixture of astonishment and bewilderment.[52] Nutting's booth remained crowded for much of the show, but many distributors worried that operators raised on electromechanical technology would not be able to service the machines and that patrons would smash them up to steal the televisions. In the end, Nutting took few, if any, orders.[53]

At this point, Ralstin and Geiman began working their marketing magic. When production of *Computer Space* finally began in late November or early December, Ralstin sent the first five machines off the assembly line to various

---

[50]While initial tests demonstrated the buttons might be too complicated a control scheme, attempts to use a metal joystick-like device for movement had failed when it proved too fragile and broke the first night that version went out on test. Goldberg and Vendel, 2012, chap. 1.

[51]Edwards, 2011.

[52]"MOA Socks 'Em in at Expo," *Cash Box*, October 30, 1971, 56.

[53]In a 1976 deposition, Nolan Bushnell said the company took no orders at the show, a sentiment echoed by Rod Geiman to Ethan Johnson. Bushnell, 1976, 312, and Geiman, 2016. Other sources indicate they might have taken at least a few.

distributors around the country to gauge its earning potential, while Geiman also placed units on his own coin route.[54] By the time full production of the machine commenced in late January/early February 1972, this ploy had generated several orders on the back of fantastic earnings reports,[55] but did little to alleviate most of the industry's skepticism of the machine. While some distributors were highly enthusiastic about the game and pushed it aggressively to good results, many others saw video as a gimmick and resisted stocking the product. In the end, the Nutting sales team had to practically force many distributors into taking the game,[56] which may have failed to sell its entire 1,500-unit production run.[57] While not strictly a commercial failure and even capable of delivering a high return on investment when placed in the right venues, *Computer Space* ultimately failed to cement a place for the video game as a viable new form of entertainment.

Perhaps the biggest problem faced by the game was its confusing multi-button control scheme and its accurate modeling of Newtonian physics, which combined to make the spaceship difficult to control. While the tech savvy individuals who hung around college campuses were able to adapt to these conditions fairly quickly as demonstrated by the game's success at the Dutch Goose, the coin-op business of the early 1970s was still primarily focused on working-class bars and taverns, where patrons were uninterested in reading pages of instructions or mastering complex controls. Introducing the public to the video game would, therefore, require a far simpler concept that was easy to learn, yet interesting enough to hold a person's attention over time. Unbeknownst to Bushnell, such a video game concept had already been in development for five years by the time *Computer Space* made its debut in October 1971 at New Hampshire defense contractor Sanders Associates.

---

[54] Goldberg and Vendel, 2012, chap. 1.

[55] "Old-Fashioned Op Scored by NA Exec," *Cash Box*, February 12, 1972, 42.

[56] Steve Bloom, *Video Invaders* (New York: Arco Publishing, 1982), 8.

[57] In his 1976 deposition, Nolan Bushnell estimated sales of 1,300–1,500 units. Bushnell, January 1976, 39.

9

1TL200
A Video Game Odyssey

On September 7, 1927, a largely self-taught electrical engineer from Idaho named Philo T. Farnsworth stood in front of a screen in San Francisco, California, upon which a small line appeared. Farnsworth called out to an assistant in the next room to rotate a slide containing an image of a triangle, and the line changed position as he did so. The slide sat in front of a special vacuum tube called an image dissector that transformed the light passing through it into an electromagnetic wave that was transmitted to the screen in the other room. While the resulting image failed to depict the entire triangle, this experiment represented the first demonstration of a fully electronic television.[1]

Farnsworth was not the first person to dabble in television. Indeed, he was not even the first to demonstrate a working system, but earlier efforts at places like Bell Labs and General Electric had been mechanical, based around a spinning disk design first invented by German university student Paul Nipkow in 1884. Farnsworth, on the other hand, had been keeping close tabs on developments in physics research since he was a teenager working on the family farm and figured the only way to generate an image with sufficient sharpness and clarity would be to manipulate it on the subatomic level through the use of a cathode-ray tube (CRT), a special type of vacuum tube invented by German Physicist Karl Braun in 1897 in which a stream of electrons passes through an evacuated glass cylinder and strikes a phosphor-coated screen to generate a point of light. By regulating the voltages of a magnetic field, Farnsworth

---

[1] Evan I. Schwartz, *The Last Lone Inventor: A Tale of Genius, Deceit, and the Birth of Television*, reprint ed. (New York: Harper Perennial, 2003), Kindle, chap. 7.

theorized, this beam could be pointed at different spots on the screen in rapid succession, thus allowing it to draw a complete picture in the barest fraction of a second. Combined with existing broadcasting technologies, this would theoretically allow a picture to be converted into a wave, broadcast into a home, and then converted back into an image again by the CRT.[2] Farnsworth's September 1927 demonstration proved that he was correct. The race was now on to bring the first television to market.

Farnsworth's most serious competition would come from the corporate powerhouse RCA, a wireless company established in 1919 by General Electric. Although founded to monopolize wireless communication in the United States after the medium had proven so crucial in World War I, RCA shifted its focus in the 1920s through the efforts of its commercial manager David Sarnoff, who was convinced that the future of wireless technology was not telegraphy, but the broadcasting of entertainment content that could be picked up by radio sets owned by the general public. Sarnoff was not the first person to hit upon this idea, but he was the first to enjoy the backing of one of the largest electrical companies in the world. Sarnoff convinced his superiors at RCA to acquire all the significant wireless patents it did not already own from AT&T and Westinghouse in exchange for RCA stock, giving the company a monopoly on radio technology.[3] When demand for radio sets took off in the early 1920s after a series of high-profile broadcasts of sporting and other public events, RCA dominated this new trade, first as the sole authorized manufacturer of radio sets and then by licensing its patents to other companies.[4]

Meanwhile, in September 1928 Philo Farnsworth demonstrated his television publicly for the first time, sparking the first media coverage of the new technology. Three months later, a researcher from Westinghouse named Vladimir Zworykin approached Sarnoff. Like Farnsworth, Zworykin had been inspired by science journals in the early 1920s to pursue an electronic television solution and had even attempted to patent a system in 1923, but failed because he proved unable to demonstrate his method. His work had to proceed in a clandestine manner, however, as it was not officially sanctioned by his employer. Zworykin came to Sarnoff came to Sarnoff in the hopes that RCA would back his research. Sarnoff immediately took to his proposal and arranged for him to come work for RCA.[5]

---

[2] Ibid, chap. 1.
[3] Ibid, chap. 2.
[4] Ibid, chap. 4.
[5] Ibid, chap. 8.

In 1930, Sarnoff was rewarded for his domination of the radio business with a promotion to president of RCA, but this period of greatest success also turned into his greatest period of struggle. The Depression was now in full swing, and radio sales were collapsing. Worse, the generally pro-business administration of President Herbert Hoover was taking such a beating for failing to prevent the economic calamity that it launched an anti-trust suit against RCA for its dominance of the radio business in an effort to mollify its critics. In the midst of these struggles, however, Sarnoff managed to establish a new centralized R&D operation in Camden, New Jersey, where Zworykin and a team of engineers toiled away trying to create a viable commercial television system that Sarnoff believed would be the future of broadcast entertainment.[6]

After years of research, RCA finally demonstrated its system in 1936, but it compared poorly to the system Farnsworth had developed concurrently. Zworykin's team decided they would need to copy elements of Farnsworth's system, but this technology had been patented. Sarnoff attempted to have these patents invalidated, but failed. In September 1939, Sarnoff was forced to concede defeat and license Farnsworth's patents to head off a potential infringement suit.[7]

In April 1939, RCA publicly debuted its first commercially available television sets at the World's Fair in New York City and began a series of experimental broadcasts. With commercial television now a reality, the Federal Communications Commission began holding hearings in the summer of 1940 to standardize the television broadcasting format. This resulted in the promulgation of the NTSC standard in 1941 that, with some modification, remained the standard in the United States for over 70 years.[8] World War II interrupted television research and manufacturing, but the need for radar displays during the war led to rapid technological developments that greatly decreased the cost of manufacturing sets at its conclusion. As the United States experienced a new period of prosperity in the 1950s, the entire country embraced television entertainment, and the percentage of households owning a television increased from just 0.6% of the population in 1946 to roughly 90% by the end of the 1950s. RCA continued to dominate the business, particularly after the sales of color televisions, for which RCA promulgated what became the broadcast standard, exploded in the 1960s.[9]

[6] Ibid.
[7] Ibid, chap. 13.
[8] Ibid.
[9] Ibid, chap. 14.

To most people, the television was merely an extension of the existing radio business with a sole purpose of receiving information broadcast by a station so as to provide a passive form of entertainment. Consequently, none of the major television manufacturers looked to transform the television into an interactive form of entertainment. Indeed, in the 40 years after Philo Farnsworth filed the first television patents in 1927, the only patent for anything approaching a television game was issued on December 14, 1948, for a device called a "Cathode-ray tube amusement device." This patent was filed almost two years earlier by engineers working for the DuMont Laboratory in Passaic, New Jersey.

Inventor Allen DuMont first became interested in television when he went to work for Lee De Forest in 1928 and first made his mark by inventing a longer lasting CRT tube in 1930 that helped make practical electronic television possible. He established DuMont Laboratory the next year to specialize in oscilloscopes, but he also introduced one of the first fully electric television sets in 1938 and established the second television network in the United States, the DuMont Network, in 1946 to promote the sale of his televisions.[10]

As a specialist in CRT technology, DuMont was always on the lookout for new applications for its equipment. These R&D efforts were overseen by Thomas Goldsmith, Jr., who became DuMont's research director in 1936 after receiving his PhD from Cornell. It was Goldsmith, along with a fellow engineer named Estle Ray Mann, who filed the CRT amusement device patent in January 1947, the first known instance of anyone proposing to use a CRT to play a game. Consisting of just a few resistors, a sawtooth generator, and a CRT, Goldsmith and Mann's game simulated firing a missile at a target, perhaps taking inspiration from Goldsmith's radar research during World War II. Using a knob, the player would guide the electron beam generated by the CRT across a screen to a target. After a certain period of time elapsed, which was adjustable by the player, the beam would defocus to simulate an explosion. If the beam defocused while on the target, it counted as a hit.[11] Despite filing the patent, however, DuMont never actually built the game. The reason for this is not clear, though DuMont was always strapped for cash during this period, so the company may have simply not had the resources to invest in a new commercial product.

[10] "Dr. Allen Balcom DuMont," *Baird Television*, accessed June 5, 2019, http://www.bairdtelevision.com/dumont.html.

[11] Thomas T. Goldsmith, Jr. and Estle Ray Mann, "Cathode-ray Tube Amusement Device," U.S. patent 2,455,992, filed January 25, 1947 and issued December 14, 1948.

Some have been tempted to label this "cathode-ray tube amusement device" as the first video game, but the device fits no definition of the term. There is no video signal, no computer, no software program, and only the simplest of electronics. There are also no graphics beyond the arc of the missile, as the targets for the system consisted of physical objects affixed to a screen. Basically, the exact same effect could have been created by mechanically controlling a flashlight shining its beam on a piece of paper. Therefore, while Goldsmith and Mann's work proved pioneering, the honor of inventing and patenting the first video game remains with Ralph Baer and his bus terminal brainstorm in the summer of 1966.

***

Rudolf Heinrich "Ralph" Baer was born on March 8, 1922, in Pirmasens, Germany. His father, a Jewish World War I veteran named Leo, ran a leather tannery supplying the many shoe factories in town, but due to the depressed economic conditions in the region after World War I, the family moved to Cologne two years after Ralph was born. As a German of Jewish descent, Ralph was subjected to increasingly anti-Semitic practices after Adolf Hitler came to power in 1933 and was expelled from school at the age of 14. He subsequently attempted to secure a job as a plumber's apprentice but was not "Aryan enough" for his potential employer, so he ended up working in an office instead, where he learned shorthand and typing and performed filing and bookkeeping tasks.[12]

In 1938, the Baer family emigrated to the United States just ahead of *Kristallnacht* and settled in the Bronx, where Ralph worked in a factory owned by a cousin earning $12 a week putting buttons on cosmetic cases until he saw an ad on the back of a magazine for the National Radio Institute and enrolled in a correspondence course in radio servicing. Upon completing the course, Ralph took a job with a radio store on Lexington Avenue handling all pickup, delivery, and servicing for the company.

In 1943, Baer was drafted into the U.S. Army as a combat engineer. Shipped overseas as part of the buildup for the Normandy landings, Baer contracted pneumonia in England and was spared going ashore on D-Day. Afterwards, he became part of a special military intelligence unit attached to Supreme Allied Commander Dwight Eisenhower's headquarters that gave

---

[12] Ralph Baer, interview by Gardner Hendrie, October 12 and November 27, 2006, Computer History Museum, https://archive.computerhistory.org/resources/access/text/2013/05/102657972-05-01-acc.pdf.

courses in identifying enemy uniforms, interrogating enemy soldiers, and identifying and handling enemy weapons.

In March 1946, Ralph Baer received his discharge from the Army, returned to New York, and secured a job fixing faulty radios for a manufacturer called Emerson. Bored after three months, Baer quit and explored avenues for continuing his education. Turned down by all the New York colleges because he had no record of his education in Germany, Baer saw an ad for a small unaccredited school in Chicago called the American Television Institute of Technology (ATIT) and enrolled in late 1946 through the GI Bill. By the time he graduated in 1949, the school had received accreditation, so Baer walked away with one of the first BS degrees in television engineering. Upon graduating from ATIT, Baer secured employment at a small medical equipment firm called Wappler Inc., but he felt the work lacked sufficient challenge and departed two years later to take a job at the defense contractor Loral Corporation. It was at Loral that Baer first suggested adding a game to a television set in 1951, but his idea was turned down.[13]

When the Loral television project ultimately stalled, Baer left the company to work for a defense contractor named Transitron.[14] In 1955, Transitron became a subsidiary of Van Norman Industries and moved to New Hampshire, which would remain Baer's home for the rest of his life. When the company hit hard times three years later, Baer left to work for another defense contractor called Sanders Associates. Specializing in electronic warfare systems, Sanders was founded in 1951 by a group of engineers led by Roydon Sanders. An electronics genius, Sanders invented the first FM Altimeter while still a college student at the Rensselaer Polytechnic Institute in the 1930s, worked for RCA during World War II, and ran Raytheon's Lab 16 in the late 1940s, where his team developed the first guided missiles.[15] By 1958, his company employed 8,000 people and enjoyed sales of $9 million a year.[16]

Sanders assigned Baer to its Equipment Design Division, where he worked primarily on a spying apparatus codenamed BRANDY designed to pick up Soviet radio transmissions in Berlin. Soon after Baer completed the project ahead of schedule, the division manager retired, so in 1966 Baer was promoted to lead the unit. It was in this context that Baer found himself sitting

---

[13] Ibid.
[14] No relation to the Wakefield, MA semiconductor company.
[15] "Royden C. Sanders," *Microwave Journal*, November–December 1958, 10.
[16] Ibid, 26.

outside that New York City bus terminal on August 31, 1966, dreaming up the first video game.[17]

On September 1, 1966, Baer drafted his four-page memo outlining his ideas for a "TV Gaming Display" that would transmit a video signal to a television through its antenna ports and incorporate an RF modulator oscillating at one of the standard TV channel frequencies so that the television could tune to the signal and display the game. He also outlined several types of games he felt would be well suited for his system such as driving games with a steering wheel controller, card games, board games like checkers and chess, basic educational software like arithmetic and geometry programs, games of chance like dice and roulette, target shooting games, and a "pumping" game in which each player presses a button rapidly to fill a vessel. On September 6, Baer drew up a rough schematic of how the device might work and specified channels 3 and 4 for its video signal, which remained the standard right up until plugging a video game console into a television no longer required an RF modulator in the 1990s.[18]

Soon after drafting these documents, Baer initiated a skunk works project to build a prototype of his new game system. While Baer could never sanction a game system as an official company project, his Equipment Design Division carried a staff of 500 people, so no one would notice or even care if Baer took an engineer or two aside and put them to work on a special project in between more important work. Therefore, he asked one of his department managers to lend him a technician to create a feasibility prototype of his TV game using vacuum tubes. The manager loaned him a man named Bob Tremblay, who in December 1966 completed the circuitry necessary to interface a Heathkit TV alignment generator with a television via an RF modulator and move a vertical line around the screen. With this feasibility prototype in hand, Baer approached the Sanders Corporate Director of Research & Development, Herbert Campman, to officially sanction the project. After viewing Baer's line-moving system in action, Campman approved further development with a modest initial budget of $2,000 for labor and $500 for materials. Sanders was now officially in the video game business.[19]

On February 12, 1967, Baer formally started work on his game system by recruiting a technician named Bill Harrison. Born in Sagamore, Massachusetts, in 1935, William L. Harrison left home in 1953 at the age

17 Baer, 2006.
18 Baer, 2005, 27.
19 Ibid, 27–30.

of 18 to join the U.S. Air Force, where he was assigned to an electronics course at Kessler Field in Mississippi so he could be trained as a ground radar repairman. After completing his tour of duty in 1957, Harrison joined Sanders Associates, where his cousin was married to one of the founders, and by 1967 he was part of the Ocean Systems Division working on a sonar buoy project. He had previously worked briefly with Baer on the BRANDY project, however, who was both impressed by his reliability and knew he had some television experience from tinkering with sets in his spare time. Therefore, Baer called one day to invite him to see his TV game prototype and to recruit him for the project. With Harrison on board, work soon commenced on the first real system prototype.[20]

Although now an official project, Baer's video game was still a highly unusual endeavor for a defense contractor to undertake, so he decided to keep the work low key by stashing Harrison in a small room on the fifth floor of the main Sanders building on Canal Street that remained locked at all times and for which only Baer and Harrison had a key. Unfortunately, Harrison had barely started development on his first prototype when he was called away for three months to work on a more important project.[21] During this lull, Baer brainstormed more game ideas with the manager of Advanced Techniques Programs within the Sanders Corporate Research and Development Department, Bill Rusch, a 1953 MIT graduate in electrical engineering who joined Sanders in 1957 after serving a tour of duty with the U.S. Army.[22] On May 10, 1967, Rusch drafted a formal memo articulating multiple game types that emerged from these brainstorming sessions, including a drawing game, two driving games set on an endless road and a circular track, a chase game, a maze game, a roulette game, several variations on a baseball guessing game in which the screen was divided into horizontal bands and the "batter" would guess in which band the "pitcher" will throw the ball, a U.S. geography map game, two target shooting games, a number guessing game, a "fox and hounds" game in which multiple pursuers chase one target, a soccer game, a golf putting game, and a horse racing game.[23]

Meanwhile, Harrison returned to the project on May 2 and implemented the pumping game outlined in Baer's first memo. In this game, the first playable on

---

[20] Benj Edwards, "Bill Harrison: The First Video Game Hardware Guru," Vintage Computing and Gaming, May 15, 2007, http://www.vintagecomputing.com/index.php/archives/319/vcg-interview-bill-harrison-worlds-first-video-game-hardware-builder.

[21] Baer, 2005, 32.

[22] William Rusch. Testimony, Magnavox Co. v. Bally Manufacturing Corp., No. 74-1030 (N.D. Ill), February 19, 1976.

[23] Baer, 2005, 32–39.

Baer's hardware, one player would furiously press a button to raise a blue square on the screen that represented water, while the other player would pound his button to lower the square. An overlay placed on top of the screen contained a drawing of the "bucket" that held the "water." If the first player could fill the bucket high enough within a time limit, he won, otherwise, the water turned red and the other player won the contest. Subsequently, Baer directed Harrison to implement four additional games, all of which required only one spot since that was all the hardware could produce. These were a second pumping game called *Firefighters*, *Color Catching*, *Roulette*, and *Car Ride*.[24] Once these were completed, Harrison built a few more components that allowed the team to retire the Heathkit equipment from the initial prototype.[25]

Once the duo had the full system up and running, Baer designed the necessary hardware to add a second dot on the screen, which Harrison implemented starting on May 22. This allowed two players to each control their own dots and led to the design of the "chase" game outlined in the Rusch memo in which one dot attempted to catch the other. This required two new features in the hardware: collision detection and the ability to make a dot disappear. Both of these functions were sketched out by Baer and then implemented by Harrison on May 25.[26] Harrison also built a light gun around this time by buying a toy gun from Sears and retrofitting it so that it could sense dots on the screen and cause them to disappear with a pull of the trigger.[27]

On June 14, 1967, Baer invited Campman back to the lab for a demonstration of the system. Though impressed by all the games, Campman particularly liked the light gun game and believed Baer now had a winning product. He, therefore, approved additional R&D funding and indicated it was time to bring senior management into the loop. The next day, Baer demonstrated the system for Royden Sanders, executive VP Harold Pope, and the entire board of directors of Sanders, who happened to be in town for a meeting. Seven games were shown: a chase game on a grid of squares called *Chess*, a freeform chase game called *Steeple Chase*, a chase game called *Fox and Hounds* that used random dot generation hardware to place multiple pursuers on the screen, *Target Shooting* with the light gun, a guessing game called

---

[24] Firefighters was a one-player variant of the original pumping game in which the player pressed the button rapidly to reduce the size of the dot to simulate fighting a fire; Color Catching was a simple guessing game where the players predicted what color would appear next; Roulette simulated the popular casino game; and Car Ride challenged the player to keep his car, represented by a dot, on a road, represented by a line.

[25] Ibid, 39.

[26] Ibid, 39–41.

[27] Edwards, 2007.

Color Wheel Game, and the two previously implemented pumping games under the names *Bucket Filling Game* and *Pumping Game.* While neither Sanders nor Pope nor all but two of the company directors were particularly impressed, Sanders and Pope conferred briefly at the end of the demonstration before formally authorizing the project with the goal of creating a commercial product that Sanders could sell itself or license to another company.[28]

In the aftermath of the successful demonstration of his system, Baer began refining it into a viable commercial product. His target retail price was just $25.00, so to reduce the part count he refocused the system around the best ideas he and Harrison had developed. Harrison removed the pumping game mechanic, which had never been particularly fun, as well as the circuits that allowed for color graphics and the placement of additional dots on the screen through a random number generator. By August 1967, Harrison had completed his scaled-down version of the system, which now only played chase and shooting games. Unfortunately, despite cutting as many corners as they possibly could, Baer and Harrison were unable to come near their target price: the system they built would have to sell for a minimum of $50.00 at retail. Baer felt his simple chase and light gun games did not provide nearly enough entertainment value to justify that price, so he put the color circuitry back into the system and tried to develop additional game concepts. When he proved unable to make the system more interesting, Campman loaned Baer his former brainstorming partner Bill Rusch. On August 18, 1967, Rusch became the third member of the Sanders TV game team.[29]

Bill Rusch, described at various times as "very different" and "a colorful character," clashed with the straight-laced Baer and infuriated him by repeatedly showing up late for work, goofing off for an hour before turning to the task at hand, taking two-hour lunches, and generally spending as little time actually working as possible. Before long, Baer was so desperate to motivate his frustrating engineer that he let him work on a pet project involving changing the octave of notes played on a guitar in addition to the TV game project. Despite these difficulties, however, there was no doubting Rusch's intelligence or creativity, which is why Baer ultimately kept him around despite the headaches. Indeed, soon after joining the team Rusch proved his value by proposing the idea that saved the entire project: adding a third, machine-controlled dot to serve as a ball for use in a game of ping pong. By November 1967, Baer's team had a video game unit that could play

---

[28] Baer, 2005, 31–44.
[29] Ibid, 44–45.

ping pong, chase, and shooting games with three controllers: a light gun for target shooting, joysticks for the chase game, and a three dial control for ping pong that controlled the horizontal and vertical movement of the player's paddle and allowed the player to manipulate the ball to put a little "English" on it. After another demo for Campman, the R&D director concurred with Baer that the system finally contained enough interesting gameplay variants to be worth selling, so Baer focused on finding a retail partner.[30]

Baer turned first to the fledgling cable industry. At the time, there were no dedicated cable channels, so cable TV was basically just an expensive way to receive the exact same channels that a person could already tune for free over the air. Unless a person lived in the mountains or in a similar environment where reception was exceptionally poor, it was hard for a consumer to justify the cost. As a result, the cable industry was struggling, and Baer felt that a novel product like a TV game could be just the thing for the industry to break out of its slump. He directed Harrison to modify the game to accept background graphics transmitted by a cable signal and contacted the largest cable provider, TelePrompter, which supplied roughly 60,000 subscribers. The idea was that the cable company could point a camera at a highly detailed view of a tennis court or some other venue which would be broadcast to the TV game to provide a background for the action. The spots generated by the hardware would then be superimposed on top. TelePrompter expressed interest, and negotiations proceeded on and off between January and April 1968. While the cable company thought the game a good idea, an economic recession left it in an untenable financial situation, and it could not afford to develop the product. Baer would need to find another partner.[31]

***

In December 1967 and January 1968, Harrison continued to work on improving the TV game and added two new ball-and-paddle variants, handball and volleyball.[32] At that point, funding for the project dried up. The same recession affecting TelePromper also hit Sanders hard, and the company scaled down from 11,000 employees to just 4,000 during this period. This also marked the end of Bill Rusch's short, but productive time on the project.

---

[30] Ibid, 45–48.

[31] Ibid, 48–49.

[32] In handball, the "net" was moved to one side of the screen and served as the wall of a handball court, while in volleyball, the centerline was modified to serve as a net. Otherwise, the gameplay remained the same as in the ping-pong game.

In September 1968, Baer secured additional funding and brought Harrison back to create another prototype that featured a rotary dial to select different game modes rather than switches as in previous versions. Still feeling they could do a little better, Baer and Harrison developed one final prototype in January 1969 that they called the "Brown Box" because Harrison wrapped the casing in self-adhesive woodgrain to make it more attractive.[33] This version included an expanded set of games, with hockey, soccer, and football joining the ping-pong, handball, volleyball, target shooting, and chase games found in previous versions.[34]

By the end of 1968, Baer and Harrison had essentially finished the Brown Box, but they were no closer to selling it. The Sanders patent attorney, Lou Etlinger, provided the solution: approach the television manufacturers. These firms were already using the components contained within the Brown Box in their TV sets, so ramping up manufacturing would be relatively simple. Additionally, the TV companies would most likely be interested in anything that could spur television sales. One by one, Etlinger invited some of the most prominent U.S. TV manufacturers – RCA, Zenith, Sylvania, General Electric, Motorola, Sears-brand manufacturer Warwick, and Magnavox – to view the Brown Box in action. While many of these companies showed some interest, Baer and Etlinger were never able to close a deal. Warwick was impressed and told Sanders to contact the buyer at Sears, but the executive refused to sell the product in his stores because he feared parents would drop their kids off in the electronics department to play the games and transform Sears into a glorified babysitter. The General Electric engineers were likewise impressed and helped set up a meeting at the company's small-color-set assembly facility in Virginia, but nothing ever came of it.[35]

The first company to view the system, RCA, ultimately proved the most enthusiastic. After attending a demonstration of Baer's technology in Nashua, New Hampshire, in January 1969, the company liked the system so much that it started negotiating a licensing agreement with Sanders in the spring. An agreement was hammered out after several months of negotiations, but Sanders backed out of the deal after deciding the terms were unacceptable. Baer appeared out of options at this point, but luckily one of

---

[33] Ibid, 52–56.

[34] They also created a golf putting game in which the player would place a joystick with a golf ball on top of it on the floor and tap the ball with a putter, after which the spot representing the ball would move based on the contact with the joystick. If the ball hit the dot representing the hole, they both disappeared. This game was ultimately cut before the system was released.

[35] Ibid, 56–57.

the RCA negotiators, Bill Enders, remained highly enthusiastic about the product. When Enders left RCA to become the director of business development operations at Magnavox, he urged his new employer to take another look at the system.[36]

***

The Magnavox Corporation originated as a partnership established in Napa, California, on March 1, 1911, called the Commercial Wireless and Development Company that brought together three individuals: Danish electrical engineer Peter Jensen, Stanford-trained electrical engineer Edwin Pridham, and San Francisco financier Richard O'Connor.[37] Jensen was initially interested in developing new technologies for wireless and telephonic communication, but ultimately developed the first loudspeaker public address system instead, which he demonstrated for the first time on December 10, 1915, in San Francisco. Jensen called his system the "Magnavox," "great voice" in Latin, which became the name of the entire company after it merged with the Sonora Phonograph Distribution Company in July 1917.[38]

Magnavox focused on loudspeaker systems initially, but after AT&T came to dominate the field in the 1920s, the company transitioned into the phonograph and radio business. Magnavox consolidated its various facilities at a new headquarters in Fort Wayne, Indiana, in 1930 before nearly falling apart during the Great Depression.[39] The firm narrowly avoided bankruptcy only through the onset of World War II and the lucrative government contracts that followed.[40] In 1950, Hungarian émigré Frank Freimann became CEO of the company and aggressively pushed it into the television business, leading to a more than ten-fold increase in sales between 1950 and 1967 from $32 million to $450 million.[41] Freiman's sudden death in 1968 left the company adrift just as component stereo equipment and small Japanese televisions began severely cutting into the sales of Magnavox's traditional console stereos and televisions housed in large wooden cabinets. New company

---

[36] Ibid, 57.

[37] Billy Malone, *The Early History of the Magnavox Company*, Magnavox Government and Industrial Electronics Company, 1989, 1.

[38] "Peter L. Jensen and the Magnavox Loudspeaker," Audio Engineering Society, accessed April 20, 2016, http://www.aes.org/aeshc/docs/recording.technology.history/jensen.html.

[39] Malone, 1989, 1.

[40] Arthur P. Stern, interview by William Aspray, July 13, 1993, IEEE History Center, https://ethw.org/Oral-History:Arthur_Stern_(1993).

[41] Frank M. Freimann, "Harvard Business School," accessed September 30, 2019, https://www.hbs.edu/leadership/20th-century-leaders/Pages/details.aspx?profile=frank_m_freimann.

president Robert Platt began an aggressive diversification program to keep
the company relevant, so Magnavox was constantly on the lookout for new
business avenues as the 1960s came to a close.

In July 1969, Bill Enders returned to Nashua for a personal demonstration of the Brown Box. Still impressed with the technology, he began heavily
lobbying his superiors to license it. This campaign culminated in a demonstration of the technology at Magnavox headquarters in Fort Wayne on
July 17, 1969, for Gerry Martin, the VP of the Magnavox Console Products
Planning Division. Martin liked the technology, but it took him months
of lobbying with Magnavox corporate before he was finally authorized to
negotiate a deal in March 1970. Nearly a year of negotiations followed,
culminating in a preliminary licensing agreement between Sanders and
Magnavox in January 1971.[42]

With a license agreement in place, further development of the Brown Box –
known within Magnavox by the product designation 1TL200 – shifted from
Baer's lab at Sanders to a team of Magnavox engineers in Fort Wayne led by
George Kent. While Baer and Harrison consulted with these engineers from
time to time, their active role in the development of the video game was now
over. Magnavox management placed an emphasis on reducing the cost of the
system, so Kent's team removed the chroma circuitry for generating color backgrounds.[43] They also chose to move away from switches or dials to select games
by including a group of plug-in circuit cards that determined how the spots and
lines generated by the system would behave to facilitate a variety of games.[44]

Magnavox originally placed the video game project under the supervision of Bob Wiles, the product manager for color televisions. In late 1971,
the system was placed in its own category under a product manager named
Bob Fritsche. A 1966 graduate of Miami University of Ohio with a degree
in marketing, Fritsche joined the U.S. Air Force right out of college, mus-
tered out in October 1970 at the rank of captain, and subsequently joined
Magnavox in the purchasing department. In September 1971, he became the
product planner on the Magnavox video game system.[45]

---

[42] Baer, 2005, 57–59.

[43] Ibid, 59–62.

[44] The inclusion of circuit cards has led some to label the system the first cartridge-based system,
though this comparison is not apt. There is no memory or game code on these cards, which merely
complete different circuit paths within the hardware itself to define the rule set for the current game.
All of the game information is contained in the dedicated hardware, and inserting a new circuit card is
really no different an act from flicking a set of toggle switches.

[45] Robert Fritsche, Testimony, Magnavox Co. v. Bally Manufacturing Corp., No. 74-1030 (N.D. Ill),
December 28, 1976, 461–462.

When Fritsche took over the project, Magnavox had just begun performing consumer playtest and marketing surveys using prototype hardware of what was now being called "Skill-O-Vision." The first, conducted in Los Angeles, proved successful, so a second survey was scheduled for Grand Rapids, Michigan, to gauge the response in a more technologically conservative part of the country. When this test also proved a resounding success, Fritsche successfully lobbied his superiors to ignore the original market projections calling for a limited production runs of 50,000 units for the first holiday season and build 100,000 units instead. In order to ensure Magnavox dealers across the country would have sufficient stock to meet market demand, the company decided to release the video game system in only 18 major markets, one metropolitan area in each of its 18 sales territories nationwide.[46]

The final version of the Magnavox video game system, now dubbed the Odyssey – a name whose origin has been lost to time – was unveiled to the company's authorized dealers in May 1972 in Las Vegas. The product was subsequently publicly unveiled at a press event hosted at Tavern on the Green in New York City on May 22. Over the next few months, Magnavox hosted shows in roughly 16 cities to allow its dealers and other interested industry parties to familiarize themselves with the product ahead of the general retail availability of the console in the fall.[47]

***

The Magnavox Odyssey hit store shelves in September 1972 at a suggested retail price of $99.95, roughly double what Baer had originally planned. The system shipped with 12 games unlocked by six circuit cards, which all centered on moving dots around the screen since the Odyssey remained capable of generating only two player-controlled dots plus one machine-controlled dot and a single line of varying height.[48] Each game required a plastic overlay to define additional graphical elements, which clung to the TV screen through static electricity.[49] The system also shipped with cards, play money, and dice to provide additional game mechanics. Despite the multiple control schemes Baer and Harrison produced, the final product shipped with only one, the three-dial control, which also incorporated a reset button that caused the dot to disappear or reappear. The overlays and packaging materials were designed by Ron Bradford of Bradford/Cout Design, which had

---

[46] Ibid, 462–481.

[47] Ibid, 476–477.

[48] Ibid, 483–534.

[49] Each overlay came in two sizes to accommodate both 18″ and 25″ televisions.

previously done creative work for Magnavox's advertising agency. Bradford also designed the games for the system in conjunction with adman Steve Lehner, which were largely based on the ball and paddle and chase games developed by Baer, Harrison, and Rusch at Sanders.[50]

While the capabilities of the Odyssey were limited, Bradford and Lehner did what they could to provide a variety of game experiences. These included *Tennis*, *Table Tennis*, and *Hockey* games in which the players knock a ball back and forth between their dots; *Ski*, in which the player guides his dot along a path on an overlay; *Cat and Mouse*, in which one player pursues the other; *Submarine*, in which one player launches the machine-controlled dot at a player-controlled dot navigating a "shipping" lane represented on an overlay; and a complicated *Football* game that uses dice and "play cards" to simulate the overall game and uses two different circuit cards to simulate individual running, passing, and kicking plays. The other games were *Simon Says*, *Analogic*, *Haunted House*, *Roulette*, and a trivia game called *States*.

Six additional games were available individually for $5.95 each or in a six pack for $24.99. These were two ball-and-paddle games, *Handball* and *Volleyball*, two racing games, *Fun Zoo* and *Wipeout*, and a complex strategy game called *Invasion* that requires the players to track their progress on a separate game board. Most of these games use the six circuit cards that shipped with the system, but *Volleyball* and *Handball* were packaged with new cards. The light gun was sold separately for $24.99 with two circuit cards to play four target shooting games, *Prehistoric Safari*, *Dogfight!*, *Shootout!*, and *Shooting Gallery*.[51]

The Odyssey initially launched in 25 markets, seven more than originally planned after Magnavox expended considerable effort to increase production capacity and build additional systems based on the favorable feedback gathered during the marketing surveys. Rather than making these systems available to retailers generally, distribution was restricted to the Magnavox network of dealers who sold the company's products exclusively, a decision made by a senior marketing VP who felt that as the world's first video game system, the Odyssey would draw customers to Magnavox dealers and therefore present an opportunity to sell them a full range of Magnavox products.[52] To support the launch of the system, Magnavox produced a national advertising campaign featuring glossy sales flyers, in-store displays, national television and radio ads, and promotional tie-ins such as a product demonstration

[50] William Cassidy, "Interview with Odyssey[2] Artist Ron Bradford," The Odyssey[2] Homepage, accessed May 30, 2019, http://www.the-nextlevel.com/odyssey2/articles/bradford.

[51] "Maggie's 'Mystery Product' – TV Fun & Games," *Weekly Television Digest*, May 15, 1972, 7.

[52] Fritsche, 1976, 495–496.

on the game show *What's My Line?* Initial results were positive as many dealers sold out their first shipments nearly instantaneously, so Magnavox increased production still further.[53] Sales soon stalled, however, and the company only sold 69,000 Odyssey consoles by the end of the year out of a production run of roughly 140,000 units.[54] Tens of thousands of unsold systems were left piled in a warehouse.[55]

Why did the system sell so poorly despite the initially positive marketing research? While impossible to say for certain, a number of factors can be identified. Certainly price had to be a major factor, as $100, equivalent to roughly $570 today, represented a significant investment in a new and unproven technology that offered relatively limited gameplay. Limiting distribution to Magnavox dealers probably also hurt, as this not only curtailed the reach of the product but also may have left consumers with the mistaken impression that the system only worked with Magnavox televisions. The initial television ads did little to dispel this confusion by showing the Odyssey hooked up to a Magnavox set. Starting in early 1973, Odyssey ads and commercials went to great pains to inform the public that the system would work with any 18" or 25" television, but by then the damage may have already been done. Furthermore, it is also likely that individual dealers failed to disclose the system's universal compatibility in their desire to sell an Odyssey system alongside a new television. Of course, it is also worth noting that the system bettered Magnavox's original market projections by nearly 20,000 units, so the performance of the system may have just been hampered by an overly excited product planner ordering the production of more systems than the market could bear.

With such disappointing sales, Magnavox seriously considered halting Odyssey production and liquidating the remaining stock, but the company stuck with the system based on positive customer feedback and continuing, though modest, retailer demand.[56] While it remained on the market for three more years, however, the Odyssey cannot really be considered a success because sales remained low and no other companies were inspired to follow Magnavox into the home video game market. Still, the Odyssey played a crucial role in the evolution of the video game industry greatly out of proportion to its commercial success after Nolan Bushnell and his cohorts at Syzygy Engineering built on Ralph Baer's concepts to create the first hit video game: *Pong*.

---

[53] "Odyssey, Magnavox's Electronic Game," *Weekly Television Digest with Consumer Electronics*, September 18, 1972, 10.

[54] Fritsche, 1976, 533.

[55] Baer, 2005, 90.

[56] Ibid, 86.

10

Ping-Pong Diplomacy

In late 1972, a simple yet exciting new game in which a small object is batted back and forth between two players began making its way into arcades and onto college campuses and had soon taken the coin-operated amusement industry by storm. Indeed, *Air Hockey*, invented by Bob Lemieux at billiards and bowling giant Brunswick by building on earlier work by Phil Crossman, Bob Kendrick, and Brad Baldwin,[1] would quickly become the single best-selling product the coin-operated games industry had seen in years, moving an astonishing 33,000 units.[2]

At the same time, a new manufacturing startup in California was beginning to experience success with a hot product of its own. For-Play Manufacturing was incorporated in the greater Los Angeles area in July 1972 by industrial engineers William Lewis, Robert Harp, and Harry Bieker with the backing of Henry Leyser, a German Jew who spent World War II stranded in a Shanghai ghetto before moving to San Francisco after the war. He became a coin route operator in the city before establishing his own distributor, A.C.A Sales and Service, in 1952.[3] At the 1972 MOA show, For-Play debuted a large light gun target shooting game built with solid-state components called the *Las Vegas Gallery* that attracted both rave reviews and brisk sales.[4] Less successful was the company's rip-off of Nutting's *Computer Space* – called *Star Trek* despite the lack of a license from Paramount – which debuted at the same show, but remains only a footnote as the second commercially released coin-operated video game.

[1] Smith, 2016, 1684–1685.

[2] Ibid, 115.

[3] "Thumbnail Sketches: Harry Leyser," *RePlay*, February 1982, 33.

[4] "Las Vegas Gallery Big on Market," *Cash Box*, December 2, 1972, 56.

The real success story of 1972, however, was a relatively new class of game making its way into the bars of the United States. A wall game consists of a lighted backglass mounted on the wall and remote control units wielded by the players. The lights on the backglass flash in sequence to simulate movement, such as a hand throwing a dart or a pitcher throwing a baseball, and the player must press the button on his remote at the right moment in the sequence to make a bullseye, hit a home run, etc. First deployed by a company called Funtronics in 1969,[5] the wall game was the top earning class of coin-operated amusement machine in 1972, narrowly beating out the usual champion, the pool table.[6]

Lost amid the hype for *Air Hockey*, For-Play, and the products of a dozen or so wall game manufacturers was a small new company with a strange foreign name that did not even attend the MOA show despite putting its first product into very limited production that November. Nevertheless, it would not be *Air Hockey* or *Las Vegas Shooting Gallery* but rather the unheralded *Pong* from the completely unnoticed Atari that would change the world.

***

Computer Space may not have set the world on fire, but it was certainly not a complete failure either, and Bill Nutting proved eager to continue the product line. As with *Computer Quiz*, he felt the next logical step was to create a two-player version of *Computer Space*, so he entered negotiations with Nolan Bushnell to develop it. Bushnell, however, was ready to be more than a mere employee. He felt that Nutting, who spent much of his time at the office tinkering with his planes, and Rod Geiman, who actually ran the company day-to-day, had little idea of how the coin-op industry worked. Consequently, he did not want to continue with Nutting Associates unless granted a financial stake in the company.[7] Bushnell asked for 33%. Nutting countered with five. Bushnell decided there was little more he could accomplish at the firm and began searching for new opportunities under the auspices of the Syzygy Company he co-owned with Ted Dabney. Not wanting the overhead and hassles involved with operating a factory, Bushnell required an alliance with one of the big Chicago firms to manufacture any games he and Dabney designed. Bushnell quickly settled on Bally, which since going public in 1969 had moved from strength to strength as revenues climbed from just over $27 million in 1969 to over $50 million by 1972.[8]

[5] "Funtronics of USA Formed to Market Electronic Game Line," *Cash Box*, May 24, 1969, 60.

[6] "1972 Amusement Machine Route Survey," *Cash Box*, September 16, 1972, 54.

[7] Bushnell, 2015.

[8] "Slot Machines Make Fortune for Him, But Not As Player," *The Modesto Bee*, January 14, 1973.

Bally CEO Bill O'Donnell's ultimate dream was to bring his company into the casino business, where Bally slots were making far more money for their owners than Bally could ever hope to make by merely selling them. In the meantime, he took steps to transform his company into a vertically integrated powerhouse with interests on every step of the coin-op chain from component manufacturing to operating. In 1969, the company purchased cabinetmaker Lenc Smith, while in 1972 it acquired Europe's largest coin-operated gambling device manufacturer, Wulff-Apparatebau. The company also established or bought distributors in Belgium, Sweden, France, Australia, and Hong Kong to provide an international reach for its products.[9]

In the amusement business, Bally's most important acquisition was the Midway Manufacturing Company, which it purchased from co-founders Hank Ross and Iggy Wolverton in 1969.[10] Since its founding in 1958, Midway had developed a reputation as a leading innovator in the U.S. coin-op space and had been quick to enter new product categories like the audiovisual games pioneered in Japan and the wall games beginning to take over the bar scene. As Bally's amusement business was still mostly confined to pinball, this acquisition provided Bally with a full line of amusement machines and demonstrated its interest in remaining at the cutting edge of new amusement trends.[11] If anyone would see the wisdom of capitalizing on an exciting new technology like video, it would be Bally.

At the MOA show in late 1971, Bushnell made the acquaintance of Gil Kitt, the founder and co-owner of Empire Distributing in Chicago, one of the largest and most prestigious distributors in the coin-op industry.[12] Though Kitt was one of the many people who thought *Computer Space* nothing more than a passing fad,[13] he was still impressed enough with its engineer to stay in touch. Therefore, when Bushnell came to Chicago in April 1972 to run a service school on behalf of Nutting Associates, Kitt arranged a meeting between him and Bally executive John Britz.[14] A company veteran who joined the original Bally as a draftsman in 1937, Britz worked on slot machine designs in the late 1930s before taking a production role in Bally's military products division during World War II. He took charge of produc-

---

[9] Marfels, 2007, 34.

[10] "Bally Acquires Midway & Lenc-Smith," *V/T Music & Games*, August 1969, 1.

[11] David Marofske, Sr., interview with the author, February 27, 2009.

[12] Empire would soon become yet another arm of the growing Bally organization as well after being purchased on December 14, 1972, as part of Bally's drive to create a network of domestic distributors to complement its international operations. "Empire to Bally Dec. 14," *Cash Box*, December 30, 1972, 147.

[13] Donovan, 2010, chap. 2.

[14] Goldberg and Vendel, 2012, chap. 2.

tion in Bally's new vending division in the 1950s, which Ray Moloney's sons sold to Seeburg in 1961 in an attempt to fund new slot machine production before the O'Donnell buyout. Britz went to Seeburg as part of the deal, but O'Donnell personally recruited him to return to Bally as general manager in 1963 to oversee engineering and production for the entire company.[15] Further promotions followed as he became senior vice president and then executive vice president of technology in 1968 and 1970, respectively. Through his long Bally career, Britz gained a reputation as one of the best production executives in the coin-op industry.

Britz proved amenable to working with Bushnell, but not while he remained associated with a competitor. Therefore, on June 5 Bushnell and Dabney tendered their resignations at Nutting Associates so they could transform Syzygy Company into a design and engineering firm that would create games for coin-op manufacturing companies and license them on a royalty basis.[16] The duo subsequently set up shop in a small startup facility at 2962 Scott Blvd. in Santa Clara, CA, a 1,700-foot facility consisting of two offices and a warehouse area accessible via a roll-up door. The partners simultaneously secured a law firm to draft articles of incorporation for Syzygy, but discovered the name was already in use. Requiring a new name, Bushnell turned to his love of *go* and chose three names that correspond with terms used in the game: *hane, sente,* and *atari.*[17] The articles of incorporation were executed on June 9, 1972, and on June 27, the California Secretary of State's office filed the articles under the name Atari.[18] The Syzygy partnership was technically rolled into the new Atari, Inc. upon its founding, though the company continued to do business as Syzygy until the summer of 1973 because Bushnell felt the name had built some recognition in the industry.[19]

Atari held few resources at its founding. Bushnell and Dabney earned some royalties from *Computer Space*, which helped fund a purchase of the coin-operated game route operated by Nutting to provide a small, yet steady source of income. The company also employed Cynthia Villanueva, a 17-year-old high school graduate who had previously been a babysitter for

---

[15] "John Britz Back with Bally as Operations Gen. Mgr.," *Billboard*, November 2, 1963.

[16] The date is fixed by a sworn affidavit Bushnell executed at Bally's request. Nolan Bushnell, "Affadavit," executed June 10, 1972.

[17] A *hane* is a move in *go* where a stone goes around one or more of the opponent's stones. A *sente* move is one which essentially compels the other player to commit to a particular follow-up move. Putting a stone in *atari* is like placing the king in "check" in the game of chess in that it refers to a situation in which a stone will be captured unless it moves to an adjacent vacant point.

[18] Goldberg and Vendel, 2012, chap. 2.

[19] Nolan Bushnell, interview with the author, August 25, 2009.

the Bushnell family. She served as the company receptionist largely to give potential customers the impression that Atari was a larger concern.[20]

Before the month of June was out, Bushnell and Dabney finalized a development contract with Bally that would pay $4,000 a month for six months starting that July. The contract called for Atari to deliver one pinball game and one video game to Bally in exchange for the funding.[21] Bushnell also negotiated a deal with Nutting to develop the two-player version of *Computer Space*.[22] Bushnell took responsibility for creating the *Computer Space* upgrade and also fooled around a bit more with the asteroid-dodging game he had briefly considered doing for Nutting,[23] Dabney tackled the pinball table, a pioneering multi-level design called *Fireball*.[24] Before long, they realized hiring a third engineer would be necessary to create the video game for Bally, so they turned to an acquaintance from their Ampex days named Al Alcorn.

***

Allan Edwin Alcorn was born in San Francisco, California, on New Year's Day 1948. An unusual combination of jock and technology nerd, Alcorn made both all-city and all-state football teams out of Lowell High School, but he also took an RCA correspondence course on radio and TV repair while in junior high school and became adept at working with electronics. By the time he was 15, Alcorn was working after school as a TV repairman for a company called S&M TV Repair. He basically ran the shop in the afternoon by virtue of being the only sober person in the building.[25]

Alcorn gained entrance to the University of California at Berkeley through his football acumen, but he quickly gave up football to focus on engineering. After his father suffered a heart attack and could no longer pay Alcorn's tuition, he was forced to pay his own way and took a job with another TV

---

[20]Cynthia started work on June 26, one day before the company incorporated as Atari. Within two months she had left the company after Bushnell refused to let her work part time while she attended college. He reversed himself a week later. At that point, she was trained to wire wrap circuit boards and eventually became a tester, staying at Atari far longer than either of its founders. "Atari's Fourth Employee," AtariGames.com, accessed May 1, 2015, http://www.atarigames.com/index.php?option=com_content& view=article&id=237%3Aataris-fourth-employee&catid=14%3Anews-articles&Itemid=5.

[21]"Royalty Agreement," contract between Bally Manufacturing Corporation and Nolan Bushnell, executed June 26, 1972.

[22]Bushnell, January 1976, 83.

[23]Bushnell, January 1976, 92–93.

[24]No relation to the Bally table of that name released in early 1972. This game featured an ambitious three-level playfield long before multi-level tables became common. Ramsey, 2012, chap. 2.

[25]Allan (Al) Alcorn, interview by Henry Lowood, April 26 and May 23, 2008, Computer History Museum, https://archive.computerhistory.org/resources/access/text/2012/09/102658257-05-01-acc.pdf.

repair shop, Hubbard and Radio Television Repair, to make ends meet. By his junior year, the pressure of maintaining good academic standing to avoid losing his college deferment from the draft at the height of the Vietnam War and the conflicts dividing the Berkeley campus as a result of the student protest movement became too much for Alcorn to handle, and he nearly dropped out. To save his education and his sanity, Alcorn opted to participate in the school's work-study program, in which students alternated between six months of classes and six months of full-time employment. He had difficulty finding a company that would take him until his mother used her connections with Ampex president Bill Roberts to secure him a position in that company's Videofile division, where he met both Nolan Bushnell and Ted Dabney.[26]

Alcorn started at Ampex in late 1968 and primarily worked with video circuitry to build synch generators for the Videofile system. In 1969, Ampex entered a period of financial difficulty and could not bring Alcorn back for a second internship, so he worked for a small company called Peripheral Technologies instead. By the time he graduated in 1971, Ampex was doing better and was able to hire him on as a full-time junior engineer. One year later, Bushnell approached him to work for Syzygy. Despite a pay cut from $1,200 to $1,000 a month and stock options Alcorn assumed would be worthless due to his lack of faith in the company's viability, Alcorn accepted Bushnell's offer. He figured it would be a fun ride, and he could always get hired somewhere else when the company inevitably failed.[27]

Shortly after hiring Alcorn, Bushnell proposed to Bally a hockey game featuring "on screen digital scoring, goals, field markings, multidirectional hockey players with sticks, goal tender, [and a] puck with computer controlled motion to simulate actual ice characteristics."[28] Bushnell realized this would be an ambitious project for a new engineer like Alcorn with no experience in video game design, so he decided to give him a simpler project first to familiarize him with the technology.

***

[26] Ibid.

[27] Ibid.

[28] Nolan Bushnell, "Letter to John Britz," July 10, 1972. The inspiration for a hockey game is not known, but there had been several coin-operated hockey games since the 1930s in which each player controlled a hockey player on either end of a playfield and batted a puck back and forth to score goals. In fact, Chicago Coin had just released the latest game of that type, *Slap-Shot Hockey*, in early 1972. Conversely, *Air Hockey* was probably not an inspiration, as Bushnell's proposal predates the public unveiling of the game.

While Bushnell was still at Nutting Associates, Bill Nutting and Rod Geiman heard that a new video game would soon be entering the home market via television company Magnavox.[29] Further learning that Magnavox would be holding a demonstration of the game for potential dealers and distributors in nearby Burlingame on May 24, Geiman decided to attend and brought Bushnell and an operator of Nutting games named Charles Fibian with him.[30] In Burlingame, Bushnell had an opportunity to play table tennis on the Magnavox Odyssey.[31] While not particularly impressed by a game that was a far cry from the sophisticated products like *Spacewar!* available on minicomputers, Bushnell realized after he hired Alcorn that it would be a perfect starter project to acclimate his new engineer to Syzygy's video game technology.

To motivate Alcorn to create the game quickly and cheaply, Bushnell lied that he had a signed contract with General Electric for a table tennis game playable on a television set for release as a consumer product. Bushnell's only directives were that the game should feature two paddles and one ball and that the score should be displayed on the screen.[32] He provided his original *Computer Space* schematics to Alcorn so he could see how to place and move spots on the screen, but they were drawn in such a screwy way that Alcorn could not follow them, so Bushnell gave him a brief tutorial instead. Armed with this knowledge, Alcorn set to work.[33]

Bushnell saw Alcorn's table tennis project as simply an exercise, but Alcorn, unaware of his boss's ruse, put his full effort into the game. Placing the basic spots on the screen and moving them around did not require much effort, but varying the angle of the ball return so it would not just travel back and forth in a straight line proved more difficult. The Odyssey – which Alcorn had never seen – accomplished this feat through a special control specifically for the ball, but this was an imperfect solution necessitated by technology limitations. Alcorn chose instead to divide his paddles into segments so that the velocity of the ball would differ depending on where it made contact with the paddle.[34] This simple change transformed Alcorn's game into something very different from what Ralph Baer and Bill Rusch had implemented on the Odyssey.

---

[29] Bushnell, January 1976, 112.

[30] Baer, 2005, 81 and Geiman, 2016.

[31] Bushnell, January 976, 113.

[32] Al Alcorn, "Story of Pong," Australian Center for the Moving Image, March 6, 2008, http://www.acmi.net.au/talks_gameon_storyofpong.htm.

[33] Al Alcorn, "First-Hand: The Development of Pong: Early Days of Atari and the Video Game Industry," Engineering and Technology History Wiki, November 13, 2009, https://ethw.org/First-Hand:The_Development_of_Pong:_Early_Days_of_Atari_and_the_Video_Game_Industry.

[34] Ibid.

Once the prototype was completed, Alcorn, Bushnell, and Dabney started playing it. They found it fun, but Bushnell thought the ball bounced around too quickly and asked Alcorn to slow it down. This made starting a good volley easier, but made the game feel too slow once they became good at knocking the ball back and forth. To balance these competing needs, Alcorn added a speed-up feature so that the ball moved faster over the course of the volley.[35] He also decided not to fix a bug that crept into the game that left a gap at the very top of the screen where the paddle could not reach because then even the best players would eventually be confronted with a ball that was impossible to return.[36] Bushnell also told Alcorn that the game should incorporate sound. He envisioned a cheering crowd, while Dabney thought there should be booing and hissing when a player missed a shot. Already well over budget for a consumer product and not adept at sound design, Alcorn refused to include complex audio, but he poked around the sync generator until he found a few simple sounds for when the ball hits the paddle and for when a player scores a point.[37]

After three months, Alcorn had completed his game,[38] which he felt was an utter failure since the cost was far too high for a consumer product.[39] For his part, Bushnell considered it a throw-away project and never intended to put it into production. Bushnell, Dabney, and Alcorn realized when they began playing the finished product, however, that Alcorn had actually produced a fun, addictive game. Therefore, they decided to place it on test in a tavern on their coin-op route called Andy Capp's that maintained a small game room featuring a handful of pinball machines and a *Computer Space* unit.[40] Owner Bill Gattis enjoyed a good working relationship with the Atari people, so he was happy to allow them to place Alcorn's machine, now called *Pong* and housed in a wooden cabinet built by Dabney, on top of a wine cask and set it next to the *Computer Space*.[41] Roughly two weeks later, Alcorn received a call from Gattis, who stated the game had suddenly stopped working. When Alcorn came around to investigate, he discovered that so many coins had been deposited into the machine that they had spilled out of the bread pan serving as a makeshift coin collector and were scattered all over the

[35] Bushnell, January 1976, 97–98.

[36] Alcorn, Australian Center for the Moving Image, 2008.

[37] Alcorn, 2009.

[38] Ibid.

[39] Alcorn, oral history, 2008.

[40] Alcorn, 2009.

[41] "RoundUp 24: Oh She's Doing Fine," *Retrogaming Roundup*, podcast audio, October 2010, http://www.retrogamingroundup.com/shownotes/2010/roundup024_2010.10.php.

circuit board. Alcorn estimated that the game had been played roughly 400 times since he last emptied the machine a week before.[42] *Pong*, it seemed, was destined to be a hit.

At the same time Alcorn was fixing the *Pong* machine at Andy Capp's, Nolan Bushnell was in Chicago demonstrating a portable prototype to Bally, which he hoped would be accepted in fulfillment of their development contract.[43] Bushnell met with John Britz and the company's head of engineering, Joseph Lally, who both found the game somewhat interesting, but refused to accept it because it was not graphically or mechanically as impressive as either *Computer Space* or the hockey game Bushnell had promised them and required two players for a game.[44] They allowed Bushnell to take it over to Midway as well, which continued to run as a largely autonomous subsidiary of Bally under the leadership of its founders, but Iggy Wolverton also turned it down. At the time, Midway was preparing to release a table tennis product as a wall game, and it was not in the market for a second one.[45] Finally, Bushnell made a stop at the MOA show currently underway in Chicago to see if Bill Nutting might be interested in the game. He not only discovered that his old employer was not interested in *Pong* at the royalty rate he demanded, but also learned that Nutting had decided to go with a different design for a two-player *Computer Space*, so Atari would not be receiving any royalties on the product.[46]

Still certain they had a winner, Bushnell and Dabney decided to manufacture twelve units of *Pong*, ten to put on location, one to send to Bally for its own evaluations, and one to keep in the shop.[47] At this stage, several improvements were made to the game. Rather than the countertop original model, the cabinet would now be a floor model typical of other arcade machines. Alcorn also sourced stronger potentiometers for the control knobs on the machine because those used in the original unit had quickly worn out through overuse.[48] Bushnell also mandated play instructions on the cabinet, which were found on most coin-op machines but usually ignored by the paying public. Alcorn came up with the simplest guidelines he could think of: "DEPOSIT QUARTER, BALL WILL SERVE AUTOMATICALLY, AVOID MISSING BALL FOR HIGH SCORE."

---

[42] Goldberg and Vendel, 2012.

[43] Donovan, 2010, chap. 2.

[44] Bushnell, January 1976, 99.

[45] John Britz, Deposition, Magnavox Co. v. Bally Manufacturing Corp., No. 74-1030 (N.D. Ill), June 25, 1974, 25–27.

[46] Goldberg and Vendel, 2012, chap. 2.

[47] Dabney, 2010.

[48] Alcorn, oral history, 2008.

Unlike *Computer Space* with its complicated controls and confusing physics, *Pong* is controlled by a single knob that can be rotated to move the paddle up and down the screen; the ball physics are straightforward, and the simple gameplay proved incredibly addictive. As a result, Atari's first ten *Pong* units achieved phenomenal earnings over the next few weeks. They were so great in fact, that Bushnell and Dabney worried that if they submitted the reports to Bally, the pinball giant would believe they were inflating the earnings in the hopes of enticing the company to take the game. They decided to cut the figures by one-third before submitting them to Bally, but even these figures were not believed. In the end, there was nothing they could do to convince Bally to take the game.[49]

By this point, Bushnell realized that *Pong* was destined to be a company-making hit no matter what Bally said and refused to let the game die in a limited test run. Although Atari had been founded solely to develop games, not build them, Bushnell decided his only recourse was to enter the manufacturing business. Both Dabney and Alcorn were opposed, as this move not only would take the company well away from its original mission, but also would be costly to boot. After an animated meeting at Andy Capp's Tavern, Bushnell was able to convince his partners that they needed to produce *Pong* themselves.[50]

Over the next few weeks, Bushnell, Dabney, Alcorn, and Dabney's brother, Doug, frantically worked to assemble 50 *Pong* machines. The work required more space than their startup facility contained, so they cut a hole in the wall into the vacant identical facility next door and presented their landlord with a *fait accompli*.[51] Circuit boards for the game were printed by a company that happened to reside just across the street, while Dabney located a cheap source for Hitachi TVs in San Francisco and used his life savings to make the down payment. Cabinets were provided by P.S. Hurlbut Woodworking, which later became one of the giants in the field of arcade cabinets. When the owner learned that Atari did not have a truck to pick up the cabinets themselves, he even delivered them at no additional cost.[52]

At the end of November 1972, Bushnell made his first sales calls to distributors. He started with Nutting's local distributor, Advance Automatic.[53]

---

[49] Dabney, 2010.

[50] Ted Dabney has claimed that it was Nolan, not him, who was hesitant to enter the manufacturing business, but Alcorn backs up Bushnell's recollections. Given that of the two Bushnell is the one with both a long history of risk taking and a track record of taxing Atari to its limits to introduce new product, Bushnell's version of events feels more credible. Kent, 2001, 45 and Alcorn, oral history, 2008.

[51] Donovan, 2010.

[52] Dabney, 2012.

[53] Kent, 2001, 53.

Lou Wolcher, an old hand in the industry who would pass away less than two months later,[54] had heard about the earnings of *Pong*, immediately placed a large order, became one of the game's earliest champions, and talked it up to other distributors.[55] Larger still was the order by Portale Automatic Sales, a relative newcomer founded in 1968 by a protégé of Lou Wolcher in Los Angeles, which stood at the heart of the California coin trade.[56] Bob Portale had been one of the few distributors to push *Computer Space* aggressively and had experienced fantastic sales as a result.[57] Therefore, he had no qualms about backing Bushnell's latest product and promptly ordered 150 units. Between Advance, Portale, and a third distributor, Bushnell sold 300 units in three sales calls in a single day.[58]

Atari's small shipping area could barely hold the 50 units the company was already assembling even after Bushnell and Dabney had doubled their space, so it soon became clear the company needed a new manufacturing facility. Fortunately, the company that owned their building on Scott Avenue also owned a larger building at 1600 Martin Avenue in Santa Clara. This building had once housed a concert hall called the Continental Ballroom where noted rock musicians like Jimi Hendrix and the Doors had performed but had more recently served as a roller rink.[59] Atari set up manufacturing in the new building in February 1973 while keeping its offices at Scott Boulevard. To fund an assembly line, the duo turned to Dabney's personal banker at Wells Fargo,[60] which ultimately funded the company through the Special Industries Group it had established in 1970 specifically to invest in high-technology companies in Silicon Valley. The group provided a $50,000 line of credit on the back of a purchase order from Portale Automatic Sales.[61] The coin-op business still largely operated on handshake agreements at the time, but Bob Portale was so excited by the prospects of the new game that he broke with convention to supply the written order.[62]

[54]"Lou Wolcher, Trade Pioneer, Dies Jan. 2nd," *Cash Box*, January 13, 1973, 34.

[55]Marcus Webb, "Atari Turns 25," *RePlay*, July 1997, Atari 9.

[56]"California Clippings," *Cash Box*, March 16, 1968, 97.

[57]"NA Honors Portale," *Cash Box*, November 4, 1972, 55.

[58]Dabney, 2012.

[59]Goldberg and Vendel, 2012.

[60]Ibid.

[61]Ted Dabney claims that Atari secured only a $3,000 loan from his banker, but both a 1976 *Business Week* article and a 1977 article in Wells Fargo's own company newsletter, *Wells Fargo Banker*, recount the involvement of the Special Industries Group and the more plausible figure of $50,000. "Atari Sells Itself to Survive Success," *BusinessWeek*, November 15, 1976, 120 and "Atari – A Big Winner in the Business of Games," *Wells Fargo Banker*, 1977.

[62]Dabney, 2012.

With cash in hand, Bushnell and Dabney began hiring employees anywhere they could find them, which largely meant local high schools and colleges and the unemployment office. This left the company with a motley collection of hippies, bikers, drug addicts, and television thieves manning an inefficient assembly line in which components were stuffed into cabinets rolled into the middle of the floor one at a time.[63] Despite these challenges, the company was able to meet its initial orders as Bushnell and Dabney personally delivered ten units at a time to Portale and others in a single small truck.[64]

In January 1973, Bushnell and Dabney hired an accountant named Fred Marincic as secretary-treasurer to manage the company books and prepared to issue the stock assigned to each partner. By this point, it was clear to everyone at Atari that *Pong* was almost certain to become a massive hit, so Bushnell took steps to consolidate his own position in the company. In his mind, Ted Dabney, while a wonderful engineer, did not have the vision or the management skills to handle the massive growth Atari was about to experience.[65] He also realized nearly all the stock of the company was tied up between the two founders and their spouses, which would make it more difficult to lure in the professional management he knew the company would soon require. As a result, he decided that Dabney had to go. On February 5, 1973, the duo held a meeting in which Bushnell asked to buy Dabney out of his shares. Dabney resisted at first, but when Bushnell threatened to transfer the assets to a new company and leave Dabney with nothing, he capitulated. While Dabney remained with the company to oversee manufacturing as vice president of production facilities, after March 1 he was no longer a partner.[66]

By March 1973, *Pong* had become a sensation on the west coast, and Atari was ready to roll the game out nationally.[67] Bushnell placed the first advertisement for the game in the March 3 issue of trade publication *Cash Box* and prepared for the orders to start rolling in. The company had taken so long to organize a national sales and manufacturing capability, however, that it soon became clear that while *Pong* was destined to be a massive success, it would not necessarily be Atari that reaped the benefits.

---

[63] Kent, 2001, 51–53.

[64] Smith, 2016, 99.

[65] Bushnell, 2009.

[66] Goldberg and Vendel, 2012, chap. 3.

[67] "Pong into National Distribution; Success for Atari, Inc.," *Cash Box*, April 7, 1973, 104.

11

The Day of the Jackal

In late 1972, a group of engineers and executives from a Sunnyvale technology company called Ramtek noticed a strange new coin-operated game called *Pong* in one of their regular hangouts, Andy Capp's Tavern. After playing the game, one of the executives, H.R. "Pete" Kauffman, attempted to move the unit and found it would not budge, presumably because it was full of quarters.[1] The Ramtek staff sensed this might be the beginning of a new popular form of entertainment and just might present a solution to its current financial problems.

Ramtek was established by a group of partners led by Charles McEwan in September 1971.[2] After graduating high school, McEwan joined the army in 1954 and received electronics training. After leaving the service in 1956, he became a field engineer for Philco in Palo Alto, California, and later transferred to the New Boston Air Force Station in New Hampshire. In 1967, he joined Data Disc Corporation, where he came to believe advances in color graphics would revolutionize the medical scanning industry. When Data Disc refused to let him work on graphics technology, he left to form Ramtek.[3]

Ramtek manufactured high-end graphic displays used in products ranging from the earliest CAT scanners to NASA's *Viking II* program. Largely funded through "bootstrapping" – i.e., plowing all the money earned back into the company in hopes of keeping revenues just ahead of expenses – the company experienced chronic shortages of cash and often teetered on the edge of collapse. Before long, McEwan decided he needed to explore other product categories to fund his primary business. As McEwan and CFO

---

[1] David Ellis, "Of Mouse Traps and Crossbows: The Exidy Story," *GameRoom*, August 2006, 48.
[2] "Articles of Incorporation," Ramtek, filed September 28, 1971.
[3] "Obituary: Charles McEwan," *The Desert Sun*, December 6, 2006.

Tom Adams, who owned a stake in Andy Capp's, brainstormed ways to keep the company afloat, their minds turned to *Pong*. Although no one in the company had any experience in the coin-op industry, McEwan realized *Pong* was an exceedingly simple piece of technology compared to the state-of-the-art display systems his company was producing and figured he could put a similar game into production quickly to generate the cash he needed.[4]

By March 1973, the month Atari's *Pong* finally debuted nationwide, Ramtek was offering its own take on the game dubbed *Volly*.[5] That same month, For-Play began shipping samples of its own *Pong* clone, which it called *Rally*.[6] A third company, Allied Leisure of Florida, also released a ball-and-paddle game that month under the name *Paddle Battle*,[7] while Midway, the Bally subsidiary that had initially passed on *Pong*, announced a licensing agreement consummated with Atari late in the previous month to produce its own version of the game.[8]

By the middle of the year, Nutting Associates had introduced *Computer Space Ball*,[9] while two Philadelphia-area firms called Amutronics and PMC Engineering had also entered the market. Amutronics was incorporated in October 1972 by Mort Bricklin and industry veteran Fred Pliner, who started as a jukebox operator in the 1930s while still in his teens and later worked as a sales executive for several companies, including Bally and Williams.[10] The company released *TV Ping Pong* in April.[11] PMC Engineering was a PC board manufacturer for companies like RCA and Control Data established in 1965 that dabbled in everything from dental x-ray equipment to photo booths on the side.[12] The company entered the market by establishing a new division called PMC Manufacturing under Amutronics co-founder Pliner and bowed *TV Table Tennis* in July.[13] Not since the debut of the first pint-ables at the beginning of the 1930s had the coin-op industry seen so many companies scramble to copy a hot new game so quickly. An incensed Nolan Bushnell labeled these companies "the jackals."

---

[4] Smith, 2016, 203.

[5] Ibid, 1364.

[6] "ACA & For-Play Introduce New Rally Video Game," *Cash Box*, March 17, 1973, 55.

[7] "Allied Leisure Pops Paddle Battle; Two Player TV Game is Big on Skill 'Collections High,'" *Cash Box*, March 24, 1973, 58.

[8] "Midway to Pop Hockey & TV Games," *Cash Box*, March 10, 1973, 56.

[9] *Computer Space Ball* had already been out for some time before June, but was not mentioned in the trades until then. "California Clippings," *Cash Box*, June 16, 1973, 58.

[10] Smith, 2016, 283.

[11] "Amutronics Bows TV Ping Pong Game," *Cash Box*, April 21, 1973, 56.

[12] Smith, 2016, 283.

[13] "Eastern Flashes," *Cash Box*, June 16, 1973, 58.

Despite stiff competition from the clone makers, Atari had a bona fide national hit on its hands by the middle of 1973. Indeed, *Pong* proved so popular the company was able to bypass certain coin-op industry conventions. Generally speaking, new games were sold to distributors on 60- or 90-day credit so they could be sold on to the operator before the distributor was forced to hand over any money. *Pong* was in such high demand that Atari succeeded in selling the game for cash up front, which was crucial for continuing to finance what was still a fragile and underfunded operation. By collecting payment immediately, Atari could buy components on credit, turn a completed machine around rapidly, and have cash on hand to pay its suppliers before its own bills came due.[14] Furthermore, the cost of components for a *Pong* unit came to around $400, and the company sold the game to distributors for just over $900, so the profit on each machine was significant.[15] Bootstrapping can be a notoriously difficult way to fund a company – just look at Ramtek – but Atari did so relatively efficiently. By the end of Atari's first fiscal year in June 1973, it brought in $3.2 million in revenue and achieved a $600,000 profit.[16]

Despite this success, manufacturing remained an absolute mess, and Atari proved completely unable to keep up with distributor demand. Ted Dabney continued to oversee production after Bushnell bought him out of the company, but he had no experience in that role and was clearly lost.[17] At the beginning of April, Bushnell hired an industrial engineer and accountant named Bill White, who had just completed an independent audit of the Atari books, as director of operations in an attempt to sort these issues out.[18] Dabney stayed on as vice president of production facilities, but this move marked the beginning of the end of his involvement in the company.

In October, Bushnell offered to renegotiate the buyout of Dabney's share of their partnership because Atari was having difficulty making the payments. He proposed Dabney acquire the assets of the coin route they had originally purchased from Nutting along with consideration on a smaller promissory note. Dabney took both the route and the Syzygy name and left Atari to run the Syzygy Game Company from a space in the Martin Avenue facility that

[14] "Atari Sells Itself to Survive Success," *BusinessWeek*, November 15, 1976, 120.

[15] Ramsay, 2012, chap. 2. Bulk purchases drove the price lower, but still brought in well over double Atari's cost.

[16] "Atari Prospectus," document created by Atari to attract institutional investors, c.1975.

[17] Alcorn, oral history, 2008.

[18] Michael Current, "A History of Syzygy/Atari," *Atari History Timelines*, last modified April 28, 2019, https://mcurrent.name/atarihistory/syzygy.html.

he leased from Atari.[19] Dabney remained on Atari's board of directors, but he never attended any meetings before leaving the board in March 1974.[20] On May 15, 1974, he sold Syzygy back to Bushnell when Atari proved unable to pay off his note once again. Bushnell then sold the firm to Atari comptroller Ted Olsen.[21] The departure of Dabney and the relinquishing of both Atari's original coin route and the Syzygy name severed the company's last remaining ties to its roots as a small engineering company intended solely to create games on a consulting basis for the big Chicago coin-op manufacturers.

In May 1973, Atari moved into a new 30,000 square-foot facility in Los Gatos, California, that consolidated the company's offices and factory in one location. The company also hired a salesman named Pat Karns away from one of its major suppliers, Cramer Electronics, to serve as its national sales manager and director of marketing.[22] By the end of 1973, the company had manufactured over 6,000 *Pong* games, but still lagged far behind market demand.[23] This gave the jackals just the opening they needed to experience success cloning Atari's hot game.

***

The most successful *Pong* clone manufacturer was also one of the first, a Florida company called Allied Leisure controlled by veteran coinmen David Braun and Ron Haliburton. Braun started in the record business in 1944 in partnership with his brother Jules by recording early R&B artists on his own label in Linden, New Jersey. In 1951, he left the music business to work for a local kiddie ride manufacturer named Mars Manufacturing. The next year, he relocated to Florida and established All-Tech Industries to manufacture kiddie rides, grips testers, and pool tables. In the 1960s, Braun designed innovative pieces that combined traditional kiddie rides with other arcade concepts like target shooting and driving games.[24]

---

[19] Bushnell, Deposition, 1974.

[20] Goldberg and Vendel, 2012, chap. 3.

[21] Nolan Bushnell, Deposition, Magnavox Co. v. Bally Manufacturing Corp., No. 74-1030 (N.D. Ill), June 28, 1978.

[22] "Karns to Atari; New Facilities to Open," *Cash Box*, May 19, 1973, and "Meet Pat Karns," *Cash Box*, August 11, 1973.

[23] Final sales figures for *Pong* are unknown. They stood at 6,000 in late 1973 and over 8,000 in mid-1974. It is unlikely they sold many more after that point, though a retrospective on the company in 1997 in trade publication *Replay* indicated the company sold as many as 12,000 units of the game. "A Red-Hot Market for Video Games," *BusinessWeek*, November 10, 1973, 212, and Robert Wieder, "A Fistful of Quarters," *Oui Magazine*, September 1974, 60, and "Atari at 25," 1997, Atari 9.

[24] Smith, 2016, 118.

Ron Haliburton came to All-Tech via Nashville, Tennessee, where he spent his teenage years building custom engines for stock cars. Through his NASCAR work, he met an older engineer who took him under his wing, and together they designed a bill changer and sold it to a Florida manufacturer. Around this time, Haliburton noticed the popularity of coin-operated games and designed a coin-operated slot car game. Although he failed to attract sufficient investment capital to build it himself, the game came to the attention of Braun, who offered Haliburton a job at All-Tech. He eventually rose to become president of the company.[25]

In January 1968, Braun retired from All-Tech and divested himself of his stock in the company, but he soon found himself back in the business on behalf of his son, Robert, who suffered from cerebral palsy and required some meaningful activity to occupy his time. To that end, in March 1968 he established a new firm in Hialeah, Florida, called D & R Braun Company with himself as chairman, his son as president, and Haliburton as secretary-treasurer and chief engineer. That November, the company changed its name to Allied Leisure.[26]

Far removed from the center of the coin-op manufacturing business in Chicago, Allied did not attempt to compete in traditional pinball or shuffle alleys or any of the standard categories of games that had been manufactured for decades. Instead the company embraced the new solid state and audio-visual machines entering the market. Allied Leisure experienced its first hit in late 1968 with *Unscramble*, a word game designed to cash in on the trivia craze started by Nutting's *Computer Quiz*. In 1970, the company experienced even greater success with *Wild Cycle*, a motorcycle game in the vein of Chicago Coin's *Speedway* that featured one of coin-op gaming's earliest soundtracks via an eight-track player attached to the machine.[27] By 1971, Allied had transformed into a publicly traded company inhabiting a 40,000 square foot facility with revenues in excess of $3.2 million.[28]

With its reputation for developing advanced audiovisual games, Allied was a logical destination for impatient distributors when Atari could not fill all their *Pong* needs. Therefore, a California distributor sent Allied one of the earliest *Pong* units in the hopes that the company would put a copy into production.[29] Allied's manufacturing vice president, Troy Livingston, took the game apart and was horrified by what he saw. While the logic of

---

[25] Ibid, 118–119.
[26] Ibid, 119.
[27] Ibid, 120–121.
[28] Allied Leisure, 1971 Form 10-K.
[29] Gene Lipkin, interview with the author, April 11, 2014.

the game was well engineered, Atari had no experience building a complete coin-operated game, so most of the components from the coin circuit to the power supply were woefully insufficient for the rigors of the arcade market. Livingston redesigned most of these parts himself, but to create a new circuit board, he turned to a Chicago company called Universal Research Laboratories (URL).[30]

URL founders Ed Polanek and Bill Olliges both worked in electronics at Ampex and Motorola, respectively, before becoming co-workers at Seeburg Corporation. They established URL in 1969 as a contract manufacturer of sound effects PC boards for the new wave of realistic driving and shooting games proliferating in the coin-operated amusement industry. Within 18 months, they had expanded into other products such as car cassette players and alarm systems, but they remained intimately connected to coin-operated games.[31] Allied contracted the firm to create its *Pong* clone in February and provided a $25,000 advance.[32]

On March 8, Allied Leisure announced its *Pong* clone, *Paddle Battle*, in the industry trades. Unlike Atari, Allied operated an efficient production line and even did much of its component manufacturing in house, so the company was able to ramp up production to 150 units a day at a time when Atari was struggling to move beyond a few dozen. Even when the big Chicago companies moved in, Allied maintained an advantage. By the time Midway's licensed clone *Winner* and Chicago Coin's *TV Ping Pong* arrived in April followed by Williams' *Paddle Ball* in May, Allied Leisure had already made enough money on *Paddle Battle* that it could instigate a price war to stay ahead of its larger competition. Then, in July the company delivered its coup de grace by releasing a four-player variant called *Tennis Tourney* that largely destroyed the market for two-player *Pong* games.[33] Therefore, while Midway sold around 7,000 units of *Winner* and Chicago Coin moved around 5,000 units of *TV Ping Pong*,[34] Allied Leisure topped them all with

---

[30]Smith, 2016, 123.

[31]"Ex-Jukebox Engineers Priming Impressive Audio Equipment Bow," *Cash Box*, August 21, 1971, 12.

[32]"Letter from Bill Olliges of URL to David Braun of Allied Leisure," February 19, 1973.

[33]Keith Smith, "Allied Leisure Industries – Designer, Jack Pearson," *GameRoom*, accessed, July 29, 2007. https://www.gameroommagazine.com/index.php?main_page=infopages&pages_id=10&zenid =d3064b67d37f361414a0663c306e4e78.

[34]Timothy Jarrell, "Like Old Man River Midway Sales Go Rollin Along," Play Meter, November 1976, 50 and Baer, 2005, 10. Note that Midway sales director Larry Berke gives a figure of 9,000 for "table tennis-type games" in "A Red-Hot Market for Video Games," *BusinessWeek*, November 10, 1973. This almost certainly includes early sales of the four-player variant *Winner IV*, as the same Berke says in the Jarrell article not only provides the 7,000 figure but also states that their highest run on a game was 8,600.

over 17,000 *Paddle Battle* units sold This represented more units than any other company, including Atari.[35] Allied's sales rose from $1.5 million in 1972 to $11.4 million in 1973, while the company's $1.6 million profit for the year looked better than the $838,700 loss posted in that prior period.[36]

***

In 1973, an estimated 70,000 coin-operated video games were sold,[37] and nearly all of them were *Pong* clones. These included both the straight copies of the original game as well as variants such as Allied's four-player *Tennis Tourney* and Ramtek's *Hockey*, in which the players control multiple paddles that represent forwards and a goalie and attempt to knock the ball into their opponent's goal.[38] According to *Cash Box*, video games were the top earning category of amusement machine despite far fewer video cabinets on location than pool tables and pinball machines.[39]

There were several factors behind video's explosive financial success. First, *Pong* games definitively cemented quarter play in the arcades by following in the footsteps of the quiz and audiovisual games in allowing just a single play for 25 cents rather than the two plays for a quarter that still persisted in pinball.[40] Furthermore, their solid-state design left video games far less prone to breakdowns than complicated pinball, driving, and target shooting games full of steppers, relays, wipers, and other electromechanical parts, meaning they spent less time waiting for repairs and more time raking in coins. Finally, video games did not carry the same stigma as pinball and pool, both of which had varying ties to gambling since their earliest days. Video units were skill-based contests clearly intended for amusement only, while their advanced technology conjured up the space race and futuristic laboratories rather than seedy back alleys and smoke-filled rooms.[41] Therefore, Video

---

[35] Smith, 2016, 123. Smith got the figure from Troy Livingston in 2001, who was reported as giving a lower figure of 12,000 at Pinball Expo in 2005. "Pinball Expo 2005," *Pinball News*, accessed 6/5/2019, https://www.pinballnews.com/shows/expo2005/index8.html. Allied engineer Jack Pearson told Smith that it sold 22,000, but it is likely he was combining sales of *Paddle Battle* and its four-player follow-up, *Tennis Tourney*. Smith, 2016, 124.

[36] Allied Leisure, Annual Report, 1973.

[37] *The Coin-Operated and Home Electronic Games Market* (New York: Frost & Sullivan, 1976), 87.

[38] Four-player *Pong* variants released in 1973 include Midway's *Winner IV*, Chicago Coin's *TV Tennis*, and Williams' *Pro Tennis*. Hockey variants include Williams' *Pro Hockey* and Chicago Coin's *Olympic TV Hockey*.

[39] "1973 Amusement Machine Route Survey," *Cash Box*, November 19, 1973, 82.

[40] "Williams' Stern Calls for Quarter Play on Flippers," *Vending Times*, June 1974, 57.

[41] "The Space Age Pinball Machine," *The New York Times*, September 15, 1974.

games were considered acceptable in other venues besides working-class bars and inner-city arcades and consequently attracted a wider clientele.

While the entire coin-op industry focused on *Pong* clones and variants in 1973, Atari made a concerted effort to expand into new genres. These efforts met with only limited success. The second game the company created was the first it conceived, Bushnell and Dabney's racing game in space. Dubbed *Asteroid* and actually implemented by Al Alcorn, the game places two players in control of spaceships that race from the bottom of the screen to the top while dodging dots representing asteroids. Each time a player reaches the top of the screen, he scores a point, while each time he hits an asteroid, he is deposited back at the bottom of the screen. Whoever scores the most points within the time limit claims victory. The players control their ships using joysticks, but can only move the ship up or down, not left or right, perhaps in an effort to avoid the confusing movement and control scheme that had dogged *Computer Space*.

Bushnell presented *Asteroid* to Bally, which accepted the game in fulfillment of Atari's development contract.[42] Bally decided not to manufacture the game itself and passed it on to Midway,[43] which agreed to pay a royalty on each unit sold. Bushnell also decided to release the game himself through Atari, which brought it to market in July as *Space Race* several months before Midway put *Asteroid* into production. A furious Midway complained, so Atari agreed to forego royalties on the game as compensation.[44] This was hardly a big sacrifice, as the game sank in the *Pong*-obsessed coin-op marketplace. Midway managed to sell only around 2,000 units of *Asteroid*, which was still more than the roughly 1,500 units of *Space Race* put on the market by Atari.[45]

Atari's next original game, *Gotcha*, faired only slightly better than *Space Race*. The idea for the game originated with Al Alcorn due to a bug in the scoring chips on the original *Pong*, which when defective would spew randomly shifting garbage across the screen. Alcorn figured these shifting patterns would make an interesting maze, so he outlined a game in which one player chases another player through the randomly changing playfield.[46]

---

[42] While Bally, or rather its Midway subsidiary, ultimately licensed *Pong*, this was a separate deal from the existing contract between Bally and Atari, so *Pong* did not fulfill that original contract as reported in some sources. Britz, 1974, 25.

[43] Britz, 1974, 34.

[44] Henry Ross, Deposition, Magnavox Co. v. Bally Manufacturing Corp., No. 74-1030 (N.D. Ill), June 25, 1974, 26.

[45] Baer, 2005, 10.

[46] Paul Drury, "In the Chair with Allan Alcorn," *Retro Gamer*, no. 83, 2010, 86.

Atari created three versions of the game, a straight black-and-white model, a version that gave the illusion of color through use of an overlay on the screen, and a full-color version that represented the first use of color graphics in a video game.[47] While the game moved 3,000 units after being launched in October, its sales paled in comparison to the hit *Pong* clones, and the game was quickly forgotten.[48]

With original product fairing so poorly, Atari embraced the ball-and-paddle market as aggressively as any of its competitors. The company released the four-player *Pong Doubles* in September in response to the collapse of the two-player market. In October, the company deployed the more innovative *Elimination*, a four-player *Pong* variant in which each player guards a goal on one side of the screen and is eliminated from play if the ball enters his goal four times.[49] Volleyball variant *Rebound* followed in February 1974, in which the players' paddles are situated at the bottom of the screen, and they attempt to hit the ball in a parabolic arc over a net. In August, the company manufactured a limited run of a game called *Puppy Pong* in which the basic *Pong* game is housed in a cabinet shaped like a doghouse to entice pediatricians to place the game in their waiting rooms. Another short-lived *Pong* experiment was *Barrel Pong*, which repackaged the game in old wine casks to provide more aesthetic appeal for higher-end venues.

By the middle of 1974, Atari had largely left the ball-and-paddle market behind as it once again moved on to other genres, but many of its competitors persisted in the category. While most of these were content to continue releasing variations on the same old products, the video game division of Ramtek, led by Charles McEwan's brother Melvin,[50] attempted to innovate in the field. In March 1974, the company released a game called *Wipe Out* featuring the same basic gameplay as *Elimination* but with the addition of a "frustration bumper" in the middle of the playfield that causes the ball to ricochet in unexpected directions. Because Ramtek did not have a well-developed nationwide distribution network, it augmented its own manufacturing run bylicensing the game to Midway, which produced it under the

---

[47] The color version only saw a very limited production run of probably fewer than 50 units. Ed Fries, "Fixing Color Gotcha," blog, May 25, 2016, https://edfries.wordpress.com/2016/05/25/fixing-color-gotcha and

[48] Today, *Gotcha* is largely remembered only for the unusual pink rubber domes that encased the joysticks in the early production models, which eccentric Atari industrial designer George Faraco designed to resemble breasts. Drury, 2010, 86.

[49] Technically, *Elimination* was produced by a secret subsidiary company called Kee Games. Atari released its version, dubbed *Quadrapong*, a few months later.

[50] Howell Ivy, interview with the author, April 10, 2018.

name *Leader*.[51] Ramtek followed *Wipe Out* with an even more innovative ball-and-paddle game in April from a new engineer named Howell Ivy.

A military veteran who spent seven and a half years in the U.S. Air Force, Ivy was stationed at the satellite test facility on Onizuka Air Force Station just outside Sunnyvale, California, in 1972 when he discovered *Computer Space*. A specialist in telemetry systems, Ivy felt he could create a video game himself and designed a *Pong* clone in his two-bedroom apartment.[52] When he finished the game, he offered it to Ramtek, which paid him $2,000 for the design and offered him a job.[53] Ivy remained in the military as he designed a ball-and-paddle variant game called *Clean Sweep* for the company over nights and weekends.

With *Clean Sweep*, Ivy's main goal was to create a more dynamic playfield featuring greater action on the screen, so rather than pit two or four players against one another, the game features just one paddle at the bottom of the screen and rows of dots arrayed across the rest of the screen. The player's objective is to clear the screen of dots by bouncing a ball off the paddle Any dots struck by the ball disappear.[54] Technically, *Clean Sweep* was quite advanced for the time. It was one of the earliest video arcade games to incorporate ROM memory, which was used to store the paddle graphic so it could be rendered with a distinctive curved shape to illustrate that the ball would launch at different angles depending on which segment of the paddle it hit. It also featured the first random access memory (RAM) used in an arcade video game to facilitate the disappearance of the dots. Released by Ramtek in April 1974, *Clean Sweep* sold roughly 3,500 units and re-entered production twice after its initial run as it continued to find success.[55]

After he completed *Clean Sweep*, Ivy left the Air Force to work for Ramtek full time as its only game engineer. He continued to pursue innovative designs with his next game, *Baseball*, which adapted the basic mechanics of the ball and paddle genre to the traditional pitch-and-bat electromechanical game, complete with multiple pitch types and controllable fielders represented as crude silhouettes. The game was initially released in a wooden cabinet that sat lower to the ground than most games of the time to give the effect of looking into a stadium from above, though the next year it was rereleased in a

---

[51] Ivy, 2018.

[52] Howell Ivy, interview with the author, July 24, 2009.

[53] Ramtek never actually released the game. Paul Drury, "In the Chair with Howell Ivy," *Retro Gamer* no. 125, 2014, 92.

[54] Ivy, 2018.

[55] Charles McEwan, deposition, Bally Manufacturing v. Williams Electronics, No. 78-2246 (N.D. Ill), January 31, 1980 and Baer, 2005, 12–13.

standard arcade cabinet as *Deluxe Baseball*. The additional complexity of the game over ball-and-paddle concepts required two circuit boards instead of one, which led to problems during the manufacturing run. The first 1,500 of roughly 2,000 units proved defective because the wooden housing containing the two boards proved too flimsy to handle the job. Ramtek ended up having to replace the wooden housing with a metal one at considerable cost.[56] As with *Wipe Out*, Ramtek licensed *Baseball* to Midway, which released it as *Ball Park*. Ramtek also licensed a third game to Midway that it did not release itself, *TV Flipper*, which debuted in December 1974.[57] In this pinball-inspired game, 20 square targets are arrayed in a 5×4 grid across the center of the screen and a series of rectangular targets are placed around the edges. Players score points by knocking out the targets.

***

The *Pong* craze was not solely an American phenomenon, as Europe embraced video games just as enthusiastically as the United States – at least for a short time. As in the United States, the European market first developed in 1973, but Atari largely ceded the continent to the clone makers because it proved unable to set up effective international distribution before the middle of the year. In Britain, Nutting Associates was one of the first companies on the scene with *Computer Space Ball*, imported by a distributor named Vic Leslie, but it was Allied Leisure's *Paddle Battle* that dominated the market after being imported by a major distributor called London Coin.[58] In France, the Amutronics clone *TV Ping-Pong* arrived first in summer 1973 and was quickly followed by a host of other games.[59] In Spain, ball-and-paddle games proved so popular for a time that they were blamed for a decline in the country's vibrant slot machine market.[60] Within four or five months, however, the markets in Europe completely saturated as operators rushed to place machines in as many locations as they could, and the demand for new games collapsed.[61]

The U.S. manufacturers were not willing to give up on Europe and soon made a second attempt to enter the market through ball-and-paddle takes on the game of soccer. Ramtek and Allied Leisure introduced the first soccer

---

[56] McEwan, 1980 and Ivy, 2018.

[57] McEwan, 1980.

[58] "U.K. Salesman High on Video," *Play Meter*, August 1976, 13.

[59] Blanchet, 2015.

[60] Manuel Garin and Victor Manuel Martínez, "Spain," in *Video Games around the World*, ed. Mark J.P. Wolf (Cambridge, MA: The MIT Press, 2015), iTunes.

[61] "U.K. Salesman," 1976, 13–14.

games in late 1973, *Soccer* and *Super Soccer,* respectively, while Atari created a game called *World Cup* specifically for Europe that launched in April 1974.[62] During this second wave of ball-and-paddle games, a small number of European companies in France, Germany, and Italy began manufacturing their own ball-and-paddle games, but in the end the market only oversaturated again as many distributors imported everything they could regardless of quality and completely flooded the market.[63] After two boom-bust cycles in rapid succession, European coin-op distributors imported video games only in small quantities over the next several years as they refocused on more traditional coin-operated equipment like jukeboxes, slot machines, pool tables, and pinball.[64]

Back in the United States, it appeared video games might suffer a similar fate. Despite its popularity, the widespread success of *Pong* and its many clones and variants in 1973 did not immediately result in the birth of a sustainable video game industry. By the end of the year, the market for ball-and-paddle games was completely saturated and demand for new product sharply declined. As 1974 dawned, a continuing global recession and an energy crisis precipitated by the oil embargo enacted by Arab countries in response to U.S. support for Israel during the Yom Kippur War served to curtail consumer spending on leisure activities, and erode demand still further.[65] As a result, coin-operated video game sales fell by over half to just 30,000 units in 1974,[66] while pool narrowly beat out video to reclaim its traditional ranking as the most profitable coin-operated amusement on location.[67]

As video appeared destined to become just another novelty product that would fade from the arcade after a year or two like so many concepts that had come before it, many of the larger manufacturers abandoned the market entirely. Williams did not release any new models in 1974, while Allied Leisure opted against re-entering the business after a devastating fire destroyed much of its factory on January 31, 1974.[68] The company was able to return to full production on coin-operated games by March after a miraculous recovery,[69] but by then Dave Braun felt that the video game market was

[62] Smith, 2016, 141.

[63] Larry Siegel, interview with the author, February 10, 2015 and "U.K. Salesman," 1976, 14.

[64] "Briton Depicts Operating Methods in UK," *Play Meter,* February 1976, 47–48.

[65] *The Coin-Operated and Home Electronic Games Market* (New York: Frost & Sullivan, 1976), 90.

[66] Ibid, 87.

[67] "Route Survey," *Cash Box,* November 2, 1974, MOA 17.

[68] "Blaze Destroys Hialeah Plant," *The Miami News,* January 31, 1974.

[69] "Hialeah Firm Will Reopen," *The Miami News,* March 1, 1974.

played out.[70] Among the well-established coin-op firms, only Midway and Chicago Coin continued to manufacture games into 1974.

With traditional coin-op venues completely saturated with *Pong* clones, some manufacturers began looking to other establishments in which to place their games. While coin-operated amusements traditionally filled working-class bars and taverns, the broad appeal of *Pong* among all classes of society engendered hope that higher-class lounges, restaurants, and hotels might host *Pong* games as well. These establishments would never accept traditional upright cabinets, however, because they would attract a transient clientele who would noisily crowd around the game without necessarily ordering any food or drinks. This would not only fail to provide the establishment with any custom, but would also discourage regular patrons from entering the premises. The solution to this dilemma was to create a sit-down table-style game that would be unobtrusive while also encouraging patrons to order food and drinks while they played. As this new style of arcade cabinet was particularly targeted at cocktail lounges, it was called a "cocktail table" cabinet.[71]

Perhaps the first person to see that cocktail tables could open up new venues for coin-operated amusements was Bob Runte. In August 1973, Runte established a company called National Computer Systems in Des Plaines, Illinois, that later changed its name to Fascination, Ltd. The company introduced its first cocktail model in October 1973, but rather than sell through distributors, who proved skeptical of the viability of the lounge market, Runte sold directly to operators through "business opportunity seminars" attended largely by affluent professionals like doctors and lawyers looking to invest their money into something tangible rather than letting it sit in the bank and be consumed by a spiraling inflation rate.[72]

A second entrepreneur named Dick Januzzi entered the business at roughly the same time as Runte by approaching Atari to build a cocktail table he could market. Always interested in expanding his business, Nolan Bushnell agreed to manufacture a test run of 200 tables in late 1973. Januzzi sold them largely through ads placed in the classified section of the newspaper.[73] Atari and Januzzi chose to terminate their arrangement after those first units,[74]

---

[70] David Braun, Deposition, Magnavox Co. v. Bally Manufacturing Corp., No. 74-1030 (N.D. Ill), June 14, 1974, 9.

[71] Gene Beley and Sonny Albarado, "Cocktails, Anyone? The Boob Tube Pays Off," *Play Meter*, April 1975, 26.

[72] Ibid, 27–28.

[73] Ibid.

[74] Januzzi claimed he cancelled his deal with Atari over quality issues, while Nolan Bushnell claimed he terminated the deal because Januzzi had not delivered full payment for the initial units.

but in March 1974 Januzzi joined with William Wasson and David Perry to establish a company called National Entertainment in San Jose California. National Entertainment became the exclusive worldwide sales agent for the most successful game of the cocktail era, *Flim Flam* by Meadows Games.

Meadows Games was a coin-operated amusement spinoff of a company called Meadows Manufacturing established by Dan Meadows in 1958 as a contract manufacturer for local electronics firms like Ampex and Western Electric. In 1966, Meadows sold the firm to employee Harry Kurek. In the early 1970s, Kurek correctly predicted that an economic recession was on the horizon and decided to diversify his operation into a "recession proof" business. He chose coin-op after learning how successful the pinball manufacturers had been in the face of the Great Depression and incorporated Meadows Games in Sunnyvale in January 1974.[75]

Flim Flam, released that August, was Meadows' first game. This four-player *Pong* variant incorporated joysticks for control rather than dials, so the paddles could move forwards and backwards as well as up and down. The paddles could also be adjusted to three different lengths to make the game easier or more challenging depending on the skill level of the player. Finally, each player had a "flim" and a "flam" button to alter the speed and course of the ball to make gameplay more unpredictable. *Flim Flam* arrived just in time to ride the wave of the cocktail boom and remained in production for nearly two full years. By the time the last unit rolled off the assembly line in July 1976, Meadows had sold nearly 12,000 units.[76]

Other companies rushed to follow the lead of Fascination, National Coin, and Meadows by introducing their own cocktail games as sales reached 10,000 units in 1974. In 1975, the number of units sold increased to 26,000, but that proved to be the high-water mark of the business.[77] Many of the cocktail manufacturers were shady fly-by-night businesses preying on a new breed of inexperienced operator through exorbitant pricing and inadequate service and support. These so-called "biz op" or "blue suede shoe" salesmen succeeded in growing the market for *Pong*-style games in the short term, but did nothing to drive innovation in the cocktail space forward. By 1975, some traditional distributors and operators began embracing the new market as well, but more companies merely led to the same market saturation that had already crippled the original ball-and-paddle market.

---

[75] Smith, 194–195.
[76] "Meadows Games: From California to the World," *RePlay*, July 1976, 28.
[77] Frost & Sullivan, 1976, 88.

***

By the mid-1970s, the coin-operated amusement industry had moved past the ball-and-paddle genre, and many of the smaller companies that had never expanded beyond that market shut down. Amutronics was bought out by PMC Electronics in 1974, while For-Play disappeared before the end of 1975.[78] PMC managed to limp along in the cocktail market long enough to spin off its video game division as PMC Industries in February 1976,[79] but it never moved beyond ball-and-paddle games and was gone before the end of the year. Perhaps the most significant loss of the period was Nutting Associates, which despite being the first company to release a video game and one of the first to release a *Pong* clone after Atari never managed to gain any traction in the new marketplace. In November 1973, Nutting attempted to make a splash with a standard four-player tennis variant called *Wimbledon* designed by a contractor named Gerald Gleason and finished by Dutch engineer Miel Domis.[80] The game incorporated a color monitor to display a bright green playfield and paddles in four different colors,[81] but adding color was not enough to jump-start the declining ball-and-paddle market. By summer 1974 Nutting was forced into Chapter 11 bankruptcy.[82]

With his company in dire straits, Bill Nutting turned to the cocktail market with a ball-and-paddle game called *Table Tennis* and did well enough to pull Nutting Associates out of bankruptcy by October 1975.[83] The company displayed two new games at the MOA show that year, but continued to struggle.[84] In July 1977, a gambling machine manufacturer based in Reno, Nevada, called A-1 Supply purchased Nutting Associates to serve as a West Coast conduit for its gray-market video blackjack machines. Nutting debuted its final video game that October: a cocktail game similar to Midway's three-year-old *TV Flipper* called *Ricochet*. By 1979, Nutting Associates had been merged into A-1 to create a new company called Sircoma, and Bill Nutting moved to Reno to serve as a production manager.[85] After nearly dying in a serious plane crash, however, Nutting connected with a group called

[78] Smith, 2016, 283.

[79] "PMC Spins Off Games Line; Bender Heads New Company," *Vending Times*, February 1976, 48.

[80] Gerald Gleason, email correspondence with the author, September 15, 2018 and "Electronics Review," *Electronics*, June 1976, 32.

[81] *Electronics*, June 1976.

[82] "What's News?" *Marketplace*, August 30, 1974, 24.

[83] Letter from Bill Nutting to Bill Gersh, reprinted in *Marketplace*, July 30, 1975, 7.

[84] While the games are not named in show coverage of the time, they were probably two cocktail ball-and-paddle cabinets called *Table Tennis II* and *Paddle Derby*.

[85] Smith, 2016, 183.

Mission Aviation that served as an air-taxi service for Christian Missionaries. Impressed with his background as a pilot and a businessman, the group hired him to manage its office in Nairobi, Kenya. When that job ended in 1985, Nutting retired to Arizona.[86] He never worked in the coin-op industry again.

***

The ball-and-paddle market may have been completely dead by 1976, but the video game itself did not vanish with it as some had predicted. While the collapse of the *Pong* market drove several companies out of the business, those that survived started broadening their reach into new genres like racing and target shooting that had traditionally been served by a wide array of electromechanical products grouped into the catch-all categories of "arcade pieces" or "novelty amusements." Distributors and operators meanwhile, followed up on the momentum of the short-lived cocktail lounge market by expanding out of traditional bar locations into a more sustainable new venue: the shopping mall.

---

[86] Petersen, 1992.

12

These Violent Delights

On October 8, 1956, a new shopping complex called Southdale Center opened in the Minneapolis suburb of Edina, Minnesota. The building was designed by architect Victor Gruen, an Austrian immigrant who decried the rise of suburban living in the United States because it isolated people in a chaotic jumble of "billboards, motels, gas stations, shanties, car lots, miscellaneous industrial equipment, hot dog stands, [and] wayside stores." Gruen determined that suburban communities required something akin to a town center to unite people in a common environment. Therefore, he conceived of a fully enclosed and climate-controlled building of two stories joined by escalators full of retail and entertainment spaces anchored by large department stores on either end and centered on a courtyard in the middle. Southdale was the first realization of this vision, and it became the archetype for a new type of community space: the suburban shopping mall.[1] By 1964, roughly 7,600 malls had opened throughout the United States. By 1972, that number had risen to 13,174.[2]

On its face, the shopping mall was a perfect venue for coin-operated games, as the high volume of foot traffic would insure a constant stream of visitors much as the old penny arcades at the turn of the twentieth century had been fed by the pedestrians of downtown thoroughfares and public squares. Unfortunately, shopping mall owners had no interest in allowing coin-operated games onto their premises, for the remaining inner city arcades held poor reputations as dirty, smoke-filled hangouts for delinquents and miscreants. In 1969, one man decided to change that.

---

[1] Malcolm Gladwell, "The Terrazzo Jungle," *The New Yorker*, March 15, 2004, https://www.newyorker.com/magazine/2004/03/15/the-terrazzo-jungle.

[2] Donovan, 2010, chap. 4.

Jules Millman had been fascinated by coin-operated amusements nearly his entire life, so after graduating from the Coral Gables campus of the University of Miami he relocated to Chicago to work for World Wide Distributors, one of the biggest coin-op distributors in the country. Once there, he was shocked at the lack of business acumen he found among operators, who basically just put the same few machines in the same few locations without sophisticated presentation or marketing yet appeared to make money despite themselves. Millman believed that if an operator put some real effort into maintaining a prime location, the business could be far more profitable.[3]

Millman's key brainstorm was to hire full-time attendants to watch over a group of games on location to make sure the facilities were clean and the patrons well behaved. Justifying the salary of an employee required a large concentration of machines in a single place. Millman's first thought was to approach airports or military bases, but he realized these were locations already well known to most operators, and he would have too much competition for real estate. He finally settled on the enclosed shopping mall as the ideal location after experiencing success operating five games at the entrance of a discount store owned by an uncle and coming to believe that retail and coin-operated amusements were a natural fit.[4]

Millman hoped to launch his new arcade operation through World Wide. When management turned him down, he left to found his own company dubbed American Amusements, Inc.[5] He began approaching malls in the Chicago area only to be turned down by every single one. Finally, he approached the Dixie Square Shopping Center in Harvey, Illinois, which was experiencing problems filling all of its space and was therefore desperate enough to take a chance on Millman.[6] The location proved immensely profitable, and when other mall owners realized what a clean and orderly enterprise Millman was running, they reconsidered and let him expand into their locations as well. By 1974, Millman and his brother Tuffy were operating roughly 20 shopping mall arcades under the name Aladdin's Castle.

Even with the new quality and cleanliness standards imposed by Millman, the shopping mall arcade would probably have never caught on if not for the fundamental changes occurring in coin-operated amusements during the same period. As quiz games, advanced electromechanical novelties

---

[3] "The Arcade Genie Makes a Wish, Creates Amusement Game Palaces," *Play Meter*, May 1975, 13.
[4] Ibid.
[5] Ibid.
[6] "Amusement Centers Shed Seedy Image," *Chicago Tribune*, April 16, 1978.

like *Periscope* and *Speedway*, air hockey, and the first video games emerged in rapid succession between 1967 and 1973, the public perception of the coin-operated amusement industry shifted as it took on a more high-tech, family-friendly image. When these games appeared in new arcade venues that felt respectable due to their clean, well-maintained, and safe environments, the industry was poised for its greatest period of growth in decades.

With shopping mall arcades becoming a new disruptive force in arcade revenues, coin-op manufacturers rushed to embrace these new venues, none more so than Bally. In 1972, the company purchased an operator of kiddie rides and games in discount stores called Carousel Time. The chain had been established by Arthur Gold and Irvin Brodsky, who met while executives at the Neisner Brothers chain of variety stores and later went into business together with four stores of their own. In 1951, they pivoted to coin-operated kiddie rides and established Carousel Industries. Within a few years, it was one of the largest operators of rides in the country.[7] Upon purchasing the company and incorporating it as Carousel Time, Inc., Bally expanded the business into shopping malls.[8] Two years later, Bally purchased American Amusements from Millman, merged it into Carousel Time,[9] and changed both the name of the company and its arcade locations to Aladdin's Castle. Bally began aggressively opening new locations and became the leader in the shopping mall arcade business over the course of the next decade.

For Nolan Bushnell, the shopping mall arcade represented one of several avenues he explored as he began expanding Atari in 1973. In February, the company opened an arcade in the relatively new Orange Mall in Los Angeles.[10] Soon after, Atari opened two more locations in the Oakridge Mall in San Jose and the Bay Fair Shopping Center in San Leandro.[11] Meanwhile, on the technology front Nolan exhorted his engineers to build elaborate new products like a 20-player version of *Gotcha* and a color version of *Pong* for the home market.[12] When VP of engineering Al Alcorn responded to an August 1973 memo regarding these engineering projects by reminding Nolan that the company did not have any money, his boss was loath to accept the excuse. In the end, 20-player *Gotcha* was never built, while a home version of *Pong* would need to wait for better technology.

---

[7] "Carousel Gets New Chi Qtrs.," *Billboard*, March 14, 1953, 78.

[8] "1972 in Review," *Cash Box*, December 23, 1972, 38–39.

[9] "Bally Acquires Overseas Distributor, Domestic Coin-Op Arcade Operator," *Vending Times*, June 1974, 61.

[10] "Pinball Machines Invade Big Shopping Centers," *Boston Herald American*, February 15, 1973.

[11] "Atari to Open Another Arcade," *Cash Box*, May 11, 1974, 50.

[12] Memo from Nolan Bushnell to Atari Engineering Department, August 3, 1973.

During this period, Bushnell realized he did not possess the managerial skills necessary to oversee the massive growth his company was experiencing. In summer 1973, he hired his brother-in-law, psychologist and business consultant Dr. John Wakefield, to serve as president and kept only the chairman of the board title for himself.[13] Wakefield subsequently recruited the general manager of Hewlett-Packard's (HP) Intercontinental Sales Division Region, Richard Mobilio, to serve as VP of Marketing. Mobilio brought several HP employees with him, most notably Leslie Oliver, who became VP of Finance.[14] In September 1973, Al Alcorn took a leave of absence to care for his terminally ill mother,[15] so early the next year Bushnell brought in another former Videofile engineer, Lloyd Warman, as his new VP of engineering.[16] Bushnell hoped his new management team would provide Atari with the necessary skills to grow into a major corporation, but in this he was disappointed. None of these men had experience in the fast-paced coin-operated amusement business, and the more rigid corporate structure they created led to a lack of effective communication across departments.[17] These issues came to a head as Atari attempted to bring its latest product to market in early 1974, a driving game called *Gran Trak 10*.

The plan for a driving game originated at a new Atari subsidiary acquired during Nolan Bushnell's expansion spree called Cyan Engineering founded by electrical engineers Steve Mayer and Larry Emmons. Like Nolan Bushnell and Ted Dabney, Mayer and Emmons spent time in the Ampex Videofile Division in the early 1970s, and Mayer even became a key source of electronic components for Bushnell and Dabney's *Computer Space* prototype by smuggling them out of the Videofile installation he was setting up for the Los Angeles County Sheriff's Department. Mayer and Emmons soon fled the collapsing Videofile Division and joined another defense contractor called Arvin Systems working on videodisc technology. They also began doing some consulting work on the side, including an ultimately fruitless project to create a remote-control version of Atari's *Pong* game.[18]

Before long, Mayer and Emmons realized that the Arvin videodisc project was going nowhere, so in February 1973 they struck out on their own. They had previously been introduced to the sons of famed engineer Charles Litton,

[13] Goldberg and Vendel, 2012, chap. 3.

[14] Richard Mobilio, interview with the author, January 21, 2019.

[15] Goldberg and Vendel, 2012, chap. 3.

[16] "Warman to Atari as VP Engineering," *Cash Box*, February 23, 51.

[17] Mobilio, 2019.

[18] Goldberg and Vendel, 2012, "Back to Our Grass Roots."

who owned an old hospital building in Grass Valley, California, a sleepy hill town near the Nevada border. The duo relocated to Grass Valley and leased a space in the building for their new consulting firm, which they eventually named Cyan Engineering.[19]

Mayer and Emmons continued their relationship with Atari after founding Cyan, and Bushnell convinced them to become his advanced R&D group so his in-house engineering staff could focus on putting games into production to meet his relentless release pace of one new game every other month. Cyan essentially became a division of Atari, although it technically continued as an independent consultancy until being formally acquired in mid-1974. The first game Cyan worked on was *Gotcha*, which it transformed from Alcorn's idea based on defective chips into a finished game. Next, the company worked on Atari's growing library of *Pong* variants before turning its attention to creating the first driving video game.[20]

While a video driving game was an obvious evolution of the electromechanical games like *Speedway* popular in the late 1960s and early 1970s, the direct inspiration for *Gran Trak 10* came from a pen-and-paper game called *Racetrack* published by Martin Gardner in his "Mathematical Games" column in the January 1973 issue of *Scientific American*. The column presented rules for calculating the movement of cars along a curvy track. After reading this article, Steve Mayer believed these game mechanics would translate well into a video game.[21] Mayer designed most of the game himself, but near the end of the project a recent hire named Ron Milner also worked on the game.[22] A veteran of the Lawrence Berkeley National Laboratory, Milner joined Cyan because he happened to be passing through town looking for work after leaving a small electronics firm in Colorado.[23]

Gran Trak 10 represented several important firsts for a video game. Previously, games like *Computer Space* that displayed more complex graphics than the simple blobs and rectangles of the ball-and-paddle genre incorporated diodes soldered onto the circuit board to create a primitive form of read-only memory (ROM). Mayer realized that depicting an entire race track on the screen would require a prohibitive number of diodes, so he incorporated the first IC ROM chip used in a video game instead. This allowed him

---

[19] The Cyan name was chosen because the color is negative red on the color chart, and the partners did not want their company to be "in the red." They also liked the idea of calling themselves "Cyantists." Ibid.

[20] Ibid.

[21] Steve Mayer, interview with Ed Fries, 2017.

[22] Steve Mayer, interview with the author, July 7, 2018.

[23] Ron Milner, interview with the author, June 25, 2018.

to store all the information for the car, track, and scoring digits on a single piece of silicon. The ROM chip was a custom design created by a small chip company called Electronic Arrays, but Atari gave it the same part number as a Texas Instruments circuit in the hopes that any company attempting to copy the game would put the wrong chip in the socket and fry the board.[24]

Another innovation present in the game was the use of an interlaced video signal, in which the CRT draws the screen in two passes by first completing all the odd numbered lines and then returning to the top of the screen to complete the even numbered lines. Previous games were rendering using non-interlaced video, in which the entire screen is drawn in a single pass, to save money by cutting down the number of required chips, but this method resulted in a lower screen resolution and increased flicker compared to a standard television signal. Mayer switched to interlaced video for *Gran Trak 10* so the movement of the race car on the screen would be much smoother.[25]

Gran Trak 10 was also the first game to incorporate a dedicated monitor rather than a modified television set with the receiver removed. At the time, the monitor industry in the United States was in its infancy, and the few companies creating products in the field were serving a small set of clients in highly specialized areas like airport arrival and departure displays and closed-circuit security systems. When the *Pong* fad hit in earnest in 1973, Chicago-based monitor manufacturer Motorola realized that a new outlet for its products was opening up and decided to market its new 19-inch XM-501 directly to the video game industry. This marked the real birth of the dedicated monitor industry and eliminated the need to convert televisions for coin-operated game use.[26]

With its sprite-based graphics, realistic car physics, and innovative controls consisting of a steering wheel, gear shift, and pedals, *Gran Trak 10* was more sophisticated than any video game currently on location. Unfortunately, these advanced features caused a host of problems with the design. Mayer's partner Larry Emmons created a complex hybrid chip containing both analog and digital components for the game sole-sourced to National Semiconductor in an effort to forestall the copying that had plagued *Pong*. National proved unable to fabricate the chip, however, and turned it into a far more expensive three-chip configuration. Furthermore, the steering wheel and pedals in the Cyan design were authentic components sourced from

---

[24]Ed Fries, "Fixing Gran Trak 10," blog, June 14, 2017, https://edfries.wordpress.com/2017/06/14/fixing-gran-trak-10.

[25]Mayer, 2017.

[26]Fries, 2017.

automotive manufacturers and were not cost effective.[27] Finally, the game proved extremely finicky and did not work well once out in the field.[28] An experienced coin-op engineer might have spotted some of these issues before they became serious, but the game was largely developed after Al Alcorn left the company. The inexperienced Lloyd Warman failed to catch the problems, which became a key factor in the near demise of Atari.[29]

Atari could have probably weathered the *Gran Trak 10* debacle save that the market for the company's *Pong* clones was drying up, and the company was losing money on an ill-advised international expansion plan. Sensing Atari was entering a period of financial distress, National Semiconductor suddenly changed its terms for the special circuits in *Gran Trak 10* to cash on delivery, and Atari could not afford to pay. The company was forced to shut down production after only a few units were released, leaving the company without a major product to sell just when it desperately needed one.[30]

Al Alcorn returned to engineering to redesign *Gran Trak 10* sans National Semiconductor circuits. Atari was able to resume production in May, but at that point another problem reared its head: due to the poor coordination fostered by Atari's new management team, the game actually sold for $100 less than it cost to build.[31] While this issue was eventually sorted out and the game ultimately became a 10,000-unit smash hit,[32] the lost revenue from the production delays and accounting errors helped plunge the company into the red. In the fiscal year ending in June 1974, Atari's revenues rose to $12 million, but it suffered a $600,000 loss.[33] With little cash on hand and banks refusing to finance the struggling firm, there was a real possibility Atari would be out of business before the end of the year. It was saved by a secret subsidiary established the year before called Kee Games.

***

In the coin-operated amusement business of the 1970s, distributors carried equipment on an exclusive basis. As the business was still oriented around the jukebox, this meant that most regions were served by two or three distributors each handling one of the major jukebox lines: Seeburg,

---

[27] Goldberg and Vendel, 2012, "Back to Our Grass Roots."

[28] "Improvement Tips Offered on Gran Trak," *Play Meter*, March 1975, 59.

[29] Goldberg and Vendel, 2012, "Back to Our Grass Roots."

[30] Kent, 2001, 95.

[31] Joe Keenan, interview with the author, August 28, 2018.

[32] Wieder, 1974, 60.

[33] Atari Prospectus, c. 1975.

Rockola, and Rowe International.[34] These distributors insisted on being the sole market supplier for any pinball or video game lines they carried and locked their operators into exclusivity deals. Therefore, Atari not only found itself out produced by many of the clone makers, but was also limited to only half – or even a third – of the market in any given region even when it could supply machines in quantity. Worse, Atari built its early distribution contacts with the help of its first customer, Advance Automatic, which was primarily a Bally distributor. While this relationship proved crucial to achieving national distribution for *Pong*, it had the side effect of locking Atari in with Bally distributorships in many major markets whether they were the most effective company in that market or not.[35] For Nolan Bushnell, this was completely unacceptable.

In search of a solution, Bushnell turned to a friend named Joe Keenan. A Philadelphia native and 1964 graduate of LaSalle University with a degree in accounting, Keenan moved to Princeton after college to sell IBM computers. After a brief stint at General Electric, he joined a startup called Applied Logic. The company moved Keenan to California in May 1969 to serve as its western regional sales manager, where he lived across the street from another recent arrival to the area: Nolan Bushnell.[36] Bushnell and Keenan became friends, and at a New Year's Eve party at Bushnell's house in 1972, Keenan played *Pong* for the first time.[37]

In 1973, Bushnell approached Keenan to help solve his distribution difficulties. Keenan remembered a story he had heard about GE buying a curling iron company and deciding not to fold the acquisition into its existing business so it could increase its market share by running two distribution networks. Keenan advocated a similar approach for Atari through the establishment of a secret subsidiary that could build a second distribution network for Atari products. Bushnell asked Keenan to run this new organization and dubbed it Kee Games in honor of his neighbor.[38]

Atari incorporated Kee on September 25, 1973, and provided an initial capital investment of $50,000. Kee also sourced most of its personnel from the parent company. Bill White, who had briefly moved from head of operations to CFO of Atari before the arrival of Leslie Oliver, became the comptroller of the company, while Gil Williams, who had just joined Atari from

[34] A fourth major jukebox company, Wurlitzer, exited the U.S. market in 1973.
[35] Keenan, 2018.
[36] Robert S. Lyons, Jr. "The Video Game Virtuoso," *LaSalle*, Winter 1983–1984, 7–8.
[37] Keenan, 2018.
[38] Ibid.

Ampex that August, became head of operations and opened the company's new factory in Santa Clara. To head engineering, Atari gave the company its number-two designer, Steve Bristow.[39]

Born in Oakland, California, on December 31, 1949, Stephen Dixon Bristow majored in electrical engineering at the University of California at Berkeley and graduated at the top of his class in 1973.[40] Like fellow Berkeley student Al Alcorn, Bristow participated in the university's work study program and interned in the Ampex Videofile Division, where he worked for none other than Nolan Bushnell. Bristow's first tour of duty at Ampex lasted from September 1969 to March 1970.[41] When he returned for a second round in early 1971, Bushnell was hard at work on what became *Computer Space* and actually tasked Bristow with building some of the circuits for the memory and motion controller boards of the prototype hardware.[42]

When it came time for Bristow to do a third tour of duty in early 1972, Ampex was experiencing financial difficulty and eliminated his position, so Bristow went to work for Bushnell at Nutting Associates instead. He started as a technician fixing faulty *Computer Space* boards, but when Bushnell and Dabney left to incorporate Atari, he took over as the company's chief engineer. In that capacity, he brought in his wife, Pati, to build the wire-wrapped prototype for Nutting's two-player *Computer Space* design and exhibited it at the MOA show in September 1972.[43] He then returned to Berkeley for his final semester of college and took a job with Atari collecting coins along the company's game route.[44] After graduating, he joined Atari full time as an engineer in June 1973 and built the four-player *Pong Doubles*. At Kee, Bristow designed the company's first game, *Elimination*,[45] which Atari also produced later in the year as *Quadrapong*.[46]

Ostensibly, Kee was an independent company that had poached Atari personnel to enter the coin-op business, but in truth Atari owned 90% of the stock,[47] Nolan Bushnell and Al Alcon sat on the company's board,[48] both companies received prototypes from Cyan with slightly different features,

---

[39] Atari History Timelines, 1969–1976.

[40] Obituary: Stephen D. (Steve) Bristow, *San Jose Mercury News*, February 26, 2015.

[41] Scott Cohen, *Zap! The Rise and Fall of Atari* (New York: McGraw-Hill, 1984), ebook, chap. 2.

[42] Drury, *Retro Gamer* 93, 33.

[43] Paul Drury, "Desert Island Disks: Steve Bristow," *Retro Gamer* no. 75, 2010, 70.

[44] Drury, 2011, 33.

[45] Drury, 2010, 70.

[46] Bushnell, 1976, 83.

[47] Keenan, 2018.

[48] Kent, 2001, 67.

and many of the PCBs for Kee Games were produced at Atari.[49] The company executed various ploys in the trades to throw off suspicion about its real relationship with its parent company. For instance, *Elimination*, was supposedly licensed to Atari to prevent a lawsuit over theft of trade secrets,[50] while the companies announced in February 1974 that Atari had purchased an interest in Kee and would provide "basic financial support."[51] At one point, Bristow even staged a phony break in at Atari to "steal" game parts while his wife distracted a security guard.[52] Although some distributors saw through these tricks, the companies were generally able to maintain the illusion of functioning as separate, squabbling entities.

Unlike Atari, however, Kee employed an experienced coin-op engineer in Bristow and a competent manager in Keenan. As a result, while Atari was failing under the weight of its foreign misadventures and manufacturing disasters, Kee Games was selling 6,000 units of its version of Atari's *Gran Trak 10, Formula K*,[53] at a profit alongside a successful two-player follow-up called *Twin Racer*. Kee thus assumed a central role in a plan to save Atari advocated by its international vice president, Ron Gordon.

Although he studied philosophy at the University of Colorado, Ron Gordon cultivated a passion for international trade. After apprenticing with several businesses, he established his own trading firm, the Multi-National Corporation, in 1963 when he was just 23 years old. Multi-National connected manufacturing operations with overseas distributors and used letters of credit collected from the overseas companies to finance the operation. All he asked for in return was a small royalty on all foreign sales.[54]

In 1973, Gordon learned about Atari from a friend and showed up one day to introduce himself to Nolan Bushnell. Gordon made his pitch, and Bushnell contracted with Multi-National to ship games to distributors across Europe. Gordon became Atari's VP of international sales, but he never actually became an employee and worked on a commission basis through Multi-National Corporation. The company sent entire cabinets overseas until Gordon realized the whole operation would be more cost effective if he shipped only the circuit boards and sourced cabinets and televisions locally.[55]

[49] Keenan, 2018.

[50] "Kee Game, Atari Pact," *Cash Box*, December 15, 1973, 42.

[51] "Atari & Kee Resume Ties," *Cash Box*, February 2, 1974, 51.

[52] Cohen, 1984, chap. 4.

[53] Baer, 2005, 10.

[54] Ron Gordon, interview with the author, June 25, 2018.

[55] Ibid.

When John Wakefield became president of Atari, he decided the company could make more money by owning its own international distribution. Therefore, he established a string of subsidiaries in the Far East starting with Atari Japan in August 1973 and continuing with Atari Pacific and Computer Games Ltd. in February 1974 in Hawaii and South Korea, respectively.[56] Wakefield tapped personal acquaintances who had no experience in the coin-op industry to run these companies and largely sent them older back stock to sell, which failed to generate much interest.[57] Consequently, these subsidiaries added significant new overhead costs while not generating many additional sales and played a significant role in Atari's financial crisis in 1974.

Despite the difficulties Atari faced in Asia, sales in Europe remained an important part of its overall business, and the company remained Multi-National's most lucrative client. Therefore, Ron Gordon had a vested interest in preventing an Atari bankruptcy. To keep the company solvent, he cosigned a loan from Bank of America and heavily lobbied Bushnell to fire Wakefield and retake control of the company.[58] Wakefield was duly dismissed after the company's disastrous fiscal 1974, and Gordon temporarily assumed the powers of the presidency to terminate the company's relatively new management team on Bushnell's behalf, sell off the international subsidiaries, and restore a positive cash flow. More importantly, he helped convince Bushnell to fold Kee Games into Atari and elevate Keenan to the presidency of the combined company.[59] Atari took full control of Kee in September 1974, which technically remained a separate subsidiary with its own game line, but with manufacturing consolidated at the Atari factory. Keenan became president of Atari, while Bushnell retained the role of chairman.[60]

In November 1974, Kee debuted its biggest game yet: *Tank*. The concept originated with Steve Bristow, who desired a return to the *Computer Space* conceit of two players shooting at each other, but without the confusing Newtonian physics that had turned off so many players. Bristow decided to ground the action by having the players drive tanks using a two-lever control scheme influenced by his experience driving a Caterpillar tractor in his youth. After developing the basic concept, Bristow turned the design over to a newly hired engineer named Lyle Rains, who set the action in a maze

---

[56] Ibid. and Atari Prospectus, c. 1975.
[57] Gordon, 2018.
[58] Ibid. and Mobilio, 2019.
[59] Kent, 2001, 68.
[60] "Atari Acquires Kee Games Factory; Keenan Prexy, Bushnell Chairman," *Cash Box*, September 21, 1974, 36.

and added mines to the playfield.[61] Debuted at the MOA show in November 1974, *Tank* took the industry by storm. Demand became so great many distributors were willing to ignore exclusivity and place the game with their operators. This marked the beginning of the end of that time-honored practice.[62] Atari produced over 15,000 units of the game,[63] contributing to earnings in fiscal 1975 of $19 million and a return to profitability.[64]

The success of *Gran Trak 10* and *Tank* spurred a new phase in the nascent video arcade game industry. While the *Pong* craze of 1973 proved merely a fad in the larger coin-op landscape, Atari's new games represented the next step in the evolution of the traditional driving and shooting games that had populated the arcade for decades. This continuity played a critical role in legitimizing the video game with skeptical distributors and operators.

Despite Atari's renewed success, the traditional coin-op manufacturers in Chicago remained spooked by the crash of the *Pong* market and stayed with their electromechanical roots. Even those few companies that remained in the video game business like Chicago Coin largely concentrated on ball-and-paddle variants for their video line while releasing a range of traditional electromechanical products. Therefore, as in the audiovisual game market of the late 1960s, it once again fell to Japanese developers and their American manufacturing partners to take the lead in spreading the video game into traditional coin-op genres.

***

In 1970, Japan hosted the first world's fair held in Asia. Dubbed Expo '70 and staged in Osaka, the event took on great symbolic importance as a recognition of Japanese resurgence following the utter destruction of World War II. It also served as a showcase for a Japanese coin-operated amusement industry that had been growing at an average rate of between 30% and 50% a year in the late 1960s due to a retail boom that prompted the rapid expansion of hotels, bowling alleys, and supermarkets, all of which tended to include a game corner on their premises.[65]

Internationally, Japanese coin-op firms also exerted their dominance. The four largest manufacturers in the country – Sega Enterprises, Taito

---

[61] Donovan, 2010, chap. 3.

[62] Cohen, 1984, chap. 4.

[63] Donovan, 2010, chap. 3.

[64] "Atari Markets 'Pong' TV Home Unit; Consumer Distribution Thru Sears," *Cash Box*, October 11, 1975, 48.

[65] "Imagination Leads to Boom in Amusement Machinery," *Business Japan*, September 1971, 51.

Corporation,[66] Nakamura Manufacturing, and Kasco – redefined the novelty game market in the late 1960s and ushered in a new era of quarter play in the United States. The audiovisual games developed by these companies sold in quantities in the United States and Europe that had not been approached by most arcade machines in years, opened up new venues for coin-operated games, and launched a technological renaissance critical to fostering a healthy environment in which the newly emerging video game could flourish.

In the early 1970s, this international influence diminished rapidly. Once American firms like Midway, Chicago Coin, and Allied Leisure began cloning the latest novelties coming out of Japan, they were largely able to force the Japanese firms out of the North American market.[67] The Japanese companies began an aggressive strategy of releasing new game concepts every four months in an attempt to stay ahead of this clone market, but these efforts proved unsuccessful.[68] The rise of the video game caused this situation to become even more untenable because few Japanese firms boasted any expertise with solid-state electronics and could therefore not effectively penetrate this new segment of the market. The rise of *Pong* also marked the end – for a time at least – of Japanese coin-op relevance abroad.

At the same time, the domestic Japanese industry began evolving in a new direction. Although games of chance like *pachinko* had been popular in Japan for decades, gambling ostensibly remained illegal in the country, cutting it off from the lucrative slot machine business active in the rest of the world. In 1964, Taito secured special permission from the government to introduce a three-reel slot machine with the capability to stop each individual reel with a button press, thus introducing an (incredibly) small degree of skill. Taito dubbed its machine the *Olympia* in honor of the 1964 Tokyo Olympics. The game ignited a brief slot machine fad but left no lasting impact. In 1970, the introduction of the gambling wall game *Rotamint* manufactured by the German company NSM spurred a new demand for stop-button slot machines, which the Japanese called *pachislot*. These machines threatened to undermine the country's coin-operated amusement business.[69]

In response to this threat, a lawyer named Katsuki Manabe who had entered the coin-operated amusement business in 1967 by establishing a manufacturer called Sigma Enterprises opened a new facility in December 1971 called the "Game Fantasia Milano." This venue replicated a luxurious casino

---

[66] The Taito Trading Company changed its name to Taito Corporation in August 1972.

[67] "Interview: David Rosen of Sega," *RePlay*, October 1975, 12.

[68] "Imagination," 1971, 54.

[69] Akagi, 2005, 56.

atmosphere and was populated by modified slot machines that accepted and paid out in tokens with no actual value, thereby providing some of the thrill of gambling without any money changing hands. The popularity of token-fed slot machines, which soon gained the moniker "medal games," skyrocketed as other entrepreneurs rushed to follow Manabe into the new market.[70] By 1974, there were 807 game centers operating 16,483 medal games in Japan.[71] Those numbers grew to 1,274 game centers operating 39,314 medal games in 1976.[72] The industry peaked in 1977 at 1,544 game centers before increasing regulation brought an end to the medal game phenomenon.[73] Game Fantasia Milano and its imitators were the first game centers in Japan not attached to an existing business like a movie theater or a bowling alley, but at this point they did not typically house traditional electromechanical and video amusements.

By 1973, there were somewhere between 500,000 and 700,000 coin-operated amusement machines on location in Japan.[74] These consisted largely of electromechanical target shooting and driving games manufactured domestically and pinball machines imported from the United States. The industry was centered in Japan's two largest metropolitan areas, Tokyo and Osaka, with machines largely spread across 200 amusement parks, 1,000 game centers, 2,755 bowling alleys, and 5,400 hotels and inns. Coin-operated machines remained a significant presence on the rooftops of roughly 500 department stores as well, but these locations were beginning to fade in importance and profitability due to their limited hours when compared to bowling alleys and game centers, which frequently operated 24 hours a day.[75]

Despite the widespread popularity of coin-operated amusements, video games penetrated Japan only slowly. Both Sega and Taito imported an Atari *Pong* cabinet for evaluation soon after its release, but Taito management saw no future in what its managers saw as an overly simplistic game and did not even bother to put it out on test. Sega did test it, however, and experienced great earnings on location.[76] The company then tasked its three-person R&D group to examine the game and produce a clone. This effort was led by Hideki Sato.

[70] Eickhorst, 21, 2002.

[71] "New Markets Being Studied for Amusement Machines," *Business Japan*, September 1975, 63.

[72] "New Game Machines Cater to Fickle Public," *Business Japan*, August 1977, 103.

[73] "ゲームマシン２０１９年６月１日号," Amusement Press, last modified December 29, 1997, http://www.ampress.co.jp/backnumber/bn1998.01.1-15.htm.

[74] "Varigated Amusement Machines Changing Almost Daily," *Business Japan*, July 1973, 44.

[75] Ibid, 47.

[76] Florent Gorges, *Space Invaders: Comment Tomohiro Nishikado a Donné Naissance au Jeu Vidéo Japonais!* (Chatillôn: Omake Books, 2018), 60–62.

The son of a sawmill and factory worker born in 1950,[77] Hideki Sato was an aimless student in high school but demonstrated aptitude in science and enjoyed crafting, so he attended Tokyo Metropolitan Industrial College to study electrical engineering.[78] While in college, he became deeply involved with an English-speaking society on campus and planned to spend some time abroad through Saitama Prefecture's Overseas Youth Cooperation Volunteers organization. When that opportunity fell through, he had to scramble to find a job. Traditional electrical engineering work did not appeal to him, but he became interested in the toy company Tomy. He applied, but because he had waited too long to begin his job search, there were no openings. Next, he turned to Sega and joined the company in April 1971.[79]

Sato dissected *Pong* with the help of the circuit diagrams included in the manual for the game and used an oscilloscope to figure out where all the signals from the chips were going and what they were accomplishing. This allowed Sega to create an exact copy of Atari's hit product.[80] Meanwhile, Taito put its own *Pong* cabinet out on test after hearing about Sega's successful test. After achieving similar results, the company began importing *Pong* boards from the United States to place in cabinets of its own design.[81] Both Sega and Taito hit the market in July 1973 with *Pong Tron* and *Elepong*, respectively. Before the end of the year, Taito followed up by importing *Space Race* to release as *Astro Race*, while Sato slightly modified the circuitry in his *Pong* clone to create the variants *Pong-Tron II* and *TV Hockey*, which Sega released in November.[82] Taito also began developing its own products late in the year, which were designed by one of the few engineers at any Japanese coin-op company possessing significant electronics expertise, Tomohiro Nishikado.

Born in 1944, the inquisitive Nishikado began conducting his own science experiments at an early age and started working with electronics in junior high school by building his own radios and amplifiers. After graduating from Tokyo Denki University in 1967, Nishikado nearly joined Sony Corporation, but he failed the final round of the company's testing process. He joined an audio

[77] Hideki Sato, interview by Hiroshi Shimizu, part 1-1, February 1, 2018, Hitosubashi University Institute of Innovation Research, http://pubs.iir.hit-u.ac.jp/admin/en/pdfs/show/2165.

[78] Hideki Sato, interview by Hiroshi Shimizu, part 1-2, February 1, 2018, Hitosubashi University Institute of Innovation Research, http://pubs.iir.hit-u.ac.jp/admin/en/pdfs/show/2166.

[79] Ibid.

[80] Hideki Sato, interview by Hiroshi Shimizu, part 2-1, February 1, 2018, Hitosubashi University Institute of Innovation Research. http://pubs.iir.hit-u.ac.jp/admin/en/pdfs/show/2167.

[81] Gorges, 2018, 62.

[82] Sato, 2-1, 2018.

engineering company called Takt instead in early 1967, but after completing his training he was not put in the development department. Bored, he quit a year later. While looking for a new job, Nishikado sometimes met up at a nearby train station with a colleague from his old job who had recently joined Taito. Although he accepted a job offer from a communications company, Nishikado felt the work his friend was doing on games sounded more interesting, so when the friend told him Taito was desperate for new engineers, he ended up joining the company's Pacific Industries division instead in 1968.[83]

While he desired placement in the development section of Pacific, Nishikado was assigned to production. After learning the fundamentals of the coin-op business by assembling machines for six months, he rotated through the quality control and technical divisions before finally moving to development in late 1969. At the time, Taito primarily copied concepts from the United States for production in the domestic market, but Nishikado wanted to create original designs. The result was a 1971 target shooting game called *Sky Fighter* in which he used mirrors to project the images of model planes in front of a sky-blue background provided by a film canister on a rotating drum. While a hit, the game cabinet proved too large for most locations, so a scaled-down sequel followed under the name *Sky Fighter II* that moved 3,000 units.[84]

Despite the success of *Sky Fighter*, Nishikado was transferred again to the department responsible for procuring materials for manufacturing. He considered quitting the company, but ultimately stayed on despite his unhappiness. Perhaps sensing his dissatisfaction, his old boss in development tasked him with learning more about TTL circuits in his spare time because they looked poised to play a significant role in the industry.[85] Therefore, when Taito entered the video game business, Nishikado returned to the development division because no other employee of the company knew how to work with IC technology.

After helping bring Taito's early imports to market, Nishikado decided he wanted to create his own games. He spent six months dissecting a *Pong* unit to learn how the integrated circuits in the game worked and then developed a modification called *Soccer*. Released in November 1973 Nishikado's game added a second paddle and a soccer goal on each side of the screen.[86]

---

[83] Gorges, 2018, 14–31.

[84] Ibid, 2018, 35–49.

[85] Ibid, 56–57.

[86] Nishikado claims *Soccer* was the first original Japanese video game. However, Hideki Sato's original *Pong* variants came out the same month as Nishikado's did, so it is not possible to say which was first.

A four-player ball-and-paddle variant called *Davis Cup* followed before Nishikado decided to move beyond simple rectangles to character graphics. The resulting game, *TV Basketball*, is still a ball-and-paddle game in which the players use dials to move paddles up and down to knock a ball into a basketball hoop, but the paddles are shaped like human figures.[87]

The same year Taito entered the video game business, it also established its first presence in the United States. Taito America opened for business in downtown Chicago in 1973 as an extension of its parent company's import-export business with a mission to sell knickknacks like ivory carvings in the United States and arrange the shipping of arcade games and jukeboxes being imported into Japan.[88] Mike Kogan appointed a man named Ed Miller to run the company. A buyer for the parent company since 1971, Miller first came to Kogan's attention after he befriended the Taito president's son, Abba, while running his own charter flight company while attending Boston University. Miller soon dropped the trinket business and began seeking American coin-op companies to which he could license games from Taito, Kasco, and other small Japanese companies. In 1974, he licensed *TV Basketball* to Midway. This was the first time a Japanese video game had been imported into the United States.[89]

Meanwhile, Nishikado observed Atari's *Gran Trak 10* and decided to make a driving game himself. Feeling that Atari's game with its twisty track and complex control scheme was too difficult to be truly enjoyable, he looked to Kasco's *Mini Drive* and a 1970 rear-projection driving game from Taito similar to *Speedway* called *Super Road 7* for inspiration. Both games involve guiding a car down an endlessly scrolling road, with *Super Road 7* incorporating the need to dodge cars that appear in front of the player. Nishikado adapted these basic gameplay elements in a video game called *Speed Race* released by Taito in November 1974 in which the player controls a large car situated in the middle of the screen moving along a straight path and dodges other cars that appear from the top of the screen. Nishikado created the illusion of movement by animating a background image of a road and modulating the speed of the oncoming computer-controlled cars based on the speed of the player.[90]

Due to the complexity of the *Speed Race* hardware, Taito needed to charge a comparably high price for the game and set it to 100-yen play rather than

---

[87] Ibid, 66–72.

[88] Paul Moriarty, interview with the author, June 10, 2016.

[89] Ed Miller, interview with the author, January 26, 2014.

[90] Gorges, 2018, 74–80.

the standard 50. Nishikado believed that players would balk at such a high price and included a dip switch to let operators set the game to either 50- or 100-yen play, but the game proved a massive hit at the higher price point. After the success of *Speed Race*, 100 yen per play became a standard that persisted in Japan for decades.[91] *Speed Race* became a hit in the United States as well after Midway licensed and released the game under the name *Wheels* and sold over 7,000 units.[92] Midway also released the game under the name *Racer* in a smaller cabinet featuring a seat in an attempt to penetrate the lounge market,[93] where cocktail-style ball-and-paddle games were becoming increasingly popular at the time. A two-player sequel followed in both markets, *Speed Race Twin* in Japan and *Wheels II* in the United States.

For his next project, Nishikado wanted to develop a video game featuring human characters and turned to a competitor for inspiration. In 1970, Sega released an elaborate electromechanical game called *Gun Fight* in which two players control cowboy figurines positioned on opposite sides of a long cabinet housing a playfield full of obstacles. Each player attempts to shoot his opponent's cowboy, who collapses when hit. Like *Periscope* and other games of this type, wipers and contacts under the playing surface register hits. In 1975, Taito released Nishikado's video take on this game, dubbed *Western Gun*, which features two cowboys rendered as blocky and squashed sprites who attempt to shoot one another while navigating a landscape dotted with rocks and cacti. The players control their characters via a large joystick with a trigger button for moving and firing and a small lever that changes the angle of the gun between three different positions. The goal is to achieve the most kills within a time limit. The game became a hit and, along with *Tank*, ushered in a new wave of one-on-one dueling video games in the arcade.[94]

***

Western Gun represented a significant milestone for the emerging video game medium: the first depiction of violence perpetrated against a human target. While pinball and other coin-operated amusements were often derided as gambling devices or frivolous pursuits designed solely to cheat children out of their allowances or lunch money, they largely avoided scrutiny for encouraging violence. This was because even those games that incorporated shooting featured targets that differed little from the abstract representations

---

[91] Ibid, 80.
[92] David Marofske, 2009, and Baer, 2005, 11.
[93] "Chicago Chatter," *Cash Box*, April 5, 1975, 29.
[94] Gorges, 2018, 88–90.

one might find at a rifle range. Computer graphics offered the prospect of a more realistic – or at least more immersive – experience and thus risked attracting more concern. *Western Gun* itself invited no controversy, perhaps due to the long-standing tradition of cowboy duels in Western films targeted at children and adults alike, but the next year a driving game created by a small coin-op manufacturer called Exidy touched off the first moral panic centered on video games.

Exidy founder H.R. "Pete" Kauffman traced his history with commercial video games back to nearly their beginning, for after spending time at the Stanford Research Institute and the Data Disc Corporation he joined co-worker Charles McEwan at his new startup, Ramtek, and numbered among those employees of the company who played the first *Pong* prototype at Andy Capp's Tavern. Convinced that video games would become a significant form of entertainment, he left Ramtek before the end of 1973 and joined with a former Ampex engineer named Samuel Hawes to establish Exidy,[95] a portmanteau of the phrase "excellence in dynamics."[96]

Kauffman lured away the Ramtek engineer who designed that company's earliest video games, John Metzler, to create products for Exidy. These consisted largely of ball-and-paddle variants marketed exclusively on the West Coast. After debuting with a ball-and-paddle game called *Hockey/Tennis*, the company experienced its first success with another ball-and-paddle game called *TV Pinball* released in December 1974. After moving into a slightly larger facility the next year, the company prepared to expand nationwide by exhibiting its lineup at the MOA show in October 1975. In addition to *TV Pinball* and a couple cocktail ball-and-paddle games, the company introduced a driving game called *Destruction Derby* in which one or two players ram into hardware-controlled cars to score points. When both *TV Pinball* and *Destruction Derby* attracted considerable interest, Kauffman realized Exidy would not be able to manufacture both in significant quantities and farmed out *TV Pinball* to Chicago Coin, which released it as *TV Pin Game*. Exidy eventually licensed *Destruction Derby* to Chicago Coin as well, which released it as *Demolition Derby*.[97]

Unfortunately, the venerable Chicago Coin was teetering on the brink of collapse. For decades, the company had largely relied on electromechanical novelty games to sustain itself, an approach that brought the company

---

[95] Smith, 2016, 210.
[96] "Exidy: Excellence in Dynamics," marketing brochure, 1981.
[97] Smith, 2016, 210–211.

its greatest success with the introduction of *Speedway* in 1969. The onset
of the video game rapidly eclipsed the novelty field, however, and like the
major coin-op companies in Japan, Chicago Coin did not possess the solid-
state engineering talent to adapt to the new medium. While the company
released a smattering of video games between 1973 and 1975 copied or contracted from other developers, it never achieved a breakout hit. In mid-1976,
Sam Gensburg hired coin-op veteran Jerry Marcus as general manager in
an attempt to turn the company around and promoted him to president in
September.[98] Marcus refocused the company's efforts on pinball, where it had
always run a distant fourth to Gottlieb, Bally, and Williams.[99] Unfortunately,
the pinball market was on the verge of transitioning from electromechanical to electronic designs as well, so the company could not compete in that
realm either. By December 1976, Chicago Dynamic Industries had declared
bankruptcy, and its assets were ultimately purchased by two banks to help
satisfy its debts. One of the oldest coin-op manufacturers was no more.[100]

Exidy entered its own period of difficulty due to the Chicago Coin bankruptcy. Throughout early 1976, Chicago Coin's version of *Destruction Derby*
was outselling Exidy's own model due to the former company's superior
manufacturing capability and distributor network, but because Chicago
Coin was in such dire straits, it proved unable to make the royalty payments
agreed upon in the licensing contract.[101] Exidy had hoped its current game
lineup could carry it through until the latter half of the year, but now the
company needed a new game as soon as possible to remain in business.

The task of creating a new video game fell to the company's new vice
president of engineering, Howell Ivy, whom Exidy hired away from Ramtek
when John Metzler left to form his own computer graphics company. With
Exidy requiring a new product immediately to stay in business, Ivy decided
the only way to quickly design a new game would be to use the existing
Destruction Derby as a base because developing a completely new concept
from scratch using TTL hardware would be too time-consuming. While this
required the gameplay to remain similar to the older game, the graphics were
stored on easily replaceable ROM chips and would be relatively simple to
replace with new images. Ivy replaced the cars with blocky stick-figures that

[98] "Marcus to ChiCoin as Gen'l. Manager," *Cash Box*, June 12, 1976, 41, and "Chicago Dynamic
Industries Appoints J. Marcus President," *Vending Times*, October 1976, 99.

[99] "Marcus to ChiCoin," *Cash Box*, 1976, 41.

[100] "Newly Formed Stern Electronics, Inc. Purchases CDI/Chicago Coin Assets," *Cash Box*,
January 15, 1977, 36.

[101] Ellis, 2006.

the players run down for points.[102] Originally titled *Death Race 98*, the name was shortened before release to simply *Death Race*.[103]

According to the promotional materials for *Death Race*, the crude stick figures being run down on the screen were not humans, but rather "gremlins" and "skeletons." To Associated Press reporter Wendy Walker, however, they looked suspiciously like people when she happened upon the game at the Seattle Center arcade. Although assured by both the arcade manager and Exidy spokesmen that the figures were monsters, she penned an article that ran in newspapers across the United States calling attention to this new level of video game violence and including quotes from a psychologist claiming such a game appealed only to the basest nature of mankind. Exidy marketing VP Paul Jacobs was given a chance to defend the company in the article, but probably did not help matters when he attempted to make light of the situation with Walker by stating that "if people get a kick out of running down pedestrians, you have to let them do it."[104]

Walker's article ran nationwide at the beginning of July 1976.[105] It garnered little attention at first, but in December a non-profit organization that promoted traffic safety called the National Safety Council declared *Death Race* "insidious," "morbid," and "sick, sick, sick" in the winter issue of its quarterly magazine, *Family Safety*. Following the article, a media frenzy developed.[106] Hundreds of newspapers ran stories over the next several months, magazines as wide-ranging as *Newsweek*, *Playboy*, and the *National Enquirer* penned features about the game, television news programs like *Today* and *60 Minutes* devoted segments to the game, and a PBS program called *Decades* declared the controversy one of the major news stories of 1977.[107] While Exidy employees performed damage control by attempting to portray the game as harmless fun and stating that they could have made something far more disgusting if violence had been their primary goal, critics felt *Death Race* trivialized

---

[102] Drury, 2014, 94.

[103] Over the years, many people have assumed the game took inspiration from the Roger Corman movie *Death Race 2000*, which had debuted a year previously and featured a similar concept of running over people for points. Everyone at Exidy who has been asked about a connection between the movie and film, including Ivy himself, has denied this. Ivy, 2009, and Smith, 2016, 212.

[104] Jacobs, for his part, claims he was misquoted. Smith, 2016, 213.

[105] The article was reprinted in several newspapers. For one example, see "Newest Game: 'Death Race,'" *Osewgo Palladium-Times*, July 3, 1976.

[106] Ralph Blumenthal, "'Death Race' Game Gains Favor, but not with the Safety Council," *The New York Times*, December 28, 1976.

[107] Smith, 2016, 212–213.

the seriousness of roadway accidents at best and promoted deviant behavior at worst.[108]

Ultimately, the *Death Race* controversy passed with little lasting effect, for even most of those observers who feared that the immersive and participatory nature of video gaming might lead to greater psychological harm than passively watching violence play out on television or in the theater had to admit they did not foresee players rushing out to mow down pedestrians after experiencing the title's crude graphics and limited gameplay. For Exidy, the controversy proved a boon, as the company gained a national profile while selling roughly 2,000 *Death Race* cabinets in the United States and another 1,000 PCBs for export overseas after a second production run prompted by its sudden notoriety.[109] These numbers still paled in comparison to the biggest coin-op hits, however, so with more prosaic ball-and-paddle, driving, and target shooting games remaining the primary sources of video game revenue, *Death Race* and the controversy it spawned soon faded into obscurity. Indeed, even as the violence debate reached its apex, arcade video games were entering a period of stagnation and were in danger of being eclipsed by a new wave of ball-and-paddle games now entering the home.

---

[108] Blumenthal, 1976.
[109] Smith, 2016, 215.

13

Homeward Bound

On May 21, 1954, Texas Instruments executive vice president Patrick Haggerty approached electrical engineer Paul Davis with a challenge: develop a portable radio using germanium transistors in lieu of vacuum tubes. At the time, the transistor was struggling to replace the venerable tube in most electronic devices, and Haggerty reasoned that so long as it only served industrial and military applications, it would never achieve high-volume production. That required a consumer product, and no electronic consumer device was more widespread than the radio.[1]

Four days after Haggerty approached him, Davis had a working prototype. As Davis's team continued to refine the design over the next few months, Haggerty attempted to locate a radio company interested in manufacturing his transistor radio but was turned down by all of them. Ultimately, TI turned to a company called Industrial Development Engineering Associates (IDEA) that marketed antenna boosters under the Regency brand name. In November 1954, IDEA released the Regency TR-1, the world's first transistor radio and the first consumer product of any kind based on solid-state technology. Although it never worked well and cost more than a tube radio of similar size and capability, the TR-1 sold 100,000 units within a year based on its novelty alone, while TI produced half as many transistors just for the radio as the entire industry had produced for all applications the year before. Although TI never earned much profit through transistor radios, the

---

[1] Robert J. Simcoe, "The Revolution in Your Pocket," *American Heritage Invention and Technology*, Fall 2004, 14.

TR-1 demonstrated one important fact: the best way to spread and improve solid-state technology rapidly was to pair it with a consumer application.[2]

In the early 1960s, TI faced a similar problem with integrated circuits, which were not being embraced despite their obvious superiority over discrete electronics. Once again, Haggerty decided to jump-start the new technology through a consumer product, so in 1965 he tasked integrated circuit co-inventor Jack Kilby with creating a handheld calculator. By 1967, Kilby's team had delivered a prototype called the Cal-Tech that contained all its functionality on just four ICs. Three years later, TI partnered with Japanese manufacturer Canon to release an improved version of the Cal-Tech as the Pocketronic.[3] A year after that, a TI spinoff called Mostek succeeded in creating a pocket calculator using only a single chip, which was debuted by another Japanese company called Busicom.[4]

Unlike the transistor radios that were initially more expensive and less capable than the technology they were attempting to supplant, the pocket calculator was far smaller and cheaper than existing designs that provided the same functionality and was immediately successful. By 1973, 7 million handheld calculators were being sold a year.[5] The first solid-state consumer electronics boom had begun. It ended nearly as quickly. In 1972, Texas Instruments broke with convention by not just suppling ICs to other companies, but actually manufacturing calculators itself. As a vertically integrated company, TI could undercut its competitors on price and touched off a ruinous price war over the next two years that cut into profitability for everyone and drove several high-profile companies out of the business entirely. By 1974, calculators that had cost $300 or more just three years prior could be purchased for only $19.95.[6] The pocket calculator was here to stay, but it would never again be such a highly profitable business.

While the calculator boom ended poorly for most of the companies involved, it exerted an important lasting effect on the semiconductor industry. The high-volume production of ICs to meet calculator demand drove down the price of the devices dramatically and led to rapid advancement in large-scale integration (LSI) circuits, the first ICs with enough power to be useful in a wide array of consumer products at a competitive price. The boom

[2] Ibid, 15–17.

[3] Guy Ball, "Texas Instruments Cal-Tech: World's First Prototype Pocket Electronic Calculator," Vintage Calculators Web Museum, accessed June 6, 2019, http://www.vintagecalculators.com/html/ti_cal-tech.html.

[4] John R. Free, "Microelectronics Shrinks the Calculator," *Popular Science*, June 1971, 111.

[5] Leonard Wiener, "Pocket Calculator Industry in Ferment," *Chicago Tribune*, September 23, 1974.

[6] Nathaniel Nash, "Shakeout Time for Calculators," *The New York Times*, December 8, 1974.

also awoke the solid-state industry to the value of designing ICs specifically for consumer applications and to the desirability of entering the consumer electronics market directly under the right circumstances. Indeed, by the time the calculator market had run its course, the major semiconductor factories were already looking for the next big thing in consumer electronics, and many of them settled on the home video game.

***

In September 1972, Magnavox released the Odyssey in the United States, which proved a sales disaster when the company only sold 69,000 of the roughly 140,000 units produced. Magnavox nearly pulled the product but relented in the face of several positive signs. Magnavox had included a customer survey card with each Odyssey and held back a game called *Percepts* as an exclusive for anyone who returned the card as an incentive to fill it out.[7] When these customer surveys began pouring in, Magnavox discovered most of their customers were happy with their purchase.[8] Magnavox dealers were also pleased because they were able to sell through much of what they actually ordered and were interested in stocking the system again for Christmas 1973. Magnavox started a new production run on the system to build an additional 27,000 units before the end of 1973 and began offering the console at half price if purchased in tandem with a new Magnavox television.[9] The product sold 89,000 units in 1973, which largely cleared out the unsold inventory.[10]

While Magnavox was happy to maintain the status quo, the company held no interest in expanding its video game product line further. In 1973, Bob Fritsche and his Odyssey marketing team envisioned a "lite" version of the console with only five games and a deluxe version with four controllers as well as a dozen or so new and updated games. In the end, no new console variations were released and only four new games came to market: *Interplanetary Voyage, Basketball, Brainwave,* and *WIN.* All four were designed by Odyssey assistant product planner Don Emry, though *WIN* and *Brainwave* were started by Bradford/Cout, the contractors that developed the initial set of games. They all used existing circuit cards save *Interplanetary Voyage,* which used a new card that added momentum to the spot. These were the last new Odyssey games released.[11]

---

[7] Fritsche, 1976, 485.

[8] Ibid, 492.

[9] Ibid, 534, and Baer, 2005, 86.

[10] Fritsche, 1976, 495.

[11] "DP Interviews Don Emry," *Digital Press,* 2004, http://www.digitpress.com/library/interviews/interview_don_emry.html.

Meanwhile, Magnavox itself was falling apart. The company's failure to transition to solid-state television technology fast enough found it losing market share by the start of the 1970s. Furthermore, a Federal Trade Commission (FTC) consent decree in 1971 forced the company to end price maintenance policies in non-fair trade states and caused price erosion in most of the United States that destroyed the company's margins.[12] In late 1972, Magnavox president Robert Platt forced Consumer Electronics Group president George Fezell into retirement and replaced him with Alfred Di Scipio from the Singer Company, who was known to be a savvy marketer.[13] Di Scipio then cleaned out most of the division's senior executive staff including Gerry Martin, the vice president who had authorized the Odyssey project back in 1971. As the company's difficulties continued, Magnavox became a subsidiary of Dutch electronics giant Philips in September 1974.[14] Odyssey was quite simply lost in all the turmoil, and Fritsche proved unable to convince his new superiors that the product was worth supporting when sales were so far below those of the company's televisions.

Nonetheless, Di Scipio's new marketing approach benefited the Odyssey. In late 1973, Magnavox sponsored a Frank Sinatra television special as a springboard to advertise its complete line of products and subsequently hired baseball player Hank Aaron, one of the most recognizable men in America as he prepared to break Babe Ruth's career home run record, as a company spokesman.[15] The increased exposure and publicity the Odyssey experienced through these marketing campaigns helped fuel a banner sales year in 1974 during which the company sold 129,000 units.[16]

In 1972, the production cost of a single Odyssey unit came to $37.00, of which roughly $5.00 represented the cost of the overlays and additional game accessories, and the rest was the cost of the electronics. Magnavox sold the system on to dealers for $65.00, who then marked it up to $99.95.[17] By 1975, rising inflation in the United States had increased the production cost of the Odyssey to $47.00, but the company could not afford to

---

[12] "George Fezell 'Retires' From Magnavox," *Weekly Television Digest with Consumer Electronics,* October 9, 1972, 7–8.

[13] Ibid, and "New Magnavox Team," *Weekly Television Digest with Consumer Electronics,* January 15, 1973, 11.

[14] "Philips Acquires Control of Magnavox," *Weekly Television Digest with Consumer Electronics,* September 23, 1974.

[15] "Magnavox's Signing," *Weekly Television Digest with Consumer Electronics,* January 28, 1974, 12.

[16] Fritsche, 1976, 495.

[17] Ibid, 571.

raise the retail price.[18] Due to the risk of the system becoming unprofitable, Magnavox began looking for cheaper parts alternatives and ultimately signed a contract with Texas Instruments in May 1974 to provide four MSI ICs to replicate the functionality of the dozens of discrete transistors and diodes in the original system.[19] Recognizing that the ball-and-paddle games that had since taken the arcade by storm were far and away the most popular games on the Odyssey, Fritsche and his team dropped the majority of the games on the system to focus solely on table tennis, hockey, and handball.[20]

Magnavox ceased production of the original Odyssey in fall 1975 and sold another 80,000 units for the year,[21] bringing total sales over five years to roughly 367,000 units. At the same time, the company introduced its new IC-based system in two configurations, the Odyssey 100 and the Odyssey 200. Both systems consisted of a single unit that attached directly to the television with no separate circuit cards or controllers.[22] The Odyssey 200, which retailed for $109.95, was the complete version of the system and shipped with three games, *Tennis*, *Hockey*, and *Smash*, the last of which was a renamed version of *Handball*. Unlike the original Odyssey, it also featured sound and a primitive form of on-screen scoring in which a rectangle advanced across the screen when a player scored a point. The Odyssey 100 was designed to prevent Magnavox being undercut in the market on price and omitted both the *Smash* game and on-screen scoring so it could retail for only $69.95.[23] Despite a late delivery on the ICs from TI that pushed the introduction of both systems back until November,[24] Magnavox sold over 100,000 units between them to stay on top of a suddenly competitive marketplace.[25] Total sales of the Odyssey 100 and 200 systems over their lifespans were just under 100,000 and 200,000 units, respectively.[26]

---

[18] Ibid, 542.

[19] Baer, 2005, 92.

[20] A secondary reason for this change was the arrival of solid-state televisions, which came in a variety of nontraditional sizes and therefore made the inclusion of universally compatible overlays difficult. Fritsche, 1976, 577–578.

[21] Baer, 2005, 92. In its final year on the market, the Odyssey was bundled with the rifle accessory and sold at a higher retail price of $110. "Two New Versions of Odyssey Were Announced," *Weekly Television Digest with Consumer Electronics*, May 26, 1975, 11.

[22] To control the games, the players used three dials built directly into the console, which corresponded to the horizontal, vertical, and "English" dials on the original Odyssey controller.

[23] Fritsche, 1976, 540.

[24] "Magnavox's Dominant," *Weekly Television Digest with Consumer Electronics*, October 20, 1975, 10.

[25] Frost & Sullivan, 1976, 98.

[26] Baer, 2005, 153.

For three years, Magnavox essentially had the home video game market to itself. Only one other company, *Paddle Battle* creator URL, marketed a home system in the United States in 1974, and that was merely to clear out unused game components after the collapse of the ball-and-paddle market in the arcades. Called *Video Action*, URL's game played the three most common arcade ball-and-paddle variants, *Tennis*, *Soccer*, and *Hockey*. The inclusion of a 12-inch black-and-white television with the system pushed the price to a decidedly non-consumer-friendly $499, and it sold poorly. URL tried again with the *Video Action II* sans TV in 1975, but the system still retailed for a cost prohibitive $299.[27]

In 1975, two new competitors emerged from an unlikely source: the novelty product business. Over the previous year, several companies in this field had experienced success bringing popular coin-operated products like pinball and air hockey into the home, and now they were ready to do the same with video games. Executive Games, established in 1968 to create novelty versions of board games like chess and backgammon, decided to capitalize on the burgeoning popularity of both *Air Hockey* and *Pong* by producing a limited run of home versions of both games in 1975.[28] The video game was developed by a group of MIT students who were part of an initiative called the MIT Innovation Center and was released as *Television Tennis* in November.[29]

In December, Executive was joined in the market by former Nashville firefighter Norvell Olive, who in 1971 established a company called General Advertising Corporation to sell novelties like key rings through bank credit card system. To enter the video game market, he established a company called First Dimension in 1975 and contracted a Massachusetts firm to build a ball-and-paddle game called the *FD-3000W*.[30] Both Executive and First Dimension kept their production runs small, but the video game market ended up growing well beyond their expectations due to the introduction of a new system by one of the leading companies in coin-operated video games, Atari.

***

In late 1973, Atari hired a man named Harold Lee as a production engineer, a role in which he took wire-wrapped prototypes coming out of Cyan

---

[27]Smith, 2016, 296–197.

[28]"Executive Games Inc.," MIT Case Study, 1977, 1–2.

[29]Ibid, 2, and "TV Tennis Game," *Weekly Television Digest with Consumer Electronics*, September 8, 1975, 11.

[30]"First Dimension," Pong Story, accessed June 6, 2019, http://www.pong-story.com/firstdim.htm.

in Grass Valley and turned them into production model PC boards that could be wired to the various other components in the arcade cabinet. Before coming to Atari, Lee had worked for Standard Microsystems, which like so many technology companies entered the calculator chip business in the early 1970s. Lee personally designed 12 chips at the company, several of which entered production.[31]

After about a year at Atari, Lee was burned out on arcade games and decided to quit.[32] Due to his chip experience, Al Alcorn asked him to continue working for the company as an independent contractor and to deliver a custom sync chip to help combat the rampant copying of Atari products by its competitors.[33] Lee decided this project was a bad idea, for by the time he completed the nine-month development cycle on the chip, Atari would have updated its technology, and the chip would be useless.[34]

While mulling over the sync chip, Lee turned to a friend from his Standard Microsystem days named Bob Brown.[35] An electrical engineer with a PhD from Stanford, Brown worked on speech recognition for five years at Rockwell before joining Fairchild Semiconductor to lay out ICs using new computer-aided design (CAD) techniques. Brown next worked on high-speed modems with a startup called Modex that was subsequently acquired by Standard Microsystems, where Brown managed CAD and IC testing.[36] At the time Lee approached him, Brown had recently become fascinated by a product called the Go Scope that generated colorful patterns on a TV when music was played into it. Using a Go Scope required a state-of-the-art hi-fi TV system that retailed for around $1,000, so Brown became interested in producing something cheaper that could be hooked into a regular television set. Combined with his work on the sync chip with Lee, this led him to ponder if *Pong* could be placed on a single chip.[37] Brown brought his idea to Lee, who decided it could be done and offered it to Alcorn in place of the sync chip.[38] Alcorn pitched Bushnell, who had indicated as far back as August 1973 that he wanted Atari to enter the home market and felt pressure

---

[31] Goldberg and Vendel, 2012, chap. 4.

[32] Ibid.

[33] Alcorn, oral history, 2008.

[34] Alcorn, 2009.

[35] "50 Most Memorable Moments," *Digital Press*, May–June 2003, 6.

[36] John Joss, "Bob Brown's Odyssey: His Invention Gives TV a '5th Dimension' – Viewer Interaction," *Silicon Valley Engineer Magazine*, June–July 1989, 16.

[37] "50 Memorable Moments," *Digital Press*, May–June 2003, 6.

[38] Steven Bloom, "Atari: From Cutoffs to Pinstripes," *Video Games*, December 1982, 41–42.

to diversify after the difficult 1974 fiscal year, and the project received the green light.[39]

Lee set to work on the chip in late 1974 under the umbrella of his contracting firm, MOS Sorcery, which was based in a cabin on a Christmas tree farm he had recently purchased in the hills outside Los Gatos. Over the next few months, Lee diagramed the chip, Alcorn's wife Katie wire wrapped it, and Alcorn debugged it and sent corrections to Lee. Once they had a working chip prototype, Lee rented time on a CAD system in East Palo Alto and spent his nights – rent being cheaper than during the day – laying out the chip with the help of Bob Brown, whom Alcorn hired into Atari from GTE Sylvania to write the testing software necessary to make sure the chips were functioning properly. By July 1975, the group had completed the chip, so Atari turned its attention to locating a manufacturer. Four local semiconductor companies were approached, and Atari chose American Micro Systems, Inc. (AMI), a spin-off from electronics giant Ford-Philco established in 1966 that specialized in creating custom circuits for outside clients.[40]

As Lee and Brown continued designing the final chip, Atari brought a wire-wrapped prototype of their *Home Pong* unit to the American Toy Fair in January 1975. Sponsored by the Toy Industry Association since 1903, Toy Fair was the premiere trade show of the U.S. toy industry and attracted thousands of buyers to the show rooms in the Toy Center on New York City's Fifth Avenue to examine the toy lines planned for the coming year and decide what and how much their stores should buy. Atari set up a small booth on the main floor of the show but failed to entice any toy buyers with a suggested retail price of $99.95 that was unpalatable to an industry that never sold a product for over $30 other than bicycles.[41] The only company that showed any interest was Tandy, proprietors of the Radio Shack chain of electronics stores, but when the buyer asked for a standard term in the toy industry called an "anticipation discount," Atari's management team,

---

[39] Like the creation of *Computer Space*, the story of *Home Pong* is complicated by vastly different tellings by its major participants. Harold Lee states that doing *Pong* on a single chip for the home was Alcorn's idea, and that Alcorn then asked him to do it. Alcorn says that he tasked Lee to do the anti-piracy sync chip, and Lee came back to him with the *Pong* chip idea. Brown says he was helping Lee on a sync chip for Atari when he had the idea for *Pong* on a chip and asked Lee if it was possible. Lee and Brown then brought it to Alcorn. Of the three stories, Alcorn's and Brown's match up on several key elements including the sync chip project and Lee being the one to pitch the idea to Alcorn, so that is the version I believe is most credible.

[40] Goldberg and Vendel, 2012, chap. 4.

[41] Kent, 2001, 81.

which had no experience with the customs and mores of the industry, turned the offer down.[42]

With the toy industry uninterested in *Home Pong*, Atari turned in desperation to Sears Roebuck, the largest retailer in the United States. Atari cold-called the company's television department at the Sears Tower only to be turned down. The television buyer did, however, connect Atari to another person at the company who had previously expressed interest in home video games, a sporting goods buyer named Tom Quinn.[43] In the winter months, the sporting goods department largely became a purveyor of indoor pastimes like table tennis and pool, and Quinn had decided that digital depictions of sports like *Table Tennis* and *Volleyball* made a video game console a natural part of the family rec room.[44] In 1974, he convinced Magnavox to let him sell the Odyssey through the vaunted Sears Catalog, but the company refused to let Sears sell the system in its stores due to its policy of dealer exclusivity. As a result, Quinn was perhaps the only retail buyer in the country actively searching for new video game product. Quinn invited Atari to demonstrate the game for the head of his department at the Sears Tower. The demo almost ended in disaster when the antenna on top of the building interfered with the signal from the console and forced Alcorn to undertake a quick modification.[45] Despite this hurdle, Atari and Sears signed a deal on March 17, 1975, in which Atari would provide *Home Pong* to Sears for the 1975 holiday season.[46]

Manufacturing a consumer product on such a large scale would require a new facility and a large influx of capital. The facility proved relatively easy: in spring 1975 Atari and Kee Games consolidated their operations into a new 65,000 square foot facility on Martin Avenue in Santa Clara, California, which left the old Kee Games factory idle. This facility was transformed into a manufacturing plant for *Home Pong*.[47] Money proved harder to come by. Despite having a purchase order from Sears to use as collateral, banks refused to lend Atari the money it required to establish a production line due to its small capital base. Atari needed an infusion of cash quickly and turned to venture capital to provide it by approaching one of the newest investors in Silicon Valley, Don Valentine.

---

[42]Goldberg and Vendel, 2012, chap. 4.

[43]Lipkin, 2014.

[44]Kent, 2001, 81.

[45]Goldberg and Vendel, 2012, chap. 4.

[46]Sears had wanted complete exclusivity on the product, which Atari refused to grant. The company did, however, guarantee that Sears would have its order filled first, so the company received Atari's entire stock for the 1975 holiday season. Lipkin, 2014.

[47]Alcorn, oral history, 2008.

Born in Yonkers, New York, Valentine studied chemistry at Fordham University and spent time in the Army as an electronics instructor before transferring to a naval base in California, which fueled a desire to spend the rest of his life in the state. After leaving the military, Valentine worked for electronics giant Sylvania from 1957 to 1960 – interrupted by a brief stint at Raytheon – before joining Fairchild Semiconductor as a salesman in the Los Angeles area. After increasing sales significantly in his territory while simultaneously taking courses at the UCLA business school, Valentine became sales manager for the company in 1962.[48]

In 1967, Valentine followed Fairchild general manager Charlie Sporck to a struggling company called National Semiconductor. Established in Connecticut in 1959 by former Sperry Rand employee Bernard Rothlein, National was a small, but generally successful semiconductor firm until a patent lawsuit filed by Sperry Rand depressed the stock price in the mid-1960s. Investor Peter Sprague took advantage of this situation to purchase a large stake in the company and become chairman of the board in 1966. Sprague wanted National to become a major player in the semiconductor industry, and he hired Sporck to transform his vision into reality. A manufacturing guru crucial to transitioning Fairchild from small-scale defense contract work to mass production for the consumer market, Sporck moved National to Santa Clara in 1968 and commenced high-volume production of linear and TTL circuits at a low cost. In the process, he instigated a price war that drove many companies out of the business and left National one of the largest semiconductor manufacturers in the world. Valentine led the company's sales force while beginning to make private investments on the side.[49]

In 1972, Los Angeles-based mutual fund company Capital Research and Management Corporation approached Valentine to manage a venture fund. With Capital's backing, Valentine left National to form Sequoia Capital. He spent the next year and a half raising money, then spent that much time again looking for suitable investments. He was determined to invest only in Northern California high-technology companies, which limited his options, but he eventually settled on Atari.[50] Although initially repulsed by its coin-op business, which continued to be associated with organized crime in the minds of many people, he loved the home business, which would be wholly

---

[48] Don Valentine. 2009, interview by Sally Smith Hughes, October 20 and December 4, University of California, http://digitalassets.lib.berkeley.edu/roho/ucb/text/valentine_donald.pdf.

[49] Ibid.

[50] Ibid.

dependent on the semiconductors Valentine felt would be the future of all technology businesses.[51]

Valentine invested $600,000 in Atari in the summer of 1975, solicited a matching contribution from Time Inc. and the Mayfield Fund, and pulled in an additional $300,000 from the Boston-based firm Fidelity Venture Associates. This gave Atari a capital base of $4.5 million and allowed the company to secure a $10 million line of credit to put *Home Pong* into production. Marketed by Sears under the "Tele-Games" label, the system incorporated the most complex LSI yet designed for a consumer product and featured both on-screen scoring and full-color graphics to provide a technological edge over competing systems from Magnavox and the novelty manufacturers. The combination of America's largest retailer and the most recognizable name in video games proved irresistible to the public, and Sears was swamped with more orders than it could fill as customers waited in long lines during the holiday season for the chance to put their name on a list that would guarantee them a system. Sears hoped to sell as many as 200,000 units before the end of the year Atari was only able to supply 85,000, which quickly sold out.[52]

In 1975, roughly 310,000 home video games were sold in the United States, and most of them were dedicated *Pong* systems.[53] Magnavox sold the greatest number of units, but Atari generated much of the consumer excitement with its technologically superior system. The market was incredibly supply constrained, so even small companies like Executive Games and First Dimension that only managed to sell a few thousand units between them took back orders for hundreds of thousands more.[54] With video games generating so much excitement from both retailers and consumers, analysts predicted a big year for the category in 1976.

Despite the apparent popularity of home video games, however, the toy industry continued to shy away from the category due to the high cost of the products. Instead, a host of consumer electronics companies that had profited from the calculator boom by importing cheap models from Taiwan and Hong Kong rushed to fill the market. These companies did not have chip design expertise, so they needed to partner with existing semiconductor companies to create their games. The early entrants into the market like Magnavox and First Dimension relied on discrete components and MSI circuits to power

---

[51] Kent, 2001, 84.

[52] *The Electronic Games Market in the U.S.* (New York: Frost & Sullivan, 1983), 24.

[53] Ibid, 26a.

[54] Maria Karagianis, "Invention's the Name of Their Game," *Boston Sunday Globe*, February 1, 1976.

their products, but once Atari deployed a console built around an LSI that offered superior gameplay at a competitive price, any company that hoped to remain viable in the rapidly expanding market would need to follow suit.

National Semiconductor was the first chip company to explore an LSI for video games. Like its main competitor in circuits, TI, National moved aggressively into building its own calculators in the early 1970s by establishing the Novus consumer products division in 1971. To run the division, Charlie Sporck tapped a salesman with deep experience in the office equipment and electronics businesses named Gene Landrum. Under Landrum's watch, National became the leading producer of calculators in the world for a brief time,[55] but it ultimately scaled back its consumer efforts when that market fell apart. Landrum departed in September 1975, but before he left, National made a bid to win the Magnavox game business with a single-chip solution superior to the multi-chip system proposed by TI in 1974. Magnavox rejected the proposal due to the larger upfront cost of the chip,[56] so National demonstrated its technology at the same 1975 Toy Fair at which Atari debuted *Home Pong*.[57] Like Atari, it found no takers.

National had initially planned to mirror the original Odyssey by using plug-in cards to allow new game designs for its basic system, but with the success of *Home Pong* and the scaled down Odyssey systems in 1975, the company chose to refocus its efforts on a dedicated unit.[58] To that end, National engineers designed a chip called the MM-57100N that played the same three games as the Odyssey 200, *Tennis*, *Hockey*, and *Squash*, but with eight-color graphics and on-screen scoring. The plan was to make the chip available to any interested company, but National also released a system called the Adversary to showcase the chip that proved a modest success in 1976 with sales of 200,000 units.[59] The firm began marketing the MN-57100N in July 1976,[60] but it was not successful because by then the home game market was dominated by a different chip originally developed in Europe.

***

As in the United States, the Magnavox Odyssey was the first home system available in Europe. It was first released via a small test market in Germany

---

[55] "Novus Was No. 1," *Weekly Television Digest with Consumer Electronics*, April 5, 1976, 13.

[56] Baer, 2005, 92.

[57] "TV Game," *Weekly Television Digest with Consumer Electronics*, March 17, 1975, 10.

[58] "Video Games Playing to Home Market," *Weekly Television Digest with Consumer Electronics*, November 24, 1975, 9.

[59] Jerry Eimbinder, "Home Electronic Game Categories," *Gametronics*, January 1977, 209.

[60] "FCC Game Approvals," *Weekly Television Digest with Consumer Electronics*, May 31, 1976, 11.

in 1973 through ITT Schaub-Lorenz before becoming widely available the next year.[61] For the general European release, Magnavox altered the game mix by removing several less popular games or games that would not work as well for an international audience and adding a few games that were sold separately in the United States.[62] While it was well received in certain markets, it ultimately failed to have much impact.

As arcade video games continued to experience popularity into 1974, the European markets birthed their own home video game manufacturers, but adoption of the new technology proved uneven. While Europe is often treated as a single entity when discussed in passing, each country is its own market with differing regulations and tastes, which makes introducing a new product like the video game difficult. These problems were further complicated in the mid-1970s by inadequate distribution systems because most Western European countries still relied upon small mom-and-pop businesses to drive their economies, and achieving significant market penetration could be extremely difficult. Only the United Kingdom and West Germany were capable of mass market distribution, so these two nations became the largest European markets for video games. France, the third largest market, was hindered by fragmented distribution, while sales in southern European countries like Spain and Italy were hampered by significantly lower television adoption rates than Western and Northern Europe.[63] Most systems distributed in the European countries were manufactured or marketed from Britain, Germany, or the Netherlands, home to Europe's most important consumer electronics firm, Philips.

The first European-designed video game system was introduced in 1974 by the British company Videomaster established by Cameron MacSween and Richard Fairhurst. A natural marketer, MacSween started in the food industry before switching to hiring out models for promotional purposes. He later teamed with Fairhurst, a market researcher for the Milk Marketing Board, to promote Barclays travelers checks in the United States. The duo beheld their first video game when they ducked into a seaside arcade in 1973 to escape the rain. Impressed by the amount of money the machine appeared to be

---

[61] "Odyssey TV Game," *Weekly Television Digest with Consumer Electronics*, September 10, 1973, 11.

[62] Magnavox removed *Cat and Mouse*, *Football*, *Haunted House*, *Roulette*, and *States*, while adding *Volleyball*, *Wipe Out*, and a reconfigured version of *Football* called *Soccer*. "Magnavox Odyssey: First Home Video Game Console," Pong Story, accessed June 8, 2019, http://www.pong-story.com/odyssey.htm.

[63] Cameron A.C. MacSween and Derek C. Martin, "Problems & Opportunities for Video Games in the European Market," *1977 Electro Conference Record* (El Segundo, CA: Electro, 1977), 61–63.

earning, they began installing the machines themselves and became one of the largest operators of video games in British pubs.[64]

Later in 1973, an engineer named Robert Palmer who had built a ball-and-paddle game that could plug into a television approached the duo. Although they were unimpressed at first, Palmer eventually won them over and joined the company as technical director in 1974. That same year, Videomaster released Palmer's game as the Videomaster Home TV Game, which played *Tennis, Football,* and *Squash* games similar to those found on the Odyssey and retailed for £70. It sold roughly 4,000 units.[65]

In 1975, Videomaster released four more systems that played varying combinations of ball-and-paddle games. The same year, a Cologne-based electronic manufacturing company founded in 1962 by Hans-Herbert and Hellmuth Türk called Interton released a system called the Interton Video 2000 that played ball-and-paddle games called *Sparring, Badminton, Tennis,* and *Super Tennis* and a spot-chasing game called *Attacke* [sic]. Like the Magnavox Odyssey, these games came packaged on discrete circuit cards, though unlike that system certain of these cartridges added graphical elements not found in the base system. While neither company sold more than a few thousand units, their entry into the market signaled the beginning of a small cottage industry of European video game manufacturing that birthed the most significant product of the dedicated console era, a ball-and-paddle LSI developed by the Scottish branch of an American electronics company called General Instrument (GI).

Established in New York in 1923, GI remained a small electronics manufacturer until the 1950s, when it began a massive acquisition spree to become a major player in a wide variety of electronic fields, including transistors. The company's main business consisted of selling electronic components to manufacturers of consumer electronics like radios and televisions, so when managers at GI's lab in Glenrothes, Scotland, learned in 1974 about the ball-and-paddle video games gaining popularity in American bars, they were intrigued.[66]

Management asked an engineer who had previously worked on television remote control chips named Gilbert Duncan Harrower if it might be possible to design a chip to play a tennis video game on a television. Harrower thought it was and agreed to work on the project on his own time because GI was not

[64]Roger Eglin, "Big Shots with a Small Screen," *The Sunday Times*, June 26, 1977.
[65]Ibid.
[66]Nate Lockhart, "Interview with Gilbert Duncan Harrower," *The Geekiverse*, January 25, 2019, https://thegeekiverse.com/interview-with-gilbert-duncan-harrower-inventor-of-the-pong-on-a-chip.

willing to invest any money. Once Harrower and his assistant Dave Coutts had a basic prototype running, GI embraced it as an official company project and put out feelers to customers about additional features.[67] These ideas were incorporated into the finished product, designated the AY-3-8500, which could play six games: four ball-and-paddle variants and two target shooting games similar to the basic rifle games found on the Magnavox Odyssey. The chip could only output black-and-white graphics, but it sold for the incredibly low price of $5.00 per chip if purchased in bulk. GI was in the process of adapting the chip to work with American televisions when it was approached by one of the few toy companies that were looking to enter the video game business, Coleco Industries.

Coleco founder Maurice Greenberg immigrated to the United States from Russia in 1911 when he was just a boy and worked for his older brother's moving company in New Haven, Connecticut. Eventually, he transitioned into the shoe findings business before moving to Hartford in 1932 and establishing the Connecticut Leather Company to supply leather products to shoe manufacturers.[68] While the company served primarily as a distributor, in 1944 Maurice's 16-year-old son Leonard convinced his father to let him open a small shop to sell handcrafted leather items. After graduating from Trinity College in 1948 with a degree in mathematics, Leonard took a job as an engineer at United Aircraft in Hartford, but quickly grew bored and joined his father's business full time in 1949. The next year, he convinced his college friend and fellow engineer Melvin Gershman to join him at the company to help fashion and operate a leather-cutting machine to produce spools of leather lacing. This initiative brought the Greenbergs into the manufacturing business.[69]

In the early 1950s, the Connecticut Leather Company took over an abandoned glove factory in Mayfield, New York, to manufacture leather moccasin kits. When the kits proved extremely popular at the 1954 Toy Fair, the company committed fully to the toy business by offering a variety of leather kits in the late 1950s backed by major licenses including Davy Crockett, Howdy Doody, and Mickey Mouse. In 1956, Leonard expanded the business into small plastic toys and then into plastic wading pools. The pools proved immensely successful, so the Greenbergs sold off their leather supply and manufacturing departments in 1961 and renamed their company

---

[67] Ibid.

[68] Antoine Clerc-Renaud and Jean-François Dupuis, *Coleco: The Official Book* (Quebec: BOOQC Publishing, 2016), 13–15.

[69] Ibid, 20–22, and Arnold Greenberg, interview with the author, June 17, 2017.

Coleco Industries. The next year, Coleco went public on the American Stock Exchange, and Maurice ceded the president and CEO roles to Leonard, retaining only the title of chairman for himself.[70]

Over the next four years, Leonard Greenberg expanded the company aggressively through several acquisitions, including inflatable backyard pool maker Kestral Corporation in 1963, leading doll carriage producer Playtime Products in 1965, and Canadian tabletop hockey and football game maker Eagle Toys in 1968.[71] During this process, Leonard leaned heavily on his younger brother Arnold, a 1958 graduate of Harvard Law School who worked at the law firm that had represented Coleco since its founding in 1932. As Coleco began to eat up more and more of Arnold's time, he decided to join the family business himself in 1966. Officially appointed Coleco's chief legal counsel, he immersed himself in all aspects of the business and discovered a knack for marketing, rising to the rank of executive vice president in 1970.[72] In the late 1960s, Coleco became the largest maker of aboveground swimming pools in the world, enjoyed record earnings, and listed on the New York Stock Exchange in 1971.[73]

Although Coleco enjoyed great success in the 1960s and experienced 12 consecutive years of record growth through 1972, the Greenbergs worried they remained too reliant on swimming pools, which as late as 1968 remained 75% of the company's sales. An acquisition spree of roughly 20 companies followed over the next five years that Coleco largely financed with short-term debt. Integrating the companies efficiently proved impossible, however, and management found itself stretched too thin.[74] The final straw came in 1973 when a snowmobile company purchased the year before proved unprofitable during a mild winter and an attempt to move into dirt bikes failed. The company posted a loss of $1.1 million for the year, the first loss in company history.[75] An executive reshuffle followed as Maurice retired, Leonard replaced him as chairman while retaining the CEO position, and Arnold took over Leonard's former role of president.[76]

[70] Clerc-Renaud and Dupuis, 2016, 22–30.

[71] Ibid, 31–39.

[72] Greenberg, 2017.

[73] N.R. Kleinfield, "Coleco Moves Out of the Cabbage Patch," *The New York Times*, July 21, 1985.

[74] "Butler, Greenberg Describe How Troubled Toy Firm 'Bounces Back,'" *Toy & Hobby World*, August 1977, 52.

[75] Kleinfield, 1985.

[76] "Leonard Greenberg Named Chairman of Coleco Industries," *Toy & Hobby World*, August 1, 1973, 10.

After two years of retrenchment, Coleco prepared to expand again and diversify into categories that sold well during the Christmas shopping season to balance its outdoor line that heavily skewed toward the spring and summer. Arnold Greenberg took note of the growing consumer electronics field and the emerging video game business and believed that if Coleco could produce a system for around $50, it might appeal to toy industry buyers.[77] The company employed no electrical engineers capable of designing such a game, so Coleco's head of product development, Bert Reiner, formed an alliance with a small Connecticut company called Alpex Computer Corporation to develop a video game hardware system.[78]

When it came time to engage a computer chip company to develop the heart of its new video game, Coleco was naturally drawn to GI because it was one of the few companies located on the East Coast rather than in Silicon Valley. Reiner arranged a meeting with representatives of the chip company, who revealed partway through his presentation that they were already developing a *Pong* chip of their own. Alpex cautioned against a GI partnership due to the company's generally poor reputation, but the AY-3-8500 sealed the deal.[79] Alpex and Coleco developed a system around the chip called the Telstar – named after the famed communication satellite launched in 1962[80] – which included only three ball-and-paddle variants out of the six games included on the chip to keep costs down so the system could retail for roughly $70.00. Coleco planned to release the system in June to coincide with Father's Day, but these plans were almost wrecked due to problems with the Federal Communications Commission (FCC).

As part of its mission to regulate the airways in the United States, the FCC requires that any device broadcasting on a radio frequency not interfere with other devices as outlined in the Federal Communications Act. Because early video game systems used an RF modulator to broadcast a video signal to a television set, they fell under the category of devices required to comply with the act and had to be tested by the FCC to ensure compliance. For most of the toy and consumer electronics companies now clamoring to enter the video game business, this was unfamiliar territory that involved navigating confusing interference standards and investing in an expensive electromagnetic interference (EMI) laboratory so as not to risk a failed test.

---

[77] Greenberg, 2017.

[78] Bert Reiner, interview with the author, May 1, 2017.

[79] Ibid.

[80] Greenberg, 2017.

Coleco had neither the expertise nor the facilities to ensure the Telstar met the FCC standards, and the unit consequently failed its test. The FCC told Coleco it could resubmit the product at the end of the week for a second round of testing, but if the Telstar failed again, it would move to the back of the line of the dozens of systems awaiting approval and Coleco would miss its launch window. Desperate to release on time, Arnold Greenberg turned to Ralph Baer, who had started a side business of consulting on electronic game designs.[81]

Baer had access to an EMI lab within Sanders Associates and was able to isolate and correct the interference problem so that the Telstar could pass its second round of FCC testing and release on schedule.[82] Even better, GI experienced such huge demand for the AY-3-8500 that it proved unable to fill all its orders in a timely fashion. Because Coleco had ordered its chips first, however, it received a full allotment.[83] Releasing into a wide-open market, the Telstar rocketed Coleco to the top of the nascent home video game industry as the company sold just under 1 million systems before the end of the year.[84]

Although Coleco was widely acknowledged as the market leader in the United States in 1976, Atari may have actually come out on top, as the company claimed it sold over a million units combined of several console models. These were now marketed directly by Atari's new consumer division in addition to its continuing relationship with Sears.[85] The main product offered by the company was an upgraded version of its original system called *Super Pong* that included full-color versions of both *Pong* and the Atari arcade game *Super Pong* and two original variants developed by Harold Lee.[86] A second console, *Super Pong 10*, added four-player variants of the games found in the *Super Pong* unit as well as a *Handball* game similar to the *Smash* game in the Odyssey 200.

Meanwhile, previous market leader Magnavox concentrated on refining the systems it released in 1975 with new low-end and high-end products.

---

[81] Baer, 2005, 139–140.

[82] Baer's help was not entirely altruistic: Sanders had been attempting to get Coleco to sign its standard licensing agreement to use its patented video game technology for some time, and Baer only agreed to help after the Greenbergs finally did so. Ibid, 140.

[83] Kent, 2001, 96.

[84] Reiner, 2017.

[85] Warner Communications, Annual Report, 1976.

[86] The original games were a reverse Pong called *Catch* in which each player controlled a paddle that took up the entire screen with just a small hole in it the size of the regular paddle and a mixed variant dubbed *Basketball* in which one player controls a small paddle and the other player controls a reversed paddle. *Super Pong* gave each player control of two paddles, placed one in front of the other, which was one fewer paddle than the original arcade game.

The Odyssey 400 contained all the functionality of the 200 model but with the addition of full on-screen scoring, while the Odyssey 500 sported full-color graphics and replaced the rectangular paddles with stick figure representations of people holding tennis rackets and hockey sticks. The two new systems retailed for $100 and $130, respectively. The company also embraced the AY-3-8500 through a system called the Odyssey 300. In addition to producing this console itself, the company made it available to other organizations through its Sentinel private label division.[87] After enjoying a relative lack of competition over the previous four years, Magnavox had to settle for third place after moving around half a million units.[88]

Behind the market leaders lurked another dozen or so companies that experienced varying degrees of success. The most prominent of these firms was a New-York-based importer of Asian products called APF Electronics established by brothers and veteran Asian importers Albert and Philip Friedman in 1968.[89] The company went public in 1972 after riding the calculator boom and jumped into video games in 1976 with an AY-3-8500-based system called the TV Fun that retailed for $90.00 and moved 400,000 units.[90]

On the other end of the spectrum was Allied Leisure, which sought to combat flagging sales of its arcade games by releasing a home system in 1976 called *Name of the Game* powered by a chip from GI competitor MOS Technology that could play four ball-and-paddle games and shipped in both a two-player and a four-player configuration. With video games in such high demand, Allied secured orders for 60,000 units, but difficulties in obtaining FCC approval delayed the system until December and resulted in cancelled orders and unsold inventory. Allied lost $3 million in the 1976 fiscal year and teetered on the edge of bankruptcy.[91]

The novelty companies that jumped into the market in 1975 continued to sell systems in 1976 as well, but neither of them survived the year. Executive Games experienced some success as *Television Tennis* reached 65,000 units

---

[87]Two companies released Sentinel products in 1976: General Home Products, which released it as the Wonder Wizard, and Gulliver Products. Sentinel operated independently from the Odyssey marketing group, which caused some tension. "More Magnavox Games," *Weekly Television Digest with Consumer Electronics*, September 6, 1976.

[88]Baer, 2005, 133.

[89]The name was derived from the brothers' initials.

[90]Benj Edwards, "Ed Smith and the Imagination Machine: The Untold Story of a Black Video Game Pioneer," Fast Company, September 2, 2016, https://www.fastcompany.com/3063298/ed-smith-and-the-imagination-machine-the-untold-story-of-a-black-vid.

[91]Smith, 2016, 305.

sold and a follow-up game called *Face Off* moved another 18,000, but what would have been huge numbers in 1975 were only modest in 1976. The company closed up shop in early 1977 rather than try to continue in the increasingly competitive business.[92] First Dimension fared worse: the company placed a large order for the discrete components to manufacture a new system in 1976 right before GI announced the AY-3-8500 and rendered the system obsolete. Norvell Olive sold out to a Tennessee businessman and politician named John Hooker, who saw an opportunity to make some quick cash, but after the purchase he learned that First Dimension had been acquiring most of its parts inventory via debt, and the company simply ran out of money before the end of the year.[93]

Overall, 3.2 million dedicated consoles were sold in the United States in 1976 with a market value of $125 million,[94] and video games were declared one of the hottest toys of the holiday season. Another 125,000 games were sold in Europe, where the United Kingdom was the largest market with sales of 50,000 games,[95] or 40% of the European total.[96] Videomaster remained the leading company and controlled roughly 80% of the British market while also exporting to the Continent.[97] Like Coleco and Magnavox, the company embraced the GI AY-3-8500 chip for its 1976 model, the Videomaster Superscore, which played all six games on the chip.[98]

With no sign of waning popularity, analysts estimated that sales in the United States could grow as high as 10 million units in 1977. Ultimately, the industry would not come close to reaching those heights because the market rapidly shifted to new platforms for games. These included not just more sophisticated consoles based on advancing chip technology, but also smaller and cheaper computers intended for personal use in the home. When the first of these so-called "microcomputers" arrived in quantity between 1975 and 1977, they were immediately capable of playing a diverse array of games developed over the proceeding decade at schools and researched labs equipped with mainframes and minicomputers useable by multiple individuals simultaneously through time-sharing.

---

[92] "Executive Games," Pong Story, accessed June 6, 2019, http://www.pong-story.com/executivegames.htm.

[93] "First Dimension," Pong Story.

[94] Frost & Sullivan, 1983, 24.

[95] "The Year That TV Videogames Took Off," *Investors Chronicle*, December 23, 1977, 953.

[96] *Electronic Games Market in Europe* (New York: Frost & Sullivan, 1981), 75.

[97] *Investors Chronicle*, 1977.

[98] "Videomaster Superscore," Pong Story, accessed June 8, 2019, http://www.pong-story.com/vm8.htm.

14

Back to BASICs

In July and August 1962, the Board of Cooperative Educational Services (BOCES) of Westchester County, New York, staged a joint workshop with IBM, the most important company headquartered in Westchester, to pursue computer automation initiatives in education. Established by state law in 1948, the BOCES system existed to help smaller school districts in New York State, particularly in rural areas, pool their resources to purchase or develop programs and services that were financially out of reach for the individual organizations. Westchester BOCES Superintendent Dr. Noble Gividen was a passionate advocate of improving outcomes at smaller schools and believed that providing a quality education in rural areas would only be possible through extensive reform. He believed that the computer had a role to play in this process.

The early twentieth century had been characterized by a rapid expansion of high schools in rural America that were patterned on existing institutions located in larger cities. As education standards and curricular demand became more complex, these small school districts were unable to keep up with city districts and their larger staffs. A wave of consolidation and the formation of intermediate school districts like BOCES for resource pooling followed, but many districts were still hampered by ineffective leadership and poorly trained staff.[1] Aware of the computer business simulations like the *Carnegie Tech Management Game* being incorporated into college curricula, Dr. Gividen believed introducing similar programs into secondary education

---

[1] Noble J. Gividen, "High School Education for Rural Youth," a report delivered to the U.S. Department of Health, Education, and Welfare Office of Education, September 1963, 2–21.

could help compensate for the weaknesses of rural teachers.[2] Residing in the same county in which IBM was headquartered provided Dr. Gividen an outlet to explore his theories.

In 1962, Gividen approached IBM about establishing an informal relationship to discuss the intersection of education and technology. This resulted in the BOCES hosting a summer workshop later that year led by Bruse Moncreiff and James Dinneen of IBM with support from Dr. Richard Wing, the curriculum research coordinator for BOCES. Ten teachers were invited to the workshop and explored the possibilities of simulated environments as a tool for classroom instruction.[3] The workshop was so well received that in December 1962, BOCES applied for a $96,000 grant for an 18-month study on methods of incorporating simulation into elementary and secondary education;[4] the cooperative research branch of the United States Office of Education gave them $103,824.[5] Two further grants later extended the program into 1967.[6]

Cooperative Research Project 1948 commenced in February 1963 under the direction of Dr. Wing, who asked nine teachers to submit plans for bringing simulations into the classroom. One of these teachers, Mabel Addis, wanted to flesh out an idea proposed by Moncrieff at the workshop. Inspired by the board game *Monopoly* and his own research into the use of computer simulation, Moncrieff proposed developing an economic model for a civilization to teach basic economic theory. He chose Sumeria as a setting because schools at the time ignored pre-Greek civilizations even as new archaeological digs in the Near East were shedding increasing light on the importance of ancient cultures found therein.[7] Addis had studied Mesopotamian civilization in college, shared Moncrieff's views, and desired to complete the game.

Addis's proposal was approved, so she worked with IBM programmer William McKay to develop a program called *The Sumerian Game* that illustrates the factors aiding the development of Mesopotamian civilization through a land management game played by a single individual. The game takes place over the reign of three kings of the Sumerian city-state of Lagash: Luduga I, Luduga II, and Luduga III. In the first reign, the player develops

[2]Gividen, 1963, 21, and "BOCES Gets $103,824 to Study Simulation," *North Westchester Times New Castle Tribune*, 1963.

[3]Richard L. Wing, "The Production and Evaluation of Three Computer-based Economics Games for the Sixth Grade, Final Report," U.S. Department of Health, Education, and Welfare report, June 1967, ii.

[4]Joan Booth, "BOCES Asks $96,000 for 'Simulation' Study," *Patent Trader*, December 30, 1962.

[5]"$103,824 Grant for Special Research," *The Brewster Standard*, March 14, 1963.

[6]Wing, 1967, ii.

[7]Ibid, 13.

farmland and grows and stores crops to balance population expansion and the stockpiling of sufficient resources to weather drought and natural disasters. In the second reign, the player changes his focus to investing his food supply into developing technology and culture. In the third reign, the player interacts with other city-states and expands through trade and military might.[8]

By 1967, BOCES and IBM had created two additional games in the vein of *The Sumerian Game* called *The Sierra Leone Game* and *The Free Enterprise Game* that applied similar mechanics to alternate scenarios. At that point, work ceased when BOCES could not secure additional grants to continue the project. According to the agreement between BOCES and IBM, the programs themselves became the property of the computer giant, which never made any real effort to promote them more widely. Under normal circumstances, this would have been the end of the *Sumerian Game* story. Instead, it was one of the opening shots in a new wave of computer game creation that accompanied projects to introduce computer-based education into secondary schools. Unlike the BOCES project, which remained localized in a single consolidated school district, most of these projects would flourish over large regions – and even entire states – thanks to the spread of networked computing through time-sharing.

***

In the early 1960s, the computer game *Spacewar!* achieved notoriety at several universities and research facilities and demonstrated the potential of computer gaming as a new entertainment medium. The game directly influenced the birth of the commercial video game industry by guiding the work of Nolan Bushnell and Ted Dabney on *Computer Space*, but not until nine years after Steve Russell and friends had originally coded it. From a commercial perspective that additional decade was required for computer technology, most notably integrated circuits, to become cheap enough to incorporate into a product intended for mass consumption. Computer labs like the RLE at MIT in which Russell coded *Spacewar!* were not bound by the same cost concerns, yet it would still be over half a decade before another computer game appeared that achieved anywhere near the same impact.

The primary factor limiting the spread of computer gaming in the 1960s was a scarcity of computer resources. Even if a university, government think tank, or corporation was lucky enough to own an interactive, real-time computer similar to the PDP-1 that birthed *Spacewar!*, these institutions would

---

[8]Richard L. Wing, "Two-Computer-Based Economics Games for Sixth Graders," *American Behavioral Scientist* 10, no. 3 (1966): 31.

still only operate a handful of computers that only a handful of people would know how to program on them. In such an environment, computing resources were simply too precious to waste on the development of entertainment software with no research purpose and little commercial prospect.

The situation changed when John McCarthy and others at MIT began exploring time-sharing in the late 1950s. With multiple users now able to access one computer simultaneously, computer time did not have to be regulated quite as strictly. Furthermore, as time-sharing opened up computer use to thousands of additional people, many academics came to believe computer programming would become an essential skill in everyday life and began looking at expanding computer instruction to a larger percentage of college, and even high school, students. Encouraging non-technical people to dabble in computer programming necessitated a new emphasis on making programming both easy and fun. The former would require new programming languages, while the latter was best accomplished through entertaining applications such as computer games.

**

The development of the first time-sharing system, the Compatible Time-Sharing System (CTSS) at MIT, evolved out of the unique computing resources available at the institution. In the early 1950s, computing was still a new and radical concept, but MIT had emerged as one of the important centers of computer research through the Whirlwind project that had pioneered real-time computing. Despite this central role in developing new computer technology, MIT faculty and staff made little use of computers to aid in their research projects.

MIT began exploring a wider introduction of computing at the university in 1950 through a committee formed by provost Julius Stratton and chaired by physicist and father of Operations Research Philip Morse. In 1954, this committee recommended that MIT establish a Computation Center on campus. At the same time, IBM began making a concerted effort to place mainframe computers in higher education facilities to develop a new generation of users of its equipment, so Morse allied with IBM to outfit the center with its latest equipment free of charge. The center opened in 1957 with the arrival of an IBM 704 computer and served not just MIT, but also a host of other schools under the banner of the New England Computation Center.[9]

---

[9] "Guide to the Records of the Massachusetts Institute of Technology Computation Center," MIT Libraries, accessed June 27, 2019, https://libraries.mit.edu/archives/research/collections/collections-ac/ac62.html.

The Computation Center proved a boon to researchers, but was quickly overtaken by demand. As the problems being fed into the machine became more complex and, consequently, also more error-prone, the wait for a successful batch processing run became longer and more frustrating. A group of professors led by Fernando Corbató and Herbert Teager, all of whom had programmed on the Whirlwind in the early 1950s, advocated for an interactive computing environment like the one they were familiar with at Lincoln Labs.[10] They were guided toward a time-sharing solution by John McCarthy, who began conducting some basic time-sharing experiments on the 704 in 1957 and wrote a key memo outlining the time-sharing concept in detail in 1959.[11] As he was primarily devoted to AI research, McCarthy turned the time-sharing experiments over to Teager.

Teager secured a National Science Foundation (NSF) grant and began putting together a plan for an elaborate time-sharing system in early 1960, but it proved overly ambitious. Corbató, meanwhile, began developing a simpler system to serve as a demonstration of what time-sharing could achieve.[12] First operational in November 1961, the CTSS allowed three users to access the Computation Center's IBM 7090 simultaneously through use of typewriters, while a fourth user could also have a program loaded into the system that would be processed during any period when the other users were inactive.[13] The success of CTSS would lead to larger and more ambitious time-sharing projects at MIT, while its main architects would spread the word of its benefits to other institutions.

One of the first people outside MIT to embrace time-sharing was Dartmouth professor Thomas Kurtz. A statistician with a PhD from Princeton, Kurtz was exposed to computing in 1951 and would have pursued a degree in computer science if one had existed at the time. In 1956, he was recruited for Dartmouth by fellow Princetonian John Kemeny, a brilliant Hungarian-Jewish émigré who worked on the Manhattan Project before he had even completed his bachelor's degree in mathematics, served

---

[10] David Walden and Tom Van Vleck, "Compatible Time-Sharing System (1961–1973): Fiftieth Anniversary Commemorative Overview," *IEEE Computer Society*, 2011, 1–2.

[11] Ibid, 7. McCarthy's memo was inspired in part by a similar paper written by AI pioneer Christopher Strachey earlier that year, but while Strachey articulated the concept of a terminal hooked up to a mainframe to serve as a debugging station, he did not envision a large network of terminals interacting with a single computer as McCarthy did.

[12] John McCarthy, "Reminiscences on the History of Time Sharing," Stanford University, 1983, http://www-formal.stanford.edu/jmc/history/time-sharing/time-sharing.html.

[13] Walden and Van Vleck, 2011, 7.

as Albert Einstein's mathematical assistant while he was in graduate school, and completed his doctorate at the age of 23.[14]

Like many New England colleges, Dartmouth relied on MIT for its computing needs. Kemeny helped facilitate Kurz's appointment as the Dartmouth liaison to the New England Computation Center, but he also felt Dartmouth would be unable to continue attracting top mathematics students if it did not own a computer itself. He convinced the university to divert some of the funding for a new mathematics building to the purchase of a small computer, the LGP-30. A vacuum tube computer in an era when the transistor was rising to prominence, the LGP-30 nevertheless stood out for its small size and interactive programming environment and presaged the arrival of the minicomputer just a few years later.[15]

While working with the LGP-30, Kemeny and Kurz came to believe that human–computer interaction would become a central part of everyday life both at home and in the workplace. They also encouraged students to experiment with the machine and work on their own projects, creating something akin to the hacker culture that was flourishing simultaneously at MIT. The professors' aim was not just to reach a small group of math and engineering students with a predilection for computer programming, however, but to teach the entire student body how to both use and program computers. This ambition was stymied by one major obstacle: the LGP-30 could only handle one user at a time.[16]

Around 1962, Kurz formally proposed to Kemeny that they should facilitate free access to computing for all Dartmouth students through time-sharing, which he learned about directly from John McCarthy at MIT. Kemeny supported this initiative and helped secure funding from the NSF to develop it. For a computer to sit at the heart of the network, they turned to an unlikely source, General Electric (GE), which had never managed to develop a significant computer division. The GE deal hinged on a computer called the Datanet-30 communications processor that proved particularly adept at routing inputs from multiple devices and could work in tandem with a GE-225 mainframe to deliver an efficient time-sharing system.[17]

---

[14] Joy Rankin, *A People's History of Computing in the United States* (Cambridge, MA: Harvard, 2018), kindle, chap. 1.

[15] Ibid.

[16] Ibid.

[17] Ibid.

Kemeny shared Kurz's vision of free computing access for all students as a necessary educational tool for the modern world, but he felt there was another major obstacle in carrying out this vision: the lack of an easy to use programming language. The machine code and assembly languages unique to any given computer required dedicated study to master, and even early high-level languages like FORTRAN assumed advanced knowledge of engineering and/or mathematics principles. Without a more accessible programming language, only Dartmouth's most technically minded students would actually be able to accomplish anything on the time-sharing network.[18]

Kurz felt a simplified version of FORTRAN would solve this problem, but Kemeny disagreed. During his experiments with the LGP-30, he had developed, in tandem with a student, a programming language called "Dartmouth Oversimplified Programming Experiment" or DOPE. While too limited to serve the needs of the time-sharing network, DOPE convinced Kemeny that, with a little effort, they could develop a language far simpler than any of the currently available options. In 1963, Kemeny and Kurz worked together to create the Beginners' All-Purpose Symbolic Instruction Code, better known as BASIC. By using natural language for many commands and building complexity in layers so the user could accomplish many programming feats by mastering simple commands before tackling more difficult instructions, BASIC revolutionized programming by allowing just about anyone to jump right into creating computer programs with little formal training.[19]

The Dartmouth Time-Sharing System (DTSS) went live in May 1964 and entered general use that fall. By October, the system could accommodate 21 simultaneous users, a number that would greatly expand over the coming years. BASIC instruction was incorporated into several first-year math courses as a series of lectures and problem-solving exercises culminating in the creation of a BASIC program by the student. This approach ensured that roughly three-quarters of all Dartmouth students would receive computer instruction in their first year at the school. Students who particularly enjoyed the experience would then be provided outlets to continue working with BASIC during their time at the institution.[20]

DTSS and BASIC democratized computer use at Dartmouth by providing the computing resources for nearly anyone affiliated with the university to create and share their own computer programs regardless of their technical

---

[18] Ibid.
[19] Ibid.
[20] Ibid.

acumen, but Kemeny and Kurz had no intention of stopping there. As they truly believed programming would become a necessary task for people of all walks of life, they felt computer education should begin in secondary school. Therefore, as they began expanding DTSS outside the confines of the Kiewit Computer Center at Dartmouth, some of their first targets were area high schools.

During the 1964–1965 school year, Kemeny and Kurz introduced tele-types to Hanover High School, a public school located just a short walk from the Dartmouth campus. The students there enjoyed programming so much that a computer club at the school counted several hundred members before the end of the year. By 1967, eight more high schools in New Hampshire, Massachusetts, and Vermont had joined the network. That same year, Kemeny established the Dartmouth Secondary School Project with another NSF grant to form the Kiewit Network, which connected 18 high schools across New England to DTSS at no cost.[21]

With thousands of high school and college students having access to a computer and being encouraged to flex their creativity by programming whatever they wanted in BASIC, it is no surprise that many games appeared on the network. Indeed, Kemeny felt encouraging game playing on DTSS was crucial to its success because engaging in a fun activity could serve as a pleasant introduction to the new technology and help alleviate fears related to using it. In the late 1960s, students wrote simulations of casino games like blackjack and poker; sports like basketball, baseball, and soccer; and adaptations of board games like checkers. Even Kemeny chipped in: on November 21, 1965, the avid football fan created a simple game called *FTBALL* to commemorate Dartmouth's upset victory over his alma mater Princeton to win the Ivy League championship.[22]

***

The DTSS project was a full partnership between Dartmouth and GE. At the 1964 Fall Joint Computer Conference, the two organizations publicized the time-sharing system and the BASIC language at a jointly operated booth. That same fall, MIT's own ambitious extension of the CTSS, dubbed Project MAC, chose a GE computer to serve as the heart of its time-sharing system, no doubt spurred by the success of DTSS. Buoyed by these contracts, GE launched a commercial time-sharing service in 1965 through a two-pronged

---

[21] Ibid, chap. 3.
[22] Ibid, chap. 2.

strategy of selling and leasing computers and opening time-sharing service centers to provide computing to individuals, small businesses, and educational organizations that could not afford to own a computer.[23]

By 1968, the highly profitable GE time-sharing operation had opened 25 locations and spurred imitation from over 20 companies. Some of these were existing firms active in other fields that rented out terminals like IBM and BBN, while others were specifically set up to offer time-sharing services like Tymshare in San Francisco, established by former GE employees in 1965, and Call-a-Computer in North Carolina. Together these corporations brought computer use to tens of thousands of individuals across the United States.

The success of DTSS, particularly with bringing computer use into secondary schools, also helped spur similar educational computer networks in other parts of the country. Many of these projects also adopted the BASIC programming language, for Kemeny and Kurz promoted it widely and made it freely available. As with DTSS, the combination of an easy-to-use programming language and a mandate for students to flex their creativity on computer terminals in a largely unstructured way ensured these systems would also sport a variety of games.

One of the first significant educational networks to emerge after DTSS was the Huntington Project, which Polytechnic Institute of Brooklyn electrical engineering professor Ludwig Braun established in 1967 with the aid of an NSF grant.[24] Like Noble Gividen and John Kemeny, Braun believed that computers would play an important role in the future of education, so between 1967 and 1970 the Huntington Project placed computers and/or time-sharing terminals in over 80 high schools in 30 Long Island, New York, school districts to explore how best to incorporate computers into the high school curriculum.[25] During the creation of the project, Braun visited Kemeny and Kurz in Dartmouth and fell in love with the BASIC programming language, which ensured it would play a key role at Huntington.[26]

Over 3,000 students gained computer access through the Huntington Project,[27] and they began creating simple games like those appearing on the DTSS. One that stands out, if only for being unusual in the context of the

---

[23] Ibid, chap. 4.

[24] Ibid, chap. 3

[25] Marian Visich, Jr. and Ludwig Braun, "The Use of Computer Simulations in High School Curricula," Huntington Computer Project, January 1974, 2.

[26] Rankin, 2018, chap. 3.

[27] Visich and Braun, 1974, 2.

usual casino and board game fare, is *High Noon*. Programmed by Syosset High School student Christopher Gaylo in 1970, this turn-based game simulates a Wild West shootout against a computer-controlled bandit named Black Bart. During each of his turns, the player has the option to move, shoot, or run away. The player and Bart have four shots apiece, and the odds of a successful hit increases the closer they get to each other. Playing the game is therefore a balancing act of moving just close enough to bring down Bart before he can shoot the player. While a simple game, *High Noon* includes brief narrative snippets to frame the action, introducing a small degree of storytelling into a medium still largely based around fast action, puzzle solving, or simulation without any context.

At the close of the first Huntington Project in 1970, Braun and his colleagues concluded, like the Westchester BOCES computing project before them, that simulations showed the greatest promise for computer-enhanced learning. Therefore, Braun secured a second grant to extend the project with a new focus on crafting educational simulations for high school students. Over the next two years, Huntington developed 17 simulations covering subjects as diverse as combating a malaria epidemic, competing to sell a product, and evaluating the damage caused by water pollutants and the effectiveness of antipollution measures.[28] These simulations were widely disseminated over the next few years and helped generate further interest in bringing computers and time-sharing terminals into secondary – and even elementary – schools.

While the Huntington Project brought computing to many schools, perhaps the most remarkable time-sharing hub in the United States was in Minnesota. That Minnesota would become such an important time-sharing center stems from its place as arguably the most important computer industry hub in the Midwest in the 1960s. IBM located a division in the city of Rochester that focused largely on mid-range computer systems, while one of the more effective of the "Seven Dwarfs" competing with IBM in the mainframe space, Control Data Corporation, was headquartered in Minneapolis. Univac and Honeywell maintained a presence in the state as well. This thriving Minnesota computer industry inspired a math teacher named Dale LaFrenz to explore brining computers into the classroom.

A native of St. Charles, Minnesota, LaFrenz attended the University of Minnesota for a time, joined the military, and then completed a bachelor's degree in math education at Mankato State. After teaching for two years, LaFrenz returned to the University of Minnesota to pursue a master's

---

[28] Ibid, 2–23.

degree in mathematics but discovered he was not suited to life as a pure mathematician. He changed course when he discovered UHigh, a high school established by the University of Minnesota College of Education in 1908 to serve as a testing ground for new teaching theories and curricular approaches. LaFrenz became a teacher at the school as he pursued his degree and remained there for five years.[29]

In 1963, LaFrenz was one of a group of UHigh math teachers who believed computers would be important to the future of education and began developing a computer curriculum for the school. A CDC employee named Bob Albrecht told them about DTSS, so they called Kemeny and were impressed to learn about a system that allowed a student one-on-one access to a computer via a teletype. Kemeny offered to bring UHigh into the Kiewit Network if the school could handle the long-distance charges. LaFrenz got a grant from GE, and UHigh connected to the Kiewit Network in 1965. The next year, Minneapolis-based Pillsbury Company purchased the new time-sharing-optimized GE-635, so UHigh left Kiewit for the cheaper local option.[30]

LaFrenz and his colleagues began evangelizing time-sharing in state educational circles, and in 1966 another University of Minnesota College of Education entity, the Educational Research and Development Council (ERDC), began taking steps to form a larger computing consortium. Like the BOCES system in New York, Minnesota had a law on the books called the Joint Exercise of Power Act that allowed local government entities, including school systems, to form combined organizations to pool money and make decisions on behalf of the member entities. The ERDC proposed that Minneapolis-St. Paul school districts join forces to purchase a time-sharing mainframe and introduce terminals at schools throughout the Twin Cities. In 1967, this initiative led to the creation of the Minnesota School Districts Data Processing Joint Board, soon renamed Total Information for Educational Systems (TIES), encompassing 18 area school districts.[31] Dale LaFrenz left UHigh to serve as head of instructional services for TIES.[32]

One of the many Minneapolis schools with a TIES terminal in the early 1970s was Bryant Junior High School in south Minneapolis. In 1971, two Carleton College math majors named Paul Dillenberger and Bill Heinemann

---

[29] Dale LaFrenz, 1995, interview by Judy E. O'Neill, April 13, Charles Babbage Institute, https://conservancy.umn.edu/bitstream/handle/11299/107423/oh315dl.pdf?sequence=1&isAllowed=y.

[30] Ibid.

[31] Rankin, 2018, chap. 5.

[32] LaFrenz, 1995.

were student teaching at Bryant while rooming with a third Carleton student named Don Rawitsch, a student teacher in American history at a school in north Minneapolis. One night, Dillenberger and Heinemann returned home to discover their roommate plotting an elaborate board game on the floor of their living room. Rawitsch was due to teach a unit on Western expansion in a little over a week, and he felt the students might find the subject more exciting if he created a board game depicting travel along the famed Oregon Trail.[33] Heinemann had taken the only computer course offered by Carleton before serving as a lab assistant for the instructor. For some time, he had been pondering creating a program allowing a user to interact with a computer through natural language, but he had been unable to brainstorm a concept. When he beheld Rawitsch trying to draw a map of the American West on a four-foot sheet of butcher paper, he suggested to his two roommates that they create the game on a computer instead.[34]

Rawitsch had already spent about a week designing the board game before his roommates became involved. He had planned to chart player movement across the map through dice rolls, while having the students draw random event cards to simulate the hardships encountered on the trail. For the computerized version, the trio translated movement into a fixed amount of progress each turn based on a speed chosen by the player, while adding the consumption of resources such as food and medicine to the mix. In place of random event cards, the programmers created a flow chart of misfortunes that could occur and tied them into the terrain that the player was traversing so that, for example, attacks by bandits would be more likely in the plains, while cold weather mishaps were most likely to occur in the mountains.[35]

Heinemann handled main programming duties on the game, and Dillenberger assisted with subroutines and debugging.[36] They programmed the game after school hours in the Bryant computer room, a small converted janitor's closet outfitted with a teletype and two chairs.[37] Most of the programming proved straightforward, but one difficulty was implementing hunting in the game, which could be used to replenish food resources. The solution came from Heinemann, who realized that BASIC could not only

---

[33] Jessica Lussenhop, "Oregon Trail: How Three Minnesotans Forged Its Path," *City Pages*, January 19, 2011, http://www.citypages.com/news/oregon-trail-how-three-minnesotans-forged-its-path-6745749.

[34] Kevin Wong, "The Forgotten History of 'The Oregon Trail,' as Told By Its Creators," *Motherboard*, February 15, 2017, https://www.vice.com/en_us/article/qkx8vw/the-forgotten-history-of-the-oregon-trail-as-told-by-its-creators.

[35] Ibid.

[36] Ibid.

[37] Lussenhop, 2011.

register inputs from the teletype, but could also register the length of time between inputs. He took advantage of this feature to make results dependent on how fast the player could accurately type the word "Bang."[38]

Dubbed *The Oregon Trail*, Rawitsch, Heinemann, and Dillenberger's game proved a hit with both Rawitsch's class and the students at Bryant Junior High. When the week-long Western expansion unit ended, however, Rawitsch copied the program onto paper tape and deleted it from the system.[39] *Oregon Trail* may not have even become a footnote in computer game history save that after he graduated, Rawitsch was drafted to fight in Southeast Asia. While he avoided military service by filing for conscientious objector status, this required him to provide two years of alternate service considered beneficial to the country, and teaching did not qualify.[40]

Meanwhile, the success of TIES in the Minneapolis area had attracted the attention of the Minnesota legislature, which mandated that the same computing services be provided to the entire state. This led to the creation of the Minnesota Educational Computer Consortium (MECC) in 1973 to provide time-sharing to all 435 school districts in Minnesota. Dale LaFrenz, who had left TIES by that point and was self-employed, played a role in building the organization and became its assistant director. One of Rawitsch's professors at Carleton College was friends with LaFrenz, so when Rawitsch needed a public service job, the professor called LaFrenz and secured him a position as a liaison between MECC and a group of community colleges. In 1974, Rawitsch thought of *Oregon Trail* and asked if MECC might be interested in distributing it on the time-sharing system. LaFrenz responded in the affirmative, and *Oregon Trail* was soon being played across the state of Minnesota.[41]

***

Once DTSS and GE proved the efficacy of time-sharing and helped spur its widespread adoption in the classroom, it did not take long for the concept to attract the attention of other major computer companies, most notably DEC. DEC realized that school consortiums were either purchasing or leasing time on expensive mainframe computers and that offering them minicomputer packages instead could drive down the cost of time-sharing for these consortiums and win a large portion of the educational computing market. The company repackaged its PDP-8 computer into a series of configurations it

---

[38] Wong, 2017.
[39] Ibid.
[40] Lussenhop, 2011.
[41] Ibid.

called EduSystems that included its own FOCAL programming language, which, like BASIC, was designed for ease of use.

DEC's entry into the marketplace proved a boon for smaller consortiums that did not necessarily have the resources of an Ivy League school like Dartmouth or an entire state like Minnesota. One good example is Project Local, one of the earliest high school computing consortiums. Local grew out of a pilot project by two Massachusetts towns, Lexington and Westwood, that were awarded a grant under the Elementary and Secondary Education Act (ESEA) to lease teletypes hooked up to Telecomp, the time-sharing service run by BBN. In 1967, a further grant allowed Lexington, Westwood, and the additional towns of Natick, Needham, and Wellesley to establish Project Local under the supervision of Robert Haven to explore the use of computers in math education and in developing problem-solving skills.[42]

For the first year, Local continued to rely on Telecomp for computer access, which proved expensive. In 1968, the consortium secured another grant that allowed it to purchase five DEC EduSystems based around the PDP-8/I minicomputer so that each town could have its own system. As the project continued to grow in the early 1970s, its size and scope expanded as it encompassed more primary and secondary schools and began developing curricular materials and training programs focused on better integrating computers in the classroom.[43]

As with all the early time-sharing networks, Project Local soon became a hub for games, several of which were novel for the time period. For example, in 1968 three students named Cram, Goodie, and Hibbard wrote a war game that recreates 14 U.S. Civil War battles using a basic rock-paper-scissors approach to determine results after the player and the computer opponent choose from one of four offensive or defensive strategies each turn. Local was also the home of one of the most significant computer games created in the 1960s, *Lunar Lander*. Its creator, Lexington High School student Jim Storer, had been captivated by the moon landing in July 1969, so when he returned to school in the fall, he resolved to program a simulation of the landing in FOCAL on the PDP-8. *Lunar Lander* tasks the player with deciding how much of his limited fuel supply to burn each turn to control the velocity of a lunar module and guide it to a safe, soft landing on the lunar surface. Although simple in concept, the game modeled the physics of lunar gravity

[42] Pamela Petrakos, "Project Local: A Classroom Project with a 13 Year History," *80 Microcomputing*, February 1981, 74.
[43] Ibid, 74–75.

and module velocity reasonably well through a set of complex equations that Storer believes were provided by his father.[44]

Storer also created his own variant of *The Sumerian Game* called *King* after discovering a scaled down version of the game called *Hamurabi* on the Project Local network. That a *Sumerian Game* variant existed on a time-sharing network when work had ceased on the game in Westchester before time-sharing became popular was due to a remarkable set of encounters. With DEC starting to focus on the education market in the late 1960s, its engineers began attending conferences to espouse the use of DEC computers in schools. At one such conference in Alberta in March 1968, Canadian DEC employee Doug Dymet gave a talk on computers in education, after which a woman described to him in detail an interesting educational game she had come across called *The Sumerian Game*. When Dymet returned from the conference, he decided to program the game as a demo for FOCAL.[45]

To serve as an effective demo, Dymet required his game to run in the smallest possible FOCAL memory configuration of 4K, so he scaled down *The Sumerian Game* by focusing on just the first phase of harvesting and storing grain to manage population growth. Not being knowledgeable about Sumerian history, he decided to change the king in the game to the more famous Babylonian ruler Hammurabi, though he misspelled it as "Hamurabi" in the game text. Once he completed the game, he published it in both the 1968 DECUS catalog and a 1970 book of FOCAL programs aimed at colleges. The official name of the Dymet version was *King of Sumeria*, but due to character limitations in program titles, it went by a variety of names, of which the most widespread was that of the featured king: *Hamurabi*.[46]

By 1970, dozens, if not hundreds, of games were being created and played on time-sharing networks and providing countless hours of entertainment to students across the United States. These were isolated pockets of game-playing, however, remaining largely disconnected from each other and unknown by the larger public. Only about 13% of American high schools were using computers for instruction, and these schools tended to be clustered in specific areas like Oregon, New England, and Minnesota.[47] Most of the country's students remained computerless. Therefore, while Lexington

---

[44]Benj Edwards, "Forty Years of Lunar Lander," *Technologizer*, July 19, 2009, https://www.technologizer.com/2009/07/19/lunar-lander.

[45]Devin Monnens, "'I Beg to Report…' The Sumerian Game 50 Years Later: The Strange and Untold Story of the World's Most Influential Text Simulation Game," unpublished draft 1.3.2, c. 2017, 8.

[46]Ibid, 8–9.

[47]Visich and Braun, 1974, 9. While not an important game creation center, the University of Oregon was another early pioneer of time-sharing networks.

students were piloting a *Lunar Lander*, Long Island kids were participating in shootouts in *High Noon*, and Minnesota school children were traversing the *Oregon Trail*, none of these games attained even the modest profile of *Spacewar!*. Within a decade, however, games like *Hamurabi* and *Lunar Lander* would become household names – at least among those who owned or worked with computers – after multiple channels for the national distribution and promotion of software emerged in the early 1970s.

15

These Are the Voyages

In spring 1951, the photography club of Malverne Junior-Senior High School in Malverne, New York, took a field trip to New York City to walk from Battery Park to 42nd Street while photographing everything in sight. One of the club's students, David Hollerith Ahl, held no passion for photography and had merely joined the club due to a crush on its sponsor. He would discover a new life-changing hobby that day, however, as the group passed through an area called "Radio Row."[1]

World War II had been won not just by legions of soldiers, but also by investment in new technologies that relied on electronic components for their operation. Amplifiers, transformers, diodes, resistors, vacuum tubes, and solenoids were produced in great quantities to feed the war effort and discarded in record numbers when it reached its conclusion. Junked electronic parts and devices filled military surplus stores and scrapyards and fueled a new wave of hobbyists interested in creating their own electronic devices. In Manhattan, much of this business clustered in "Radio Row" on the site later occupied by the World Trade Center. As Ahl perused the bins of discarded components lining the street, he became the latest convert to the world of electronics.[2]

In 1956, Ahl graduated high school and matriculated to Cornell University on a full scholarship provided by the Grumman Aircraft Engineering Corporation. Cornell installed its first computer the next year, and Ahl took both available computer courses. He also spent his summers working in Grumman's computer group. In 1961, Ahl matriculated to the Graduate

[1] John J. Anderson, "Dave Tells Ahl – The History of Creative Computing," *Creative Computing*, November 1984, 67.
[2] Ibid.

School of Industrial Administration at Carnegie-Mellon, where he wrote portions of the *Carnegie-Tech Management Game* and helped port it from machine language to FORTRAN.[3]

After two years in the military, Ahl became a computer programmer for a market research company. In 1969, he joined the Educational Systems Research Institute in Pittsburgh, where he wrote computer simulations aimed at predicting the success of vocational school students. He also began taking night courses at the University of Pittsburgh to earn a Ph.D. in educational psychology. He was only a few credits and a dissertation short when he took a job in 1970 with DEC to perform market research on educational computing.[4]

Ahl spearheaded DEC's move into education by developing the EduSystem bundles largely responsible for bringing PDP-8s into the high school setting. He also became one of the company's lone champions of BASIC and made sure the language would run on PDP systems alongside DEC's preferred FOCAL. To further entice schools to adopt a DEC minicomputer for their time-sharing needs, he scoured the country for programs that might interest both students and teachers. Some would come bundled as part of an EduSystem, while others would be printed in a newsletter he started called *Edu* that reached a circulation of 20,000 within 18 months. In launching *Edu*, Ahl took his first step toward becoming one of the key individuals in the dissemination of many of the first iconic computer games.[5]

***

The spread of time-sharing in the late 1960s created the first environments in which computer game creation was not merely tolerated, but openly encouraged. From *FTBALL* at Dartmouth to *Lunar Lander* at Lexington to *Hamurabi* at DEC, students, instructors, and professional programmers created and played games as part of a larger initiative to further technical education and computer-assisted instruction. These communities rarely intersected, however, and none of these games initially attained national recognition.

In the early 1970s, a new group of evangelists arose who operated outside of any particular time-sharing network, felt the entire United States was on the brink of computerizing, and wanted people from all walks of society to

---

[3] Ibid, 68–70.
[4] Ibid, 70.
[5] Ibid.

be prepared for this revolution. They established newsletters and magazines designed to keep the general public abreast of the latest developments in computing, and they embraced the BASIC programming language as the simplest method to empower average people to start programming on their own. Through these efforts, some of the more accomplished programs developed in BASIC – including many games – gained national exposure for the first time.

No single game illustrates the methods through which computer games began to disseminate nationwide in the early 1970s than the tactical combat game *Star Trek*. In 1971, a high school senior named Mike Mayfield began visiting the computer center at the University of California campus in his native Irvine. UC Irvine owned two computers at the time, a Sigma 7 mainframe and a DEC PDP-10 hooked up to a vector display, for which a port of the ubiquitous *Spacewar!* had been installed. Mayfield was teaching himself BASIC out of a book at the time and decided to create his own version of the game. Unfortunately for Mayfield, his access to the computer lab was not exactly authorized, and the time-sharing account he was "borrowing" only provided access to the Sigma 7, which lacked a display. Instead, he would have to output his program to an ASR-33 teletype terminal, by far the most common output device for time-sharing systems in the late 1960s and early 1970s when CRT terminals were a rare commodity.[6]

Mayfield was also a fan of the pioneering science fiction television show *Star Trek*, which had been cancelled in 1969 after three seasons but was just entering a second, more successful life in syndication. Mayfield and several friends began brainstorming how they might implement a combat game based on *Star Trek* on the Sigma 7. Their ideas were stymied by the limitations of the teletype, for virtually any real-time combat game they could think up would simply be impractical on a system that only outputted on rolls of paper. Finally, they decided they could at least have the teletype print out a map of a section of space to provide a static view of a tactical combat situation.[7]

Over the course of several weeks, Mayfield implemented *Star Trek* on the Sigma 7. As an unauthorized user, he did not have any personal disk space on the system, so he printed a paper tape copy at the end of each day and reloaded the program the next day so he could keep working.[8] The final product is a

---

[6] Mike Mayfield, interview with Ethan Johnson, June 3, 2017.

[7] "Star Trek," Games of Fame, accessed June 9, 2019, https://gamesoffame.wordpress.com/star-trek.

[8] Ibid.

tactical combat game in which the player controls the *U.S.S. Enterprise* and is tasked with ridding the galaxy of Klingon ships. The *Enterprise* has a limited amount of energy to accomplish this task, which is expended through movement, discharging weapons, and bolstering shields. This energy can be replenished at a starbase. The galaxy is divided into quadrants, each of which can be occupied by several Klingon ships or a starbase. Klingons do not move during encounters but do fight back. They can be destroyed with phasers, which always hit but decrease in power over distance, or photon torpedoes, which never lose potency but must be precisely aimed.

Once Mayfield completed his game and wiped it from the Sigma 7 for the last time, it should have been relegated to the dustbin of history like so many early programming experiments. It persisted because of Mayfield's new HP-35 calculator. As he engaged with his new toy in 1972, he made trips to the local HP sales office and at some point mentioned his *Star Trek* game. In 1964, HP had entered the computer business through the purchase of a small company called Data Systems, Inc., and by 1972, it was a major player in the minicomputer market. Like DEC, HP aggressively marketed its HP 2100 series of time-sharing computers to schools. It also maintained a library of contributed programs that were available upon request. While most of these programs were educational, there were several games. The HP employees at the sales office offered to let Mayfield program on their HP 2000C computer on the condition that he convert his *Star Trek* game to HP BASIC. HP included the program in its software catalog with credit given to "Centerline Engineering," a name Mayfield concocted for a non-existent company.[9]

In summer 1973, David Ahl discovered Mayfield's *Star Trek* game.[10] By that time, he was no longer working on educational systems at DEC after having been laid off earlier in the year, but he managed to remain with the company in its R&D division. While working on the RSTS time-sharing system for the PDP-11, Ahl compiled a book of the many games he encountered over the past two years, all of which he converted into DEC BASIC. In July 1973, DEC published this book as *101 BASIC Computer Games*.[11]

In his book, Ahl brought together for the first time in a single package some of the most popular programs on various time-sharing systems. Many of these were simple number-guessing games with names like *BAGLES*, *BULCOW*, and *STARS*. Others were logic puzzles (*TOWER*); Nim variants

---

[9] Ibid.
[10] Ibid.
[11] Anderson, 1984, 72.

(*NIM*, *EVEN*, *23MTCH*); educational drills (*CHIEF*, *MATHD1*, *TRAIN*); and simple simulations of sports, board, dice, or casino games (*BASBAL*, *BASKET*, *BLKJAC*, *CHECKR*, *FOOTBL*, *MNOPLY*, *POKER*, *ROULET*, *TICTAC*, *YAHTZE*). Still others were not games at all, rendering character-based portraits of everything from Snoopy to the Playboy bunny or informing people on what day of the week they were born. Doug Dymet's *Hamurabi* was included, as were many games from Project Local such as *Civil War*, *King*, and *Lunar Lander*.[12] Finally, Ahl included the recently discovered *Star Trek*, which he dubbed *SPACWR*.

In early 1974, a Westinghouse employee named Bob Leedom discovered *SPACWR* in Ahl's book and implemented it on his company's Data General Nova 800 minicomputer. After converting it to Data General BASIC, Leedom and some of his friends improved the game. In the original, commands were entered by selecting a number, but Leedom replaced these with easy-to-remember three-letter combinations. He also improved navigation, maneuvering, and fire control and added movement to the Klingon ships. Finally, to add more flavor to the game he included status reports by crew members such as Spock and Uhura. Once this version was complete, Leedom sent a letter describing the game to one of the first nationwide personal computing newsletters, *People's Computing Company*, circulated from Menlo Park, California.[13]

***

People's Computing Company was the brainchild of Bob Albrecht, the person who informed Dale LaFrenz about BASIC at UHigh and one of the first people to bridge the gap between computing professionals and ordinary people. Albrecht first worked with computers at the Aeronautical Division of Honeywell in Minneapolis in the 1950s. He was an avid skier, so when the Burroughs Corporation had an opening in its computer division in Colorado, he moved west. After spending time at a Denver-based company called Martin Aerospace, he moved on to Control Data Corporation (CDC), which had just opened a new Denver office.[14]

One of Albrecht's jobs at CDC was teaching programming to new hires who had received insufficient instruction prior to joining the company. In spring 1962, he had a life-changing experience when asked to speak to the

---

[12] Identified as *HMRABI*, *CIVILW*, *KING*, and *ROCKET*, respectively.

[13] "Star Trek," Games of Fame.

[14] John Markoff, *What the Doormouse Said: How the Sixties Counterculture Shaped the Personal Computing Industry* (New York: Viking, 2005), 205–206.

math club at George Washington High School. At the end of his presentation, he asked the students if they would be interested in learning programming and was shocked by their enthusiastic response. He began teaching
students how to program on a CDC 160, one of the earliest minicomputers, and grew impressed at how easily students took to programming compared to his employee trainees. In the process, he discovered a new calling of
empowering students to work with computers.[15]

In 1963, CDC purchased the computer division of California-based
Bendix Corporation. Bendix had been marketing a smaller, low-cost computer called the G-15 that CDC felt could be introduced to schools and
sent Albrecht to California to explore this possibility. While CDC ultimately
decided to phase out the G-15 instead, the trip to San Francisco gave Albrecht
the opportunity to meet Sid Fernbach at the Lawrence Livermore Laboratory.
An early computing pioneer, Fernbach believed both that computers would
come down drastically in price and that it was important to teach children
how to use them. This encounter helped crystallized Albrecht's desire to
make computing available to the masses.[16]

Soon after his meeting with Fernbach, Albrecht transferred back to CDC
headquarters in Minneapolis, but he spent most of his time on the road evangelizing computer use by teaching groups of students how to program and
emphasizing how quickly they were picking it up. He also learned of BASIC
and became one of its most enthusiastic adherents. Before the end of 1964, he
left CDC and turned to freelance writing. Figuring he might as well pursue
his new profession in a less frozen environment, he moved to San Francisco
in 1966.[17]

In the late 1960s, San Francisco was in the throes of the counterculture
movement. While this movement took many forms, some of which were
decidedly anti-technology, there existed a small group of technophiles who
took to the counterculture and its desire for equality, social justice, community activism, and human progress and saw the computer as a great equalizer
that would give ordinary people the power to change the world. Albrecht
fit right in with this ethos and became affiliated with the Midpeninsula
Free University, a commune that offered free instruction in anything that
an individual was interested in teaching. He also met a former economics
consultant with the Stanford Research Institute named Dick Raymond,

---

[15] Ibid, 206–207.
[16] Ibid, 207.
[17] Ibid, 207–208.

who was looking to establish a nonprofit foundation to explore alternative education. Albrecht helped Raymond establish the Portola Institute, which, among other endeavors, served as the publisher for noted counterculture figure Stewart Brand's *Whole Earth Catalog*.[18]

Through the Portola Institute, Albrecht connected with a Woodside High School teacher named LeRoy Finkel who shared his passion for educating students in computer use. Together, they founded a computer book publishing company called Dymax as a for-profit spin-off from Portola and wrote a series of books about programming in BASIC.[19] Initially headquartered in a warehouse in Redwood City, Dymax moved to a shopping mall in Menlo Park so it could establish a People's Computer Center (PCC) in which anyone could access a terminal hooked up to a time-sharing service. Soon after, Albrecht acquired a PDP-8 from DEC in trade for some technical writing so Dymax could run its own service.[20] By 1971, the PCC was a magnet for area youths interested in learning more about computing.[21]

Albrecht did not just want to inspire a few local students; he wanted to create a movement. He knew that time-sharing setups were becoming increasingly common in schools around the country, and he wanted to create a publication that would both document the rise of this new time-sharing revolution and bring together its disparate elements in order to further its growth. To that end, he launched a newsletter in October 1972 called the *People's Computer Company* named in honor of the counterculture rock icon Big Brother and the Holding Company. The counterculture ethos of the publication was evident from the cover of the first issue, which stated the purpose of the newsletter was to free the computers that were being used against people by the military-industrial complex and empower people to use them instead for the good of humanity.[22]

People's Computer Company embraced BASIC as the medium of this new computer revolution and from its inception featured listings for computer programs written in the language that subscribers could type into their own computers, many of which were games. As with *101 Basic Computer Games* most were simple logic puzzles or guessing games, but some were more interesting. The most noteworthy game to come out of the newsletter was a

[18] Ibid, 208–209.
[19] Levy, 2010, 168.
[20] Markoff, 2005, 211.
[21] Levy, 2010, 168.
[22] Ibid, 169.

hide-and-seek style game called *Hunt the Wumpus* programmed by Gregory Yob and published in November 1973.

Wumpus traces its origins to a series of hide-and-seek games using a Cartesian coordinate plain. The original version of the game, simply titled *Hide and Seek*, was created in 1972 by high school students taking part in a University of Pittsburgh computer education initiative called Project SOLO. This simple game presents a Cartesian coordinate grid upon which three points are occupied. The player must determine the *x*, *y* coordinates of each occupied spot. Each time the player types in a set of coordinates, he is given a clue as to how far away he is from one of the occupied spots on the grid. The goal is to find all three objects in as few moves as possible.

Bob Albrecht did his best to keep abreast of all the computer education projects across the United States and reported on them whenever he could. Indeed, the simulation programs created by the Huntington Project were featured in the inaugural issue of the *People's Computer Company*. Albrecht learned of the activities of Project SOLO as well and enjoyed the *Hide and Seek* game so much that he created two Cartesian coordinate games of his own, *Hurkle* and *Mugwump*, that he published in the third issue of his newsletter in 1973.[23] Yob was hanging around the PCC during this same time frame and observed people playing the game, but personally found it boring and decided to create something better.[24]

For his own stab at a hide-and-seek game, Yob moved from a flat, Cartesian plane to his favorite geometric solid, the dodecahedron. Each vertex of the shape represents a room in a series of interconnected caves, while each line denotes a path between two rooms. A creature called the "wumpus" inhabits this cave network and will devour the player if he is in the same room. The player wins through killing the wumpus by shooting an arrow into the room it inhabits. If the player shoots an arrow into an empty room, the wumpus moves to a new location. When the player enters a room, he is informed if the wumpus is in an adjacent room, so the goal of the player is to triangulate the position of the wumpus by mapping out the caves and only shooting when he is certain which room contains the beast. Other obstacles like bottomless pits and bats add additional challenge.[25]

Once *Hunt the Wumpus* hit the PCC time-sharing network, it quickly became the most popular program on the system. With games proving

---

[23] *People's Computer Company*, vol. 1, no. 3, 1973, 8.

[24] Gregory Yob, "Hunt the Wumpus," *Creative Computing*, September–October 1975, 51.

[25] Ibid, 51–52.

so successful, Albrecht published a book of computer games in December 1974 called *What to Do After You Hit Return*.[26] The book largely retread the same ground as Ahl, complete with its own versions of *Star Trek*, *Hamurabi*, *Civil War*, and *Lunar Lander*, but it also included games particular to the PCC like *Hunt the Wumpus*. Albrecht continued promoting interesting game developments in his newsletter as well, which is why Bob Leedom, wrote a letter to the *People's Computer Company* describing the improvements he made to the Mayfield *Star Trek* game.

Albrecht did not follow up with Leedom and continued to promulgate the original Mayfield *Star Trek* in later printings of *What to Do After You Hit Return*, but David Ahl did. Ahl subscribed to Albrecht's newsletter and had even included *Hurkle* and *Mugwump* in *101 BASIC Computer Games*. He read about Leedom's version of *Star Trek* in *People's Computing Company* and called the programmer to ask for a copy of the code to feature it in his newest publishing venture, *Creative Computing*.

In 1974, David Ahl finally left DEC for good. The impetus for his departure was a rejection by the Operations Committee of two prototypes he was working on that repackaged the PDP-8 and the PDP-11 in a manner that promoted their use as personal computers. The Operations Committee split right down the middle on the proposal, with the engineers feeling it was a wonderful idea and the marketers being completely against it. It fell to Ken Olsen to break the tie, and he turned it down because he did not see value in marketing a minicomputer for use by a single individual when the entire industry was embracing the idea of universal access to time-sharing terminals.[27]

Ahl moved to Morristown, NJ, and took a job with AT&T as its education marketing manager, but he had no intention of leaving his personal computing evangelism behind. At the National Computer Conference in June 1974, he announced his intention to publish a new magazine called *Creative Computing*. While several computer trade publications existed, hobbyist electronics magazines often covered developments in computing, and a handful of newsletters like the *People's Computer Company* circulated, *Creative Computing* would be the first magazine dedicated solely to personal computer use by hobbyists and enthusiasts.[28]

---

[26] *What to Do After You Hit Return or P.C.C.'s First Book of Computer Games* (Menlo Park, CA: People's Computer Company, 1974).

[27] Anderson, 1984, 72.

[28] Ibid.

Ahl promoted the magazine throughout the summer, and by 1974, he had netted 600 subscribers. Rather than print just 600 copies of the first issue, Ahl deliberately overprinted to the tune of 8,000 copies and sent the extra 7,400 to libraries and school systems at no charge.[29] Officially dated December 1974, the inaugural issue featured articles describing how computers were being used around the country, suggestions for new ways to use computers, reviews of computer-related products, and a type-in listing for a game called *Depth Charge* that played like the old hide-and-seek games except on a cube rather than a flat plane. Subsequent issues continued to feature new games, and the Leedom version of *Star Trek* was featured in the fourth issue in May 1975 as *Super Star Trek*.

Circulation numbers remained low for *Creative Computing* over those first few issues and only reached 2,500 by August 1975. Soon after, subscriptions skyrocketed, so that by 1978 the magazine had over 60,000 subscribers and reached nearly $1 million in revenue, allowing Ahl to quit his day job at AT&T to devote his full attention to the magazine.[30] The reason for this windfall was that by 1978 computing was no longer solely the purview of the student in the computer lab or the enthusiast who lived near a time-sharing center, for computers had finally entered the home.

---

[29] Ibid, 72–74.
[30] Ibid, 74.

16

Micro Machines

On July 18, 1968, a new semiconductor firm called NM Electronics incorporated in Silicon Valley. The founders were two of the "Traitorous Eight" who left Shockley Semiconductor to establish Fairchild Semiconductor a decade before: integrated circuit co-inventor and Fairchild general manager Robert Noyce and Fairchild director of R&D Gordon Moore. Key financial support came once again from Arthur Rock, who became the company's chairman of the board.[1] Unhappy with their generic name, Noyce and Moore soon renamed the company by combining the words "integrated electronics" to form Intel Corporation.

When Fairchild Semiconductor was established in 1957, it was technically an independent company founded with an investment from Fairchild Camera & Instrument (FCI). FCI controlled the company through a voting trust and retained the right to purchase it any time before it achieved three straight years of earnings of $300,000.[2] The company exercised that right in September 1959.[3] FCI president John Carter invested in Fairchild Semiconductor because he felt his company had become too dependent on defense contracts that had grown scarce since the end of the Korean War, and he looked to diversify into a wide range of new fields.[4] By 1965, Fairchild Semiconductor dominated the transistor business due to its invention of the planar process, but most of its profits were squandered to buy companies in fields ranging from printing supplies to home movie cameras that were not so successful.[5]

---

[1] Malone, 2014, 51
[2] Berlin, 2005, 88–89.
[3] Ibid, 112.
[4] Ibid, 84.
[5] Ibid, 120.

In 1966, Fairchild Semiconductor began to fall apart. Years of failing to reinvest profits into the company left its manufacturing facilities woefully underequipped, so as demand for semiconductors began to rise on the back of UHF televisions and the space program, Fairchild found itself unable to keep up. Worse, FCI refused to grant stock options or other incentives to top employees, who began leaving to join one of the many semiconductor companies popping up all over the Valley to meet the burgeoning demand for silicon.[6] Although FCI relented and began offering options after the defection of Charlie Sporck to National Semiconductor in early 1967, managers at Fairchild Semiconductor were so fed up with their parent company by this point that it did little to stem the tide.

In 1967, FCI posted its first loss in a decade as John Carter's poor management finally caught up with the firm. The FCI board formed a committee to evaluate the financial performance of the company, and Carter resigned before it could oust him. Richard Hodgson, the FCI executive principally responsible for the deal establishing Fairchild Semiconductor, succeeded him, but was himself quickly fired in February 1968 after the same committee that drove out Carter convinced Sherman Fairchild made a mistake in appointing Hodgson because they did not approve of his plans for growing the firm.[7]

In 1965, Robert Noyce had been elevated to a group vice presidency overseeing multiple divisions of FCI. Over the next few years, he lobbied management to restructure the entire organization around semiconductors and shed most of the other subsidiaries that had performed so poorly. As the leader of FCI's most profitable division, many predicted Noyce would be given the chance to implement his plan as Fairchild's next CEO, but the board passed him over, citing his relative inexperience in a high-level management position. This was the last straw for Noyce, who convinced Moore to leave Fairchild Semiconductor so they could establish Intel together.[8]

Meanwhile, the time-sharing terminal business was entering a new phase. At MIT's long-running Project MAC, the prevailing consensus in the late 1960s was that user access to a time-sharing mainframe would be enhanced by CRT displays. Therefore, the graphics research group of the project worked with the school's Electronic Systems Laboratory under the leadership of computer graphics pioneer John Ward to develop a cheap CRT terminal. They achieved

---

[6] Malone, 2014, 29–31.

[7] Bo Lojek, *History of Semiconductor Engineering* (New York: Springer, 2007), 159–160.

[8] Berlin, 2005, 150–153.

a breakthrough after discovering a new type of storage tube developed by oscilloscope manufacturer Tektronix in 1968 that used two electron guns to create a form of screen memory. Project MAC incorporated the tube into its new Advanced Remote Display Station (ARDS), the first effective low-cost graphical computer terminal.[9] Tektronix was so impressed that it released a commercial terminal based on the ARDS in 1969, the Tektronix 4002.

While the Tektronix storage tube method could create intricate images on a screen, it suffered from numerous limitations. One of the most significant was that it could not scroll characters, as redrawing the screen was an all-or-nothing proposition. While later Tektronix terminals implemented the ability to scroll a tiny portion of the screen at the bottom of the display, this limitation made storage-tube-based terminals unsuited for replacing the industry standard ASR-33 teletype terminal for basic input and output. The ASR-33 suffered from its own drawbacks, however, as it was slow and noisy and consumed reams of paper. In 1968, a company emerged that offered a new solution for the terminal industry.

NASA engineers Phil Ray and Gus Roche established the Computer Terminal Corporation (CTC) after sensing that with the moon landings imminent their engineering work at the government agency was reaching its natural conclusion. Ray had recently read an article about one of the first LSI shift registers and realized integrated circuits were about to become both far cheaper and more versatile. He convinced Roche they should go into business together to create a product incorporating microchips. Unsure what product to build around an LSI at first, they found their niche when an acquaintance informed them the Associated Press was searching for a CRT-based replacement for its teletypes.[10]

The main stumbling blocks in creating a decent CRT terminal had been the lack of cost-effective memory, both for the storing alpha-numeric characters and for drawing the screen. The arrival of LSI technology changed that. Datapoint contracted with TI for the first practical character generator chip to hit the market and learned from a sales rep about a new 256-bit shift register developed by Fairchild that was being second sourced to the new Intel Corporation. These chips formed the heart of the Datapoint 3300 that CTC released in October 1969. While not the first CRT terminal, the 3300 featured a sharp, flicker-free screen in contrast to most existing

[9] "Project MAC Progress Report V: July 1967–July 1968," Massachusetts Institute of Technology, c.1968, 72–77.

[10] Wood, 2012, chap. 2.

models that were fuzzy and jittery. It could also scroll and accommodate a 72-column display rather than the typical 40, making it compatible with the industry standard ASR-33.[11]

The arrival of low-cost CRT terminals spurred the creation of new computer games featuring proper graphics. At Dartmouth, Tektronix provided one of its first 4002 terminals to the DTSS in 1969.[12] One of the first individuals to work with the display was a physics professor named Arthur Luehrmann who believed computer graphics to be a useful learning tool. In addition to various modeling programs, he developed a game called *Pot Shot*, in which two players control artillery batteries on either side of the screen.[13] The players take turns shooting at each other, recalculating the angle of their guns before each shot. A mountain stands between the two players that can be set to a varying height, and the game calculates wind speed and direction as well.[14] Tektronix began using the program as a demo for its terminals under the name *Artillery*,[15] after which it spread rapidly.

Another terminal that prominently featured a game was the GT40 released by DEC in 1973. DEC contracted a former employee named Jack Burness to write a demo for the terminal highlighting its capability to display line art and update the screen in real time. An avid space program aficionado, Burness had been exposed to one of the many variants of Jim Storer's text-based *Lunar Lander* program and thought a graphical version would be a good fit for the GT40. Burness visited MIT, where the actual lunar module was partially designed, to acquire accurate data on the weight, fuel burn rate, and other characteristics of the actual module. He then created a lunar landscape displayed from a side view full of jagged peaks and small valleys upon which the player attempts to land his module in real time by managing burn rate, velocity, and fuel as in the text version. Bundled with the GT40 under the name *Moonlander*, it soon became nearly as popular as its text-based cousins.[16]

***

With the success of the 3300, Ray and Roche felt the next logical step was to emulate the IBM 029 keypunch, the primary device used to create

---

[11] Ibid, chap. 3.

[12] "Tektronix Ad," *Scientific American*, March 1976, back matter.

[13] David Ahl, "Editorial," *Creative Computing Video & Arcade Games*, Spring 1983, 4.

[14] "Letters to the Editor," *People's Computer Company*, September 1974, 22.

[15] Arthur Hu, "How I Helped Create Angry Birds," Blogspot, May 9, 2011, http://hu1st.blogspot.com/2011/05/how-i-helped-create-angry-birds.html.

[16] Edwards, 2009.

punched cards for IBM mainframes. The CTC engineers also felt it would be worthwhile to incorporate additional functions not possible on a standard keypunch like basic error correction and information validation. Adding these features meant that the proposed Datapoint 2200 could not just be a hardwired CRT replica of another device like its predecessor, but would need to be reprogrammable to take on additional tasks. In effect, this so-called "intelligent terminal" would itself be a small computer.[17]

CTC hired electrical engineers Harry Pyle and Vic Poor to layout the processor for the 2200. Ray and Roche insisted the resulting terminal be roughly the same size as an IBM Selectric typewriter to appeal to corporate America, meaning the design needed to be slimmed down to as few components as possible. Poor approached Intel to help design chips for the machine, at which point Intel engineer Stan Mazor suggested doing away with TTL hardware and producing a full-fledged 8-bit processor on a single chip.[18] This idea came to Mazor because he was already working on a similar design for the Japanese calculator manufacturer Busicom.

In 1968, Busicom had begun designing a new desktop calculator called the 141-PF. Unlike other calculators of the time that functioned entirely through hardwired logic, the 141-PF was designed to execute many tasks in software so the hardware could be easily adapted for use in other projects. This approach would have been unthinkable less than a decade before, but in 1964 a new transistor fabrication process called metal oxide semiconductor (MOS) entered commercial use that offered the possibility, at least in theory, of designing a single microchip divided into multiple regions dedicated to an arithmetic unit, a control unit, I/O management, RAM and ROM memory caches, and power control, essentially a complete computer architecture on a single sliver of silicon.[19]

By 1969, multiple technology giants from RCA to IBM were attempting to develop this theoretical microprocessor, but Busicom approached Intel to complete the 141-PF, both because it was one of the few semiconductor firms not already committed to a calculator company and because the Japanese electronics community held Robert Noyce in particularly high esteem for his role in the invention of the integrated circuit. Busicom did not believe semiconductor technology was yet sufficiently advanced to reduce a computer to

---

[17] Wood, 2012, chap. 4.

[18] Ibid, chap. 5.

[19] The MOS process was first developed at Bell Labs in 1959, but the first commercial MOS IC was not released until 1964.

a single chip, but it hoped Intel could provide a microprocessor system spread across a dozen custom chips.[20]

Intel assigned an engineer named Marcian "Ted" Hoff to oversee the project, who quickly concluded it would be an abject failure. By the time Busicom delivered the final specs for the calculator, it had morphed into an unwieldy 12-chip monstrosity to carry out a wide array of special functions, each of which incorporated five times the number of transistors found on a typical calculator chip. Inspired by the PDP-8, which sported only a small instruction set but could be programmed to undertake a wide variety of tasks, Hoff proposed a general-purpose design based around a single-chip CPU and three support chips that could carry out complex instructions through subroutines rather than specialized hardware. Together with Mazor, who had greater software expertise, he developed the basic framework for a 4-bit computing chip.[21]

After working in near-complete secrecy for several months, Hoff presented his microprocessor concept to Busicom, which gave its approval in October 1969. Hoff and Mazor had to be pulled off the project soon after to deal with problems in Intel's memory business, so design had not actually begun by the time Poor and Mazor discussed an 8-bit processor for Datapoint.[22] Once again, Mazor and Hoff defined the specs for the chip, after which Intel hired Hal Feeney in March 1970 to design it. Though it was conceived second, the Datapoint chip became the first microprocessor to enter the design phase as the 1201 microprocessor.[23]

Progress on the 1201 was sporadic at first due to resources being diverted to the stalled Busicom project. In April 1970, Intel lured Italian engineer Federico Faggin away from Fairchild to complete the 4-bit chip, which it dubbed the 1202. A few days later, a Busicom representative named Masatoshi Shima came to Intel to review progress on the 1202. Expecting a nearly finished project, Shima was horrified to discover that design work had barely even begun. He remained in California to assist Faggin in completing the chip, which was rebranded the 4004 after Faggin argued the chip should have a more distinctive name.[24] Delivered on an exclusive basis to Busicom in March 1971, the 4004 became generally available in November after the collapse of the desktop calculating market led Busicom to renegotiate its

---

[20] Berlin, 2005, 183–185.
[21] Malone, 2014, 148–151.
[22] Ibid, 151–153.
[23] Wood, 2012, chap. 6.
[24] Ibid.

agreement with Intel to allow the semiconductor company to market the chip to other companies.[25]

Once the 4004 finally hit the market, Feeney concentrated on completing the 1201, which debuted in April 1972 as the 8008 microprocessor to draw attention to the fact it incorporated twice as many bits as the 4004.[26] By then, CTC had long since completed the prototype of the 2200 using a TTL-based processor after deciding not to wait for Intel to finish the 8008. Released in June 1970, the 2200 was billed as a terminal, but was in fact capable of performing many operations without being hooked into a mainframe and was therefore the first example of a new computer category: the microcomputer.[27]

The announcement of the 8008 led other organizations to start work on their own microcomputer projects. In 1972, a researcher named Bill Pentz at Sacramento State University led a team that built a small computer intended for storing medical records nicknamed the Sac State 8008, but it never moved beyond the prototype phase after being deemed not cost effective.[28] That same year, French computer scientist François Gernelle accepted a commission from the *Institut National de la Recherche Agronimique* (INRA) to develop a microcomputer for process control in crop evapotranspiration measurements.[29] The INRA microcomputer was commercialized by Gernelle and his business partner, a French entrepreneur of Vietnamese descent named André Truong Trong Thi. The duo released the computer through their R2E company as the Micral N in early 1973, but it sold few units. While intelligent terminals like the Datapoint 2200 experienced success, the 8008 was slow, inefficient, and difficult to program effectively and therefore too limited to form the heart of a useful microcomputer for research or business purposes. Consequently, the development of the earliest commercially successful microcomputers were undertaken not by a university research team or a major corporation, but rather by a series of small companies established to cater to the hobbyist electronics market.

***

[25] Malone, 2014, 170–171.

[26] Ibid, 182.

[27] Wood, 2012, chap. 7.

[28] Daniel Terdiman, "Inside the World's Long-Lost First Microcomputer," CNET, January 8, 2010, https://www.cnet.com/news/inside-the-worlds-long-lost-first-microcomputer.

[29] "How Agronomy and IT Made the World's First Microcomputer," INRA, April 18, 2016, http://institut.inra.fr/en/Overview/Historical-milestones/1970s/Toutes-les-actualites/How-agronomy-and-IT-made-the-world-s-first-microcomputer.

By 1970, the hobbyist community was mostly involved in HAM radio operation, model rocketry, or soldering together kits of radio transceivers, calculators, remote control cars, and similar electronic devices. To keep up to date on the latest developments in this admittedly niche field, hobbyists relied on a small number of periodicals that advertised the latest electronic kits, gave tips on building and operating devices, profiled hobbyists and their exploits around the country, and provided a forum for enthusiasts to share their own tips and opinions.

With the arrival of the first microprocessors, electronics hobbyists began expressing interest in a computer kit in the hobbyist magazines. In September 1973, one of these publications, *Radio-Electronics*, published an article from frequent contributor and Goodyear Aerospace engineer Don Lancaster describing a low-cost kit of his own design called the TV Typewriter that converted a standard television set into a 32-column computer terminal. While merely a terminal to hook into a time-sharing service, the arrival of the TV Typewriter helped raise demand for a computer kit to a fever pitch.[30]

At *Popular Electronics*, the hobbyist magazine with the largest subscriber base, new editorial director Arthur Salsberg saw the TV Typewriter article and vowed to do it one better by delivering the first computer kit. He and technical editor Les Solomon began scouring their contacts for a suitable design, but every submission they received was either poorly made or not capable enough to be of interest. Solomon began exhorting his best regular contributors to submit designs and finally acquired a kit with potential from a small company called Micro Instrumentation Telemetry Systems (MITS).[31]

Air Force officers Ed Roberts, Forest Mims III, Stan Cagle, and Robert Zaller founded MITS in Albuquerque in 1968 as a side business to produce small kits for model rocket hobbyists. In 1969, Roberts bought out his partners and moved the company into calculators with the intent of involving the hobbyist community in the burgeoning market by selling programmable calculators in kit form. By 1974, the calculator price wars had left MITS on the brink of bankruptcy, so Roberts shifted his focus to a computer kit.[32] His timing was perfect: in April 1974, Intel released the Faggin-designed 8080 microprocessor that corrected the more serious flaws of the 8008 and appeared viable for a home computer. Other kit makers avoided the new processor because of a prohibitively expensive $360 per unit price, but Roberts

---

[30] Paul Freiberger and Michael Swaine, *Fire in the Valley: The Making of the Personal Computer*, 2nd ed. (New York: McGraw Hill, 2000), kindle, chap. 2.

[31] Ibid.

[32] Forest M. Mims III, "The Altair Story," *Creative Computing*, November 1974, 17–26.

committed to a high-volume order and received a discounted price of $75 a chip.[33]

The computer was still far from completion when *Popular Electronics* began its search for a kit, and Solomon decided to go with an 8008-based "computer trainer" created by a man named Jerry Ogdin. His plans changed in July 1974 when *Radio-Electronics* scooped his magazine once again with an 8008 kit computer called the Mark-8 from Jonothan Titus. *Popular Electronics* still had an opening to innovate, however, as the Mark-8 was not a complete self-contained kit, but rather a booklet that described how to assemble a computer by combining components the builder would have to locate and acquire himself. *Popular Electronics* could still debut the first fully contained computer kit, but Salsberg and Solomon dumped the Ogdin project because a competing 8008 product would not make the big splash they desired.[34]

At this point, Solomon turned to Roberts and asked if his 8080-based machine could be priced at under $500 and be ready in time for the January issue, typically the company's best-seller of the year. Roberts agreed to the conditions and began designing the computer in earnest. Many of his design choices were guided by existing minicomputer design, especially his desire for expandability by plugging circuit boards into the motherboard in order to expand the memory or allow for new operations. With this goal in mind, fellow engineer Bill Yates laid out the motherboard using a 100-channel bus to allow signals from up to 16 daughter boards to reach the processor.[35] Roberts, Yates, and a third designer named Jim Bybe were able to complete the computer by October 1974. It went on sale that December. Originally the kit was designated the PE-8, but Solomon thought the name boring. His assistant technical editor, John McVeigh, provided the solution when he opined that the launch of the computer was akin to a stellar event and should

---

[33] Freiberger and Swaine, 2000, chap. 2. Some sources indicate that Roberts received such a good deal by accepting cosmetically blemished chips, but this appears to have been nothing more than a rumor started by some Intel sales reps to explain to disgruntled customers why Roberts got such a low price.

[34] Ibid. Technically, one fully contained computer kit had reached the market by this point, the SCELBI-8H, which was first advertised in a publication called *QST* in March 1974. The computer was built by Nat Wadsworth, a General Datacomm employee who learned of the 8008 microprocessor in 1973 at an Intel seminar. He established Scelbi that August, which stood for "Scientific, Electronic, and Biological." The computer did not sell well largely because Wadsworth could not dedicate much time to promoting it do to health problems. Stephen B. Gray, "The Early Days of Personal Computers," *Creative Computing*, November 1984, 12–13.

[35] Freiberger and Swaine, 2000, chap. 2.

be named after a star. He chose the 12th brightest star as seen from Earth, Altair.[36]

Priced at $397 and backed by the *Popular Electronics* January 1975 cover story, the Altair was soon the darling of the electronic kit industry. Despite many limitations, including faulty parts, difficult assembly, a primitive interface consisting merely of switches and lights, and a lack of memory that required all programs to be reentered every time the computer was shut off, the hobbyist community, hungry for personal computers, eagerly embraced the new machine. Originally guaranteeing delivery of each computer sold within 60 days, Roberts was soon just scrambling to keep pace with orders as news of the kit spread through the hobbyist community by word of mouth. By February 1975, MITS had already received 1,000 kit orders. By May, over 2,500 computers had been delivered.[37] Three months later, the number doubled to 5,000.[38] MITS went from a company of around ten employees and a $250,000 debt to a profitable concern that employed over 90 people and still had difficulty meeting demand.

***

As the Altair install base grew, several entrepreneurs realized a new industry was taking shape around the machine. One of the earliest companies formed to serve the Altair market was Micro-Soft, established by Paul Allen and Bill Gates in April 1975. Natives of Seattle, Washington, Gates and Allen were first exposed to computers as teenagers in 1968 when Lakeside, the private preparatory school they attended, leased a teletype machine to access a GE-635.[39] Gates, the brilliant and competitive son of a lawyer and a prominent civic activist, took an immediate interest in programming in BASIC on the teletype.[40] Allen, two years older, was already interested in computers before the terminal arrived but never had the opportunity to program on one before. They met in the teletype room and bonded over a shared love of programming.[41]

---

[36]Mims, 1984, 27. A more fanciful story, almost certainly false, relating to the naming of the Altair often told by Solomon himself claimed that the name came from Solomon's daughter after she watched an episode of *Star Trek* in which the Altair star system was mentioned.

[37]"MITS Altair Ad," *Digital Design*, June 1975.

[38]"Are They Real?" *Byte*, October 1975, 81.

[39]Paul Allen, *Idea Man: A Memoir by the Co-Founder of Microsoft* (New York: Portfolio/Penguin, 2011), 27.

[40]Stephen Manes, *Gates: How Microsoft's Mogul Reinvented an Industry – and Made Himself the Richest Man in America*, (New York: Touchstone, 1994), kindle, Chap. 2.

[41]Allen, 2011, 1.

The mother of one of Bill Gates's classmates, Monique Rona, was also the corporate secretary for a new commercial time-sharing service called the Computer Center Corporation, or C-Cubed. The company purchased a DEC PDP-10 mainframe but was not required to pay for it during an "acceptance test" period during which the corporation made sure the computer met its specifications. Rona knew about the student programming group at Lakeside and wrote to the school to enlist the aid of some students to come in on Saturdays to hunt for bugs in exchange for free computer time. Gates and Allen signed on and put the machine through its paces until the trial period ended. Afterwards, Lakeside switched to C-Cubed for its time-sharing needs, and Gates and his friends continued to program on the PDP-10 at the school. As they now had to pay for the privilege of using the computer, they hacked into C-Cubed's system to gain free time. When they were discovered, they were banned from using the computer for an entire summer.[42]

C-Cubed went bankrupt in early 1970, so Lakeside contracted with another time-sharing service. The new organization did not have a PDP-10, which Gates and his friends preferred, but Gates soon discovered an Oregon company called Information Sciences, Inc. with a PDP-10, and the group once again hacked into a system for free computer time. Once they were caught, they took a different approach by offering to create a payroll program for the company under the guise of the Lakeside Programmers Group consisting of Gates, Allen, and two other students. The group managed to complete the program in late 1971, by which time Allen had left for college.[43]

When Intel released the 8008 microprocessor, Allen convinced Gates they should build a computer system around it. After a year of work, they completed a traffic analysis machine in 1972 and established a company called Traf-O-Data to sell it. The company lurched along until 1974 but experienced little success. In fall 1974, Gates matriculated to Harvard, which kept him close to Allen, who was working for the computer company Honeywell in Boston. In December, Allen saw the ad for the Altair in *Popular Electronics*, and the duo resolved to create a version of BASIC for the machine.[44]

Gates called Ed Roberts at MITS and lied that he and Allen had a completed Altair BASIC ready to go that they could demonstrate in two or three weeks. After six weeks furiously coding on an emulator, Allen delivered the final product to MITS personally and was relieved to see it worked on an

[42]Manes, chap. 2.
[43]Ibid, chap. 3.
[44]Ibid, chap. 4.

actual Altair. A month later, Allen accepted a position at MITS as director of software.[45] In July 1975, Gates and Allen signed a formal licensing contract with MITS, which required them to come up with a name for their partnership. They chose Micro-Soft.[46]

While Micro-Soft established a niche in software, most companies that entered the Altair market did so through hardware, particularly expansion boards. Expandability had been one of Roberts' primary mandates for the computer during its design, but he had planned to keep the board business for himself. When the initial MITS memory expansion boards did not work properly, however, the market was left wide open for competition. The first person to step into that void was Bob Marsh, one of several crucial links between the computer evangelism birthed out of the San Francisco counterculture movement, the hobbyist electronics community, and the newly emerging microcomputer industry.

An engineering student at UC Berkeley, Marsh dropped out in 1965 to travel Europe, but ultimately returned to finish his degree. In 1971, he met a fellow engineer named Gary Ingram with whom he became involved in the hobbyist scene. Ingram also helped him get a job at an importer of dictation equipment called Dictran International, where he rose to the rank of chief engineer. By 1974, Marsh was unemployed, but still active in the hobbyist community. He was particularly interested in computer terminals after being inspired by the Lancaster TV Typewriter. Therefore, he answered a call for interested parties to meet and discuss a terminal project being organized by counterculture figure and computer evangelist Lee Felsenstein.[47]

A Philadelphia native, Felsenstein followed a similar path to Marsh: enrolling in, dropping out of, and ultimately graduating from UC Berkeley with a degree in electrical engineering. Indeed, the two men overlapped at the school. Unlike Marsh, Felsenstein also became heavily involved in the Free Speech Movement and served as the "military editor" for the counterculture newspaper *Berkeley Barb*. In 1971, Felsenstein became affiliated with an initiative called Project One established by architect Ralph Scott and housed in a San Francisco warehouse. This project was a technological commune in which professionals could teach courses on any subject they desired and demystify technology for the general public. Felsenstein joined

[45] Ibid, chap. 5.
[46] Allen, 2011, 90–91.
[47] Freiberger and Swaine, 2000, chap. 4.

a group called Resource One within the commune to operate a time-shared XDS-940 computer donated by Transamerica Corporation.[48]

In 1973, Felsenstein developed an offshoot of Resource One called Community Memory that installed free time-sharing terminals in the San Francisco area on which people could post notices and exchange messages, essentially the first electronic bulletin board system. These terminals frequently broke down, however, and were not user friendly for the untrained. Felsenstein endeavored to build a more user-friendly CRT terminal he dubbed the Tom Swift Terminal, hence the meeting he organized that Marsh attended. The terminal project never went anywhere, but Marsh did talk with Felsenstein about establishing a company together to build electronic products. Felsenstein was uninterested in a partnership, but he agreed to split the rent on a garage while taking on freelance projects. Marsh, meanwhile, planned to build digital clocks. Both their plans changed with the announcement of the Altair in January 1975.[49]

The arrival of the Altair sent shockwaves through the San Francisco computing evangelist community and particularly excited a peace activist and computer instructor named Fred Moore. While Felsenstein was building Community Memory, Moore was taking a similar approach to community activism minus the computers. Using the *Whole Earth Catalog* as a base, he connected people with similar interests by maintaining a mailing list based on which concepts in the catalog appealed to them. He ultimately decided he would need to computerize the whole system, so he began learning how to program by hanging around the Stanford Medical School computing center while simultaneously attempting to acquire his own computer for his information network. His search eventually led to Bob Albrecht, who agreed to let him harness the resources of the PCC.[50]

Moore was not a particularly adept programmer, but while at the PCC he did acquire Albrecht's passion for teaching young people about computers. He soon became a regular fixture at the organization, taught classes on programming, and helped with other projects.[51] As he took on more responsibility, tensions between him and Albrecht flared due to Albrecht's desire to retain complete control. This resulted in a split in 1975 in which Albrecht retained the publishing of the *People's Computer Company* newsletter, while

---

[48] Levy, 2010, 154–161.
[49] Freiberger and Swaine, 2000, chap. 4.
[50] Markoff, 2005, 295.
[51] Levy, 2010, 198.

the computer education and outreach portion of the organization became a new corporation called the People's Computer Center.[52]

After learning of the Altair, Moore wanted to offer a set of classes on building a microcomputer. He remained reliant on Albrecht for funding after the corporate split, however, and their relationship was continuing to deteriorate. Therefore, when Moore broached his class, Albrecht refused to fund it. Undaunted, Moore decided to cultivate a new enthusiast community, and in early 1975 he circulated a flyer with a simple message: "Are you building your own computer? If so, you might like to come to a gathering of people with like-minded interests."[53]

The first meeting of the Amateur Computer Users Group, soon better known as the Homebrew Computer Club, was held on March 5, 1975, in the garage of Gordon French, another PCC associate Albrecht originally hired to write some assembly language programs, but who like Moore had fallen out with him over the management of the organization. Despite the animosity, Albrecht attended the meeting and displayed his recently acquired Altair computer. Felsenstein and Marsh also attended the meeting, and Marsh was so inspired by the Altair that he decided on the spot to form a company to create expansion boards for the computer. He corralled Gary Ingram into his scheme, and the duo formed Processor Technology in April 1975 to produce two I/O boards and a 4K memory expansion board for the Altair.[54]

Expansion boards became a lucrative business for Processor Tech and several other companies, much to the chagrin Roberts. To counter these interloper companies, MITS took several steps including attempting to shut them out of Altair shows and dealers and only selling Micro-Soft BASIC as part of a bundle with a memory board. The former efforts were unsuccessful, while the latter merely led to widespread piracy of BASIC.[55]

***

The Altair was the best-selling microcomputer of 1976, but by the middle of the year MITS faced competition from over a dozen kit producers based all over the country. Most of the computers they released copied the bus structure of the Altair, eventually designated the S-100, thus creating an early industry standard. These firms were generally established by hobbyists and released kits for that community, and none of them threatened the

---

[52] Ibid, 299.

[53] Ibid, 300–302.

[54] Freiberger and Swaine, 2000, chap. 4.

[55] Ibid, chap. 2.

Altair's market share as they faced many of the same problems that had previously plagued MITS such as manufacturing difficulties, shipping delays, and defective parts. MITS did not face a true competitor in the computer marketplace until a company called IMS Associates appeared that combined more professional management with a desire to expand outside of the hobbyist market.

IMS founder Bill Millard started in the computer business as a sales rep for IBM before taking a government job in the late 1960s as manager of data processing for the city of San Francisco. Millard founded IMS in 1973 as a consulting firm that helped businesses determine their computing needs and match them with appropriate hardware and software solutions. The company took a different turn in early 1975 when a New Mexico auto dealer asked Millard to find a low-cost computer system on which he could do his accounting.[56]

Learning of the new Altair, Millard hatched a scheme to buy the cheap microcomputers in bulk from MITS and assemble them for resale to businesses. When Roberts appeared unwilling or unable to provide Millard what he needed, he established his own computer company, IMSAI Manufacturing, as a subsidiary of IMS. The result of these efforts was the IMSAI 8080, an Altair clone designed by Joe Killian and released in late 1975 that started to reach the market in mass quantities by fall 1976. While still a kit like the Altair, the IMSAI 8080 was targeted at businesses rather than hobbyists and featured several enhancements over its competitor, including a better power supply and more expansion slots. With a professional management team and an enthusiastic sales force, IMSAI became the number two computer company behind MITS.[57]

As IMSAI and other companies entered the market with computers based on the Altair bus, Roberts found his grip on the expansion board market slipping even further. He did authorize one company to create its own board in this period, however, because it offered a graphical capability for the Altair. Cromenco was founded in 1974 by Stanford graduate students Harry Garland and Roger Melen who, like Roberts, were regular contributors to *Popular Electronics*. As an inner circle contributor to the magazine, Melen saw the first Altair computer in Solomon's basement before it was released and bought the second Altair that MITS sold. He and Garland began adapting a camera they had designed, called the Cyclops, to be compatible with

[56] Ibid, chap. 3.
[57] Ibid.

the computer with Roberts' blessing, but soon abandoned that project to create a circuit board they called the Dazzler that allowed the Altair to display graphics on a color television.[58]

Cromenco was not the only company to enter the Altair graphics market. Working as a contractor for Processor Tech, Lee Felsenstein developed a board for the Altair called the VDM-1 that outputted character-based black-and-white graphics and was announced at roughly the same time as the Dazzler.[59] He then answered a call from Les Solomon to complete the first "intelligent terminal" kit, a microcomputer that – unlike the Altair – would feature a keyboard and video output to a television right out of the box. The result was a Processor Tech kit called the Sol-20 that Solomon featured in the July 1976 issue of *Popular Electronics* before it became generally available in November.[60]

In addition to pioneering microcomputer graphics, Cromenco and Processor Technology also pioneered the sale of games for microcomputer platforms. From the beginning, games played an important role in promoting microcomputer sales as one of the few viable activities on the limited machines. Indeed, because MITS embraced BASIC through its partnership with Micro-Soft, a wide variety of games existed for the Altair from practically the moment it was released. Time-sharing classics like *Lunar Lander*, *Hunt the Wumpus*, *Hamurabi*, and *Star Trek* were easily adaptable to the array of microcomputers on the market, and David Ahl ensured these games remained in the public consciousness by pivoting his *Creative Computing* magazine toward microcomputer owners and continuing to push games within its pages. Both *101 BASIC Computer Games* and the PCC's competing *What to do After You Hit Return* also remained in print and provided dozens of additional options.

The release of the Dazzler display board and the Sol-20 with its built-in video capability spurred their creators, Cromenco and Processor Technology, to develop and sell their own games that not only took advantage of the displays, but could also be loaded into memory through cassettes or paper tape instead of having to be typed in by the user. Cromenco may have been the first company to offer individual games for sale when it began advertising a version of the PDP-1 classic *Spacewar!* on paper tape for the Dazzler in

[58] Ibid, chap. 5.
[59] Levy, 2010, 242–243.
[60] Ibid, 244–247.

October 1976 at a price of $15.00.[61] Meanwhile, Processor Tech began advertising programs written by a hobbyist named Steve Dompier in December 1976 for use with the Sol-20. Gamepac 1 included a program called *Target*, in which the player controls a gun battery at the bottom of the screen represented by an arrow and attempts to shoot down alien ships flying across the top of the screen represented by alphanumeric characters. Processor Tech also sold a second Dompier-created game called *Trek-80*, which was a real-time graphical variation of the Mayfield *Star Trek* game.[62]

The introduction of the microprocessor paved the way for small, affordable computers and teased a world in which complex simulations and games could be enjoyed in the comfort of one's own home. Early computer systems like the Altair and IMSAI were underpowered, however, and the earliest microcomputer games were barely distinguishable from the text-based games that preceded them on time-sharing networks. The microprocessor exerted a more immediate tangible impact on the coin-operated amusement industry, where the arrival of the Intel 4004 and 8080 processors allowed for new game possibilities in the mid-1970s.

---

[61] Keith Smith, "Preliminary Report: Was The Devil's Dungeon the First Commercial CRPG and What Was the First Commercial Microcomputer Game?" The Golden Age Arcade Historian, October 22, 2015, http://allincolorforaquarter.blogspot.com/2015/10/preliminary-report-was-devils-dungeon.html.

[62] "Sol Computer Ad," *Byte*, December 1976, 74–75.

17

Solid State of Mind

On September 26, 1974, Bally executive vice president of technology John Britz led a delegation to Milwaukee and was ushered into a room at the offices of Dave Nutting Associates containing two Bally *Flicker* pinball tables that Dave Nutting had received from the company the month before. The two tables looked identical save for one tiny detail: the typical scoring reels on one machine had been replaced by a readout composed of light-emitting diodes (LEDs). Nutting demonstrated both machines, noting how they played and behaved exactly the same. Then came the dramatic reveal as the games were opened, and the one with the LED readout contained just a small circuit board connected to a few wires as opposed to the rat's nest of wires, relays, steppers, and other parts one would expect to find in a pinball cabinet. The shocked Bally executives immediately began searching the room for the giant computer that must have been running this specially modified machine only to discover that all the components were arrayed on that single board inside the nearly empty cabinet. The future of pinball had arrived.

The *Flicker* demonstration came at the end of a period of transition for Dave Nutting. His original coin-operated amusement manufacturing company, Nutting Industries, entered bankruptcy in 1971 following the failure of its educational subsidiary,[1] after which he established a new firm with his head of manufacturing, Dan Winter, called Milwaukee Coin Industries or MCI.[2] The new company released an updated version of Nutting Industries' *Red Baron* filmstrip target shooting game called *Super Red Baron* that incor-

[1] Nutting, 2017.
[2] In *Cash Box*, Dave Nutting announced the move to MCI as merely a name change for Nutting Industries, but he has stated in more recent interviews that Nutting Industries went bankrupt and MCI was a separate company.

porated electronic sound alongside a few minor updates and subsequently developed several variations on the theme over the next two years with names like *Flying Ace*, *Blue Max*, and *Desert Fox*.[3]

The novelty game business proved volatile, so Nutting began searching for a steadier revenue source. Pinball was still considered the staple of the industry even with the advent of the first video boom and seemed a likely choice, but Nutting did not believe he could break the stranglehold of the big Chicago companies unless he came up with a novel approach. Therefore, he decided to explore a solid-state pinball design. Through his ill-fated Modec subsidiary at Nutting Industries, Nutting had experience deploying solid-state machines, so in late 1973 he asked one of his engineers, Duane Knudtson, to adapt that technology to create a solid-state version of MCI's latest game, *Airball*, a novelty piece in which the player guides a ball through various targets by manipulating a column of air. The prototype never worked properly, so the game was released using traditional electromechanical components instead.[4] Undeterred, Dave Nutting continued to attack the problem with a new hire named Jeff Frederiksen.

Born on July 5, 1944, Jeffrey Ellis Frederiksen attended St. Thomas College in Minnesota for three years as a math and physics major before transferring to the University of Milwaukee to pursue electrical engineering and computer science. He left school after a year to join the U.S. Air Force in 1966. Beginning his service as a communications technician, Frederiksen later became a keypunch operator for a mainframe on an Air Force base in southern Turkey. Frustrated by the lack of error-checking capability on the computer, he requested a program be created to handle the task. The base could not commit resources to the project, so a technician gave Frederiksen a programming handbook and told him to do it himself.[5]

Frederiksen left the Air Force in 1970 and took a job with a firm called Radio Communications as a technician repairing two-way radios while finishing his computer science degree part time at the University of Milwaukee. In 1973, while working for another communications firm called Ken-Com, he began consulting for MCI as it looked to diversify out of its filmstrip games into solid-state products. In October 1973, he joined MCI full time and designed a game called *The Safe*, in which the player turns the dial on

---

[3] Former MCI employees Keith Egging and Dan Winter remember MCI doing a limited run on a *Pong* clone as well, but this has not been corroborated by any other sources.

[4] Nutting, 1983, 570–572.

[5] Paul Thacker, "Jeff Frederiksen Interview (Part 1)," *Bally Alley*, September 29, 2011, http://www.ballyalley.com/ballyalley/interviews/Jeff_Frederiksen_Interview.txt.

a mockup of a safe door built into the cabinet in an attempt to crack the combination within a time limit.[6] Within three weeks of joining MCI, Dave Nutting asked him to start preliminary work on a solid-state pinball game and a solid-state update to the *IQ Computer*. Both would be powered by a microprocessor.[7]

By January 1974, Frederiksen's work on a solid-state game system had progressed sufficiently for him to convince Dave Nutting to buy an Intellec 4 development system from Intel so he could build a complete solid-state pinball hardware around a 4004 microprocessor. The Intellec was still relatively new and hard to come by, but Nutting secured one by convincing his Intel rep that his firm was an advanced R&D unit for Bally.[8] At this point, Frederiksen told Dave that continuing to work on both a pinball machine and a quiz game would not be possible, so they decided to concentrate on the *Super IQ Computer* because it could serve as a superior testbed for their theories on how to incorporate a 4004 into a coin-op machine. The quiz game was completed and demonstrated for Bally in June 1974, but the company was not interested in manufacturing the product.[9]

Soon after the Bally demonstration, Nutting found himself changing companies once again. Back in 1972, MCI's marketing director, John Ancona, suggested a new tactic to compensate for flagging sales of the company's novelty game products: emulating Aladdin's Castle by opening a chain of shopping mall arcades under the name Red Baron. Before long, MCI controlled roughly 20 arcades stretching from Ohio in the east to Arizona in the west. By mid-1974 these arcades had proven so profitable that the company's investors decided to terminate game development and transform MCI into an arcade chain.[10] An operating company did not require a game designer, so Nutting was asked to leave.[11] He formed a new partnership with Frederiksen called Dave Nutting Associates (DNA) to continue designing games, which he funded by entering into a development contract with Bally.[12] For the next three months, the solid-state pinball system became the primary focus at DNA, with the ultimate goal of presenting a complete working system to its new corporate benefactor.

---

[6] Jeff Frederiksen, testimony, Bally Manufacturing v. Williams Electronics, No. 78-2246 (N.D. Ill), January 3, 1983, 63–64.

[7] Nutting, 1983, 586.

[8] Donovan, 2010, chap. 4.

[9] Nutting, 1983, 587–590.

[10] Donovan, 2010, chap. 4.

[11] Nutting, 2017.

[12] Nutting, 1983, 582.

While the Bally executives who attended the *Flicker* demonstration in September were impressed by the Nutting system, the company ultimately decided it should develop its own solid-state hardware in house rather than pay DNA a royalty. Therefore, nutting needed a new partner to bring a solid-state game to market and turned to John Bilotta, a distributor who had been mentoring him in the coin-op business going back to the introduction of the *IQ Computer* in 1967. Bilotta introduced him to an Arizona company called Mirco Games.[13]

Mirco Games was a subsidiary of an electronic testing equipment manufacturer called Mirco founded by former General Electric employees John Walsh, Bruce Kinkler, and Bob Kessler in 1971.[14] Before founding Mirco, Walsh worked for GE in Germany, where he was exposed to one of the most popular coin-operated amusements in France, Germany, and Italy: table soccer, also known as foosball. In 1967, he started a side business with another GE employee named Dick Raymond to ship foosball tables to the United States. Soon after, Raymond returned to the United States and established Arizona Automation to serve as a distributor for the foosball tables that Walsh continued to import from Germany.[15]

In 1971, importing tables became less economical after the devaluation of the German Mark, so Raymond began building his own tables domestically. Meanwhile, Mirco started looking for additional sources of revenue to fund its primary business and purchased Arizona Automation in 1973 to enter the coin-op business.[16] The company's first video games, *Champion Ping Pong* and *Challenger*, were uninspiring two- and four-player ball-and-paddle games that did not perform well at first, but after the company converted *Challenger* to a table-top format, Mirco rode the cocktail boom to success.[17]

After the introduction by Bilotta, Mirco signed on to produce a pinball game based on the Nutting system, though it chose to make its own modifications, including the use of a Motorola rather than an Intel processor. The resulting game, *Spirit of '76*, attracted intense interest and large orders at the 1975 MOA show, but the game was still in the prototype phase, and Mirco suffered through various technical difficulties and production delays. While a few units were made available in November, they often failed to work correctly, so the company had to shut down production. By the time

---

[13] Nutting, 2017.
[14] Smith, 2016, 286.
[15] "The Table Soccer Phenomenon," *RePlay*, February 28, 1976, 17.
[16] Ibid.
[17] Smith, 2016, 287–288.

Mirco resumed shipping in March 1976, many distributors had cancelled their orders, so the company only sold 140 units.[18] The solid-state pinball revolution was placed on hold. In the meantime, the microprocessor had a transformative impact on coin-operated video games.

***

In 1975, pool topped the inaugural earnings chart of the new coin-operated amusement trade publication *RePlay*, narrowly beating out pinball and finishing well ahead of video games.[19] While arcade video games recovered somewhat from the market collapse in 1974, sales did not return to the heights of 1973, with an estimated 53,000 units sold.[20] Atari dominated the market with sales of 25,000 units, while Midway ran a distant second at 10,000. Next came Allied Leisure – newly returned to video games after taking a year off – at 7,500, followed by Ramtek at 4,000 units. Between them, these four companies controlled over 85% of the coin-operated video game market.[21]

The big hits of the year were Atari's *Tank* and Midway's *Wheels*, while the single biggest earner on location was likely a massive racing game Atari deployed through its Kee Games subsidiary called *Indy 800*. Housed in a $4.66 \times 4.66 \times 7.25$-foot cabinet that accommodated two players on each side for a total of eight, the game incorporated a color monitor so that each player's car could be distinguished by a different color. Supporting eight players required eight circuit boards, which pushed the cost for operators to buy a cabinet to nearly $9,000, but the game proved capable of taking in over $300 a week on average and reached earnings as high as $5,000 in a single month in some locations. Due to the immense size and cost of the game, Atari planned to manufacture only 200 units, but when those sold out quickly they built more.[22] Even so, the production run remained low compared to other games.

In 1976, arcade video game sales surged to levels not seen since 1973 as the widespread adoption of the microprocessor allowed manufacturers to overcome the realistic limits of TTL hardware and displace the electromechanical

---

[18] Ibid, 289–290.

[19] "Replay Route Analysis," *RePlay*, October 1975, 38. Replay was launched in October 1975 by veteran coin-op industry journalist Ed Adlum, who had covered the amusement beat for *Cash Box* since 1964. In *Cash Box*'s own survey for 1975, pinball narrowly beat out pool for the top spot. Both surveys placed pinball and pool well ahead of video games. "1975 Amusement Machine Route Survey," *Cash Box*, October 18, 1975, C20.

[20] Frost & Sullivan, 1976, 87. This figure does not include the sale of cocktail-style games, which were estimated at 26,000.

[21] Ibid.

[22] Smith, 2016, 150.

novelty game market. Early driving games and target shooting games like
Gran Trak 10 and *Tank* had been hampered by restrictions on the number
of moving objects that could appear on the screen at once, as more gameplay elements meant more circuits, bigger boards, higher costs, and greater
service headaches. In contrast, microprocessor-based games could transfer
some, though not all, of this burden to software. This allowed manufacturers to reduce the cost and size of game boards and introduce more sophisticated gameplay and smoother animations than games created solely in TTL
hardware.

Jeff Frederiksen at DNA pioneered the use of microprocessors in coin-
operated video games by improving on his pinball system. Initially,
Frederiksen attempted to use the same 4-bit 4004 processor found in the
Flicker machine only to discover it was not powerful enough to drive a display. He turned to the 8080 microprocessor instead. Frederiksen created a
hardware system around the chip in which a frame buffer housed in dynamic
RAM contained the instructions used by the monitor's CRT to draw images
on the screen, with the microprocessor providing instructions on which individual pixels would be active in each frame. This system, the first bit-mapped
display created outside of high-end computer research labs, allowed for more
elaborate graphics and smoother movement and animation than any video
game yet released.[23]

After Frederiksen completed his system, he turned to one of his former
instructors at the University of Wisconsin named Richard Northouse to rec-
ommend programmers. Northouse funneled the company two of his students, Tom McHugh and Jaime Fenton.[24] While Fenton worked on a home
conversion of the Bally pinball game *Fireball*, McHugh joined Dave Nutting
on a project to redesign *Western Gun*, which Bally subsidiary Midway had
recently licensed from Taito. While the executives at Bally and Midway
were pleased with the overall concept of the Japanese game, they were less
impressed with the squashed, cartoony graphics they felt would not go over
well with an American audience. DNA's new microprocessor system appeared
to provide a perfect solution to this problem.

Dave Nutting designed the new version of *Western Gun* himself and
handed off his concepts to McHugh to implement on Frederiksen's hardware
system.[25] The duo redid the graphics so the cowboys were more realistically

---

[23] Thacker, 2011.

[24] Fenton transitioned from male to female in the late 1990s. At the time of the events in question,
she presented as male and went by her birth name, Jay.

[25] Tom McHugh, interview with Ethan Johnson, April 20, 2017.

proportioned and eliminated the fixed playfield of rocks and cacti. Instead, one cactus appears on the screen before the first kill, then two after the second, then three after the third, and so on up to a maximum of six, which are slowly replaced by trees in later rounds. After five kills, a stagecoach also begins moving across the center of the screen to serve as an additional obstacle. Each time a player is killed, the words "Got Me!" appear over his head. The controls are reversed from the original, with a small eight-way joystick providing movement and a large lever used to change the angle of the gun. Though a slower paced game than its Japanese counterpart, the superior graphics and animations of the DNA version, dubbed *Gun Fight*, proved a huge draw, and the game was a sizable hit for Midway that sold 8,600 units.[26]

In 1976, DNA developed four more games for Midway using Frederiksen's system. These included *Tornado Baseball*, in which the player graphics are superimposed onto a painted model of a baseball diamond through use of a mirror; *Amazing Maze*, in which the player navigates a complex maze drawn from over 1 million patterns within a time limit; and a target shooting game called *Sea Wolf*, programmed once again by Tom McHugh based on a design by Dave Nutting. Derived from earlier electromechanical target shooting games like *Periscope* and Midway's own *Sea Raiders*, *Sea Wolf* challenges the player to peer through a periscope and fire at ships and other objects moving across the screen at various speeds in order to score as many points as possible within a time limit. Capable of earning over $200 a week consistently for weeks on end, the game proved so popular that Midway brought it back for a second production run in early 1977 after it had been discontinued.[27] The company ultimately produced 10,000 units of *Sea Wolf*, making it one of the best-selling video arcade games of the 1970s.[28]

The fourth and final game DNA developed in 1976 was a driving game called *280 Zzzap*. Unlike early driving games like *Gran Trak*, *Speed Race*, and *Demolition Derby* that portrayed the game world from a bird's eye perspective, *280 Zzzap* took advantage of the microprocessor to present the action from a first-person perspective instead, with smoothly animated white rectangles outlining an undulating road. The basic idea for this game did

[26] Jarrell, 1976, 50. *Gun Fight* is usually identified as the first microprocessor-based video game, but there is another candidate for that distinction called *PT-109* by Mirco Games, in which four players control boats and attempt to shoot each other while navigating a playfield full of islands, mines, and other obstacles. Mirco debuted the game at the same MOA show that Midway bowed *Gun Fight*, but which one shipped to distributors first is not known. Unlike *Gun Fight*, *PT-109* was not successful. Smith, 2016, 288–289.
[27] "Sea Wolf Back on Midway Line," *RePlay*, March 1977, 60.
[28] Bloom, *Invaders*, 1982, 16.

not come from DNA, however, but originated with a German named Reiner Foerst.

An engineer with both a master's and doctor of engineering degree from the Institute of Technology in Darmstadt, Foerst was working at a German wire manufacturer called Trakus in 1971 when he took notice of early driving simulators, which consisted of a computer hooked up to a projection screen and the controls of a car for the purpose of training individuals in motor vehicle operation. Foerst became fascinated with the engineering behind these simulators and built one of his own. With both computers and displays being prohibitively expensive, he used analog circuitry and light-bulbs to achieve a primitive driving effect.[29]

With the advent of the *Pong* craze in 1973, Foerst adapted his prototype to incorporate a monitor, though the machine remained largely analog. After completing two prototype units in 1975, Foerst attended the International Exhibition for Coin-Op Games in Berlin in March 1976 to display them under the name *Nürburgring 1*. The game generated some interest at the show, but due to a lack of money to fund a full assembly line, Foerst was only able to produce machines at a rate of one per week. By the time he had split from Trakus to form his own company to sell the game in September 1976, only 30 units had been sold.[30] This meant copying by a more well-equipped factory was inevitable.

The first company to notice *Nürburgring 1* was a small American manufacturer called Micronetics, which grew out of a game repair shop called Amusement Device Engineering established by Bill Prast and Steve Holder in early 1974. In June 1974, the duo founded a new company called Digital Games to enter the booming cocktail market and experienced immediate success by selling over 7,000 units of various ball-and-paddle games.[31] When that market collapsed, the company entered a period of financial difficulty, so in June 1976 the owners wound it up and established Micronetics to replace it.[32]

Digital Games/Micronetics made several attempts to break out of the ball-and-paddle market but were largely undone by a lack of engineering or manufacturing experience. This situation changed in August 1976 when the company dispatched a recently hired engineer named Ted Michon to Germany to fix a defective shipment of its latest game, *Air Combat*. While in

---

[29] Smith, 2016, 189–191.
[30] Ibid.
[31] Ibid, 185–187.
[32] Ibid, 191.

Germany, Michon saw one of the few *Nürburgring 1* units at a bowling alley in Düsseldorf. By chance, Foerst himself was showing off this unit to his sons, and the two engineers ended up discussing the inner workings of the machine. When he returned to the United States, Michon created a digital version of Foerst's game.[33]

With Micronetics continuing to face an uncertain future, company management decided to license the game to Midway, which debuted its version at the newly renamed Amusement and Music Operators Association (AMOA) show in October. Designed by Jamie Fenton at DNA, the Midway game incorporated a microprocessor that allowed the white rectangles outlining the road to scroll quickly and smoothly to provide a better sense of speed than previous driving efforts. Midway originally planned to call its version *Midnite Racer*, but it secured a licensing deal at the last minute to name it *280 Zzzap* after the Datsun 280Z automobile. Micronetics also showed its version of the game at the AMOA under the name *Night Racer* and released it in December, but the company folded soon after.[34]

Atari also embraced the microprocessor in 1976. Like DNA, the company began experimenting with microprocessor technology in 1974. That year, Steve Mayer and Larry Emmons at Atari's Cyan Engineering subsidiary launched a project to replace the electromechanical parts in a pinball machine with solid-state components. They began converting an old pinball game called *El Toro* to a solid-state design before switching the project to a Bally table called *Delta Queen* in the middle of the year.[35] The game was tested at a local pizza parlor, but Cyan proved unable to iron out all the technical glitches, so no game based around the system was released.

Meanwhile, Atari began hiring programmers so it could transition to microprocessor-based video games. The first programmer, Tom Hogg, was hired in 1975 and began working on an eight-player version of *Tank* as a follow-up to the highly lucrative, yet prohibitively expensive, *Indy 800*. Dubbed *Tank 8*, the game fit on a single circuit board rather than the eight required for its predecessor because every element no longer had to be rendered in hardware. Hogg also produced a microprocessor-driven trivia game called *Quiz Show* that debuted alongside *Tank 8* in April as

[33] Ibid, 189.
[34] Ibid, 191–192.
[35] Stephen Bristow, deposition, Bally Manufacturing v. Williams Electronics, No. 78-2246 (N.D. Ill), August 5, 1982, 12–14.

the company's first microprocessor-based products.[36] Atari's second programming hire, Dave Sheppard, tackled the company's answer to Midway's *Tornado Baseball*, dubbed *Flyball*, and then turned his attention to Atari's version of *Nürburgring 1*,[37] which became a modest hit under the name *Night Driver* and sold roughly 2,100 units.[38]

Atari's most successful game among its early microprocessor releases was a variation on *Gran Trak 10* dubbed *Sprint 2*, which was designed by *Tank* creator Lyle Rains and programmed by Dennis Koble. While conceptually similar to previous games in the *Gran Trak* series, *Sprint 2* broke from convention by removing both the brake pedal and the ability to drive in reverse and added a fourth gear to transform the game from one of maneuver into one of pure speed that emphasized drifting around the curves of the track. The incorporation of a microprocessor allowed not only for smoother animation, but also for the addition of three computer-controlled race cars that moved around the track in a pseudo-random fashion. These cars served as additional obstacles rather than opponents, and the goal of the game remained completing as many laps as possible within a time limit.[39] Released in November 1976, *Sprint 2* moved an astonishing 8,200 units and remained one of the top earning games on location for three years.[40] Despite this success, *Sprint 2* was not Atari's biggest hit of the year. That honor went to the last significant TTL hardware game released: a ball-and-paddle variant called *Breakout*.

---

[36] Smith, 2016, 221. Both games were released under the Kee Games label, which persisted for several years after the merger with Atari as the company continued its fight against distributor exclusivity. The Kee engineering group was also kept separate until Atari split into consumer and coin-op divisions in 1976, and the Atari and Kee teams merged. Frank Ballouz, interview with the author, July 28, 2009, and Keenan, 2018.

[37] Smith, 2016, 228.

[38] "Atari Arcade Production Numbers," internal document with release dates, prices, and units sold, c. 1999.

[39] "The Making of Sprint 2," *Retro Gamer*, no. 89, 2011, 38–39.

[40] Atari Production Numbers, c. 1999.

18

Breaking Out in Japan

In May 1975, a new player appeared in the coin-operated video game industry called Fun Games, Inc. The founder of the company, Oberto Alvarez, was a banker forced to leave Cuba in 1962 due to his opposition work against Cuban leader Fidel Castro. After arriving in the United States, he took a job as a janitor at the Corrobilt Container Company in Alameda County and rose to become VP of wood products. Corrobilt built shipping containers for coin-op manufacturers, providing Alvarez his introduction to the amusement industry. Like Harry Kurek at Meadows, he decided to establish his own coin-op manufacturer because the industry appeared recession proof.[1] The key employees of Fun Games, salesperson Pat Karns and engineer Larry Leppert, defected to the firm from Atari after becoming fed up with the chaos, financial difficulties, and politicking that marred Atari during the John Wakefield presidency.[2]

Leppert originally left Atari to work for a carnival supplier called Mar-Quin looking to break into the video game industry, and he illegally took several Atari schematics, circuit boards, and ROMs with him. When Mar-Quin folded soon after, Leppert joined Fun Games instead, where he completed the process of copying *Tank* using his pilfered Atari materials to develop a clone called *Tankers*.[3] The next year, Leppert used the same technique to develop *BiPlane*, which copied an Atari game called *Jet Fighter* that applied the one-on-one gameplay of *Tank* to aerial combat. *BiPlane* proved to be a far bigger hit than *Jet Fighter*, but such flagrant theft of trade secrets

---

[1] Smith, 2016, 192.

[2] Satish Bhutani, interview with Ethan Johnson, July 12, 2016.

[3] "Atari Wins Fun Games Litigation," *Cash Box*, April 3, 1976, 54. Leppert had worked on a carnival trailer mobile arcade project at Atari, so this is probably how he first met the people at Mar-Quin.

resulted in a lawsuit from Atari that put an end to Fun Games' copying. Unable to compete with original ideas, the company collapsed and merged with Meadows Games in 1977.[4]

One of the more unremarkable games released by the company in its brief lifespan was a 1975 ball-and-paddle collection called *Take Five*. Despite *Pong*-style games being completely blasé at that point, Fun Games updated it later in the year with two more games to create a new compilation called *Take Seven*. Meadows considered *Take Seven* interesting enough to re-release after purchasing Fun Games, but it left little impact on the marketplace. Included in this update was a new *Pong* variant called *Bust Out*, in which the player bounces a ball off a paddle situated on the right side of the screen to break bricks arrayed on the left side of the screen. Like Fun Games' other products, *Bust Out* was also an Atari design adapted into a finished game, but unlike the forgettable *Take Seven*, it would mark an important turning point in the industry when it was released in early 1976 under the name *Breakout*.[5]

***

By 1975, Atari was back on its feet after the disastrous Wakefield era and blazing a unique trail through Silicon Valley. Perhaps in response to the corporate atmosphere that had pervaded in 1973–1974, Nolan Bushnell penned a manifesto espousing his hopes for the firm going forward in which he described Atari as a collection of dedicated people who could be friends outside of the corporate hierarchy and push the company forward together. This was not just empty corporate jargon: the Atari of the mid-1970s took on something of a frat house atmosphere as marijuana smoke filled the air, beer busts celebrated the end of the working week on Friday afternoons, and men and women working at the company paired off into relationships lasting anywhere from a few days to several years.[6] The executive staff socialized after work and on the weekend, while board meetings were often held in the hot tub at Bushnell's house in Los Gatos. When the company opened a new engineering building in 1978, it featured its own hot tub that saw alternating use by men and women during the week but was co-ed on Fridays.[7]

---

[4] Smith, 2016, 192–194.

[5] Ibid.

[6] Goldberg and Vendel, chap. 3 and chap. 6; Smith, 2016, 244.

[7] Cecilia D'Anastasio, "Sex, *Pong*, and Pioneers: What Atari Was Really Like, According to the Women Who Were There," Kotaku, February 12, 2018, https://kotaku.com/sex-pong-and-pioneers-what-atari-was-really-like-ac-1822930057.

The culture of Atari largely reflected the ages and personal beliefs of the participants. At the time, engineering jobs continued to be largely associated with either the military-industrial complex only beginning to fade in importance as the Vietnam War inched toward its conclusion or corporate behemoths like IBM that valued conformity over individuality. Atari offered a place for a new breed of engineer exposed to the student protest and women's liberation movements prevalent on Bay Area college campuses and desirous of avoiding working on guided missiles or the massive mainframes that calculated the kill ratios in Vietnam. Young, idealistic, and perhaps a little distrustful of authority, these individuals were naturally drawn to a company like Atari that not only pedaled fun rather than destruction, but also encouraged flexible hours, relaxed dress codes, open avenues of communication across all levels of the company, equal opportunity for advancement based on merit, and a great deal of freedom in the game development process.

Nolan Bushnell set the tone at Atari with his outsized personality, gregarious nature, and insatiable curiosity. He also took the lead in developing the party-like atmosphere that pervaded Atari culture, reasoning that a bunch of young men and women working long hours to develop new video game product would appreciate the ability to blow off steam at work just as much as traditional corporate perks.[8] While the day-to-day mundanities of running a corporation proved anathema to him, he gladly sold the Atari vision to investors and the press and nurtured the best ideas coming from his engineering staff while making them feel valued. Nothing delighted Bushnell more than walking through the engineering labs to see all the cool new games under development. He often could not resist contributing his own ideas, however, forcing Al Alcorn and Steve Bristow to watch him like a hawk and remind their engineers that Nolan did not manage R&D and engineering. Nolan's ideas would be forgotten in a few days anyway as he became excited about the next big thing.[9]

Keeping the company on track fell to company president Joe Keenan. Unlike his predecessor, Keenan was not that much older than the rest of the team and understood the value of keeping a loose atmosphere. Unlike Bushnell, however, he was a competent administrator who could keep the day-to-day operation of the company flowing smoothly. While Atari placed a lot of emphasis on having fun, Keenan made sure that all departments were working hard and hitting targets before engaging in extracurricular activities.

---

[8] Bushnell, 2009.
[9] Kent, 2001, 87–89.

In its first few years, Atari did not employ any staff with extensive experience in the coin-op business, but that changed in late 1974 when the company hired Gene Lipkin, whose father, Sol, was a celebrated coin-op salesman with American Shuffleboard. Although Lipkin initially attended Ball State University in Indiana, he dropped out to enter the coin-op industry by working for a distributor and became the sales manager of Allied Leisure in 1970.[10] He grew disenchanted with the company during the *Pong* boom when a promised per unit commission on the smash hit *Paddle Battle* failed to materialize and departed the company to join Atari in late 1974 as a director of special projects because he was enamored with a multi-game arcade kiosk being developed by the company.[11]

In March 1975, Pat Karns departed Atari as part of the Fun Games defection, and Lipkin moved into his former sales role while picking up the VP of Marketing title as well.[12] With his extensive contacts in the industry and his skill as a dealmaker, Lipkin played a key role in stabilizing Atari's sales over the next few years, as did his friend Frank Ballouz, a former salesman for copier company AB Dick whom Lipkin hired into Atari as sales manager in mid-1975.[13] Lipkin and Ballouz possessed a keen sense for what games would be successful in the marketplace and were not afraid to kill games in development early if they looked to be losers, which helped Atari release a steady stream of modest hits throughout the rest of the 1970s.

Lipkin also introduced new marketing sophistication to the coin-op business by hiring Carol Kantor as manager of marketing services in 1976.[14] At the time, the only real market research that coin-op manufacturers engaged in was putting their prototypes out on test in local arcades and measuring the coin drop. This gave the manufacturers a good idea as to whether a game would be successful in the marketplace, but they never explored why a particular game did well or fared poorly. Kantor may well have been the first true market researcher in the history of the coin-op industry, and she frequented local arcades to speak with players and discover what they really liked and

---

[10] John Hubner and William F. Kistner, Jr., "What Went Wrong at Atari," *Infoworld*, November 23, 1983, 152, and "From the Sunshine State," *Cash Box*, March 13, 1970, 72.

[11] "Atari Welcomes MOA Conventioneers," *St. Pong Revisited*, November 1974, 1, and Lipkin, 2014.

[12] "Atari's Karns Resigns; Establishes New Company," *Vending Times*, May 1975, 52, and "Atari Promotes Lipkin to Marketing Vice-President," *Vending Times*, May 1975, 56.

[13] Ballouz, 2009.

[14] Several secondary sources indicate that Kantor joined Atari in 1973, but this is inaccurate. The trades noted her hiring in 1976, and Kantor confirmed to me in an interview that she was hired by Gene Lipkin, who did not even join the company until 1974 and did not run marketing until 1975. "Atari Appts. Kantor Mktg. Research Mgr.," *Cash Box*, August 7, 1976, 45 and Carol Kantor, interview with the author, March 9, 2017.

hated about the games on the market. She would then pass this information along to the engineers to help them refine their games. While this new practice was looked upon with skepticism at first, the results were so useful that Kantor soon had a whole team of market researchers reporting to her.[15]

New game ideas at Atari came from a variety of sources, but one particularly fruitful practice initiated in this period was for the entire engineering staff to attend off-site retreats dedicated solely to brainstorming new game ideas. These retreats started at a local Holiday Inn before moving to Pajaro Dunes.[16] The best ideas would be compiled in a book for future reference, and engineers could bid for projects in which they were particularly interested. One such project that Bushnell particularly championed was yet another take on the ball-and-paddle genre brainstormed in January 1975 and inspired by the Ramtek game *Clean Sweep* from 1973. The idea was to keep the screen-clearing gameplay of the original, but to turn the dots of the game into a solid field of obstacles off which the ball would ricochet even as it knocked them off the screen.[17] While Bushnell truly believed this concept would be a winner, none of his engineers proved willing to work on the game due to the collapse of the ball-and-paddle market. Therefore, Bushnell and Bristow took the unorthodox step of giving the project to a mere technician, a loud-mouthed, filthy, often obnoxious 20-year-old named Steve Jobs.

***

Steven Paul Jobs was born on February 24, 1955, to Joanne Schieble and Abdulfattah Jandali and adopted at birth by Paul and Clara Jobs. Paul, a former Coast Guard sailor working as a collection agent, moved the family to Mountain View, California, in 1960. He instilled a deep love of design and craftsmanship in his adopted son through his hobbies of woodworking and refurbishing and selling used cars. It was through automobiles that Jobs first became exposed to electronics, but it was living in the heart of the region quickly developing into Silicon Valley that allowed his interest in technology to flourish as towns like Mountain View filled up with engineers and other technology experts.[18]

After a move to nearby Los Altos, Jobs attended Homestead High School, where in addition to continuing his studies in electronics he began hanging

---

[15] Kantor, 2017.

[16] Cohen, 1984, chap. 5.

[17] Bristow, Steve, "Grass Valley Conference," 1-11-75, memo to Nolan Bushnell and Al Alcorn, January 14, 1975.

[18] Walter Isaacson, *Steve Jobs* (New York: Simon & Schuster, 2011), ebook, chap. 1.

out with the counterculture crowd and experimenting with LSD.[19] After graduation in 1972, he matriculated to Reed College in Oregon and cultivated an interest in Eastern Mysticism and Zen Buddhism. Bored at Reed, he dropped out soon after arriving but continued to hang around, adopted a hippie lifestyle, and started walking around barefoot, following extreme vegetarian diets, and rarely bathing because he believed his diet would prevent body odor. In February 1974, he returned to Los Altos and managed to secure a job as a technician at Atari by walking into the lobby and refusing to leave until he was hired.[20]

None of the engineers at Atari liked Jobs, whom they perceived as arrogant and opinionated and who usually smelled terrible, but Nolan Bushnell saw something in this brash, yet intelligent and philosophical young man and placed him on a night shift so he would not have to interact with many people. In April, Jobs left the company to travel to India with his college friend Dan Kottke to further his quest for spiritual enlightenment.[21] He convinced Atari to pay his air fare as far as Europe in return for delivering a fix to one of Atari's latest games to distributors in Germany and Italy.

After seven months in India and 12 weeks of primal scream therapy in Oregon, Jobs returned to Atari with a shaved head and saffron robes in early 1975 and wrangled his old job back.[22] He continued making frequent trips back to Oregon but often needed additional funds to make the journey. Perhaps remembering how Atari helped him the last time he traveled, Jobs went to see Joe Keenan, claimed a guru he needed to meet would be visiting Oregon soon, and asked if he could do something to earn some extra money. The day before, Bushnell had sketched out for Keenan on his blackboard the recently brainstormed *Clean Sweep*-style game that had failed to generate much enthusiasm. Sensing an opportunity to build Bushnell's pet game project, Keenan took Jobs to Bushnell's office to show him the sketch and offered Jobs a bonus if he could engineer the game with fewer chips than the typical hardware of the day.[23] Jobs took the assignment, but he did not really

---

[19] Ibid.

[20] Ibid, chaps. 3 and 4.

[21] Ibid, chap. 4.

[22] Isaacson, chap. 4, and Jeffrey S. Young, *Steve Jobs: The Journey is the Reward* (Chicago, IL: Scott Foresman, 1988), kindle, chap. 5.

[23] Keenan, 2018. Other sources state Jobs needed the money to attend the apple harvest at the commune, but the timeline for the game's creation was fixed by internal Atari documents and Homebrew Computer Club newsletters as occurring sometime between January and March 1975, which seems an odd time to harvest apples. Keenan's recollections about a guru make more sense.

possess the engineering skill to put together a complete arcade game. He did, however, count among his friends a brilliant engineer named Steve Wozniak.

Born August 11, 1950, in San Jose, California, Stephen Gary Wozniak came by his fascination for engineering honestly, as his father worked on defense projects such as guided missiles at Lockheed and tutored his precocious son in electronics from an early age.[24] In 1960, Wozniak read an article about the pioneering ENIAC computer, began immersing himself in Boolean logic, and fantasized about having a computer of his own someday.[25]

Like Jobs, Wozniak attended Homestead High School, where he took an advanced electronics course and participated in a work study program at Sylvania once a week in which he learned FORTRAN and programmed a computer for the first time.[26] He also discovered minicomputers and began designing his own on paper.[27] Upon graduation, he matriculated to the University of Colorado at Boulder, but left in 1969 after being placed on academic probation and being disciplined for using university computers to run a series of mathematical programs and print the results, which ran his class well over budget for computer time. He returned home to San Jose and enrolled at De Anza Community College while continuing to design computers in his spare time.[28]

After a year at De Anza, Wozniak quit school and gained employment at a small computer company called Tenet. Using parts from his employer, Wozniak built his first computer prototype with the help of a younger friend named Bill Fernandez, which they called the "Cream Soda Computer" in honor of their beverage of choice during the project. This may have been one of the first personal computers built, but it was accidentally destroyed when a reporter from the *Peninsula Times* came by to do a story and stepped on the power supply. After the completion of the project, Fernandez told Wozniak that he should meet a classmate of his at Homestead who shared Wozniak's love of practical jokes and building electronics named Steve Jobs.[29]

The two Steves bonded immediately over a shared love of pranks and electronics and Bob Dylan, and they soon embarked on an entrepreneurial scheme together. In September 1971, as Wozniak prepared to return to school at Berkeley, he read an article in *Esquire* about the practice of "phone phreaking," in which individuals created devices called "blue boxes" that

---

[24] Steve Wozniak and Gina Smith, *iWoz* (New York: W.W. Norton, 2006), 12–13.

[25] Ibid, 32–33.

[26] Ibid, 49–51.

[27] Ibid, 54–55.

[28] Ibid, 67–71.

[29] Ibid, 85–88.

could emulate the tones of the routing signals used by AT&T in its long-distance network to place free calls.[30] Wozniak and Jobs decided to construct their own blue box together, after which Jobs suggested they sell it. This illegal venture ended quickly when a potential buyer robbed them at gunpoint in the parking lot of a Sunnyvale pizza parlor.[31]

In January 1973, Wozniak secured a position at HP designing calculators. Soon after, he was introduced to video games through a *Pong* unit at a local bowling alley. Wozniak now had a new fascination, and he decided to build his own version of the game. After studying how televisions and video signals worked, he crafted a complete *Pong* unit out of 28 chips, a remarkably small number for the time. To further enhance his version, he added a feature that caused words like "Hell" and "damn" to appear on the screen when the player missed the ball. By the time he had finished the game, Jobs was working at Atari, so Wozniak showed it to some of the engineers while visiting his friend one day. Al Alcorn offered him a job on the spot, but as far as Wozniak was concerned, he already had his dream job at HP designing circuits, and he never planned to leave.[32]

While Wozniak turned down the opportunity to work at Atari, he loved playing the company's games, and Jobs would sneak him in at night so he could play the latest arcade hits for free. It was in this context that Jobs asked Wozniak to implement the game Bushnell sketched out for him. There was an additional catch, however: due to the impending guru visit, Jobs told Wozniak that they had to complete the job in just four days. Wozniak decided he was up for the challenge.[33]

Over the next four days, Wozniak designed the layout of the hardware during the day, and Jobs produced the wire-wrapped circuit boards based on these designs at night as Wozniak spent a few hours playing *Gran Trak 10* while waiting to test the newest revision. When the four days were over, both Steves had contracted mononucleosis, but the game was completed using a mere 45 chips, an astoundingly low number in a time when TTL games usually required more than a 100.[34] Jobs paid Wozniak half of the design fee for the game, but he did not tell his friend about the bonus for removing chips and kept all that money, several thousand dollars', for himself.[35]

---

[30] Ibid, 93.
[31] Isaacson, 2011, chap. 2.
[32] Ibid, 139–143.
[33] Ibid, 144.
[34] Ibid, 144–148.
[35] Kent, 2001, 72–73.

Atari accepted Wozniak's schematics and wire-wrapped prototype, but had to completely reengineer the game for release. Although Wozniak's design was efficient, it was also idiosyncratic and impossible for Atari's technicians to understand for testing purposes. He also failed to complete several features, including coin control and sound, while also incorporating several components like an LED readout for the score that were not suitable to a coin-operated product. Atari engineer Gary Waters used Wozniak's work as a base but discovered several glitches in the logic and received permission to use a typical Atari layout, thus largely negating the chip savings that Wozniak had engineered. He also added proper on-screen scoring, sound, and a two-player mode to the game.[36] Once the redesign was complete, Atari released *Breakout* in May 1976.[37] It proved to be a smash hit and sold over 11,000 units.[38] As popular as the game was in the West, its impact was even greater when it reached Japan later in the year through the Nakamura Manufacturing Company.

***

Atari had been interested in releasing its products in the lucrative Japanese coin-op market since its earliest days, so John Wakefield established Atari Japan in August 1973.[39] Wakefield placed Kenichi Takumi in charge of the company, a salesman who graduated from Japan's prestigious Waseda University and spent time at National Cash Register and The Ohio State University.[40] From its inception, the company was beset with a host of problems stemming largely from both Atari's unfamiliarity with the Japanese market and Takumi's own lack of experience in coin-op, including an inability to pass product through customs or attract local operators to take their games.[41] Takumi finally approached Masaya Nakamura in early 1974 to ask Nakamura Manufacturing to serve as a distributor. Nakamura was already thinking about global expansion now that his firm was one of the largest coin-op manufacturers in the country and readily agreed.[42]

---

[36] Goldberg and Vendel, 2012, chap. 4.

[37] "Happy Birthday Breakout," *Atari Coin Connection*, May 1977, 1.

[38] Atari Production Numbers, 1999.

[39] Atari Prospectus, 1975. Some sources peg Atari Japan on international sales VP Ron Gordon, but Gordon himself says he had nothing to do with the Far Eastern expansion. This feels plausible because establishing subsidiaries goes against Gordon's consistent strategy of working through local partners. Gordon, 2018.

[40] Goldberg and Vendel, 2012, "Atari's Growing Pains."

[41] Alcorn, oral history, 2008, Kent, 2001, 74–75, and Kazuhisa Maeno, "Namco: Maker of the Video Age," *Journal of Japanese Trade & Industry*, no. 4, 1985, 39.

[42] Maeno, 1985, 39.

Even with Nakamura's help, Atari Japan continued to fall apart as employee theft ran rampant, and Takumi simply stopped coming into work. Leadership of the company fell to its general manager, Hideyuki Nakajima, an ambitious executive who had left the employment of the Japan Art Paper Company because he knew he would never be more than a faceless cog in a machine at the large and venerable papercraft firm. Nakajima possessed an unusual entrepreneurial spirit for a Japanese salaryman, so when his brother, a lawyer helping to setup Atari Japan, told him about the new coin-op subsidiary, he leapt at the chance to be involved. Now its de facto leader with Takumi's departure, he began putting some of his own money into the company to keep it afloat and asked Nolan Bushnell to give him time to right the ship. Unfortunately, Atari was in the midst of the financial woes that almost destroyed the company and could not afford to wait for a turn around.[43]

Selling Atari Japan would be crucial to fixing Atari's cash flow problems, so the firm required a sizable return on the sale. Ron Gordon, still acting as a fixer for Bushnell at the time, approached both Sega and Taito about a deal, but neither was willing to offer much considering the poor showing made by Atari's games in the country. Next, Gordon approached Nakamura to see if he might take Atari Japan off his hands. At first, Nakamura refused. While a major player in the Japanese market, Nakamura Manufacturing was still a relatively small company with a market capitalization of just ¥80 million, far less than Gordon's asking price. But Nakamura understood that even though electromechanical games still ruled Japan at that time, video was the future of the industry. Gordon convinced Nakamura that he may never have another chance this good to break into the new medium, and Nakamura agreed in July 1974 to meet Atari's ¥296 million ($1.18 million) asking price for Atari Japan.[44]

The Atari deal called for Nakamura to pay the full amount by October 1974, but he quickly realized he would be unable to meet that obligation. A two-day negotiation followed in August, after which Bushnell and Gordon relented since they had no other good options for selling the business and allowed Nakamura to pay $550,000 immediately and $250,000 a year for three years.[45] Nakamura managed to acquire loans from several banks despite the general unwillingness of the financial sector in Japan to deal with coin-operated amusement companies and completed the purchase by assuming a

---

[43] David Sheff, *Game Over, Press Start to Continue: The Maturing of Mario* (Wilton, CT: CyberActive Media Group, 1999), ebook, chap. 11.

[44] Gordon, 2018; Maeno, 1985, 39.

[45] Ibid.

debt that would take two years to pay off.[46] Atari Japan remained a separate subsidiary of Nakamura Manufacturing under Nakajima, who ultimately stayed on despite a reluctance to work for another established firm after Nakamura elevated him to a vice presidency in Nakamura Manufacturing and charged him with boosting international sales.[47]

Over the next two years, Nakamura released several Atari games in Japan and experienced some success with products like *Tank*, but this was the height of the medal game fad, and video games failed to have a large impact in the coin-op marketplace. By 1976, the Japanese government was beginning to crack down on medal games, and the coin-op industry was on the lookout for something to replace them. *Breakout* did not appear to be the answer at first, as distributors at the annual Japanese Amusement Show were far more interested in Taito's import of Midway's *Tornado Baseball*,[48] but its simple yet addictive gameplay and requirement for only one player helped it slowly gain popularity until Nakamura proved unable to keep up with demand.[49] This led other companies to create their own versions of the game, including some that had never been involved in the industry before.

The first Japanese company to release a *Breakout* clone was a *pachinko* manufacturer called the Universal Sales Company. Founder Kazuo Okada grew up poor and fatherless in the aftermath of World War II but managed through hard work and perseverance to gain entry to a Japanese technical college and become an expert on vacuum tubes. In roughly 1963, Okada discovered an old jukebox in a trash pile and realized he could use his knowledge of vacuum tubes to repair it. He subsequently established a jukebox repair business and over the course of six years amassed savings of roughly ¥20 million, a significant sum for an entrepreneur in Japan at that time.[50]

In 1967, Okada began installing and operating jukeboxes, leading him to use his life savings to establish the Universal Lease Company in 1969. In July 1970, he started a manufacturing division in order to produce *pachinko* machines.[51] He discovered that manufacturing required a different skill set than operating, however, and ran out of money within two years. With no banks willing to lend to a coin-op company, Okada convinced some of his

---

[46]Maeno 1985, 39;Sheff, 1999, chap. 11.

[47]Sheff, 1999, chap. 11.

[48]Akagi, 2005, 111.

[49]Kent, 2001, 75.

[50]Gillian Tett, "Pinball Wizard Steps Out: Profile Kazuo Okada, Aruze," *Financial Times*, August 28, 2000.

[51]Akagi, 2005, 223.

fellow manufacturers to extend him credit to keep the company afloat until it finally reached profitability.[52] After *Breakout* became successful, a jukebox vendor named Takeshi Miyajima asked Okada to manufacture a version for him. Released as *Scratch* in early 1977, Universal's game helped kick the *Breakout* fad into high gear by paving the way for other companies to release their own machines.[53]

As *Breakout* and its imitators found success in Japan, leading coin-op company Taito struggled with a new problem: the decline of its traditional jukebox business. The culprit was a new type of coin-operated music player called a *karaoke* machine into which a patron could insert a ¥100 coin to sing along with the backing track of a popular song. The inventor of *karaoke*, Daisuke Inoue, was working as a club musician in Kobe when a regular customer asked him to record piano accompaniment for several songs. The salaryman made the request because he would be meeting business clients out of town and would be expected to sing, but he felt only Inoue's arrangements made him sound any good. This worked out so well for the businessman that he asked Inoue for more recordings, leading Inoue to envision the *karaoke* machine. Released as the Juke 8 in 1971, Inoue's machine achieved sales of 25,000 units within a year. As Inoue never patented his system, he was soon joined by a host of imitators as *karaoke* quickly became a national pastime.[54] In this environment, the jukebox was quickly displaced.

To regain a foothold in the bar market, Taito experimented with a new type of arcade cabinet called a "table-top" or "TT" model, a flat, sit-down cabinet that would allow a player to eat or drink while playing the game housed within. This approach was similar to the cocktail table design several U.S. manufacturers had adopted to expand the *Pong* market into high-end establishments, which had not infiltrated Japan in large numbers.[55] Due to its popularity, Taito decided to make its *Breakout* clone the first game it released in a TT cabinet. Deployed in 1977, *T.T. Block* took the industry by storm as some establishments rushed to replace all their tables with TT

---

[52] Gillian, 2000.

[53] Akagi, 2005, 111.

[54] Daisuke Inoue and Robert Scott, "Voice Hero: The Inventor of Karaoke Speaks," The Appendix, December 3, 2013, http://theappendix.net/issues/2013/10/voice-hero-the-inventor-of-karaoke-speaks. The term "*karaoke*" is derived from the phrase *kara okesutura*, which means "empty orchestra." The use of this term is said to date to 1952 when a theatrical troupe in Osaka replaced its orchestra with a machine after the musicians went on strike.

[55] A few cocktail cabinets were imported into Japan during the height of the boom that were largely placed in hotel lobbies, but they did not catch on. Yoshiki Shinozaki, "Space Invaders Provides Thrills for Game Enthusiasts," *Business Japan*, July 1979, 129.

games due to the incredible revenue they generated.[56] TT cabinets extended video games into Japanese clubs, snack bars, and coffee and tea houses for the first time, thus greatly expanding the reach of arcade video games and helping them become a significant force in the Japanese coin-op industry for the first time.[57]

For the Nakamura Manufacturing Company, which changed its name to Namco in early 1977,[58] the entry of Universal, Taito, and other firms into the market was problematic. Atari continually proved unable to ship enough units for Namco to meet demand, thus providing an opportunity for these other companies to establish a foothold in the marketplace. The success of *borokuzushi*, or block-busting, games also attracted the attention of several *yakuza* clans, organized crime syndicates that ran many of the less savory business enterprises in the country. Indeed, Nakamura himself was approached by a *yakuza* representative who promised to make his competition problems go away if he would only cut the clan in on his business. Wanting nothing to do with organized crime, Nakamura travelled to Europe to make a personal appeal to Nolan Bushnell at a trade show for more supply, but he found the Atari boss hung-over and in no state to make a deal. Feeling out of options, Nakamura decided to break his contract with Atari and begin making his own PCBs of the game, fully bringing Namco into the video game manufacturing business. This decision left Namco poised to become one of the most important coin-op manufacturers in Japan as the video game industry matured.[59]

***

By 1978, government crackdowns on medal games, long tarnished by gray market operators who would allow players to exchange tokens for prizes, had brought Japan's biggest coin-operated amusement fad to a halt. Japan's four largest coin-op manufacturers, Sega, Taito, Namco, and Kasco, responded to these new market conditions in different ways. Taito focused on importing the latest video games from American companies like Midway, Exidy, and Meadows, supplemented by a small amount of internal video game development led by its original video game engineer, Tomohiro Nishikado. Namco

---

[56] Taito, 2010.

[57] Shinozaki, 1979, 129.

[58] Namco, a contraction of Nakamura Manufacturing Company, had been used as a brand name on Nakamura coin-op products since 1972, but the company did not formally change its name to Namco, Ltd. until early 1977.

[59] Kent, 2001, 75–77.

remained focused on its Atari video game business and domestic electro-mechanical output but began researching the possibility of developing its own video games as well. In contrast, Kasco chose to focus exclusively on electromechanical games, a decision largely driven by the company's lack of expertise in solid-state design and inability to attract an outside partner for collaboration.[60] Kasco never would fully commit to the video game industry, and the firm slowly faded in importance.[61]

Japan's top coin-op manufacturer, Sega, followed a slightly different path from its competitors. After Gulf & Western purchased the company from David Rosen, Marty Bromley, and partners in 1969, Rosen made a point of becoming close with both G&W CEO Charles Bludhorn and G&W president Jim Judelson. Impressed by Rosen's ambition and drive, they offered him an opportunity to form a new Far Eastern conglomerate that could rival G&W's holdings in the West. Gulf & Western Far East Pacific was created in Hong Kong in 1970 with Rosen as president and Sega Enterprises as a subsidiary, but the era of conglomerating was rapidly ending, and the market conditions in Asia at the time did not lend themselves to this scheme. In 1974, G&W wound up the company so that Bludhorn and Rosen could take Sega public in the United States instead.[62]

Rather than take Sega public directly, G&W employed an elaborate scheme centered on its many subsidiary companies. One such firm, Consolidated Brands, owned just over 53% of a publicly traded cosmetics firm called the Polly Bergen Company that had been transformed into a shell corporation when its cosmetics business was sold off to a rival firm in 1973. In March 1974, G&W carried out a reverse stock split to increase its holdings in Polly Bergen to 95%, shifted ownership of Sega Enterprises, Ltd. to the former cosmetics firm as a subsidiary company, and renamed Polly Bergen to Sega Enterprises, Inc. Rosen became chairman, CEO, and president of the new parent company.[63] A G&W executive with extensive experience in the consumer electronics business named Harry Kane, who had joined Sega as executive vice president in 1972, took over the day-to-day operations of Sega Enterprises, Ltd. in Japan.[64]

---

[60] The Company almost created a video game hardware system in 1973 in partnership with consumer electronics powerhouse JVC called the Playtron that would have incorporated a color monitor and hardware capable of generating animated sprites in a period when both were rare in the industry. A change in leadership at JVC killed the project. Kasco, 2001.

[61] Ibid.

[62] Kent, 2001, 341–342.

[63] Sega Enterprises, Inc., Annual Report, 1974.

[64] "Sega Enterprises," *Weekly Television Digest with Consumer Electronics*, June 28, 1976, 12.

By 1974, Sega was bringing in revenues of just over $23 million with a profit of $2.4 million. Most of this income came from the Operations Division, which placed roughly 20,000 Sega arcade games in 7,000 locations throughout Japan. Sega also continued to import Rock-Ola jukeboxes and Williams pinball machines for distribution and to operate the Rosen Enterprises network of movie theater gun corners. To supplement these locations, Sega established a chain of game centers patterned on the Sigma Enterprises "Game Fantasia Milano" that offered medal games and similar amusements.[65]

Sega remained a major manufacturer of coin-operated games as well, which were built at a 135,000 square foot facility near the Haneda Airport in Tokyo. Sega expended most of its efforts on the medal game market and achieved notable successes with a console roulette wheel machine called *Faro* and an elaborate horse racing game called *Harness Race*.[66] The company also began developing its own video games by adapting the light gun technology it had been using for the electromechanical games in its gun corners for years to create target shooting games incorporating light-sensitive gun-shaped controllers called *Balloon Gun* (1974) and *Bullet Mark* (1975). Its first video hit, however, was baseball game called *Last Inning* (1975). Finally, Sega was the only Japanese company to manufacture a complete range of coin-op amusements after introducing Japan's first domestically produced pinball machines in 1971.[67]

With business booming in Japan, David Rosen was eager to expand his operations into the United States. In May 1974, the company opened its first U.S. office under the auspices of Sega Finance VP Malcolm Kaufman.[68] In early 1975, Rosen reached a preliminary agreement with the financially troubled Seeburg Corporation to purchase its Williams Electronics subsidiary, but the deal fell through.[69] That July, Rosen established a new subsidiary called Sega of America in Redondo Beach, California, centered around a 50,000 square foot factory that could build Sega games for the American market.[70] *Bullet Mark* was the first game built at the factory, but it proved a flop with North American operators due to the gigantic size of the cabinet. A scaled-down version called *Tracer* was therefore developed and released the next year.

---

[65] Sega Annual Report, 1974.

[66] Ibid.

[67] Akagi, 2005, 143.

[68] "Sega Opens Office in Los Angeles," *Cash Box*, May 11, 1974, 50.

[69] "Sega, Seeburg Agree in Principle to Sega Acquiring Williams Firm," *Play Meter*, March 1975, 45.

[70] Sega Enterprises, Inc., Annual Report, 1975.

In 1976, Sega turned its attention to driving video games to capitalize on the massive success of Taito's *Speed Race* in Japan. In February, the company deployed a game called *Road Race* designed by Hideki Sato that featured the same basic gameplay as *Speed Race* but used circuitry that directly manipulated the monitor to distort the picture and give the illusion of a winding road for additional challenge.[71] In August, the company released a variant called *Man T.T.* that replaced the cars with motorcycles and the steering wheel control with handlebars that vibrate after a collision, the first instance of haptic feedback in a video game. In November, the game was rebranded for the North American market as *The Fonz* to capitalize on the popularity of the motorcycle-riding bad boy of the hit television sitcom *Happy Days*, produced by another Gulf & Western subsidiary, Paramount Television.

As the licensing agreement for *The Fonz* indicates, David Rosen was keen on turning the U.S. market into an important profit center for Sega. He was also convinced of the necessity of cultivating North American engineering talent for his company's arcade games. His Japanese staff was still primarily focused on electromechanical game design, so he sought to hire engineers with solid-state and computer engineering experience in the United States who could collaborate with his engineers back in Japan on new technology.[72] In 1976, Rosen appointed Sega Enterprises, Ltd. executive VP Harry Kane as the new president of Sega of America and brought in Dane Blough from General Instrument to replace him as EVP and COO of Sega Enterprises.[73] He also hired an RCA engineer named Richard Norwalt with an extensive background in solid-state circuits and advanced display design as vice president of R&D. One of the first fruits of this R&D effort was a microprocessor-driven quiz game called *Tic-Tac-Quiz* deployed in December 1976.

Sega also looked for other ways to penetrate the North American market outside of coin-op game manufacturing and R&D. In July 1975, the company purchased a 50% stake in a company called Kingdom of Oz that operated four arcades in California shopping malls.[74] That number rose to six by March 1976 when Sega made Kingdom of Oz a wholly owned subsidiary and renamed the arcades "Sega Centers."[75] In June, Sega expanded into consumer electronics by purchasing the assets of Muntz Manufacturing,

[71] Sato 2-1, 2018.

[72] "Interview: David Rosen of Sega," *RePlay*, October 1975, 14.

[73] "Sega Announces Appointments for Three," *Play Meter*, June 1976, 37.

[74] Sega Annual Report, 1975.

[75] Sega Enterprises, Inc., Annual Report, 1976.

a producer of projection television systems that the company marketed under the Sega-Vision brand name.[76]

By the end of fiscal 1978, it was clear that Sega's expansion into North America was not working. The television manufacturing business proved a complete disaster and was suspended in early 1978, while a downturn in the U.S. market for coin-operated video games left the company with excessive inventory and a sharply curtailed release schedule. Only the arcade operations, by now expanded to a dozen locations, turned a profit, but only after suffering through three years of losses. Therefore, while the Japanese arm of the company continued to perform well and overall revenues increased from $23.9 million in 1975 to $37.2 million in 1978, profits steadily trended downward from $2.6 million in 1975 to just $347,000 in 1977 before stabilizing at $1.9 million in 1978.[77] These difficulties did not hit just Sega, but the entire coin-op video game industry as the solid-state revolution begun by *Spirit of '76* and *Gun Fight* in 1975 contributed to a revitalization of the game of pinball.

---

[76] "Gulf & Western Enters Home Electronics," *Weekly Television Digest with Consumer Electronics*, June 21, 1976, 9.

[77] Sega Enterprises, Inc., Annual Report, 1978.

19

Chasing the Silver Ball

On May 17, 1969, MCA Records released the latest record by The Who in the United States. Called *Tommy*, the album represented a departure from previous LPs consisting of largely unconnected three-minute pop songs, instead presenting a complete "rock opera" that told the story of the eponymous troubled boy – rendered deaf, dumb, and blind by a traumatic event in his childhood – as he attempts to overcome his condition and reach spiritual enlightenment.

While grappling with the story of the album, The Who guitarist and *Tommy* composer Pete Townsend shared an early assembly with noted music critic Nik Cohn, who felt it focused too exclusively on heavy spiritual themes and required a lighter selection to balance the composition. Cohn suggested that *Tommy* be particularly good at a game. Townsend turned to pinball because Cohn was an aficionado of the coin-operated amusement and composed a new song for the album called "Pinball Wizard."[1]

Released as a single in advance of the full album on March 7, 1969, "Pinball Wizard" shot up the charts in both the United States and the United Kingdom, peaking at 19 and 4, respectively, in the two countries. Pinball and rock & roll had already been tied together in the public mind through the close association of the jukebox and the pin game in bars and taverns and the reputation of both mediums as havens for rebellious or delinquent youth. "Pinball Wizard" rendered this connection even more explicit. The opportunities for cross-promotion appear obvious today, but at the time licensing was simply not done in pinball, and the Depression-era executives still running all the major coin-op manufacturers in the late

---

[1] "The Who's Pete Townsend Shares the Story Behind 'Pinball Wizard,'" Guitar World, May 19, 2017, https://www.guitarworld.com/artists/acoustic-nation-whos-pete-townshend-shares-story-behind-pinball-wizard.

1960s were probably barely aware that The Who or their rock opera existed. In 1975, Columbia Pictures announced an adaptation of *Tommy* to the silver screen with an all-star cast that included Ann-Margaret, Tina Turner, and an up-and-coming piano rocker named Elton John. This time, the rock opera caught the attention of a relatively new member of the sales team at third-largest pinball manufacturer Bally named Tom Nieman.

Tom Nieman graduated from the University of Michigan in 1972 with a degree in radio, television, and film but had difficulty finding a job in his chosen field. When Nieman's good friend and son of Bally CEO Bill O'Donnell, Jr. learned of his plight, he arranged a job for Nieman with Bally's Carousel Time operating subsidiary. The company briefly tried Nieman as a service tech before employing him as a delivery truck driver. While out on delivery, Nieman would analyze the locations on the route to determine which were well run and which were not and share his observations with the staff at Carousel Time. Before long, this led to a full time job analyzing routes for the operator. Shortly after Aladdin's Castle was merged into Carousel Time, Nieman moved to sales at Bally corporate, where his job was to move excess inventory of the company's pinball machines.[2]

As Nieman became more immersed in the pinball world, he came to realize that the teenagers who played pinball also drove the movie and record businesses and wondered why no pinball manufacturers had taken advantage of this fact. He particularly felt that Bally should explore synergy with *Tommy* because it referenced Bally in the song *Pinball Wizard*. Nieman mentioned this fact to long-time Bally executive Herb Jones, who showed him a letter the company had received from the company that published The Who's music asking for permission to use the Bally name in the song. Jones had never heard of the band and did not act on the letter, but with The Who apparently interested in dealing with Bally on some level and the *Tommy* movie just announced, Neiman was inspired to pursue a license for a pinball machine.[3]

Despite being unable to generate any enthusiasm for a licensing deal within Bally, Nieman made a series of phone calls to Columbia Pictures over the next few weeks until he connected with Barry Lorrie, the executive responsible for making licensing deals related to *Tommy*. Lorrie loved Nieman's plan and concluded an inexpensive licensing deal. Bally management continued to show resistance but eventually gave Nieman leave to move

---

[2] "Show 54," *TOPcast*, podcast audio, March 2008, http://www.pinrepair.com/topcast/showget.php?id=54.

[3] Ibid.

forward with a limited budget. Working from nothing but a script and a few still photos, Nieman collaborated with designer Norm Clark and artist Dave Christensen to create a table dubbed *Wizard* that sported a colorful playfield and backglass intended to capture the spirit of the movie.[4]

Under Nieman's direction, Bally and Columbia debuted *Wizard* alongside the movie in several media markets and gave away several units via promotions to generate interest. The two companies also collaborated on advertising materials, such as a flyer featuring film co-star Ann-Margaret posing with the machine. These tactics helped generate enormous demand for the game from fans eager to imitate the movie's titular character, leaving Bally in the enviable position of merely needing to supply cabinets rather than solicit orders.[5] Released in May 1975, *Wizard* became a 10,000-unit blockbuster to deliver the best showing by a pinball machine since the Great Depression.[6]

With *Wizard* proving a phenomenal success, Nieman found himself under pressure to produce another hit. Turning to the *Tommy* movie for inspiration once again, Nieman felt that Elton John left the largest impression on the audience and called the singer's management – with whom he had previously interacted during promotional work for *Tommy* – to pitch an Elton-themed machine. John loved the idea, so Bally created a table in 1976 called *Capt. Fantastic and the Brown Dirt Cowboy* that owed more to John's character in *Tommy* than his latest album and moved 16,000 units to prove the sales of *Wizard* were no fluke.[7] With these successes, licensed tables became a staple of the pinball industry as all the major manufacturers began emulating Bally. These tables held an appeal with young people from all walks of life that pinball had not experienced in decades and transformed the game into a mass market phenomenon no longer limited to bars and arcades, but now also found in drug stores, candy shops, and other mainstream venues. This in turn helped pinball gain a new acceptance in society.

Even before the debut of *Wizard*, the elimination of the last gambling elements in pinball, the introduction of new coin-operated amusements like quiz games and video games unburdened by any gambling stigma, and the rise of the family-friendly shopping mall arcade significantly altered the public's perception of coin-operated amusements as a front for organized crime and engendered hope among operators that the games might be operated

---

[4]Ibid.

[5]Richard Meyers, "Pinballyhoo: How Pinball Was Hyped into Respectability," *Videogaming Illustrated*, February 1983, 41.

[6]Bueschel, 1988, 241.

[7]Ibid, 242; Show 54, 2008.

legally all around the country. They experienced their first major victory in 1974 when the California Supreme Court upheld a lower court ruling issued in 1972 calling for the ban on pinball in the city of Los Angeles to be overturned,[8] a decision that hinged largely on testimony from pinball pioneer Harry Williams that demonstrated pinball had evolved over the decades into a game of skill.[9]

Operators brought a similar suit against New York City in 1975, but proved unsuccessful in overturning the city's 30-year-old ban, so they adopted a different strategy.[10] With New York mired in a fiscal crisis and in desperate need of income, the city had been raising mass transit fares, scaling back city services, and levying taxes on everything from shoe shines to haircuts. In this climate, local operators approached City Councilman Eugene Mastropieri of Queens to introduce a repeal on the city's decades-long ban on pinball so the city could generate revenue by requiring license fees of $50 per machine.[11]

An avid pinball player himself, Mastropieri waged a long campaign that culminated in a hearing before the city council consumer affairs committee on April 2, 1976. At the hearing, an associate editor for *Gentleman's Quarterly* researching a book on the history of pinball named Roger Sharpe played a Gottlieb table called *Bank Shot* to illustrate that pinball had long since left behind the pure randomness that had motivated Mayor LaGuardia to attack the game in the 1930s and 1940s and had morphed into a game of skill.[12] Satisfied by the demonstration, the committee unanimously voted to lift the ban,[13] and Mayor Abraham Beame signed the bill officially authorizing the operation of pinball machines within city limits on August 1.[14] Chicago, the center of the pinball industry and the last major holdout, almost legalized the game the same year, but a powerful city councilman named Ed Burke delayed the bill in committee due to fears about organized crime. The bill finally passed in early 1977.[15] After over four decades of operation, pinball had finally shed its seedy, mafia-controlled image, and the future of the game looked bright.

The introduction of the first solid-state pinball machines cemented the game's renewed position as the leading game in the coin-op industry. While

[8] "Cal. Supreme Court Scores for Trade," *Cash Box*, August 10, 1974, 48.

[9] "L.S. Legalizes Flippers; 1939 Law 'Unconstitutional,'" *Cash Box*, February 26, 1972, 45.

[10] "N.Y. Upholds Pinball Ban," *Cash Box*, November 8, 1975, 39.

[11] Tom Buckley, "Pinball Goes Electronic," *The New York Times*, January 23, 1977.

[12] Kent, 2001, 89–90.

[13] "New York City Council Votes 6-0 to Lifet City's Pinball Ban," *Cash Box*, April 17, 1976, 39.

[14] "Beame Signs Bill, Pinball Machines Are Legal Again," *The New York Times*, June 2, 1976.

[15] Smith, *Chicago Reader*, 2018.

early efforts like Mirco's *Spirit of '76* failed for a variety of reasons, Bally introduced its internally produced solid-state system in its December 1976 game *Freedom*. While that game only had a moderate run of 1,500 units because it was a conversion of an existing electromechanical game, in February 1977 the company released its first original solid-state game, *Night Rider*, which sold 7,000 units. Even greater success followed with *Evel Knievel* in July, which sold 14,000 units off the back of the daredevil's extraordinary popularity.

In September, Bally released *Eight Ball*, which highlighted the advantages of transitioning to solid state as the first pinball machine to incorporate scoring memory. While previous multi-player pinball games could keep track of each player's score, they could not transfer any score multipliers accumulated through play from ball to ball. *Eight Ball* could remember the state of the board when a player's turn ended and pick right back up where the player left off in the next round. This capability helped transform the game into a sensation, and it set yet another new post-war record with sales of 20,320 units.[16] With these games, Bally cemented its position as the number one pinball company in the world.

***

The rising fortunes of solid-state pinball in the late 1970s came at the expense of other forms of coin-operated amusement, particularly video games. In 1976, coin-op video game revenues peaked as *Sea Wolf, Gun Fight, Breakout*, and *Sprint 2* led a robust group of games that sold somewhere between 70,000 and 75,000 units.[17] This performance obscured underlying problems, however, as operators became more selective in the video equipment they would buy, the secondary market for used games largely collapsed, and several smaller manufacturers went out of business.[18]

In 1977, the coin-op video game market declined as sales dipped to around 50,000 units.[19] While most companies in the industry embraced the microprocessor, the driving, dueling, and shooting gallery games produced that year failed to generate the same sales or excitement as their predecessors. For the next two years, the popularity charts of both *Replay* and competing trade publication *Play Meter* remained clogged with games that premiered in 1976. The average weekly earnings of video games fell behind both pinball

---

[16] Bueschel, 1988, 244.

[17] Institute of Electrical and Electronic Engineers, *1977 Electro Conference Record: Presented at Electro 1977, New York, NY, April 19–21, 1977* (New York: Electro, 1977), 46.

[18] Gene Beley, "Business Preview '77: One Western Opinion," *Play Meter*, January 1977, 22.

[19] *The Video Game Industry: Strategic Analysis* (New York: Sanford C. Bernstein & Co., 1982), 63.

and pool,[20] while overall revenues came to just over $334 million, which put the category in second place behind pinball's massive $1.4 billion take.[21]

Atari remained the leading arcade video game manufacturer with an estimated 44% market share.[22] Compared to the dual successes of *Sprint 2* and *Breakout* in 1976, however, sales of individual games were modest. The two biggest successes were the company's latest entries into the popular target shooting and racing genres, *Starship 1* and *Super Bug*. Programmed by Ron Milner at Cyan Engineering, *Starship 1* took its primary inspiration from the television show *Star Trek*. It incorporated a first-person perspective and forward scrolling starfield inspired by the main viewscreen of the USS *Enterprise* to give the player the sensation of flying a ship through space while shooting at ships and space monsters inspired by the show.[23] *Super Bug*, programmed by new hire Howard Delman based on a design by Lyle Rains, featured the same basic gameplay as Atari's previous driving games, but this time with a zoomed in view, larger, more detailed graphics, and both horizontal and vertical scrolling – a rare feature in games of the period – to depict a larger course. The two games sold roughly 3,500 units apiece.[24]

In 1978, Atari remained the market leader, though its share declined to 29%.[25] The company's biggest hit of the year grew directly out of the development of *Super Bug*. When the game became successful, the next logical step was to create a two-player version. This proved impossible because the car remains fixed in the center of the screen at all times while the track scrolls around it.[26] The solution came from Steve Mayer at Cyan Engineering, who was interested in exploring cooperative play and developed the idea of having two players drive a hook-and-ladder truck, which has a second steering wheel in the rear due to the vehicle's length.[27] After the basic parameters of the game were laid out at Cyan, Howard Delman and hardware engineer John Ray completed the game. Called *Fire Truck*, it requires one player to sit down in the arcade cabinet and control the front of the engine, while the other stands behind him and uses his own steering to control the rear section. Together, the players guide their fire engine around a scrolling playfield while

---

[20] Vending Times Census of the Industry, July 1981, 63–66.

[21] Ibid, 56.

[22] Bernstein, 1982, 66.

[23] Milner, 2018.

[24] Atari Production Numbers, 1999.

[25] Bernstein, 1982, 66.

[26] Scott Stilphen, "DP Interviews Howard Delman," *Digital Press*, 2011, http://www.digitpress.com/library/interviews/interview_howard_delman.html.

[27] Mayer, 2018.

keeping it on the road and avoiding oil slicks. Deployed in June 1978, *Fire Truck* was the first video game in which two players played together cooperatively rather than competitively and sold around 4,000 units.[28]

The second biggest manufacturer in the coin-op video game business remained the Midway Manufacturing subsidiary of Bally, the only major Chicago coin-op company that took the video segment of the coin-op market seriously throughout most of the 1970s. Unlike Atari, Midway relied almost exclusively on outside developers to create its products. The most significant of these firms remained Dave Nutting Associates, responsible for the hits *Gun Fight* and *Sea Wolf* in 1975 and 1976, respectively. Over the next two years, DNA's – and by extension Midway's – most significant games were sequels to those two products. In 1977, DNA created *Boot Hill*, which enhanced *Gun Fight* with improved graphics and a colorful backdrop of a stereotypical Western town. As in *Tornado Baseball* the year before, the company created this backdrop by sculpting the town in plastic and then incorporating a mirror into the cabinet to superimpose the computer graphics over top of it. For a brief time, this mirroring technique became a popular method to create elaborate graphical elements beyond the capability of coin-op hardware.

The next year, DNA hardware designer Jeff Frederiksen finished an important upgrade to the company's microprocessor-driven hardware system. While the introduction of microprocessors greatly simplified PC board design by allowing many functions to be executed in software, early microprocessor-based arcade systems still required a great number of TTL circuits for display elements, I/O controls, and sound. To further simplify board design, Frederiksen reduced all these circuits to their own chips that could work in tandem with the processor.[29]

Frederiksen's original board was developed around the 8080 microprocessor created by Federico Faggin at Intel. In 1974, Faggin left Intel to establish his own company called Zilog with fellow Intel engineer Ralph Ungermann. Faggin planned for the company's first product to be a single-chip microcontroller, but quickly realized margins would be slim in the crowded market. Therefore, he worked with Ungermann and Masatoshi

---

[28] Frost & Sullivan, 1979, 176. While unit sales for the game are not recorded, it is noted as the third highest selling game of the year between *Space Wars* and *Sea Wolf II*. Other sources indicate that *Space Wars* sold 4,000–5,000 units that year and *Sea Wolf II* sold about 4,000 units, which allows a rough estimate of *Fire Truck*'s sales. Atari also created a single-player version called *Smokey Joe* because the full *Fire Truck* cabinet proved too large for many street locations. *Smokey Joe* is identical to the original game save that one player controls the truck by himself. Stilphen, 2011.

[29] Thacker, 2011.

Shima to develop a microprocessor called the Z80. Released in 1976, the Z80 was both cheaper and more capable than the Intel 8080 but maintained complete compatibility with the chip. As a result, it eclipsed Intel's earlier designs and remained one of the most popular processors of the 8-bit era.[30]

For his new coin-op hardware, Frederiksen paired the Z80 with a custom-made graphics chip built by American Micro Systems that allowed for full-color graphics at what was then considered high resolution, 320 × 204.[31] The first game created using this new system was *Sea Wolf II*, which played similarly to the original but featured colorful graphics and more ships and torpedoes on the screen at one time thanks to its advanced hardware. While not as big a seller as the original due to the generally depressed video game market, *Sea Wolf II* became one of the biggest video game hits of 1978 and sold 4,000 units.[32]

Behind Midway came Exidy,[33] which rode the *Death Race* controversy to an increased national profile and larger distribution network. Like Atari and Midway, Exidy moved to embrace microprocessor-driven hardware in the wake of the success of *Gun Fight*. VP of engineering Howell Ivy led the push to adopt the new technology, as he had been working with microprocessors since developing a solid-state pinball prototype based around the 4004 processor for Ramtek in late 1974.[34] When others at Exidy proved skeptical of the new technology, Ivy purchased a 6502 processor from MOS Technology with his own money to demonstrate the capabilities it possessed.[35]

For his first microprocessor-driven game, *Car Polo*, Ivy decided to make a splash by incorporating a full-color display, still highly unusual in the industry at the time due to the expense. Essentially a soccer match between four cars of different colors set against a bright green background, the game left little impact on the marketplace. A bowling game called *Robot Bowl* followed and experienced more success, remaining a top-ten earner on location for two years, but Ivy's microprocessor-based hardware experienced its real breakthrough when he decided to liven up the game of *Breakout* with a new variant called *Circus*.

---

[30] "Chip Hall of Fame: Zilog Z80 Microprocessor," *IEEE Spectrum*, June 30, 2017, https://spectrum.ieee.org/tech-history/silicon-revolution/chip-hall-of-fame-zilog-z80-microprocessor.

[31] Thacker, 2011.

[32] Kent, 2001, 102.

[33] Frost & Sullivan, 1979, 176.

[34] The game, called *Lucky Dice*, sported programming by Ivy and a playfield design by Bob Jonesi. Ramtek ultimately declined to release the game due to the high cost of establishing a pinball manufacturing line. McEwan, 1980.

[35] Smith, 2016, 216.

Circus retained *Breakout's* basic conceit of bouncing one object off another to clear the top of the screen of targets, but it added sophistication to the experience by transforming the solid rows of bricks into colorful balloons moving across the screen,[36] the paddle into a seesaw, and the ball into two acrobats launching each other into the air. While the characters were little more than stick figures, their limbs flailed comically in the most impressive display of animation yet seen in a coin-operated video game. The added charm captured the attention of the industry when the game debuted at the 1977 AMOA Expo and spurred brisk sales as Exidy ramped up production to 100 units a day and resorted to storing cabinets in the parking lot as they ran out of space in their building.[37] By the end of its run, *Circus* sold over 7,000 units to become the best-selling game of 1978 and inspired its own round of clones.[38] Like *Breakout*, *Circus* also proved a big hit in Japan, where it was licensed by Taito as *Acrobat* for release in both an upright and table-top version and was widely cloned by other manufacturers as video continued to assert itself in the country's shifting coin-op marketplace.

***

Rounding out the top five coin-op manufacturers were two relative newcomers to the business both based in the San Diego area: Gremlin Industries and Cinematronics. A science enthusiast from a young age, Tennessee native and Gremlin co-founder Frank Fogelman studied engineering at East Tennessee State in the heart of Appalachia in the late 1940s and early 1950s, interrupted by a stint in the U.S. Navy during the Korean War. Well versed in electronics during his military tour of duty, he gained employment with a Tennessee TV company after leaving the service. A visit to a friend in California led him to fall in love with a state in which it did not rain all the time.[39] After bouncing around several companies in San Diego and Los Angeles, he established his own firm in San Diego in 1959 called Aeromarine Electronics that focused on temperature controls for spacecraft and missiles and later expanded into marine navigation aids. The company fell on hard times in the mid-1960s when Fogelman developed a battery-powered phone that two different manufacturing firms he contracted ended up stealing from him to make on their own.[40]

---

[36] Unlike in *Car Polo*, the color in *Circus* was achieved using overlays.
[37] Ellis, 2006, 49.
[38] Frost & Sullivan, 1979, 182.
[39] Frank Fogelman, interview with Ethan Johnson, November 18, 2016.
[40] Smith, 2016, 249.

Frustrated at his lack of control over the entire production process, Fogelman established a small contract electronics firm in 1970 with a friend from the aerospace industry named Carl Grindle. The duo decided to name their company after themselves as "Grindleman Industries," but when they went to incorporate, the people they were working with in Delaware to set up the corporation misheard them say "Gremlin Industries" over the phone, and the name stuck. Over the next two years, Gremlin produced products ranging from integrated circuit testers to the French fry timers used by the Jack-in-the-Box fast food chain.[41]

Most of the early employees of the company came from Grindle's former firm, Cohu Electronics, including the VP of engineering, Jerry Hansen. One day in 1972, a customer approached Hansen with a broken wall game and asked him to fix it. This was at the height of the wall game boom in the coin-operated amusement industry, and Hansen was shocked to learn from the customer that despite the primitive circuitry and limited gameplay of the unit, it was immensely profitable. Hansen figured he could create a better wall game himself and set to work designing a baseball variant called *Play Ball*. Released in 1973, the game proved a hard sell at first as the wall game market was in the midst of collapse, but the quality of the product won through, and it became such a massive success that Gremlin abandoned its other products to focus exclusively on coin-operated games.[42]

Gremlin followed *Play Ball* with a skeet-shooting-themed wall game called *Trapshoot* that once again proved a hit. The company was beginning to run into trouble, however, because the circuit boards of the game were fairly complicated and straining the limits of TTL hardware. Hansen knew he would need to transition to a microprocessor-driven system, but no one at the company had the necessary programming expertise. A solution emerged when Hansen attended a presentation by chip company Signetics and met an engineer named Lane Hauck.[43]

A math and physics major who loved technology, Hauck became a computing convert in the early 1970s when he beheld some of the earliest minicomputers. Hauck worked for Lockheed at the time and lobbied heavily for the firm to purchase a PDP-8. When the company refused, he shelled out $5,500 to buy one for himself. Soon after, he moved to San Diego to work for Spectral Dynamics and placed the computer in his back bedroom. He began

---

[41] Ibid, 249–250.
[42] Ibid, 250–251.
[43] Ibid, 251–252.

playing games on the machine to help him understand the new technology and became particularly fascinated with the logic game *Moo*, a computerized version of the code-breaking game Bulls and Cows. Eager to share the game with his friends, he built a custom circuit board roughly the size of a hand-held calculator dedicated to playing the game.[44]

Hauck followed his *Moo* handheld by constructing a computer the size of a bread box that could hook into a television to play blackjack. This contraption impressed Fogelman and Hansen when Hauck invited them to his home after their chance meeting at Signetics. They commissioned Hauck to create a new wall game for them, and he drafted a plan for a game called *FoosWall* that incorporated an Intel 8008 microprocessor.[45] Gremlin offered him a job, and he completed the game with help from George Kiss, the son of a former co-worker.[46]

By 1976, Gremlin controlled 95% of the wall game market, but it was clear the coin-operated world was moving in a different direction. Hauck lobbied hard to enter the video game business, but Hansen and Fogelman demurred because they were hesitant to enter a volatile field in which their expertise was limited. Undeterred, Hauck began tinkering with a video game board on his own time in the hopes of winning them over. To test the system, he programmed a random walk process, a mathematical object that models the path of a succession of random steps. After watching an arrow move around the screen for a time, he got bored and decided to add a wrinkle to the exercise: the arrow could not visit the same square twice. After watching the arrow become trapped after a few steps, he realized he had a viable game idea.[47]

Hauck and Kiss further developed this concept into a two-player game called *Blockade*, in which each player controls a cursor that moves around the screen while leaving a trail behind. Running into the trail of either cursor causes the player to crash and his opponent to score a point. The first player to score six points wins the game. Fogelman and Hansen were impressed with the game and agreed to put it out on test at a local miniature golf center. When the earnings from the prototype proved substantial, Gremlin brought the game to the AMOA show in November, alongside a four-player variant called *CoMotion*.[48]

---

[44] Jeannette DeWyze, "San Diego's Gremlin: How Video Games Work," *San Diego Reader*, July 15, 1982.

[45] Ibid.

[46] Ibid, and George Kiss, interview with the author, August 14, 2018.

[47] Smith, 2016, 253.

[48] Ibid, 254.

Blockade proved the hit of the show and generated orders for 3,000 units. Unfortunately, Gremlin had never produced a video game before, so by the time it could bring the game to market it faced an array of clones, including *Barricade* from Ramtek, *Bigfoot Bonkers* from Meadows, *Checkmate* from Midway, and *Dominos* from Atari. Gremlin did patent the concept and sued some of these companies for infringement, but the process of working through the courts moved too slowly to provide the company relief. With Gremlin unable to keep up with manufacturing, it lost most of its orders. The gameplay ultimately proved relatively unpopular with the public anyway, so the concept was essentially dead by the end of 1977.[49]

Gremlin rebounded from the *Blockade* disappointment with a string of modestly successful games, but failed to score a major hit over the next two years. Consequently, sales lagged behind the company's rapid growth, particularly after bad winter weather in 1977 prevented many of its games from reaching distributors. While the company pulled through, the exact same thing happened in 1978 and left the company teetering on the edge of collapse.[50] Fortunately, this was the period Sega was looking to improve the performance of its North American operations. Gremlin appeared a good fit due to its expertise with microprocessors, so in September 1978 Sega purchased Gremlin to serve as its primary R&D and manufacturing hub in North America.[51]

As Gremlin struggled to come up with a major hit after its misadventure with *Blockade*, its crosstown rival released one of the biggest games of 1978. Cinematronics was established in 1975 in Kearny Mesa, California, as a sideline business by two San Diego Chargers football players, Gary Garrison and Dennis Partee. The origins of the firm are a bit hazy, but it appears to have been formed to penetrate the cocktail *Pong* market that was already starting to fade by that date. Partee and Garrison apparently had no desire to manage their company day-to-day, as they acquired a third partner, a former beet farmer with a knack for salesmanship named Jim Pierce, to serve as president. Over the next two years, the company lost money as neither its cocktail *Pong* game nor a knock-off of Exidy's *TV Pinball* called *Flipper Ball* sold well.[52]

Despite these early difficulties, Pierce resolved to transform the company into a success. In mid-1976, he hired Cinematronics' first game designer,

[49] Smith, 2016, 254–255.

[50] Ibid, 258.

[51] "Gremlin Acquisition Boosts Sega Profile in U.S. Market," *Cash Box*, October 28, 1978, 72–74.

[52] Smith, 2016, 270–271. Cinematronics apparently attempted to offer its *Pong* game in the home as well in 1976 according to a newspaper ad, but no details have emerged about this product.

Robert Shaver, who produced a game called *Embargo* that played similarly to *Blockade* and its many clones but featured graphics of ships and mines. In early 1977, Pierce joined with a mortgage company owner named Ralph Clarke to buy out Garrison's share of the company and hired a veteran of recently defunct manufacture Chicago Coin named Bob Sherwood as his sales manager, providing the company with experienced coin-op management for the first time.[53] The key to the company's turnaround, however, was a deal Pierce made with an MIT graduate named Larry Rosenthal to bring an accurate and cost-effective rendition of *Spacewar!* to the arcade for the first time.

An electrical engineering prodigy, Larry Rosenthal built his first circuit when he was four and earned a HAM radio license at 11. He was first exposed to computing in 1967 as a junior in high school as part of a group of students allowed to program on an IBM 360 computer owned by Sandoz Pharmaceutical once a week. Rosenthal first saw the game *Spacewar!* in May 1968 while paying a visit to MIT as a 17-year-old high school senior freshly accepted by the university. While the encounter proved memorable, he did not play the game again during his years at the school. After graduating in 1972 with a BS in electrical engineering, Rosenthal travelled across the country to the University of California at Berkeley to complete a master's degree. That Christmas, he paid a visit to MIT and beheld a *Computer Space* unit in the student union. Rosenthal was shocked, but not due to amazement over this new technology. Rather, he was disdainful because he could not understand why the birthplace of *Spacewar!* would host such a primitive derivative of the landmark computer game.[54]

After completing his masters in June 1973, Rosenthal was uncertain what to do with his life. A professor at MIT offered him a lab job, but he loved California and was not sure he really wanted to head back east. After spending the summer contemplating his situation, he resolved to remain in California and create a home version of *Spacewar!* based on his memories of seeing the game five years before. At the time, the only microprocessors on the market were Intel's 4004 and 8008 models, which were not powerful enough to drive a display, so Rosenthal built his own custom computer out of TTL logic. When it came time to hook up the system to a television, however, he discovered the spaceships looked terrible at the standard resolution of 320×256. To make the game viable, Rosenthal would need to incorporate a vector display.[55]

---

[53] Ibid, 271–272.

[54] Kevin Butler, "Space Wars," *Old School Gamer Magazine*, September 2019, 14.

[55] Smith, 2016, 273.

Since the invention of the television in the 1920s, the standard method of creating a picture using a CRT has been to generate a raster image in which the electron gun rapidly traverses the entire screen from top to bottom, one horizontal line at a time, to produce a complete image as a collection of pixels. In contrast, a vector scan system aims the electron gun at a single point and then provides it a vector in order to draw a line before deflecting the beam in another direction, allowing it to draw wireframe models. This method is far too slow to draw an image that fills the entire screen like a television picture, but because the whole screen does not have to be redrawn in each frame, it allows the creation of individual shapes and models at a higher resolution than a comparable raster scan. While no longer necessary due to the capabilities of modern displays, vector monitors were often used to create high-end computer graphics in the 1970s and 1980s. They were not used in early arcade video games, however, because the monitors cost tens of thousands of dollars.[56]

By using a standard television rather than a monitor and cutting a few corners in areas that did not matter for a video game, Rosenthal managed to cobble together a working vector graphics system that could sell for just $2,000 and programmed a version of *Spacewar* to run on it. In December 1976, he put his game out on test in a Berkeley arcade called the Pinball Palace owned by a friend, where it became a smash success that collected $500 in ten days. Nonetheless, trying to find a manufacturer for the game proved exceedingly difficult. Rosenthal met a Bally engineer at a Bay Area game conference and invited him to see the game at its test location. The engineer was impressed and invited Rosenthal to Chicago to demonstrate his technology, but the Bally executives were unhappy that the game used a multi-button control scheme rather than a joystick and offered a paltry 0.5% royalty, so Rosenthal turned them down.[57]

Rosenthal began lugging a prototype of his hardware around the Bay Area in a suitcase to provide demonstrations to distributors but continued to find no takers. Finally, he approached an arcade cabinet manufacturer called Tempest Products and asked them to help him form a company to manufacture and market the game. The Tempest executives were impressed, but they had just been bought out by Ramtek and could therefore not provide Rosenthal the support he needed. They did, however, call in an attorney to help Rosenthal work out a deal somewhere else, which is how the game landed at Cinematronics.[58]

---

[56] Ibid, 274–275.

[57] Ibid, 275–277.

[58] Ibid, 277.

By early 1977, Cinematronics was desperate for a hit, so not only did Jim Pierce agree to manufacture the game and give Rosenthal a 5% royalty, he also allowed Rosenthal to retain the rights to his vector hardware technology, which he had patented back in 1975.[59] Cinematronics debuted the game at the AMOA show in October 1977 under the name *Space Wars* in a calculated effort to ride the popularity of the recently released film *Star Wars*. The game became a surprise hit of the show and generated $2 million in orders. The struggling manufacturer teetered on the brink of bankruptcy and did not have the funds, facilities, or expertise to deploy a product on a massive scale, so to ramp up production Pierce installed a new management team in early 1978 led by Tom Stroud, a veteran operator in Indiana and California who had most recently been running Par Tee Golf in San Diego. Stroud bought out remaining co-founder Dennis Partee's share of Cinematronics to become a co-owner of the company.[60]

Pierce and Stroud tapped veteran coin-op salesman Bill Cravens as their new marketing director, who worked his distributor contacts in Los Angeles to raise the money needed to keep the firm running while *Space Wars* was built. He also brought in an old friend and Atari veteran named Kenneth Beuck to whip the assembly line in shape. By February, Cinematronics was producing 75 units of the game a week, which did not come close to meeting demand. In April, the company added more manufacturing space before moving to a new larger facility in June. With its fantastic graphics and engaging competitive gameplay alongside a renewed interest in space combat themes after the success of *Star Wars*, *Space Wars* became the biggest video game hit the industry had seen since *Breakout* in early 1976. By the end of 1978, Cinematronics had manufactured between 4,000 and 5,000 units and remained in full production of the game.[61] By the end of its run, the company had produced over 7,000 units of *Space Wars*,[62] which became the first video game not made by Atari or Midway to top the operator polls of both *Replay* or *Play Meter* and remained a top ten earner into the middle of 1980. The success of the game was an outlier in this period, however, as video continued to lose ground to pinball.

***

In 1978, video game collections declined from an estimated $334 million in 1977 to $304 million. Units on location also declined from 173,700 to

---

[59] Reports that Rosenthal demanded a 50% royalty appear to be greatly exaggerated.

[60] Ibid, 278–279.

[61] Frost & Sullivan, 1979, 184.

[62] Smith, 2016, 279–281.

164, 600.[63] *Space Wars* was the top earning game on location, but the next two best earners were *Sprint 2* and *Sea Wolf,* both of which debuted in 1976. Few games released over the preceeding two years offered more than cosmetic changes or minor gameplay tweaks over previous top earning games and therefore proved unable to sustain earnings for more than a couple of months. Operators consequently became more selective in their purchases, and sales of new games stagnated at around 62,000 units.[64] According to a survey conducted by *Replay* in the fall, 47% of operators planned to buy fewer video games in 1979, while just 28% planned to buy more.[65]

In addition to lack of innovation the main factor in the decline of coin-operated video games was the phenomenal rise in the sale of pinball machines spurred by the introduction of solid-state hardware that promised fewer maintenance headaches and more flexible scoring mechanics to completely transform the game. The average weekly take of a pinball game hovered somewhere between $50 and $65 in 1978 to become the highest earning game on location for the first time in years, far beyond video, which earned in the low $40 range, and even beating out the usual champion, the pool table. While no video game reached sales of 10,000 units in 1978, Bally alone introduced seven machines that would ultimately reach that figure, the most popular of which was a *Playboy*-themed game that debuted in December and sold over 18,000 units. In 1979, over 200,000 pinball machines were sold to set a post-war industry record.

Even Atari, the originator of the coin-operated video game industry, realized it would need to evolve to stay relevant in the new business climate. In early 1976, the company established a pinball division under the auspices of manufacturing VP Gil Williams, which debuted its first table, *The Atarians,* at the MOA show that November. Over the next two years, Atari focused on building solid-state pinball machines with extra wide playfields in an attempt to stand out from the competition. The company also stepped up its efforts in the home, where the microprocessor was poised to lead a technological revolution just as great as the one currently sweeping through the arcade.

---

[63] Vending Times Census of the Industry, 1981, 63.

[64] *Home & Coin Operated Electronic Games* (New York: Frost & Sullivan, 1979), 177.

[65] Smith, 2016, 338

20

Putting the F in Fun

On August 10, 1968, the board of Fairchild Camera & Instrument named Dr. C. Lester Hogan the new president and CEO of the company, filling a vacancy dating back to the dismissal of Richard Hodgson that February. The head of the semiconductor business at Motorola, which he grew from a small operation to the second largest chip manufacturer in the world, he came in with a mandate to revitalize the Fairchild Semiconductor operation that had been providing most of the company's profits for several years but was falling behind technologically as those profits were invested in other businesses. In a symbol of this new focus, Hogan moved FCI headquarters from Syosset, New York, to Mountain View, California, in the heart of Silicon Valley.[1]

Over the next two years, Hogan dismantled virtually all FCI's businesses not related to the manufacture of solid-state components and electronics while pouring money into modernizing of Fairchild Semiconductor's manufacturing facilities.[2] While sales increased significantly as a result, the company failed to turn a profit initially as a recession devastated the semiconductor industry. Consequently, Fairchild proved unable to transition from bipolar circuits to MOS circuits, lost significant ground to its competitors, and began hemorrhaging cash.[3] Although the company eventually returned to profitability, the failure to upgrade its product line marked the beginning of its long decline. In 1974, Hogan resigned as president due to lingering health issues from a botched operation several years before and turned the company over to his protégé Wilf Corrigan, one of seven Motorola employees dubbed "Hogan's

---

[1] Lojek, 2007, 162–164.
[2] Fairchild Camera and Instrument Corporation, Annual Report, 1968, and Fairchild Camera and Instrument, Annual Report, 1969, and Lojek, 2007, 168–169.
[3] Young, 1998, 133.

Heroes" who followed their boss from Motorola to take senior management positions at Fairchild.[4] Corrigan followed the example of Texas Instruments and National Semiconductor to bring Fairchild into consumer electronics. By 1974, the calculator market was largely played out, so Corrigan focused on the latest consumer electronic fad: the digital watch.

Digital watch technology, in which the display is formed using solid-state components, was made possible by the invention at TI in 1962 of a special type of diode, the light-emitting diode, or LED, that generates light when a suitable voltage is passed through it. A decade of enhancement and miniaturization followed before the Hamilton Watch Company introduced the first electronic digital watch in 1972, which at $2,100 was prohibitively expensive for most people. As with the pocket calculator, however, consumer electronics and semiconductor companies knew it would be just a matter of time until digital watches dropped in price precipitously.[5] Corrigan brought FCI into the field by purchasing a watch circuit startup called Exetron in 1975 to form the heart of a new consumer electronics division at the company.[6] To run the new division, Corrigan tapped Greg Reyes, a 1962 graduate of Rensselaer Polytechnic Institute who worked at National Semiconductor and Motorola before following Corrigan to FCI in 1968. Before moving to consumer electronics, he had spent the last few years running Fairchild's discrete electronics group.[7]

Fairchild released its first watches in July 1975.[8] The next year, TI introduced its TI-500 LED watch sporting a plastic case allowing it to retail for only $20. As in calculators, a race to the bottom on price developed that destroyed most of the companies in the business.[9] By 1976, FCI was the second-largest digital watch producer behind TI,[10] but consumers were already tiring of them, leading to massive overstocks at Christmas and deep discounts at the beginning of the next year. When TI subsequently cut the price of its cheapest watches to $10 in spring 1977, the opportunity for FCI

[4]C. Lester Hogan, interview by Rob Walker, January 24, 1995, Stanford University, https://searchworks.stanford.edu/view/zm237vn0430.

[5]Joe Thompson, "Four Revolutions, the Lost Chapter: A Concise History of the LED Watch," Hodinkee, February 26, 2018, https://www.hodinkee.com/articles/four-revolutions-led-watches.

[6]"Watch watch," *Weekly Television Digest with Consumer Electronics*, April 28, 1975.

[7]*Dun & Bradstreet Reference Book of Corporate Managements* (New York: Dun & Bradstreet, 1977), 455.

[8]Fairchild Camera and Instrument Corporation, Annual Report, 1975.

[9]Thompson, 2018.

[10]"Fairchild's Problems: More Than Watches," *Business Week*, August 15, 1977, 116.

to make money in the business had passed.[11] By then, Fairchild had already embraced the latest hot consumer electronic product: the video game.

***

In 1976, an estimated 3.2 million dedicated video game consoles were sold in the United States as the demand for *Pong*-style games continued unabated from the previous year.[12] For a variety of reasons, this represented only around one-third of consumer demand. General Instrument struggled all year to produce sufficient quantities of its industry-leading AY-3-8500, particularly after a November strike at its main manufacturing plant. Sales were further hampered when prominent Japanese OEM electronics manufacturer Systek entered bankruptcy late in the year and could not supply product to its American partners, most notably the electronics importers Lloyd's and Unisonic.[13] Additionally, several U.S. firms that planned to release a system in time for the holidays were hampered by a failure to receive FCC approval for their hardware. If not for these factors, analysts believed the market could have absorbed as many as 10 million units. Faced with such overwhelming consumer interest and analyst estimates of another 7–10 million in sales for 1977, the leading companies in the business – Coleco, Atari, and Magnavox – each readied a new line of dedicated consoles for the next holiday season alongside a host of smaller companies.

As the Telstar only played three of the six games present on the GI AY-3-8500 chip, Coleco focused on new variants incorporating different sets of games. Because of the success of that first product, the company decided to market all these new variations under the Telstar name.[14] The primary model for the year was the Telstar Alpha, which added a squash game called *Jai-Alai* to the lineup of the original system and retailed for just $40. Coleco also released a color version of the Alpha called the Telstar Colormatic for $50 and a deluxe model called the Telstar Ranger that shipped with two detachable controllers as well as a separate light gun to play the two target shooting games on the AY-3-8500 chip for $60. Finally, Coleco deployed its first four-player unit, the Telstar Galaxy, which retailed for $60 and could play eight games in full color.[15]

Magnavox, meanwhile, abandoned its custom chip designs from the previous two years and embraced the GI chip line with three new systems, the

[11] Victor K. McElheny, "The Shakeout in Digital Watches," *The New York Times*, September 21, 1977.
[12] Frost & Sullivan, 1983, 24.
[13] "RCA Game Approved," *Weekly Television Digest with Consumer Electronics*, November 29, 1976, 11.
[14] "Coleco Reports Great Success with Telstar; Plans to Beef Up Promotional Spending," *Playthings*, October 1977, 34.
[15] "Coleco's Plug-In Game," *Weekly Television Digest with Consumer Electronics*, February 21, 1977, 11.

Odyssey 2000, 3000, and 4000. Both the 2000 and 3000 used the AY-3-8500 chip like the Odyssey 300 the year before but added the *Squash* game on the chip to the tennis, hockey, and practice mode games found in the earlier system. While both the 2000 and the 3000 shipped with the same games, they featured different controllers, and only the 3000 included difficulty settings to adjust ball speed, paddle size, and ball angle. The 4000 incorporated the new AY-3-8600 that added another four ball-and-paddle games including basketball and gridball. It also featured color graphics.

While Coleco and Magnavox concentrated on exploiting GI chips in 1977, Atari forged ahead with its own designs. These included *Ultra Pong* and *Ultra Pong Doubles* systems that featured 16 ball-and-paddle variants for two or four players, respectively, as well as more innovative systems like *Video Pinball*. Retailing for $99, *Video Pinball* may have been the most sophisticated dedicated console yet produced, as it incorporated RAM memory in order to feature several pinball-like games in which the targets could change color and a port of the hit arcade game *Breakout.*

With a diverse array of new systems coming to retail, the market for 1976 models collapsed. By spring 1977, systems that retailed for $70–$80 the previous holiday season could be found for half that price as retailers cleared old stock in anticipation of newer models. Concern began to grow that the video game business might soon follow the calculator and watch businesses that started out so promising but fell apart in relatively short order.[16] The obvious solution was to develop more sophisticated games with more interesting gameplay than *Pong*, but moving beyond ball-and-paddle and simple target shooting games proved tricky due to increasing complexity straining the limits of LSI circuits. The first company to try was URL, still hanging in the market with its Video Action series despite generally lackluster sales. In late 1976, the company released a system called Indy 500 that added two new driving games to the tennis and hockey games from its Video Action III console released earlier in the year after the Video Action II had to be taken off the market for failing FCC testing.[17] Indy 500 combined the discrete circuits of Video Action III with the new driving mechanics on a two-chip set mounted on a single substrate produced by chip manufacturer Omnetics. The promise of home driving games spurred orders from several major department stores of around 60,000 units, but the chip proved difficult to manufacture, yields

---

[16] Peter Weaver, "Mind Your Money: Video Game Prices Are Going Down the Tube," *The Modesto Bee*, March 24, 1977.

[17] "Everybody's Playing Games," *Weekly Television Digest with Consumer Electronics*, January 12, 1976, 11.

were low, and URL could not bring the system to market in sufficient quantities for the holiday season. In mid-1977, the company filed for bankruptcy.[18]

GI attempted to address the variety problem by releasing a new line of chips in 1977 that each played a set of games derived from the latest hits in the arcade. These included its new *Pong* chip, the AY-3-8600, that played eight ball-and-paddle games and two target shooting games; Roadrace (AY-3-8603), which played a series of driving games; Submarine (AY-3-8605), which played target shooting games similar to Midway's *Sea Wolf*; Wipe-Off (AY-3-8606), which played variations of *Breakout*; Tank Battle (AY-3-8700), which played variations on *Tank*; and Cycle (AY-3-8760), which played variations of a 1975 Atari coin-op game called *Stunt Cycle* that tapped into the popularity of daredevil motorcyclist Evel Knieval by challenging the player to jump a motorcycle over a group of cars.[19]

In the United States, the only significant company to adopt the new wave of LSI chips from GI and its competitors was Coleco. In addition to producing its line of ball-and-paddle games, the toy company also continued its relationship with Ralph Baer by entering into a development contract with Sanders Associates. Baer assembled a small team led by a co-worker named Dunc Withun that helped Coleco develop three of its systems, the Telstar Alpha and two non-ball-and-paddle products.[20] The first, *Telstar Combat*, was powered by the AY-3-8700 chip from GI that played four variants of the hit arcade game *Tank* and replicated the dual joystick controls of that game.[21] The second system, the *Telstar Arcade*, took advantage of a chip from GI competitor MOS Technology called the MPS-7600 that came in four variations that each played a different ball-and-paddle, driving, and target shooting game. The system itself is a triangular base unit with a different control scheme on each side – paddles, a steering wheel, and a light gun – into which one of four triangular cartridges can be inserted. Each cartridge contains a different MPS-7600 variant sporting three games. The first shipped with the system, which retailed for $79.99, while the other three sold separately for $25 each.[22]

---

[18] Smith, 2016, 297–298.

[19] "Pong in a Chip," Pong Story, accessed June 8, 2019, http://www.pong-story.com/gi.htm.

[20] Baer, 2005, 142.

[21] "Telstar Combat," Pong Story, accessed June 8, 2019, http://www.pong-story.com/coleco_combat.htm.

[22] "Telstar Arcade," Pong Story, accessed June 8, 2019, http://www.pong-story.com/coleco_arcade.htm. Some have been tempted to label the *Telstar Arcade* a programmable console, but in truth, this description is not accurate, as there is no CPU in the base unit and no microprocessor in the cartridges. Instead, the LSI in each cartridge is paired with a different group of custom circuits in order to produce the different game effects.

While GI and Coleco focused on a hardware-based cartridge solution, a small Connecticut company called the Alpex Computer Corporation focused on a software solution instead. Alpex founder Norman Alpert worked as an engineer at an AMF R&D facility in Stamford, Connecticut, until the bowling company decided to move it North Carolina in 1969. Not wanting to relocate, Alpert and several other engineers at the facility formed Alpex in Stamford and entered into a partnership with mailing-equipment company Pitney Bowes to develop an electronic cash register system. That partnership fell apart in 1973 as larger companies like IBM and NCR entered the field, forcing Alpert to lay off most of his staff and leaving his company in desperate need of a new product. Fellow AMF alum William Kirschner believed Alpex should enter the video game business.[23]

Kirschner received approval to start a video game project in early 1974, which he decided should incorporate a microprocessor. He hired a former co-worker at AMF and Alpex named Lawrence Haskel to program the software for the system, which they dubbed Remote Access Video Entertainment, or RAVEN. Haskel, an avid video game player since seeing a Magnavox Odyssey demonstration unit in a department store, programmed a ball-and-paddle hockey variant, a tic-tac-toe game, a simple target shooting program, and an art program that allowed the player to draw lines on the screen. As the game library increased, Kirschner and Haskel realized interchangeability would be ideal. Inspired by their Intel 8080 development kit and its erasable-programmable read only memory (EPROM) chips, they decided to house each game on a ROM attached to a circuit board with a sturdy pin connector that could interface with the microprocessor system.[24]

Once the duo had a prototype in place, they shopped the system around to television manufacturers Sylvania, Zenith, RCA, and Motorola, all of which turned them down. They decided to pivot to semiconductor companies next since they were beginning to launch their own consumer products divisions and approached a contact at Fairchild who used to supply them with parts. The contact passed their info to Greg Reyes, who thought the system might have merit. Reyes sent a team to Stamford to evaluate RAVEN led by former Novus general manager Gene Landrum and a Fairchild engineer named Jerry Lawson.[25]

---

[23] Benj Edwards, "The Untold Story of the Invention of the Game Cartridge," Fast Company, January 22, 2015, https://www.fastcompany.com/3040889/the-untold-story-of-the-invention-of-the-game-cartridge.

[24] Ibid.

[25] Ibid.

Born December 1, 1940, and raised in Queens, New York, Gerald Anderson Lawson began experimenting with amateur radio when he was 13 and started making house calls to repair TVs at 16. After attending Queens College and City College of New York, Lawson worked at several East Coast defense contractors before taking a job with Kaiser Electronics in Palo Alto. Around 1970, he moved on to Fairchild as a field engineer helping other companies integrate Fairchild products into their designs.[26] Lawson took an interest in video games after seeing *Computer Space* and getting to know the Atari engineers as they worked on *Pong*.[27] When Fairchild deployed its first microprocessor, the F8, in 1975, Lawson built his own coin-operated game around it in his garage to prove that a microprocessor could drive a display.[28] Called *Demolition Derby*,[29] the game attracted interest from a small local coin-op company called Major Manufacturers that placed it out on test in a pizza parlor and may have exhibited it at the 1975 MOA, but Major folded and the game never received wider distribution.[30] When Fairchild learned that Lawson had created the game, he was tapped to lead its evaluation of the Alpex home video game project.[31]

After viewing the prototype, Lawson helped Kirschner and Haskell make changes to its design, most notably by swapping out the 8080 microprocessor for a Fairchild F8. He also worked to simplify the control scheme. The prototype used a keyboard due to the complex hockey game, which allowed the players to move their paddles in all four directions and change the angle as well. To condense these functions into a game controller, Lawson created a thumbstick that could be pushed in four directions, rotated like a dial, and pressed like a button. Meanwhile, Gene Landrum wrote a marketing report delivered to Fairchild in November 1975 called "Business Opportunity Analysis: Alpex Video Game" advocating a move into the video game space. Impressed by the report, Greg Reyes officially brought Fairchild into the business.[32]

[26] Benj Edwards, "Jerry Lawson, Black Video Game Pioneer," *Vintage Computing and Gaming*, February 24, 2009, http://www.vintagecomputing.com/index.php/archives/545/vcg-interview-jerry-lawson-black-video-game-pioneer.

[27] Ibid.

[28] Donovan, 2010, chap. 6.

[29] No relation to the Exidy/Chicago Coin game of the same name.

[30] Major Manufacturers was founded by a furniture salesman named Bill Kinsel after he filled in for a friend at a San Francisco coin-op show in 1974 and saw how profitable the coin-op video game business appeared to be. Major deployed a *Pong* clone called *Fascination* and a cocktail game called *Lunar Module* but went out of business in late 1975 or early 1976. Smith, 2016, 330.

[31] Lawson, 2009.

[32] Edwards, 2015.

Fairchild announced its deal with Alpex in February 1976, which gave Fairchild the exclusive rights to market a video game based on the company's technology for four years.[33] By now, Lawson was hard at work alongside an industrial engineer who used to work for National Semiconductor named Nicholas Talesfore to define the form factor of the console. During this process, they confronted a serious problem: they had no idea how to allow for the insertion and removal of cartridges. While removable ROM had been gaining traction for industrial applications, there had never been a consumer product designed to swap out ROM memory chips, and the implications of constantly plugging and unplugging them into a circuit board had never been seriously explored. The Fairchild team needed to develop a system that allowed for easy insertion and removal while protecting the connectors and avoiding surges that might fry the entire system.[34]

To solve these problems, Talesfore turned to one of his former co-workers at National Semiconductor named Ron Smith. Smith developed a solution consisting of a special connector on the motherboard sporting flexible metal pins that would rotate to connect with gold-plated contacts on the game circuit board, after which a separate locking mechanism would hold the cartridge in place so it could not be jostled loose and break the connection. To protect the electronics on the circuit board from physical harm, Talesfore created a bulky plastic housing inspired by 8-track cassette tapes.[35] With the insertion problem solved, Talesfore finished the outer casing of the console, which he designed to look like a high-end stereo component, in time to debut what Fairchild was now calling the Video Entertainment System (VES) at the June 1976 Consumer Electronics Show (CES).[36]

Midway through the CES show, Jerry Lawson departed to bring the system to the FCC for testing. It promptly failed. What followed was a multi-week ordeal to shield the hardware sufficiently to pass the test, which in turn required constant changes to the assembly line as the hardware underwent a series of minor tweaks and modifications.[37] Fairchild had hoped to begin shipping systems to dealers in August but did not receive FCC approval until late October.[38] The process also delayed the completion of the first games for the system: Fairchild had planned to ship three games at launch,

[33] *Electronic Games & Personal Computers* (Cleveland, OH: Predicasts, Inc., 1979), 4.

[34] Edwards, 2015.

[35] Ibid.

[36] "Games New CES Star," *Weekly Television Digest with Consumer Electronics*, June 21, 1976, 13.

[37] Tom Maher, *Silicon Valley Road* (College Station, TX: Virtualbookworm.com Publishing, 2005), 112.

[38] "Fairchild Game Okayed," *Weekly Television Digest with Consumer Electronics*, October 25, 1976, 11.

but in the end could only manufacture one in sufficient quantities for the holidays.

Fairchild finally launched the VES in late November 1976 at a price of $150. The release started with a limited rollout in JC Penny and Montgomery Ward department stores serving select markets before expanding to roughly 40 markets before the end of December.[39] Two games were built into the system, *Tennis* and *Hockey*, while six additional games were sold on three cartridges, which Fairchild called Videocarts. Videocart-1, the only one to make it into stores in quantity,[40] contains four simple games: *Tic Tac Toe*, a one paddle ball-and-paddle game called *Shooting Gallery*, a drawing program called *Doodle*, and a drawing variant called *Quadra-Doodle* in which the machine itself creates the patterns. Videocart-2 features a *Tank* clone called *Desert Fox* and the same *Shooting Gallery* found on Videocart-1, while Videocart-3 contains a *Blackjack* game. While the system was generally well received, Fairchild could only manufacture the system in limited quantities due to the FCC testing delay and sold just 40,000 units before the end of the year.[41]

In 1977, the VES received a new name, the Channel F,[42] and rose in price to $170 due to increased manufacturing costs related to passing the FCC test. The company also worked diligently to develop new games. Since the system had to be sold essentially at cost due to the FCC situation, Fairchild would have to realize virtually all of its profits from software. In January 1977, the number of available Videocarts doubled to six.[43] Two of the new games, *Spitfire* and *Space War*, are one-on-one dueling games. *Spitfire* is based on *Jet Fighter* and sports a primitive AI for one-player action. *Space War* bears little resemblance to its namesake as two players fight to deplete each other's energy, which can be recharged by visiting a starbase located in each corner of the screen. The third new game, *Math Fun I*, is an educational cartridge

[39] "Game plans: Magnavox," *Weekly Television Digest with Consumer Electronics*, December 6, 1976, 11.

[40] "Other New Games," *Weekly Television Digest with Consumer Electronics*, January 17, 1977, 12.

[41] *The Electronic Games Market in the U.S.* (New York: Frost & Sullivan, 1983), 34.

[42] There is some confusion regarding the Channel F name. Many sources claim the name was changed from the VES to Channel F because of the impending arrival of the Atari Video Computer System, or VCS for short. This is certainly not true, as the VCS remained a complete secret before its unveiling at the June 1977 CES, and Channel F advertisements have been discovered as early as January 1977. The system was, however, also advertised as the VES during this time period. According to Nick Talesfore, the name change was the suggestion of a marketing consultant right before launch, so there was simply not time to change over all the marketing materials. Thus, the VES name continued to persist until at least the middle of 1977. "Nicholas F. Talesfore," FND Collectibles, accessed June 10, 2019, http://www.fndcollectables.com/NINTENDO/NES_C_thru_D/SHIPPING/VIDEO_GAMES/INTELLIVISION/working_interview_notes.html

[43] "Other New Games," 1977, 12.

with basic addition and subtraction problems. Four more cartridges were released over the summer: *Math Fun II* with multiplication and division problems, *Magic Numbers* with variants of *Mastermind* and *Nim*, *Drag Race*, and *Baseball*. By the holidays, 12 cartridges were available with the addition of *Backgammon/Acey Ducey* in October and *Maze* in November 1977.[44]

As Fairchild began pushing its video game system heavily, its digital watch business began to fall apart. Although Fairchild remained the number two watch company in the United States in 1977, it began losing millions of dollars on watches every quarter as profitability evaporated across the entire category. In response, Wilf Corrigan split the Consumer Products Group into two separate division reporting directly to him. The Time Products Division took over the digital watch business and continued to limp along until it was closed in 1979 without ever turning a profit. Former Consumer Products Group Vice President Greg Reyes took charge of the Video Games Division, which did a brisk business in the early part of 1977. Despite what looked like a solid market, however, Corrigan and Reyes opted for a conservative production run so as not to be caught with excess inventory in the event of a market downturn like the one they experienced in the watch business.[45]

***

At the beginning of 1977, Fairchild faced its first competitor in the programmable console space: consumer electronics giant RCA. Once the undisputed leader in television technology, RCA entered a period of decline in the 1960s as long-time company leader David Sarnoff slowly ceded control to his son Robert, who became president in 1965, CEO in 1967, and finally added the role of chairman in 1970 after the elder Sarnoff retired. Like Charles Bludhorn at Gulf & Western, Robert diversified his company through conglomerating, acquiring companies as disparate as book publisher Random House, car rental company Hertz, rug maker Coronet, and food processing operation Banquet Foods. He also expanded the company's efforts to challenge IBM in the mainframe computer space, a disaster that cost RCA $490 million in write-offs when the computer division closed in 1971. With profits in decline due to these missteps, Robert Sarnoff was ousted by the board of directors in 1975.

The closure of the computer division did not end RCA's research into computer technology, as it retained a sizable semiconductor division and its extensive R&D operation in Princeton, New Jersey. Indeed, with the end of

---

[44] "Fairchild on Games," *Weekly Television Digest with Consumer Electronics*, October 24, 1977, 12.

[45] "Fairchild's Problems," 1977, 116.

development on mainframe computers, the engineers who had been working on these products for the last few years were able to refocus their efforts on the exciting new technological breakthroughs being achieved in integrated circuits. One of these engineers, Joseph Weisbecker, felt that ICs were becoming complex enough to power low-cost computers devoted to education and entertainment and dedicated himself to bringing RCA into the emerging video game business.

Joseph A. Weisbecker was born on September 4, 1932, in Audubon, New Jersey. Interested in electronics from an early age, he constructed his own tic-tac-toe-playing computer in 1951 while still in high school. After finishing his electrical engineering degree at Drexel University in 1956, he became a key member of the team that designed RCA's earliest mainframe computers. Weisbecker was particularly interested in uses for electronics in education, so in 1964 he invented a cheap plastic toy marketed as *Think a Dot* that introduced basic computer concepts and became a big hit that sold over 500,000 units.[46]

Before shutting down its computer systems division, RCA made one last effort to save it by moving everyone to new facilities in Marlboro, Massachusetts in 1969. Uninterested in moving to New England, Weisbecker realized that remaining employed as an engineer by RCA in New Jersey would require being hired by the RCA Labs R&D division, so he began brainstorming potential projects he hoped would capture the attention of one of the managers there. His ultimate goal was to use any project that the company took on as a Trojan horse to keep RCA in the computer business.[47]

Figuring RCA would continue its integrated circuit business for at least a few years despite the end of its computer work, Weisbecker built a prototype personal computer system constructed from TTL hardware called FRED – short for Flexible Recreational Educational Device – and began showing it to colleagues. The project caught the attention of the manager responsible for integrated circuit projects at RCA Labs, Jerry Herzog, who hired him in 1970 and suggested they work together to incorporate the basic functionality of FRED into a microprocessor. Herzog further suggested they use a relatively new chip fabrication process RCA had played a key role in pioneering called complementary metal-oxide-semiconductor (CMOS) that was becoming an industry standard because transistors fabricated using the process consumed

[46] "Joseph A. Weisbecker (1931–1990)," Cosmac Elf, accessed June 10, 2019, http://www.cosmacelf.com/history/joseph-weisbecker.html.

[47] Joyce Weisbecker, interview with Kevin Bunch, 2018.

far less power – and therefore also generated far less heat – than standard MOS components.[48] Herzog and Weisbecker completed a two-chip version of the FRED system dubbed the 1801 in 1975, after which other engineers in the labs consolidated all the functionality onto a single microprocessor, the 1802, in 1976.

As the 1802 project gained support within RCA, Weisbecker continued his own work at home to create a low-cost computer system based around the chip. Uncertain what division of the RCA conglomerate might ultimately take an interest in the system, Weisbecker tinkered with multiple FRED configurations with a variety of recreational and educational uses. He then launched a two-pronged assault to generate enthusiasm within the company by bringing these designs into the Labs so that his co-workers could play around with them while publishing articles on his hardware in professional and hobbyist journals.[49] Weisbecker and his colleagues could not convince the RCA consumer products division to bring FRED to retail, so they explored bringing it to the arcade through a coin-operated version that replaced cassette tapes with ROM cartridges. While some of the games created for the system, such as a one-on-one fencing game, were imaginative for their day, they were ultimately too simple to appeal to the arcade market.[50]

In 1976, RCA's Distributor and Special Products Division agreed to market a version of FRED for home use that accepted ROM cartridges, which was originally designated the Home TV Programmer before taking the name Studio II.[51] A new set of games was developed for the system, most of which were programmed by a new hire named Andy Modla. Weisbecker's daughter, Joyce, also contributed a couple games as an independent contractor. RCA hoped to have the system on the market in time for Christmas 1976, but engineering and production delays forced the company to adjust its release schedule.[52]

The RCA Studio II debuted in February 1977 at $150 through a test market in four cities, Oklahoma City, Indianapolis, Spokane, and Portland, Maine. Encouraged by the results of the test, RCA expanded to 19 markets in March and went nationwide by June.[53] Four programs were built directly

---

[48] Ibid.

[49] Ibid.

[50] Atari Archive, "Archive Annex Episode 1: RCA, FRED, and the Studio II," YouTube video, posted September 6, 2018, https://www.youtube.com/watch?v=o35y6W9hI-o.

[51] "Home TV Programmer," *Weekly Television Digest with Consumer Electronics*, October 11, 1976, 11.

[52] "RCA to Test-Market ROM Cartridge Game," *Electronic News*, January 10, 1977.

[53] "RCA's Video Game a Success in 4 Test Areas; Color Put Off," *Home Furnishings Daily*, April 18, 1977.

into the system, *Addition*, *Bowling*, *Doodle*, and a driving game similar to *Speed Race* called *Freeway*. Three additional games were available at launch on cartridges: *Space War*, a simple target shooting game for one or two players completely different from both the PDP-1 classic and the Channel F game of the same, and two more educational cartridges called *TV Schoolhouse 1* and *Fun with Numbers*.[54] By the middle of the year, two more cartridges were added: *Pong* clone *Tennis/Squash* and *Baseball*.[55] *TV Schoolhouse II* and *Blackjack* arrived in September.[56]

While FRED had been ahead of its time in the mid-1970s, the Studio II could not claim the same distinction in early 1977. Like all previous FRED prototypes, the system featured only black-and-white graphics rather than the full color of the Channel F, while it also betrayed its computer roots through an awkward keypad control system built directly into the unit rather than the detachable paddle and joystick controllers becoming common on both dedicated and programmable systems. As a result, the Studio II appeared unable to mount a credible challenge to the Channel F. Fairchild's first real competitor appeared later in 1977, when leading video game company Atari finally brought its own programmable game to market.

---

[54]"RCA Has Video Game," *The Trentonian*, April 2, 1977.
[55]"RCA's Video Game a Success, 1977."
[56]"Game Plans," *Weekly Television Digest with Consumer Electronics*, September 19, 1977, 11.

21

Hey Stella

On April 15, 1974, the Magnavox Corporation filed a lawsuit in the Federal District Court for the Northern District of Illinois, Eastern Division for patent infringement related to its Odyssey home video game system. Named in the suit were four companies that had released coin-operated ball-and-paddle video games – Atari, Bally, Allied Leisure, and Chicago Dynamic Industries – alongside one of the country's largest coin-op distributors, Bally subsidiary Empire.[1] A second suit filed in August targeted Seeburg Industries, its coin-operated games subsidiary, Williams Electronics, and another large Chicago-based distributor, World Wide.[2] In 1975, a third lawsuit targeted Sears over the Atari-made *Pong* consoles it marketed for home use.[3]

As a veteran engineer at a major defense contractor, Odyssey creator Ralph Baer accumulated broad experience patenting new inventions and thoroughly documented the creation of the Odyssey from his first proposal in 1966. Baer subsequently filed for a series of patents between 1969 and 1974. The most important of these, issued in 1973 as US3728480, described in detail Baer's plans for a "television gaming and training apparatus."[4] A second patent filed by co-worker Bill Rusch and issued in 1975 as USRE28507 described a game in which a machine-controlled dot collides with a player-controlled dot and

---

[1] Complaint for Patent Infringement, Magnavox Co. v. Bally Manufacturing Corp., No. 74-1030 (N.D. Ill), April 15, 1974. This filing was preceded by a filing in New York by Bally subsidiary Midway attempting to have the patents invalidated, which was superseded by the April 15 case. Complaint for Declaratory Relief, Midway Mfg. Co. v. Magnavox Co., No. 74-1657 (S.D. NY), April 12, 1974.

[2] Complaint for Patent Infringement, Magnavox Co. v. Seeburg Industries, No. 74-2510 (N.D. Ill), August 30, 1974.

[3] "Legal Battle Royal," *Weekly Television Digest with Consumer Electronics*, December 1, 1975, 9.

[4] Ralph Baer, "Television gaming and training apparatus," U.S. Patent 3,728,480A filed March 22, 1971, and issued April 17, 1973.

changes its vector.[5] These two patents together constituted a legal claim for having invented the concept of the video game generally as well as *Pong*-style ball-and-paddle games in particular.

As Sanders Associates derived its primary video game income via licensing its technology to other companies, management was keen that anyone marketing a product similar to the Odyssey pay a licensing fee and/or a royalty for the privilege. When the *Pong* boom started in the arcades, however, no company did so. Under Sanders' agreement with Magnavox, it was the television company's duty to bring any lawsuits: hence the spate of patent infringement suits wending their way through the Federal Court system by 1975.

One-by-one, the defendants in these three patent lawsuits, which were ultimately consolidated into a single case, began to fall away. Allied Leisure argued improper venue to remove itself, which bought the Florida company a short reprieve before Magnavox sued it in its home state in 1976, resulting in a settlement in early 1978.[6] Bally decided to settle in May 1976,[7] while Chicago Dynamic Industries went bankrupt before the case could be decided, though it technically remained a party to the suit. At Atari, Nolan Bushnell initially desired to fight the suit, incensed that Magnavox claimed that what he considered his superior arcade technology owed anything to Ralph Baer's more primitive home system, and launched a countersuit in California in 1975 seeking to invalidate the Magnavox patents that was consolidated into the Chicago case as well.[8] Atari ultimately decided continuing the fight in court could be financially ruinous,[9] so on June 8, 1976, the company settled.[10]

Seeburg and what remained of Chicago Dynamic continued to fight Magnavox to the bitter end and lost in court in early 1977. The presiding judge in the case, John Grady, declared Ralph Baer's '480 patent the "pioneering patent" in video game technology and set a precedent that any company that created a game using a video signal in which a machine-controlled symbol collided with a player-controlled symbol and changed vector would run afoul of the '507 patent.[11] These judgments insured that Sanders would collect

[5]William Rusch, "Television Gaming Apparatus," U.S. Patent RE28507E, filed April 25, 1974, and issued August 5, 1975.

[6]"Tandy & Allied Leisure," *Weekly Television Digest with Consumer Electronics*, February 6, 1978, 9.

[7]"RCA into Games," *Weekly Television Digest with Consumer Electronics*, May 24, 1976, 12.

[8]Complaint for Declaratory Judgement, Atari, Inc. v. Magnavox Co., No. 75-1442 (N.D. Cal.), July 11, 1975.

[9]Kent, 2001, 46–47.

[10]Non-Exclusive Cross License for Video Games, agreement between Atari and Magnavox, June 8, 1976.

[11]"Case: The Magnavox Co., et al. V. Chicago Dynamic Industries, et al.," Patent Arcade, June 2010, http://patentarcade.com/2010/06/case-magnavox-co-et-al-v-chicago.html.

millions of dollars in licensing fees from companies all over the world before the patent finally expired in the early 1990s.

Atari's settlement agreement with Magnavox called upon the video game company to pay $1.5 million in two installments to license Ralph Baer's patents in perpetuity. The company also agreed to provide detailed information on any technology it developed for any product manufactured or available for sale by June 1, 1977.[12] The latter term may have led Atari to delay its entry into the emerging programmable console market, but at the June CES in 1977 the company unveiled the product that would propel it into the next generation of video games, the Video Computer System, or VCS.[13]

***

As *Home Pong* inched toward completion in summer 1975, Steve Mayer and Ron Milner at Cyan Engineering discussed how best to continue Atari's move into the home market.[14] They discerned that if *Home Pong* proved successful, the next logical product would be *Tank*, at the time one of the most popular coin-op games on the market. Doing that game would require a more sophisticated IC than the one used for *Pong*, and the thought of designing a new microchip every time Atari wanted to produce a new game was not palatable at all.[15]

Mayer saw another way forward. Inspired by Hewlett-Packard's pocket calculator line, in which the primary difference between business and scientific variants was a different ROM chip inside a standard form factor, Mayer envisioned creating a base unit containing a microprocessor into which the company could plug in ROM chips containing individual games. This would provide Atari with a universal hardware standard and allow the company to design each new dedicated console game in software rather than through LSI

---

[12] Agreement between Atari and Magnavox, 1976. Most companies paid royalties rather than a flat fee. Coleco's license, which was probably typical, called for $100,000 against a 5.5% royalty on net sales of the first 100,000 units followed by a sliding scale down to 3% of net sales on units above 350,000. "Magnavox Game Suit," *Weekly Television Digest with Consumer Electronics*, December 13, 1976, 11.

[13] Al Alcorn has stated that Atari kept the system a secret until the June CES so it would not have to share info on it with Magnavox, as the show was held right after the deal expired. Other former Atari executives are not so sure. Furthermore, Magnavox's patent attorney, Thomas Briody, testified that Atari did share information on the system pursuant to the agreement. Alcorn, oral history 2008, and Thomas Briody, testimony, Magnavox Company v. Activision, Inc., No. 82-5270 (N.D. Cal), 1985, 99–100. It is possible Atari disclosed general information on the VCS while it was under development to ensure it did not violate the settlement, but did not have to disclose specific technical details since it was not being offered for sale to distributors and retailers until after June 1.

[14] Marty Goldberg, "Inside the Atari 2600," *Retro Gamer*, no. 103, 2012, 27.

[15] Hans Reutter, "PRGE 2017 – Ron Milner – Portland Retro Gaming Expo," filmed October 21, 2017, YouTube video, posted November 2, 2017, https://www.youtube.com/watch?v=CbaAgAAY77U.

circuits. After developing this basic idea, Mayer came to the same realization as Wallace Kirschner at Alpex that if they were putting individual games on interchangeable ROM chips, they might as well just release the base unit and let consumers switch out games themselves.[16]

As Mayer and Milner began sketching out the design of their new system, with Milner focusing on hardware and Mayer on software, they realized keeping the retail price around their target of $200 would limit the budget for the microprocessor at its heart to perhaps no more than $30.[17] This put the whole project in jeopardy, as in their survey of the emerging microprocessor industry they were unable to find any that sold for less than $100. The solution arrived in the form of a letter mailed to Cyan advertising a new processor debuting publicly at the upcoming Western Electronics Show and Convention (Wescon) created by a team led by Chuck Peddle.[18]

A graduate of the University of Maine, Chuck Peddle entered the computer industry in 1961 at General Electric, where he worked on time-sharing and electronic cash register designs for nearly a decade until GE exited the computer industry in 1970. After briefly working at two startups he co-founded that focused on cash registers and word processing, respectively, Peddle took a job at Motorola in 1973 to help finish the company's first microprocessor, the 8-bit 6800. Afterwards, Peddle was tasked with evangelizing the 6800 to potential customers. While the new chip generated enthusiasm, there was disappointment in some circles due to the chip's $300 price tag. While this was a reasonable price for companies looking to replace the processing power of an entire computer, some engineers hoped to use the chip as a microcontroller and were disappointed that doing so would not be cost effective. Peddle realized a potential market existed for cheaper microprocessors for use in computer peripherals, appliances, and similar devices, but when he proposed that Motorola create a low-cost version of the 6800 to meet this demand, he was rebuffed. Peddle, therefore, decided to pursue this chip himself.[19]

In order to proceed on his own, Peddle required an existing semiconductor company that could develop and manufacture his design. After several companies turned him down, Peddle reconnected with a former co-worker at GE named John Paivinen, co-founder and president of a firm called MOS Technology. Established in Valley Forge, PA, in 1969 as a subsidiary of Allen-Bradley to bring the industrial manufacturing company into the

---

[16] Mayer, 2018.
[17] Ibid.
[18] Goldberg, 2012, 29.
[19] Brian Bagnall, *Commodore: A Company on the Edge* (Winnipeg: Variant Press, 2010), 2–9.

semiconductor industry, MOS had become the largest independent supplier of chips to the calculator industry by the mid-1970s. Paivinen was happy to take on Peddle's new project, so Peddle and seven members of his design team left Motorola in August 1974 and moved east. After just under a year of work, they completed their low-cost microprocessor in June 1975 and laid it out in two versions,[20] the 6501, which had the same pin layout as the 6800 for socket compatibility and cost $20, and the 6502, which featured a different layout and cost $25. Knowing the industry would likely greet the announcement of such cheap CPUs with skepticism, Peddle decided to debut them at the Wescon show in September 1975.

Shortly before the show, Peddle began running ads in industry trades announcing that the new 6502 processor would be available for purchase on the floor of the Wescon show for $25.[21] When the Wescon organizers learned of the ad, they responded by banning sales on the show floor to forestall a flea market atmosphere. Unperturbed, Peddle set up shop in a hotel room and stationed a small booth on the floor of the show to point people to where they could buy the chip.[22] Mayer and Milner were two of his many customers that day, and after evaluating the chip they called Peddle the next day to express interest in using it in their game system. After a brief negotiation, they concluded a deal with Peddle to use the MOS Technology 6507 microprocessor, a slightly more limited version of the 6502 that sold at a far cheaper price, and its supporting chips at a cost of $12 a set.[23] With a CPU now in place, Mayer and Milner began assembling a prototype of their new system.

As Mayer and Milner turned to their video game project in earnest, they were guided by one simple principle: include as much functionality as possible in the hardware, but never at the expense of a competitive price point. This philosophy led them to move as many capabilities out of the hardware and into software as they could. The 6507 was synchronized to the television scan rate and created the display only one or two lines at a time in lieu of a frame buffer; the less important background images were rendered at a much lower resolution than moving objects, and vertical synchronization was moved out of hardware entirely, all in an effort to cut down on video memory.[24] Indeed, with DRAM still incredibly expensive in 1975, the duo

---

[20] Ibid, 10–19.

[21] The 6501 was never released because a lawsuit by Motorola forced MOS to remove it from the market.

[22] Ibid, 32–35.

[23] Ibid, 35–36.

[24] "Design Case History: The Atari Video Computer System," *IEEE Spectrum*, March 1983, 45.

initially decided to include only 64 bytes of system memory, though after realizing the cost savings from using a 6507 rather than a 6502 they doubled the memory to 128 bytes. This was still a paltry amount of memory, but they could simply not afford to include more.[25]

Mayer and Milner assumed a limited lifecycle for their system and only built in the functionality required to play all of Atari's major arcade hits to that point: *Pong*, *Pong Doubles*, *Quadrapong*, *Gran Trak 10*, *Tank*, and *Jet Fighter*.[26] Therefore, it could only generate five sprites, two 8-bit sprites to represent players and three 1-bit sprites to represent two missiles and a ball.[27] These sprites could be one of 128 colors and placed anywhere on what was essentially a 160×192 playfield.[28] They could be superimposed against a background image up to 40 bits wide that could alternately be mirrored to show the same 20-bit wide image on each half of the screen. These graphical tricks insured that simple games like *Pong* or *Tank* could be housed within 2K of ROM, so the duo designed the system to address up to 4K of ROM memory. Addressing more ROM was deemed too expensive to remain within the desired price point for the system and its attendant cartridges.

By the beginning of December 1975, Mayer and Milner had completed a rough prototype of the system and created a simple adaptation of *Tank* to play on it.[29] That month, they hired a third team member named Joe Decuir. A Berkeley grad with a master's degree in biomedical engineering, Decuir had been interested in computers since high school and purchased his own 6502 processor at the same Wescon as Mayer and Milner. Decuir helped debug the *Tank* game and assisted in the development of a gate-level proto-type of the hardware incorporating a breadboard full of integrated circuits to mirror as closely as possible the custom graphics and sound chip Atari would have to design for the final system.[30] He also provided the name for the pro-totype of the chip, which the team dubbed Stella after the brand of bicycle Decuir rode to work every day. Before long, the codename Stella was applied to the entire console project.[31]

---

[25] Mayer, 2018.

[26] Ibid.

[27] The term "sprite" as referring to a predefined block of pixels had not yet been coined in 1975. Atari called its objects "player-missile graphics."

[28] Due to the way the VCS drew the screen without a bitmap, there were not technically any pixels being turned on and off, but there were essentially 160×192 different spots on the screen where a sprite could be placed.

[29] Goldberg, 2012, 30.

[30] Scott Stilphen, "DP Interviews Joe Decuir," *Digital Press*, 2005, http://www.digitpress.com/library/interviews/interview_joe_decuir.html.

[31] Goldberg, 2012, 31–32.

With Stella's basic features established by February 1976, Joe Decuir was pulled out of Cyan and set up shop at a new Atari facility on Division Street in Sunnyvale separate from the rest of the company's microelectronics department to turn the prototype into a viable product away from prying eyes.[32] The most important task was completing the custom graphics and sound chip needed for the system, which was beyond the expertise of anyone working at Cyan or Atari. It fell to R&D VP Al Alcorn and microelectronics director Bob Brown to find someone who could complete the chip, but it was their *Home Pong* partner Harold Lee who presented the solution, telling them that only Jay Miner of Synertek could execute the design.[33]

Born in May 1932 in Prescott, Arizona, Jay Glenn Miner graduated from high school in Southern California and then joined the U.S. Coast Guard. He received his first formal electronics training through a six-month course at the Coast Guard Electronics Technician School in Groton, Connecticut, and then joined the North Atlantic Weather Patrol to service radar stations and radio installations on remote islands. After three years of this work, he enrolled at the University of California at Berkeley with a major in electrical engineering and graduated in 1958 with a focus on the design of generators and servomotors. In 1964, Miner was hired by Fairchild spin-off General Micro Electronics and helped design the first MOS calculator chip. In 1973, he left the company and co-founded Synertek, where he served as the principal chip designer.[34] By that time, he was already considered one of the best designers in the field.

Synertek served as the primary source of LSI chips for Atari's dedicated console systems,[35] so setting up a meeting proved simple. Convincing the company to give up its best chip designer proved harder. Alcorn, however, had an ace up his sleeve. Atari president Joe Keenan had insisted that the only way he would allow his engineers to use the 6507 in their video game system rather than a Motorola 6800 was if they set up a second source for the chips, a standard practice in the electronics industry to reduce dependence on a single company in the volatile semiconductor market. Atari worked out a deal for Synertek to serve as that second source. Alcorn reminded Synertek that if Atari's video game system proved successful, it would be receiving orders for vast quantities of chips over the next few years, and he got his man.[36] Miner worked

---

[32] Golderg and Vendel, 2012, chap. 5.

[33] Kent, 2001, 99.

[34] Brian Bagnall, *Commodore: The Amiga Years* (Winnipeg: Variant Press, 2017), 3.

[35] Although, the original *Home Pong* LSI was developed by AMI, the chip company got cold feet about entering mass production and only produced a limited run. Synertek took over production and became Atari's main chip supplier.

[36] Alcorn, oral history, 2008.

with Joe Decuir and a mathematician Alcorn met after giving a talk named Larry Wagner to reduce Stella's breadboard full of parts to a chip labeled the Television Interface Adapter (TIA). Meanwhile, Atari began drawing up plans for putting Stella into production via its new consumer electronics division.

***

With the success of *Home Pong* in 1975, Nolan Bushnell and Joe Keenan decided at the beginning of 1976 to split Atari into two divisions. Marketing VP Gene Lipkin became the general manager of the new coin-operated games division, while a former employee of National Semiconductor's Novus division named Sheldon Ritter took control of a new consumer electronics division.[37] These entities would exercise complete control over product development, sales, marketing, and manufacturing in their respective spheres. At Atari Consumer, Malcolm Kuhn and Michael Shea were hired as directors of sales and marketing, respectively. To fill out his product development team, Ritter hired a group of former Novus employees led by his former co-worker John Ellis as VP of Engineering. Former Novus general manager Gene Landrum was also retained as a consultant and created a market analysis and product planning strategy document to help define the Stella system – playing a similar role as he had for Fairchild on their Channel F console – that he delivered in May 1976.[38]

Based on Landrum's report, Ellis began drawing up the final production specs for Stella, while remaining mindful of the potential costs. Landrum recommended the system ship with several built-in games like the Channel F, but the required ROM chips were deemed too expensive. The report also mirrored the Channel F in calling for sound generated by speakers located within the console itself, but engineers Niles Strohl and Wade Tuma, who designed the RF modulator for the system, realized they could easily run the sound through the modulator to the television speakers instead. Making this modification not only provided better sound, but also reduced the audio part cost from $10 to a mere 25 cents.[39] Solving the cartridge insertion problem proved trickier until Atari hired an industrial engineer named Doug Hardy who had worked with Ron Smith at Fairchild on the cartridge mechanism for the Channel F. Although Hardy used a different system to avoid running afoul of Fairchild's patents, his solution was informed by the work done by the Fairchild team.[40]

---

[37] "Trade Personals," *Weekly Television Digest with Consumer Electronics*, February 2, 1976, 12.
[38] Goldberg and Vendel, 2012, chap. 5.
[39] Ibid.
[40] Edwards, 2015.

The case for the console was created by industrial designer Fred Thompson, who joined Atari in 1975 to refine the case design for *Home Pong*. Thompson referenced the aesthetics of component stereo equipment and developed a form factor that could be cradled in a lap because he figured the insertion and removal of cartridges, the need to set several toggle switches to select game modes, and the short length of the cords on the controllers would require the players to stay close to the console. The primary controller, a joystick and button set into a square base, was designed by Kevin McKinsey for a *Tank* console that Atari developed as a backup in case the VCS did not work out.[41] The system also shipped with a pair of paddle controllers that could be plugged into a single controller port.

In late 1976, microelectronics director Bob Brown began assembling a software team to create games for the console. Larry Wagner was tapped to lead the new group, and he also put the finishing touches on the *Tank* game that Joe Decuir had implemented as a test program during hardware development, which now went by the name *Combat*. Decuir, meanwhile, implemented *Pong* on the system under the name *Video Olympics*.[42] Because both games were relatively simple, Wagner and Decuir enhanced them via the addition of multiple game modes to increase replay value. *Combat* included parameters like bouncing bullets, invisible tanks, and a bank shot variant in which a tank could only be destroyed by a bullet that bounced off a wall first. It also included several variations on the coin-op game *Jet Fighter*. *Video Olympics* shipped not only with *Pong*, *Super Pong*, and *Pong Doubles* ports, but also with *Quadrapong*, soccer, hockey, volleyball, and basketball variants.

In August 1976, Brown and Wagner hired their first dedicated Stella programmer, Larry Kaplan. Kaplan had initially matriculated to UC Berkeley in spring 1968 with plans to major in biochemistry, but because he arrived in the middle of the school year, he was unable to start his core courses until the next fall. His academic advisor was a member of the faculty of the brand new computer science department, so he encouraged Kaplan to take a programming class as an elective that spring as part of a larger strategy to boost enrollment in computer courses so that the university would not shut down the nascent department. That summer, Kaplan took a work-study job with the U.S. Forestry Service as a statistician to help pay for his schooling and worked with both calculators and computers. After taking several more

[41] Tim Lapetino, *Art of Atari* (Runnenmede, NJ: Dynamite Entertainment, 2016), 296–300.

[42] Curt Vendel, "Interview with Joe Decuir," Atari Museum, accessed June 29, 2019, http://www. atarimuseum.com/articles/joedecuir.html.

programming courses over the next two years, he dropped out of school in 1970. After getting married and being drafted, he returned to Berkeley as a computer science major to secure a deferment and graduated in 1974.[43]

After graduation, Kaplan took a job with Control Systems Industries to work on a computerized power grid for the Missouri River for the Bureau of Reclamation in Missoula, Montana.[44] Already familiar with microprocessors because he had taken a course programming the Intel 4004 after Berkeley alum Ted Hoff donated several chips to the university,[45] Kaplan became interested in the emerging home computer market and bought an Altair 8800 to fool around with. In 1976, Kaplan saw an Atari ad in the *San Jose Mercury News* seeking programmers, and he beat out roughly 100 applicants for the job of Atari's first consumer programmer largely on the strength of his interest in, and familiarity with, home computers.[46]

For his first game, Kaplan chose to convert the 1975 Atari coin-op game *Anti-Aircraft*, in which two players shoot at airplanes flying overhead to score the most points. Creating a target-rich environment proved challenging because Stella was designed to display only five objects on the screen at one time. Fortunately, Jay Miner included a register called "H-move" within the TIA architecture that allowed Stella to calculate the horizontal motion of objects between frames. Kaplan discovered that since the system had to be aware of the horizontal position of objects on each line of the display during the rendering of a frame due to the way vertical draw was synchronized to the CRT, the H-move could be executed more than once per frame to update the position of objects line by line in horizontal bands. The upside of this quirk was that sprites could be reused as the screen was being drawn, and multiple objects could thus be rendered using the same character so long as they appeared in different horizontal positions.[47] Kaplan took full advantage of this capability to not only faithfully recreate *Anti-Aircraft*, but also to include naval variants that mimicked hit arcade games like *Sea Wolf* and shooting gallery variants that allowed the players to move their gun batteries along the bottom of the screen while replacing ships and planes as targets with clowns and animals. In light of these many variants, Atari called the game *Air-Sea Battle*.

[43] Larry Kaplan, interview with the author, September 3, 2018.
[44] Scott Stilphen, "DP Interviews Larry Kaplan," *Digital Press*, 2006.
[45] Kaplan, 2018.
[46] Stilphen, 2006.
[47] "Design Case History," 1983, 46.

In January 1977, Atari hired a second programmer named Bob Whitehead. A native of the Santa Clara Valley, Whitehead majored in computer science and mathematics at San Jose State University and then took a job with defense contractor GTE Sylvania, where his boss was future Atari microelectronics director Bob Brown. Brown remembered Whitehead as a quick learner with microprocessor experience and personally called to offer him a job at Atari.[48] Whitehead adapted the first-person space shooter *Starship 1* as his first project under the name *Star Ship*. Like the other early programmers, Whitehead incorporated several variants into the game, including a take on the early Atari arcade game *Space Race* and a primitive version of the *Lunar Lander* computer game.

In February 1977, Atari hired the final two programmers of the original VCS group, Alan Miller and Gary Palmer. In addition to creating games, both men played a crucial role in improving the development environment for creating new games. At the time, the programmers were required to input all their code using a teletype that could only display one line at a time connected to a time-sharing computer in Oakland. They debugged the software using a simple modified KIM-1 board adapted by an electrical engineer named Ed Riddle. Miller had experience working with PDP-11 minicomputers, and he successfully lobbied jointly with Kaplan to convince Atari to acquire PDP development systems. Palmer, meanwhile, designed proper debugger stations to replace the KIM boards. Palmer subsequently developed an educational cartridge called *Basic Math*, while Miller created a clone of the arcade game *Blockade* under the name *Surround*.[49]

Three more cartridges rounded out the Stella launch lineup. Original debugger designer Ed Riddle decided to try his hand at programming and developed a *Gran Trak*-style driving game called *Indy 500* based on a design started by Wagner.[50] With its overhead view and twisty curves, the game was unsuited to either the joystick or paddle controllers slated to ship with the system, so Atari packaged a rotary controller with the game that looked similar to the system's paddle controllers but could be rotated a full 360°.[51] Kaplan and Whitehead, meanwhile, each completed a second game, a *Wheels* clone called *Street Racer* and a *Blackjack* game, respectively.

***

[48] Bob Whitehead, interview with the author, February 2, 2016.
[49] Al Backiel, "DP Interviews Alan Miller," *Digital Press*, 2003.
[50] Scott Stilphen, "Ed Riddle Interview," Atari Compendium, 2017.
[51] *Indy 500* was the only game to ever use this controller.

As work progressed on Stella in 1976, Nolan Bushnell and Joe Keenan realized they did not possess the financial resources to complete the hardware and software and build inventory for the 1977 holiday season. While the company was now profitable, most of its reserves were tied up in inventory for the 1976 Christmas season, leaving little cash on hand. Bushnell hoped to take the company public to raise additional funds, but he became spooked when a soft market led his underwriter to believe they would not get nearly as large a return as hoped in an initial public offering.[52] Don Valentine, who in addition to being the principal venture investor in Atari also sat on the company board, pushed Bushnell to sell the company instead, promising they could achieve a similar payout to what they could expect on the open market. The board drew up a list of 40 or so companies active across a wide range of technological and entertainment fields and split them up among its members to put out feelers for a sale. For Valentine, there was only one choice that made sense based on his prior history of investments with the company: Warner Communications.[53]

Warner mastermind Steven Jay Ross was born in 1927 in Brooklyn and grew up in impoverished circumstances after his father was ruined in the Great Depression. In 1953, he married Carol Rosenthal, whose father owned a large funeral home called Riverside Memorial Chapel. Two years later, Ross went to work for Mr. Rosenthal as a funeral director. Ever the businessman, when Ross realized that the funeral home limousines were idle in the evening, he received permission from his father-in-law to start a rental business on the side.[54] In 1959, Mr. Rosenthal started a joint venture called Abbey Rent a Car that leased parking garage space from a company called the Kinney Parking Company. Ross helped nurture this business, which grew so successful that it began supplanting the garage business, making its owners unhappy. Ross provided the solution: merge Riverside and Kinney into a single firm that he would take public. The organizations merged as the Kinney Service Company in 1960, which went public in 1962 with Ross as president.[55]

The 1960s were an era of conglomerating, and the skillful dealmaker Ross began expanding his company. In 1966, he capped off his first series of acquisitions with a $25 million purchase of National Cleaning Contractors, instantly doubling the size of the firm that was now called Kinney National

[52] Bushnell, 2015.

[53] Keenan, 2018.

[54] Connie Bruck, *Master of the Game: How Steve Ross Rode the Light Fantastic from Undertaker to Creator of the Largest Media Conglomerate in the World* (New York: Simon & Schuster, 1994), kindle, chap. 1.

[55] Ibid.

Service. The next year, his friend and former employee Kenneth Rosen introduced him to Ted Ashley, owner of the Ashley Famous Talent Agency. By now, Ross was looking to expand out of Kinney's core businesses and had identified the leisure and entertainment industries as potential growth fields. Ashley initially had no desire to associate with someone in the funeral, parking, and janitorial business, but Ross won him over in a half-hour meeting that stretched to three hours and purchased the company. After consummating the deal, Ross was promoted to co-CEO of Kinney National Service.[56]

The purchase of the Ashley Famous Talent Agency focused Ross's attention on entertainment, and he made overtures to acquire Warner-Seven Arts, the parent company of Warner Records and the Warner Brothers movie studio. Initially rebuffed because Warner already had a deal in place with another company, Ross acquired the company in 1969 for $64 million after the original deal failed to receive government approval due to anti-trust problems.[57] With the era of the conglomerate nearing its end, and the Kinney parking business facing a price fixing scandal, Ross spun off all the non-entertainment assets of the business into a new firm called National Kinney Corp in 1972. Ross assumed the roles of chairman, CEO, and president at Kinney National, which he renamed Warner Communications.[58]

While putting together the Warner-Seven Arts deal, Ross relied heavily on entertainment analyst Emmanuel "Manny" Gerard. After graduating from Brown University and attending Harvard Business School, Gerard cut his teeth as an analyst with Wood Struthers & Co. in the late 1950s. Although he was rotated between a number of industries, he gravitated toward entertainment and founded his own boutique firm focused on that market with Alan Roth in 1961. After his consulting work on the Warner deal, Ross asked him to join Warner in 1974, where his mission was to seek out acquisitions in the entertainment business.[59] In 1976, Gerard became one of four members of a new "Office of the President" established by Ross to run Warner Communications and serve as the interface between the parent company and its subsidiaries, which Ross encouraged to run almost entirely independent of central oversight.[60]

---

[56] Ibid, chap. 2.

[57] Ibid.

[58] Ibid, chap. 3.

[59] "The Return of Manny Gerard," *Barron's National Business and Financial Weekly*, May 14, 1990.

[60] The other members were Ken Rosen, who helped facilitate the Ashley Famous sale, David Horowitz, a lawyer who had been the general counsel for Columbia Pictures, and Jay Emmett, who had run a company called the Licensing Corporation of America acquired by Kinney and later became a close friend and confidant to Ross. Bruck, 1994, chap. 3.

In early 1976, Gerard received a telephone call from Gordon Crawford of Capital Research on behalf of Don Valentine.[61] Crawford simply asked if Gerard would be interested in "a technology-based entertainment company, growing rapidly." Gerard replied in the affirmative. After flying out to see the Atari facilities in person, Gerard penned an analysis for Warner in which he boldly proclaimed that he had "seen the future, and its name is Stella." Convinced the console would become a massive hit, he encouraged Warner to buy the company.[62]

Negotiations began in earnest in spring 1976 but were complicated by several factors. Atari CFO Bill White grew severely ill during negotiations and was forced to limit his involvement, while an attempt by National Semiconductor to sell its moribund Novus consumer division to Atari was misread by Warner as a move by National to buy Atari. In July, an article appeared in a local newspaper describing Nolan Bushnell's recreational activities that included a picture of him in a hot tub with a lady friend. Nolan's ex-wife, Paula, whom he had divorced in 1974, was so enraged by the article that she threatened to rescind their divorce agreement. Doing so would force Atari to restore her 25% stake in the company, so Warner worked with Nolan and Paula to forge a new agreement in which she agreed to surrender her ownership stake or any future profits from the company. After surmounting these obstacles, Warner purchased Atari in October 1976 for $28 million. Nolan Bushnell and Joe Keenan remained in their positions as chairman and president, respectively, and were promised near-complete autonomy, though they now reported to Manny Gerard. Warner began investing money into Atari so it could bring Stella to market.[63]

***

Atari began shipping Stella to retailers as the Video Computer System (VCS) in July 1977 at a suggested retail price of $190.[64] *Combat* came packaged with the system, while the other eight launch titles were available for $20.00 each, save for *Indy 500*, which cost $40.00 due to the included rotary controllers. Sears also marketed the console under its own Telegames brand as the Video Arcade and packaged it with *Air-Sea Battle* under the name *Target Fun*.[65]

---

[61] Capital Research was the company that funded Valentine's Sequoia Capital at startup.

[62] Manny Gerard, interview with the author, September 5, 2017.

[63] Goldberg and Vendel, 2012, chap. 5.

[64] "Games – Déjà vu Sets In," *Weekly Television Digest with Consumer Electronics*, October 17, 1977, 10.

[65] Over the first two years of the VCS life cycle, Sears marketed all Atari games under alternate names.

The console sold 340,000 units,[66] but the launch was beset with problems that limited overall profitability. Manufacturing difficulties led to defects and delays, blown delivery schedules, and an unacceptably high return rate.[67] Storms on the East Coast delayed overland shipments even further,[68] while the chip shortages that had plagued the console industry since the start of the *Pong* boom in 1976 further hampered Atari's ability to manufacture cartridges in sufficient quantities to meet demand.[69] Atari attempted to compensate by continuing to run the assembly lines practically right up to Christmas, but retailers were not interested in ordering product past the beginning of December. Atari got stuck with unsold inventory sitting in warehouses that would not be viable until the next Christmas season, as high ticket items like video game consoles remained a seasonal product.[70] Despite a 35% increase in revenue and the highest sales in the industry by dollar volume, the consumer division lost money.[71]

Overall, the video game market proved disappointing in 1977. While dedicated console sales increased to 5.5 million units worth $230 million,[72] they fell below estimates of 7–10 million.[73] Dollar volume also suffered due to deep discounting during the holidays intended to clear out stock so as not to repeat the situation at the beginning of the year when retailers proved unable to sell remaining inventory after the previous Christmas.[74] Programmable sales topped out at around 450,000 units,[75] which also lagged analyst expectations. Both Fairchild and Atari attributed the shortfall to chip shortages. Worse, prices eroded rapidly during the holidays because retailers were terrified that they would not be able to sell excess stock come January 1 because of their experience with dedicated consoles the year before.[76] Atari led the way in the programmable market with its 340,000 VCS systems, while Fairchild, with its conservative approach to the market, sold around

---

[66] Warner Communications, Annual Report, 1977.

[67] Tristan Donovan, "The Replay Interviews: Ray Kassar," Gamasutra, April 29, 2011, https://www.gamasutra.com/view/feature/134733/the_replay_interviews_ray_kassar.php.

[68] Bushnell, 2009.

[69] Warner Communications, 1977.

[70] Malcolm Kuhn, interview with the author, July 9, 2013.

[71] Warner Communications, 1977.

[72] Frost & Sullivan, 1983, 24.

[73] "Games and Computers," *The Emporia Gazette*, December 21, 1977.

[74] "How the Two Big TV Toys are Faring," *Broadcasting*, 1978, 80.

[75] Frost & Sullivan, 1979.

[76] "Games – Retail Confusion," *Weekly Television Digest with Consumer Electronics*, December 12, 1977, 10.

100,000 units.[77] RCA did so poorly with its antiquated Studio II – even after dropping the retail price to $90 in early December[78] – that it shut down production entirely in February 1978 and sold its remaining stock to Radio Shack. The company had been working on a full-color Studio III and had even begun design work on a Studio IV,[79] but these projects were cancelled as RCA left the video game business behind.

In the dedicated console market, cheaper models did well, while advanced systems in the $70–$100 price range faltered.[80] Coleco remained the market leader with sales of 1.75 million units, but an East Coast dockworkers strike left the company unable to ship its entire inventory in time for the Christmas buying season, and it barely eked out a $1.7 million profit for the year. Forced to liquidate leftover stock in early 1978, the company took a $22.3 million loss and exited the video game industry[81] In the process, it scrapped plans to release a new cartridge-based system called the Telstar Game Computer.[82] APF took second place by selling around 1 million units of its latest TV Fun models. Atari came in third with around 510,000 units sold,[83] and Magnavox rounded out the major companies by moving 400,000 units of its 1977 models.[84]

As the dedicated console video market fell apart on the low end of the video game market, the microcomputer industry looked poised to take a giant step forward and settle in as a new alternative to video games on the high end of the market. At its inception, the industry targeted hobbyists and electronics enthusiasts who desired to build their own computers. Now, in 1977 several companies were preparing to release the first fully assembled microcomputers.

---

[77] Frost & Sullivan, 1979.

[78] "Games – Retail Confusion," 10.

[79] G.B. Herzog, "Fred Systems," internal progress report on Studio III and Studio IV, c. 1977.

[80] "Changing Games Market," *Weekly Television Digest with Consumer Electronics*, January 16, 1978, 9.

[81] Michael Rosenbaum, "Gamesmanship: Coleco Industries' Electronic Toys are Doing Just Fine," *Barron's National Business and Financial Weekly*, March 16, 1981.

[82] Despite the name, the Telstar Game Computer was not programmable. Like the Telstar Arcade, there was no CPU and each cartridge contained its own LSI.

[83] Frost & Sullivan, 1976, 8.

[84] Baer, 2005, 133.

22

Meet Me at the Faire

On April 16, 1977, the first annual West Coast Computer Faire opened at the San Francisco Civic Auditorium. The primary organizer of the event was Jim Warren, yet another individual who stood at the intersection of technology and the counterculture in 1970s Silicon Valley. For ten years, Warren had been a math teacher at the Catholic women's College of Notre Dame in Belmont, California, until he was asked to leave in 1967 due to the increasing publicity of the nudist parties he was holding at his house. Looking for something new to occupy his time, Warren took up programming on the advice of a friend.[1]

While doing contract programming for the Stanford Medical Center under the name Frelan Associates, Warren fell in with the Midpeninsula Free University, a counterculture educational organization that maintained a course catalog that anyone could contribute any topic to so long as they paid a $10 registration fee. These classes would then be offered free of charge in ad hoc classrooms around the region. Warren served three terms as the general secretary of the university and founded and edited a newsletter for the organization called *The Free You*.[2]

Through this work, Warren met Bob Albrecht and Dennis Allison of the People's Computer Company, who were looking to expand their publishing operations. Albrecht and Allison were receiving an increasing number of submissions on programming tools and programming languages but did not want to feature these topics in their newsletter for fear of harming the publication's accessibility to non-technical people. Instead, they asked Warren

---

[1] Freiberger and Swaine, 2000, chap. 6.
[2] Jim Wolpman, "Alive in the 60s: The Midpeninsula Free University," Midpeninsula Free, accessed June 10, 2019, http://midpeninsulafreeu.com.

to edit a limited three-issue magazine devoted to a new version of BASIC submitted by two programmers in Texas that fit into 2K of memory called Tiny BASIC. *Dr. Dobb's Journal of Tiny BASIC Calisthenics and Orthodontia* debuted in January 1976 and proved so popular that publication continued well past its planned three-issue run under the more general name *Dr. Dobb's Journal of Computer Calisthenics and Orthodontia*.[3] *Dr. Dobbs* was the first magazine devoted entirely to microcomputer software.

Alongside programming articles, *Dr. Dobbs* provided reports on an emerging new trend in 1976: computer fairs. These events were generally organized by local computer clubs and provided a space where attendees could listen to talks by noted figures in the nascent microcomputer industry, check out the latest available computers and peripherals, and meet up to share their knowledge and enthusiasm with each other. The earliest fairs were primarily held in the Midwest or on the East Coast, which Warren considered an affront because he felt the most interesting developments in microcomputing were occurring on the West Coast. When he complained about this fact to the editor of the Homebrew Computer Club newsletter, Bob Reiling, the duo decided they should organize a Bay Area fair themselves.[4]

After being rebuffed by Stanford, Warren approached the San Francisco Civic Auditorium to serve as a venue for what he envisioned as a "Renaissance faire" for computer geeks. He almost scuttled the whole thing when the auditorium quoted a rental price of $1,200 per day. After breaking down the numbers with Reiling, they decided that if they could attract 60 exhibitors and 7,000 attendees, they would break even and perhaps realize a small profit. Warren worked tirelessly to promote the event by convincing topflight local companies like Processor Technology and Cromemco to attend, soliciting the largest hobbyist and evangelist groups like Homebrew, the Southern California Computer Society, the People's Computer Company, and the People's Computer Center to serve as sponsors, and starting a newsletter called the *Silicon Gulch Gazette* solely to promote the event.[5]

At the time of the West Coast Computer Faire, the most successful fairs in the country were attracting around 4,000 people. Warren and Reiling figured the concentration of computer enthusiasts in Silicon Valley would

---

[3] Freiberger and Swaine, 2000, chap. 6. The name "Dobbs" was a combination of the first names of Albrecht and Allison. "Orthodontia" was a reference to an in-joke at the PCC about "overbytes." It became the longest running of the early computer magazines, publishing in print monthly until 2009 and persisting online through 2014.

[4] Levy, 2010, 267–268.

[5] Ibid, 268–269.

allow them to attract 7,000 people. They were blown away when thousands of people formed five huge lines around the entrances to the auditorium and waited more than an hour to enter the show floor without complaint. Nearly 13,000 people attended the two-day event.[6]

The huge crowds at the West Coast Computer Faire served notice that the market for microcomputers had spread beyond a few hobbyists tinkering with electronics in their basements or garages. This realization in turn attracted mass-market electronics companies to explore the microcomputer market more seriously and set the stage for a new generation of fully assembled computers designed not for the hardcore computer hacker, but for the average consumer. The event also served as the coming out party for the most significant computer gaming platform of the late 1970s: the Apple II.

***

The genesis of Apple Computer was the same seminal event that launched Processor Technology and encouraged a host of hobbyist projects: the March 1975 inaugural meeting of the Homebrew Computer Club. As the call went out to interested parties, an HP engineer named Allen Baum saw a flyer advertising the meeting on a bulletin board at work and brought along his high school friend and fellow HP employee Steve Wozniak.[7] At the time, Wozniak had started tinkering with a time-sharing terminal design and hoped to connect with other terminal enthusiasts at the meeting.[8] He felt out of place when talk turned to microprocessors because he had not kept up with their development. As the meeting continued, he realized that the Altair computer everyone seemed excited about was like the Cream Soda Computer he had built several years before save that the TTL hardware had been largely replaced by a single microchip. Inspired, Wozniak decided to start a new computer project.[9]

Wozniak's computer borrowed features from several sources. His basic plan was to merge the computing capability of a system like the Altair with the terminal he was developing. This meant it would support a keyboard for input rather than switches. From the calculators he designed at HP, Wozniak borrowed the idea of incorporating a small ROM chip to store a

---

[6] Freiberger and Swaine, 2000, chap. 6.

[7] Wozniak and Smith, 2006, 152.

[8] Wozniak would complete his terminal in late 1975 and sell it to a time-sharing company called Call Computer founded by Lockheed Engineer Alex Kamradt in 1974 after using the proceeds from selling a house to purchase a minicomputer. Wozniak and Kamradt met at the Homebrew Computer Club. Young, 1988, chap. 6.

[9] Wozniak and Smith, 2006, 152–156.

simple monitor program in memory so that the computer would be ready to accept commands immediately after powering up. Finally, Wozniak drew on his love of video games to incorporate video output to a standard television. Choosing a processor for the computer proved challenging due to the expense. After briefly considering the Motorola 6800, Wozniak pivoted when he saw advertisements for the 6502 debut at the September 1975 Wescon. As the 6502 was similar to the 6800 but available at the cheaper price of $25, Wozniak attended the show and purchased one to serve as the heart of his new machine.[10]

Wozniak created his computer to share with his new friends at Homebrew and provide an entrée into being more involved in that community,[11] so he gave schematics away for free. His friend Steve Jobs, who began attending Homebrew meetings periodically after Wozniak showed him the computer, noticed that while many attendees were taking copies of the schematics, few of them possessed the requisite skill to assemble the computer. Jobs suggested he and Wozniak form a company to build the computer boards themselves to sell as kits. Although he could not see a viable business, Wozniak agreed to go along with the idea.[12] The name for their venture came as Wozniak drove Jobs home from the airport after he returned from one of his frequent journeys to the commune in Oregon. Jobs was partaking of one of his fruitarian diets and had been participating in the apple harvest at the farm, so he suggested the name Apple Computer.[13]

Wozniak and Jobs formally established Apple on April 1, 1976, with each partner taking 45% of the firm. The other 10% was granted to Ronald Wayne, an older engineer whom Jobs befriended at Atari and recruited into the company both because he had experience starting his own slot machine company years before and because Jobs felt it would be valuable to have on older hand to adjudicate disagreements between Wozniak and himself. Within 11 days, however, Wayne judged the whole venture too risky and sold his entire stake for $2,300.[14]

As Wozniak and Jobs began showing off the completed computer in early 1976, they attracted the attention of entrepreneur Paul Terrell. In December 1975, Terrell had become one of the first Altair dealers in the country and established a store in Mountain View called the Byte Shop. MITS dropped

[10] Ibid, 157–161.
[11] Ibid, 157.
[12] Ibid, 172.
[13] Isaacson, 2011, chap. 5.
[14] Ibid.

him when he violated the company's policy on dealer exclusivity, but Terrell shifted to IMSAI computers to great success and began franchising his operation to create the first national computer store chain. Terrell agreed to buy 50 computers, but only on the condition that they came fully assembled rather than as kits. This condition transformed the Apple I, as Jobs and Wozniak named their computer, into one of the first microcomputers available preassembled, though this distinction merely meant all the components were soldered onto the board and the buyer would still need to purchase a keyboard, power supply, and case separately. In July 1976, Apple began advertising the Apple I in magazines, and Jobs and Wozniak started making deals with other local computer stores to carry it. Roughly 200 were sold over the next few months at a price of $666.66.[15] By then, Wozniak was already dreaming up the next model.

The Apple I was an exercise in adapting Wozniak's existing TV Terminal quickly to have something available to show the Homebrew Computer Club. The Apple II was reengineered from the ground up to deliver enough speed and audiovisual capability to play a flawless adaptation of *Breakout*. Once again powered by the 6502, the computer incorporated faster RAM and could output bitmapped 4-color graphics at a resolution of 280 × 192 or 16-color graphics at a resolution of 40 × 48.[16] It could also produce simple sounds through an onboard speaker and supported paddle controllers. As Wozniak was putting the finishing touches on the computer, he was also completing a version of the BASIC programming language for the Apple I, so he resolved that the Apple II would ship with what he named Integer BASIC loaded in ROM to serve as a simple operating system. Like the Altair, the computer also included slots for new circuit boards to expand its capability.

In August 1976, Jobs and Wozniak brought the Apple I to the Atlantic City Computer Festival, where it was overshadowed by Lee Felsenstein's Sol-20 due to the latter computer's sleek case. Jobs realized the Apple II could not just be a board like its predecessor: it would need to have a case, an integrated keyboard, and a power supply too. He contracted with a fellow Homebrew attendee named Jerry Manock to produce a foam-molded plastic case and with former Atari engineer Rod Holt for a revolutionary power

---

[15] The price was a 33% markup over their costs of $500 a computer. According to Wozniak, the relationship to the Biblical number of the beast was coincidental, as both he and Jobs had been unaware of its religious significance. Wozniak and Smith, 2006, 180.

[16] Technically, the programmer could chose from one of two sets of four colors each in hi-res mode. As black and white were repeated in each set, this gave the computer six different colors in that mode, but only four could be on the screen at once.

supply design that generated significantly less heat than other models and became an industry standard.[17]

With its integrated case and keyboard, the Apple II required a greater financial investment to bring to market than the Apple I, so Jobs and Wozniak started looking for funding. Jobs brought the computer to Nolan Bushnell and Joe Keenan at Atari, but the company had its hands full closing the Warner deal and trying to prepare the VCS for launch, so they declined to invest. Bushnell did, however, introduce the duo to Don Valentine. Valentine also declined to put money in initially because he could tell Jobs knew nothing about selling in the mass market or about putting together a business plan. He suggested they bring a more experienced executive on board and recommended Mike Markkula.[18]

A trained engineer with a sharp analytical mind, Armas "Mike" Markkula was recruited into the Fairchild Semiconductor marketing department from Hughes Aircraft in 1966.[19] He did not join the exodus of talent to the "Fairchildren" initially despite several offers, but in 1971 he relented in the face of continued decline at Fairchild and took a job as North American marketing manager at Intel.[20] In 1975, Markkula retired at only 33 years old after being passed over for the top job in sales and marketing. He could afford to do so because his Intel stock options had made him a multimillionaire.[21]

For the next 18 months, Markkula served as a business consultant one day a week while indulging in hobbies and volunteer work until Valentine called to suggest he check out Apple.[22] When he arrived at the Jobs family garage, Markkula was blown away by the Apple II not only for its capabilities but for the elegant design of the PC board.[23] He ended up writing a business plan for the company and investing himself. On January 3, 1977, Apple Computer incorporated with Jobs, Wozniak, and Markkula each taking a 26% share.[24] Markkula served as chairman of the board and head of marketing but did not want to run the day-to-day affairs of the company, so he hired a good friend from his Fairchild days named Michael Scott to serve as president.[25]

---

[17] Isaacson, 2011, chaps. 5 and 6.

[18] Ibid, chap. 6.

[19] Leslie Berlin, *Troublemakers: Silicon Valley's Coming of Age* (New York: Simon & Schuster, 2017), 45–49

[20] Ibid, 53–54.

[21] Ibid, 151–152.

[22] Ibid, 153–155.

[23] Ibid, 206–210.

[24] The rest of the shares of the company were set aside to grant to management hires.

[25] Ibid, 229–234.

Worried that a larger firm like Texas Instruments or IBM might eventually wake up to the potential of the microcomputer market, Markkula decided a slick corporate image would be key to positioning the Apple II as a new standard in microcomputing. To that end, he contracted with the Regis McKenna agency, known as the premiere high-tech marketing/PR firm after helping Intel launch its line of microprocessors. The firm developed a new rainbow-colored logo for the company and built a booth for the Apple II's debut at the West Coast Computer Faire.[26] Full-page color ads began appearing in June 1977, the same month the Apple II began shipping in a configuration with 4K of memory, two paddle controllers, and an audio cassette interface for $1,298.

Apple hoped to make a splash at the West Coast Computer Faire, but it was only sporadically covered by the press that attended the event. While the Apple II featured impressive capabilities, this power came with a prohibitively high price that turned off many potential customers.[27] Instead, the darling of the event was a second fully assembled computer that outdid Apple by including a monitor while still selling for under $1,000. This computer was developed by 6502 creator MOS Technology for its new parent company, Commodore International.

***

Commodore co-founder Idek Jacek Trzmiel was born in Poland on December 13, 1928.[28] After the German conquest of Poland in September 1939, the Jewish Trzmiel family was forcibly relocated to the Litzmannstadt Ghetto in Lódz, where Idek worked in a garment factory until the ghettos were liquidated in 1944. The Trzmiels were shipped to the Auschwitz concentration camp, though after just a few days Idek and his father were assigned to a work crew that built new satellite facilities for the Neuegamme concentration camp around the city of Hanover. The elder Trzmiel died in the camps; Idek was liberated by U.S. forces in April 1945.[29] He stayed in Europe for two years finding work where he could and married a fellow camp survivor named Helen Goldfarb in July 1947. Four months later, the Hebrew Immigrant Aid Society (HIAS) paid for ocean liner tickets so the couple

---

[26] Ibid, 238–240.

[27] Bagnall, 2010, 101.

[28] Due to World War II, there is contradiction among what few records survive from Tramiel's early days. Other sources indicated that he was born in 1927 and that his last name may have been Tramielski.

[29] D. Schmüdde, *Jack and the Machine: An Interactive Documentary*, accessed June 7, 2019, http://www.jackandthemachine.com/jack-tramiel.

could immigrate to the United States. Upon arrival, Idek took the name Jack Tramiel.[30]

The Tramiels settled into a HIAS building in New York City, and Jack worked as a handyman at a lamp store while learning English from the movies.[31] In 1948, he joined the U.S. Army and served two tours, first as a cook from 1948–1950, and then as a typewriter repairman for less than a year in 1951–1952. In between the two stints and after leaving the Army for good, he worked as a repairman at the Ace Typewriter Company in New York, where he befriended fellow employee Manfred Kapp. In 1954, Tramiel and Kapp established a used typewriter business before buying a company in the Bronx called the Singer Typewriter Company to sell new and used machines.[32]

Tramiel and Kapp soon began importing Italian adding machines from a company called Everest that were particularly well received in Canada. They proceeded to convince the manufacturer to give them exclusive Canadian rights and relocated to Toronto in 1955 to establish Everest Office Machines. In 1958, they added a line of portable typewriters from Czechoslovakia and incorporated a new company on October 10 called the Commodore Portable Typewriter Company. While the typewriters were successful, Commodore experienced a constant cash flow crisis as it attempted to import them in sufficient quantity to meet demand. At first, they relied on factoring, a process in which accounts receivable are sold to a third party at a discount to generate short-term cash. Looking for better terms, in 1959 Tramiel and Kapp sold a portion of Commodore to Atlantic Acceptance Limited, one of the largest financing companies in Canada. Atlantic president C. Powell Moran became the chairman of Commodore and funded its further growth through loans. In 1962, the company went public under the name Commodore Business Machines.[33]

In 1965, Atlantic Acceptance suddenly collapsed after a routine deposit was rejected for insufficient funds. A subsequent investigation by the Canadian Royal Commission revealed Atlantic had been falsifying its financial records for years to acquire loans that were then funneled into a web of subsidiaries in which Morgan held a personal stake. Most of this money was then either lost in poor business ventures or pocketed for personal gain.

---

[30] Bagnall, 2010, xiii.

[31] Carol J. Loomis, "Everything in History Was against Them," *Fortune*, April 13, 1998, http://archive.fortune.com/magazines/fortune/fortune_archive/1998/04/13/240847/index.htm.

[32] Zube, "Commodore Nowhere Near the Edge or Commodore Before Commodore," Personal website, March 25, 2007, http://www.cs.colostate.edu/~dzubera/commodore2.txt

[33] Ibid.

The Atlantic Acceptance collapse remains the largest financial scandal in Canadian history, and Commodore was stuck in the middle of it. Tramiel and Kapp evaded punishment because the Commission could not find concrete evidence of wrongdoing despite heavy suspicion; Morgan was spared jail time only because he died of leukemia in 1966.[34]

Despite emerging from the Atlantic Acceptance debacle legally intact, Commodore teetered on the edge of bankruptcy. No financial institution wanted to touch a company tainted by a serious financial scandal, but a Canadian investor named Irving Gould took a chance on the firm and bought a controlling share in 1966. Tramiel remained as president, while Gould became the chairman. Gould sold off the Commodore factory to reduce debt, so Tramiel contracted with Ricoh to produce adding machines in Japan.[35]

While overseas, Tramiel saw some of the earliest electronic calculators and pivoted Commodore into the new market by making deals with Japanese firms like Casio to manufacture calculators that he could sell under the Commodore name.[36] In 1969, Commodore began manufacturing its own calculators again using a chip from Texas Instruments, and the next year it relocated to Palo Alto, California, in the heart of Silicon Valley. By 1973, Commodore had become a major force in handheld calculators with factories in California, Virginia, and England and offices in Japan. In 1968, the company realized a profit of $130,000 on sales of $4.1 million. By 1973 those numbers had grown to $1.3 million and $32.8 million, respectively.[37]

In 1974, Commodore began to decline in the wake of TI's entry into the calculator market. Unable to compete on price with its vertically integrated competitor, Commodore took a loss of $4.4 million in 1975. Tramiel responded by closing the Virginia factory and the Japanese office and tightening payment terms for customers. Meanwhile, Gould incorporated a new parent company as Commodore International in the tax-free Bahamas for which Commodore Business Machines and its international sales offices became subsidiaries. Tramiel felt Commodore would need to vertically integrate like TI to survive and decided to buy a chip company.[38]

---

[34] Ibid.

[35] Subrata M. Chakravarty, "Albatross," *Forbes*, January 17, 1983, 47.

[36] Ibid., 48.

[37] "Commodore International Ltd. History," Funding Universe, accessed June 10, 2019, http://www.fundinguniverse.com/company-histories/commodore-international-ltd-history.

[38] Ibid.

Meanwhile, MOS Technology parent Allen-Bradley was growing increasingly unhappy with its chip subsidiary as anticipated synergy never occurred and the calculator chip business took a massive hit during the price wars. Rather than liquidate the firm, Allen-Bradley let the founders buy it back for next to nothing.[39] MOS remained in a perilous state, however, due both to a continuing lawsuit with Motorola over the 6501 and 6502 processors and the death spiral of the calculator market. Consequently, the company agreed to be acquired by Commodore in September 1976.[40]

At the time of the purchase, 6502 lead designer Chuck Peddle already had one foot out the door. While bringing the 6502 to market in 1975, Peddle decided the team should build a simple development system for the chip in order to entice users. The result was a $30 package containing a ROM chip sporting a debugger and monitor program and a photocopied set of instructions describing how to build the machine, called the Terminal Interface Monitor, or TIM. MOS co-founder Don McLaughlin felt TIM was not user friendly and advocated for a second design that morphed into the Keypad Interface Machine, or KIM-1, that was sold as a PC board complete with a calculator-style keypad and LED readout.[41] Although the KIM-1 was envisioned as a development system, Peddle was surprised to discover some customers were buying it for use as a simple computer. He eventually realized this behavior was due to increasing interest in microcomputers among a less technically savvy group of consumers who did not want to assemble a kit. Peddle resolved to build a computer for that market.

At first, MOS management was supportive of Peddle's computer initiative, but as losses continued to mount, it withdrew its backing. Peddle was ready to leave MOS, but then Jack Tramiel bought the company. Commodore VP of engineering Andre Souson proved more receptive to Peddle's computer and agreed to help him pitch Tramiel on the project. The Commodore owner still only had eyes for the calculator business despite his setbacks, so Peddle and Souson pitched the microcomputer as the next evolution of the HP-65 programmable calculator. Tramiel understood this concept had potential and placed Peddle in charge of bringing Commodore into the computer business.[42]

From his days at GE, Peddle was intimately familiar with the time-sharing mainframes used by institutions like Dartmouth, and he resolved to develop

[39] "Mergers & Acquisitions," *Weekly Television Digest with Consumer Electronics*, April 21, 1975, 14.
[40] Bagnall, 2010, 57.
[41] Ibid, 25–30.
[42] Ibid, 59–62.

a computer that could provide an experience akin to using a CRT terminal on a system like the DTSS.[43] This meant building a machine that could drive a character-based CRT display, integrating BASIC in ROM memory, and shipping a complete package with a keyboard and a monitor. Peddle contracted with Micro-Soft for a 6502 version of BASIC in October 1976 and considered buying Apple to jump-start hardware development. When Jobs and Tramiel could not come to terms, Peddle began working on the prototype himself with an engineer named Petr Sehnal.[44]

While Peddle designed the computer, Andre Souson thought up a name for it. Sousan wanted a three-letter designation to fit in with the TIM and KIM-1 and decided on PET due to the Pet Rock fad currently sweeping the United States. He then added the number 2001 to the name as an homage to the Stanley Kubrick science fiction film *2001: A Space Odyssey* to convey a futuristic vibe. Peddle decided the letters should also stand for something, so he coined the phrase Personal Electronic Transactor.[45]

The Commodore PET 2001 was announced at the January 1977 CES at a price of $495, a shockingly low price for a computer that shipped with both a monitor and a keyboard.[46] The low price was largely possible through vertical integration, as not only could Commodore buy 6502 chips at cost, but the company was also able to use a calculator keyboard it had already designed rather than contracting with an external company. The keyboard situation was not perfect, however, as the calculator-style keys did not allow for touch typing.

That March, Commodore exhibited the PET publicly for the first time at the Hanover Fair in Germany. Its North American debut came the next month at the West Coast Computer Faire, by which time the price had risen to $595.[47] When not showing off the prototype at trade shows, Peddle scrambled to finish the design with a team that consisted of Sehnal and Bill Seiler on hardware and John Feagans and Jack Tramiel's youngest son, Leonard, on software. The two biggest changes during this period were a shift from a molded plastic to a metal case because it could be created by a Commodore office furniture subsidiary in Canada and an additional model with 8K of RAM that retailed for $795.[48]

---

[43] Ibid, 75.

[44] Ibid, 70–71.

[45] Ibid, 78–80.

[46] Ibid, 84.

[47] Ibid, 85, 99.

[48] Some sources indicate Commodore never shipped a 4K model because it had insufficient memory to operate properly, but the trades indicate the 4K model was offered. "PET's Progress," *Weekly Television Digest with Consumer Electronics*, December 19, 1977, 9.

The PET prototype was complete by the June CES, but Commodore still had cash flow problems due to the stumbling calculator business and could not afford to begin production. Noting the demand for the computer at the trade show, Tramiel began taking preorders right away to fund manufacturing. By sending Commodore a check for $795, a customer was guaranteed delivery of a system within 90 days. The ploy worked, and PETs began rolling off the assembly line in September 1977.[49]

In 1977, Apple sold several hundred computers, while Commodore sold a few thousand. Not only did Commodore beat the Apple II on price, but the company also had well-established distribution networks in both the United States and Europe, while Apple Computer was still getting on its feet. The Apple II was technically superior to the PET in many ways, but Wozniak, for all his brilliance at circuit design, was not a trained engineer. His eccentric approach to hardware creation was looked down upon to an extent in the hobbyist community, which influenced the portrayal of the Apple II in the computer magazines that tended to extoll the PET while ignoring Wozniak's creation.[50]

The PET was also more user friendly in several ways. For one thing, the BASIC Commodore licensed from Microsoft was more versatile than the Integer BASIC Wozniak had created himself. More significantly, the PET shipped with a display while the Apple II did not even ship with an RF modulator to allow the user to hook it up to a TV or monitor himself. This was because like so many video game manufacturers, Apple ran afoul of the FCC. Rather than pack the computer with shielding and increase an already steep price, the company claimed the computer was intended for an industrial setting, where interference regulations were less strict, rather than for home use. Including an RF modulator would have called attention to the deceit, so it was sold separately. This was hardly a problem for the hobbyist community but made the computer more difficult to assemble for the general public.[51] While price and ease of use propelled Commodore ahead of Apple, the PET was still only the second-best-selling fully assembled computer of the year. The best seller was the TRS-80, a product of electronics retailer Radio Shack and its parent company, the Tandy Corporation.

***

Friends Norton Hinckley and David Tandy established the forerunner of Tandy Corporation in 1919 in Fort Worth, Texas, as a shoe findings business

---

[49] Bagnall, 2010, 110–111.
[50] Ibid, 113–114.
[51] Ibid.

called the Hinckley-Tandy Leather Company. After an initial period of prosperity, Hinckley-Tandy managed to weather the Depression despite a few close calls, but leather rationing during World War II almost killed the business. To survive, the firm started supplying leather to the government for use in therapeutic craft projects for recuperating servicemen. After the war, David's son Charles pushed the firm more aggressively into leather crafts. This did not sit well with Hinckley, who felt leatherwork crafts were a fad and remained focused on the shoe findings trade. Hinckley and Tandy ultimately decided to part ways, and on May 31, 1950, David and Charles incorporated a new firm called the Tandy Leather Company.[52]

By 1955, Tandy was the largest supplier of leather kits in the country, and Charles Tandy engineered an acquisition by a Boston-area tannery company called American Hide and Leather because it had a listing on the New York Stock Exchange. A renamed Tandy Industries became a subsidiary of American Hide and Leather. The deal turned sour almost immediately when the new parent company changed its name to General American Industries and began an unsuccessful conglomerating initiative in which it used Tandy's profits to shore up bad business decisions in other areas. A power struggle ensued in 1957 that ended in 1960 with Charles Tandy in full control of the parent. He moved General American Industries to Fort Worth and renamed it the Tandy Corporation.[53]

Now that Tandy was a public company, Charles Tandy felt pressure to grow revenue for the shareholders. He targeted the consumer electronics market for expansion, both because he felt it would become a growth industry and because the do-it-yourself hobbyist ethos complemented his existing leathercraft business. After being rebuffed by two electronics chains, Tandy purchased a nearly bankrupt Boston chain of nine stores called Radio Shack in 1963 and turned the company around by reducing inventory to a small number of specialty items for do-it-yourself hobbyists, switching to a policy of only carrying private label products backed by strong quality guarantees and national advertising, and aggressively opening new stores across the United States. Within two years, the company had returned to profitability.[54]

In the early 1970s a boom in the popularity of citizen band (CB) radios drove Tandy's sales and profits to record heights despite a nationwide

[52] Irvin Farman, *Tandy's Money Machine: How Charles Tandy Built Radio Shack into the World's Largest Electronics Chain* (Chicago, IL: The Mobium Press, 1992), 8–38.
[53] Ibid, 59–83.
[54] Ibid, 113–173.

recession. The company expanded to 3,865 retail outlets with plans to continue opening new locations aggressively. Electronics were now the most important part of Tandy's business by far, so in 1975 all the other product areas – including the original leathercraft business – were spun off into two new corporations. Tandy now consisted solely of the Radio Shack electronics stores and the manufacturing companies that produced product for them.[55]

In 1976, the CB radio bubble burst, and Tandy was left scrambling for new products to sustain its continued growth.[56] At the same time, a new manufacturing VP installed in 1975, John Roach, began bulking up Tandy's engineering capability to develop new products that could overcome the Radio Shack reputation for old-fashioned electronics. Roach planned to push hard into the calculator market; a Radio Shack buyer named Don French proposed a different idea. French had been buying and assembling early computer kits since the Mark 8 appeared in *Radio Electronics* in 1974, and he felt the do-it-yourself nature of these kits fit perfectly into the Radio Shack product line. French faced resistance from the sales and marketing side of the company, but found a champion in Roach,[57] a math and physics major in college who had done some programming in graduate school and was originally hired by Tandy in 1967 to manage its data processing department.

During a swing out to the West Coast to procure CB radio and calculator parts, Roach and French stopped at National Semiconductor to learn about its SC/MP microprocessor. The marketing manager for the chip was unavailable, so they were briefed by an engineer named Steve Leininger who had already been experimenting with using the SC/MP in a CRT terminal. When the meeting ended, they asked Leininger if there were any computer stores nearby, and he directed them to the Byte Shop. When they arrived at the store later that day, they were surprised to see Leininger behind the counter. An avid microcomputer fan and member of the Homebrew Computer Club who moonlighted as a clerk at the store, Leininger walked the executives through the products currently on the market. Impressed after these two meetings, Roach asked if Leininger would consider a consulting gig on a Tandy computer project.[58]

When he returned to Fort Worth, John Roach asked his head of engineering, Jack Sellers, to set up an interview with Leininger. When Roach checked

[55] Ibid, 365–381.
[56] Ibid, 390–398.
[57] Ibid, 399–400.
[58] David Welsh and Theresa Welsh, *Priming the Pump: How TRS-80 Enthusiasts Helped Spark the PC Revolution* (Ferndale, MI: The Seeker Books, 2013), 1–2.

back in after a month, he learned that Sellers had chosen to ignore the suggestion. Roach flew Leininger down to Texas immediately on a Saturday and hired him to design a kit to bring Radio Shack into the computer business.[59] Leingier began designing the kit in May 1976 with Don French, who defined many of the computer's features.[60]

Despite being hired for his SC/MP experience, Leininger told Roach they should build the machine around the 8080. He later pivoted to the Z80 after a visit from a Zilog sales rep. Like Commodore, Tandy prioritized keeping costs down, so the computer incorporated only 4K of RAM and 1K of video RAM, which limited the machine to black-and-white character-based graphics at a resolution of 64×16. Leininger felt it important to include a monitor as well despite the cost edict and managed to do so by using a converted black-and-white television from RCA that was available at a substantial discount because the model had been discontinued.[61]

Management hoped to sell the kit for $200, but Leininger did not believe he could create a decent machine for less than $500. This nearly killed the project, as Radio Shack had a history of customers returning kits that were "defective" due to assembly errors, so asking a customer to spend $500 on a product that may not work right when assembled due to user error seemed like a bad idea. Radio Shack's head of merchandising, Bernie Appel, suggested they create a preassembled computer instead, and Radio Shack president Lew Kornfield agreed this was the best course of action.[62] Kornfield and Charles Tandy remained uncertain about the viability of a microcomputer and set the initial production to 1,000 units, though they quickly upped the run to 3,000 in order not to lose money on startup costs.[63] They figured that if the computer was a flop, it could at least be put to work in Radio Shack stores for inventory tracking or bookkeeping.

Leininger completed a prototype of what Tandy called the TRS-80 before the end of January 1977. Unlike Apple and Commodore, Tandy did not attend the West Coast Computer Faire three months later, but coverage of the long lines waiting to enter the venue gave the company some hope its computer might be successful after all.[64] On August 3, 1977, Tandy officially

---

[59] Farman, 1992, 401.
[60] Welsh, 2013, 3.
[61] Ibid, 4–5.
[62] Farman, 1992, 402–403.
[63] Ibid, 405–406.
[64] Welsh, 2013, 1.

unveiled the TRS-80 at a press event at the Warwick Hotel in New York City and revealed it would ship complete with a cassette drive, keyboard, and monitor for just $600.[65] The entry of one of the country's largest electronics chains into the microcomputer market with a relatively cheap product drove acceptance of the computer as a general consumer product, and before the end of the year articles began appearing stating that a future in which a computer sat in every home was now on the horizon and Radio Shack was leading the way. This coverage led in turn to increasing public interest in the TRS-80 and a large volume of orders.[66]

The first TRS-80 units came off the assembly line in the middle September 1977. By November, the system was on back order.[67] With its extensive retail network and marketing reach, the system gained greater exposure than either the Apple II or the Commodore PET and surpassed both computers in sales. By the end of 1977, the company had shipped 5,000 computers and still had unfilled orders for thousands more.

***

The release of the Apple II, Commodore PET, and TRS-80 in 1977 signaled a new phase for the microcomputer industry as kit computers from companies like MITS and IMSAI, known more for unreliable products and poor delivery schedules than consumer-friendliness, were supplanted by larger, professionally managed companies. In 1978, the microcomputer began its transition from a hobbyist toy to a home accessory. While still not a mass market item, the personal computer garnered extensive press and increasing sales. Tandy led the way with sales of 100,000 units for its TRS-80 computer. Commodore was a distant second with its PET computer at 25,000 units sold. Apple followed just behind with 20,000 units of its more expensive Apple II. IMSAI, the former market leader in the kit world, sold just 5,000 units.[68] It would be gone before the end of 1979.

Due to their limited memory and primitive cassette drives, the PET, Apple II, and TRS-80 were not useful for most business or productivity functions. Therefore, one of the primary uses for all three computers was playing games. Games had also been a major selling point of the kit computers from MITS and others, but because these machines were targeted at hobbyists who wanted to create their own programs, no computer game

---

[65] Farman, 1992, 406–408.

[66] Ibid, 409–416.

[67] Ibid, 410.

[68] "Radio Shack Dominated," *Weekly Television Digest with Consumer Electronics*, February 5, 1979, 11.

publishers emerged to support them. Instead, computer users tended to copy games from book or magazine type-in listings or trade programs they had developed or modified themselves with each other. Now that less technical people who did not necessarily want to develop programs on their own were buying computers, a new computer game industry began to emerge.

23

Micronauts

In 1973, engineers Charles Muench and Terry Hughey formed a company called Intelligent Systems Corporation (ISC) in Norcross, Georgia. Muench previously founded a company called Integrated Systems that manufactured remote alarm and control equipment for the electric utility industry, and Hughey had served as his director of R&D. Muench sold the profitable company to Esterline Corporation in early 1972 and departed a year and a half later. Now he was back in business with the intent of building a color terminal for the time-sharing market.[1]

In February 1976, ISC introduced the Intercolor 8001, an intelligent terminal kit driven by an Intel 8080 processor with 4K of RAM and an 80 × 25 full-color display that cost $1395.[2] In December 1976, IS began selling a $1,295 add-on for the terminal called the Compucolor 8001 with an additional 8K of RAM, Microsoft BASIC, and an 8-track tape reader to turn the terminal into a full-fledged computer.[3] While expensive, the Compucolor 8001 was the first microcomputer kit with an integrated monitor and keyboard capable of outputting graphics in full color. One of the major selling points was that it could play games such as *Star Trek*, *Lunar Lander*, *Hangman*, and *Pong*.[4]

In October 1976, Muench bought Hughey out of ISC because his partner wanted to pursue the high-end graphics market, while he wanted to continue in the low-end microcomputer market.[5] He designed a new fully assembled

---

[1]Cathryn Jakobson, "The Man Who Never Wanted to Be President," *Inc.*, September 1, 1981, https://www.inc.com/magazine/19810901/1015.html.

[2]Intercolor 8001 ad, *Byte*, February 1976, 71.

[3]Intercolor 8001 ad, *Byte*, December 1976, 7.

[4]Compucolor 8001 ad, *73 Magazine*, January 1977, 210.

[5]Jakobson, 1981.

computer released in late 1978 as the Compucolor II that integrated a floppy disk drive in lieu of the 8-track tape drive in the 8001 because the company discovered the tape wore out quickly.[6] By using a smaller 13-inch monitor and ditching the terminal functions, Muench was able to bring the cost down compared to the 8001, but it still cost $1,495 for a system with 8K of RAM, $1,795 for 16K of RAM, and $2,395 for the maximum of 32K of RAM. Due largely to its cost, the Compucolor II never caught on and was discontinued in 1980 so ISC could refocus on the high-end terminal market.[7]

The Compucolor 8001 was probably the first computer advertised with a significant emphasis on its game-playing capabilities. In June 1977, two more computers debuted with the support of ads that emphasized games. The first was the Noval 760 developed by the engineers at Gremlin Industries but marketed by a separate subsidiary called Noval Inc. led by Gremlin VP of Engineering Jerry Hansen because Gremlin president Frank Fogelman was not fully behind the product.[8] Built around an 8080 processor, the computer shipped with 16K of RAM, a 12-inch monitor that could be upgraded to full color, a tape drive, a printer, and significant expansion capabilities. It also shipped with several flawless conversions of Gremlin arcade games like *Blockade* and the *Seawolf* derivative *Depth Charge*. The complete package was contained within a wooden desk, which raised the price to $2,995 and guaranteed it would not be successful.[9]

The other computer that began advertising that June, the Apple II, fared better than the Compucolor or Noval products even though sales remained modest over the first year. Nevertheless, as the cheapest fully assembled computer on the market capable of bitmapped color graphics, it supported a small game developer ecosystem, as did its less graphically capable but better selling competitors, the TRS-80 and Commodore PET. While games for microcomputers did not threaten video game consoles as the primary outlet for electronic entertainment, the companies established between 1977 and 1979 laid the groundwork for a thriving computer game ecosystem that would flower at the start of the 1980s.

***

[6] "Compucolor," *Merchandising*, January 1979, 76.

[7] Jakobson, 1981.

[8] John Craig, "Around the Industry," *Kilobaud*, May 1978, 21, and Fogelman, 2016.

[9] Noval 760 ad, *Byte*, June 1977, 81–84. A version designed for schools called the Telemath that shipped with educational software was slightly more successful after it was adopted by the San Diego School District. Smith, 2016, 257–258.

The earliest games for the new wave of fully assembled computers that arrived in 1977 were released by the computer manufacturers themselves. At Commodore, Leonard Tramiel created several games as he debugged the PET hardware.[10] The first games for the system, available for $11.00 each, included ports of the classic BASIC programs *Lunar Lander, Wumpus, Kingdom*, and a *Star Trek* variant called *Spacetrek*; card games *Black Jack* and *Draw Poker*; and a ball-and-paddle game called *Target Pong* in which the player places bumpers around a playfield to guide a ball to a target.[11] The TRS-80 shipped with a game cassette featuring blackjack and backgammon programs.[12] The next year, Tandy released a cassette called *Games Pack I* featuring *Tic-Tac-Toe, Checkers, Hamurabi*, a version of *Lunar Lander* called *Space Taxi*, and *Star Pilot*, a target shooting game inspired by the Death Star assault in the movie *Star Wars*.

Both the PET and the TRS-80 displays were character based, so the graphics in these early games were practically non-existent. In *Space Pilot*, for example, the sides of the trench and the enemy ships are rendered with a combination of dashes, brackets, and asterisks. The Apple II, by contrast, could generate bitmaps and shipped with *Breakout* on a cassette tape as befit Wozniak's initial goal of creating a computer that could play the game. A user reference manual released in early 1978 contained type-in listings for several more programs, including *Pong* and *Star Trek*.[13]

Perhaps the first computer game offered for sale not released by a hardware company was *MicroChess*. Its author, Peter Jennings, was a British-born Canadian who became so enamored with electronics he started building his own simple computers when he was 11 years old. In junior high school, he learned how to program in FORTRAN by reading a book and performed his first calculations at the University of Waterloo for a science fair project. Jennings planned to become a physicist, but after he completed his master's degree in 1971, he learned that jobs were becoming scarce in the field as the U.S. government cut back in the aftermath of the Moon landing. Jennings decided to earn an MBA instead.[14]

After business school, Jennings worked for Gulf Oil for a few years, but he left to join a time-sharing company called Comshare in order to have greater

[10] Bagnall, 2010, 92.

[11] Commodore PET ad, *Popular Mechanics*, August 1978, 17.

[12] Jimmy Maher, "The Trash-80, Part 3," The Digital Antiquarian, June 14, 2011, https://www.filfre.net/2011/06/the-trash-80-part-3.

[13] *Apple II Reference Manual* (Cupertino, CA: Apple Computer, 1978).

[14] Peter Jennings, 2005, Interview by Sellam Ismail, February 1, Computer History Museum, https://archive.computerhistory.org/resources/access/text/2013/05/102657922-05-01-acc.pdf.

access to a computer. When the first microcomputer kits appeared, Jennings was intrigued, but they were too expensive for him. That changed in April 1976 when he learned about the KIM-1 from MOS Technology, which he subsequently bought. Back in high school, he had become interested in chess and developed a primitive system that could execute several standard openings and play a few moves.[15] Now with a more capable computer, Jennings programmed a complete chess AI largely based on the classic chess book *My System* by Aron Nimzovich.[16]

Figuring at the very least he had an interesting novelty product on his hands someone could use to show off his computer, Jennings decided to sell *MicroChess*. He began advertising the game for the KIM-1 in computer magazines in November 1976 and formed a company called Micro-Ware Limited in April 1977.[17] By summer 1978, Jennings had ported *MicroChess* to many of the popular computer systems of the day, including the S-100 bus standard, the TRS-80, and the PET. At this point, Jennings was introduced to a man named Dan Fylstra.

After graduating from MIT with an electrical engineering degree in 1975, Fylstra worked for a company called Intermetrics, where he met a regular contributor to *Popular Electronics* named Carl Helmers who introduced him to the emerging microcomputer market. The duo established their own magazine devoted to microcomputer hardware called *Byte* that debuted its first issue in September 1975 with Helmers as editor and Fylstra as associate editor. Fylstra returned to school to get his MBA and engaged in market research on the microcomputer industry as part of his coursework. Upon graduating in 1977, he established Personal Software.[18] Helmers put Jennings in touch with Fylstra, who asked to add *MicroChess* to his software catalog. Jennings became a partner in Personal Software, and *MicroChess* became the company's first major hit. The game sold more than 50,000 units by 1979, mostly of the TRS-80 version that Radio Shack picked up for both its catalog and its stores.[19] Other TRS-80 games sold by the company in 1979 included a real-time version of the classic *Star Trek* game called *Time Trek* and a version of the arcade game *Blockade*.

MicroChess soon had competition from a chess program called *Sargon* developed by the husband and wife team of Dan and Kathleen Spracklen.

[15] Ibid,

[16] Peter Jennings, "Microchess," Peter Jennings personal website, accessed June 9, 2019, http://www.benlo.com/microchess.

[17] Ibid.

[18] Burton Grad, "The Creation and the Demise of VisiCalc," *IEEE Annuals of Computing*, July-September 2007, 22.

[19] "Some Straight Talk About Your First Million," *SoftSide*, August 1979, 4.

A math major in college, Dan learned how to program after taking a job with McDonnell Douglas after graduation. Three years later, he took a job with UNIVAC in the San Diego area. An avid chess player in college, Dan toyed with the idea of programming a chess algorithm from time to time but did not seriously consider doing so until he went to an early MITS sales convention in San Diego in 1975. Dan was not interested in assembling his own computer so did not buy one of the kits, but he did start plotting out a chess program on paper in anticipation of fully assembled computers arriving at some point in the future.[20]

The Spracklens ultimately purchased a Z80-based computer called the WaveMate Jupiter III that was not really a microcomputer but rather an industrial control system that cost several thousand dollars. Kathleen, a programmer in her own right, began playing around with graphics on the system and added visuals to Dan's chess program. After the husband and wife team completed the crude program, they brought it to the second West Coast Computer Faire in March 1978 to compete in a tournament of chess AI. Their program, dubbed *Sargon*, won the tournament.[21]

Later that year, the Spracklens started advertising the program listing for *Sargon* in *Byte* at a cost of $15.00. Thanks to the free publicity from winning the tournament, orders began pouring in. In 1979, the book publisher Hayden entered the computer software business and offered a deal to the Spacklens to publish their program as a book. Soon after, Hayden also released it on cassette tape for the TRS-80 and Apple II. Before the end of the year, the Spracklens created an improved version of the program that Hayden published as *Sargon II*.[22]

***

By the end of 1979, a handful of companies had emerged alongside Personal Software and Hayden Books as a cottage industry developed to provide games for microcomputers. The most prolific of these companies was also the first, a firm based in the Los Angeles area called Softape. The lynchpin of the company was William Smith, who first became interested in computers around 1977 after seeing an article in *Popular Electronics* about building an S-100 computer and decided to construct one with his friend

---

[20] Danny and Kathleen Spracklen, 2005, interview by Gardner Hendrie, March 2, Computer History Museum, https://archive.computerhistory.org/resources/access/text/2013/05/102701977-05-01-acc.pdf.

[21] Ibid.

[22] Ibid.

Dave Mosher. Through the experience, the duo decided there might be a market for protective cases for hobbyist computers and formed a company called International Computer Accessories to market plexiglass cases for IMSAI computers and other popular brands.[23]

Mosher also owned another business that supplied fish and aquarium supplies to pet stores. Through this job he met a fellow salesman named Gary Koffler, who also happened to be an Apple II enthusiast. Mosher introduced Koffler to Smith, leading the two to collaborate on a program together called *Rollin' on the River*. Koffler started trading the game in local Apple II circles, where it attracted the attention of a talented programmer named Bill DePew. Subsequently, Smith, Koffler, and DePew decided to go into business together to sell both hardware and software products for the Apple II and established Softech in 1977. Soon after, the trio discovered a San Diego company already went by that name, so they renamed the firm Softape after the storage medium for their programs.[24]

Softape's business plan was to collect the best programs being traded in hobbyist circles or published in magazines as type-in listings into cassette collections called "modules" to simplify the process of locating and acquiring new programs. Customers would pay a $20 membership fee for the ability to order any module they desired at a cost of $2 each. The first module contained three games. *Saucer War* by DePew places two blocky ships on either side of the screen with an asteroid field between them. Using the paddle controllers, the players can move their ships up and down to line up a shot on the opposing player. Whoever depletes his opponent's energy first wins. *Digital Derby*, also by DePew, allowed the player to bet on the results of a horse race.[25]

The third game in the set was written by outside author Gary Shannon. Shannon first learned how to program when he was fresh out of high school in 1963 from a neighbor who worked for IBM. He subsequently attended a programming school in Los Angeles and did contract work installing IBM computers. Shannon then took a job with California State University Northridge while pursuing a master's in computer science but dropped out of the program because he felt it lacked real-world relevance. Around the same time, he discovered the Apple II, became addicted to game programming, and took a job with Rainbow Computing in Los Angeles, one of the

---

[23] Keith Smith, "Softape History, Part I," The Golden Age Historian, November 20, 2014, http:// allincolorforaquarter.blogspot.com/2014/11/softape-history-part-i-plus-review-of.html.
[24] Ibid.
[25] Ibid.

earliest computer stores. Shannon contributed programs to multiple early companies. For Softape's first module, he programmed *Advanced Dragon Maze*, a chase game in which the player must escape a randomly generated maze that slowly fills in on the screen as the player moves through it while avoiding a dragon that pursues him.[26] Picturing said dragon is mostly left to the player's imagination, as it is represented by a red rectangle.

Over time, Softape decided that some of its games were worth standalone releases. These included several games by Shannon such as *Jupiter Express*, in which the player navigates a ship through an asteroid field, and an adaptation of the board game *Othello*. They also released multiple games by the company's most prolific contributor, Bob Bishop. A physics major at the University of Wisconsin at Madison, Bishop first became interested in programming when he read through a FORTRAN textbook to pass the time while working a summer job in the school's science library. Bishop earned his master's at UCLA and then worked for Xerox and the NASA Jet Propulsion Laboratory. In 1975, he saw the ads for the earliest kit computers and decided to buy one. Bishop ended up buying an Apple I in 1976 and created one of the few games developed for it, a *Star Trek* variant published in the magazine *Interface Age* in May 1977.[27]

When the Apple II appeared, Bishop wanted to upgrade, but the computer was out of his price range. He visited Apple and met with both Steve Wozniak and Mike Markkula, who agreed to sell him an Apple II at a lower price if he traded in his Apple I. Bishop received his computer in July 1977 and immediately wrote a game called *Rocket Pilot*, a *Lunar Lander* variant in which the player has to take off on one side of a mountain and land on the other side.[28] Bishop published the game in the January 1978 edition of another magazine called *Kilobaud*. Bishop followed the program with a third-person target shooting game called *Saucer Invasion*, a first-person target shooting game called *Star Wars*, and a game called *Space Maze*, in which the player must navigate a ship through a maze without crashing into the walls. Softape eventually published all four of these programs alongside several other games by Bishop.[29]

---

[26]Keith Smith, "History of Softape, Part 2," The Golden Age Historian, December 24, 2014, http://allincolorforaquarter.blogspot.com/2014/12/history-of-softape-part-2.html.

[27]KansasFest, "Bob Bishop's KansasFest 2011 Keynote Speech," YouTube video, posted May 18, 2012, https://www.youtube.com/watch?v=FlsHGmijFP0.

[28]Ibid.

[29]In the early days of microcomputer software publishing, deals were not always exclusive, so Bishop's four original games were also sold by a New Jersey publisher called Powersoft established by a man named Jim Powers in 1978. Based on the copyright dates, the Powersoft versions probably appeared first, though this cannot be certain.

***

Softape was most likely the first dedicated publisher of Apple II software, but the most prolific company in the late 1970s was Programma International. Programma founder David Gordon grew up in Brooklyn until his family moved to Los Angeles when he was 18 years old. After graduating from California State University Los Angeles with a master's degree in accounting in 1964, he bounced around as an auditor for major entertainment companies like Warner Brothers and Paramount Pictures. In 1977, he became aware of the burgeoning microcomputer industry and placed orders for both a PET and a TRS-80. He cancelled both when he saw the Apple II and its superior graphics.[30]

Over the next year, Gordon visited every computer store, attended every user group meeting, and introduced himself to every Apple II enthusiast he could find in his quest to acquire as many Apple II programs as possible, gaining a reputation as one of the most prolific software pirates of his day. In 1978, he befriended a man named Mel Norell who ran a company called Programma Associates that sold software for a Motorola 6800-based microcomputer called the Sphere, a short-lived computer developed in Utah that may have been the first sold with an integrated keyboard and monitor. Gordon had already considered turning his obsession into a business, so he collaborated with Norell to establish Programma International.[31]

Programma gathered software submissions in all areas from utilities to productivity software, but one of its most successful areas was games. Examples include *Laser Turret*, in which the player controls a laser in the middle of the screen and uses the paddle controller to rotate it to strike targets that appear from the edges of the screen, and *Pirates*, an artillery duel style game in which the player must sink an approaching pirate ship by destroying the masts and hitting the hull before the ship destroys the fortress upon which the player's cannon rests.

More impressive games came from Chris Oberth, an early Apple II user inspired to become a computer programmer after reading Ted Nelson's *Computer Lib/Dream Machines* in 1974. His first computer experience came on the PLATO system, which he encountered while a student at Wright Junior College and DeVry University in Chicago. He subsequently purchased an Apple II and learned how to program on it by typing in games from

---

[30] David Hunter, "Exec: Datamost, Inc.," *Softalk*, July 1983, 58.
[31] Ibid, 60.

magazines like *Creative Computing* and *Interface Age.*[32] Oberth contributed the games *Phasor Zap* and *3-D Docking Mission* to Programma. *Phasor Zap* is a shooting game in which the player uses the Apple II's paddle controller to move a targeting reticule around the screen to shoot enemy ships that converge on the middle of the screen and fire at the player if not destroyed in time. *3-D Docking Mission* requires the player to navigate an asteroid field and dock with a space station before he runs out of fuel. While two-dimensional, the game world is displayed in split screen from a top view and a side view simultaneously to provide a three-dimensional effect.

***

The first microcomputer games written between 1976 and 1978 were limited in several ways. The PET and the TRS-80 only supported character graphics, limiting games to basic shapes and symbols. The Apple II supported a bitmapped screen, but a lack of hardware sprites meant creating graphics-intensive games that also played at a decent speed was difficult. These problems were compounded by both limited RAM and the limitations of the original Integer BASIC that shipped with the computer, which lacked the ability to do floating point calculations. Most early games stuck with the system's "low-res" graphics mode, which offered 16 colors, but only at a screen resolution of 40×48. This made for large, blocky pixels and objects rendered as basic geometric shapes. "Hi-res" mode offered a resolution of 140×92 but required at least 12K of RAM. As many early Apple users did not own systems with that much memory, most games released in the 1970s stuck with low-res graphics to maximize their customer base. Both low-res and hi-res games running at any speed were beset by constant flickering.

Due to the limited graphical capabilities of the leading microcomputers, they were not suited to the fast-paced action games dominating the arcade. Instead, many of the earliest successful microcomputer programs revolved around exploration and puzzle solving, taking their lead from a new pen and paper game sweeping through college campuses and computer hobbyist circles called *Dungeons & Dragons.*

---

[32] Smith, 2016, 699–700.

24

Critical Role

On August 23, 1969, the second annual Lake Geneva Wargames Convention –
Gen Con for short – opened in Lake Geneva, Wisconsin. The convention
was started the previous year by the International Federation of Wargamers
(IFW), a hobbyist club established by Pennsylvania teenager William Speer
in January 1966 as the U.S. Continental Army before changing its name in
May 1967. The club sought to connect enthusiasts of miniature and tabletop
wargaming, a hobby that made up for its small fan base through the fervent
devotion of its adherents. As few cities boasted a large circle of wargamers,
organizations like the IFW kept members abreast of new developments in the
hobby, provided matchmaking services for play-by-mail games, and linked
individuals who were interested in taking the hobby a step further and developing their own rules of play.[1]

In July 1967, the IFW held its first convention in Speer's hometown of
Malvern, Pennsylvania, which flopped because few people opted to make the
trek to the East Coast. The club nearly folded after being stuck with a large
catering bill from the event, but it persevered under the leadership of new
president Scott Duncan. In 1968, the group tried again, but this time opted
to hold the convention in the Midwest, both because it was more centrally
located, and because many wargamers hailed from that part of the country. The vice president of the IFW, Gary Gygax, offered to front a portion
of the cost on the condition the convention was held in his hometown of

---

[1] Peterson, 2012, chap. 1.1.

Lake Geneva, a resort community popular with residents of Chicago and Milwaukee.[2]

Gen Con attracted nearly 100 people, so a second convention was planned for 1969. Almost 200 people attended this time, including a group of wargamers from Minnesota led by a college student named David Arneson. Ironically, the Arneson group was not there to meet people from other parts of the country, but to find some fellow Minnesotans to swell their own ranks. In the niche world of wargaming, Arneson and his friends decided they would have more luck meeting fellow Twin Cities wargamers by driving eight hours to a gathering in another state as opposed to scouring their own community. Arneson met Gygax at the event, and the two bonded over their mutual interest in Napoleonic-era naval games. They promised to stay in touch and to collaborate on a set of naval rules together.[3]

In 1971, this collaboration produced a naval miniatures game called *Don't Give Up the Ship* published in four parts in the hobbyist magazine *International Wargamer* before receiving a printed release the next year through Guidon Games, a boutique publisher run by Gygax's friend Don Lowry.[4] Guidon also published a Medieval miniatures ruleset developed by Gygax called *Chainmail* that became particularly popular with Arneson's group in Minnesota, spurring a second collaboration with Gygax on a product that introduced a revolutionary new game that defined not just the future course of the board game industry, but of the video game industry as well: *Dungeons & Dragons*.

***

Military miniatures have existed for as long as humanity has possessed the technology to produce small figurines, but their widespread adoption dates to the eighteenth century, when a Nuremburg pewter artisan named Johann Gottfriend Hilpert used the leftover metal from tableware production to create flat figures mounted on broad stands to commemorate the victories of Frederick the Great during the Seven Years' War. After a brief interruption due to the Napoleonic Wars, Nuremberg became the center of a military miniature industry that grew increasingly popular as the nineteenth century progressed.[5]

---

[2] Ibid.

[3] Ibid, chap. 1.3.

[4] Ibid, chap. 1.7.

[5] Ibid, chap. 3.1.5.

Military miniatures were not linked to wargaming activities at this time: they were intended primarily for display or as cheap toys for children. After the Franco-Prussian War and the accompanying rise of international interest in German kriegspiel, a small group of British enthusiasts took the first halting steps toward linking toy soldiers and rulesets designed to use them to simulate military engagements. The writer Robert Louis Stevenson, for instance, played a series of wargames using miniatures while living in Davos, Switzerland, over the winter of 1881–1882.[6] Undoubtedly, other individuals were crafting rules for their own private war games in the same period, though none of them were published.

In 1893, a British toymaker named William Britain, Jr. introduced a new type of metal figurine that was three-dimensional rather than flat but could be produced cheaply due to a new manufacturing process. Toy soldier fever swept Britain over the next two decades, and the first published rulesets for miniatures wargaming appeared. The foremost of these was developed by noted author H.G. Wells, who took great delight in sharing in the play activities of his two young children and crafted a set of rules suited for structured play with their toy soldiers that were suitable for adults. He called his ruleset *Little Wars* and syndicated it from December 1912 in *Windsor Magazine* before publishing it as a booklet in 1913.[7]

Little Wars did not spark a civilian wargaming revolution in its own time, as pretend wars were soon overtaken by the horrors of two actual globe-spanning conflicts. It did gain adherents, however, most notably a group of miniatures collectors that established the British Model Soldier Society (BMSS) in 1935. Although dedicated to collecting generally rather than wargaming specifically, *Little Wars* was a common topic of conversation in the society's newsletter, and one of its members, Captain J.C. Sachs, developed a new set of rules derived from *Little Wars* that incorporated twentieth-century military equipment not found in the original rules.[8]

With World War II safely in the distance, *Little Wars* was reprinted in the mid-1950s, and members of the BMSS began publishing their own custom rulesets in their newsletter once more. Though the organization remained primarily British, some of its roughly 400 members resided in other countries, including the United States. American wargaming enthusiast Jack Scruby grew emboldened by a survey conducted by the BMSS indicating that at least

---

[6] Ibid.
[7] Ibid.
[8] Ibid, chap. 3.1.6.

a quarter of its membership was interested in wargaming and launched a new quarterly publication in 1957 called *War Game Digest*. Through his magazine, Scruby built the first community dedicated specifically to wargaming.[9]

Miniature wargaming was destined to remain a niche hobby due to the time and expense required to field large armies, but another form of wargaming gained a measure of popularity in the 1960s. The architect of this movement was Charles Roberts, an enlisted reservist with aspirations to become a full-time soldier. In 1952, Roberts became a commissioned officer in a National Guard unit and applied for a Competitive Tour of Duty, a posting that would allow him to convert his guard commission into a regular army commission. Taking his training seriously, Roberts decided to enhance his study of military principles through board games that could simulate a variety of tactical and strategic scenarios to complement his field exercises. No such games existed at the time, so Roberts created his own.[10]

With the Korean War winding down, the Army ended the Competitive Tour Program, and with it Roberts's aspirations of joining the regular army. He found his board game to be a valuable tool, however, and published it in 1954 under the name *Tactics* through a venture he named The Avalon Game Company after the town in Maryland where he lived. Assembling games in his garage and selling them through mail order, Roberts essentially broke even on sales of roughly 2,000 units.[11] This initial foray into publishing convinced him there was a market for his products, so in 1958 he entered the business full time with a revised version of his game called *Tactics II* and a recreation of *Gettysburg*. He also incorporated his business that year as Avalon Hill after discovering that his original company name had already been taken.[12]

In 1961, Avalon Hill released an updated version of *Gettysburg* that replaced squares on the game board with hexes. The publicity surrounding the centennial of the Civil War helped generate interest in the game, and it sold 140,000 copies over the next few years. Sales of other games remained modest, however, and a recession in the early 1960s coupled with the rise of discount stores to prominence drove many Avalon Hill's distributors out of business. The company was nearly forced to declare bankruptcy, but Roberts

[9] Ibid, 3.1.7.

[10] Charles S. Roberts, "Charles S. Roberts in his own Words," CSR Awards, accessed March 11, 2015, https://www.alanemrich.com/csr_pages/articles/csrspeaks.htm.

[11] Ibid.

[12] *The Avalon Hill General Index and Company History* (Baltimore, MD: The Avalon Hill Game Company, 1980), 6.

reached a deal to hand it over to his largest creditors in December 1963: his box designer, Smith Box Company, and his printer, Monarch Services, owned by Eric Dott. J.E. Sparling became the new president of Avalon Hill and cut expenses to the bone to keep the company going.[13] One of Roberts's last acts before departing his company was to lay plans for a bimonthly magazine called *The General* that advertised Avalon Hill products, featured columns on game strategy and design, and provided a directory of wargamers to help subscribers locate opponents. *The General* proved a critical nexus for wargaming enthusiasts around the United States and facilitated the creation of clubs like the IFW to birth a national fandom out of a niche hobby.[14]

Although most wargamers focused on the Napoleonic Wars or the twentieth century, there were a small number of adherents who preferred the Ancient and Medieval periods. One game that gained popularity with this set in 1967 was *The Siege of Bodenburg*, which was created by New Jersey hobby store owner Henry Bodenstedt and serialized in a magazine called *Strategy & Tactics* founded as a competitor to *The General* that same year. This miniature war game depicted a fictional siege of a German fortress by invading Turks and was developed to boost the sale of miniatures Bodenstedt carried in his store. While not the first Medieval miniature game, it became significant after a demonstration at the first Gen Con ignited a new interest in miniatures wargaming for avid Avalon Hill war-game player Gary Gygax.[15]

***

Born July 27, 1938, in Chicago, Illinois, Ernest Gary Gygax moved with his family to Lake Geneva, Wisconsin, when he was eight years old. An avid player of card and board games from the time he was five, Gygax also enjoyed his father's bedtime stories of magic-wielding heroes and exploring the tunnels under the abandoned Oakwood Sanitarium.[16] As a teenager, Gygax immersed himself in the sword and sorcery fantasy and pulp fiction authors of the day such as H.P. Lovecraft, Firtz Leiber, Jack Vance, and Robert E. Howard.[17]

A poor student more interested in games than academics, Gygax dropped out of high school at 17 and enlisted in the Marines. When he was medically

---

[13] Ibid, 7–8.

[14] Peterson, 2012, chap. 1.

[15] Ibid, chap. 1.3.

[16] David Kushner, "Dungeon Master: The Life and Legacy of Gary Gygax," Wired, March 10, 2008, https://www.wired.com/2008/03/dungeon-master-life-legacy-gary-gygax.

[17] Michael Witwer, *Empire of Imagination: Gary Gygax and the Birth of Dungeons & Dragons* (New York: Bloomsbury, 2015), 40.

discharged months later, he took a job as a shipping clerk in Chicago. In 1958, Gygax experienced two significant life events: he married his childhood friend Mary Jo Powell, and he played Avalon Hill's *Gettysburg* for the first time.[18] The game inspired a fierce passion for wargaming, and he began consistently playing Avalon Hill games on evenings and weekends.

At Mary Jo's encouragement, Gygax attended night school at Wright Junior College to complete his high school education. In 1962, he secured a job as an underwriter for the Fireman's Fund and moved his family back to Lake Geneva.[19] In 1966, he joined the IFW and became a frequent contributor to both *The General* and the small fanzines popping up all over the country.[20] His tireless advocacy of wargaming and interest in collaborating with nearly anyone who was developing their own ruleset led to his central role in organizing the Gen Con convention at which *Siege of Bodenburg* was demonstrated.

Inspired by the Medieval miniatures game, Gygax built his own sand table in his basement in 1969 and formed a local wargaming group dubbed the Lake Geneva Tactical Studies Association (LGTSA). Members included his childhood friend Donald Kaye, a local teenager named Robert Kuntz, and a college student named Jeff Perren. Despite his youth, Perren had been involved with the hobby for years and had contributed articles to Jack Scruby's pioneering *War Games Digest*. He shared Gygax's newfound love for Medieval wargaming and even developed his own simple ruleset for recreating the battles of the period.[21] Gygax, meanwhile, began beating the drum for a comprehensive set of Medieval rules in the various magazines and fanzines of the day and established with Kuntz a new organization called the Castles & Crusades Society to link Medieval enthusiasts that counted 40 members within a year. Gygax edited a fanzine for the organization called the *Domesday Book* in which he published a set of Medieval rules based on the rules Perren brought with him to the LGTSA.[22]

In 1970, Gygax lost his job as an underwriter.[23] At first, Gygax hoped this would become an opportunity to work on creating games full time, though this was not realistic with the small size of the hobby and his need to support a wife and six kids. He became a cobbler, which at least allowed

---

[18] Ibid, 43–50.
[19] Ibid, 53–57.
[20] Peterson, 2012, chap. 1.1.
[21] Ibid, chap. 1.3.
[22] Ibid, chap. 1.4.
[23] Witwer, 2015, 83.

him to work from home and gave him extensive opportunities to continue indulging in his hobby.[24] In this he was aided by Don Lowry, a military history enthusiast and former Air Force Officer running a prominent mail-order hobby shop out of Belleville, Illinois. Lowry started publishing rulesets with the aim of boosting miniature sales, which proved successful enough that he established a small publishing firm called Guidon Games. Gygax published several games with Lowry, most notably an update to the Medieval ruleset he had collaborated on with Jeff Perren.[25]

Released in 1971 as *Chainmail*, the latest edition of the Gygax and Perren's rules included a special 14-page supplement in the back added by Gygax that provided rules for depicting battles in fantasy settings, particularly the world of J.R.R. Tolkien's *Lord of the Rings* saga. Why exactly these rules were included is lost to history, but Gygax was an avid reader of fantasy and had been trying to gauge interest in a ruleset to depict Tolkienesque battles over the previous couple of years. The supplement was roundly criticized by the majority of the wargaming establishment, presumably due to its deviation from history and incorporation of the fantastic, but it did gain some adherents, notably Gygax's new friend Dave Arneson.[26]

***

Born October 1, 1947 in Hennepin County, Minnesota, David Lance Arneson received his introduction to wargaming the same way Gygax did, through the Avalon Hill *Gettysburg* game, which his parents bought him in the early 1960s. In 1965, he put out a call for opponents in *The General* that led him to the Twin Cities Military Miniatures Group (TCMMA). Founded by David Wesely, the TCMMA engaged in traditional war gaming, but also experimented with other styles of play. One of its more interesting variants was a Napoleonic game developed by Wesely called *Braunstein*. Wesely had been interested in the Napoleonic period for some time and had adapted his own ruleset from the classic Charles Totten military training game *Strategos* that he named *Strategos N*. One of the key elements that Wesely borrowed from that game was the concept that any action could be attempted by the players, after which a referee would decide how successful these actions would be based on an application of the rules. In the context of the original

---

[24] Peterson, 2012, chap. 1.11.
[25] Ibid, 1.5.
[26] Ibid, 1.6.

Strategos, this "anything is possible" approach applied strictly to military actions, but in *Braunstein* Wesely took this concept in a new direction.[27]

At its core, the *Braunstein* scenario was a typical miniatures engagement between French and Prussian forces over the control of the small fictional town of *Braunstein*. In order to give other members of the TCMMA a chance to participate, however, Wesley allowed them to assume the roles of various townsfolk such as the local lord, a radical student supportive of the French Revolution, and the chancellor of the local university. While none of these players commanded military units, they were free to determine the actions of their characters with little restriction, with Wesley acting as referee and determining whether they were successful or not. *Braunstein* ended without any military action taking place, but the players, including Arneson, had so much fun they clamored for more. Wesley ran several more campaigns, which were all referred to as "Braunsteins" even though they featured different time periods and locales to denote them as games with a large cast of characters and open-ended objectives.[28]

In late 1970, Dave Wesley's Army Reserve unit was called up, so Arneson took over the running of the *Braunstein* games. By now, Arneson had joined the Castles & Crusades Society and become more involved with Medieval wargaming. In early 1971, he decided to run a *Braunstein* in which combat would be adjudicated by the *Chainmail* ruleset. Informed by his love of author Robert E. Howard's books and the *Chainmail* fantasy supplement, Arneson decided his new Braunstein would take place in a fantasy setting called *Blackmoor*.[29]

The first *Blackmoor* game revolved around defending the Barony of Blackmoor from the marauding forces of the "Egg of Coot." In this sense, it was a traditional miniatures war game, but as in previous Braunsteins each player took on a role in the campaign, and not all of them were martial. The assembled players had such a good time that when the campaign ended, they desired further adventures in Blackmoor. Arneson not only obliged, but also decided to both provide continuity in regard to events taking place in the game and allow the players to improve certain core abilities of their characters through the accrual of "experience points." By appending

---

[27] Ibid, 1.9.

[28] Ibid.

[29] Ibid. Members of the Castles & Crusades Society would claim "fiefdoms" as befit the organization's focus on feudal times. Arneson called his fiefdom the "Barony of Blackmoor," which leant its name to his *Braunstein* campaign.

character advancement to the existing *Braunstein* formula of allowing players to attempt any action, Arneson created a new type of game.[30]

Subsequent *Blackmoor* campaigns continued to focus on combating external threats, but over time a secondary activity evolved. The centerpiece of the barony was a Sicilian castle model Arneson used as the central hub for the game. The scale of the castle was too small for all the activities Arneson wanted to set there, however, so he began mapping out an elaborate series of caverns and dungeons beneath it,[31] inspired in large part by the British horror movies developed by Hammer Films. In between fights with the forces of Egg of Coot and other marauders, players would descend into these caverns to fight monsters and acquire treasure. These activities became so popular that some players began focusing more on dungeon exploration than the primary campaign objectives.[32]

In fall 1972, Dave Arneson travelled once again to Lake Geneva to meet with Gygax, who had read reports of *Blackmoor* in the fanzines and wanted to play it for himself. Also tagging along was fellow TCMMA member Dave Megarry, who had distilled the dungeon exploration of *Blackmoor* into a board game called *Dungeons of Pasha Cada*. Gygax and several other members of the LGTSA played both games. Gygax was taken with both the character progression and dungeon exploration aspects of *Blackmoor* and asked for a copy of the rules.[33]

Unlike Gygax, Arneson was less enamored with creating complete rule systems as he was with developing ad hoc solutions and additions on the fly as new situations presented themselves. As a result, *Blackmoor* did not have a ruleset so much as a series of notes on courses of action that built off the foundation of *Chainmail* but were not integrated in a systematic way. Using these notes as a base, Gygax typed up a complete ruleset for a fantasy game that incorporated multiple players each taking on the role of a single hero, differing character traits based on the hero's chosen profession or "class," dungeon exploration, the ability to upgrade to more powerful equipment, and character progression based on the accumulation of experience points over multiple play sessions.[34]

---

[30] Ibid., chap. 1.10

[31] Jeremey L.C. Jones, "Interview with Dave Arneson," *Kobold Press*, April 9, 2009, https://koboldpress.com/interview-with-dave-arneson.

[32] Peterson, 2012, chap. 1.10

[33] Ibid.

[34] Ibid, chap. 1.11.

The rules continued to evolve throughout early 1973 as Gygax tried them out on the LGTSA and Arneson used them in his continuing *Blackmoor* campaign. Although technically a collaboration, Gygax asserted more and more control over the process as development continued and incorporated Arneson's input less and less. In mid-1973, Gygax completed a second draft that was twice the length of his initial version. Now that the ruleset was close to completion, it required a name. Gygax began experimenting with word pairings like "Swords & Spells" and "Men & Magic" and polled his friends and acquaintances on which sounded best. The consensus choice was *Dungeons & Dragons*.[35]

Gygax began looking for an outlet to publish his new fantasy game but could find no takers. In the past, Gygax had released product through Guidon Games, but Lowry moved to Belfast, Maine, in 1972, and his company never recovered its financial footing. Gygax also approached Avalon Hill but was rebuffed because the game was just too different from the successful games on the market. Gygax was not sure where to turn next but discovered a new path forward at Gen Con VI. Unlike in past years, the convention was not sponsored by the IFW – which was in the process of falling apart – but by the LGTSA. When the convention proved successful despite the lack of national backing and publicity it had enjoyed in the past, Gygax and his friend Donald Kaye decided to form their own company to publish *Dungeons & Dragons* themselves. In honor of the LGTSA, they named their company, formally established on October 1, 1973, Tactical Rules Studies, or TSR.[36]

Despite establishing a company together, Gygax and Kaye were unable to begun producing *Dungeons & Dragons* right away. Over the course of development, the game had expanded to fill three booklets, and TSR did not have the money to publish such an elaborate product. They published a set of English Civil War rules authored by Gygax and Perren called *Cavaliers & Roundheads* in the hopes of raising the necessary funds, but the game sold poorly. TSR was saved by another member of the LGTSA named Brian Blume. A tool and die maker and avid Avalon Hill wargamer, Blume joined the LGTSA in 1973 after becoming impressed at the organization's work in putting on Gen Con VI. A believer in the future of fantasy gaming, Blume agreed to fund the initial print run in exchange for a one-third stake in TSR.[37]

---

[35] In later years, Gygax associated the choice of name with a family member, but which one changed in the telling between his wife and one of his daughters. It is more likely the name was a consensus pick.

[36] Ibid.

[37] Ibid.

Dungeons & Dragons went on sale in February 1974 at a cost of $10 for the three booklets.[38] At first, the game garnered little attention despite Gygax's attempts to publicize it in various fanzines. The turning point came at Gen Con VII in August when Gygax was able to demonstrate the game for the larger wargaming community for the first time. *Dungeons & Dragons* became the talk of the show, and many of the 300 attendees bought rulesets to take back to their own communities.[39]

By the end of October 1974, the first print run of 1,000 copies had sold out. TSR did a second run of 2,000 copies in November, which lasted until May 1975.[40] As the decade progressed, D&D slowly but steadily grew in popularity as more rules supplements were released and the game struck a chord with not just wargaming clubs, but also groups of students on college campuses across the United States. As had occurred with war games, a gaming culture coalesced around the game as individuals formed local clubs, created their own rules modifications and scenarios, and kept current with national trends and events through *Dragon Magazine*, launched by TSR in 1976. Members of this new gamer culture were often attracted to computer programming with its own complex system of rules that could be shaped by the programmer, so it was not long before these individuals were applying the concepts of *Dungeons & Dragons* to computer programs as well.

---

[38] Technically, the first copy was sold via mail order at the end of January, but it did not really go on sale until February. Ciro Alessandro Sacco, "An Interview with Gary Gygax," *OD&DITIES*, February 2003, 10.

[39] Peterson, 2012, chap. 5.3.

[40] Alessandro, 2009 10.

25

Adventure Time

In early 1976, a new game appeared on the few computers connected to the nationwide Department of Defense computer network called the ARPANET. The author of the program was William Crowther, a physics major with a degree from MIT who spent ten years at Lincoln Labs working on real-time control systems and then moved to defense contractor BBN, where he did important work on the ARPANET. Crowther was also an active rock climber and caver, as was his wife, Patricia, who gained a measure of fame in caving communities in 1972 by navigating a tiny, narrow passageway to prove the Flint Ridge Cave system in Kentucky connected to the Mammoth Cave, making it the largest cave complex in the world. Crowther integrated his caving with his computer work by spending evenings at BBN plotting out caving routes on a mainframe.[1]

In mid-1975, the Crowthers divorced, and Will was separated from his two young daughters. Looking for a way to remain connected to them, he created a computer program combining his caving hobby with the new game he had been playing recently with a group of friends at BBN, *Dungeons & Dragons*.[2] Crowther developed a series of rooms based on the layout of the Colossal Cave in the Bedquilt Section of the Mammoth Cave complex and populated it with five treasures to collect, an axe-wielding dwarf that wandered the labyrinth, and three puzzles solvable by finding items within the caverns and using them in the right place and manner to proceed.[3]

---

[1] "Will Crowther," oral history, March 1994.
[2] Ibid.
[3] Dennis G. Jerz, "Somewhere Nearby Is Colossal Cave," *Digital Humanities Quarterly*, vol. 1, no. 2, 2007, http://digitalhumanities.org/dhq/vol/001/2/000009/000009.html.

As computer terminals capable of more than character-based graphics were still rare in the mid-1970s, Crowther's game was entirely text based. Each room featured a description of the environment and allowed the player to interact with certain objects by typing nouns and verbs into a text parser. Because it was created for use by his daughters rather than fellow computer programmers, Crowther used plain language commands such as "Go South" and "Get Lamp" rather than the more complex inputs usually required to accomplish anything on a computer. Crowther wrote his game in FORTRAN on a DEC PDP-10 computer, a mainframe released in 1966 that gained popularity in the 1970s due to its time-sharing operating system, TOPS-10. Due to filename length restrictions, he named the game *ADVENT.* It also went by *Colossal Cave* after the location in which the game takes place. It has gone down in history as *Adventure.*

When Crowther completed *Adventure,* he uploaded a copy to the ARPANET at BBN and left on a month-long vacation.[4] In his absence, the game started spreading around the country. One location that took to *Adventure* right away was Stanford, where the Medical Center owned a PDP-10 connected to the ARPANET. One of the many graduate students who tried his luck at the game was John Gilbert, who then brought his friend Don Woods to the center to play the game.[5] The son of a computer designer and a programming prodigy who sold his first computer program to Honeywell at 12 years old,[6] Woods was intrigued by the game and converted it to work on the time-sharing system at the Stanford Artificial Intelligence Laboratory. In the great tradition of computer hackers going back to *Spacewar!* at MIT, Woods felt that while *Adventure* was an interesting program, there was room for improvement.

Crowther conceived of *Adventure* as a game of treasure collecting and puzzle solving, but he placed the greatest emphasis on exploration as befit his caving activities. He also likely abandoned the game before completion, as several exits from the later rooms did not work, and one even had an "under construction" sign placed next to it.[7] Woods decided to complete the game and bring the treasure collection to the fore by implementing a point system for completing tasks and developing a new primary objective of acquiring 15 treasures through a combination of exploration and inventory-based

---

[4] Crowther, 1994.

[5] Ibid.

[6] "The Adventure Begins: Origin of the Text Adventure Game," *Retro Gamer,* no. 31, 2006, 54–55.

[7] "Observations About Crowther's Original Adventure (1975)," Renga in Blue, March 7, 2011, https://bluerenga.blog/2011/03/07/observations-about-crowthers-original-adventure-1975.

puzzle solving and returning them to the small brick structure in the forest at which the player begins his descent into the labyrinth.

While Crowther's *Adventure* contained some fantastic elements like the dwarf, Woods incorporated additional fantasy tropes based on his love of author J.R.R. Tolkien. He also modified a few basic gameplay systems, added many new rooms, and designed several new antagonists. Some of his more notable additions were the need to replace the batteries in the lamp that is crucial to navigating the dark caves, a thief who wanders the caves and picks up items the player needs, and a dragon the player must slay in his quest to collect all the treasures.[8]

Woods started improving on the Crowther version of the game in early 1977 and released it into the wild a few months later.[9] The game's mix of exploration and puzzle solving proved unlike anything most computer programmers had seen before, and it soon became a phenomenon at computer centers across the United States.[10] Anecdotal stories have been told of development projects being set back by several weeks as programmers abandoned their work until they had solved *Adventure* by gathering all 15 treasures and accumulating all 350 available points. By the end of 1977, *Adventure* was just as ubiquitous as *Star Trek* and *Lunar Lander* on time-sharing networks. Over the next two years, the game played a key role in the development of the new computer software industry emerging on the microcomputer platforms.

***

The earliest *Adventure*-style game for a microcomputer was created by Lance Micklus, a studio engineer for Vermont's public television station who first experienced *Adventure* on a computer at the University of Vermont, with which the station was affiliated. He noticed the game was popular with the students, but only played it a little himself. When he purchased a TRS-80, he began recreating the games he saw at the university and developed a simple *Adventure* derivative called *Treasure Hunt* that he submitted to the TRS-80

---

[8] Jerz, 2007. The dragon puzzle is perhaps the most infamous in the game. The player must type "kill dragon," after which the game displays the phrase "With what? Your bare hands?" If the player answers "Yes" to what appears to be merely a sarcastic retort, he slays the dragon.

[9] Ibid. Earlier sources put the release of the game in 1975 or 1976, but Jerz and Woods discovered Crowther's original dated source code, and Woods now concurs with this timeline.

[10] There is one known program that predated *Adventure* and featured exploration of a series of rooms using simple commands called *WANDER*. As the original 1974 source code is lost, it is impossible to ascertain how the program functioned at launch, and it is possible the later versions that are preserved were influenced by *Adventure*. Regardless, it only achieved limited distribution, and Crowther has confirmed he did not see it before creating his game.

Software Exchange, a mail order service maintained by the TRS-80-focused *SoftSide Magazine*, in October 1978.[11] Micklus submitted several more games to the exchange, but never turned game design into a career. The man who created the first widely disseminated microcomputer adventure game, Scott Adams, did.

Born July 10, 1952, Adams beheld his first computer on a class field trip to the University of Miami when he was 8 years old.[12] Adams was only able to view this machine through glass doors, but it left an impression. He later attended North Miami High School while it was participating in a pilot program with the University of Miami in which a single time-sharing terminal was placed in the math department of the school. Adams was allowed to use the terminal and fell in love with programming.[13] Before long, he started coming to school early and staying late to work with the machine.

After graduating high school in 1970, Adams attended the Florida Institute of Technology (FIT). Requiring a job for extra income, Adams hoped for a placement in the school's computer lab, but could only secure an appointment as a clerk. Once his programming experience became known, however, he rose to become the chief programmer on the school's accounting system. In 1975, Adams left school to work for RCA as a space object information analyst and was posted to a satellite facility on Ascension Island off the coast of Africa. Adams took a leave of to complete his B.S. in computer science at FIT in 1976.[14] After completing his degree, Adams was assigned to another radar station on Antigua in the West Indies. The computer at the station was only needed during the day, so at night Adams would fool around on it and play games, including a version of the Mayfield *Star Trek* game. Adams converted this game so that rather than using a teletype to display the galaxy, he could use the radar screens hooked up to the computer instead.[15]

After nine months on Antigua, Adams returned to Florida to work at RCA's Cape Canaveral division before taking a job at a small systems programming company in nearby Melbourne, Florida. While there, he met

[11] Jimmy Maher, "A Few Questions for Lance Micklus," The Digital Antiquarian, July 1, 2011, https://www.filfre.net/2011/07/a-few-questions-for-lance-micklus, and "TRS-80 Software Exchange Market Basket," *SoftSide*, October 1978, 53. Note that while the game was clearly inspired by *Adventure*, it was exceedingly primitive and did not implement a real parser.

[12] Ron Mitchell, "Scott Adams: Adventuring with Atari," *Antic*, July 1983, 12.

[13] "GameSetInterview: Adventure International's Scott Adams," GameSetWatch, July 19, 2006, http://www.gamesetwatch.com/2006/07/gamesetinterview_adventure_int.php.

[14] Mitchell, 1983.

[15] "ANTIC Interview 25: Scott Adams, Adventure International," *ANTIC*, Podcast audio, March 16, 2015, http://ataripodcast.libsyn.com/antic-interview-25-the-atari-8-bit-podcast-scott-adams.

Alexis, a psychology major at Miami-Dade Community College. The duo met because Alexis was helping run a computer-driven dating service to which Scott submitted his information. Three months later, they were married. The couple moved to Central Florida, where Scott got a job as a programmer with telecommunications manufacturer Stromberg Carlson.[16]

Adams was involved with the hobbyist microcomputer scene early on and purchased a Sphere computer for which he programmed an adaption of the Atari coin-op hit *Tank* and built custom controllers to play it. After joining Stromberg Carlson, he graduated to the TRS-80 and formed a local user group dedicated to the computer. Adams liked making his own games on the system and was considering creating a program requiring the player to use language in some fashion. At that point, a copy of *Adventure* appeared on the mainframe at his employer. Adams stayed after work for an entire week to beat the game and decided to create something similar on the TRS-80.[17]

Shoehorning a game like *Adventure* onto a microcomputer with just 16K of memory was not an easy task and required a few sacrifices. While the structure of Adams's game, which he also called *Adventure*, follows the basic Crowther/Wood conceit of descending into an underground labyrinth to gather treasures, the landscape is much smaller. As with the original game, the player moves through rooms, interacts with objects, and solves puzzles through two-word commands, but the parser in the game is more limited than that found in the original *Adventure*. Furthermore, to cut down on memory requirements, the parser does not actually check for whole words, but just the first three letters.[18] Despite these limitations, Adams was able to create reasonable approximation of *Adventure* on a TRS-80.

Adams showed off his *Adventure* to his user group, and the members suggested it was good enough to sell. As the few extant computer game companies on the West Coast were focused primarily on Apple II software, Adams submitted the program to *SoftSide*, which advertised *Adventure* in its January 1979 issue at a cost of $24.95.[19] *Creative Computing* also began selling the

---

[16] Mitchell, 1983.

[17] RSS Bot, "Important People Who Shaped the TI99/4A World–Scott Adams," AtariAge Message Board, December 12, 2015, http://atariage.com/forums/topic/246996-important-people-who-shaped-the-ti-994a-world-scott-adams.

[18] This quirk can lead to some humorous encounters. One of the game's more infamous puzzles involves startling a bear so that it falls off a ledge. In later versions of the game, one way to do this is to "Scream" at the bear, after which "the bear is so startled he falls off the ledge." As only the first three letters matter, the player can technically perform other acts instead such as "screw bear."

[19] "New Arrivals, TRS-80 Software Exchange," *SoftSide*, January 1979, 28. *Backgammon* and *3-D Tic Tac Toe* programs by Adams were advertised in the same issue at a cost of $7.95.

game through its software label in its February 1979 issue at a more modest
$14.95. The ads attracted the attention of a Radio Shack franchise owner in
Chicago named Manny Garcia who contacted Adams directly to order 50
copies. Adams filled the order by packing each tape in a baby bottle liner
with a business card stapled to the top.[20]

At first, Scott's new venture did not sit well with Alexis. As he spent every
weekend and evening working on his *Adventure* game, she finally snapped
and placed all his disks in the oven and informed him his programming
exploits were over until he spent some time with her. She had meant to
destroy the disks but forgot to turn on the oven.[21] Once the game was completed and looked to be saleable, Alexis reconciled with Scott and contributed
ideas for his next game, *Pirate Adventure*, which was inspired by the books
Treasure Island and *Robinson Crusoe*.[22] Both the TRS-80 Software Exchange
and Creative Computing Software began selling both games on a single cassette, so to differentiate the two, they started advertising them as *Adventure,
Pirate* and *Adventure, Land*. Within months, the original game started going
by the name *Adventureland*.

Adams released six more "Adventure" games before the end of 1979, by
which time "adventure" was fast becoming the label for a whole genre of
games that combined text commands entered via a parser, exploration, item
collection, and inventory-based puzzle solving. *Mission Impossible, The Count*,
and *Strange Odyssey* were all written by Adams himself, while *Voodoo Castle*
and *Mystery Fun House* were collaborations between himself and Alexis.
The sixth game, *Pyramids of Doom*, was a fan submission by a programmer
named Alvin Files who reverse-engineered Adams's game engine. *Pyramids*
was a traditional treasure hunt in the *Adventure* mold, while *Voodoo Castle*
introduced a rudimentary story with an objective to lift a curse affecting a
count. *Mission Impossible* added the wrinkle of a finite time limit to complete
objectives, while *The Count* broke new ground by introducing a day-night
cycle in addition to a time limit and having certain key plot developments
occur only at specified times over the course of the four-day game.

Adams continued selling all his games through the magazine publishers,
but he also started to receive an increasing number of direct requests from
retailers to ship them units wholesale. This finally forced the couple to relocate
operations in October 1979 from a spare bedroom in the Adams house to a

---

[20] Robert Levering, Michael Katz, and Milton Moskowitz, *The Computer Entrepreneurs* (New York:
NAL Books, 1984), 117.

[21] Ibid, 116–117.

[22] Paul Drury, "The Making of Pirate Adventure," *Retro Gamer*, no. 89, 2011, 48.

small retail location. Since they now operated from a building with a storefront, Scott and Alexis decided to undertake software operations in the rear of the space and run a retail store called the Adventure International Computer Center out front to sell both their own games as well as those from other programmers. Scott concentrated on churning out new product, while Alexis, who before her marriage had managed a chain of restaurants in Miami and sold cookbooks and recipes via mail order, managed the business.[23]

***

While Scott Adams was bringing the exploration and puzzle-solving of *Adventure* to microcomputers, several other programmers began supplying dungeon crawls directly inspired by *Dungeons & Dragons*. The earliest commercial microcomputer game bearing any resemblance to *Dungeons & Dragons* was *Devil's Dungeon* by Charles Engel. A professor of math education at the University of South Florida in Tampa, Engel released a booklet containing type-in listings for ten programs called *Stimulating Simulations* in 1977 and followed it up in early 1978 with a 15-page booklet containing *Devil's Dungeon*. In this text-based game, the player proceeds through a series of numbered rooms to fight monsters to earn gold and experience points. Only two stats are tracked, strength and speed, which can be improved by spending points.[24]

As it was text-based and contained almost no character development, *The Devil's Dungeon* barely qualifies as an offshoot of *D&D*. In late 1978, a programmer named Don Worth created a more complex take on the game called *Beneath Apple Manor*. Worth first learned how to program as an undergraduate at the University of California, San Diego in 1967. In 1968, he transferred to UCLA and got a job writing software for an IBM System/360 connected to the APRANET. During that time, Worth and his friends developed a turn-based space strategy game called *FRON* to play on the computer. After graduation, Worth took a job with the university. An avid wargamer from a young age, Worth took to *Dungeons & Dragons* upon its release and became the dungeon master of his group of friends. In 1978, he split the cost of buying an Apple II with a friend with whom he would trade the computer back and forth every two weeks. During his time with the machine, Worth learned Integer BASIC and began work on a game that emulated the dungeon exploration of *Dungeons & Dragons*.[25]

---

[23] Levering et al., 1984, 117.

[24] Smith, 2015.

[25] David Craddock, *Dungeon Hacks: How NetHack, Angband, and Other Roguelikes Changed the Course of Video Games* (Canton, OH: Press Start Press, 2015), kindle, chap. 1.

In crafting his game, Worth was inspired by Gary Shannon's *Dragon Maze*, which was included as a type-in program in the reference manual for the Apple II. Worth borrowed the random maze generation and exploration elements of that game but crafted a multi-level dungeon containing chests with equipment and treasure guarded by a variety of monsters with different attributes and capabilities. The player's abilities are defined by the strength, dexterity, and intelligence traits of *D&D*, but they serve as ability pools that are depleted by performing certain actions. Strength, for example, can be spent to bash open locked doors or fight monsters, while casting spells depletes intelligence. Play proceeds in turns, with the player taking an action such as moving or attacking and then all the monsters taking their own actions. Players can restore their ability pools by resting, but the monsters continue to move around the dungeon as the player does so. The goal of the game is to locate the golden apple on one of the lower floors of the dungeon. Worth released *Beneath Apple Manor* in November 1978 through a company he founded called The Software Factory.[26] It was the first of two dungeon crawls released for the Apple II at the tail end of 1978. The other was developed by a Seattle-based programmer named Bill Clardy.

A science enthusiast as a child, Clardy was introduced to computers when he took an introductory programming course in the summer of 1970 right after he graduated high school. For his class project, he wrote a Nim variation called *21 Matches*. Clardy matriculated to Rice University in Texas as a double major in electrical engineering and mathematics because the school did not yet have a computer science department.[27] He discovered both *Chainmail* and *Dungeons & Dragons* while at the school and became particularly enamored with serving as a dungeon master. Upon graduating in 1974, Clardy worked for Boeing as an electrical engineer, but while he found the work interesting, his first love was programming. When the first microcomputers appeared, he fooled around with the TRS-80 and then bought an Apple II in August 1978.[28]

Like Don Worth, Clardy was attracted to the type-in listing for Gary Shannon's *Dragon Maze*. After entering the simple game into memory, Clardy began rewriting it to add more complexity and incorporate elements from *Dungeons & Dragons*.[29] The resulting game, dubbed *Dungeon Campaign*, was

---

[26] Ibid.

[27] Robert Clardy, *Cyber Jack: The Adventures of Robert Clardy and Synergistic Software* (Apple Puget Sound Program Library Exchange, 2017), 1–2.

[28] Ibid, 7–11.

[29] Ibid, 13.

like *Beneath Apple Manor* in that it featured randomly generated dungeon mazes populated by treasure to find and monsters to fight. Unlike the dozens of levels of *Beneath Apple Manor*, however, *Dungeon Campaign* features just four per playthrough. The player's objective is to reach the exit of the lowest level while collecting as much treasure as possible. As an additional challenge, the game retains the maze chase gameplay from *Dragon Maze* in the form of a boss monster on each level that pursues the player.

Rather than controlling a single character as in Worth's game, players of *Dungeon Campaign* control a whole army consisting of 13 soldiers, an elf who can locate secret doors, and a dwarf who helps map the dungeon. The party members are not capable of independent actions, however, and merely serve as a stand in for hit points. If the player loses his entire party, the game ends. As in *Dungeons & Dragons* the characters improve their abilities over time, though their only attribute is strength. In December 1978, Clardy established Synergistic Software to market *Dungeon Campaign* and began pedaling it to computer stores in the Seattle area where he lived. After several months, it had sold a few dozen copies.[30]

The first dungeon crawl to achieve significant sales was developed by a company called Automated Simulations. The founder of the company, Jim Connelley, began working with computers while studying math and physics at the University of Pittsburgh, where he also played some of the early mainframe games like *Lunar Lander* and *Star Trek*. After a stint in Naval Intelligence, he worked as a programmer and engineer in Silicon Valley at companies like Westinghouse and GTE. An avid wargamer, Connelley joined a gaming group in Mountain View and introduced it to a game he started playing in college, *Dungeons & Dragons*. Before long, he was serving as the dungeon master for a regular group of players.[31]

Connelley learned about the emerging microcomputer market from co-workers at GTE, but he was never interested in assembling a computer himself. When Commodore announced the fully assembled PET, however, he purchased one in early 1978 and created a program to help run his *D&D* campaign. He also programmed a few simple games on the system. After a time, he decided to create a game that combined his love of war games with the basic principles of the classic *Star Trek* game. Called *Starfleet Orion*, Connelley's game aped the tactical combat of *Star Trek* with its need to balance energy between multiple systems but played out on a larger scale as

---

[30] Ibid, 15–17.
[31] Jim Connelley, interview with the author, July 6, 2018.

two players pitted whole fleets of ships with different characteristics against each other.[32]

Connelley did all the programming on *Starfleet Orion* himself, but to design ships and create combat scenarios, he enlisted the help of a member of his *D&D* group named Jon Freeman, who had been working as a freelance writer for several years.[33] In fact, Freeman was introduced to Connelley's *D&D* group because one of the other players, Susan Lee-Merrow, had worked with him to write a user manual for a chip fabrication company.[34] While he struggled in the profession at first and had to supplement his income by doing word processing, he managed to publish a science fiction novel and a reference work called *A Player's Guide to Table Games*, which led to steady work as a frequent contributor to *GAMES Magazine* and a consultant to several game companies.[35] When Connelley learned of Freeman's writing and design activities, the programmer brought him into the development of *Starfleet Orion*.

Starfleet Orion was written between August and December 1978. Around Thanksgiving, Connelley formed Automated Simulations in anticipation of selling the game and granted shares in the company to Freeman. Although the game was originally created on the PET, it launched first on the TRS-80 due to that computer's much larger install base. As both the PET and the TRS-80 only supported a character-based display, the graphics were primitive, with ship represented as numbered dots and explosions rendered as asterisks. The game sold decently based on the modest standards of the day, but sales were inhibited because it required two players. Incorporating a computer opponent had not even occurred to Connelley, because he considered a game to be a contest between two players. Once he realized his mistake, he collaborated with Freeman on an update to the game called *Invasion Orion* that allowed a single player to challenge the computer.[36]

In 1979, Connelley and Freeman brought *Starfleet Orion* to a San Mateo, California, *D&D* convention called DunDraCon The attendees were nonplussed, because what they really wanted was a *Dungeons & Dragons*-style game. This spurred Connelley to develop a game engine for a dungeon crawl. Freeman once again provided the game design, while another member

---

[32] Ibid.

[33] Ibid.

[34] Susan Lee-Merrow, interview with the author, August 30, 2017.

[35] James Hague, "Jon Freeman & Anne Westfall," Halcyon Days, March 1997, https://dadgum.com/halcyon/BOOK/FREEFALL.HTM.

[36] Connelley, 2018.

of the *D&D* group, a teacher named Jeff Johnson, pitched in on level and enemy design.[37]

As *Dungeons & Dragons* consists of a core rules system and individual modules that send players on professionally designed dungeon crawls, Connelley created a core game engine that could be used to script individual game scenarios. Connelley and Freeman envisioned designing a whole line of games using the engine, so they united their dungeon crawl products under the banner of a brand called "Dunjonquest." The first game in the series was called *Temple of Apshai*.

In *Apshai*, the player creates a character using the standard *D&D* attributes and then descends into one of four levels to fight monsters, gather treasure, find new equipment, and gain experience. The action unfolds in a pseudo-real-time manner: the player and the monsters take turns performing actions, but if the player is idle too long, the monsters continue to take turns on their own. In addition to tracking health, the game also tracks player fatigue, which is expended by taking actions. If the player's fatigue rating reaches zero, he must stop and rest, which can leave him at the mercy of the monsters.

Unlike *Beneath Apple Manor* and *Dungeon Campaign*, *Apshai* is modeled on a canned *D&D* module, so the levels are not randomly generated. Because the TRS-80 can only display primitive graphics assembled from basic characters and 64 blocky, abstract graphical tiles, the team also borrowed from the design of *D&D* modules by including descriptions of each room in the accompanying instruction book to provide ambience that could not be conveyed through graphics alone.

In many ways, *Apshai* was less a coherent game than a series of scenarios. The dungeon consists of four levels, but the player can play through them in any order, and they are not connected to each other. Instead, the player returns to the "Inn" between delvings, which doubles as the character creation area. Furthermore, due to the limitations of the hardware and the cassette medium on which the game was initially sold, the player is unable to save progress through the dungeon and must manually keep track of his statistics and equipment to enter again at the start of a new play session. Indeed, nothing stops the player from outfitting a character with the highest attribute scores and best equipment right from the start if he so desires.

Released in August 1979, *Temple of Apshai* quickly proved successful, and Automated Simulations released two additional dungeon crawls based

---

[37] Ibid.

on the same system before the end of the year: *The Datestones of Ryn* and *Morloc's Tower*. As both were smaller games than *Apshai*, they were marketed as "MicroQuests" and sold for half price. The dungeon in *Datestones* consists of just a single level, but new urgency is added to the game by imposing a 20-minute time limit on the player. *Morloc's Tower* consists of six small levels and imposes a 45-minute time limit.

***

By the middle of 1979, the computer game market remained tiny because the overall install base of Apple II, TRS-80, and PET computers remained small. In this time period, a game was considered a success if it sold just a few hundred or a few thousand copies. Most of the companies remained part-time ventures, as their owners could not afford to quit their jobs and support themselves and their families solely through making games. Nevertheless, computer game sales were outpacing those of other types of programs like business and productivity software, so it was clear that as the number of computer owners continued to increase, computer games would become another significant electronic entertainment field alongside coin-operated games and home consoles. In the meantime, video game consoles faced a new challenge at the low end of the electronic games market in the form of cheap portable games with LED displays that players could hold in their hands.

26

Power in the Palm of Your Hand

In 1936, a young couple from Denver, Colorado, moved to California to seek their fortune. Ruth Mosko, the youngest of ten children of Polish immigrants, took a job as a stenographer with Paramount Pictures. Her boyfriend, Isadore "Izzy" Handler, an aspiring artist whom Ruth met in 1932 at a dance when they were both 16 years old, followed her to enroll in the Art Center School in downtown Los Angeles. Though her family disapproved of the match, Ruth married Izzy in 1938 and subsequently convinced him to start going by his middle name, Elliot.[1]

Elliot found a job designing light fixtures to put himself through school, where he learned about new plastics like Lucite and plexiglass. Intrigued by the materials, he began building Lucite furniture in his spare time to fill his and Ruth's apartment. Ruth felt the furniture was of high enough quality to sell and convinced her husband to drop out of school and quit his job so they could manufacture furniture under the name Elliot Handler Plastics. Elliot built the products, and Ruth sold them.[2]

Elliot later branched out into giftware and then costume jewelry, attracting the attention of a prominent Los Angeles jeweler named Zachary Zemby. The duo formed a partnership called Elzac in 1941.[3] Elliot led design efforts, while his friend Harold "Matt" Matson, the shop foreman at his old lighting fixture company, ran manufacturing. Wartime shortages created challenges, and Elliot began having disagreements with Zemby and three new investors

---

[1] Ruth Handler and Jacqueline Shannon, *Dream Doll: The Ruth Handler Story* (Stamford, CT: Longmeadow Press, 1994), 21–33.

[2] Ibid, 35–41.

[3] Ibid, 41.

brought in by his partner. Matson grew sick of the infighting and left in 1944.[4]

Ruth, meanwhile, had given up sales for motherhood after the birth of her daughter Barbara in 1941. Anxious to get back into business, she visited Matson after he quit Elzac. Elliot, Ruth, and Matt agreed that Matt could build picture frames based on old designs by Elliot and sell them in partnership with Ruth. Although Elliot himself would remain at Elzac, the trio named the new company by combining letters from "Matt" and "Elliot" to spell Mattel. As tensions increased at Elzac, Elliot let Zemby and his other partners buy him out in 1945 so he could join Matt and Ruth at Mattel.[5]

Before long, Elliot began combining leftover wood from the frames with plastic scraps to construct dollhouse furniture, thus bringing Mattel into the toy business.[6] Although profitable in its first year, the company hit a snag in 1946 when a competing company put out a more detailed line of doll furniture that drove Mattel out of the business. In 1947, the company experienced its first hit with a plastic toy instrument called the "Uke-A-Doodle," but once again, another company introduced a competing product at a lower price. Although Mattel weathered the crisis, the constant financial worries were too much for Matson, who sold his share in the business to Ruth's sister.[7] The next year, the company experienced another hit with a plastic piano and incorporated as Mattel, Inc.

Mattel continued as a moderately successful toy company until 1955, when the Handlers took a risk that transformed the entire industry. In the early twentieth century, the toy business was strictly seasonal with products bought almost exclusively around Christmas, so firms spent virtually no money advertising their products. The rise of television in the early 1950s created both opportunities to create tie-in products with popular programs as well as the prospect of peddling toys directly to children year round through commercials.

In 1955, the television network ABC approached Mattel with an offer to sponsor a 15-minute segment of the new "Mickey Mouse Club" show from The Walt Disney Company for 52 weeks in exchange for $500,000. That figure represented virtually Mattel's entire net worth, but the Handlers decided to accept the offer and worked with the Carson/Roberts advertising agency to create a commercial for a new automatic cap gun called the "Burp Gun."

[4]Ibid, 57–58.
[5]Ibid, 58–61.
[6]Ibid, 61.
[7]Ibid, 66–70.

Backed by the commercial, the gun set a new annual sales record and helped usher in a new era of television promotion and year-round sales for the toy industry.[8] Mattel expanded its line of guns over the next two years to take advantage of the popularity of TV westerns, and sales reached $14 million by 1959. The company's biggest hit was yet to come.

On a family trip to Europe in 1956, the Handlers encountered a German novelty doll called Lilli based on a German comic strip character known for her loose morals, skimpy clothing, and gold-digging schemes. While dolls had been a fixture of the toy industry for decades, they were typically sculpted as babies or small children, and play centered on childcare and motherhood. Indeed, Lilli herself was intended not for children to play with, but for adults to exchange as a gag gift. Ruth Handler saw something more. When her daughter Barbara was younger, Ruth noticed she enjoyed pretending her paper dolls were teenagers or adults rather than young children and saw an untapped market for a teenage plastic doll. When she asked her designers to craft such a doll, they said it could not be done for technical reasons. Now armed with Lilli, she ordered them to try again. The result was a teenaged doll supported by a line of clothing and accessories released in 1959 called Barbie.[9]

An instant smash success, the Barbie line transformed Mattel into the number one toy company in the world and paved the way for a public offering in 1963. With sales reaching $100 million by 1966, Ruth Handler felt that delivering further growth for the shareholders would require both increased toy production and diversification outside the toy business. To further these goals, the Handlers hired Seymour Rosenberg, one of the most respected acquisition specialists in the country, as executive vice president and CFO.[10]

Rosenberg spearheaded the acquisition of five companies between 1968 and 1971 under the banner of the "World of the Young" initiative designed to take Mattel beyond toys into other forms of children's entertainment. This brought the company into pet products (Metaframe), playground equipment (Turco), magnetic tape production (Audio Magnetics Corp.), the motion picture industry (Radnitz/Mattel Productions), and theme parks (Ringling Brothers and Barnum & Bailey Circus, which was building Circus World in Florida). Meanwhile, the company realized another monster toy hit in 1968

---

[8] Ibid, 83–86.

[9] Ibid, 1–12. Barbie was named after Barbara Handler. Barbie's boyfriend, introduced in 1961, was named after Elliot and Ruth's son Ken.

[10] "Mattel Tells Troubles in Toyland," *The Milwaukee Journal*, November 17, 1975.

with its line of Hot Wheels cars and posted five straight years of record earnings to close out the 1960s.[11]

After two years of brisk sales, interest in Hot Wheels started to fade in 1970. A September fire at a Mexico plant further stunted growth, so while Mattel remained profitable, the company was poised to miss its earnings targets and fall short of record profits for a sixth straight year. To compensate, executives at Mattel booked future orders as revenue to deliver another year of record results and inflate the company stock price.[12] As the Hot Wheels line took another sharp dip the next year and a West Coast shipyard strike prevented Mattel from delivering much of its inventory onto store shelves for the 1971 Christmas shopping season, the company recorded the first annual loss in its history.[13]

Mattel's spate of acquisitions made it difficult for the Handlers to manage the company effectively, so in 1969 they initiated a three-year plan to divisionalize.[14] This process culminated in 1972 with the formation of an operating committee consisting of CEO Elliot Hander, President Ruth Handler, and four senior vice presidents: Arthur Spear, Ray Wagner, John Jones, and Robert Ehrlich, who replaced the retiring Rosenberg as CFO. A new Mattel Toys subsidiary was also formed with Ruth Handler as president, Spear as EVP of operations, Wagner as EVP of marketing, and Ehrlich as CFO.[15] Mattel Toys was further subdivided into four divisions: toys, dolls, wings and wheels, and games.

Restructuring Mattel resulted in increased overhead costs, and losses continued to mount in 1972 as several of Mattel's recently purchased subsidiaries proved unprofitable. Nevertheless, Mattel issued a press release in February 1973 stating it had turned a corner and was poised for recovery. Three weeks later, the company was forced to issue a correction stating that it would record another loss in fiscal 1973 and that the earlier release should be disregarded.[16] This strange behavior prompted both a class-action lawsuit by shareholders and an SEC investigation, after which years of inventory manipulation came to light.

For the next two years, Mattel was consumed by legal struggles. Responsibility for navigating this crisis fell to Arthur Spear, an MIT-educated

---

[11] Ibid.

[12] Handler and Shannon, 1994, 162–163.

[13] "Mattel Reports First Loss in History," *Playthings*, May 8, 1972, 19.

[14] Handler and Shannon, 1994, 134–135.

[15] "Mattel Revamps Structure, Establishes Toy Division," *Playthings*, September 1972, 35.

[16] Handler and Shannon, 1994, 167.

engineer who joined Mattel in 1964 to run manufacturing. He became president of the company in 1973 when the Handlers resigned all their executive positions save for co-chairmen of the board as they came under investigation for the financial irregularities.[17] Spear managed to clear the company's short-term debt and restructure its long-term debt.[18] He also sold several non-profitable and/or debt-ridden divisions like Audio Magnetics,[19] Turco,[20] and the Ringling Brothers Circus.[21]

In August 1974, Mattel signed a consent decree with the SEC requiring the appointment of additional outside directors, only to suspend trading on the New York Stock Exchange the next month when the extent of the financial transgressions became evident. A second consent decree followed in October in which enough outside directors were appointed to constitute a majority. In October 1975, the Handlers resigned from the board, severing their last significant ties to the company they founded.[22] Less than a month later, Mattel settled its shareholder suits for $30 million.[23] With its reputation ruined and its finances in tatters, Mattel needed a hit desperately, and the electronic game market just beginning to coalesce around Atari's *Home Pong* seemed like a promising avenue to help turn the company around.

*** * ***

The rise of the home video game proved a challenge for the toy industry. While nominally within its purview as an entertainment product popular with children, a video game was both more expensive than a typical toy and built upon technology outside the comfort zone of the typical toy buyer. As a result, early video games were just as likely to be found in sporting goods and electronics departments as mixed in with other toys.[24]

This situation began to change when Coleco entered the industry with its Telstar line. As an established toy company, Coleco already did most of its business through toy department buyers, so it continued to rely on them when marketing its video games. New Magnavox video game product

[17] "Mattel Lists Major Shifts in Officers," *Playthings*, May 4, 1973.

[18] "Business and Finance," *Toy & Hobby World*, March 1975, 30.

[19] "Mattel Agrees to Sell Audio Magnetics," *Toy & Hobby World*, August 20, 1973, 10.

[20] "Mattel Closes Sale of Turco," *Toy & Hobby World*, February 4, 1974, 26.

[21] Peter Fiero, "Gulf Oil Subsidiary to Buy Circus World," *Lakeland Ledger*, January 23, 1974.

[22] "Mattel Elects A.S. Spear; Meason is Named President," *Playthings*, September 1978.

[23] "Mattel to Settle Lawsuits Out of Court," *Playthings*, December 1975, 15.

[24] Milton Schulman, "Toy Industry Enters Electronic Age; Promising Market is Still Unshaped," *Toy & Hobby World*, September 1976, 1.

manager John Helms, who took over from Bob Fritsche in November 1975,[25] also courted toy buyers by bringing the Odyssey product line to Toy Fair in 1976 as he looked to continue expanding distribution out of the exclusive Magnavox dealer network.[26] While video games remained split between multiple departments that year, it was clear they would play a significant role in the future of the toy industry.

Even as toy buyers became comfortable with a higher priced product, designing the games remained beyond the expertise of most toy companies, and the risk of failure with such an expensive offering proved daunting. As the price of LSI circuits began to fall, some of these firms saw an opportunity to create simpler games that retained the high-tech allure of the video game while retailing at a more traditional price point. This approach was particularly favored by the major players in board games, as well as by the severely wounded Mattel. By 1978, non-video electronic games developed by these companies would become so popular that it appeared they might supplant video games entirely.

While Art Spear navigated Mattel through its legal and financial difficulties, Ray Wagner, who became president of Mattel Toys in 1972,[27] and his marketing vice president, Ed Hamowy, attempted to keep the company relevant in its core business. Part of their strategy to combat flagging sales of its key toy lines was to hire new managers out of the traditional packaged goods business who could jump-start product development and marketing. One of these new hires was a young marketing executive named Michael Katz.

A graduate of Cornell University with an MBA from Columbia, Katz spent time in product marketing and brand management with companies like Lever Brothers and Foremost Foods. He then took an account manager role at the McCann Erickson ad agency in San Francisco but grew unhappy in the role. A headhunter recruited him to Mattel as director of new product category marketing, where his mandate was to explore new product categories and introduce products in areas where the company had not previously been successful. Games were a traditional weak spot for Mattel, and pocket calculators had become ubiquitous over the last few years, so during a brainstorming session Katz asked the head of electronics development at Mattel Toys, Richard Chang, to create a calculator-sized electronic game using LEDs.[28]

---

[25] "Trade Personals," *Weekly Television Digest with Consumer Electronics*, November 24, 1975, 12.
[26] "Video Games Sweeping Toy Field," *Weekly Television Digest with Consumer Electronics*, February 23, 1976, 9.
[27] "Mattel Lists Major Shifts in Officers," 1973.
[28] Michael Katz, interview with the author, August 1, 2014.

Chang responded to the challenge by developing a simple obstacle avoidance concept in which parallel strips of red LEDs light up in sequence to simulate movement from top to bottom or side to side. The player controls his own LED that can move between strips to avoid the oncoming lights. Chang worked with a graphic designer named David James to theme this setup around several activities including baseball, auto racing, and football. Focus groups indicated that football held the greatest appeal, but Mattel management decided to develop the auto racing concept first because Chang was continuing to make refinements to the hardware that would be beneficial to the football concept.[29] To develop the LSI required to power the final product, Chang approached Rockwell International, a conglomerate with a chip design operation in Southern California. Rockwell assigned an engineer named Mark Lesser to the project, who converted one of Rockwell's existing calculator chips to meet the needs of a game and programmed the racing theme in the 511 bytes of memory available to him on the chip.[30]

In fall 1976, Mattel Toys hired a marketing executive named Edward Krakauer as VP of New Business Development, further strengthening a team the company hoped would put Mattel back on track.[31] Like Katz a veteran of the food products industry, where he was vice president of consumer products marketing for Hunt-Wesson, Krakauer took over the marketing of the handheld line in February 1977 as the head of a new Mattel Electronics unit.[32] Results were not promising at first. Mattel offered a first look at its *Auto Race* and *Football* games at the January 1977 Consumer Electronics Show, but the industry was skeptical of the products, in large part because Mattel had never been successful in games. Krakauer tried again at the June CES, where alongside *Auto Race* and *Football* he showed a third game called *Missile Attack* that changed the *Auto Race* format so that the player attempted to collide with approaching LEDs to simulate shooting down missiles launched at New York City.[33] Once again, he was unable to generate much enthusiasm.

Despite the lackluster reception, Mattel secured parts for 500,000 units and prepared a massive fall advertising campaign. *Auto Race* arrived first in May 1977 and underperformed, causing Sears to significantly cut back on its orders for the whole line and forcing Mattel to halt production at

---

[29] Katz, 2014.

[30] Scott Stilphen, "DP: Interviews Mark Lesser," *Digital Press*, 2007, http://www.digitpress.com/library/interviews/interview_mark_lesser.html.

[31] "People," *Playthings*, October 1976, 95.

[32] "Trade Personals," *Weekly Television Digest With Consumer Electronics*, February 21, 1977, 12.

[33] "Mattel's Missile Attack Viewed at Chicago Electronics Show," *Playthings*, August 1977, 31.

100,000 units.[34] Another blow came when the NBC television network refused to air commercials featuring *Missile Attack* because it thought children might believe that if they failed at the game, New York City would actually blow up.[35] Once *Football* debuted, however, it proved a hit during the Christmas season.

In 1978, Mattel sold over 1 million units of *Football*.[36] Another Mattel handheld introduced that year, *Basketball*, also topped a million units. These successes occurred despite fierce competition with the former leader of the dedicated video game console market, Coleco. After its disastrous 1977 holiday season, Coleco cancelled most of its video game development, but prepared to move forward in the same electronic handheld market as Mattel. Leading these efforts was the company's new head of electronic game development, Eric Bromley.

A philosophy graduate of Syracuse University, Bromley was teaching logic at Utica College in New York when the first solid-state games entered the arcade. Looking for something more lucrative than a philosophy teaching gig, Bromley followed the advice of a colleague and used his logic knowledge to create an electronic dart game and attempted to sell it as a coin-operated product. While the game was not successful, Bromley parlayed the experience into a job at Midway Manufacturing working on coin-operated games.[37]

Bromley joined Coleco in 1976 when the Telstar was nearing completion and became one of the primary designers for the company's growing electronic game line. After Mattel debuted its *Football* game, he started work on his own version that included several enhancements, most notably the ability to throw passes. Coleco planned to market the game exclusively through Sears, but during a demonstration of the prototype unit an executive tripped over and broke it, and Sears declined to buy. Coleco released the game under its own label in 1978 and sold 3 million units by the end of its run to pull the company back to profitability after its disastrous flirtation with video games.[38] Helping fuel these sales was the first head-to-head advertisement

[34]"Trivia and Stories," Handheld Museum, accessed June 11, 2019, https://www.handheldmuseum.com/Mattel/Trivia.htm. Several sources have *Auto Race* coming out in 1976, but this appears unfounded. The toy trades indicate the game was displayed for the first time at the January 1977 CES, and ads for the game did not start appearing in newspapers until May 1977.

[35]*Missile Attack* was pulled and reworked as a science fiction title originally called *Space Alert* and ultimately rebranded as a licensed tie-in with the new TV series *Battlestar Galactica* in 1978.

[36]"Toying with Electronics," *Weekly Television Digest with Consumer Electronics*, February 26, 1979, 10.

[37]"Electronic-Games Race," *The New York Times*, December 14, 1980. Note that Bromley is referred to pseudonymously as "Bill," but in context it is clearly him.

[38]Rusel DeMaria, *High Score Expanded*, (New York: CRC Press, 2018), 37.

in the electronic game field in which Coleco placed *Electronic Quarterback* side-by-side with Mattel *Football* to highlight its more robust list of features.

While Mattel and Coleco battled it out in the electronic handheld realm, two board game giants introduced slightly larger electronic games designed for play on a tabletop. The first was Parker Brothers, established as the George S. Parker Company in 1885 by its 18-year-old namesake. In 1883, George had grown tired of the moral lessons integral to the board games of the day and started peddling a banking-themed game of his own design intended solely for amusement rather than ethics education. Intending to become a journalist, he instead established his own company to continue marketing games after being forced to quit his job due to a severe bronchial infection.[39] For the next 80 years, the firm, which became Parker Brothers after George's brother Charles joined in 1888,[40] remained a family owned company best known for its jigsaw puzzles and board games, particularly *Clue, Risk, Sorry,* and the most successful board game of all time, *Monopoly.*

In 1952, George Parker died, and his son-in-law Robert Barton took control of Parker Brothers.[41] Barton began a massive expansion of the company into other areas of the toy business that led to rapid growth but also caused a continual cash crunch. By 1966 it became clear that to keep growing Barton would have to secure investment partners, go public, or sell out to another company. A suitor soon emerged in the form of General Mills, a cereal company looking to diversify in the age of conglomerates. Barton resisted at first, but his son Randolph saw a General Mills acquisition as an opportunity to modernize the company through new manufacturing and marketing techniques and pushed for a sale. Barton finally relented – largely due to his desire to retire – and sold Parker Brothers to General Mills in 1968 for $47.5 million. His nephew, Edward Parker, became president, while Randolph – who generally went by Ranny – became executive vice president.[42]

In 1974, Edward Parker, who was dying of lung cancer, ceded the presidency to Ranny Barton.[43] Barton swiftly fired or demoted several top executives and appointed a new set of MBAs to enact the manufacturing and marketing reforms he had long desired. Barton was determined to double his

[39] Philip E. Orbanes, *The Game Makers: The Story of Parkers Brothers from Tiddlywinks to Trivial Pursuit* (Boston, MA: Harvard Business School Press, 2004), 4–7.

[40] Ibid, 11.

[41] Ibid, 125–126.

[42] Ibid, 146–152.

[43] "Parker Bros. Names Ed Park Chairman, Barton President," *Toy & Hobby World*, October 1, 1973, 1.

company's sales within a short period and expressed a willingness to embrace any product that could further this goal.[44]

In 1975, a husband and wife team of astrophysicists from Harvard named Robert and Holly Doyle approached the head of R&D at Parker Brothers, Bill Dohrmann, to propose creating an electronic game utilizing a microprocessor that could provide a challenging computer opponent for the player. Dohrmann demurred, both because he believed the company lacked the necessary expertise to enter the field and because he was unimpressed with the prototypes the Doyles had created. After video games took off in 1976, Dohrmann changed his mind and brought the Doyles back in.[45]

The Doyles' offerings remained unremarkable, but Dohrmann selected a board/electronic game hybrid in which the players take on the role of destroyer captains attempting to locate a submarine maneuvered by the computer for further development. Released in late 1977 under the clunky name *Code Name: Sector*, the game proved a flop due to an overly challenging computer opponent and an excessive $50 price tag. Despite this setback, Dohrmann realized that with Mattel's *Football* handheld proving a hit during the holiday season with simpler mechanics and a cheaper price, Parker Brothers could not ignore the market and would need to try again.[46]

Dohrmann funded a new effort by the Doyles to create a fully electronic game for 1978. The result was a tic-tac-toe playing machine called *3-T*. Management felt a pen-and-paper adaptation lacked enough excitement to be a hit electronic product but used it as a base to develop a more elaborate toy. The final product, dubbed *Merlin*, was shaped like a phone handset and played not just tic-tac-toe, but also four additional games largely created by an industrial designer named Arthur Venditti that involved pressing buttons in response to combinations of light and sound. With its distinctive shape and expansive feature set, *Merlin* became a smash hit in 1978 and sold 700,000 units.[47] Despite this success, it was not the most popular electronic toy of the year. That distinction went to a product from Parker Brothers' oldest competitor in the board game industry, Milton Bradley.

Milton Bradley was established by a draftsman of that name in 1860 to sell lithographs of his own design. Looking for other uses for his lithograph machine, Bradley was inspired by an evening playing an old English board game with best friend and future company president George Tapley to invent

---

[44]Orbanes, 2004, 165–166.

[45]Ibid, 171–173.

[46]Ibid, 173.

[47]Ibid, 173–174.

a distinctly American board game. Combining the traditional chess board with a narrative based on Puritan tradition, Bradley designed the *Checkered Game of Life* and nearly single-handedly birthed the board game industry in the United States. By 1920, the company was well established as a maker of games and educational supplies, but soon after it entered into a long decline exacerbated by the Great Depression. Desperate to avoid bankruptcy the board of directors brought in prominent Springfield, Massachusetts, businessman James Shea to turn the company around in 1941.[48]

After restructuring debt, modernizing facilities, and literally burning mounds of back stock, Shea revived Milton Bradley through government war contracts for a universal joint for landing gear of his own design, wooden gunstocks, and a collection of games for soldiers at the front. Shea also returned the company to a leading position in board games through new products such as *Chutes and Ladders* (1943), *Candy Land* (1949), *Concentration* (1959), and an update to Bradley's original game called *The Game of Life* (1960). An even bigger hit arrived in 1966 called *Twister*, which struck a chord with adults and sold 3 million copies within a year after talk show host Johnny Carson and actress Eva Gabor played it together on an episode of *The Tonight Show*.[49]

In 1967, Shea ceded control of Milton Bradley to his son, James Shea Jr., who joined the company in 1949 after attending the Wharton School of Business.[50] In 1977, the younger Shea decided to enter the burgeoning electronic games business but took a conservative approach through adapting the board games *Mastermind* and *Battleship* as *Comp IV* and *Electronic Battleship*, respectively. When these games proved successful, Milton Bradley looked to expand into more original fare. Its flagship product in 1978 came not from its own designers, but from video game pioneer Ralph Baer.

After his experience developing the Brown Box prototype that became the Magnavox Odyssey, Baer convinced management at Sanders to let him focus on designing entertainment products to license to other companies. His first few attempts ended unsuccessfully. In 1974, he tried to bring Sanders into the coin-op business using circuitry Bill Rusch had created for the Brown Box, but could not be debugged in time to incorporate into the Odyssey. The circuits added velocity sensitivity to the ball physics, which meant that friction

[48] "Milton Bradley Company History," Funding Universe, accessed June 10, 2019, http://www.fundinguniverse.com/company-histories/milton-bradley-company-history.

[49] Ibid.

[50] Jim Kinney, "James J. Shea Jr., Former Milton Bradley Chief, Dies at 87," Masslive, January 16, 2013, https://www.masslive.com/news/2013/01/james_j_shea_jr_former_milton.html.

could be modeled so that, for example, a spot representing a hockey puck could gradually slow down as it traveled across the ice. Baer incorporated this circuitry into three coin-operated ball-and-paddle games called *Skate-N-Score*, *Hit-N-Run*, and *Pro Soccer* and placed them out on test. Although the games performed well, Sanders decided against entering the coin-op business because it fell so far outside its area of competency.[51] A second attempt to enter the business through video-based horse racing gambling games in partnership with printer company Centronics also failed in 1975.[52]

Baer shifted his focus to the home market by reaching an agreement to become an outside designer for Marvin Glass & Associates. Established in 1941 by its namesake, Marvin Glass had become legendary in the toy industry thanks to a string of hits it sold to major toy firms that included Rock 'em Sock 'em Robots, Lite Brite, and the board games *Operation* and *Mouse Trap*.[53] Marvin Glass passed away in 1974 and was succeeded at the firm by a group of general partners led by Anson Isaacson,[54] who embarked on a massive expansion of the firm's efforts both inside and outside the toy industry and put Baer on the payroll to design electronic toys while still maintaining his day job at Sanders.[55] In July 1976, Isaacson and two others were killed by a disgruntled employee in a tragic murder-suicide, but Baer's deal continued under Isaacson's successor, Jeffrey Breslow.[56]

Baer first attempted to bring Marvin Glass into the video game business with a football game in April 1976, but the company was unable to find any takers.[57] That fall, he took a different tact after he and his principal contact at the company, Howard Morrison, beheld an Atari coin-operated game called *Touch Me*.[58] Released in 1974, *Touch Me* is not a video game, but a pattern memorization game featuring a panel of four buttons that are each a different color. The game plays a series of sounds each accompanied by one of the buttons lighting up. The player must press the buttons in the same sequence to continue, with the sequences becoming longer and more complex as play continues.

---

[51] Baer, 2005, 93–100.

[52] Ibid, 121–122.

[53] "Marvin Glass, Toy Designer, Dies at 59," *Playthings*, January 21, 1974, 11.

[54] "Marvin Glass' Successor to Maintain Company Image," *Playthings*, April 1974, 64.

[55] Baer, 2005, 138.

[56] "Isaacson of Glass is Dead at 56; Breslow Succeeds in Post," *Playthings*, September 1976, 21.

[57] Baer, 2005, 122–124.

[58] Baer claims he saw the game at the 1976 AMOA show, but this seems highly unlikely considering the game was two years old at that point. Certainly none of the coin trades at the time mentions Atari featuring the game at the show, though no exhaustive list of games demoed that year exists. It is more likely that Baer saw a unit on location.

Baer and Morrison were not impressed with *Touch Me* because the form factor was unappealing and the sounds were hideous, but they believed it was built on a solid concept. Baer decided to transform it into an attractive home product and achieved a breakthrough when he decided the sounds should be musical notes instead of beeps. After perusing a children's encyclopedia, he realized that one of the simplest musical instruments, the bugle, could only play a limited number of notes on a harmonic scale, meaning that the notes could be played in any order without sounding dissonant. Adopting the same principle to the memorization game instantly made the product more appealing than *Touch Me*.[59]

After sorting out the basic concept in conjunction with Morrison in late 1976 and receiving the go ahead from Jeffrey Breslow, Baer began developing his take on *Touch Me* in January 1977 under the name *Feedback* with assistance from Sanders employee Lenny Pope. To power the game, Baer chose the TMS-1000 microprocessor, a 4-bit processor released by TI in 1974 that was fast becoming an industry standard for simple electronic games due to its reasonable price.[60] In July 1977, Marvin Glass brought the game to Milton Bradley, which requested the company add difficulty levels and some alternate game modes. Once these changes were made, Milton Bradley began focus testing in September and discovered kids were often hesitant to gather around the machine. They determined this was due to a square form factor in which the players were supposed to sit at the corners of the device. The company built a round prototype, and children began flocking to the machine in tests.[61]

In November, Milton Bradley greenlit the project under the name *Simon* and projected an initial run of 300,000 units.[62] Gameplay remained similar to *Touch Me*, with up to four players taking turns repeating from memory a series of note patterns generated by the game by pressing the four colored buttons in sequence. At Toy Fair in February 1978, *Simon* was overshadowed by an electronic spaceship toy Milton Bradley exhibited alongside it called *Star-Bird*, but once it entered production in March, units began disappearing from store shelves almost as fast as the company could make them.[63]

[59] Paul Drury, "The Making of Simon," *Retro Gamer*, no. 73, 2010, 50.

[60] Ibid.

[61] Terry Atlas, "Simon Says: Ho, Ho, Ho, New Electronic Game is 'the Season's Hit,'" *Elyria Chronicle-Telegram*, December 22, 1978.

[62] Ibid.

[63] Sales were likely aided by the November 1977 release of Steven Spielberg's *Close Encounters of the Third Kind*, in which scientists communicate with a circular alien spacecraft through a combination of lights and sounds. Baer, 2005, 173.

By July, Milton Bradley realized it was going to blow through its initial sales target and began adding more shifts and hiring more workers to increase production. By the end of the year, the game had sold 1 million units with no end to its popularity in sight and looked to become the most popular toy the industry had seen in years.[64]

In 1977, sales of electronic games, led by *Comp IV* and Mattel *Football*, reached $58 million. In 1978, as *Football, Basketball, Electronic Quarterback, Merlin,* and *Simon* all sold in huge quantities the number climbed to $180 million and could have easily been higher if not for a memory chip shortage and an underestimation of demand by the toy industry.[65] This rapidly growing business threatened to displace a video game industry already beginning to struggle. With electronic handhelds cannibalizing the low end of the market and microcomputers threatening the high end, the programmable console manufacturers were caught in a difficult position as the retail community took a conservative approach to ordering while waiting to see how the public would react to the array of electronic options now available. This situation exerted a profound impact on every company that remained in the console market, including the market leader, Atari.

[64]Atlas, 1978.
[65]Frost & Sullivan, 1983, 27–28.

27

The King is Dead, Long Live the King!

In November 1978, Warner Communications held its annual budget meeting in New York City. As chairman of Atari, Nolan Bushnell represented the subsidiary before a group of Warner executives to discuss strategies for the coming year. What should have been a straightforward presentation quickly devolved into a shouting match.

The past year had not been one of Atari's finest. After chip shortages, production delays, and late deliveries had partially spoiled the 1977 Christmas season for the new Video Computer System (VCS), Atari found itself with unsold systems sitting in warehouses. Atari consumer sales director Malcolm Kuhn was ordered to clear out the back stock at the start of the new year, but when he pointed out that retailers were not going to stock the expensive video games again until Christmas, he was fired and replaced by Don Thompson.[1]

At Warner Communications, Steve Ross and Manny Gerard worried that their Atari investment was about to blow up in their faces. Gerard continued to believe in the VCS, but it was now clear that while Atari was good at engineering, it lacked experienced leadership in manufacturing, finance, and marketing.[2] Finance resolved itself as Bill White stepped down as CFO due to health problems and was replaced by Dennis Groth of Arthur Anderson, who had been serving as an independent auditor of the Atari books.[3] To shore up marketing and production, Ross and Gerard discussed bringing in an outside consultant to spend some time in the Atari Consumer Electronics

---

[1] Kuhn, 2013.
[2] Cohen, 1984, chap. 7.
[3] Dennis Groth, interview with the author, February 10, 2017.

Division. They were unsure who to approach for this task until Bill Sarnoff, the head of Warner's book publishing division, suggested his friend Ray Kassar.[4]

Raymond Edward Kassar was born on January 2, 1928, in Brooklyn, New York. His father, Edward Wahid Kassar, was of Assyrian decent and immigrated with his family from Syria in 1911. The family controlled silk mills in Patterson, New Jersey, but lost everything in the Great Depression, so Edward worked a variety of jobs from handyman to cab driver to support the family. Ray graduated high school at 16 and matriculated to Brown. Due to World War II, the university implemented accelerated semesters, and he graduated in 1948 at age 20.[5]

At Brown, Ray roomed with Robert Love, whose father, Spencer, was the founder and chairman of textile conglomerate Burlington Industries. They became friends, and at a Christmas party at Spencer Love's Palm Beach house in 1947, Spencer offered him a job and the dean of Harvard Business School offered him a scholarship. Ray started at Burlington in 1948 as a trainee moving from mill to mill in North Carolina for nine months and worked at Burlington for two years before taking an official leave of absence to attend Harvard.[6] When he returned to Burlington with his MBA in 1953 after two years at Harvard and one in the Air Force, he became a sales trainee in New York for the Galey & Lord high-fashion cotton clothing subsidiary.[7] With an eye for fashion and a mind for marketing, Kassar rose to manager of the Industrial and Diversified Fabrics Division of Burlington in 1954.[8] Presidencies at Burlington Narrow Fabrics and Burlington Decorative Fabrics followed in 1956 and 1957, respectively, before he rejoined the parent company in 1959 as the youngest vice president in its history.[9]

Kassar worked closely with Spencer Love until his mentor died of a heart attack in 1962. Whispers had been circulating for some time that Kassar owed his rapid rise solely to his close relationship with Love, so incoming CEO Charlie Myers demoted him, and he had to prove his value to the corporation all over again.[10] Despite this setback, by 1970 he was an executive vice

[4]Gerard, 2017.

[5]Lucinda Watson, *How They Achieved: Stories of Personal Achievement and Business Success* (New York: John Wiley & Sons, 2001), 94–95.

[6]Ibid, 95.

[7]Harold S. Taylor, "Burlington Officer Calls It 'Home Fashions'," *The New York Times*, April 9, 1972.

[8]"Two Promotions Announced in Affiliates of Bur-Ind," *Burlington Daily Times-News*, February 15, 1957.

[9]Ibid, and Taylor, 1972.

[10]Watson, 2001, 96.

president overseeing all the home furnishing subsidiaries of the company.[11] In 1974, Kassar was one of three candidates to become the next chairman and CEO of Burlington. Although he was the youngest candidate by more than a decade, he also oversaw the most profitable portion of the firm. Despite this, he did not get the job. Sensing he would never be given a shot at the top spot, he resigned his position and established his own boutique firm, R.E. Kassar Corp., to import cotton shirts and dresses from Egypt.[12]

When Bill Sarnoff approached Kassar on behalf of Warner about running the Atari Consumer Electronics Division, he had no interest in leaving the East Coast to manage a high-technology company, but he agreed to take a meeting with Gerard.[13] After listening to Manny talk for four hours,[14] he was still not convinced, but he agreed to come out to California for a few weeks subject to certain conditions, including not giving up his own company, working at Atari only a couple days a month, and being able to commute to Sunnyvale from an apartment in San Francisco via a chauffeured car, both of which would be provided by Warner. He figured Gerard would turn him down, but Warner agreed to all his terms.[15]

Kassar started his consulting gig as president of the Consumer Electronics Division in March 1978 and was dismayed by what he saw.[16] Financial controls were poor, marketing was non-existent, quality control was lacking, and inventories were high. Nevertheless, like Gerard before him, he was fascinated by the VCS and convinced of its future potential. Therefore, he committed to working at Atari full time and sold his business. Over the next several months, Kassar devoted himself to improving quality control and company infrastructure while developing a proper advertising campaign for the VCS.[17]

Meanwhile, the programming staff of Bob Brown's microelectronics department continued to expand throughout the year, and the number of available cartridges for the VCS more than doubled to 20. Having already ported most of the significant coin-operated games on the market to the system in 1977, the 1978 lineup included only two more: *Breakout* and a clone of *Gun Fight* called *Outlaw*. Two sports games were also introduced, *Home Run* and *Basketball*, as were two one-on-one dueling games, a *Tank*-like game

[11] Taylor, 1972.
[12] Watson, 2001, 97.
[13] Ibid.
[14] Donovan, 2011.
[15] Watson, 2001, 97.
[16] "People," *Playthings*, February 1979, 20.
[17] Watson, 2001, 98.

called *Slot Racers* and a port of the mainframe classic *Space War*. Rounding out the lineup were a *Hangman* cartridge – the first to use a 4K ROM rather than 2K – a capture-the-flag-style game called *Flag Capture*, and three games created for a new "keyboard" controller consisting of two number pads introduced to counter the encroaching threat of the microcomputer. These were a memory matching game called *Hunt & Score*, a guess-the-number game called *Codebreaker*, and *Brain Games*, which featured several math games and two variants of *Touch Me*.[18]

On September 15, 1978, during the World Heavyweight Championship fight between Muhammad Ali and Leon Spinks, Atari launched its 6-million-dollar advertising campaign for the holiday season developed by the new ad agency Kassar secured for the company, Doyle, Dane, Bernbach. The centerpieces of the campaign were three 30-second TV spots unified by the slogan "Don't Watch TV Tonight, Play It" featuring a host of celebrities including Pete Rose, Pele, Billie Jean King, Bobby Riggs, Kareem Abdul-Jabbar, Carol Channing, Jack Palance, Gene Rayburn, and Don Knotts. Commercials subsequently aired during major sporting events, the premiere of the television series *Battlestar Galactica*, and other high-profile programs. Alongside the television blitz, full-page ads appeared in *People*, *Playboy*, *TV Guide*, *US Sport*, and *Penthouse* magazines.[19] Kassar and his management team instructed Atari's sales reps to follow up the ads aggressively as manufacturing worked diligently to produce 800,000 units of the VCS for retail.[20]

But 1978 was the year that handheld electronic games were in and video games were out. The collapse of the dedicated console market after the 1977 holiday season and the emergence of electronic handheld and tabletop games convinced retailers that the video game fad was over and that the programmable systems on the market like the Fairchild Channel F and the VCS were destined to fail. Retailers were still happy to stock programmable systems and their attendant cartridges, but they were determined not to repeat 1977, when overstocking of dedicated consoles led to drastic price cuts, unsold inventory, and greatly reduced profits.[21] By late summer, Atari had shipped over

[18] "Atari Introduces Seven Cartridges," *Merchandising*, May 1978, 58, and "Atari," *Merchandising*, June 1978, 48.

[19] "Atari Launches Campaign; Promotes Video Games," *Playthings*, October 1978.

[20] Donovan, 2011, and Bloom, "Cutoffs," 1982, 46.

[21] "Cutback in Games," *Weekly Television Digest with Consumer Electronics*, August 21, 1978, 9.

400,000 systems, but then orders virtually stopped. With nearly 400,000 systems sitting in warehouses, Atari looked set to lose money again.[22]

While Kassar was working long hours to sell the VCS, Nolan Bushnell and Joe Keenan were often nowhere to be found. Newly wealthy from the Atari deal, Bushnell purchased the former Folger mansion in Woodside, California, and began tacking long vacations onto business trips. Both he and Keenan stopped paying as close attention to the day-to-day operations of the company, basically letting Kassar in consumer and Gene Lipkin in coin-op run their businesses without much oversight. Bushnell would periodically show up to make pronouncements, however, which would prompt a frustrated Gerard to tell him he could "not rule the company by the divine right of kings."[23]

For Bushnell's part, he was not happy with the direction the company was taking. The solid-state pinball division established two years before had failed to be the innovative operation he had hoped for and could not compete with the Chicago companies on costs, and he was ready to shut it down. Atari was preparing to enter the emerging home computer market as well, but Bushnell was not certain Gerard and Warner were really prepared to make the financial investments necessary to break into a new product category. Most of all, he disagreed with Warner about the future of the VCS.[24]

When Atari launched the VCS in 1977, it maintained high profit margins on both hardware and software.[25] The logic was that consumers would probably only buy two or three of the eight additional games available, thus necessitating a decent financial return on the hardware as well. In reality, the average consumer bought between three and four cartridges, and some were purchasing every title available.[26] A single cartridge cost only around $4.00–$5.00 to produce and sold for $20. Even accounting for the cuts taken by distribution and retail, this represented an enormous margin on each unit sold. Bushnell felt it would be better to cut the price on the VCS and reduce hardware profit margins to further stimulate software sales.[27]

At the November 1978 budget meeting, Bushnell stated that it was time to cut the price of the VCS and start looking toward its eventual replacement.

---

[22] Bloom, 1982.

[23] Gerard, 2017.

[24] Cohen, 1984, chap. 7.

[25] While some have assumed that Atari sold hardware close to cost, multiple sales and marketing executives have pointed to high hardware margins. Michael Moone, interview with the author, May 13, 2013, Bill Grubb, interview with the author, July 24, 2014, and Bob Faught, interview with the author, January 21, 2019.

[26] Bushnell, 2009.

[27] Cohen, 1984, chap. 7.

To the room full of shocked Warner executives, most of whom did not follow the Atari business closely, this sounded like Bushnell wanted to give up on the VCS business entirely and liquidate the product.[28] Gerard pushed back, arguing that a steep price cut would devalue the system in the eyes of consumers and lead to the end of the Atari consumer business. Bushnell responded that Gerard had no feel for the consumer electronics business at all. When the shouting finally died down, it was clear something would have to be done in response.[29]

The next day, a shaken Steve Ross called Gerard into his office and asked him what they should do. Gerard told him all they could do was wait. They had only a few weeks until December 25, and they could not do anything to alter the course of the Christmas season even if they wanted to. On December 26, the VCS would either be sold out across America, thus proving retailers had underestimated consumer demand for video games, or the shelves would still be full, and the retailers would take the liquidation decision out of Atari's hands anyway. All that was left to do was see how Atari and a diverse array of competitors would fair with the general public.[30]

**

The rise of the handheld market spelled a definitive end to the dedicated console market, though several companies continued to lurch through it over the course of 1978. Total unit sales collapsed from 7 million to 1.6 million, while dollar volume was cut nearly in half from $210 million to $120 million.[31] Coleco led the depressed market as it deployed the final two units of the Telstar line: the Telstar Marksman, which did the previous year's Telstar Ranger one better by shipping with a rifle controller instead of a pistol, and the Telstar Colortron, which was identical to the Telstar Alpha system released the previous year save that it sported color graphics and better sound.[32] The company saw its revenues on video games decline from $49.8 million to just $4.6 million and exited the video game business for good to focus on its new line of successful electronic sports games.[33]

Those companies that remained committed to the video game business in 1978 generally attempted to stay relevant by dropping the dedicated

---

[28] Kent, 2001, 111.

[29] Cohen, 1984, chap. 7.

[30] Donovan, 2010, chap. 6.

[31] Frost & Sullivan, 1983, 26–26a.

[32] "13 New Electronic Games Featured by Coleco Industries," *Playthings*, April 1978.

[33] Frost & Sullivan, 1983, 25.

console segment and concentrating solely on programmable systems. The one exception was APF, which remained the second largest producer of dedicated systems behind Coleco while deploying a programmable unit based around the Motorola 6800 processor called the MP-1000. Released in fall 1978 at $180, the system shipped with a simple built-in target shooting game called *Rocket Patrol.* Six cartridges were sold separately: *Catena, Hangman, Bowling, Baseball, Blackjack*, and a *Breakout* clone called *Brickdown.* Although the system could generate colorful graphics through use of a Motorola 6847 video display generator, the simplistic games did not endear themselves to the public, and the console sold few units.

For video game pioneer Magnavox, leaving the dedicated console market behind nearly meant dropping out of the video game industry entirely. In 1978, the company planned to release a new dedicated console called the Odyssey 5000 based on a chip by Signetics, a Fairchild spinoff that Magnavox parent Philips purchased in 1975. The system would play 24 different games largely consisting of ball-and-paddle variants, but also included primitive tank and helicopter games in the vein of *Tank.* With the collapse of the dedicated console market, the product was cancelled.[34] Instead, the company half-heartedly continued work on a programmable console in partnership with Intel.

Stan Mazor, the co-designer of Intel's first microprocessors, had been interested in the potential for computers to play games since seeing *Spacewar!* on a PDP-1 at the Fall Joint Computer Conference in Las Vegas in 1964. While working on the 4004, Mazor and Hoff told management at Intel that video games were a potential market for microprocessors and even had an engineer named Glenn Louie recreate *Spacewar!* using the 4004 chipset, but they were unable to convince management to promote that application of its processors. Nevertheless, as Intel continued producing newer and more powerful chips, the company kept tabs on the consumer electronics market to source potential clients. Mazor headed up the company's effort to place its chips in these products, so a field rep in Chicago put him in touch with the Magnavox console design team led by Gene Kale.[35]

To power its programmable system, Magnavox settled on the Intel 8048 processor, a microcontroller containing a 1.79 MHz 8-bit processor, 1K of ROM and 64 bytes of RAM. A separate RAM ship provided an additional

[34] "Magnavox Odyssey 100-5000 Systems," Pong Story, accessed June 30, 2019, http://www.pong-story.com/odyssey_other.htm.

[35] Stan Mazor, interview with Ethan Johnson, October 21, 2018.

128 bytes of memory. Magnavox also commissioned Intel to develop a custom graphics chip for the system. Kale and his team defined its functionality, and Intel engineer Peter Salmon designed the chip with the help of Sam Schwartz and Gary Bastian. Mazor served as the project manager for the chip and as the liaison between the two companies.[36]

The resulting 8244 chip could display only four sprites, but as on the Atari VCS, these could be reused multiple times on different lines to populate the screen with more objects. Unlike the VCS, it also had a built-in character generator that stored an additional 64 objects, of which 12 could be on the screen at one time. Many of these were letters and numbers, but a few were common objects such as trees and people. The chip could also generate a background grid of lines divided into segments that could be turned on and off independently to represent walls and other obstacles.

Magnavox planned to release its programmable system in late 1977, but bugs in the 8244 forced the company to delay the release to 1978. In the meantime, Philips, which had never been happy with the video game business it inherited with its Magnavox purchase, decided to pull the plug on the entire project in August 1977. John Helms brought in Ralph Baer to brief senior management on how lucrative the video game business had been for some of Sanders' other partners like Coleco and managed to save the system.[37] Soon after, Helms left the company, and the video game division was merged with the laserdisc and video tape recorder business to form a new "interactive devices" division under an executive named Mike Staup.[38]

The Magnavox programmable system, originally announced in June 1978 as the Odyssey Computer Video Game System,[39] finally began shipping to retailers in September as the Odyssey².[40] Unlike competing systems from Atari and Fairchild, it was positioned as both a video game system and a cheap educational computing device and therefore featured not only joystick controllers, but also a built-in membrane keyboard. It retailed for $180 with one cartridge containing three games: a *Speed Race* clone called *Speedway*, a *Gran Trak* clone called *Spin-Out*, and a word scramble game using the keyboard called *Crypto-Logic*. *Golf, Basketball, Football, Blackjack*, and a cartridge combining an educational game called *Math-a-Magic* and a *Simon*

[36] Ibid.

[37] Baer, 2005, 184–185.

[38] Mike Staup, Testimony, Atari, Inc. v. North American Philips Consumer Electronics Corp., No. 81-6434 (N.D. Ill), November 30, 1981, 226.

[39] "Magnavox," *Merchandising*, June 1978, 56.

[40] "Magnavox has started," *Weekly Television Digest with Consumer Electronics*, September 25, 1978, 12.

clone called *Echo* were also available at $20 each. Magnavox managed to ship around 100,000 systems by the end of the year,[41] but sales were inhibited by late FCC approval, which kept the system out of the major department store chains that remained responsible for the bulk of video game sales in 1978.[42]

While Magnavox explored the fringes of the low-end computer market, arcade giant Bally fully embraced it with a console-computer hybrid. Like many of Bally's video game projects in this period, the concept originated at Dave Nutting Associates. DNA began planning for a programmable console in 1975 as Jeff Frederiksen developed the Z80-based upgrade to his microprocessor arcade hardware, and development began in early 1976 using a scaled down version of that system.[43] As with Frederiksen's original coin-op video hardware, the system could not generate hardware sprites and instead drew the entire screen as a bitmap. This necessitated 4K of RAM to display eight colors drawn from a palette of 256 at a screen resolution of 160×102 at a time when semiconductor memory was expensive,[44] but the company was able to negotiate a relatively good price because it was already one of the largest purchasers of RAM chips in the world to power its coin-operated games.[45]

Unlike its competitors, DNA included an 8K ROM chip on the system that not only contained several built-in games, but also a primitive operating system that functioned as an application programming interface (API). While Frederiksen and another engineer named Terry Coleman developed the hardware, programmer Jamie Fenton led the team that developed the software.[46] The team wanted to include an eclectic mix of games for the built-in product, so the console incorporated an action game (*Gun Fight*), a strategy game (a port of Midway's *Blockade* clone *Checkmate*), a casual product (a doodling program called *Scribbling*), and an educational program (a calculator). To play these games, DNA designed a pistol-grip controller inspired by the hand controllers of the Channel F that featured a trigger button in the grip and a plastic dial on top that could be tilted in eight directions for movement or rotated to control a paddle.[47]

---

[41] Frost & Sullivan, 1979, 8.

[42] "Cutback in Games," 1978, 9.

[43] Jamie Fenton, interview with the author, March 25, 2019.

[44] Technically, the system could only display four colors, but the screen could be divided in half, with a different 4-color palette used on each side.

[45] Fenton, 2019.

[46] Fenton transitioned from male to female in the late 1990s. At the time of the events in question, she presented as male and went by her birth name, Jay.

[47] Fenton, 2019.

DNA parent Bally planned to release the system as the Bally Home Computer Library in late 1977 through its new consumer division led by Bob Wiles, the former Magnavox color TV product manager who initially had responsibility for the Odyssey until it was spun out into its own unit. Electronics mail order firm JS&A signed on to sell the system in its catalog, while the Montgomery Ward department store chain agreed to sell it at retail. By July 1978, Bally planned to introduce a keyboard unit including more RAM and a dual cassette tape drive that would turn it into a full-fledged computer.[48]

JS&A began running ads for the Bally Home Computer Library in September 1977 alongside two cartridges: one featuring a port of *Tornado Baseball* alongside *Tennis, Hockey,* and *Handball* ball-and-paddle games and the other sporting two educational games called *Elementary Math* and *Bingo Math*.[49] The console did not ship that year, however, because like most of the programmable console makers and early microcomputer companies, Bally ran afoul of the FCC and its interference standards. Even after these issues were resolved, the company experienced delays from its chip suppliers that caused Montgomery Ward to cancel its order.[50] JS&A began accepting orders from customers in the fall as planned, but the extra shielding needed to pass FCC testing led to overheating problems that rendered the first batch of consoles defective. Bally was unable to start manufacturing until December 1977,[51] and JS&A was unable to begin delivering units to customers until early 1978. Then, Bally discovered one of the chips in the console was defective, and it was forced to halt production again until May.[52] Due to the manufacturing issues with the base unit, Bally cancelled the computer add-on despite displaying a functioning prototype at the January 1978 CES. The system was also renamed the Bally Professional Arcade, likely to not call attention to the company's failed computer ambitions.

By fall 1978, Bally was able to start delivering consoles in quantity, though its distribution only reached about 60% of the United States.[53] Eight game cartridges were available, with the two titles advertised in 1977 joined by a driving cartridge featuring the games *280 Zzzap* and a *Wheels* port called *Dodgem*; a

---

[48] "Bally Gets FCC OK," *Weekly Television Digest with Consumer Electronics,* December 19, 1977, 9.

[49] The decision to lump all the ball-and-paddle products together stemmed from the Magnavox patent lawsuits. The DNA team figured that putting all the potential patent-violating games on one cartridge would limit their exposure. Fenton, 2019.

[50] "Bally Gets FCC OK," 1977, 9.

[51] "Bally Game Report," *Weekly Television Digest with Consumer Electronics,* October 2, 1978, 13.

[52] "Bally Again Shipping Programmable Games," *Merchandising,* May 1978, 14.

[53] Frost & Sullivan, 1979, 29.

one-on-one dueling cartridge with *Tank* and *Jet Fighter* clones *Panzer* and *Red Baron*; a target shooting cartridge incorporating *Seawolf* and *Missile*; a cartridge featuring a *Breakout* clone called *Brickyard* and a *Circus* clone called *Clowns*; a *Football* cartridge; a card game cartridge featuring *Blackjack*, *Poker*, and *Acey-Deucey*; a board game cartridge with *Checkers* and *Backgammon*; and a word game cartridge containing *Letter Match*, *Spell 'N Score*, and *Crosswords*. While the computer add-on did not materialize, the company released a BASIC cartridge in October that allowed users to create their own simple programs that could be saved to cassette with the help of a separately sold tape interface. Bally managed to ship an estimated 75,000–80,000 units of the Bally Professional Arcade by the end of the year,[54] but most of them remained unsold.

Meanwhile, Fairchild experienced its own ups and downs in the business. After the price difficulties the company experienced with the Channel F in 1977 due to the need for additional shielding to pass FCC testing, the company redesigned the system and deployed the new model in late 1978 as the Channel F II. Externally, the most notable changes were detachable controllers and sound passed through the television speakers. Internally, a new LSI replaced most of the discrete components in the system to bring costs back under control and allow Fairchild to drop the system back to the launch price of $150.[55] New games for the year included a ball-and-paddle variant called *Dodge It* in which the players have to avoid a bouncing ball; a version of the board game *Battleship* called *Sonar Search*; a *Breakout* clone called *Pinball Challenge*; an *Air-Sea Battle* clone called *Torpedo Alley*; and depictions of *Hangman*, *Bowling*, and *Checkers*. Fairchild also advertised a "keyboard" controller like the one released for the VCS, but it never shipped.

By the middle of the year, Fairchild was considering exiting the video game business entirely in the face of its continued poor showing in consumer electronics generally and digital watches in particular. Perhaps sensing the current corporate climate, video products division VP Greg Reyes departed the company in June 1978.[56] His replacement, Richard Bohnet, continued his predecessor's conservative approach to the market, though the company did run a brief advertising campaign beginning in mid-November centered on print and TV ads featuring comedian Milton Berle.[57] Fairchild sold roughly 150,000 units on the year, slightly more than it did in 1977.[58]

[54] Ibid, 28.

[55] "Computers & Games," *Weekly Television Digest with Consumer Electronics*, June 19, 1978.

[56] "Personals," *Weekly Television Digest with Consumer Electronics*, June 12, 1978, 14.

[57] "Cutback in Games," *Weekly Television Digest with Consumer Electronics*, August 21,1978, 9.

[58] Frost & Sullivan, 1979, 8.

That modest total fell slightly below expectations, as Fairchild was forced to lower its forecasts in the face of the same retailer resistance encountered by Atari. In all, roughly 700,000 programmable systems were sold in 1978,[59] far fewer than previous estimates of nearly a million.[60]

***

Despite the obstacles faced by video game companies in 1978, once the Christmas results were in it was clear to executives at Atari and Warner Communications that the VCS was, in fact, a hit. Not only did the 400,000 units accepted by retailers virtually sell out, but software sales also doubled as the average consumer bought five games per system sold. Ross and Gerard credited Ray Kassar for the success and asked him to stay on at Atari as president of the whole company. Kassar refused. The hard-nosed, no-nonsense Kassar did not get on well with the more laid-back upper management of the company with its 5:00 PM marijuana gatherings and hot tub board meetings. Kassar told Gerard that for him to stay, Bushnell would have to go.[61] Bushnell's behavior at the November budget meeting made the decision easy.

On December 28, 1978, Manny Gerard stripped Nolan Bushnell of his position as chairman and co-CEO of the company he co-founded with Ted Dabney in June 1972. Joe Keenan was elevated from president and co-CEO to chairman of the board, and Ray Kassar assumed the roles of president and CEO. Warner announced Bushnell would be retained as a creative consultant, but he quickly rejected that role and departed the company for good. Keenan lasted less than a year before following him out the door, after which Kassar added the title of chairman as well.[62]

The company Kassar inherited weathered the retail crisis of 1978, but it still lost money for the second year in a row, and its future was not assured. The coin-operated video game market remained stagnant, the pinball division was still a disaster, and the VCS continued to face stiff competition from the ascendant handheld electronic game manufacturers and the looming microcomputer business. Within a year, however, the company – and indeed the entire video game industry – would find itself on the brink of a new golden age of prosperity. This reversal of fortune stemmed largely from the release of a new Japanese video game called *Space Invaders*.

---

[59] Frost & Sullivan, 1983, 35.
[60] "Programmable Video Game," *Weekly Television Digest with Consumer Electronics*, April 2, 1979, 14.
[61] Watson, 2001, 98.
[62] Goldberg and Vendel, 2012, chap. 7.

28

Japanese Invaders

On May 25, 1977, the science fiction movie *Star Wars* debuted on 32 screens in the United States. The film was a labor of love for director George Lucas, who decided in 1971 to film a "space opera" in the fashion of the old *Flash Gordon* movie serials after finishing his current picture, the surprise hit *American Graffiti*.[1] The writing took Lucas a torturous three years,[2] the filming nearly killed him, and the first cut was a disaster devoid of energy. Lucas was convinced he had created a massive flop.[3] The special effects, however, proved amazing thanks to new technologies and techniques pioneered by Lucas's own special effects company, Industrial Light and Magic (ILM), and his wife Marcia recut the movie to give it both energy and heart. Although the initial release was small, word of mouth spread like wildfire so that before the end of the week practically every showing was greeted by lines stretching around the block. *Star Wars* was not just a hit: it was a cultural phenomenon.[4]

The impact on the entertainment industry was immediate. The NBC television network commissioned a science fiction television series from producer Glen Larson called *Battlestar Galactica* that debuted in fall 1978 to a 42 share in the Nielsen ratings; Paramount greenlit a *Star Trek* movie reuniting the original cast, and Disney resurrected a stalled project called *The Black Hole*. In toys, General Mills subsidiary Kenner revolutionized the action figure with a line of 3¾ inch *Star Wars* figures that were in such high demand that they not only sold out in 1977, but Kenner also sold IOU certificates

[1] Michael Kaminski, *The Secret History of Star Wars* (self-pub., ebook, 2008), 45.
[2] Ibid, 116.
[3] Ibid, 137.
[4] Ibid, 142.

guaranteeing the buyer four figures early in the next year. The shortages returned for the holidays in 1978.

In coin-operated video games, the leading genres continued to be driving games and target shooting products with predominantly military themes, but there were signs that this might be changing. *Space Wars* topped the lists of both best-selling and highest-earning games of 1978, and *Starship* continued to do decent business as well. *Star Wars* appeared to have primed the coin-op industry for a breakout science fiction hit, and the Taito Corporation provided it.

***

Taito engineer Tomohiro Nishikado was responsible for some of the earliest Japanese video game hits between 1973 and 1975 but had been stuck in something of a rut since. After finishing *Western Gun*, Nishikado decided to translate his hit electromechanical game *Sky Fighter* to video. Released as *Interceptor* in March 1976 after six months of development, this adaptation broke new ground graphically through enemy planes animated using sprites of different sizes to give the illusion they were coming closer to or flying away from the player. The game also incorporated special circuits to blur the sprites representing background clouds to give them a more realistic look than otherwise possible at the low-graphic resolution of the day. These tricks required relatively costly hardware, yet the game did not attract players in large numbers and became an expensive flop.[5]

Meanwhile, Taito secured a cabinet of DNA's *Gun Fight*, which introduced Nishikado to the microprocessor. While he was not impressed with the gameplay changes DNA made to his *Western Gun*, he recognized the microprocessor would revolutionize game design and began an extensive study of the DNA hardware.[6] Soon after Nishikado completed *Interceptor*, the company received a *Sea Wolf* cabinet too, and this time Nishikado was impressed with both the hardware and the gameplay. Management asked him to analyze the game, but not long after starting he was pulled off the project for six months to work on a four-player racing game called *Fisco 400* partially inspired by the massive *Indy 800* from Atari. Once Taito released the game in early 1977, Nishikado returned to his microprocessor experiments.[7]

As Nishikado explored the microprocessor, *Breakout* became a massive hit. Management asked Nishikado to develop a product that would surpass *Breakout* in the marketplace, and the engineer decided that meeting this

---

[5]Gorges, 2018, 92–95.
[6]Ibid, 90–91.
[7]Ibid, 100–101.

challenge required a focus on simple, yet addictive gameplay first and graphical sophistication second.[8] Nishikado began his new design by analyzing what made *Breakout* fun and determined it was the feeling of satisfaction that came with clearing the entire screen of objects. He decided to keep this core mechanic, but with fresh gameplay.[9] Likening the abstract ball and paddle to missiles fired from a mobile launcher and the bricks to targets, he decided to create a game in which the player controls a launcher that can move left and right across the bottom of the screen and shoots at a grouping of targets arrayed at the top of the screen.[10]

Without having to keep a bouncing ball on the playfield, Nishikado's play concept lacked excitement, so he came to a crucial decision: to keep the game unpredictable and challenging, the targets would shoot back at the player. He also decided to replace the ubiquitous timer present in shooting gallery video games, but to maintain a sense of urgency a time limit provides by having the targets descend one line at a time. If any targets reached the bottom of the screen without being destroyed, the player would lose.[11] Outside of a few one-on-one dueling games like *Computer Space* and *Jet Fighter* that allowed for one or two hardware-controlled opponents, no one had created a game where objects on the screen could harm the player. By allowing targets to attack the player and eliminating the timer, Nishikado created a new paradigm in video games.

Nishikado decided the playfield would consist of an array of 55 targets arranged in five rows, but defining these objects proved challenging due to the limited hardware available. Nishikado tried tanks first, but he could not animate them convincingly. Planes appeared to be a good possibility but having them descend in a block formation rather than zooming all around the screen seemed unnatural. Nishikado finally settled on human foes because they could be animated easily, but Taito president Mike Kogan had often remarked he did not like people being targets in games, so Nishikado was afraid the concept would be rejected.[12]

Star Wars broke the impasse. After the movie became a massive hit in the United States and a Japanese release was announced for June 1978, Nishikado deduced that space games would be in high demand right around the time his game would hit the market. Therefore, he changed the humans to aliens. These were not based on anything in *Star Wars*, but rather on the

---

[8] Ibid, 104.
[9] Ibid, 113.
[10] Ibid, 115.
[11] Ibid, 115–116.
[12] Ibid, 116–117.

octopus-like Martian invaders from a film adaptation of H.G. Wells's *War of the Worlds* that Nishikado had seen as a child. For variety's sake Nishikado rounded out the *War of the Worlds* design with several aquatic-themed aliens of his own. In homage to these creations and in honor of a recent hit single called "Monster" by the pop duo Pink Lady, Nishikado named his game *Space Monster*.[13] Nishikado did not realize that Taito had already produced an electromechanical target shooting game called *Space Monster* several years earlier, but management remembered and requested a new name shortly before release. After considering dozens of options, the company decided on *Space Invaders*.[14]

As Nishikado began moving and animating his alien invaders, he soon came up against the limits of the hardware. He had hoped to move the entire group of aliens in a block, but processing limitations forced him to move them one at a time instead. Although this happens in rapid succession to give as close an impression of block movement as possible, the limitation on the number of movements per processing cycle meant that the aliens could only advance slowly. Nishikado realized, however, that as the number of targets decreased, he would be able to move the remaining targets faster. He decided the aliens would descend faster as targets were eliminated, creating an even greater sense of urgency for the player as his session continued. Nishikado further increased the difficulty over the course of play by having each successive wave of creatures start one line closer to the player than the one before it.[15]

In deference to the challenges presented by his new game mechanics, Nishikado provided the player some respite from the encroaching hordes through four bunkers he could hide behind for protection, but which would slowly be whittled away by the aliens. He also borrowed the pinball convention of giving the player multiple plays on a single coin – in this case three – and rewarding extra plays for a certain score – in this case 5,000 points. To provide additional scoring opportunities, he added a UFO that would fly across the top of the screen periodically and could be destroyed for extra points. With score playing an integral role, Nishikado decided to display the highest score achieved on the machine next to the player's current score.

Nishikado's hardware was limited to black-and-white graphics, but Taito used several tricks to provide a little color. Colored strips of cellophane

---

[13] Ibid, 120.
[14] Ibid, 129–130.
[15] Ibid, 121–122.

attached to the monitor create three bands of color, one at the top for the score and the UFO, one through middle where the aliens descend, and one at the bottom for the bunkers and the player's missile battery. Cabinet artist Kazuo Nakagawa envisioned the game taking place on the moon as humanity mounts its last defense against the aliens before they reach Earth, so he drew a moonscape as a background image for the action.[16] The monitor was recessed in the bottom of the cabinet, and the computer graphics were superimposed on top of the moonscape through use of a mirror.[17]

Space Invaders took Nishikado over ten months to finish, an extended development cycle for a late 1970s arcade game.[18] This was largely because he needed six months just to develop the programming tools to create the game in the first place, as Japan was still well behind the United States in working with microprocessor technology.[19] Indeed, development proved so frustrating that he completed two other games, *TT Soccer* and *Super Speed Race V*, between stints working on his shooting game.[20]

Another reason for the extended development was that Nishikado created virtually the entire game himself. While this had been common in the early TTL era, even early microprocessor-based games divided hardware and software development between two people at the very least. The only element Nishikado did not complete himself was the sound,[21] which was developed by a fresh university graduate named Michiyuki Kamei. Nishikado and Kamei were inspired by the tension-inducing score of the movie *Jaws* in creating a recurring loop of four notes that played continuously over the action and sped up as the number of aliens decreased and the remaining foes descended faster and faster.[22]

On June 16, 1978, Taito unveiled *Space Invaders* to distributors alongside a more traditional light gun target shooting video game called *Blue Shark*. The reception was not promising. At the time, most coin-operated video games provided a predictable play time per coin, usually through a fixed time increment or a competition that ended when one player reached a certain number of points. Games were generally tuned to give around 90 seconds of play time, with the possibility of gaining more time by attaining a specific score.

[16] Ibid, 124.

[17] The moonscape only appeared in the upright cabinet version of the game. Taito also released a tabletop version that did not have a background.

[18] Ibid, 133.

[19] Jonti Davies, "The Making of Space Invaders," *Retro Gamer*, no. 62, 2009, 54.

[20] Gorges, 2018, 126.

[21] Davies, 2009, 54.

[22] Gorges, 2018, 123–125.

In *Space Invaders*, play was regulated like pinball with a certain number of attempts per coin. This meant a novice player might run through his three tries within the first few seconds, and perhaps become so frustrated he never puts another coin in the machine again. Operators feared the game would bring in a poor return on investment.[23]

Space Invaders went on sale in July 1978 in both upright and tabletop format to little fanfare and even smaller sales. A few longstanding Taito operators placed orders for a machine or two out of respect for their relationship, but most units were placed in Taito's own locations. In all, the company probably sold no more than 500 cabinets. Once it reached the young players in the coffee houses and gun corners, however, it became a phenomenon.[24] Few video games had ever managed to impart a true feeling of danger or thrill, so the intense battle for survival as lasers flew and aliens approached faster and faster in time to a relentlessly pounding musical accompaniment injected new excitement into a relatively staid medium. Furthermore, the inclusion of a high score display gave players a new challenging opponent to overcome: fellow players. Nabbing the top score on a machine became an obsession for many, and the competition fueled a constant flow of ¥100 coins deposited into an exponentially growing number of *Space Invaders* cabinets.[25]

By August 1978, *Space Invaders* was the talk of the Japanese coin-op world. By September, Taito could no longer keep up with orders for the game. Manufacturing of all other products was immediately halted so that Taito's entire factory capacity could be devoted to *Space Invaders*. It was still not enough. By October, Taito was taking out ads in trade publications apologizing that not everyone could get as many units of the game as they had hoped.[26] Counterfeiting and cloning ran rampant to fill the void, so to prevent unauthorized manufacturers from taking over the market, Taito sublicensed manufacturing of the game to some of its competitors.

***

One of the first companies Taito brought on to produce *Space Invaders* was Shin Nihon Kikaku – which translates into English as "New Japan Project" – an electronics manufacturer established by former boxer Eikichi Kawasaki

---

[23] Ibid, 132.

[24] Ibid, 133.

[25] Nishikado almost certainly borrowed the high score tracking from Midway's *Sea Wolf*, which was most likely the first video game to record the highest score achieved on the game. Unlike *Space Invaders*, however, the *Sea Wolf* high score could be reset by the player at any time by pressing a button on the cabinet. Therefore, it did not engender a score tracking culture like *Space Invaders* did.

[26] Gorges, 2018, 136.

in 1973. When *Breakout* became a massive hit in Japan, Shin Nihon Kikaku created a version called *Micon Block* that launched in April 1978 and was powered by a microprocessor rather than TTL hardware.[27] The game proved so successful that the firm incorporated three months later and shifted its focus to games. Two other firms were brought in to manufacture *Space Invaders* before the end of 1978: Logitec and Sammy Industries.[28] Logitec – not to be confused with the Swiss consumer electronics company Logitech – was a brand name used by Kanto Electronics, a manufacturing company originally established in 1963 to manufacture CRTs for televisions. Sammy Industry was established in 1975 by coin-op industry veteran Hajime Satomi.

The son of a salaryman who at age 40 became an entrepreneur by establishing a tofu and konnyaku wholesaler in Tokyo, Satomi knew by the time he was in college that he wanted to start his own business too, an unusual aspiration in Japan. In his third year of university, he borrowed money from his parents and opened a bar. The next year, he met a group of men involved in coin-operated amusements and joined with them to establish a game machine sales and leasing company for which he served as representative director. The company failed within a year.[29]

Figuring he could do better as a manufacturer, in 1965 Satomi became managing director of his father's company, changed the name from Tokyo Nutrition Foods to Satomi Co. Ltd., and established a new amusement manufacturing division. Satomi rode the 1960s crane boom to great success and then caught the medal game wave in 1973 by manufacturing "arrange ball" machines, a cross between a *pachinko* machine and a bingo pinball. These machines were marketed under the "Sammy" brand name. After being caught up in a major fraud case, Satomi Co. entered bankruptcy, but Satomi was able to keep the amusement business going by establishing a new company in 1975 called Sammy Industry. The company remained primarily a producer of medal and *pachinko* machines; manufacturing *Space Invaders* for Taito was its first foray into video games.[30]

In early 1979, Taito added two more manufacturers as it desperately tried to keep pace with demand: Jatre and IPM.[31] Jatre was an import-export company and a big player in the medal game business, while IPM was one of the

---

[27] Akagi, 2005, 237.

[28] Ibid, 156.

[29] "This Person at This Time: Sammy Chairman Hajime Satomi," P-Landmark, accessed December 20, 2009, http://www.p-landmark.com/news/2542.aspx.

[30] Ibid.

[31] Akagi, 2005, 156.

largest coin-operated game operators in Japan. Its founder, Kenzo Tsujimoto, was born in 1940 and worked in his family's wholesale food business after graduating high school while studying accounting in his spare time.[32] In 1966, he left the family business due to the dramatic effect supermarkets were beginning to have on wholesalers.[33] Tsujimoto moved to Osaka to open his own confectionary products store and soon began selling cotton candy machines as well. In the late 1960s, he began seeing *pachinko* machines targeted at children in candy stores and became an operator in April 1969 under the name IPM Trading Company, which stood for International Play Machines. This business proved so successful that Tsujimoto was able to incorporate the company in 1974 as IPM Co. Ltd.[34]

IPM became the fourth largest operator in Japan, trailing only the big factory operations Taito, Sega, and Namco. Tsujimoto achieved this position by operating only a small number of titles but deploying them in large quantities, often as the exclusive operator of the game. When one of his exclusives became a hit, other operators would approach him about placing the game as well, which brought Tsujimoto into the distribution business. In late 1977, IPM made the leap from distribution and operation to manufacturing during the block-busting boom through a game called *Block Out* that moved 35,000 units. With a wide distribution reach and large factory operation, IPM was a natural partner for Taito in the distribution of *Space Invaders*.[35]

Unlike the first three licensees, both Jatre and IPM released slightly different takes on *Space Invaders* under alternate names. Jatre called its game *Spectre*, and it featured both smoother animation and slightly faster gameplay. The IPM version, dubbed *IPM Invader*, incorporated a color monitor as opposed to colored cellophane strips and sold 50,000 units.[36] Even with all these companies providing support, Taito still could not satisfy customers and took the highly unusual step of entering a secret agreement with Atari to manufacture *Space Invaders* games in the United States and ship them over to Japan.[37]

***

[32] "Profile: Chairman and Chief Executive Officer Kenzo Tsujimoto," Capcom Investor Relations, accessed June 8, 2019, http://www.capcom.co.jp/ir/english/company/views_ceo.html.

[33] "Game Maker Capcom's Head Takes on Wine-Making in California," iStock Analyst, March 24, 2009, http://www.istockanalyst.com/article/viewiStockNews/articleid/3141868.

[34] Akagi, 2005, 233.

[35] "Tsujimoto – Capcom's 'Toy Maker' – Talks about Video Business & Video Philosophy," *RePlay*, December 1985, 85–86.

[36] Ibid, 86.

[37] Lipkin, 2014.

By the middle of 1979, there were an estimated 280,000 video games in location in Japan. An estimated 230,000 were "Invader games." Taito and its licensees were responsible for roughly 200,000 of these cabinets, while the rest were created by cloning operations that took advantage of the unsettled status of computer software under Japanese copyright law.[38] The rapid spread of the game was aided by several factors. The decision by Taito to license additional manufacturers allowed the company to fill the market faster than it could have done on its own, and the wide array of bootleg versions saturated the market even further. These companies were able to ramp up production unusually fast because a major recession caused by the oil embargo shock in 1973 caused a significant downturn in the Japanese consumer electronics business. Monitors, ICs, and other components began piling up in warehouses, so when *Space Invaders* came into such high demand, these component manufacturers suddenly had an outlet for their surplus stock and the game was not subject to the typical shortages plaguing a surprise hit electronic product.[39]

The boom was also aided by the previous success experienced by table-top block-busting games in opening up new venues like coffee houses and snack bars. Fully two-thirds of *Space Invaders* cabinets were placed in coffee houses, where some owners ordered five or ten units at a time and replaced all their tables with video games. What had once been small coffee shops were now "Invader Houses," the first establishments in Japan devoted exclusively to video games. As demand continued unabated, *pachinko* parlors, medal game centers, and even small retail shops converted to Invader Houses as well.[40]

Space Invaders became a cultural phenomenon that transcended age groups and spurred fierce competition for high scores. Players desperately chased tips and rumors of strategies to become better players; national tournaments held by Jatre and other companies attracted large crowds, and Taito even published a 61-page book entitled *How To Play Space Invaders* in 1980 that may have been the first video game strategy guide. Perhaps the greatest testament to the game's widespread appeal was the disappearance of Japan's supply of ¥100 coins into the machines. The coins became so scarce that the Japanese mint ordered a temporary increase in production, while members

---

[38] Akagi, 156.
[39] Shinozaki, 1979, 129.
[40] Akagi, 156.

of the Imperial Diet negotiated directly with Taito to get coins out of games and back into circulation faster.[41]

Space Invaders became so popular it even transcended the video game medium. Taito authorized merchandise like stickers, pencils, notebooks, t-shirts, and even potato chips emblazoned with the iconic *Space Invaders* alien designs, while in 1980 a novelty group called Funny Stuff released a single called "Disco Space Invaders" that sampled the game and lent itself to a new dance that briefly took over the Tokyo club scene. Early electronic music acts in Japan like Yellow Magic Orchestra drew inspiration from its minimalist score and sound effects.

In June 1979, the Invader boom ended almost as quickly as it had begun. At the time, game centers and Invader houses were open 24 hours a day and carried a reputation as being dark, smoke-filled hangouts for gangs and other unsavory individuals. The unprecedented popularity of *Space Invaders* among children consequently set off a moral panic at the highest levels of Japanese society that led to attacks on the game as causing juvenile delinquency and corrupting the youth. The Japanese coin-operated amusement industry realized that if it did not take steps to regulate access to the game, it would likely face extensive regulation from the Imperial Diet.[42]

On June 2, 1979, the principle trade organization of the industry, the All-Japan Amusement Park Association (JAA), issued a directive called the "Declaration of Invader Type Game Machine Operational Controlled Management" that called for Invader games to only be installed at facilities with an attendant, for children under 15 to be barred from playing the game without parental accompaniment, and for anyone under 18 to be forbidden from entering an establishment after 11:00 PM. While these were voluntary guidelines, the JAA worked with the National Police Agency to compel enforcement almost as if they had the effect of actual laws. These new restrictions had a chilling effect on Invader games as earnings dropped and the sale of new cabinets ground to a halt.[43]

***

---

[41] Miller, 2013. The 100-yen shortage caused by *Space Invaders* has been dogged by persistent claims that it is but an urban legend. *Game Machine*, the trade publication of the Japanese coin-op industry, reported the story of shortages and increased production in 1979, but it appears to have been at most a temporary bump. Later reports that the Japanese Mint tripled production of the coin due to extreme nationwide shortages are almost certainly exaggerations.

[42] Akagi, 2005, 160–161.

[43] Ibid, 161–162.

The sudden collapse of the Invader market left the many companies that had thrived by cloning *Space Invaders* in desperate need of new product. This void was partially filled by a new game from Sega's Gremlin subsidiary in the United States called *Head On*. Gremlin engineer Lane Hauck developed the initial idea for the driving game, in which the playfield consisted of a series of fixed lanes radiating from the center of the screen full of dots two players must collect to score points. The players' cars would drive in opposite directions and could only change lanes at the four compass points, so the challenge was to pick a lane with a lot of dots to collect while trying not to end up in the same lane as your opponent and causing a collision. The player with the most points at the end of a set time limit would win.[44]

Once Hauck had the basic concept running, he realized his game suffered from a fatal flaw: if one player ended up with a significantly higher score than his opponent, he would stop driving around to collect dots and would instead continually crash into the other player to maintain his scoring advantage until time ran out. Hauck's solution to this problem was to adapt the game for one player and have the hardware control the second car. Now, the player would try to collect all the dots on the screen while avoiding the computer-controlled car, which was programmed to seek him out.[45]

Once Hauck and programmer Bill Blewett finished *Head On*, they received one important piece of feedback from Sega's designers in Japan: with *Space Invaders* currently all the rage without a time limit, the Japanese suggested Hauck remove the timer from *Head On* as well.[46] This final tweak allowed *Head On* to become a score-chasing game on par with *Space Invaders* and helped it become a significant hit when it reached Japan in April 1979. Like Taito with *Space Invaders*, Sega licensed the game to a small number of companies for manufacture, providing a needed outlet for firms suffering from the slowing of the Invader market.

Perhaps the most notable *Head On* manufacturers outside of Sega itself were Irem and Data East.[47] Irem was the new name of Tsujimoto's IPM Co. as of July 1979, a change necessitated by a threatened lawsuit by IBM over their similar names.[48] As with *Space Invaders*, Irem did not just copy the Sega board, but created its own enhancements to the game. In addition

---

[44] DeWyze, 1982.

[45] Ibid.

[46] Ibid.

[47] Akagi, 2005, 192.

[48] As IPM stood for "International Play Machines," Irem stood for "International Rental Electronic Machines." Tsujimoto, 1985, 85.

to full-color graphics, the company added letters that would be uncovered when the player collected certain dots. If the player ran over these letters in sequence to spell "Irem," he scored additional points.

Data East also took a different approach to producing the game. Company founder Tetsuo Fukuda graduated from Tokai University with an electrical engineering degree and joined a maker of electronic measuring equipment called Nomura Electric Machinery as the head of new business in 1970. In 1974, he developed a light gun system that brought Nomura into the coin-operated amusement space. Fukuda left the company in 1976 to establish Data East, which likely gained its name because its most successful early business was importing and selling measuring machines. He also served as a subcontractor of electronic parts for fax machines and early dedicated video game consoles, but with less success.[49]

Data East's first coin-operated game was a 1977 medal game called *Jack Lot* incorporating elements of blackjack. In early 1978, the company entered the video game business with its own version of *Breakout* called *Super Break*. The company continued its video game business with a *Circus* clone called *Balloon Circus* and then combined both games into a special "2 in 1" cabinet to great success. In late 1978, Data East introduced its own take on *Space Invaders* called *Space Fighter* that featured color graphics, more enemies per row, and a bonus UFO that required multiple hits to destroy.[50] In 1979, Data East not only became a licensee to produce *Head On*, but it inspired Sega to use a 2 in 1 cabinet for its own games. Sega released a cabinet containing both *Head On* and its own *Space Invaders* clone, *Space Attack*.[51]

With the first game proving so popular, especially overseas, Hauck and Blewett developed a sequel, *Head On 2*, which Sega released in late 1979 and again licensed to other companies. The primary new features of the second game are special "U-turn lanes" on the outer part of the track allowing the player to turn around even when not in a straightaway and additional computer-controlled cars in later stages up to a maximum of four. Blewett programmed these cars with distinct personalities so they each chase after the player in their own way.[52]

Head On and its sequel arrived in Japan during a transitional period for Sega. Since being acquired by Gulf & Western, Sega Enterprises, Ltd. had been run by a series of vice presidents from the United States who were strong

---

[49] Ibid, 239.
[50] Ibid.
[51] Ibid, 192–193.
[52] Bill Blewett, interview with Ethan Johnson, August 20, 2018.

in finance and administration, but less competent in sales, marketing, and R&D.[53] In these areas, the company depended a great deal on the head of the sales department, Shunichi Shiina, but in May 1975 he died suddenly,[54] and his successors were not so adept at tracking trends in the coin-op market-place.[55] While the company remained profitable, R&D entered a period of decline and a lack of innovative new product caused Sega to lose its top spot in the Japanese coin-op industry to Taito during the *Space Invaders* boom.

Purchasing Gremlin helped put the company back on track due to the American company's comfort and familiarity with new technologies like microprocessors, but Sega still lacked a dynamic individual who could lead sales and R&D efforts in Japan. That changed in January 1979 when Sega acquired a coin-op distributor that specialized in import-export operations called Esco Trading solely to offer a leadership position at Sega to its president, Hayao Nakayama.

Born in May 1932, Hayao Nakayama was the son and grandson of doctors and was expected to follow his forbearers into that profession. Unfortunately, Nakayama was not fond of science, was not possessed of dexterous hands, and could not stand the site of blood. By his second year at Chiba University, Nakayama knew he would never be a doctor. When he told his father, he was cut off from all financial support by his family. Needing a steady paycheck, Nakayama worked part time as a tutor and English interpreter until he saw a want ad from a jukebox distribution company called the V&V Hifi Trading Company owned by Jewish Lithuanian entrepreneur Samuel Vilensky and his brother.[56] Nakayama essentially became an assistant to the Vilensky Brothers and eagerly learned every aspect of the coin-op business. After a time, Nakayama was given permission to start a sales department for V&V and was soon supervising four people.[57]

When coin-operated games surged in popularity in the late 1960s after the introduction of *Periscope*, Nakayama advocated that V&V enter the wider coin-operated amusement industry, but Samuel Vilensky had died in 1963, and his more conservative younger brother refused to do so. Therefore, Nakayama left the company in 1967 with four members of the sales team to operate Esco Trading out of a small apartment in Shibuya. Esco became

---

[53] Akagi, 2005, 190.

[54] Ibid, 42.

[55] Ibid, 190.

[56] Teppei Akagi, *Sega vs. Nintendo: The Future of Multimedia Wars* (Tokyo: Japan Management Association, 1992), 83–85.

[57] Hironao Baba, *Nintendo Who Is Frightened by Sega* (Tokyo: Yale Publishing Company, 1993), 32–33.

the first real coin-op distributor in Japan by buying in bulk from smaller domestic manufacturers that lacked their own well-developed sales forces and international concerns not already dealing with one of the big Japanese factories and then selling them on to operators.[58]

David Rosen first tried to recruit Nakayama into Sega to run Japanese operations in 1975 after shifting his office to Los Angeles. At that time, Nakayama was not interested.[59] After Taito supplanted Sega as the largest coin-operated manufacturer in the country, Rosen approached him again. By now, Nakayama had grown tired of just being a distributor and wanted to have a hand in the development of games as well.[60] Therefore, when Rosen offered him complete control of sales, marketing, and R&D, he agreed to come on board. He became a representative director and one of the two executive vice presidents at Sega Enterprises, Ltd. While technically a co-equal with his fellow EVP, Duane Blough, and answerable to Rosen back in the United States, Nakayama quickly established himself as the de facto leader of Sega Enterprises, Ltd.

Upon joining Sega, Nakayama focused primarily on increasing manufacturing efficiency and rebuilding R&D.[61] When he arrived, the Japanese R&D staff numbered 45 people, but they had not come up with a real winner for some time. Nakayama increased the staff to 70 people and personally led a series of brainstorming sessions to develop a new game concept. The result was a new driving game christened *Monaco GP* that built on the basic gameplay of Taito's *Speed Race* series, in which a car drives along a straight road while avoiding other cars, but with a more dynamic track featuring bridges where the road narrows, slippery areas covered in ice, and dark tunnel sections in which visibility of most of the road is obscured. Released in November 1979, *Monaco GP* became an enduring hit despite being the last significant video game released without a microprocessor. In the United States, it never became the number one game on location but remained on the earnings charts into 1987, making it easily the longest sustained money maker of any video arcade game released in the 1970s or 1980s.[62]

***

While *Head On* and its sequel softened the blow of the Invader collapse, they did not entirely mitigate its effects. The negative impact was particularly

[58] Ibid, 38.
[59] Ibid, 39–40.
[60] Ibid, 42.
[61] Ibid, 43–44.
[62] Smith, 2016, 509.

felt by Taito and its official licensees, which were stuck with a surplus of game boards. In 1980, Jatre entered bankruptcy,[63] while Irem was forced to sell out to one of its principle component suppliers, monitor manufacturer Nanao.[64] Taito cleared stock by releasing half a dozen games using the *Space Invaders* hardware but could not conjure up another hit. In September 1979, the company tried a sequel, *Space Invaders Part II*, which incorporated a color monitor and the ability for the high scorer on the machine to enter his name to be displayed at the top of the screen during every play session. The game had nowhere near the impact of the original and was overshadowed by a new *Space Invaders* derivative from rival manufacturer Namco.

Namco entered the video game business through the distribution of Atari products in Japan, but despite touching off the first video game boom in the country through the release of *Breakout*, its internal development activities remained focused on electromechanical games. In the mid-1970s, the company produced some of the last significant games in the "realistic" or "audiovisual" category of electromechanical games that had risen to prominence a decade earlier with Namco's own *Periscope* but had since been supplanted by the video game. Its most notable product in this category during the period was the 1976 racing game *F-1* that took *Speedway*-style projection racing games to their natural endpoint by zooming in on the action to provide a nearly first-person perspective as the player speeds around a circular racetrack. The game did so well that Atari even licensed it for release in the United States. Namco followed *F-1* in 1977 with the last significant electromechanical game it, or indeed any company, produced in this time period: a target shooting game called *Shoot Away*, in which one or two players aim shotgun-shaped controllers at clay pigeons projected onto a screen.

Two men brought Namco into the video game business: Shigeichi Ishimura and Toru Iwatani. A 1976 electrical engineering graduate from Doshisha University, Ishimura had trouble finding employment due to the depressed state of the Japanese electronics industry following the 1973 oil crisis. While browsing through recruiting pamphlets, he became intrigued by a picture of a *Space Race* circuit board in a Namco ad and applied to the company. He did double duty for the firm by contributing to the score display of *F-1* and the control system of *Shoot Away* while also taking primary responsibility for the maintenance of the Atari video games the company was placing on location

---

[63] "Game Machine, February 1, 2000 issue," *Amusement Press*, last modified January 17, 2000, http://www.ampress.co.jp/backnumber/bn2000.02.01.htm.

[64] Akagi, 2005, 162.

through its Atari Japan subsidiary. As he worked on these machines, he also
began studying and dissecting the PC boards to create his own video game
hardware system.[65]

Toru Iwatani joined Namco in 1977. Creative from a young age, he developed jack-in-the-boxes, practical joke devices, and board games to amuse
himself as a child. As a teenager, he discovered pinball in bowling alleys
and lounges and fell in love with the game. After he graduated from Tokai
University with a degree in telecommunications engineering,[66] Iwatani had
no idea what he wanted to do with his life, but like Ishimura, he was attracted
to the Namco recruiting ads because of the company slogan "Creating Play."[67]
Iwatani hoped to create pinball games for the company and was disheartened
to learn that Namco only imported its tables from the United States rather
than making them itself. He ended up serving as a technician repairing Atari
video game circuit boards, which inspired him to shift his focus to designing
a video game.[68]

The same year that Iwatani joined the company, Ishimura wrote a report
on video games for Namco management and recommended the company
buy the necessary development equipment to enter the video game business.
Masaya Nakamura gave him the green light, so he worked with Iwatani to
develop the company's first product. While Ishimura created the hardware
and handled programming duties, Iwatani completed the design of the game
based on an idea by fellow Namco engineer Akira Osugi to combine the
popular *Breakout* with elements of pinball.[69] Released as *Gee Bee* in 1978,
Ishimura and Iwatani's game moved 10,000 units but was not as successful as
this sales total would indicate. The game debuted in August just before *Space
Invaders* fever swept the nation, so many of the units never left their shipping crates as locations turned away from any product that did not involve
shooting aliens.[70] Iwatani followed up with two similar games, *Bomb Bee* and
Cutie Q, but neither of them could even match the performance of *Gee Bee*.

[65] Fumio Kurokawa, "Narratives of Video Games Part 4: Shigeichi Ishimura," 4Gamer, March 17,
2018, https://www.4gamer.net/games/999/G999905/20180313040.

[66] Akagi, 2005, 197.

[67] Patrick Scott Patterson, "Icons: Toru Iwatani Gave the World the Gift of Pac-Man," Syfy Games,
April 8, 2016, https://syfygames.com/news/article/icons-toru-iwatani-gave-the-world-the-gift-of-pac-
man-patrickscottpatterson.

[68] "The Development of Pac-Man," Glitterberri's Game Translations, 2003, https://www.glitterberri.
com/developer-interviews/the-development-of-pacman.

[69] "Interview with Toru Iwatani, Namco Bandai 'The First Video Game Beginning Part 2',"
Bandai Namco Entertainment, March 6, 2019, https://www.bandainamcoent.co.jp/asobimotto/page/
videogame2.html.

[70] Kurokawa, 2018.

Meanwhile, one of the company's premiere electromechanical engineers, Kazunori Sawano, reluctantly turned his attention to video games after the Invader boom. Born in 1951, Sawano was an indifferent student as a child, but enjoyed painting, woodworking, and mechanical devices, so he matriculated to Omori Industrial High School with a focus on electrical engineering.[71] Sawano's ambition was to enter the motion picture industry, but he was unlikely to receive any job offers as a fresh high school graduate. He was also interested in the workings of electromechanical coin-operated games like Kasco's *Indy 500*, so a teacher showed him a Nakamura Manufacturing brochure and urged him to apply.[72]

Sawano joined Nakamura Manufacturing in April 1970 and entered its newly established development department. His first project was a 1971 airplane shooting game called *Zero Sen* that he created in conjunction with one of the company's original game designers, Kenichi Muramatsu. He then created several medal games, a 1973 driving game in the vein of *Indy 500* called *Formula-X*, and the hit game *Shoot Away*.[73]

After the success of *Space Invaders*, Namco president Masaya Nakamura personally tasked Sawano with creating the definitive follow-up to the game. Sawano began by undertaking a comprehensive study of *Space Invaders* and decided that its basic mechanics – the player moving left and right along the bottom of the screen and rows of targets arrayed at the top of the screen – were critical components to keep. He did want to change the venue, however, as having become a fan of *Star Wars* he wanted to depict a battle in open space rather than one focused on the surface of a planet. This meant removing the bunkers and adding a scrolling starfield to the background to give the sensation of flight through the cosmos.[74]

To further the illusion of continuous movement through space, Sawano did not want to reuse the basic attack pattern of *Space Invaders*, with the enemies descending en masse one line at a time. In developing an alternate attack pattern, he was inspired by a 1956 Japanese movie called *Admiral Yamamoto and the Allied Fleets*. During the climactic scene of the movie, in which Yamamoto is assassinated, the American P-38 fighter planes are depicted as swooping down from above to attack Yamamoto's plane and its escorts. Sawano decided to incorporate a series of similar swooping patterns

---

[71] Zek, *Galaxian Genesis: The History of Kazunori Sawano* (Gee Yume Area 51, 2017), 27–28.
[72] Ibid, 28–30.
[73] Ibid, 46–69.
[74] Ibid, 117–119.

for his alien ships.[75] He also decided these attacks should be accompanied by a distinctive noise, and he hounded the game's sound programmer until he felt they had achieved the perfect effect.

Having individual ships break formation required a more sophisticated coin-op hardware than *Space Invaders*, so Ishimura developed a powerful new system around the Z80 processor and custom graphics hardware that allowed for 15 sprites per scanline that could be rendered with up to four colors each. Toshio Kai programmed the game based on Sawano's design and developed the enemy attack patterns. The sprites were drawn by Yoshiaki Nakama. The original designs looked exactly like the TIE Fighters from *Star Wars*, but Sawano and Nakama ultimately decided to develop enemy designs that were a hybrid of machine and organic components. Originally, Sawano planned to have asteroids fly across the screen to provide additional obstacles, but he decided this made the game too difficult.[76]

Toshio Kai named the game *Galaxian*, which he envisioned as a term for a galactic warrior in the same way that someone who plays music is called a musician.[77] Released in November 1979, the impressive graphics, smooth and challenging gameplay, and carefully calibrated difficulty curve of the game attracted players looking for something new after the end of the Invader boom. By December, Namco realized it would be unable to keep up with demand and licensed several companies, including former *Space Invaders* manufacturers Irem, Logitec, and Sammy. Namco even farmed out manufacturing to the other major Japanese factories, Sega, Taito, and Sigma Enterprises, though they were not allowed to sell the game themselves.[78]

Head On and *Galaxian* saved the Japanese coin-operated video game industry by emerging from the chaos caused by the demise of *Space Invaders* and proving the industry could deliver a string of hits rather than just creating a passing fad based on a single massive game. Meanwhile, the Invader boom had spread to the worldwide market, and coin-operated video game manufacturers in the United States were soon faced with the same challenge of determining whether video games could grow beyond *Space Invaders* and dethrone the solid-state pinball machines currently dominating the industry.

---

[75] Ibid, 119.
[76] Ibid, 119–120.
[77] Ibid, 124.
[78] Akagi, 2005, 186.

29

Deep Impact

On November 2, 1976, voters in the state of New Jersey decided by a slim margin to legalize gambling in Atlantic City. Once a jewel of the East Coast known for its beaches, luxury hotels, and thriving night club scene, Atlantic City had fallen on hard times in the aftermath of World War II as the spread of the automobile and suburban living changed summer holiday patterns. Lawmakers were convinced gambling was the key to revitalizing the famed boardwalk, and voters agreed to allow the city to become the Las Vegas of the East.

As the only locale in the United States outside Nevada to legalize gambling, Atlantic City appeared the best venue for Bally chairman and CEO William O'Donnell to fulfill his dream of owning a casino. While Bally had a stranglehold on over 90% of the slot machines in use in Nevada, selling these machines did not rake in nearly as much money as operating them. O'Donnell had been hesitant to enter the casino business in Nevada, however, because he feared existing casino owners would see the entry of their leading supplier as a major threat and look for alternatives. Atlantic City was virgin territory.

In June 1977, Bally established a subsidiary called Bally Park Place with the intent of operating a casino of that name in Atlantic City. The company subsequently leased the Marlborough-Blenheim Hotel and purchased the Dennis Hotel, tearing down the former and renovating the latter to build what the company promised would be the most luxurious development on the boardwalk. Bally Park Place was completed in 1979 and merely needed to acquire a gaming license to open. The New Jersey Casino Control Commission refused to grant one.[1]

---

[1] Stephen Piccolo, "Gaming in Atlantic City: A History of Legal Gambling in New Jersey, Part 3," Museum of Gaming History, accessed June 10, 2019, http://museumofgaminghistory.org/mogh.php?p=article&a=55.

In taking control of the assets of the old Lion Manufacturing in 1963, O'Donnell relied primarily on financing from well-connected former vending machine distributor Sam Klein and representatives of the coin-op distributor Runyon Sales. Runyon was fronted by Abe Green and Barnett Sugerman, but their silent financial partner was Gerardo "Jerry" Catena, one of the bosses of the Genovese Crime Family. Catena was awarded stock in the new Lion Manufacturing, directly linking the firm with organized crime. O'Donnell claimed ignorance of this arrangement and bought out the underworld figure in 1964 when it came to light.[2]

The Catena buyout ended Bally's direct association with criminal elements, but indirect links persisted. Klein, Bally's largest shareholder and its executive VP, had a long history of ties to Catena dating back to 1960, when he nearly went into partnership with Catena, Green, and Sugerman to purchase a vending company on behalf of Lou Jacobs, another figure with questionable ties who helped finance the Lion purchase. Klein also tapped his connections to finance the early growth of the new Lion Manufacturing organization through loans from the Teamsters Central States, Southeast and Southwest Areas Pension Fund, which itself was suspected of underworld ties. As Bally sought a permanent gaming license from the Nevada Gaming Commission in 1976, an investigation revealed that Klein still consorted with Catena. Nevada refused to grant a license until Klein resigned from the corporation and agreed to divest his shares.[3] Klein resigned that August and agreed to sell all his shares in the corporation by 1980.[4]

O'Donnell had a degree of plausible deniability regarding the Catena situation, but during the New Jersey investigation, another former Bally shareholder was closely scrutinized, Dino Cellini. Cellini became a Bally distributor in 1964, first in the Bahamas and later in Europe, and continued to distribute for the company until 1973. He remained a Bally shareholder until his death in 1978. Cellini was a close associate of key mob figure Meyer Lansky and operated casinos on his behalf in the Caribbean. Even though Cellini's ties with Bally were smaller than Catena's, there was no

---

[2] Recchi, 1979. There is some dispute regarding O'Donnell's knowledge of the Catena connection. During subsequent investigations, O'Donnell always claimed ignorance and appears not to have been seriously challenged on this point. Barnett Sugerman's son Myron, who wrote a book about his experiences in the coin-op world, claims that O'Donnell came to Runyon Sales specifically for an introduction to Catena, who could bring in more wealthy backers to finance the Lion purchase. Myron Sugerman, *The Chronicles of the Last Jewish Gangster: From Meyer to Myron* (Amazon Digital Services, 2017), kindle, chap. 2.

[3] Recchi, 1979.

[4] "Faced with Quiz, Bally Exec Quits," *Chicago Tribune*, August 27, 1976.

way O'Donnell could deny them. Combined with the Klein dealings, the Teamster loans, and a letter written by O'Donnell in 1968 that appeared to suggest bribing the Kentucky legislature to legalize bingo pinball games, the Cellini connection led New Jersey to deny a license.[5]

In December 1979, Bally made a deal with the commission to grant a temporary license in exchange for O'Donnell stepping down as chairman and CEO. O'Donnell figured his ouster would be temporary as he worked to clear his name, but a year later the commission issued its final ruling that a permanent license was contingent on O'Donnell cutting all ties with the firm and divesting his shares.[6] O'Donnell had achieved his dream of a Bally casino, but at the cost of control of the company he had worked so hard to build into a global powerhouse.

Robert Mullane became the new chairman and CEO of Bally. A Harvard Business School graduate, Mullane worked in securities in Chicago from 1956 until joining Bally in 1971. He spent years in Europe running Belgium-based Bally Continental before returning to the parent company in 1978 to run its global distribution operations. More bottom-line oriented and less wedded to pinball and slot machines than his predecessor, Mullane planned to transform Bally into a diversified entertainment company. In this he was helped by a sudden surge in profits from the video game business of subsidiary Midway Manufacturing as it rode the success of its latest Japanese import, *Space Invaders*.

***

Taito prepared to bring *Space Invaders* to the United States not long after it debuted in Japan. The company planned to market it through its own Taito America subsidiary, but when the game became a phenomenon in Japan and location testing indicated it was going to be a massive hit in the United States as well, management worried that Taito America was too small to supply the market with cabinets quickly. Not wanting a repeat of the developing situation in Japan where clones were taking a good chunk of the market, Taito turned to its old distribution partner Midway to deploy the game.[7]

As in Japan, *Space Invaders* debuted in the United States to little fanfare. First displayed by Midway at the AMOA show in November 1978, the game received positive notices in the trades, but was not treated as revolutionary or

---

[5] Recchi, 1979.
[6] "Game Turns Sour in N.J. for Bally's Ex-Chairman," *Chicago Tribune*, December 28, 1980.
[7] Smith, 2016, 372.

even voted the best game of the show. For the remainder of 1978, orders were low due to the generally depressed state of the video game market and the hesitation of distributors and operators to take on new product. By February 1979, the game had proven itself an earnings juggernaut, and orders began to pour in. By March, *Space Invaders* had surpassed *Sea Wolf* as Midway's highest selling video game of all time.[8]

By the beginning of spring, *Space Invaders* was a bonafide hit; by summer it was a phenomenon. With school out and children free to chase high scores all day long, demand reached new heights. The game became a must-have item at street locations like taverns, restaurants, and convenience stores that had generally stuck to pinball previously,[9] while arcade operators often installed banks of six to eight machines, an unprecedented act in an industry that thrived on variety.[10] In May, Midway released a cocktail version to chase high-end lounges, reviving a location that had all but disappeared in the United States after the collapse of the *Pong* cocktail market with its unscrupulous "biz op" con artists in 1975.[11] Midway showed the game again at the 1979 AMOA, and it was one of the hits of the show despite being in production for a year.[12] The company vowed to keep producing units as long as demand continued and was still doing so when the AMOA show rolled around again in 1980. Final sales were between 60,000 and 70,000 units, by far the biggest sales for a coin-operated game in the United States since the earliest days of the pinball boom in the 1930s.

The explosive popularity of *Space Invaders* did not signal on its own that video games were poised to supplant pinball and pool to become the new top game in American coin-operated amusement spaces. Just because every arcade needed a *Space Invaders* cabinet or six did not mean operators were going to invest in other titles. Indeed, there were similarities to the *Pong* boom and bust just a few years before in which a single game and its clones and variants took complete control of the market for over a year only to collapse.

While Midway was thriving with *Space Invaders*, many of the other American factories were falling apart. At Ramtek, which in 1975 had been one of the most powerful video game companies in the coin-op space, game

---

[8] "Chicago Chatter," *Cash Box*, March 3, 1979, 76.

[9] Frank Manners, "Coin Machine Industry 1979: Midwest Year End Summary," *Cash Box*, December 29, 1979, 106.

[10] "Chicago Chatter," *Cash Box*, March 3, 1979. 76.

[11] "Chicago Chatter," *Cash Box*, June 16, 1979, 58.

[12] "Chicago Chatter," *Cash Box*, November 24, 1979, 54.

sales had been dropping compared to its core computer graphics business for several years. In 1975, the company had sales of $6 million, of which $4 million was in games. In 1976, revenues rose to $6.8 million, but only a bit over $2 million of that was in games. That ratio remained similar over the next two years as the game division began losing money.[13] In 1978, Ramtek went public, and Charles McEwan concluded the volatile game space was no place for a company expected to deliver consistent quarterly results to shareholders. Ramtek sold its games division in 1979 to its manager, Mel McEwan, who continued to do business as Meltec with one of the last games developed at Ramtek, a combination of target shooting and skee ball called *Boom Ball*. Meltec remained in business for over two decades, but never entered the video game business.[14]

Meanwhile, the former king of the cocktail market, Meadows Games, was also fading fast. In 1976, Meadows invested its profits from the wildly successful *Flim-Flam* game into a new factory in Sunnyvale and a new European final assembly facility in London. A slew of games in the traditional upright market followed including a *Blockade* clone called *Bigfoot Bonkers*, an elaborate take on *Tank* called *Lazer Command* in which each player can switch between 15 armored vehicles scattered around a maze to do battle, and a ball-and-paddle game called *Ckidzo* that implemented inertia. The company even hired Atari co-founder Ted Dabney, who did not stay long, and purchased Atari game cloner Fun Games in 1977. None of the Meadows games became hits as distributors became more selective in their video game purchases, and Harry Kurek sold his over-extended company to holography company Holosonics in September 1978. Holosonics hired Exidy marketing director Paul Jacobs to run Meadows, but after he was done paying off the company's debts, there was no money for R&D. Jacobs himself left after just a few months, and the company was shut down before the end of 1979.[15]

Proving that *Space Invaders* was not just another flash in the pan like *Pong* would require the coin-op industry to develop follow-up products that were just as successful in sales but differed in gameplay. Midway enjoyed great success in 1980 with both *Space Invaders Part II* and a licensed version of *Galaxian* from Namco that moved 45,000 units, but these were just variations on the same theme. The feature of these games that seemed most likely to sustain an industry was their high-score tracking, which encouraged

---

[13] McEwan, 1980.
[14] Smith, 2016, 209.
[15] Ibid, 197–199.

competition between players. Two 1979 releases combined refinements to the high-score concept and gameplay that diverged from the *Space Invaders* formula to turn a fad into the dominant coin-operated amusement category.

The first of these games, *Star Fire*, was manufactured by Exidy, but developed by a group of freelancers led by Ted Michon. The lead developer for the short-lived Digital Games and Micronetics companies, Michon established an R&D firm called Techni-Cal in 1977 after the collapse of Micronetics and secured a game development contract with Midway, which still relied primarily on outside developers to create its video games. After joining forces with two former Caltech classmates, he changed the name of the company to Technical Magic. Like Nishikado at Taito, the group decided to ride the *Star Wars* mania gripping the United States to create a target shooting game set in space.[16]

Michon knew attracting *Star Wars* fans to his game would require a state-of-the-art audiovisual experience, so he developed his own Z80-based system that interfaced with a color monitor. Color was still rare at the time due to the expense of the monitors, and early games that had experimented with it, like Exidy's *Car Polo* and Atari's *Indy 800*, had used converted televisions rather than an actual monitor long after that practice had ceased with black-and-white games.[17] Color monitors were just starting to come down in price by 1977, however, and Michon managed to locate a relatively cheap one.

As Michon developed the hardware and his girlfriend Susan Olsen worked on art for the game, Technical Magic hired another Caltech alumnus named David Rolfe to do the programming. The trio built a game in which the player maneuvers a targeting reticule on the screen and attempts to shoot down enemy ships that look exactly like the TIE Fighters in Star Wars. The enemy ships can shoot back at the player, but the game is not regulated by lives as in *Space Invaders*. Instead, play is regulated via a time limit that can be extended by scoring a certain number of points or by inserting more coins, an early example of buy in, which eventually became a standard practice of allowing the player to front-load playing time by inserting more money. As the player destroys more ships, both the difficulty level and the point value of the ships increases. If an enemy ship hits the player, the difficulty and point values reset.

Michon and crew presented *Star Fire* to Midway, but the coin-op giant was not impressed. A long period of tweaks to all aspects of the game followed,

---

[16] Ibid, 551–552.
[17] Ivy, 2018.

but nothing satisfied the company. When the game was finally rejected, Michon found a more willing partner in Exidy.[18] Not only did the company agree to produce *Star Fire*, it also designed an immersive sit-down cabinet with a large speaker in the seat to give the player the illusion of sitting in an actual cockpit. Exidy debuted the game at the 1978 AMOA show, where it garnered more attention than *Space Invaders* in some circles. Upon release it lagged that game in sales, but still became one of the top 10 earners of 1979.

Near the end of development on *Star Fire*, as the team struggled with Midway's mandates to increase the appeal of the game, Michon and Rolfe had a philosophical discussion about what players hoped to get out of games. Rolfe suggested that they like the opportunity to be remembered, which led the duo down the path of memorializing high scores. Unlike *Space Invaders*, the duo decided not just to record the top score, but to include a table with multiple high scores on it. They also implemented a system allowing a player to enter his initials next to his score.[19] These enhancements promised a new phase in score chasing in which elite players could be easily identified and individuals could better track how their skills compared to other players at their location. While *Star Fire* proved only a minor hit in the end, these enhancements gained widespread acceptance after being incorporated into Atari's answer to *Space Invaders*, *Asteroids*.

***

While Taito was introducing *Space Invaders* at the 1978 AMOA show, Atari was introducing a breakthrough game of its own. Steve Bristow and Lyle Rains had been trying to develop an arcade football game since their Kee Games days but had been stymied primarily by the cost of the hardware needed to display enough objects on the screen simultaneously. As Atari embraced microprocessor hardware in the late 1970s, which could offload some of the object display burden to software, a football game finally appeared within reach. Rains developed a new motion control circuit further modified by engineer Dave Stubben to create something Atari called MOC-16, which stood for Motion Object Control, 16 objects.[20]

Programmer Mike Albaugh served as the project leader on a new attempt at a football game originally dubbed *Monster Man Football*. In addition to

---

[18] Scott Stilphen, "DP Interviews: David Rolfe," *Digital Press*, 2004, http://www.digitpress.com/library/interviews/interview_david_rolfe.html.

[19] Ibid.

[20] Mike Albaugh, "Atari Football History," coinop.org, December 30, 2002, https://www.coinop.org/features/football.

supporting seven players on a side thanks to Stubben's circuitry, the game
also incorporated what may have been the first example of a true scrolling
playfield, which allowed the action to unfold on a full 100-yard football field
larger than a single screen. The movement of most of the players – depicted
as X's and O's in the style of a playbook – is dictated by a series of canned
plays developed by Bristow and Rains based on actual football strategies. The
player controls one team member and either attempts to advance down the
field if on offense or intercept the player with the ball if on defense.[21]

Atari management wanted to use joystick controllers for the game, but
Albaugh insisted on a trackball, a control consisting of a ball in a socket containing sensors to detect movement along horizontal and vertical axes. The
benefit of using the trackball in the game was providing a sense of momentum as the player rapidly spins the ball to propel his player down the field, but
the downside was that it was an expensive piece of technology. Atari coin-op
benefitted from its own machine shop, so Albaugh set mechanical engineer
Jerry Lichac to solve the expense problem. Meanwhile, Sega released a soccer
game called *World Cup* that incorporated a trackball, proving a cost-effective
design was feasible. Albaugh got his way.[22]

Albaugh's game debuted at the AMOA show in 1978 under the name
Atari Football after an attempt to secure an NFL license failed. Its fast-paced
action and smoothly scrolling playfield made *Football* one of the hits of the
show, and it quickly moved over 10,000 units.[23] In ordinary times, it would
have been the top earning game of 1979, but it had to settle for a distant
second place behind the *Space Invaders* juggernaut. Overcoming Taito and
deploying the next big hit would require both new gameplay ideas and new
technologies.

Topping *Space Invaders* became the province of Lyle Rains, who in late
1978 was promoted to head of electrical engineering and game development
for the Atari Coin-Operated Games Division. Rains appreciated the action
and tension of *Space Invaders* but found restricting the player to the bottom
of the screen limiting. In 1976, he had developed the concept for a game
called *Planet Grab* that combined the movement and shooting of *Computer
Space* with a competition to conquer planets scattered about the playfield by
colliding with them.[24] The game never entered production because it ended
up not being fun, but with the success of *Space Invaders*, Rains decided to

[21] Ibid.
[22] Ibid.
[23] Atari Arcade Production Numbers, 1999.
[24] Lyle Rains, "Planet Grab (Invasion) Game Description," Atari pitch document, June 7, 1976.

combine the movement of *Computer Space* with the "shoot everything on the screen approach" of *Space Invaders* to modify the premise of *Planet Grab* so that instead of capturing rocks in space, the player destroys them.[25] Rains brought his concept to one of Atari coin-op's more talented programmers, Ed Logg.[26]

Born in Seattle in 1948, George Edward Logg discovered computers when his high school acquired a Bendix G15. In junior college, Logg fooled around with an IBM 1400 series mainframe and programmed chess and slot machine simulations. He matriculated to Berkeley to study math and computer science and then did a master's degree in mathematics at Stanford. He had planned to complete a PhD as well, but his love of programming won out, and he left the school to take a job at Control Data Corporation in Sunnyvale.[27]

An avid game enthusiast, Logg played a variety of computer games at Berkeley and both *Spacewar!* and the Pitts and Tuck *Galaxy Game* at Stanford. At Control Data, he spent a lot of time digesting the games available on early time-sharing systems and converting them to other programming languages. He also enjoyed arcade games immensely and built a custom computer that could play *Sea Wolf.* This feat particularly impressed Atari, where he applied for a job after a colleague jumped ship for the game maker and encouraged him to come along. In 1978, Logg was hired as a programmer in the coin-op division.[28]

Logg's first project was a *Sprint* variant called *Dirt Bike* featuring handlebar controllers that never entered production. Next, he undertook an update of *Breakout* that entered production in September 1978 as *Super Breakout* and featured three new variations on the original game, including one where the bricks descend as the game continues in a similar manner to the aliens in *Space Invaders.* The game became a modest hit with around 4,800 units sold. After developing a flop called *Video Pinball* and doing some programming on *Atari Football,* Logg took on Rains's new target shooting project, which gained the name *Asteroids.*[29]

---

[25] Paul Drury, "Making of Asteroids," *Retro Gamer*, no. 68, 2009, 25.

[26] Ed Logg remembers the inspiration for the game being a prototype that featured an asteroid in the middle of the screen that players would always shoot at even though it could not be destroyed. What game this would be is not clear, but it does not appear to be *Planet Grab.* It's possible that Logg is remembering Cinematronics' *Space Wars,* which does feature a small indestructible asteroid that zooms around the screen.

[27] Bloom, *Invaders,* 1982, 64.

[28] Paul Drury, "Desert Island Discs: Ed Logg," *Retro Gamer* no. 29, 2006, 76.

[29] Richard Rouse III, *Game Design Theory & Practice,* 2nd ed. (Sudbury, MA: Jones and Bartlett Publishers, 2005), ebook, chap. 6.

Rains presented the basic parameters of the game to Logg as flying a ship around the screen using a similar control scheme to *Computer Space* and shooting at asteroids until the whole screen is cleared. Logg added two wrinkles of his own. First, to stop the player from just floating around the screen not engaging targets, he decided that a flying saucer would appear periodically and take shots at the player. Second, he decided to force the player to think strategically by having larger asteroids break into smaller asteroids when the player shoots them.[30]

Logg also advocated for a hardware change. At the standard raster display of 320×224, the player's ship would be little more than a blob. This presented a problem since rotating the ship to aim at asteroids was a key feature of the gameplay. Logg decided he would need a higher resolution and advocated for a vector system like the one Cinematronics used in *Space Wars*, which would allow a resolution of 1,024×768.[31] Fortunately, Cyan Engineering had recently developed a prototype in response to the release of *Space Wars*, which was turned into a functional arcade hardware by Atari coin-op engineers Howard Delman and Rick Moncrief.

To test the new hardware, Delman decided to create a port of the popular computer game *Lunar Lander*. Atari had attempted to develop a version of the game once before in 1975, but it had been scrapped before entering production.[32] Now with a powerful vector-based hardware, Delman and programmer Rich Moore took another shot, basing much of their work on the 1973 graphical version *Moonlander* that Jack Burness created for DEC. As in the computer versions, the game challenges the player to balance thrust, fuel, and the effects of lunar physics to safely land a module on the moon. Unlike the computer game, Delman and Moore took advantage of the Atari mechanical shop to incorporate a big analog lever the player could push forward on and ease off to increase and decrease thrust.[33] Released in August 1979, the game became a minor hit that sold 4,800 units,[34] which would have been considered an excellent total before *Space Invaders* redefined the industry.

Meanwhile, Logg continued to work on *Asteroids*. As a veteran *Spacewar!* player, he carefully tweaked the physics of the game to achieve just the right balance of friction and inertia to give the sensation of flying through space

---

[30] Drury, 2009, 25–29.

[31] Ibid.

[32] "Current Engineering Assignments," Atari internal memo, February 12, 1975.

[33] Paul Drury, "Making of Lunar Lander," *Retro Gamer*, no. 79, 2010, 40–43.

[34] "Atari Production Numbers," c. 1999.

without making the ship overly difficult to control. He also copied the multi-button control scheme of *Computer Space* as well as the hyperspace function of *Spacewar!* and *Galaxy Game* that could help the player escape a tight spot. To capture the same sense of tension found in *Space Invaders*, Delman created a simple two-note pattern that sounds like a heartbeat and speeds up as the player clears the screen of rocks. Finally, after seeing Exidy's *Star Fire*, Logg copied its high-score table and the ability of players to enter their initials next to their score.[35]

When *Asteroids* was put out on test, Atari coin-op sales manager Don Osborne noticed that it not only earned well, but it was also attracting the exact same players pumping all their quarters into *Space Invaders*.[36] Sure that *Asteroids* represented the hit Atari needed to counter *Space Invaders*, the company rushed the game into production in late 1979 and packed the first round of units in repurposed *Lunar Lander* cabinets. At the AMOA show, however, it went over like a lead balloon, and Atari took no orders. Osborne responded by giving several distributors free sample cabinets to put on location for two weeks. He was confident that once the game was on location, it would prove the high-earning game he expected.[37]

When Atari released *Computer Space* in 1971, its Newtonian physics and multi-button control scheme confounded players and inhibited sales. When *Asteroids* adopted the same approach in November 1979, it became a smash hit. *Space Invaders* had not only conditioned players to accept more difficult gameplay, but also normalized the idea that a player may need to play a game multiple times to master it and earn a top score. These players were also looking for a new challenge a year after the debut of *Space Invaders*, and *Asteroids* offered an intense alternative to the Taito game. By February 1980, *Asteroids* had already become the best-selling coin-op game in Atari's history.[38] In May, Atari released a version of the game in a smaller cabinet it dubbed a "cabaret" to push into the restaurant and convenience store market that *Space Invaders* opened to video games the year before.[39] That summer, *Asteroids* dethroned *Space Invaders* as the top earning game on location. Remaining in production until March 1981, the game ultimately sold 70,000 units worldwide.[40]

---

[35] Drury 2009, 20–29.
[36] Cohen, 1984, chap. 9.
[37] Ibid.
[38] "'Asteroids' Becomes Best Selling Video Game in Atari History," *Cash Box*, February 23, 1980, 43.
[39] "Atari Reveals New Cabinet Design," *Cash Box*, May 24, 1980, 43.
[40] Bernstein, 1982, 70.

In 1980, Atari delivered yet another innovative take on the shooting genre called *Missile Command*. The idea for a missile game had been percolating around the company for several years since Steve Bristow had become enamored by a Nutting Associates game called *Missile Radar* that received a limited release around 1974, and he periodically brought up the concept at brainstorming sessions.[41] The immediate inspiration to finally design the game came when Atari coin-op President Gene Lipkin saw a magazine article in 1979 discussing the possibility of a satellite-based defense system against nuclear weapons and thought a game about tracking and intercepting nuclear weapons on a radar screen could be an interesting concept.[42]

Lipkin's game idea was assigned to programmer Dave Theurer under the name *Armageddon*. A psychology major in college after first dabbling in chemistry and physics, Theurer learned how to program in FOCAL to speed up the process of analyzing statistics for his major. After college, he took a job with defense contractor Bunker Ramo in Connecticut, where he fell in love with *Pong* after playing it in a bar. Theurer moved on to National Semiconductor in the mid-1970s and then joined Atari just a few months later after his boss left National for the company and invited him along. His first game was a *Football* derivative called *Atari Soccer* that he hated working on. *Armageddon* proved more suited to his lifelong interest in blowing things up.[43]

Theurer quickly ditched the radar screen and instead depicted a landscape full of cities the player must defend from incoming nuclear missiles. At his disposal are three bases that can launch missiles that explode when they reach the portion of the screen the player has targeted with a movable crosshair, taking out any enemy targets in close proximity. Having worked with a trackball on *Atari Soccer*, Theurer incorporated one into *Armageddon* to control the movement of the crosshair. To fire missiles, the player presses one of three buttons corresponding to one of the three bases. At first, only single missiles fall from the sky, but as the game progresses, they are joined by planes, satellites, rockets that split into multiple warheads, and smart bombs with a limited AI programmed to avoid player shots. The player only receives a limited number of missiles per round and therefore must target

[41] Many sources have doubted Bristow's *Missile Radar* story, as little evidence exists that it was released. Atari corporate documents held by the Strong Museum of Play indicate that Atari did purchase a unit from distributor C.A. Robinson for evaluation purposes, however, which lends credence to Bristow's recollections. Steve Bristow, "Decisions Reached 11-6-74," Atari internal memo, November 7, 1974.

[42] Lipkin, 2014.

[43] Morph, "Blowing Things Up," Dreamsteep, accessed November 20, 2008, http://dreamsteep.com/writing/71-interviews/46-blowing-things-up.html.

enemy warheads strategically to maximize the number destroyed per missile. Once all the player's cities are destroyed, the words "The End" appear on the screen, and the game is over.[44]

After going through several name changes, *Armageddon* was finally released as *Missile Command* in June 1980. With the need to coordinate fire from three missile bases and many incoming objects to track at once, the game represented another difficulty leap compared to *Space Invaders* and *Asteroids* to provide an exhilarating new challenge for the high-score chasers. Though not as successful as either of those products, it still moved 20,000 units and became one of the top earning games of the year.

The same month *Missile Command* debuted saw a significant management shakeup at Atari coin-op. The division had avoided much upheaval in the aftermath of Ray Kassar's appointment as Atari CEO since it was both well run and profitable, but now Gene Lipkin decided to bring in a new executive named Joe Robbins. A World War II veteran, Robbins entered the coin-op industry in 1945 after leaving the Army by joining a Seeburg distributor called Atlantic New York Corporation as its salesman in Connecticut. He fell in love with the business and moved on to S.L. London Music Company in Milwaukee in 1948 so he could be nearer the industry hub in Chicago.[45]

In 1955, Robbins joined the Empire Coin Machine Exchange, a Chicago outfit established by Gil Kitt and Ralph Sheffield in 1941 with a territory in Illinois, Indiana, and Chicago. The company had expanded rapidly in the late 1940s, but in 1951 Sheffield left to form his own distributorship, and it had never quite recovered. Robbins became the company's sales manager and expanded the firm aggressively by working out deals to carry nearly every major line. He was rewarded with a partnership in the firm in 1961.[46] In this role, he expanded the company into Europe with fantastic results and gained a reputation as one of the major tastemakers in the industry. In December 1972, Bally purchased Empire, and Robbins joined the parent company's board of directors. He left the board in 1978 to assume the presidency of Empire. In that capacity, he forged Empire and two other distributors purchased by Bally, Advanced Automatic in San Francisco and R.L. Jones Company in Boston, into the Bally group, a distribution operation that blanketed the entire United States.[47]

---

[44] Darran Jones, "The Making of Missile Command," *Retro Gamer* no. 88, 2011, 62–65.

[45] "The American Amusement Machine Charitable Foundation Honors Joe Robbins," event program, March 10, 1990.

[46] "Coinman of the Month: Joe Robbins," *Play Meter*, June 1977, 8.

[47] American Coin Machine Charitable Foundation, 1990.

Lipkin brought Robbins into Atari as co-president of the coin-op division in the hopes that he could build a distribution network similar to the Bally Group for Atari. Lipkin's plan had been to keep most responsibilities for himself, but it soon became clear that Robbins was interested in exerting authority over more than just distribution. A power struggle ensued as both presidents attempted to guide the division. Lipkin, already disillusioned by the new Kassar regime, grew tired of the politics and left in August 1980. Robbins was left in full control of Atari coin-op.[48]

Robbins's tenure as president was short and largely defined by his handling of a hit game Atari released in October 1980 called *Battlezone*. The project began in mid-1979 as Atari's engineers debated what types of games they should make with the company's new vector hardware. In addition to a higher screen resolution, one of the principle advantages of vector graphics was that wireframe models could be generated more efficiently than raster images, which opened the possibility of putting three-dimensional objects into a game. Engineering decided to use the vector generator to update the one-on-one dueling games *Tank* and *Jet Fighter* by bringing them into the third dimension.

A hardware engineer who joined Atari in 1976 named Morgan Hoff served as the project manager for the tank game, which was initially called *First-Person Tank* and later *Future Tank* before the company settled on the name *Battlezone*. Jed Margolin designed the hardware, which not only made use of the vector generator, but also of a bit-sliced computer called the "Math Box" created by Dan Pliskin and Mike Albaugh that handled the 3D calculations. Ed Rotberg programmed the game. A Chicago native, Rotberg initially attended Northwestern University to study chemistry, but lost interest in the field after taking an organic chemistry class.[49] He later transferred to the University of Michigan to study computer engineering, where for a senior project he created a graphical version of the classic *Lunar Lander* game on a PDP-9 with a vector display.[50] After working at TI and Rockwell, Rotberg answered an ad in *Infoworld* to come work for Atari in 1979. His first project was a *Baseball* game built on the Atari *Football* hardware, after which he joined the *Battlezone* project.[51]

---

[48] Lipkin, 2014.

[49] Bloom, *Invaders*, 1982, 68.

[50] James Hague, "Ed Rotberg," Halcyon Days, March 1997, https://dadgum.com/halcyon/BOOK/ROTBERG.HTM.

[51] Bloom, *Invaders*, 1982, 68–69.

Battlezone spent well over a year in development due to the new hardware and programming techniques required to create a smoothly animated 3D game. It probably would have taken even longer if not for Rotberg's disciplined approach to creating a data structure for adding game elements. He began by creating stationary objects to put on the playfield, then developed the perspective of the player's field of view and a camera system to figure out how the player would move around the world. Only then did he add his first moving object, an enemy tank, to the game.[52] The programmers of *Battlezone*'s sister project, the aerial combat game *Red Baron*, took a different approach and ended up finishing several months after *Battlezone* despite starting first.

Battlezone depicts a spartan world of geometric objects in a first-person view, with the player's tank represented by a heads-up display. Using a two-lever system like that found on the original *Tank cabinet*, the player moves through the world while avoiding obstacles and exchanging shots with enemy vehicles. At first, only simple tanks appear, which are later joined by flying saucers to increase the challenge by forcing the player to pay attention to enemies on two different planes. More intelligent "super tanks" and missiles eventually appear to increase the difficulty even more. To help orient the player in the 3D world, a radar at the top of the screen shows the location of nearby enemies in relation to the player. Early versions of the cabinet incorporated a periscope viewer to give the illusion of peering out of a tank, but this was subsequently removed.

When *Battlezone* went out on test in early 1980, it became Atari's first game to pull in over $500 in a single week. Anticipation was therefore high when it premiered in November 1980. At first, the game did not disappoint as it became the number two earning game on location in late 1980. After the initial rush, marketing director Frank Ballouz sensed the game had reached market saturation and recommended halting production. Robbins, who had little manufacturing experience, decided to keep producing units. In early 1981 demand collapsed as a new wave of hit games emerged,[53] and Atari was forced to discount the cabinet from $2,100 to $1,500. The company ultimately dropped the price to $725 to clear out remaining inventory.[54] Therefore, while the game moved an impressive 15,000 units, it created a financial crisis at Atari coin-op that played a key role in Robbins resigning in mid-1981.[55]

***

---

[52] Craig Grannell, "Making of Battlezone," *Retro Gamer*, no. 59, 2009, 52–53.
[53] Ballouz, 2009.
[54] "Atari Production Numbers, c. 1999."
[55] Ballouz, 2009.

In 1979, with *Space Invaders* taking the United States by storm and *Football* packing away quarters, video game coin drop in the country nearly tripled to $968 million. This total still trailed pinball by $1 billion as the solid-state market peaked.[56] In 1980, with *Space Invaders* joined by *Asteroids, Galaxian, Missile Command,* and *Battlezone,* video coin drop eclipsed pinball for the first time while nearly tripling for the second straight year to $2.8 billion.[57] Total units on location increased exponentially as well, from 164,600 in 1978 to 232,800 in 1979 to 540,600 in 1980.[58] Midway and Atari dominated the market, each taking a roughly 33% share in both 1979 and 1980. Coming in a distant third both years with around 10% of the market was Sega/Gremlin,[59] largely thanks to *Head On,* which was popular even though it did not hit the same heights as in Japan; *Monaco GP*; and *Astro Fighter,* a Data East shooter distributed by Gremlin in the United States that switched up the *Space Invaders* format by featuring multiple waves of enemy ships with different attack patterns.

For the first time, video games were not only leading the industry, but doing so with a diverse array of products featuring full-color graphics, impressive sound effects, challenging gameplay, and intense competition focused on placing initials on a high-score table. After years of being treated as a fad, video games could no longer be ignored by even the most conservative industry figures. As the video arcade game entered its golden age, the success of *Space Invaders* and its ilk also led a resurgence of video games in the home.

---

[56] Vending Times Census of the Industry, 1981, 56.
[57] Ibid.
[58] Ibid, 63.
[59] Bernstein & Co., 66.

30

Home Invasion

On February 11, 1980, the 87th annual Toy Fair opened in New York City, and some of the biggest stars of the show were a diverse array of handheld electronic games. In 1979, electronic game sales had exploded from $180 million in 1978 to $720 million, which translated into 16 million units sold.[1] Now every company in the toy business was scrambling to take a piece of the action.[2] Over 300 electronic games were displayed at the show. Mattel, which experienced great success with an update to its *Football* game in 1979, showcased updates to its basketball and soccer handhelds, while Coleco debuted a new series of head-to-head sports games that could be played by two people. Parker Brothers followed up its smash hit *Merlin* with a unit called *Split Second* that challenged the player to complete six different games in as short a time as possible. Milton Bradley continued to push its extremely popular *Simon*, the best-selling electronic game of 1979, alongside a game called *Milton* that featured speech.[3]

Analysts remained bullish on the handheld market for 1980 and expected sales to double once again. In contrast, the video game was increasingly seen as a stagnant product category destined to be displaced by electronic games on the low end and microcomputers on the high end. Indeed, one of the major arguments of video game companies in 1979 was that video games were a user-friendly steppingstone to a full-fledged home computer. All the major programmable console makers were acting to be sure they did not miss the home computer transition.

---

[1] Frost & Sullivan, 1983, 27–28.
[2] "Varied Marketing Strategies Key Growth of Electronics," *Playthings*, April 1980, 48.
[3] "Added Features Increase Attraction to Still Growing Electronics Field," *Playthings*, March 1980, 50–51.

When all was said and done, handheld factory sales did grow in 1980, but only to $1 billion.[4] As happened with calculators, watches, and dedicated video game consoles, increasing competition and improving technology drove a rush to the bottom on price and glutted the market with cheap products.[5] Video game sales, meanwhile, surged, growing from $233 million in retail sales in 1979 to $493 million in 1980.[6] While this still placed the video game market behind the electronic handheld market in total sales, it was catching up fast. The main instigator and benefactor of this surge was Atari, which continued to grow its commanding market share in the programmable console space and enjoyed complete dominance by the end of the year.

***

Atari's rise to power began in 1979 as it embarked on a new era under the watch of Ray Kassar. Although the VCS ultimately proved popular during Christmas 1978 despite retailer reluctance to stock it, the company still lost money on the year and owned a backlog of roughly 300,000 units sitting in warehouses. Kassar's first order of business was to clear out this backstock. To do so, he embarked on a campaign to turn video games into a year-round business rather than just a Christmas item. Atari launched a $2 million advertising campaign in the first quarter of 1979 focusing on its cartridge lineup and increased the number of available games from 20 to 32 by the middle of the year.[7]

As it had in 1978, Atari's programming team developed games in a diverse array of genres, though it was becoming more difficult to brainstorm new concepts. The lack of new coin-op hits left only secondary titles to port to the VCS such as a target shooting game that was essentially a reverse *Breakout* called *Canyon Bomber*, the prototyped but never released coin-operated game *Human Cannonball*, and a parachuting game called *Sky Diver*. The company also expanded its sports, board, and casino game lines with *Football, Bowling, Miniature Golf, Backgammon, Video Chess, Slot Machine*, and a collection of card games called *Casino*.[8] Of these games, *Video Chess* was the most surprising considering the limited VCS hardware and was driven by a consumer complaint that a chess piece was pictured on the VCS box despite no chess game being available for the system. Larry Wagner, the former manager of

[4] Frost & Sullivan, 1983, 33.

[5] Donna Leccese, "Electronic Toys Play Tough," *Playthings*, April 1981, 40.

[6] Frost & Sullivan, 1983, 23.

[7] "Electronics Overviews 1979," *Merchandising*, January 1979, 48.

[8] "Atari Adds 10 New Game Program Cartridges," *Playthings*, February 1979.

the VCS programmers, who now worked in an advanced projects group managed by Bob Brown, undertook the programming of the game and partnered with a chess master named Julio Kaplan to create as convincing an algorithm as possible on such a primitive system.[9]

Meanwhile, Bob Whitehead in the VCS programming group developed a new graphical technique that allowed all the pieces on the board to be displayed. Due to hardware limitations, the VCS can draw only five sprites on a scanline, so all 32 chess pieces could not be displayed at once at the start of the game. Larry Kaplan had already demonstrated that sprites could be reused multiple times on the screen via the "H-move" technique, but this only worked on vertical bands rather than horizontal. Whitehead realized that by drawing a different pattern of sprites on every other line, he could effectively double the number of objects on a horizontal band. Because this left noticeable gaps in objects that created a visual effect akin to viewing an object by peeking through a set of open blinds, this programming trick came to be known as the "Venetian blinds" technique.[10]

Selling video games as a year-round product fell to Atari's new VP of sales and marketing, Don Kingsborough. The son of an Oklahoma farmer who moved his family to California in 1940, Kingsborough lived in public housing for much of his childhood. Popular and personable in high school but not particularly studious, he attended the University of California at Berkeley in 1967 to avoid being drafted to fight in Vietnam. Upon graduation, he became a salesman for Westwood Pharmaceuticals and discovered a natural talent for relating to and negotiating with customers.[11] After a stint at Learjet, Kingsborough formed his own sales rep company in 1976 called DK Associates.[12]

Through a contact at Wells Fargo, Kingsborough was introduced to Atari as it began marketing its dedicated consoles in 1976 and secured the Northern California territory for DK Associates.[13] As one of the firm's more successful reps, he was brought into the company in early 1979 to replace Michael Shea and Don Thompson, who left in the wake of Bushnell's dismissal.[14]

---

[9] Larry Wagner, interview with Kevin Bunch, August 25, 2018 and Craig Nelson, interview with Kevin Bunch, 2019. Julio Kaplan also contributed to the *Backgammon* program, which was developed by Craig Nelson in the same advanced projects group as Wagner.

[10] "Design Case History," 1983, 49.

[11] Anthony Ramirez and Sarah Smith, "Top Gun in the Toy Business," *Fortune*, March 2, 1987, http://archive.fortune.com/magazines/fortune/fortune_archive/1987/03/02/68727/index.htm.

[12] Don Kingsborough, interview with the author, April 29, 2013.

[13] Ibid.

[14] "Consumer Electronics Personals," *Weekly Television Digest with Consumer Electronics*, January 8, 1979, 12.

Kingsborough's mandate was to move backlogged inventory by whatever means necessary, and his natural skills at discovering and meeting customers' needs played a critical role in making Atari's sales push a success.

With Atari's backstock woes largely solved by the middle of the year,[15] Kingsborough returned to his rep company, and Kassar brought in Black & Decker marketer Bill Grubb to take his place. A more traditional corporate executive, Grubb brought an understanding of product development and branding along with distribution contacts from a diverse array of retail outlets. When he arrived, Atari still did almost 50% of its business through Sears, probably in part because Kassar had more experience dealing with department stores from his Burlington days. Grubb and his right-hand man, national accounts manager and fellow Black & Decker alum Mark Bradlee, brought order and uniformity to the company's network of sales reps and distribution partners and pushed Atari products into mass market retailers like Walmart, Kmart, and Toys R Us.[16]

For the Christmas season, Atari increased co-op advertising dollars available to retailers, cut the price of the VCS by ten dollars to $180,[17] and launched promotions giving consumers who bought a VCS and returned the warranty card in the third quarter a voucher for five free Warner Records albums. Anyone who did so in the fourth quarter received coupons good for $2.50 off on five specific games.[18] These moves stirred retailer interest, and Atari sold out its entire stock of systems by early November.[19] Consumer interest was piqued by a major fall advertising campaign that ran through Christmas week on top-rated television shows like *Charlie's Angels, Dukes of Hazzard, Monday Night Football*, and the *Tonight Show*.[20] For the year, the company moved roughly 600,000 VCS systems, bringing the install base to a little over 1.3 million.[21]

Atari practically had the market to itself. After a lackluster year in 1978, Fairchild scrapped plans to introduce three new games at the January 1979 CES and was out of the video game business by April.[22] Leftover stock was sold to a firm called Zircon International that liquidated most of it during

[15]"Games & Computers," *Weekly Television Digest with Consumer Electronics*, June 11, 1979, 12.
[16]Grubb, 2014.
[17]Atari Programmable Game Price Cut 8%, *Merchandising*, July 1979, 103.
[18]They were *Black Jack, Basic Math, Flag Capture, Space War*, and *Surround*, which were presumably five of the worst-selling games on the console. "Atari ad," *Merchandising*, October 1979, 12.
[19]"Atari Has Sold Out," *Weekly Television Digest with Consumer Electronics*, November 5, 1979, 11.
[20]"Atari Saturates Airwaves with Video System Ads," *Playthings*, February 1980.
[21]Frost & Sullivan, 1983, 36.
[22]"Programmable Video Game," *Weekly Television Digest With Consumer Electronics*, April 2, 1979, 14.

the 1979 Christmas season. By then, Fairchild was no longer independent. Due to the erratic results of its consumer electronics ventures and its failure to transition to new semiconductor technologies, the company was losing money and its stock price was depressed. This made the firm a tempting takeover target, and a battery and ball bearing manufacturer looking to expand into electronics called Gould, Inc. made an aggressive offer. Wanting nothing to do with Gould, Fairchild sued to halt the takeover on antitrust grounds.[23] When that did not work, Fairchild CEO Wilf Corrigan turned to oil field services company Schlumberger Limited to serve as a "white knight." Schlumberger bought the company in October 1979 and continued to operate it as a subsidiary until 1987, when it was sold to National Semiconductor. It never again played a significant role in video games.

Meanwhile, Bally continued in the industry, but just barely. Early in the year, the company ended its home pinball line, which had never been profitable.[24] It introduced six new games for the Professional Arcade, most notably a port of the arcade game *Amazing Maze* and a *Football* program significantly more advanced than similar games on competing platforms.[25] It also teased the computer expansion again at CES only to once again decline to release it. By the middle of the year, the system had only achieved lifetime sales of 28,000 units, and Bally had yet to realize any profit.[26] The company remained in the business through the end of the year, but new CEO Bob Mullane was not interested in continuing to back a losing product. In August 1980, Bally sold the rights to the Bally Professional Arcade to a Columbus, Ohio, startup called Astrovision for $2.3 million.

Magnavox also nearly exited the business as Philips continued to show reluctance to continue in the video game industry. In fact, the company shut down all internal game development partway through the year as new Consumer Electronics Division President Kenneth Meinken, who took over the division after Alfred Di Scipio suddenly resigned in April 1978,[27] attempted to stem Magnavox's losses in consumer electronics. VP of Interactive Devices Mike Staup felt the industry still harbored great promise, however, and was able to keep game development going through an outside contractor named Ed Averett.[28]

---

[23] "Fairchild is Suing," *Weekly Television Digest with Consumer Electronics*, May 14, 1979, 14.
[24] "Bally is Leaving," *Weekly Television Digest with Consumer Electronics*, January 8, 1979, 9.
[25] "Bally," *Merchandising*, February 1979, 44.
[26] "Computers Score as Games," *Weekly Television Digest with Consumer Electronics*, January 15, 1979, 12.
[27] "Meinken to Magnavox," *Weekly Television Digest with Consumer Electronics*, May 1, 1978, 14.
[28] Staup, 1981, 233–234.

An electrical engineer with bachelor's and master's degrees from the University of Tennessee, Averett served in the army for two years and then took a job in marketing at Intel. As part of the sales and support staff for microprocessors, Averett became aware of the Odyssey² project and decided to leave Intel in April 1977 to become a freelance developer for the system alongside his wife, Linda, who was also an engineer. At the January 1978 CES, Averett approached Staup, and they agreed to enter a game development relationship.[29] The Averetts created most of the 11 games Magnavox introduced in 1979, including a maze game called *Take the Money and Run*, a shooting game called *Invaders from Hyperspace*, an obstacle avoidance game called *Alpine Skiing*, and a sports cartridge combining hockey and soccer games that featured two teams of stick figures rather than the typical ball-and-paddle gameplay.[30] Bolstered by its lineup of unique games, the Odyssey² was the only credible competitor to the VCS in 1979, but it still only moved 125,000 units.[31]

*** *

In 1979, Atari commanded approximately 80% of the cartridge market, but only 4 million total games were sold.[32] Home video games at the time generally fell into four categories: sports games that were too complicated to emulate well on current hardware; educational games that may have pleased parents but were of no interest to children; adaptations of existing pen-and-paper, board, and casino games that did little to improve on playing the original versions; and ports of coin-operated games sporting limited gameplay that held up better in a 90-second arcade session than in an extended home marathon. While certain games like Atari's *Combat* or Fairchild's *Spitfire* provided a few thrills when played against another person, most of the output of the six principle console producers was simply not that interesting.

While home games could not match coin-operated games in audiovisual quality and interesting control schemes, they did possess one attribute that set them apart: the ability to play for hours on end without having to constantly deposit quarters into a machine. Early console games remained tied to the arcade and its short play times and did not attempt to harness this aspect of home gaming, but in 1979, an Atari programmer named Warren Robinett changed that.

[29] Ed Averett, Testimony, Atari, Inc. v. North American Philips Consumer Electronics Corp., No. 81-6434 (N.D. Ill), November 30, 1981.

[30] "Magnavox," *Merchandising*, October 1979, 66.

[31] Frost & Sullivan, 1983, 37.

[32] Ibid, 36.

Born in 1951, Joseph Warren Robinett, Jr. first encountered computers through a partnership between his high school and the University of Missouri in which the students wrote programs that were sent to the university for execution. At age 16, he attended a National Science Foundation summer math camp that cemented his desire to pursue an education in mathematics and computer science. Robinett matriculated to Rice University in Texas, where he designed his own major, computer applications to language and art, by taking a lot of programming and art courses. He then attended the University of California at Berkeley and earned his master's degree in computer science with a specialization in computer graphics in 1976.[33]

Robinett joined Atari in November 1977 as part of the second wave of VCS programmers hired by the company. Soon after completing his first game, the *Combat* variant *Slot Racers*, he was introduced to the text-based *Adventure* game at SAIL by a roommate who was a Stanford graduate student. Robinett decided to adapt the game to the VCS as his next project. When he proposed the game to the new head of the VCS programming group, an older engineer from Lockheed named George Simcock, it was rejected because Simcock could not see how a game that took up hundreds of kilobytes on a mainframe computer could be squeezed into a 4K cartridge. Robinett ignored his boss and began working on the adaptation anyway.[34]

Robinett began by distilling *Adventure* down to its core elements, which he saw as moving through a series of interconnected rooms to collect objects. To replicate this gameplay on the VCS, he decided that each room should take up the entire screen and that using the joystick to move off the edge of the screen in one of the four cardinal directions would substitute for the movement commands of the text *Adventure* and bring the player into another room. Likewise, running into an object would allow the player to pick it up in lieu of a text command. *Adventure* implemented an inventory system, but Robinett believed that leaving the action to sift through a collection of items was not conducive to an exciting console experience, so he decided the player would only be able to carry one item at a time. Knowing he would need to save his limited number of player sprites for objects and obstacles, he used the ball sprite for the player's avatar, which was consequently rendered as a featureless yellow square.[35]

---

[33] Jaz Rignall, "'Could they fire me? No!' The Warren Robinette Interview," US Gamer, January 2, 2016, https://www.usgamer.net/articles/warren-robinett-interview.

[34] Ibid.

[35] Ibid.

After about a month of work, Robinett had a basic prototype in place in which the square could move between the rooms of a maze and collide with objects. At this point he revealed his work to Simcock, who was not happy to be disobeyed Dejected, Robinett took a month off even though he was told there was no guarantee the company would hold his job. When he returned, he learned that marketing loved his prototype. Robinett use his technology to create a Superman game, as Atari desired a tie-in product for the *Superman* movie being developed by Warner Brothers.[36] Robinett resisted until a compromise was reached to have another programmer, John Dunn, turn the prototype into a *Superman* product while Robinett continued to build his *Adventure* game.[37] Released in 1979,[38] the *Superman* game incorporated the multi-screen movement and object interaction developed by Robinett but featured unremarkable gameplay.

Meanwhile, Robinett spent four months barely working on *Adventure* at all. His prototype featured a castle that the player could only explore after acquiring a key and a dragon that could chase the player, but though the multi-screen world was revolutionary, the limited gameplay was not fun. He finally broke the stalemate by changing the interaction between the dragon and the player by adding a sword that could slay the dragon. He then expanded the world by creating two more castles, two more keys, and two more dragons. In response to a bug that could cause a player to drop an item in an unreachable spot, he also added a magnet that can pull in a nearby object.[39] Rounding out the items is a magic bridge that allows the player to pass through certain walls, which was an homage to a magic rod that extended a bridge in the original text-based game.[40] Late in development Robinett added a bat that can pick up items and move them to another part of the maze to add an element of randomness to the proceedings. The objective of the game became locating an enchanted chalice being held in one of the three castles and bringing it safely to a fourth castle.[41]

During the period Robinett worked on *Adventure*, dissent was brewing in the programming group over recognition for developing hit games. Both

[36] Robinett, Warren, *Making the Dragon: How I built the first action-adventure game, planted the first easter egg, and helped launch the video-game revolution*, unpublished draft 1.0.3, 2019.

[37] Warren Robinett, *Inventing the Adventure Game: The Design of Adventure and Rocky's Boots*, unpublished manuscript, 1984, ebook, chap 3.

[38] "Atari," *Merchandising*, June 1979, 90.

[39] Rignall, 2016.

[40] Robinett, 1984, chap. 3.

[41] Robinett called this chalice the "Holy Grail," but marketing changed it to the more generic enchanted chalice.

Atari and its competitors preferred to keep the identities of their programmers a secret for fear of headhunting and would not allow them to be credited on their projects. This incensed the skilled game developers who worked long hours to brainstorm game ideas, complete every aspect of the product from game mechanics to graphics and sounds, and develop the programming tricks and shortcuts that extended the capabilities of the VCS far beyond what its designers had thought possible. As an act of rebellion, Robinett decided to leave his signature in the game.[42]

Deep in the final castle, Robinett placed a room only accessible using the magic bridge. Within this room lies an item one pixel in size colored the same gray as the background of most of the game. If that pixel is brought to a specific room in the world, a solid wall becomes passable and the player can enter a new room with the words "Created by Warren Robinett" displayed across the screen. Robinett figured Atari would eventually discover the message and remove it so that no consumer would ever see it, but at least he left his mark.

Robinett left Atari shortly after completing the design of *Adventure*, and Atari released the game in early 1980.[43] By 1981, Atari had received reports about the hidden room. Management was furious, but there was little they could do since Robinett had already departed the company and was not receiving any royalties. Unlike the marketing department, the new head of the VCS programming group, Steve Wright, saw the hidden room as an opportunity. He realized that players would probably enjoy searching out hidden secrets in games and likened the act of doing so to participating in an Easter egg hunt. Wright began encouraging all his programmers to put what he called "Easter eggs" in their games and began publicizing their existence in the press. While not the first game to include a secret, *Adventure* defined the concept of Easter eggs and led to their widespread adoption not just in video games, but in all forms of media.[44]

---

[42] Rignall, 2016.

[43] Some sources give a release date of 1979 based on Robinett's recollections of completing the game that year. All evidence points to an early 1980 release. Sam Derboo, "Adventure, a game released in the year of wedontknow," Hardcore Gaming 101 Blog, July 17, 2012, http://blog.hardcoregaming101. net/2012/07/adventure-game-released-in-year-of.html, and "Electronic Toys Zing Out Loud and Clear During CES," *Playthings*, March, 1980, 102.

[44] The first game to include a secret accessible through a hidden command was most likely the Fairchild Channel F game *Spitfire*, in which programmer Michael Glass hid his name. Due to a hardware limitation, however, the secret text was not accessible on the system. A handful of other secrets also preceded the Easter egg *Adventure*, but none of them were widely discovered or publicized. RT-55J, "I found an Easter egg from 1977," Select Button, August 7, 2019, https://selectbutton. net/t/i-found-an-easter-egg-from-1977/8828.

***

When Ray Kassar was elevated to CEO of Atari in January 1979, it created a crisis for the Consumer Electronics Division, which was now leaderless. While individual actors like Bill Grubb kept the division on track in their areas of responsibility, other managers were not pulling their weight and gaps were appearing in middle management as the company grew rapidly. In mid-1979, Kassar hired an older lawyer named Don Winn to run Consumer, but he was overmatched in the job and barely lasted five weeks.[45] In November, Kassar tried again with an executive named Michael Moone.

A graduate of Xavier University in Cincinnati with degrees in political science and economics, Moone joined toymaker Mattel right out of college in 1969 as an account manager.[46] In 1971, he moved on to Milton Bradley as a national accounts manager for subsidiaries Whiting and Amsco Industries, which produced crafts and dolls, respectively, as well as for select accounts in the Game Division. In 1974, he was promoted to assistant division manager of Whiting.[47] After his mentor at Whiting, George Ditomassi, became general manager of the Game Division, Moone became Ditomassi's assistant in 1976 and was promoted to national sales manager in 1978.[48]

Moone was first recruited for Atari in early 1978 to serve in the role Ray Kassar ultimately filled, but he turned down the job both because he was worried that Atari had still not fully embraced the programmable market over dedicated consoles and because he had not been in a high-level management job long enough to prove to himself he was up to the task. In early 1979, Ditomassi became senior vice president for marketing at Milton Bradley, and Moone succeeded him as vice president and general manager of the Game Division.[49] By the time Atari approached him again in late 1979, he felt more confident in both himself and Atari's place in the market and also felt certain he had topped out at Milton Bradley, so he took the job.[50]

Upon joining Atari, Moone immediately began cleaning house by firing underperforming managers and staffing up the division in areas it was deficient. The division's biggest weakness was its inability to deliver product in a timely manner to distributors and retailers, so Moone focused on smoothing out the entire product development and production cycle. He then harnessed

---

[45] Grubb, 2014.
[46] Moone, 2013.
[47] "People," *Toy & Hobby World*, November 1974, 42.
[48] "People," *Playthings*, April 1978, 98.
[49] "People," *Toy & Hobby World*, February 1979.
[50] Moone, 2013.

his talent for building personal relationships to visit all the toy retailers he had worked with during his Milton Bradley days and reassure them that Atari would be a more reliable partner in the future. He also worked to convince them that video games could become a year-round product category.[51] He was greatly aided in the latter task by the imminent arrival of Atari's conversion of the hit coin-op game *Space Invaders*.

While Atari had converted nearly all its own coin-operated games of any popularity to play on the VCS by the end of 1979, it had never occurred to any company in the industry to license another company's product for release. This was not really an oversight, as there had probably not been a game worth licensing before Taito's coin-op juggernaut. Warner executive Manny Gerard changed that after noticing on one of his many visits to Atari how popular *Space Invaders* was with the engineers in the employee game room. Hit by a sudden brainwave, he marched over to Ray Kassar's office and told him they needed to license the game right away. Kassar saw the value immediately and negotiated a deal with Taito to release the game on the VCS.[52]

When it came time to program the game, management was surprised to discover there was a version already in development by Rick Maurer, who joined Atari from Fairchild after the semiconductor firm shut down its video game development. While casting about for a first project to do at Atari, Maurer played *Space Invaders* in the arcade and was instantly hooked. He received permission to create a version for the VCS and implemented most of the gameplay over the course of several months.[53] The finished product played remarkably closely to the arcade game because Maurer discovered that the H-move technique Larry Kaplan developed to reuse sprites across multiple horizontal lines could be strobed to repeat sprites within the same line as well since the system did not have any screen memory and would not realize that sprite had already been used. This technique had limited utility because it could only be used to replicate identical objects moving vertically in unison, but it was perfect for the descending rows of aliens in *Space Invaders*.[54] The only downside was that the game suffered from a high amount of flicker. Despite the quality of the game, however, no one else in the group played it much, and it was not slated for production.

---

[51] Ibid.

[52] Gerard, 2017.

[53] "Reminiscing from Richard Maurer," Giant List Archive, January 5, 1999, https://dadgum.com/giantlist/archive/maurer.html.

[54] Nick Montfort and Ian Bogost, *Racing the Beam: The Atari Video Computer System* (Cambridge, MA: MIT Press, 2009), 73.

Maurer turned his attention to a second game called *Maze Craze* based on a maze game developed for the Channel F while Maurer was at Fairchild. When Kassar closed the *Space Invaders* licensing deal with Taito, Maurer dusted off his prototype, fixed the flickering graphics, improved the alien art and the sound effects, and created several gameplay variations. Atari released the game in March 1980 and spent $1 million on a television advertising campaign in major media markets focused on the game.[55] The company also offered the game for $30 rather than the old standard of $20, taking advantage of its brand recognition to establish a new price point necessary to combat inflation and an increased cost of materials.

Although Maurer's *Space Invaders* features somewhat blocky graphics and only 36 aliens instead of 55, it captures all the basic elements of the arcade game, including the bunkers, bonus flying saucers, and slowly descending aliens that increase in speed as they are destroyed. This made it not only a fun and challenging game but also an excellent practice platform for high score chasers able to save their quarters by honing their skills at home. As a result, the game not only became the hottest selling cartridge for the VCS in short order, but it also spurred new sales of the system, which the company returned to its original suggested retail price of $190 on April 1.[56] Bolstered by a multi-million dollar advertising campaign that began after Labor Day, *Space Invaders* sold 1.25 million units before the end of 1980, while the VCS moved over 1 million units to nearly double its install base to over 2 million. This meant roughly half of all VCS owners purchased *Space Invaders*.[57]

For the year, Atari captured 67% of the console market and 79% of the cartridge market by dollar volume. Magnavox, despite spending $1 million on its first significant advertising campaign for the Odyssey,[2] could only capture roughly 10% of the market, selling 160,000 units of its console.[58] Most of the rest of the market was seized by a newcomer to the business: toy company and electronic handheld powerhouse Mattel, which adopted a different strategy from Atari that factored in the burgeoning market for computers in the home.

---

[55] "Atari Completes Promotion for Video Computers," *Playthings*, June 1980.
[56] "Electronic Games," *Weekly Television Digest with Consumer Electronics*, February 11, 1980, 10.
[57] Frost & Sullivan, 1983, 38.
[58] Ibid, 39.

31

Intelligent Television

On August 9, 1977, a group of engineers from Cyan Engineering and the microelectronics department of the Atari Consumer Division promulgated the basic parameters for a new hardware project codenamed Colleen after spending several months brainstorming the next step for Atari after the VCS.[1] While Atari's first programmable console was only just being launched, the pace of video game development had progressed rapidly between 1975 and 1977 from simple dedicated consoles to full-fledged programmables, and the Atari engineers worried the VCS would already be obsolete after just three years on the market. During the same period, the microcomputer market began its transition from kits to fully assembled systems suitable for the general consumer. Atari now faced a dilemma: should its new system be a more advanced video game or a home computer? When presented this question, Nolan Bushnell and Joe Keenan decided it should be both.[2] "Colleen" was the result: a new home system planned to ship in two configurations as both an entertainment machine and a serious computer.

Jay Miner once again led the design of the new Atari system, ably assisted by Joe Decuir. One of the primary areas they wanted to upgrade compared to the VCS was its graphics capability by including more RAM and a frame buffer to allow for a bitmapped screen. As a bitmap was not necessarily the best option to render graphics in all situations, they also decided to incorporate character-based graphics and boost the machine's sprite-generating capability.[3] To achieve these graphics, Miner and Decuir designed two new chips.

[1] Goldberg and Vendel, 2012, "Technical Report: Atari's Entry into Home Computers."

[2] Mayer, 2018.

[3] Vintage Computer Federation, "VCF East 2019 – Joe Decuir – Atari 800 Series Computers: 40 Years," filmed May 5, 2019, YouTube video, posted May 6, 2019, https://www.youtube.com/watch?v=dlVpu_QSHyw.

The new ANTIC chip was designed to control the background graphics, which could either be bitmapped or character based. The chip could also switch graphics modes on the fly as it drew the screen so that, for example, a player score could be displayed at the top of the screen in a character-based mode while the main playfield was portrayed as a bitmap. The second chip was an improvement on the video chip in the VCS called the CTIA, which provided the colors for the background graphics from a palette of 128 and generated up to four 8-bit player objects and four 2-bit missile objects that could be superimposed on the background and update independently from the rest of the screen. The combination of these two chips would allow for fast action gameplay set against detailed, colorful backdrops.[4]

As breadboarding began on the chips, a brainstorming meeting was held at Pajaro Dunes on November 29 in which the specifications for the two systems were finalized. The computer system, which retained the name "Colleen," would feature 4K of RAM, a built-in keyboard, four controller ports, an audio cassette interface, and a serial interface allowing it to connect to peripherals like printers and disk drives. The low-end system, dubbed "Candy," would be a pure video game console lacking the serial interface or keyboard, though it would be possible to connect a keyboard through two of the controller ports.[5]

By January 1978, a large team was tackling the chips for the system under the leadership of Jay Miner, including Joe Decuir and Francois Michel on the ANTIC, George McLeod on the CTIA, and Doug Neubauer on the POKEY chip designed to handle paddle control and keyboard inputs as well as audio. The architectures of both Colleen and Candy were largely complete by the middle of the year, and in November they acquired their official names: the Atari 400 and 800 Personal Computer System.[6] Atari revealed the 400 and 800 to the world at a press conference in New York on December 14 at which Nolan Bushnell emphasized their capabilities as game machines. The company announced the computers would be available in August 1979 and priced at $500 for the 400 and $1,000 for the 800.[7] The line between video games and home computers had already begun to blur and now looked like it might disappear entirely.

**

---

[4] Ibid.
[5] Goldberg and Vendel, 2012, "Technical Report: Atari's Entry into Home Computers."
[6] Ibid.
[7] "New CES Products," December 18, 1978.

By 1978, the transition from kits to fully integrated computers like the TRS-80 and Apple II appeared to presage a world in which pure video game systems would be supplanted by home computers that could play all the same games and balance the checkbook too. This line of thinking produced the Bally Professional Arcade and the Odyssey², which both promised to offer certain features of a home computer like a keyboard or a tape drive as either a core component of the system or an add on and were marketed as intermediate products to ease the transition to a home computer. It also spurred APF, still hanging in the programmable market despite negligible market share, to release a docking station in 1979 called the Imagination Machine to transform its MP-1000 game console into a home computer through the addition of 8 KB of RAM, a tape drive, and a keyboard at a cost of $499. Atari did little to reposition its system as a computer, merely supplying "keyboard" controllers for the VCS in 1978 and a *Basic Programming* cartridge developed by Warren Robinett in 1979, but it was also developing its 400 and 800 computers.

For Mattel Electronics, the emergence of console-computer hybrids presented an opportunity to enter the video game space by establishing its own niche through a system featuring better graphics than competing systems from Fairchild and Atari while offering longer and richer gameplay experiences. In May 1977, Mattel Electronics head Ed Krakauer worked with Richard Chang and David Chandler from the Mattel Toys Design & Development Department to define the basic parameters of such a system, after which Chandler was charged with developing it.[8]

Chandler began by surveying the current state of video game chip technology. At the time, National Semiconductor was just breadboarding a new graphics chipset that appeared promising but was expensive at $46.00 per unit. At the June CES, Chandler examined two more chipsets, one from MOS Technology that did not incorporate sprites and a chip created by Stephen Maine of General Instruments called the Standard Television Interface Adapter, or STIC, that was cheap at $25.00 a pop, but lacked graphics RAM. Over the next couple of months, Chandler worked with National to develop a simplified version of its chip and with GI to add video RAM and make a few minor modifications to STIC. These changes altered the price of the two chips to $33.00 and $30.00, respectively. Chandler decided to go with the National chipset, but the meeting to close the deal in August turned into a

---

[8] David Chandler, "Intellivision History and Philosophy," internal company memo, c. 1982.

panicked National telling Mattel that entering the video game business was no longer a good idea.[9]

Mattel Toys President Ray Wagner decided to place the console project on hold, but Chandler remained in contact with GI. After GI delivered a more positive report on the state of the video game industry in October, Wagner reinstated the project with a mandate to have something ready to show at Toy Fair in February 1978.[10] With little time to complete a prototype, Chandler approached a firm called APh Technological Consulting Company established by Caltech graduates Glen Hightower and John Denker in 1975 to connect Caltech students with businesses that could benefit from their services.[11] APh had already been working on Mattel's handheld line; now it turned its attention to developing the software for what was currently being called the Mattel Electronics Cartridge Video Game.

Hightower assigned David Rolfe, late of Technical Magic, to develop an Exec program for the system to handle basic software functions. Needing a game to test the Exec, Rolfe also began developing a baseball game at the same time. Graphics were provided by David James, the Mattel designer who supplied the art for the Mattel handheld games as well. Drawing on his experiences developing *Star Fire* for Exidy, Rolfe developed routines for moving objects around the screen, creating sound and music, loading graphics from RAM, and other essential elements of creating a video game to ease the burden on the creators of individual titles. For Toy Fair, where Mattel displayed its technology behind closed doors, Rolfe created a basic running man demo to highlight the capabilities of the system.[12]

After Rolfe finished the Exec, APh hired four Caltech students to program the first round of games for the system.[13] In May, Mattel announced it would unveil the Mattel Electronics Cartridge Video Game at the June CES, and that a limited release would follow in the fall at a wholesale price of $160.[14] Just a few weeks later, delays in completing the chipset at GI forced Mattel to cancel the unveiling and scratch a 1978 release entirely.[15]

In September 1978, Mattel Electronics was elevated from a marketing unit to its own division within Mattel Toys. Ed Krakauer remained with the division as its general manager, while another executive, Jeffrey Rochlis,

[9] Ibid.

[10] Ibid.

[11] "Alumnus Designs Devices for the Deaf," *Caltech News*, April 1975, 2.

[12] Stilphen, 2004.

[13] Ibid.

[14] "Mattel's Video Game," *Weekly Television Digest with Consumer Electronics*, May 15, 1978, 10.

[15] "Mattel Game Scratched," *Weekly Television Digest with Consumer Electronics*, June 12, 1978, 13.

was elevated to the presidency.[16] A theater major in college, Rochlis spent three years in the Army before breaking into the advertising business with Benton and Bowles in 1970. After spending time as an account supervisor at McCann-Erickson, he became the vice president of marketing for the Aurora Products Division of Nabisco in 1973. In late 1976, Krakauer recruited Rochlis to serve as marketing director for new business development at Mattel Toys.[17] In this role, he was integral to marketing Mattel's handheld game line and championed the programmable console project with upper Mattel management.

In December, Rochlis announced the full extent of Mattel's console plans. In addition to a base console expected to retail for $230, the company planned to introduce a keyboard add on that would turn the system into an entry-level computer for a total cost of $500.[18] The plan was to have the system on the market by the second quarter of 1979, but in truth Mattel was unlikely to meet this release schedule because the STIC and RAM chips for the system were still not ready.

The console was publicly unveiled at the January 1979 CES. By the June CES, the retail price of the system had risen to $250 and deliveries were promised by August.[19] That month, Mattel announced GTE Sylvania would be manufacturing the system,[20] which was now being called the Intellivision, a combination of the words "Intelligent Television." Production was subsequently delayed to September. In October, the console was still nowhere to be seen as Mattel announced a final price hike to $275 and the imminent start of test markets in New York, Chicago, Los Angeles, San Francisco, Philadelphia, Baltimore, and Washington, DC.[21]

In November, Mattel finally had to admit that Intellivision would not roll out in large numbers in 1979. While the chipset was finally ready to go, GI had not yet been able to ramp up production and produce it in large quantities.[22] Rather than multiple test markets across the United States backed by print and television advertising as originally planned, Mattel's manufacturing partner Sylvania introduced a limited number of units under its own name through a single department store chain, Gottschalks headquartered in

[16] "Consumer Electronics Personals," *Weekly Television Digest with Consumer Electronics*, October 2, 1978, 14.

[17] "People," *Playthings*, January 1977, 71.

[18] "Computer Games," *Weekly Television Digest with Consumer Electronics*, December 4, 1978, 11.

[19] "TI Computer at CES," *Weekly Television Digest with Consumer Electronics*, May 21, 1979, 13.

[20] "Sylvania to TV Games," *Weekly Television Digest with Consumer Electronics*, August 27, 1978, 10.

[21] "Mattel Hiked Prices," *Weekly Television Digest with Consumer Electronics*, October 15, 1979, 10.

[22] "Mattel Delay," *Weekly Television Digest with Consumer Electronics*, November 12, 1979, 11.

Fresno, California. Mattel and Sylvania partnered with the store because they could not guarantee how many systems would reach retail, and Gottschalks proved an understanding partner.[23] Mattel sold 50,000 systems on the year.[24]

Upon release, the Intellivision was powered by a 16-bit GI CP1610 microprocessor with a 10-bit bus. The heart of the unit was the oft-delayed STIC chip, capable of a display resolution of 159 × 96, colorful tiled backgrounds of up to 16 colors, and the generation of eight hardware sprites, which GI called MOBs. Like the Odyssey², the system stored a set of alphanumeric characters and basic shapes in a ROM chip, but it also included 512 bytes of graphics RAM to allow individual games to load custom graphics into memory. Additional system memory included 352 bytes of system RAM and 240 bytes of scratchpad RAM to temporarily store calculations. The Exec occupied two 2K ROM chips of its own. Sound was provided by a programmable sound generator (PSG) capable of outputting three channels.

Four games were available for the system at launch, *Las Vegas Poker & Blackjack*, which was bundled with the system, *Backgammon*, *Math Fun*, and a *Tank* variant called *Armor Battle* featuring colorful background graphics and varying movement speeds on different types of terrain. To control these games, Mattel developed a novel controller consisting of a directional pad in the shape of a disk that allowed movement in 16 directions, four action buttons on the sides of the controller, and a 12-button keypad to perform special functions in individual games. To help players keep track of special commands, each cartridge that used the keypad shipped with an overlay outlining the commands for each button.

In March 1980, Mattel executed a limited launch of the Intellivision under its own name in select department stores around the country.[25] Full nationwide distribution began that August.[26] Mattel supported the system with television advertising in select markets that emphasized its potential as a cheap, easy-to-use computer.[27]

By the end of 1980, 19 games were available for the system. To raise the profile of these products, many of them sported licenses from organizations relevant to the subject of the game, the first widespread use of licenses in the video game industry. *Baseball* was rebranded *Major League Baseball*, while *Backgammon* was renamed *ABPA Backgammon* after a backgammon

[23] Ed Krakauer, interview with the author, October 7, 2016.

[24] Frost & Sullivan, 1983, 36.

[25] "Video, home entertainment systems play the price is right," *Playthings*, April 1980, 54–55.

[26] Chandler, 1982.

[27] "Mattel Charts Intellivision Debut," *Advertising Age*, January 14, 1980, 75.

player's association. Other branded games in the launch lineup included *NFL Football, NBA Basketball, NASL Soccer, PGA Golf, NHL Hockey,* and two education titles sponsored by The Electric Company, *Math Fun* and *Word Fun.* Other titles included *Checkers, Horse Racing, Las Vegas Roulette, Tennis, Auto Racing,* and two action-strategy games that combine movement on a strategic map with arcade-style combat, *Space Battle* and *Sea Battle.*

The long delay in bringing the Intellivision to market took its toll on the Mattel Electronics staff. The company originally hired Malcom Kuhn as sales director soon after his dismissal from Atari, but he left the company mid-1979 as he grew frustrated at the continued delays in getting the Intellivision to market.[28] In mid-1980, Mattel Electronics Marketing VP Tim Huber left the company as well. The exodus reached its high point in the fall when both Jeff Rochlis and Ed Krakauer left the company. Rochlis left to create a new electronic game company with the Doyles, who had brought Parker Brothers into electronic games, while Krakauer returned to consulting. These defections wreaked havoc with Mattel's sales and marketing plans and contributed to low-consumer awareness and sluggish sales. The situation was exacerbated by a high defect rate on the first manufacturing run and the initial positioning of the product as a low-cost home computer despite the keyboard component still being nowhere in sight.

In September 1980, Joshua Denham assumed the presidency of Mattel Electronics.[29] A Mattel veteran who joined the firm in 1965,[30] Denham had at various times run distribution and Far East operations and since 1972 had been serving as VP of Operations for Mattel Toys,[31] where he played a critical role in holding the company together alongside Ray Wagner as the legal drama surrounding the Handlers unfolded in the mid-1970s. In his operations role, Denham became intimately familiar with the electronic handheld business,[32] making him a logical choice to succeed Rochlis and Krakauer at Mattel Electronics.

Denham's new VP of sales and marketing was Frank O'Connell, a Cornell graduate with broad experience in consumer product marketing who knew Ed Krakauer from their shared time in the food products industry. O'Connell's first move on joining the company was to run market research

---

[28] Kuhn, 2013.

[29] "Denham Appointed President of Mattel Electronics," *Playthings*, October 1980, 92.

[30] "Denham Becomes New President at Mattel Electronics," *Toy & Hobby World*, September 1980, 28.

[31] "Mattel Lists Major Shifts in Officers," 1973.

[32] Denham, *Toy & Hobby World*, September 1980.

on Intellivision and its main competitor, the VCS. In the process, he discovered that consumers were not particularly interested in the Intellivision as a home computer but did see it as a superior video game machine to the VCS due to its improved graphics.[33] O'Connell and Denham decided the best way to proceed was a series of head-to-head commercials showcasing the superior graphics of the Intellivision vis-à-vis the VCS.[34]

Head-to-head advertising had recently made waves in the toy industry in December 1979 when Coleco ran a commercial comparing *Electronic Quarterback* to Mattel's *Football* game to point out the advanced features of its handheld compared to the older Mattel model.[35] That commercial notwithstanding, comparative advertising was simply not done in the toy industry at the time. Indeed, when Denham brought the concept to the advertising agency, it initially refused to produce such an ad and tried to convince Denham that it was a terrible idea. Denham responded that he was leaving on a four-day trip to Japan, and when he returned, he would have a comparative concept or would be looking for a new agency.[36]

Once the concept was in place, Mattel Electronics required a spokesperson to lead the commercial. Someone recommended George Plimpton, who had become a minor celebrity as a literary critic and sportswriter known for his erudition and adventurous spirit. O'Connell called Plimpton, who turned out to be an avid gamer. O'Connell brought some games to Plimpton's club, and the duo played them all night. Plimpton agreed to do the commercials on the spot, though formal negotiations still had to go through Plimpton's agent. In the end, Plimpton agreed to do the ad for an incredibly reasonable rate.[37]

Denham and O'Connell felt they had one real shot to turn around perception on Intellivision before it became the latest in a long line of also-rans in the programmable console market. Therefore, they convinced Mattel it was critical to blanket the airwaves during the holiday season and secured a $3.5 million advertising budget.[38] Starting in late November,[39] millions of Americans watched as Plimpton walked up to two screens demonstrating Atari's and Mattel's baseball and football programs side-by-side. The Atari products featured crude, mostly black backgrounds and a small number of

---

[33] Frank O'Connell, interview with the author, July 13, 2016.
[34] O'Connell, 2016, and Joshua Denham, interview with the author, February 28, 2017.
[35] "Coleco Airs Football Comparison Spot," *Playthings*, February 1980, 29.
[36] Denham, 2017.
[37] O'Connell, 2016.
[38] Frost & Sullivan, 1983, 39.
[39] Ibid.

flickering players, while the Mattel games sported colorful playfields and sharp, well-animated character graphics. Plimpton declared Mattel the winner, and many consumers could not help but agree.

The Plimpton commercials had an immediate impact on sales of Intellivision, which by the end of the year sold out its complete stock of 190,000 units alongside 1 million cartridges. This gave Mattel roughly 20% of the console market by dollar volume and 11% of the cartridge market.[40] While it still trailed Atari, it looked set to become the biggest threat to the market leader's total dominance. Meanwhile, a second threat was brewing as Atari suffered a series of defections by members of its programming staff who pioneered a new concept in video game development: the third-party software publisher.

---

[40] Frost & Sullivan, 1983, 39.

32

Active Television

In September 1978, Atari's computer project faced a crisis. The company had publicly announced it would introduce the Personal Computer System at the January CES, but the programmers hired to develop its operating system (OS) had failed to provide a working piece of software. Project leader Jay Miner could tell the OS would not be ready for the debut of the computer absent drastic action. George Simcock, the head of the VCS programming group, saved the day by volunteering three of his own programmers to complete the job: Alan Miller, Larry Kaplan, and David Crane.[1]

These three were not chosen randomly; they were some of the finest programmers working on the VCS. Kaplan, the first VCS programmer hired, had figured out the trick for displaying more sprites on the screen using H-move. Miller, a North Carolina native with an electrical engineering degree from UC Berkeley, specialized in large-scale computer systems in college and worked extensively with hardware before joining Atari, developing a control system for a lumber mill, doing computer contracts with NASA, and working for National Semiconductor.[2] His 1978 *Basketball* game for the VCS was a graphical marvel by the standards of the system, with reasonably human-looking players dribbling and shooting in a one-on-one competition.

Kaplan and Miller were part of the first batch of programmers hired to work on the VCS. David Crane joined in the second wave. A native of Indiana, Crane began dabbling with electronics when he was 12 years old and once built an unbeatable tic-tac-toe machine for a science fair. He was also an avid game player who often modified the rules of the board games that he played with his friends. After graduating from DeVry School of Technology

---

[1] Backiel, 2003.
[2] Bloom, *Invaders*, 1982, 50–51.

in Phoenix, Arizona, he took a job with National Semiconductor designing linear circuits, where he worked with Alan Miller.[3] They remained in touch after Miller joined Atari, as they lived in the same apartment complex and often played tennis together. In mid-1977, Miller asked Crane to proofread an Atari job ad, and Crane decided to apply.[4] He joined the programming group in fall 1977 and created three games, *Outlaw*, *Canyon Bomber*, and *Slot Machine*.

Over the course of 12 grueling weeks, Miller, Kaplan, and Crane wrote and debugged a complete operating system for the Personal Computer System with a little assistance from fellow VCS programmer Ian Shephard, former VCS programmer Gary Palmer, and a consultant named Harry Stewart.[5] They also selected a BASIC for the system, choosing a firm called Shephardson Microsystems rather than Microsoft because Kaplan did not like that the company's 6502 BASIC had been machine converted from the 8080 version rather than coded from scratch.[6] The trio also developed some of the first games for the system, with Miller contributing a port of his *Basketball* game and Kaplan providing a port of *Super Breakout* and a drawing program called *Video Easel*.[7]

Kaplan, Miller, and Crane finished their work on the OS just as Ray Kassar was assuming control of Atari as CEO. The beginning of his tenure was marked by a freeze on much of the company's short-term R&D and design work so the company could focus on exploiting the VCS and bringing the 400 and 800 Personal Computer Systems to market. This decision sent shockwaves through the Atari product development apparatus. Bob Brown, who had been eased out as director of microelectronics in 1978 and placed in charge of an R&D group called the advanced projects division,[8] left the company in January when his department was cut.[9] Larry Wagner, who also worked in the advanced projects group, followed him out the door. In February, Jay Miner also departed, unhappy that Ray Kassar would not let him begin work on a 16-bit computer design because the company had not even brought its 8-bit computers to market yet, and Kassar wanted a better sense of where Atari would fit into the new market before authorizing

---

[3] Ibid, 51.

[4] Crane, 2018.

[5] Backiel, 2003.

[6] Kaplan, 2018.

[7] Crane also developed a product that bundled a port of *Canyon Bomber* with a take on the classic mainframe *Artillery* game, but it was not released at that time.

[8] Crane, 2018 and Nelson 2019.

[9] Bloom, "Cutoffs," 1982, 48.

a next-generation project.[10] His fellow chip designer, Joe Decuir, departed a few months later to start his own company after becoming interested in network communications technology and sensing he would not be given the opportunity to pursue the field at Atari.[11]

Many of the VCS programmers were also unhappy because the removal of Brown from a management role and the elimination of the microelectronics group in 1978 had placed them under the jurisdiction of consumer engineering, where most of the management and staff were analog and industrial engineers rather than digital hardware experts and did not appear to fully understand complex digital computer systems or appreciate what the programmers were accomplishing on the VCS. They were also unhappy with their financial compensation. In 1977, there had been talk with Joe Keenan and Bob Brown of a bonus pool generated from VCS hardware and software sales. When the VCS struggled a bit and the consumer division lost money, those promises were quickly forgotten. In the aftermath, a written bonus plan was created in 1978 based on hitting a set of vaguely defined goals, but no money was ever paid out.[12] A few top programmers were given bonuses under the table in early 1979 after mounting discontent, but the raw feelings remained.[13]

Lack of recognition also stung some of the programmers. In the VCS group, a single programmer created a game from start to finish. This meant not only developing the concept and gameplay and writing the code, but also providing all the graphics, sound effects, and music. The job was made even more difficult by the limitations of the VCS hardware, which required a programmer to count cycles and implement clever tricks in order to make a system designed to play only *Pong* and *Tank* recreate the latest arcade hits. This turned out to be a rare skillset, and the top programmers in the VCS division took pride in their accomplishments. Management recognized this talent to an extent, but Atari feared headhunters poaching the best programmers for the competition and denied the programmers individual recognition.

These tensions came to a head when marketing promulgated a list of the best-selling VCS titles of 1978. The purpose of the list was to indicate what types of games were proving most successful and to encourage the programmers to create similar products in the future. For Alan Miller, Larry Kaplan,

---

[10] Goldberg and Vendel, 2012, chap. 7.

[11] Ibid.

[12] Backiel, 2003.

[13] Tristan Donovan, "The Replay Interviews: David Crane," Gamasutra, January 3, 2011, https://www.gamasutra.com/view/feature/134618/the_replay_interviews_david_crane.php.

David Crane, and Bob Whitehead, the list revealed that between them they developed product responsible for roughly 60% of total cartridge sales even though Kaplan, Crane, and Miller had spent the last few months working on the computer OS, and Bob Whitehead was largely stuck trying to wrangle *Video Chess*. Under these circumstances it was hard to swallow making only around $30,000 a year and not even being allowed to have their names on the boxes.[14]

Alan Miller, perhaps the most business minded of the group, decided to do something about it. Arguing that top VCS programmers had special talents and generated enormous value for the company, Miller presented Simcock with a compensation scheme based on practices in the book publishing and record industries that would provide them both recognition and a modest royalty. Simcock brought the plan to consumer engineering VP John Ellis, who agreed to take it to Kassar. For a time, it appeared a deal would be reached, but in the end Kassar shot it down.[15]

The exact reasons for Kassar's dismissal of Miller's royalty plan are not known, but they appear rooted in his experience in the textile industry. The former Burlington executive had worked with designers for much of his life, but only on everyday commodities like home furnishings and towels. In this context, the designer was an important cog in product development but was not singled out vis-á-vis the rest of the production staff. In a subsequent meeting between Kassar, Miller, Crane, Kaplan, and Whitehead, the CEO emphasized that the programmers were part of a team alongside the people on the production line and the sales and marketing staff, and he did not feel it appropriate to single out their contributions in the way they wanted.[16] For Miller, this was the last straw. Figuring the four could do better on the open market than continuing to make cartridges for Atari, he proposed they start their own company.[17]

To launch this scheme, Miller contacted Decuir to learn what law firm he had used to organize his new startup. Decuir referred him to Art Schneiderman of Wilson Sonsini Goodrich & Rosati, a firm that was fast building a reputation as the premiere law firm for startups in Silicon Valley. At this point, Miller and his companions were unsure exactly what business to pursue. Ideas included serving as a contract developer for a console company like Atari or Mattel or entering the emerging computer software

---

[14] Ibid.
[15] Kent, 2001, 191.
[16] Donovan, "David Crane," 2011.
[17] Crane, 2018.

business as a publisher.[18] Schneiderman changed the course of their plans – and indeed of the entire video game industry – when he introduced them to a marketing executive looking to establish his own computer game startup named Jim Levy.

***

Born in November 1944 in Shreveport, Louisiana, James Harmon Levy showed some aptitude in math as a high school student, so he matriculated to Carnegie-Mellon University in 1961 to study electrical engineering. After three semesters, he realized the career path was not for him, but he was successful in several management courses, so he switched majors and remained at the school until 1966 to earn both BS and MS degrees in Industrial Management and Industrial Administration.[19] After graduation, Levy worked for Hershey Chocolate Corporation for two years as a marketing manager before moving to Time, Inc. as the assistant business manager of Time Magazine. In 1970, he established a new publishing venture for Time called Time Life Audio to produce entertainment and information content on audio cassette for the home, business, and school markets.[20]

After three years at Time Life Audio, Levy moved to San Francisco to manage a Time subsidiary called Haverhills involved in mail order merchandising. Around 1975, Levy left Time for GRT Corporation. Established in 1965 as General Recorded Tape, GRT was one of several companies that emerged in the late 1960s to release popular music on the new magnetic media of 8-track cartridge and compact cassette. As the major record labels were interested only in the vinyl market, they would license their music to companies like GRT rather than engage with audiocassette production and sales themselves. Levy joined GRT to start a new mail order marketing division and later became first manager and then VP of business affairs.[21]

In late 1977, a group of executives led by Vern Rayburn approached Levy with a plan to create a computer software subsidiary at GRT since the cassette tapes the company traded in were the same medium on which computer games were published. Levy played a key role in helping them establish a software publisher named the G-2 group, which emerged as one of the few bright spots for GRT as its traditional cassette music business declined due

---

[18] Whitehead, 2016.

[19] Jim Levy, interview with the author, July 21, 2014.

[20] James Levy, testimony, Magnavox Company v. Activision, Inc., No. 82-5270 (N.D. Cal), 1985, 137–138.

[21] Ibid, 138.

to the record labels gradually reasserting control of their audio cassette rights in response to the proliferation of component stereo systems with tape decks. As GRT spiraled toward bankruptcy, Levy developed a business plan in early 1979 to purchase G-2 and spin it off as an independent company.[22]

To fund the G-2 purchase, Levy turned to the same Art Schneiderman working with Miller and company, whom he had worked with on several deals at GRT. Schneiderman worked in the same building as pioneering venture capitalist Bill Draper, who had co-founded the first venture fund in Silicon Valley in 1958 and now managed a firm he co-founded in 1964 called Sutter Hill, and got Levy a meeting with him.[23] When Levy attended the meeting, he learned that Draper owned a TRS-80 and was frustrated by the lack of quality software for the computer. The venture capitalist gladly agreed to fund Levy's acquisition attempt.[24]

With Draper's backing, Levy attempted to negotiate the buyout with GRT, but management was busy trying to save the firm, and in late May 1979 he was told no one would negotiate with him. The next month GRT collapsed. Meanwhile, Levy called Schneiderman over Memorial Day weekend to relay the bad news. Days later, Schneiderman called Levy to arrange a meeting that same afternoon with Kaplan, Miller, Whitehead, and Crane, who required both an experienced executive and funding to launch their proposed startup. By the end of the meeting, all parties agreed to explore working together.[25]

Over the next few weeks, Levy and the Atari programmers met frequently to continue feeling each other out on the specifics of their partnership. By late July, they had decided to work together and focus their efforts on developing and publishing software for the VCS. Levy wrote a business plan over the next few weeks and delivered it to Sutter Hill on August 23, 1979. In this plan, Levy did not present the potential enterprise as a technology company, but rather as a creative company developing product for a new entertainment medium. He also defined the company's product area as software for home computer systems generally, though he acknowledged that the short-term plan was to focus on the most developed platform, the Atari VCS.[26] Despite requiring double the investment as Levy's previous proposal of buying out GRT, Sutter Hill agreed to fund the venture.[27]

---

[22] Ibid, 138–139.
[23] Art Schneiderman, interview with the author, May 31, 2019.
[24] Levy, 2014.
[25] Ibid.
[26] Levy, 1985, 141–147.
[27] Levy, 2014.

In summer 1979, the four Atari programmers began leaving the company one by one. Larry Kaplan was the first to depart in June,[28] followed by Alan Miller and David Crane in August. Bob Whitehead stayed the longest, as the family man did not want to jeopardize his livelihood until he was certain the company was moving forward.[29] On the advice of counsel, none of them took any materials when they left to avoid credible accusations of stealing trade secrets.

Even as the programmers began to depart Atari, there was no guarantee they would end up joining Levy. In fact, Alan Miller, the most gung-ho among the group about creating a new company, nearly backed out of the venture at one point because he worried Levy was "not entrepreneurial enough" to make it successful.[30] The financial arrangements also gave some pause. Sutter Hill was willing to provide several hundred thousand dollars' worth of financing, but most of it was in the form of a loan. The company also demanded that each founder make a substantial upfront investment in the firm, and that they each take a pay cut from their Atari salaries, which were already slightly low for an engineer in the Valley.[31] After evaluating the risks and potential rewards, Crane, Miller, and Whitehead decided to see the plan through.

At the last second, Larry Kaplan dropped out. In the weeks leading up to the incorporation of the firm, the Atari programmers met with other suitors, including Chuck Peddle at Commodore. Peddle convinced Kaplan that rather than go through the hassle of starting a company, reverse engineering hardware, and setting up manufacturing and distribution, he should work with Commodore, where all of this would be provided. Kaplan joined a startup supported by Commodore working on speech recognition software, but after a couple of months it was clear the company was going nowhere, so Kaplan returned to the fold in December 1979. Because he joined late, his stock award was half that of the other three founding programmers.[32]

One of the more difficult tasks for the founders ended up being naming the company. In the business plan, Levy referred to it as "Video Computer Arts," but this was merely a place holder indicating the mission of the company and was never intended as a final name. After some deliberation, Levy decided to call it "Computervision" to signify that the company was

---

[28] Kaplan, 2018.
[29] Whitehead, 2016.
[30] Levy, 2014.
[31] Backiel, 2003.
[32] Kaplan, 2018.

developing product that merged a computer with a television set, but this name was already in use by another company.[33] During a brainstorming session to generate a new name, Levy focused on the interactive nature of the company's products by combining the words "active" and "television" to name the company Activision.[34]

Activision incorporated on October 1, 1979.[35] The company's first order of business was to ensure it could deliver product for the VCS in a way that did not violate Atari's rights to the system. Even before the company incorporated, Levy began working closely with an intellectual property attorney named Aldo Test to determine the most likely grounds upon which Atari might sue Activision for infringement.[36] They agreed the major sticking point would be the design of the cartridges, as Atari had taken out two patents related to their mechanical engineering and design.[37] These patents constituted Atari's main bulwark against unauthorized publishing on the VCS, and the company felt confident that they would keep competing companies off its system.

Once Activision incorporated, Levy contracted with an injection-molding plastics expert who had previously worked on the early Atari cartridges named Howard Mullin to help develop a working cartridge that would not run afoul of the Atari patents. Mullin in turn brought in the designers of the Fairchild Channel F cartridges, Ron Smith and Nick Talesfore, to design the Activision cartridge.[38] Smith determined that the primary mechanism on which the patent hinged was a door that opened to expose the edge connectors on the cartridge when it was inserted into the VCS. While intended to protect the internals of the cartridge, Smith and Talesfore determined after extensive testing that the cartridge worked just fine without that door, and it would be safe to remove it.[39]

While Mullin, Smith, and Talesfore designed a new cartridge, David Crane led efforts to reverse engineer the VCS. As the programmers were careful not to take anything with them from Atari, including development materials, he started by buying a VCS at retail and opening it up. Once he did so, he discovered an unused 24-pin ROM port on the board, which had presumably been included due to the original marketing plan for the system

---

[33] Levy, 1985, 146–147.

[34] Levy, 2014.

[35] Levy, 1985, 150.

[36] Ibid., 145–146.

[37] Ibid., 148.

[38] Howard Mullin, interview with the author, May 14, 2019.

[39] Levy, 2014.

calling for one or two games being built into the hardware. Crane soldered a zero-insertion force (ZIF) socket to the board and burned simple programs onto EPROM so he could observe how the system reacted to various inputs. Within just a few weeks, he had assembled a programming manual for the machine.[40] He then fashioned a development system consisting of a small, custom-built 6502 computer that plugged into the VCS cartridge slot and could interface with a PDP-11 minicomputer. The system was affectionately called the "blue box" for its blue sheet metal enclosure.[41]

Meanwhile, Levy began putting the company infrastructure in place. In November, he hired a recently dismissed plastics sales rep whom Mullin knew named Clifton Crowder to build a sales and distribution infrastructure. In January 1980, he hired an executive at a small Bay Area manufacturing company named Allan Epstein to run operations. When the January 1980 CES rolled around, the company was not ready to announce any product, but Crowder took meetings at the show to begin constructing a sales network.[42]

On January 31, Activision received a letter signed by Ray Kassar warning that if the company took advantage of any Atari trade secrets to violate any Atari patents, it could expect a lawsuit.[43] In May, Atari sued Activision for $20 million. In early 1981, Atari filed an amendment to its suit asking for $1 million in punitive damages alongside its other requested remedies.[44] Thanks to the sound legal advice of Schneiderman and Test and the careful reverse engineering and cartridge design work by Crane, Mullin, Smith, and Talesfore, Atari did not have a leg to stand on, and the companies settled in December.[45]

Activision announced its first four games in March 1980 and released them in July. These were *Boxing* by Bob Whitehead, *Dragster* and *Fishing Derby* by David Crane, and *Checkers* by Alan Miller.[46] While all four games featured simple gameplay, they sported fantastic graphics relative to other VCS games because the programmers realized their products would need to stand out from the Atari lineup visually in order to entice consumers to buy from the new company.[47] For instance, *Boxing*, played from an overhead

---

[40] Crane, 2018.

[41] DillyDylan, "The Blue Box: David Crane on Early Atari Inc.," Gaming Alexandria, May 12, 2019, https://www.gamingalexandria.com/wp/2019/05/12/the-blue-box-david-crane-on-early-atari-inc.

[42] Levy, 2014.

[43] Levy, 1985, 155.

[44] "Atari Seeks Punitive Damages from Activision," *Playthings*, April 1981, 32.

[45] "Atari, Activision Arrive at Settlement," *Toy & Hobby World*, January 1982.

[46] "Activision Profile 1982," promotional brochure, 1982, 6.

[47] Crane, 2018.

perspective, featured large sprites and smooth animations, even if the boxers looked a little like crabs. The cream of the crop was arguably *Dragster*, a take on a 1977 Atari arcade game called *Drag Race*, in which one or two players race cars presented in a side view on a split screen. The game sold roughly 500,000 copies and provided half of Activision's first-year revenues.[48]

Activision released four more games before the end of its first fiscal year. In December 1980, the company introduced Kaplan's first game, *Bridge*, as well as a *Skiing* game by Whitehead. In March 1981, these were joined by Miller's *Tennis* and *Laser Blast* by David Crane.[49] Once again, Crane's game led the field. *Laser Blast* was born of a desire to emulate the popular shooting games in the arcade like *Space Invaders* and *Missile Command* but reversed the action by placing the player above the surface of a planet to shoot at turrets on the surface. Crane did this because he felt too many shooting games focused on defending a planet, so he wanted a game where the player recaptured his planet instead. Crane also achieved a new technical breakthrough when he figured out how to reposition the "ball" sprite on every line to give the illusion of a continuous laser blast emanating from the player's ship.[50] With slick gameplay derived from the biggest arcade hits, *Laser Blast* became the first Activision game to sell 1 million units over its lifetime.[51]

Levy kept his promise to promote the game designers, combining practices from the music and book publishing industries to provide them recognition. Each game box identified the designer of the game on the back, while the instruction manual included tips and tricks from the designer on how to master the game accompanied by a headshot and a signature. This not only promoted the designers but created a dialogue and sense of connection between them and their player base. This sense of shared experience with Activision games was further amplified through a clever marketing ploy emulating the score chasing currently dominating the arcade. For most games, the company established a point or time limit threshold for a player to aspire to achieve. If the player reached the goal and submitted a photograph of his television screen as proof, Activision would mail him a patch to commemorate the achievement.

---

[48] "David Crane on 'Dragster,'" Gamegrid, accessed December 12, 2007, http://www.gamegrid.de/activision.php.

[49] Activision Profile, 1982, 6.

[50] "David Crane on 'Laser Blast,'" Gamegrid, accessed December 12, 2007, http://www.gamegrid.de/activision.php.

[51] James Capparell, "Activision's James Levy: A Software Success Story," *ANTIC*, June 1984, 27.

In its first fiscal year, Activision achieved sales of $6.5 million and a profit of $744,000 while grabbing an estimated 5% of the video game market.[52] The company was poised to do even better in fiscal 1982 as home video game sales surged to new heights, driven by a series of massive hits in the coin-operated space that briefly turned video games into the most profitable entertainment category in the United States.

---

[52] Activision Profile, 1982, 6.

33

Guardians of the Galaxy

In April 1976, longtime coin-op industry executive Sam Stern retired.[1] Save for a brief stint at Bally between 1969 and 1971, Stern led the Williams Electronic Manufacturing Company, renamed Williams Electronics in 1967, from 1959 and presided over a sustained period of innovation that left it the number two pinball company behind first Gottlieb and then Bally. The later years of his tenure also coincided with a great deal of corporate upheaval.

In 1964, Williams became a subsidiary of Seeburg Corporation, the conglomerate formed by Delbert Coleman and Herbert Siegel to dominate the coin-operated music, vending, and amusement manufacturing industries. In May 1965, Coleman brought a new protégé into Seeburg named Louis Nicastro, a Columbia University graduate and New York financier who rose from mail boy to senior auditor of the Bowery Savings Bank and then spent a decade at Inland Credit. Four months after joining the company, Nicastro was promoted to executive vice president of Seeburg. In 1966, he became president and chief operating officer.[2]

By 1968, Seeburg had purchased a few more companies, but had basically topped out its growth potential. At that point, Coleman and Nicastro sold their shares in the company to Commonwealth United Corporation,[3] a conglomerate that started in real estate in 1961 and entered the television and movie production business in 1967. Commonwealth subsequently purchased the rest of Seeburg to turn it into a wholly owned subsidiary. Coleman left the firm, while Nicastro became chairman of Seeburg and president of Commonwealth United. He resigned the latter position in April

---

[1] "Sam Sterns Retires," *Cash Box*, April 10, 1976, 40.
[2] Earl Paige, "Nicastro From Bank's Mail Boy to Carrying CUC Mail," *Billboard*, March 14, 1970, 42.
[3] "N.Y. Company Plan to Buy Seeburg Told," *Chicago Tribune*, August 28, 1968.

1969 under mysterious circumstances. Not long afterwards, Commonwealth shares collapsed after it could not pull together the capital for another acquisition, and it was revealed the company was fast losing money as its entertainment investments did not pan out.

Nicastro added the role of CEO at Seeburg in August 1969 and was invited back to Commonwealth as CEO in January 1970 following a power struggle over the future direction of the company.[4] He began deconglomerating by spinning out Commonwealth's real estate and insurance companies to refocus the firm solely on entertainment. Revenues at Seeburg continued to outpace the rest of the organization, but the company lost money for the first time in its history in 1969 and 1970, in part because it had trouble securing credit to buy parts due to Commonwealth's difficulties with the banks. Through a refinancing deal, Nicastro brought Seeburg back to profitability in 1971 and then established a new independent company in 1972 called Seeburg Industries. In December 1972, Seeburg Industries acquired Seeburg Corporation from Commonwealth.[5]

The separation from Commonwealth did not end the trouble at Seeburg, for in the early 1970s the jukebox business was collapsing in the United States. Wurlitzer exited the business in 1973, which led to product dumping that severely impacted Seeburg's bottom line. Nicastro almost sold Williams to Sega in 1975 when the Japanese company was looking to establish a base of operations in the United States, but the deal fell through. In 1977, Nicastro decided to sell the jukebox business instead. After all its distributors turned down the opportunity to purchase the business, Nicastro almost reached a deal with its Japanese agent, Taito, but this deal collapsed at the last minute just like the Sega deal two years before because Mike Kogan was leery of taking on the company's debts.[6] Nicastro ended up spinning off the jukebox business into a separate company named Seeburg Corporation in 1977 that became a subsidiary of yet another firm called Consolidated Entertainment, Inc. owned by his sons.[7] To distance Seeburg Industries and the original Seeburg Corporation from the money-losing jukebox business, he changed the names of the firms to Xcor International and Xcor Corporation, respectively.[8]

---

[4] "Name Nicastro to Presidency of Com. United," *Chicago Tribune*, January 14, 1970.

[5] "Seeburg Industries," *Chicago Tribune*, December 29, 1972.

[6] Ed Miller, 2014.

[7] Len Ackland, "Xcor Healthier Financially After the Sale of Its 'Parent,'" *Chicago Tribune*, March 5, 1980.

[8] Louis Nicastro, deposition, Bally Manufacturing v. Williams Electronics, No. 78-2246 (N.D. Ill), August 1, 1979, 11. There is no meaning to the name "Xcor," which was chosen off a list provided by the company's PR firm.

Stern retired during this latest turmoil, but soon discovered he did not enjoy sitting around all day and desired a new project to occupy his time. His son, Gary, provided one. A regular at the Williams factory since he was a young child, Gary first worked for the pinball company as a summer employee in the stockroom when he was 16 years old. In subsequent summers he also worked in the inventory, human resources, accounting, and design departments. After graduating from Tulane University in 1967 with an accounting degree, Gary decided he was done with school, but his father convinced him to study law, and he received a law degree from Northwestern University in 1971.[9]

By the time he graduated law school, Gary's father worked for Bally, so he joined the firm as a law clerk specializing in slot machine law. In 1973, he followed his father back to Williams and took on a variety of jobs under the title assistant to the president, including managing the company's new attempt to challenge Bally in the slot machine business. Williams never managed to compete successfully in slots, so after his father retired, Gary departed in 1976 and formed a company with a friend to deliver free-to-play slot machines to Canada. When his mother told him that his father needed something to get him out of the house, Gary and his brother, a physician named David, purchased the assets of Chicago Coin out of bankruptcy in 1976 and formed a new pinball company called Stern Electronics.[10] The brothers financed the purchase through a $2.7 million loan from Drovers Bank and $500,000 in private financing, including a sizeable contribution from Stern family friend and Service Games founder Marty Bromley, who was awarded half the firm's voting stock.[11] Gary served as president of the new company, while his father generally worked half days as an advisor.[12]

Stern released its first pinball games in early 1977, which were a combination of new designs and Chicago Coin backstock. The company quickly ran into difficulty because the industry was shifting to solid state, yet Stern only had the capability to create electromechanical designs. Another longtime Stern family friend, Bally CEO Bill O'Donnell, came to the rescue by providing a Bally table and giving his blessing to reverse engineer it to develop a solid-state system in return for royalties.[13] To create its solid-state machines, Stern contracted with URL, the firm that helped Allied Leisure break into

---

[9] Gary Stern, interview with the author, November 10, 2014.
[10] Stern, 2014.
[11] Maurice Barnfather, "Is Playboy's Luck Running Out?" *Forbes*, May 11, 1981, 59.
[12] David Stern was a silent partner and took no part in the running of the business. Stern, 2014.
[13] Stern, 2014.

the video game market with *Paddle Battle*. URL was undergoing its own challenges at the time due to both the failure of its recently established coin-operated video game manufacturer, Electra, and its Video Action home video game line, so Gary Stern shepherded URL through bankruptcy proceedings and purchased the company.[14]

Stern realized its first hit in March 1978 with a solid-state game called *Stars* that sold just over 5,000 units. By 1979, Stern had become the number four pinball company with around 23,000 units sold, many of them shipped to international markets. While this modest total put the company well behind Bally (80,000 units), Williams (60,000 units), and Gottlieb (46,000), Stern was profitable and ready to expand. In 1980, it bought cabinet manufacturer August J. Johnson Co. and purchased Seeburg Corporation out of bankruptcy from the Nicastro family for $1.5 million to enter the jukebox business.[15]

The Seeburg bankruptcy had a negative effect on Xcor, which still had close ties and some financial stake in the company. Combined with disruption of its vending machine manufacturing operations due to a tornado, Seeburg's difficulties left Xcor with a $2.4 million loss in fiscal 1979.[16] Williams remained profitable, so Nicastro engineered another spinoff. On March 5, 1981, Xcor sold 20% of Williams' stock in a public offering and used the proceeds to pay down its debt.[17] Then on May 29, the company distributed the remaining shares among its own shareholders, making the pinball company independent again for the first time in 17 years.[18] Louis Nicastro remained the CEO and ran the firm from his native New York, where he had relocated in 1973.

Neither Williams nor Stern were initially interested in video games. Williams had jumped on the ball-and-paddle bandwagon back in 1973 just like everyone else, but had not released any games since 1974, while Stern ignored the video game business entirely in its first three years of operation. By 1980, no coin-operated amusement manufacturer could ignore video. As video game coin drop hit $2.8 billion, pinball's take fell from nearly $2 billion in 1979 to just shy of $1.7 billion and appeared poised to drop further as demand for new pinball machines sharply declined.[19] Both Williams and Stern introduced video games before the end of 1980, and the releases of

[14] Smith, 2016, 487–488.
[15] Ibid, 476.
[16] Xcor Corporation, Annual Report, 1979.
[17] Xcor Corporation, Annual Report, 1980.
[18] Williams Electronics, Annual Report, 1981.
[19] Vending Times Census of the Industry, 1981, 62.

both companies played a critical role in the further growth of coin-operated video games in 1981.

**

Williams' video game activities sprang directly from its work to develop a solid-state pinball machine. Shortly before he left the company in early 1976, Sam Stern began putting out feelers about developing a solid-state hardware. Subsequently, Louis Nicastro reached agreements with National Semiconductor and Rockwell International to each take a stab at developing such a system. National put its head of microprocessor system development, Mike Stroll, in charge of its efforts.[20] Nicastro took a liking to Stroll and hired him into Seeburg Industries in October 1976 to serve as VP of Technology and continue work on the solid-state system in house.[21] Stroll brought three engineers into Williams to finish the system: Ron Crouse, Dave Poole, and Ken Fedesna.[22] They developed a system based around the Motorola 6800, while a second team at Seeburg also worked on a prototype after National Semiconductor showed off its SC/MP processor. The Seeburg project was ultimately abandoned in favor of the Williams system.[23] In May 1977, the Williams team tested its system by converting five *Grand Prix* games to solid state and putting them out on test,[24] after which Williams deployed its first mass-produced solid-state game, *Hot Tip*, in September.[25]

In December 1977, Stroll became president of Williams Electronics.[26] He immediately began expanding the pinball division by bringing in new designers and engineers comfortable working with solid-state technology, of which the most notable was Steve Ritchie. A native of San Francisco, Ritchie joined the Coast Guard after graduating high school in 1967 to avoid service in Vietnam but ended up being sent there anyway. After leaving the service, he became an electronics technician and joined Atari in 1974 as an assembly-line worker. An avid pinball player since he was a child, in 1976 Ritchie asked for a transfer to the company's new pinball division. Once there, veteran

---

[20] Nicastro, 1979, 62–63.

[21] "Stroll to Seeburg," *Cash Box*, 12-4-1976, 41. The month is given as October in Nicastro, 1979, 63.

[22] Alphonse Gregg, testimony, Bally Manufacturing v. Williams Electronics, No. 78-2246 (N.D. Ill), March 19, 1984, 2362–2364.

[23] Tony Miller, "Engineering," Tony Miller personal website, accessed December 3, 2008, http://home.pacbell.net/fmillera/engineering.htm.

[24] "Grand Prix," The Internet Pinball Database, accessed June 7, 2019, https://www.ipdb.org/machine.cgi?id=5647.

[25] "Hot Tip," The Internet Pinball Database, accessed June 7, 2019, https://www.ipdb.org/machine.cgi?id=3163.

[26] "Stroll's New Williams Prexy," *RePlay*, December 1977, 7.

pinball designer Bob Jonesi took Ritchie under his wing and taught him how to design a pinball playfield. He subsequently designed two tables for the company, *Airborne Avenger* and *Superman*.[27]

Shortly before the release of *Superman* in 1978, Ritchie met Stroll and accepted an offer to come work for Williams.[28] His first game for the company, *Flash*, introduced a continuous background noise that rises in pitch and increases in tempo the longer the player keeps his ball on the playfield. This effect created a similar degree of tension and excitement as the background music in *Space Invaders* to provide a pinball experience almost as exhilarating as the hit video game. Released in January 1979, *Flash* set a new sales record for Williams by moving 19,500 units and remained a top moneymaker for three years.

Later in 1979, another former Atari pinball division employee joined Ritchie at Williams. Eugene Peyton Jarvis was born on January 27, 1955 in Palo Alto, California. As a boy, he discovered pinball in the backroom of a local haunt called Johnny's Smoke Shop, which became a favorite pastime. In high school, he saw his first computer on a school trip, and while hanging around the Stanford University student union, he watched college students try their hand at the *Galaxy Game*. Despite a burgeoning interest in technology, when Jarvis matriculated to UC Berkeley in 1973, he majored in biochemistry. Before long, he switched his major to computer science and began writing programs on a CDC 6400 computer. He also started playing marathon sessions of *Spacewar!* on an old IBM mainframe hooked up to an oscilloscope in the basement of the university physics lab.[29]

Shortly before Jarvis graduated, Atari came to campus to conduct interviews. He sat down with representatives of the company, but never heard back. Upon graduation, he took a job with Hewlett-Packard, but quit after just three days because he could not stand his assignment to help write a COBOL compiler. At that point, Atari finally called out of the blue and offered him a job as a programmer in the pinball division. Within two weeks, a series of departures and transfers left him head of programming for the entire division.[30]

Jarvis felt Atari's tables had good play appeal, but they were plagued by unreliable hardware and manufacturing difficulties. By 1979, dealing with

[27] Russ Jensen, Pinball Expo '97 (Part 2), Pinball Collectors Resource, accessed June 7, 2019, http://www.pinballcollectorsresource.com/russ_files/expo97-2.html.

[28] Ibid.

[29] Chris Kohler, "This Game Industry Pioneer Never Gave Up on the Video Arcade," *Wired*, December 18, 2013, https://www.wired.com/2013/12/eugene-jarvis-pioneer.

[30] Ibid.

these challenges left Jarvis burned out, so he quit.[31] He spent a few months in South America and worked for his father for a time but found he missed the coin-operated amusement industry, so when Ritchie called a few months later to say there was a job waiting if he wanted it, Jarvis joined Williams.[32] His first project was to create the sound for *Gorgar*, the first pinball table to incorporate speech. Next, he served as the programmer for Ritche's *Firepower*, the first solid-state pinball game with a multi-ball feature. While *Firepower's* sales of 17,400 units lagged slightly behind *Flash*, it was arguably more successful, as it remained the top earning pinball table for a year after its January 1980 release and stayed in the top five for another year after that.

Once *Space Invaders* took hold of the marketplace, Mike Stroll organized a new skunk works team headed by Ken Fedesna in late 1979 to bring Williams into the video game business. Composed of a combination of new hires and engineers from the pinball division, the group was placed in the building that previously housed the company's defunct slot machine operations to keep it free of distraction.[33] Jarvis had fallen for *Space Invaders* hard, so he asked to join the group.[34]

The Williams video game team did not want to copy what came before: they desired to set a new standard. Therefore, in developing a video game hardware system they stuffed it with state-of-the-art components. The processor was a 6809, Motorola's latest 8-bit chip that incorporated some 16-bit features. A second processor, the 6808, drove the sound on the system. Perhaps most significantly, at a time when color was still a rarity in the arcade the Williams hardware could generate 16 colors on screen at once from a palette of 256.

As the hardware came together, Jarvis led efforts to create the company's first game. His first concept was basically *Space Invaders*, but with the added ability to shoot diagonally. It was not fun. Next, Jarvis looked to the latest arcade hit, *Asteroids*, and created a game with a rotating turret that shot at targets, but without high-resolution vector graphics the game looked terrible, and this idea was also set aside. For his next idea, he combined the two. One feature the Williams team liked about *Asteroids* was that if you flew off the screen in one direction, you would reappear on the opposite side of the screen. Jarvis thought it might be fun to have the screen scroll instead to reveal a larger playing area. To avoid the graphical problems that came with rotating an object, he decided to have the ship move horizontally only

[31] Walter Lowe, Jr., "What Sort of Man Invents Defender?" *Playboy*, March 1982, 230.
[32] Bloom, *Invaders*, 1982, 60.
[33] Smith, 2016, 477.
[34] Kohler, 2013.

and then basically turned *Space Invaders* on its side to have the player shoot at objects appearing from the right side of the screen. As in *Asteroids* these objects included rocks that would break into smaller pieces when hit.[35]

After roughly six months of work, Williams now had a game concept, but it still was not fun. Jarvis's old pinball partner, Steve Ritchie, checked out a build and suggested that the player should be able to turn around to move in both directions instead of just left to right, but even adding this feature did not really increase playability of what the team was now calling *Defender*. Jarvis's next move was to add friendly objects on the screen that the player needed to avoid shooting to break up the monotony of blasting everything in sight. A planetary surface was duly implemented with little astronauts running around. Next, Jarvis ditched the asteroids and introduced alien ships that land on the planet to abduct the astronauts, changing the paradigm of the game from just blasting targets in space to protecting a population. Subsequently, he decided that rather than an astronaut just disappearing when abducted, it would be carried to the top of the screen and turned into an evil mutant if the player did not blast the lander that had grabbed it. Finally, the game started to feel like a winner.[36]

Defender debuted at the AMOA show in October 1980. The game looked spectacular thanks to its vibrant colors and beautiful algorithmically generated explosions implemented by teenage prodigy Sam Dicker, who also programmed the sound. It was also hellishly difficult to play. Jarvis came from the pinball world and borrowed the conventions of that game in which activity is happening all over the playfield and the player must prioritize targets and bring order to the chaos. Unlike pinball and its two flipper buttons, however, *Defender* is controlled with a two-way joystick that moves the ship up and down and five buttons: a thrust button for movement, a reverse button to change direction, a fire button, a button to deploy a screen clearing smart bomb, and a hyperspace button that works as in *Spacewar!* and *Asteroids*. In addition to complex controls, a variety of enemy types swarm all over the screen and move randomly rather than in learnable patterns. A typical player may not even last five seconds on his first quarter, and even with score chasing reaching the height of popularity, distributors and operators at the show thought the game too hard to attract significant business in the arcade.[37]

[35] Craig Grannell, "The Making of Defender," *Retro Gamer*, no. 55, 2008, 34–39.
[36] Ibid.
[37] Smith, 2016, 482.

When the first sample shipments of *Defender* started reaching locations in December 1980, the AMOA attendees were proven wrong.[38] By now, the top *Space Invaders* and *Asteroids* players had learned tricks and exploits that allowed them to play for hours on a single quarter, and they required a new challenge to test their increasingly impressive skills. By spring 1981, *Defender* had dethroned *Asteroids* as the top earning game in the United States. It remained in production all year and ultimately sold 55,000 units.[39]

Defender was not the first scrolling video game, as it was preceded by multiple driving games that depicted a constantly shifting road or track, as well as the Atari *Football* game with its 100-yard field. Even other shooting games had incorporated scrolling elements to good effect, such as *Galaxian* with its starfield. *Defender* felt different, however, because it took place within the boundaries of a complete world occupying more than one screen of real estate with a distinct and fixed geography through which the player had near complete freedom to navigate his vessel. *Defender* also cemented the need for a game to have color graphics to stand out in the arcade. In fact, its appearance at the AMOA prompted frantic last-minute changes to another game that premiered at the show, the first original Stern Electronics video game, *Berzerk*.

***

When Stern decided to enter the video game business in 1979, the company asked its URL subsidiary to put a game together. Organizing a team fell to Tony Miller, a former Seeburg and Dave Nutting Associates engineer. While at DNA, Miller had created the original version of the keyboard add-on for the Bally Professional Arcade, and when it ended up being scrapped, he grew disillusioned and left the company to become the chief engineer at URL. When told to staff up for the video game project, he poached some of his former co-workers,[40] notably Terry Coleman, who designed many of the custom chips in the Bally Professional Arcade, to develop the hardware, and Alan McNeil to design and program the game.[41]

A native of Chicago, Alan McNeil attended the Chicago campus of the University of Illinois to study art and architecture but fell in with the crowd working with the university's revolutionary PLATO educational time-sharing

---

[38]"Chicago Chatter," *Cash Box*, December 20, 1980, 44.

[39]Bernstein, 1982, 70.

[40]Tony Miller, "Stern/Seeburg," Tony Miller personal website, accessed December 3, 2008, http://home.pacbell.net/fmillera/stern_seeburg.htm.

[41]Adam Trionfo, "Programmers of the Bally Arcade/Astrocade Built-in Programs," Bally Alley, August 17, 2016, http://www.ballyalley.com/faqs/Programmers%20of%20the%20Astrocade%20Built-In%20Programs.txt.

system and took a minor in computer science. After graduation in 1975, he spent a year as a PLATO research associate and then took a job with the Itty Bitty Machine Co., Chicago's first microcomputer store.[42] In 1977, he joined DNA, where he programmed *Boot Hill*, *Sea Wolf II*, and the *Gunfight* adaptation built into the Bally Professional Arcade.[43] Bored working on extensions of other people's projects, he asked Dave Nutting for the opportunity to create his own video game but was turned down because Dave thought he needed to acquire more experience first. He joined URL in 1979 upon the promise that once he worked on a pinball hardware, he could develop a video game.[44]

In designing Stern's first video game, McNeil was inspired by a game written in BASIC called *Chase* that he had encountered as a type-in program in one of the early computer magazines. In this game, the player is deposited in a room with several hazardous obstacles scattered about and several robots that want to kill him. Each turn, the player moves one space, after which all the robots move along the shortest path to the player. If one of the robots touches the player, he dies, but if one of the robots collides with an obstacle or another robot, it is destroyed. Therefore, the player must carefully plan his moves to cause these collisions.

The developer of *Chase* is unknown, but it appears to have originated on the DTSS at Dartmouth.[45] In about 1975 or 1976, a computer engineer working on a ballistic missile submarine program for the U.S. Navy named Bill Cotter visited Dartmouth, discovered the DTSS, and played the game.[46] At the time, Cotter was looking for programs to help his co-workers feel more comfortable using their time-shared Honeywell 6,000 mainframe, so he ported *Chase* to run on the computer.[47] He also submitted the program to *Creative Computing*, which featured it in the January–February 1976 issue.[48]

[42] Alan McNeil, Résumé, Alan McNeil personal website, accessed February 1, 2018, http://a9k.info/Resume.html.

[43] Berzerk Interview, Alan McNeil personal website, accessed February 1, 2018, http://a9k.info/qna.html.

[44] Craig Grannell, "The Making of Berzerk," *Retro Gamer* no. 47, 2008, 48–49.

[45] Certain listings for the game credit prolific DTSS programmer Mac Oglesby as the creator, but he denies authorship. ErikH2000, Re: Robots/Daleks, Caravel Games Forums, February 28, 2006, http://forum.caravelgames.com/viewtopic.php?TopicID=9376.

[46] ErikH2000, Re: Robots/Daleks, Caravel Games Forums, April 1, 2016, http://forum.caravelgames.com/viewtopic.php?TopicID=9376&page=1. Cotter is not 100% positive that he saw the game at Dartmouth, but he is reasonably certain. billcotter, Re: Robots/Daleks, Caravel Games Forums, April 2, 2016, http://forum.caravelgames.com/viewtopic.php?TopicID=9376&page=1.

[47] ErikH2000, 2016.

[48] "Chase," *Creative Computing*, January–February 1976, 75–76.

It subsequently appeared in *Kilobaud* in February 1977,[49] *Dr. Dobb's Journal* in a graphical version for S-100 systems in May 1977,[50] and the book *More BASIC Computer Games* by David Ahl in 1979.[51] In 1980, a variant called *Escape!* appeared in a book of TRS-80 programs that added a tank alongside the robots.[52]

When McNeil first saw *Chase* is not clear, but regardless, he decided a real-time version would make a great coin-operated video game.[53] Once he implemented it, however, he discovered it was too difficult because the robots zeroed in on the player before he had a chance to force them to collide with each other. To even the odds, he gave the player a laser pistol to fight back, but the robots were still overwhelming. Finally, he created an algorithm to generate a series of connected randomly generated mazes for the players to navigate through. This inhibited the movement of the robots enough so that the player had a chance to kill them.[54]

While no two mazes in individual play sessions of *Berzerk* are alike, each one is created through a random number generator and a seed, so the player can return to previous rooms. To prevent the player from loitering in a cleared room, McNeil added an invincible bouncing smiley face that relentlessly chases the player until he moves on, a form chosen because he could not stand the ubiquitous yellow smiley face appearing on t-shirts and other paraphernalia at the time.[55] Tony Miller named the face "Evil Otto" after the office manager at DNA, Dave Otto, who was infamous for enacting policies that grated on the engineering staff.[56]

One aspect that set McNeil's game apart on its debut was the incorporation of speech. This feature was not originally planned but was added after a salesman tried to sell a new sound chip to URL originally intended for use in applications for the blind. The limited memory on the chip led to a robotic sounding voice that perfectly fit the theme of the game. The team recorded several nouns and verbs that could be paired together resulting in phrases

---

[49] "Chase!" *Kilobaud*, February 1977, 48–49.

[50] Joseph Jay Sanger, "The Game of Chase for 8080/VDM," *Dr. Dobbs Journal of Calisthenics and Orthodontia*, May 1977, 208–214.

[51] David Ahl, *More BASIC Computer Games* (New York: Workman Publishing, 1979), 26–27.

[52] J. Victor Nahigian and William S. Hodges, *Announcing: Computer Games for Business, School, and Home for TRS-80 Level II BASIC* (Cambridge, MA: Winthrop Publishers, 1980), 46–52.

[53] McNeil claimed to see it in *Byte*, but that appears to have been one of the few magazines not to feature a variation of the game. Grannell, 2008, 49.

[54] Ibid.

[55] Ibid, 49–50.

[56] Allen Brunsen, Tony Miller Interview, bb.vg-network.com, accessed December 3, 2008, http://bb.vg-network.com/interviews/tminterview.html

like "Humanoids must not escape!" and "Chicken, Fight Like a Robot" if the player just ran from room to room without destroying anything. The speech chip was used to good effect in the game's attract mode too, during which it would exclaim "Coin detected in pocket!"[57]

One aspect of the game that did not impress was its monochrome graphics. Stern opted not to go with color due to the expense, particularly since plenty of hit games had shipped in black and white. Once company executives saw *Defender* at the 1980 AMOA in October, they realized their mistake.[58] It was too late to do a proper color generator because the game was so close to shipping, but the hardware engineers developed a color overlay system that could generate 16 colors but could only produce a single color within a four-by-four band of pixels. This meant individual sprites were limited to a single color, and if two objects of different colors got too close to each other the color of one object would bleed into the other, a phenomenon known as "color clash."[59]

McNeil named his game *Berzerk* in honor of the *Berserker* series of science fiction novels by Fred Saberhagen that depict a struggle with an army of killer robots developed by a long extinct race.[60] Released in November 1980, the game became a sizeable hit for Stern with sales of 15,000 units.[61] It spent a few months as a top-five earning video game in early 1981 but was ultimately surpassed by another shooting game that Stern licensed from the Japanese company Konami.

***

Konami co-founder Kagemasa Kozuki was born in November 1940 in Kyoto and studied economics at Kansai University. Upon graduation in 1966, he took employment with the Osaka branch of Nippon Columbia as a salesman for the company's jukeboxes. In March 1969, he established his own jukebox rental and repair business in conjunction with his co-worker, Tatuso Miyasako, who oversaw record supply at the Osaka branch, and Miyasako's friend Yoshinobu Naka, who worked at a local record store. They named their company by combining the first syllable of each of their last names to spell "Konami."[62]

---

[57] Grannell, 2008, 52.

[58] Tony Miller, message posted to newsgroup alt.games.video.classic, October 18, 1994, http://home.hiwaay.net/~lkseitz/cvg/berzerk.html.

[59] Grannell, 2008, 53.

[60] Ibid, 49.

[61] Stern Electronics, memo with manufacturing dates and sales figures of Stern games, c. 1982.

[62] Akagi, 2005, 227.

In 1973, with the Japanese jukebox business in decline, Konami changed its business to manufacturing amusement machines. The firm incorporated as Konami Industry Company but lost Miyasako, who preferred to remain in the record business. In December 1975, two major Japanese coin-operated amusement operators, Maru Sansho Co. in Kobe and Kato Amusement Industry in Nagoya, jointly formed a company called Leijac to sell coin-operated games and sub-contracted Konami to manufacture its products. The company experienced its first big success with a roulette-style medal game called *Piccadilly Circus* and continued developing medal games into the early 1980s.[63]

As with so many other Japanese coin-op companies, Konami and Leijac entered the video game business by developing a series of *Breakout* clones, in this case *Block Yard* in 1977 and *Destroyer* and *Super Destroyer* in 1978, the latter of which incorporated a microprocessor. *Space Invaders* clone *Space King* and *Gee Bee* clone *Rich Man* followed in 1979 before the collapse of the Invader market seriously impacted Maru Sansho, causing it to sell its interest in Leijac to Konami in August 1979. This spurred Kato to follow suit, so the sales company became a subsidiary of Konami, which was now an independent manufacturer. The company began making original, yet still derivative products including a *Space Invaders* variant called *Kamikaze* and a *Star Fire*-like game called *Star Ship* in 1979 and a game simply titled *Maze* in 1980 that appears similar to Midway's *Amazing Maze*.[64]

In early 1980, Konami became an official Namco licensee to manufacture and sell *Galaxian*. This not only benefitted the company financially in the short term, but also gave it access to the *Galaxian* hardware system, which was more sophisticated than anything Konami had used in its own games.[65] The Konami development department under Shokichi Ishihara adapted the hardware for its own use and began work on a new shooting game called *Scramble*.

Nothing is known about the development of *Scramble*, but it appears to combine elements of the games *Defender* and *Astro Fighter*. Released by Data East in October 1979, *Astro Fighter* is a *Space Invaders* clone that introduced two innovations. First, the game divides the action into five individual stages. Each of the first four stages consists of a fight with a group of enemy ships. These four groups are not identical like the waves in *Space Invaders* or *Galaxian*, but instead vary in their look, number, and attack pattern.

---

[63] Ibid.
[64] Ibid, 227–228.
[65] Ibid, 186.

The last stage is a fight with a larger command ship that takes multiple hits to kill. The second innovation of the game is the incorporation of a fuel bar that serves as a timer. While the game still regulates play through lives, the player must also complete all five stages before the fuel bar runs out. Once the command ship is destroyed, the game starts over from the first stage on a higher difficulty level.

For *Scramble*, Konami appears to have borrowed the stage progression and the fuel bar from *Astro Fighter* and melded it with the new horizontally scrolling playfield of *Defender*.[66] *Scramble* took this mechanic a step further by implementing forced scrolling so that the player's ship hurtles through the game world. Another difference between *Scramble* and previous shooting games is that rather than the action taking place either in open space or high above the surface of a planet, it takes place directly above a mountainous terrain and within the narrow confines of an enemy base. As such, colliding with the walls, ceiling, or the ground destroys the player's ship. The player also must contend with enemies both on the ground and in the air, so his ship has two modes of attack. The standard fire button shoots at objects in front of the player, while a second button launches missiles at the ground to destroy enemies and blow up tanks that replenish the fuel gauge. Once the player passes through all five stages, he must complete a brief sixth stage by destroying an object at the center of the enemy base. Then, as in *Astro Fighter*, the game starts over again at a higher level of difficulty.

Scramble debuted at the London Amusement Trades Exhibition in January 1981 and started shipping in Japan that March. It became an instant smash success in its home country, which caused serious issues for Konami because it was a small company with slight manufacturing capacity.[67] Cloning began running rampant within months, much of it undertaken by the *yakuza*, and Konami ended up caught between competing clans as the drama unfolded.[68] It also spawned more legitimate derivatives that adopted that adopted the game's forced scrolling through multiple stages, but featured slightly different game play like Universal's *Cosmic Avenger* and *Vanguard* from SNK. To combat the clones and derivatives, Konami rushed a sequel into production

---

[66] It remains an open question whether *Defender* inspired *Scramble*. The timeline is tight, as *Defender* was not unveiled publicly until October 1980, and *Scramble* first appeared at a trade show in January 1981. In his book chronicling the history of the Japanese industry, Masumi Akagi recounts that Kozuki stared at *Defender* for a long time at the 1980 AMOA. Whether this cryptic statement means he was taking it all in to copy it or was surprised to see a game incorporating similar ideas to *Scramble* is anyone's guess. Akagi, 2005, 230.

[67] Akagi, 2005, 229–230.

[68] Ibid, 289–290.

called *Super Cobra* that debuted just five months after *Scramble*. The new game replaced the player's spaceship with a helicopter, doubled the number of stages, and added a few new enemies but otherwise it played the same as its predecessor. Because of the high number of stages, *Super Cobra* also introduced the capability for the player to continue the game right where he left off after losing all his lives by inserting another coin. To forestall clone makers, Konami entered a deal with Sega to have the larger company manufacture the game.[69]

In the United States, Konami licensed *Scramble* to Stern. The relationship between the two companies began in 1980 when a man named Barry Feinblatt, who ran an import-export company called Universal Affiliated International, showed some Konami games to Gary Stern just as his company was planning to enter the video game business.[70] *Kamikaze* became the first video game Stern released in June 1980 under the name *Astro Invader*. It sold 5,000 units. Stern also manufactured a quirky Konami game called *The End*, a *Space Invaders* clone in which the bunkers protecting the player are composed of *Breakout*-style bricks that the enemy creatures steal to spell the word "end" at the top of the screen. When the word is completed, the game is over. The game was not a success.[71]

Stern began shipping *Scramble* in April 1981. Within two months, it was the top earning game in the country. Though its stay at the top was short, it moved over 15,000 units in less than a year. Stern licensed *Super Cobra* as well, which moved another 12,000 units after its release in July.[72] Buoyed by its video game success, Stern's revenues rose from $28 million in 1979 to $40 million in 1980 to a whopping $108 million in 1981.[73]

Stern was not the only video game manufacturer to experience such rapid financial growth, for in 1981, the entire industry took off like a rocket. After hitting $2.8 billion in 1980, coin drop nearly doubled to $4.9 billion in 1981. The number of units on location also skyrocketed from 541,000 to 1.1 million.[74] The industry was not just huge, it was now the most popular location-based entertainment activity in the United States, with twice the revenue of all the Nevada casinos put together, nearly twice the domestic box office of Hollywood, and three times the earnings of Major League Baseball,

[69] Ibid, 231.
[70] Stern, 2014.
[71] Stern, production memo, c. 1982.
[72] Ibid.
[73] "Stern Celebrates Fifth Anniversary Armed with Multi-Product Spread," *RePlay*, March 1982, 17.
[74] Vending Times Census of the Industry, July 1982, 64.

the NFL, and the NBA combined.[75] *Defender, Berzerk, Scramble,* and *Super Cobra* all played their role in this remarkable transformation of what just a decade before was still regarded by some as a shady business controlled by mobsters, but the most important product that brought video games well and truly into the mainstream was a simple maze game starring a yellow circle with a sliver removed.

---

[75] John Skow, "Games People Play," *Time,* January 18, 1982, 51.

34

Pac-Man Fever

On May 9, 1977, a new eatery opened on Winchester Boulevard in San Jose called Chuck E. Cheese's Pizza Time Theater. The establishment catered to younger children and featured three main attractions: pizza, a robot stage show, and a large arcade. The organization behind Pizza Time was the Restaurant Operating Division of Atari, Inc.

Nolan Bushnell truly believed in the video game as a new entertainment medium for men, women, and children of all ages, but all age groups did not have equal access to coin-operated games in the 1970s. When *Pong* launched in 1972, the prime venue was the working-class bar, which served a predominantly adult male clientele. When Jules Millman pioneered the shopping mall arcade, teenagers now had a place to play too, but younger children were still left out. As Atari considered expanding its arcade operations in the mid-1970s, Bushnell decided creating a family-friendly space would be the way to go.

Because arcades still suffered from a sleazy reputation and were not considered appropriate venues for young children, Bushnell decided to present his new operation to the public as a restaurant. Families would come to eat the food, and while they waited, their kids could hit the arcade games. Logically, the best food to serve would be something that takes time to prepare to maximize the time spent in the arcade, so Bushnell settled on pizza. Bushnell was also guided toward a pizzeria after eating at a chain called Pizza and Pipes that featured live music played on an old Wurlitzer movie organ. Bushnell thought a floor show would be a good way to lure in parents and keep them entertained while the kids were in the arcade, but he did not want to use live musicians.[1] Inspired by the Enchanted Tiki Room at Disneyland,

---

[1]Cohen, 1984, chap. 15.

in which animatronic birds appeared to sing prerecorded music, he decided to craft a show around a robotic band.[2]

Bushnell figured Cyan Engineering would be able to design the animatronics easily enough, but no one in the company had the artistic skills to develop the characters. Atari President Joe Keenan found what he thought was a perfect model when he attended the International Association of Amusement Parks and Attractions (IAAPA) trade show in Atlanta in 1974 and saw a vendor peddling what he believed to be an animal mascot suit in the style of the Warner Brothers cartoon character Wile E. Coyote. At the end of the show, Keenan bought the suit and brought it back to Grass Valley as a model for the animatronics. When he later called to check on the progress with the "coyote," the engineers at Cyan told him it was a rat.[3]

To develop his pizza arcade concept, Bushnell tapped former National Semiconductor executive Gene Landrum. After Landrum consulted on the VCS, Bushnell brought him into Atari with the intent of giving him a high-level position in the company's new consumer electronics division, but with the VCS still a year away from launch, he asked Landrum to do a business plan for the restaurant-arcade combination in the meantime. When Landrum presented the plan, Bushnell and Keenan were so impressed that they asked him to open the first location. Landrum protested because he had no experience in the restaurant or arcade fields, but he ultimately accepted a position as general manager of the new Restaurant Operating Division.[4]

Landrum was responsible for developing the entire concept for the venue from the floor plan to the stage show to the type of crust to use on the pizza.[5] His first major task was corralling the mascot. Keenan's rat costume had been lingering around the company for some time and even showed up in random Atari publicity photos such as the June 1976 groundbreaking ceremony for the company's new headquarters building in the Moffet Park district of Sunnyvale.[6] Landrum did not feel a rat was an appropriate mascot for the arcade, not only because of the negative connotation of rats and food, but also because they are predatory creatures. A mouse would work much better, but Disney already had the market for mice mascots cornered. Therefore Landrum worked with an artist named Harold Goldbranson to develop a

[2] Benj Edwards, "Robots, Pizza, and Sensory Overload: The Chuck E. Cheese Origin Story," Fast Company, May 31, 2017, https://www.fastcompany.com/40425172/robots-pizza-and-magic-the-chuck-e-cheese-origin-story.

[3] Keenan, 2018.

[4] Edwards, 2017.

[5] Gene Landrum, interview with the author, November 19, 2015.

[6] "Atari Plant Ground Broken," Play Meter, July 1976, 45.

hybrid mascot with characteristics of both animals. When it came time to name the new creature, Landrum suggested a three-syllable name with a similar patter to Mickey Mouse. He ultimately chose Chuck E. Cheese.[7]

Another important consideration in developing the space was how to keep it kid friendly by excluding older teenagers. Landrum's solution was not to allow anyone over a certain age into the establishment without an adult. For teenagers, the thought of having a parent present as they played coin-operated games would not be palatable at all, and they were sure to look elsewhere. Landrum had signs posted declaring that 16-year-olds were not allowed without a parent. At first, Bushnell was nonplussed at the turning away of potential customers, but he eventually came around on Landrum's idea and expanded on it by ordering the signs changed to exclude all teens without adult supervision.[8]

When Pizza Time opened in May 1977, it proved an immediate success. Warner Communications, however, was not impressed. The conglomerate bought Atari as a video game company not as a restaurant operator, and Manny Gerard believed getting too involved in this sideline would be an unprofitable distraction. When Bushnell asked for permission to open a second location, Gerard turned him down. Bushnell kept lobbying to expand the operation, so in 1978, Warner agreed to sell the business to him for $500,000. Bushnell incorporated it as Pizza Time Theater, Inc. and served as chairman and CEO of the company while retaining his positions at Atari. Landrum left Atari to become president and COO of Pizza Time. In fall 1978, they opened a second, much larger, location in San Jose with a massive two-story arcade.

When Nolan was removed from Atari, he redoubled his efforts to grow Pizza Time Theater and incentivized Gene Landrum to open as many stores as possible.[9] In 1979, the company opened three additional locations. Growing much larger would require an influx of capital from investors, so in October 1979, Bushnell lured Joe Keenan away from his largely ceremonial position as chairman of Atari to serve as president of Pizza Time because the seasoned executive would be more capable of attracting investment than Landrum.[10] Landrum remained with the firm as executive vice president and continued to oversee the firm's expansion into new locations. In 1980, he opened another 20. Then, the company decided to offer franchises to accelerate its expansion and to engage in co-op advertising with franchisees

---

[7] Landrum, 2015.
[8] Ibid.
[9] Keenan, 2018.
[10] Bushnell, 2015.

to increase the profile of the business nationwide. By the end of 1981, there were over 90 locations.

Pizza Time Theater represented the first serious attempt to expand coin-operated video games beyond their traditional male teenage audience. While a sound idea in principle, this approach was not necessarily destined for success as the *Space Invaders* boom took hold in the arcades. Because score chasing became a prime motivator during the boom, manufacturers released a string of increasingly more difficult shooting games that threatened to alienate all but the most hardcore players of video games. By 1981, however, Pizza Time was an unqualified success as video arcade games became a mainstream entertainment medium embraced by children and adults of both sexes and diverse socio-economic backgrounds. This apex for the industry spawned largely from a single game introduced by Namco and its North American manufacturing partner Midway.

***

As Namco designer Toru Iwatani began work on his next game in 1979 following *Gee Bee* and its sequels, he set himself two primary goals. Stung by the failure of *Gee Bee*, which he put down to its difficulty, he planned to develop a simpler game that could gain more traction.[11] He also noticed that game centers and Invader houses were largely dominated by men, with women only entering if they were with a boyfriend or a larger mixed group. As the centers were dark and noisy, he did not believe they were palatable to girls and wanted to create a game that couples could enjoy together or that girls might even want to play on their own.[12]

Iwatani started the design process by narrowing down the game concept through focusing on what he felt were prime activities enjoyed by women. Examples he came up with included fashion, fortune telling, going on dates, and eating.[13] As tabletop machines were common in cafés at the time, Iwatani homed in on the latter activity and shaped his concept around the verb "to eat" (*taberu*) by creating a character that would move around the screen devouring food.[14] Because he wanted the game to appeal to both sexes, Iwatani decided not to create a realistic character but to embrace instead

---

[11] "Interview with Toru Iwatani," 2010. Bandai Namco Entertainment, March 6, 2019, https://www.bandainamcoent.co.jp/asobimotto/page/videogame2.html.

[12] Chris Kohler, "Q&A: Pac-Man Creator Reflects on 30 Years of Dot-Eating," *Wired*, May 21, 2010, https://www.wired.com/2010/05/pac-man-30-years.

[13] Ibid.

[14] "The Development of Pac-Man," 2003.

the aesthetic of a social movement popular among girls in Japan at the time called *kawaii*.[15]

The term *kawaii*, which roughly encapsulates the concept of "cuteness," derives from the phrase *kawayushi*, which literally translates as "one's face is aglow" and denotes the concept of blushing. In Japanese culture, there is a connotation between blushing and being small, vulnerable, and loveable, hence the association of the term with being "cute." The *kawaii* movement originated in the 1970s as part of a larger rebellion by students and young people against traditional Japanese culture with its strictly defined roles and stern aesthetics and involved teenage girls embracing styles of dress, makeup, and presentation that emphasized a childlike demeanor and innocence. In *kawaii* art, this translated into deformed characters, often with large heads out of proportion with their bodies, giant, innocent eyes, and bright visuals.[16]

Kawaii transformed from a social movement into a lucrative business through the intervention of a company established in 1960 by Shintaro Tsuji called the Yamanishi Silk Company. In 1962, Tsuji began producing rubber sandals with flowers painted on them and soon realized that his cutest designs became his best sellers. He started hiring cartoonists to create adorable characters to adorn his merchandise. In 1973, Tsuji changed the name of his company to Sanrio,[17] a combination of *sanri*, an alternate reading of the kanji for Yamanishi, and the characters for "ou," which in Japan can represent the sound a person makes when excited. In 1974, an artist named Yuko Shimizu created an anthropomorphic white kitten wearing a blue dress and a red bow for Sanrio called Hello Kitty. First appearing on a clear plastic purse, Hello Kitty arrived at the height of the *kawaii* movement and gained instant popularity. Similar cute characters followed as Sanrio successfully commercialized *kawaii*.

In his new game, Iwatani incorporated *kawaii* styling by rendering the main character as a cartoony version of a mouth. The kanji for mouth, *kuchi*, is shaped like a square, which informed the basic design for the character, but Iwatani ultimately rounded out his design after being struck by the image of a pizza with one slice removed.[18] The team discussed adding additional facial

---

[15] Donovan, 2010, chap. 7.

[16] Bill Seigs, "Kawaii as Revolution? What's Behind the Famous Japanese Phenomenon," Kawaii Sekai, July 19, 2017, http://kawaiisekai.com/what-is-kawaii.

[17] "Sanrio Company, Ltd. History," Funding Universe, accessed June 10, 2019, http://www.fundinguniverse.com/company-histories/sanrio-company-ltd-history.

[18] Susan Lammers, *Programmers at Work: Interviews with 19 Programmers Who Shaped the Computer Industry* (Redmond, WA: Tempus Press, 1989), ebook, chap. 16. Iwatani has gone back and forth on the pizza story, which does feel like a "too good to be true" situation. It is his official story of record though, so absent contradiction I will take his word for it.

features like eyes to the design, but Iwatani decided that simplicity was the best course of action. He named both the character and the game *Puckman* to evoke the onomatopoeia for the sound a person makes while eating, which in Japanese is "paku-paku."[19]

Once he had a character, Iwatani surrounded him with food to eat, but this did not make for much of a game. At this point, Iwatani almost certainly observed *Head On* with its lanes and dot collecting, for he added structure to his game by placing the character in a maze stocked with pellets to eat. The game remained uninteresting with nothing to do other than moving around and collecting pellets, so Iwatani livened up the action by adding antagonists.[20] To keep with the *kawaii* aesthetic, these were cute ghosts like the main character in a manga Iwatani enjoyed as a child called *Little Ghost Q-Taro* and rendered in four different bright colors to enhance their appeal to women.[21]

To retain the simplicity and casual appeal central to his game concept, Iwatani ordered programmer Shigeo Funaki to program each ghost to follow a set pattern and to advance and retreat in waves so the game would not become overwhelmingly stressful. The red ghost always chases behind the player; the pink ghost always tries to position himself in front; the blue ghost switches between those two modes of attack and sometimes retreats from the player; and the orange ghost chases behind the player but retreats if he gets too close.[22]

Several other features were added to enhance the basic game. To break up the monotony of gathering pellets, Iwatani included bonus items that appear briefly near the center of the maze and can be collected for additional points. To allow the player to feel powerful from time to time, four "power pellets" were placed in the maze that when eaten turn the ghosts blue and allow the player to eat them and temporarily remove them from the playfield. This feature was inspired by the titular character of the King Features *Popeye* cartoons, who gained strength by consuming a can of spinach.[23] Finally, to give the player the occasional respite, Iwatani and Funaki created a series of three "intermissions," funny little animated vignettes that play occasionally after the player clears the maze of dots.[24]

---

[19] Ibid.

[20] Ibid.

[21] Patterson, 2016.

[22] Lammers, 1989, chap. 16. In the North American version of the game, the ghosts are given the names Blinky, Pinky, Inky, and Clyde.

[23] Craig Grannell, "The Making and Remaking of Pac-Man," *Retro Gamer*, no. 61, 2009. 29.

[24] Patterson, 2016.

Iwatani and a team of five people that included Funaki, sound designer Toshiro Kai, and hardware engineer Shigeichi Ishimura, spent roughly 17 months developing *Puckman*. This unusually long development cycle stemmed from the trial-and-error approach the team employed to lock down the feature set, the difficulty of creating the algorithms for the ghost attack patterns, and the trying process of perfecting the intermissions. On May 22, 1980, the game finally went out on test at a movie theater in Shibuya to a muted response. While couples and casual players enjoyed the game, the core game center audience did not. As the casual players only engaged with the game for short stints, *Puckman* looked to be a minor hit at best.[25]

Puckman went on sale in Japan in July 1980 and did acceptable, but not spectacular, business.[26] As *Puckman* featured simple controls – a joystick to move the title character around the maze was the only input – and overly cute characters out of step with currently popular products in the United States and Europe, Iwatani doubted the game would be released internationally. In the end, Namco offered the game to its North American partners alongside three others: an update on Atari's *Tank* called *Tank Battalion*, a cutesy *Galaxian* derivative called *King & Balloon*, and a driving game called *Rally-X*.

Namco felt *Rally-X* held the most promise for foreign markets. Like *Puckman*, the gameplay is clearly derived from *Head On*, but instead of collecting many dots the player must gather a small number of flags contained within a multi-screen maze while avoiding other cars – two at first and up to eight in later rounds. Play is regulated by lives, but the car only has a limited amount of fuel and slows to a virtual halt if it runs out. The player can deploy a smokescreen to temporarily stun the chasing computer opponents at the expense of additional fuel. At a time when games were largely set against black backgrounds and sported limited sound, *Rally-X* featured a full-color playfield that scrolled in four directions and a continuous musical accompaniment more complex than the four repeating notes in *Space Invaders*. With stellar audiovisual presentation and challenging gameplay, Namco thought the game would appeal to American score chasers more than cutesy, casual *Puckman*.

Namco looked to license its four new games to multiple companies and met with Atari, Midway, and a small pinball company looking to break into video called Game Plan.[27] Namco offered *Puckman* to Atari first, but

[25] Kohler, 2010.

[26] Grannell, 2009.

[27] Game Plan was established as a subsidiary of a company called AES Systems in 1978 because AES president Lee Goldboss was a pinball fan. It went under in 1982 without every making an impact in pinball or video games.

the two firms were not on the best of terms at that moment, and *Asteroids* production was still going strong, so Gene Lipkin turned it down.[28] At that point, Namco decided to offer Midway and Game Plan two games each. Ken Anderson of Game Plan and David Marofske of Midway flipped a coin to decide who would pick first. Anderson won and took *Tank Battalion* and *King & Balloon*; Marofske was saddled with *Puckman*.[29]

Before Midway released *Puckman*, Namco changed the name after Namco America employee Satish Bhutani pointed out vandals could easily change the "P" in the title to an "F" on the cabinet marquee with unfortunate results.[30] To keep with the "paku-paku" inspiration, the company called the North American release *Pac-Man*. Midway debuted both *Pac-Man* and *Rally-X* at the 1980 AMOA show, where the same buyers that declared *Defender* too hard declared *Pac-Man* too cutesy.[31] As with *Defender*, the prognosticators were wrong.

If *Space Invaders* was a phenomenon, then *Pac-Man* was an apotheosis. While *Defender* brought the hardcore players into the arcade in record numbers and became the top earning game of 1981 in traditional locations, *Pac-Man* brought in everyone else and opened new locations. With its simple controls, colorful characters, and addictive gameplay, the game appealed to children, young professionals, and women turned off by the violence and/ or intense difficulty of a *Missile Command* or a *Defender*. Midway and Atari started the push into convenience stores with *Space Invaders* and *Asteroids*, but *Pac-Man* cemented a place for video games in those locations and led a coin-op video invasion of supermarkets, movie theaters, fast food joints, ice cream parlors, newsstands, and dozens of other establishments with a few square feet of floor space to spare.[32] Arcades were not immune to the game's charm either and usually hosted five or six *Pac-Man* cabinets, if not more.[33]

Midway sold 96,000 *Pac-Man* cabinets in North America, shattering the record for the bestselling coin-operated amusement in the United States.[34] In a time when the average coin-op video game was taking in $186 a week, the

---

[28] Lipkin, 2014.

[29] Smith, 2016, 430.

[30] Bhutani, 2016.

[31] Reports that *Rally-X* was considered one of the best games at the show while *Pac-Man* was ignored appear not to be true, as none of the show reports in the trades paid much attention to *Rally-X*.

[32] Phillippa K. Mezile, "Video-Game Mania," *The Washington Post*, March 11, 1982, and Katya Goncharoff, "Video Games: A Glutton for Globs…And Quarters," *The New York Times*, November 15, 1981.

[33] Goncharoff, 1981.

[34] Bernstein, 1982, 70.

average *Pac-Man* game was raking in around $240 and not experiencing the typical drop-off in earnings after a few weeks on location. In prime locations, the game could earn as much as $500 a week.[35] While still a score-chasing game in the vein of a *Space Invaders* or *Defender*, the game represented a paradigm shift in video game presentation. While games featuring spaceships blasting aliens would continue to be a significant presence in the coming years, *Pac-Man* demonstrated there was also a place for cartoony graphics, distinctive protagonists, and gameplay based on dodging obstacles and collecting items rather than just blowing up everything in sight.

While *Pac-Man*'s simplicity and colorful characters helped bridge the gap between women and coin-operated video games, once they started playing, they often enjoyed a variety of games.[36] While the complex controls of *Defender* may have been a turn off for many, the right combination of pleasing visual aesthetic, deep gameplay with strategic and problem-solving elements, and elegant control systems could attract women to just about any genre. No game proved that point better than Atari's big 1981 hit: *Centipede*.

***

Centipede began life as "Bug Shooter," a concept in a book full of game ideas for which no one has ever taken credit. The book contained all the designs of merit that emerged from the periodic brainstorming sessions the Atari Coin-Op Division held at Pajaro Dunes and other off-site locations at which anyone could present a concept. These could be simple themes, more concrete proposals with some sketches backing them up, or even occasionally a fully thought out project with hardware, controls, and other features already defined. The large group would split into smaller groups to debate about and improve on various concepts, and the best would be immortalized in the book for potential further development.[37]

The Bug Shooter concept excited one of Atari's newest employees, Dona Bailey. While not particularly good at math, Bailey possessed both a faculty with language and an artistic sensibility. As a psychology major at the University of Arkansas, Bailey discovered programming while working with a calculator in a statistics class and found the discipline fascinating not for its mathematical dimensions, but for the need to adapt a language to solve puzzles. After graduation, Bailey pursued programming through 18 months

---

[35] Goncharoff, 1981.
[36] Mezile, 1982.
[37] Rouse, 2005, chap. 6.

of graduate work in statistics and three years as a researcher. Seeking nicer weather, she moved to California in 1978 and worked for General Motors as a programmer for the cruise control system on the 1981 Cadillac Seville. She did not find the work fulfilling.[38]

In 1980, Bailey heard the song *Space Invader* from the debut album of The Pretenders, which sampled the sound effects from *Space Invaders*. Bailey asked a friend where the name of the song came from and ended up in a dive bar playing the tabletop version of the game. Bailey realized that programming a video game was like her current work except with a greater artistic element and decided to break into the business. Atari hired her in June 1980. She was the only female engineer in the coin-op division.[39]

Bailey was assigned to the team managed by Ed Logg, who had been promoted since completing *Asteroids*. Logg turned her loose on the brainstorming book to pick an idea for her first game. Most of the games revolved around the space shooters prevalent at the time, which did not interest Bailey, but her eye was drawn to the bug shooter concept, which was described as a multi-segmented creature that the player shoots at.[40] Because this would be her first project, Logg defined the basic parameters of the game, which consisted of a centipede snaking its way back and forth across the screen from top to bottom, where the player was situated as in *Space Invaders*. Scattered across the screen would be blocks – later changed to mushrooms – that would cause the centipede to change direction and drop one line closer to the player. As in *Asteroids*, Logg also added a second object that would pose a more direct threat to the player to keep him moving, in this case a spider.[41] He also adapted the multi-button control scheme of that product for the game.[42]

Once Logg completed the game design, Bailey began programming. As the arcade hardware was less capable than the massive computers she had worked with at GM, she found the project difficult at times. Logg ended up programming about half the game himself after ditching his management position to get back into the trenches. The game proved uninteresting at first until director of engineering Dave van Elderen suggested that the player be able to shoot the mushrooms. This added a new layer of strategy to the game,

---

[38] David Koon, "Centipede Creator Teaches at UALR," *Arkansas Times*, November 19, 2015, https://arktimes.com/entertainment/ae-feature/2015/11/19/centipede-creator-teaches-at-ualr.

[39] Ibid.

[40] Darran Jones, "Creating Centipede," *Retro Gamer*, no. 141, 2015, 87.

[41] Rouse, 2005, chap. 6.

[42] Jones, 2015, 88.

especially after Logg used the excuse to introduce two more bugs: a flea that adds more mushrooms to the playfield in a random distribution and a scorpion that poisons the mushrooms.[43] If the centipede collides with a poison mushroom, it abandons its usual movement pattern to make a beeline for the player.

In addition to programming roughly half of *Centipede*, Bailey contributed two significant design wrinkles of her own. The first was a change in control scheme. As she was not an adept game player, she had difficulty adapting to Logg's multi-button controls. When engineer Steve Calfee noticed this, he suggested swapping in a joystick for movement in place of buttons. While this was an improvement, Bailey did not think joystick control was that fun. Next, they tried a trackball, which Bailey felt worked perfectly.[44] Her other major contribution was the color scheme for the graphics. Bailey wanted the bugs and mushrooms to really pop against the black background of the game and felt the standard color palette used in most coin-operated games did not do the trick. She asked her technician to fiddle with the hardware to look for alternatives and had him stop when he hit upon a striking set of pastels. Bailey then proceeded to create multi-colored insects and mushrooms that featured two complimentary colors, one for the outline and one to fill in the shape.[45] The result was some of the most vibrant visuals seen in an early 1980s arcade.

Released in June 1981, *Centipede* was the perfect complement to *Pac-Man*. Once the easier game lured a broader segment of the population to the arcade and hooked them on video games, *Centipede* came along with its amazing visuals and strategic mushroom management to keep them coming back for more. Not only was *Centipede* recognized as just the second coin-operated video game to entice women in large numbers, but it also became the second best-selling arcade game Atari released, topping out at over 50,000 units.[46] Within weeks of its debut, it was one of the top-five earning games on location. By November, it had passed *Pac-Man* and sat just behind *Defender* in the number two position.

With *Centipede* leading the way, Atari captured nearly 25% of the coin-operated video game market in 1981 by unit sales, lagging only Midway, which cornered roughly 30% of the market with its *Pac-Man* juggernaut.

---

[43] Rouse, 2005, chap. 6.

[44] In interviews, Ed Logg has taken credit for the trackball, which he had worked with previously on an update to *Atari Football*. Bailey told a detailed story about choosing to use one to *Retro Gamer*, which feels plausible. It is possible that Logg was the one to suggest trying the trackball when she was looking for an alternate control scheme. Jones, 2015, 88, and Rouse, 2005, chap. 6.

[45] Jones, 2015, 88.

[46] Atari Arcade Production Numbers, 1999.

Williams had the third largest market share on the strength of *Defender* alone at 11%. Between them, these top three companies cornered 66% of the market.[47] Just as *Pac-Man* cemented Bally's place at the top of the coin-operated world, so too would the game have the same impact on Atari's fortunes in the home.

---

[47] Bernstein, 1982, 66.

35

Blue Skies

In fall 1980, Atari, Inc. dispatched the president of its coin-operated games division, Joe Robbins, to Japan to meet with Masaya Nakamura of Namco. Ever since Nakamura made the decision to manufacture *Breakout* on his own in contravention of his licensing agreement with Atari, relations had been strained between the two firms.[1] Robbins, who conducted extensive international business during his time with Empire Distributing and had a solid rapport with Nakamura, was dispatched to smooth things over.

When Namco bought Atari Japan in 1974, it was granted the exclusive right to distribute Atari's coin-operated games in Japan for a period of ten years.[2] After the *Breakout* situation, Atari began dealing with other companies and granted Sega and Taito the rights to produce upright and tabletop versions, respectively, of *Asteroids* and *Missile Command*. When Atari refused to stop licensing to other firms, Namco sued.[3] Robbins was sent to Japan to help negotiate a resolution, but he was specifically instructed not to sign anything. Instead, he settled the case.

Robbins's actions in Japan stunned Atari management, and "who shot JR" jokes began circulating around the company in reference to the infamous cliffhanger that had recently ended a season of the television show *Dallas*. Combined with the *Battlezone* manufacturing debacle, signing the settlement with Namco probably cost Robbins his job. Atari ultimately profited from the settlement, however, as it gave the company certain rights to Namco coin-operated games in the home. At the time of the deal, Namco games had

[1] Lipkin, 2014.

[2] Sheff, 1999, chap. 11.

[3] "Game Machine October 15, 2000 issue" Amusement Press, last modified October 9, 2000, http://www.ampress.co.jp/backnumber/bn2000.10.15.html.

been largely unsuccessful in the United States, so this hardly seemed worth the insubordination, but it paved the way for Atari to conclude a deal in April 1981 to acquire the console and home computer rights to the megahit *Pac-Man*.[4] As in the arcade, the arrival of *Pac-Man* in the home represented the apex of an industry that had experienced rapid growth over the previous year.

***

Just as the coin-operated video game hit a significant new level of popularity in 1980, so too did the home market reach fantastic new heights in 1981. Total revenues for the U.S. market nearly tripled from $475 million to $1.45 billion despite the country being in the throes of a recession.[5] Consumers purchased roughly 4.6 million consoles and around 34.5 million cartridges, an average of over seven games per console.[6] By the end of the year, 9% of U.S. households that owned a television also owned a programmable video game console.[7]

Atari remained the dominant console company by far, capturing 65% of the market by dollar volume as it sold an estimated 3.1 million units of the VCS.[8] Sales were boosted through a $40 million advertising campaign and by a low price compared to the competition, as retailers began consistently selling the system in the $130–$140 range despite the lack of an official price cut from Atari, choosing to sacrifice hardware margins to capture rapidly expanding software sales.[9] In 1980, Atari had achieved fantastic results with its port of the hit Taito arcade game *Space Invaders*, so for 1981, the company continued to focus on bringing some of the biggest games in the coin-op world into the home. Fortunately for the company, two of the biggest arcade games of 1980, *Asteroids* and *Missile Command*, were developed in house. Unfortunately, they both featured additional complexity over *Space Invaders*, which had already tasked the VCS nearly to its limit. Thankfully, even after

---

[4]The story of Robbins acquiring the rights to *Pac-Man* has been widely told within the coin-op industry (see, for example, Al Alcorn's recollections in Kent, 2005, 208 and the summary of Robbins's life in the American Amusement Machine Charitable Foundation brochure, 1990). Whatever he signed did not settle the whole issue, however, as Atari general counsel Skip Paul signed the actual license agreement for *Pac-Man* in April 1981 (see license between Namco America and Atari Inc. for the home rights to *Pac-Man*, dated April 27, 1981). It is unlikely Robbins and Alcorn are fabricating or misremembering the entire story, so the settlement must have played a role, it is just not entirely clear what that was.

[5]Frost & Sullivan, 1983, 39.

[6]*Software Strategies: The Home Computer and Videogame Marketplace* (Boston, MA: The Yankee Group, 1984), 3.

[7]Frost & Sullivan, 1983, 39–40.

[8]Ibid, 40, and The Yankee Group, 1984, 3.

[9]Frost & Sullivan, 1983, 40.

the Activision defection, the company still employed two talented programmers in its VCS programming group named Brad Stewart and Rob Fulop.

Brad Stewart graduated with a psychology degree from the University
of Pittsburgh in 1972, but had more credits in computer science, for which
the school lacked an undergraduate degree at that time. After working for
the Ford Motor Company in both Michigan and California for two years,
Stewart joined Atari in May 1977 as one of the first hires after the original
group that developed the launch titles for the VCS. After working on an unreleased hardware project for a time, Stewart prepared to program his first VCS
game just as the programming group decided to port *Breakout* to the console.
Both Stewart and fellow programmer Ian Shepherd wanted the project, so
they decided it would go to whichever programmer achieved the highest score
on a *Breakout* cabinet in the break room. Stewart won and coded the game.[10]

After completing *Breakout*, Stewart turned his attention to *Asteroids*.
The most significant problem in porting the game to the VCS was the large
number of objects that needed to be placed on the screen. Even with all the
previously invented tricks like the H-move or venetian blinds, there did not
appear to be a credible way to display a dozen or so independently moving
objects to recreate the chaotic *Asteroids* playfield. Stewart's solution was to
"flicker" the graphics, that is, rapidly switch between two sets of graphical elements on every other frame. Stewart discovered that when this technique was executed properly, it was possible to switch between the two sets
of graphics quickly enough that it only registered as a subtle flashing of the
objects on the screen.[11] In this way, Stewart was able to put a large number of
rocks up on the screen in a diverse array of colors.

As the game neared completion, one other problem reared its head: the
complex collision detection calculations could not be completed within
the number of available cycles. This problem could be solved by storing
the collision data in tables but doing so would cause the size of the game
program to exceed 4K, the maximum amount of memory the VCS hardware could address. Stewart and fellow programmer Bob Smith used every
trick they could think of to cram the game into 4K, but they could not
do it.[12] Fortunately, a group of engineers in the semiconductor group led

---

[10] Scott Stilphen, "DP Interviews: Brad Stewart," *Digital Press*, 2001, http://www.digitpress.com/
library/interviews/interview_brad_stewart.html.

[11] "An Interview with Atari 2600 Developer and Imagic Co-Founder Rob Fulop," *Paleotronic*,
March 29, 2019, https://paleotronic.com/2019/03/29/an-interview-with-atari-2600-developer-and-
imagic-co-founder-rob-fulop.

[12] Hans Reutter, "PRGE 2016 – Atari Programmers – Portland Retro Gaming Expo," filmed October
22, 2016, YouTube video, posted October 29, 2016, https://www.youtube.com/watch?v=P3bA2dnefV0.

by Carl Nielsen had developed a method for bank switching on the VCS, a technique that allowed the system to switch between multiple blocks of memory so that even though it is never addressing more than 4K at a time, it can draw from a larger pool of ROM. Bank switching allowed Stewart to program *Asteroids* in 8K of memory to solve the collision detection problems.[13]

Asteroids was planned as the big holiday release for 1980, but the complexities of fitting the whole game onto a cartridge resulted in a delay.[14] Instead, Atari unveiled *Asteroids* at the 1981 Winter CES in Las Vegas alongside three other cartridges, *Othello*, *Video Pinball*, and *Warlords*.[15] Aside from *Asteroids*, *Warlords* was the most interesting game of the set. A two-to-four-player competitive game, it was programmed by Carla Meninsky, a Stanford psychology major who worked with the computers in the school's neuroscience group to model the human brain. After college she tried to interest companies in letting her build computer animation systems for them and fell in with a group from SAIL with similar ideas. The SAIL people roomed with Atari's Warren Robinett, who arranged an interview for her with George Simcock at Atari.[16]

Meninsky was hired by Atari to advance her computer animation work, but with the recent Activision defection, she was asked to write VCS games instead. Given a list of previously brainstormed game ideas, she chose to create a clone of the arcade hit *Head On*, which Atari released as *Dodge 'Em*.[17] For her next game, she returned to the list and chose a competitive *Breakout* concept originally submitted by industrial engineer and graphic designer Roger Hector.[18] *Warlords* allows up to four people to play using the Atari paddle controllers, of which two could be plugged into a single port on the console, and places each in control of a paddle protecting a castle in one corner of the screen made of *Breakout*-style bricks with a "king" inside. The ball represents a fireball that will destroy any bricks it hits. Players use their paddles to deflect the ball to destroy the other players' castles and kill the king inside.[19] Last man standing wins. *Warlords* proved the most exciting VCS multi-player experience since *Combat* back in 1977.

[13] Stilphen, 2001.

[14] Paul Drury, "Desert Island Disks: Dennis Koble," *Retro Gamer* no. 107, 2012, 90.

[15] "Games Hit Jackpot at Winter CES," *Playthings*, March 1981, 96.

[16] Will Nicholes, "A Conversation with Carla Meninsky," November 12, 2011, https://willnicholes.com/interviews/CarlaMeninsky.htm.

[17] Ibid.

[18] Roger Hector, interview with the author, August 26, 2014.

[19] An alternate game mode allows the player to "catch" the ball by holding down the button on the controller and then release it.

While Stewart toiled on *Asteroids*, his friend Rob Fulop tackled *Missile Command*. A native of Oakland, California, Fulop was introduced to computing in 1974 when his alma mater, Skyline High School, installed a terminal hooked up to a computer at the Lawrence Hall of Science. The first program he wrote flipped a coin 100 times and tabulated the results. After that, he wrote a version of Nim and a "Boy Analyzer" designed to entice girls to come to the lab by inviting them to type in the name of a boy at the school and get a printout describing his qualities as a boyfriend.[20]

Because of his experiences with the terminal at his high school, Fulop attended the University of California, Berkeley and majored in electrical engineering. Fulop had been designing simple games since he was a child, so when he saw an advertisement for a summer programming job at Atari in 1977 during his junior year of college, he applied. Fulop spent the summer in the company's pinball division, so when he graduated in 1978, he called the company looking for a permanent job. While there were no openings in the coin-op division, he was hired into the Consumer Electronics Division to program games for the VCS.[21]

Fulop's first project was a port of the minor Atari coin-op hit *Night Driver*. He then ported *Space Invaders* to the Atari 400 and 800, but because he did not want to create a straight up copy of an existing game again, he radically altered the presentation by changing the art for the alien ships, altering their formation, and having them fly in from a giant rocket on the side of the screen. Marketing was nonplussed with the changes, but Atari still shipped the game. After learning of Stewart's flickering graphics technique while the two were eating lunch together, Fulop decided to employ it to port *Missile Command* to the VCS. Stung by criticism of his *Space Invaders* game, he decided not to deviate in any way from the coin-op game and managed to create a version nearly identical to the original.[22]

Although *Asteroids* debuted at CES in January 1981, it did not hit retail until August. *Missile Command*, meanwhile, arrived on store shelves in May. Combined with continuing strong sales of *Space Invaders* the two games propelled Atari to a dominant 70% share of the cartridge market by dollar volume. Indeed, *Space Invaders*, *Asteroids*, and *Missile Command* accounted for 40% of the cartridges Atari sold that year.[23] Overall, the Warner Communications

---

[20] Fulop, *Paleotronic*, 2019.

[21] "Rob Fulop (Atari) – Interview," Arcade Attack, March 24, 2017, https://www.arcadeattack.co.uk/rob-fulop.

[22] Fulop, *Paleotronic*, 2019. While Fulop's recreation of the game was as faithful as the hardware allowed, it was not perfect. Most notably, the player only controls a single missile base instead of three.

[23] Frost & Sullivan, 1983, 40.

Consumer Electronics Division, which consisted primarily of Atari, surged to $1.2 billion in revenue and income of $287 million as the parent company recorded the best fiscal year in its history with over $3 billion in revenue and income over $226 million.[24]

Meanwhile, Mattel Electronics was just coming into its own after the advertising campaign featuring George Plimpton turned sales of the Intellivision around at the end of 1980. In 1981, the company spent another $15 million on George Plimpton commercials as it continued to focus on the graphical superiority of the system.[25] This led to a bit of controversy as Atari hit back with a commercial of its own featuring a smug boy imitating Plimpton and pointing out that Atari has *Asteroids, Missile Command,* and *Warlords,* while Intellivision does not. Mattel countered with a new Plimpton commercial showcasing its own space shooters like *Space Battle* and two new games called *Space Armada* and *Astrosmash.* After this commercial aired, Atari complained to the broadcast standards departments of all three television networks – ABC, CBS, and NBC – and NBC ended up pulling both the Atari and Mattel commercials in early December.[26] Despite – or perhaps because of – the controversy, Mattel Electronics more than quadrupled its Intellivision sales to 900,000 units in 1981 and took a 27% console market share by dollar volume.[27] Midway through the year, Mattel spun the division out of Mattel Toys so that it reported directly to the president of the entire company.[28]

In 1979 and 1980, Mattel relied entirely on APh to design and program games for the Intellivision, but with the system proving a success, Mattel Electronics president Josh Denham created an in-house programming group. As at Atari, these programmers were forced to keep their identities a secret to prevent poaching by other companies, but they gained a collective name when *TV Guide* ran a profile on the Mattel Electronics programmers in its June 19, 1982 issue and dubbed them the "Blue Sky Rangers."

The first two Blue Sky Rangers, Mike Minkoff and Rick Levine, were already working on handheld games for Mattel Electronics when the group was being formed and transferred to Intellivision. Levine, a former teacher with a math degree from UCLA, became involved in the early hobbyist

[24] "Warner Sets Financial Records," *Playthings*, April 1982, 15, and "Video Leads Charge in Games Battle," *Playthings*, April 1982, 49.

[25] Ibid.

[26] "Atari-Intellivision TV Battle," *The New York Times*, December 14, 1981.

[27] Bernstein, 1982, 18, and Frost & Sullivan, 1983, 40.

[28] "Mattel Electronics Becomes Separate Unit," *Toy & Hobby World*, September 1981.

computer scene and purchased a Sol-20 in 1977. He wrote several games for the computer, including a simulation he used in a psychology class to teach students about different types of stress.[29] He subsequently returned to school at University of California Irvine and completed a computer science degree in 1981. While still in school, he learned Mattel was making games and wrote the company asking for a job so he could support himself while earning his degree. He and Minkoff, a 15-year veteran of Mattel who started in data processing before transferring to Mattel Electronics, were sent to APh to learn how the Intellivision worked and start game development. Levine was an avid bowler and had created a bowling handheld for Mattel, so he and Minkoff built on that product to create *PBA Bowling* as their first game.[30]

After Intellivision had been on the market for a year, it became clear to management that while the console supported some wonderful sports games, it was suffering in comparison to the VCS because it lacked any decent action games like those currently gobbling quarters in the arcade. Mattel attempted to tackle this problem on several fronts. APh developed a cartridge informally named *Some of Theirs* that copied some of Atari's most successful early coin-op games. These included variants of *Tank, Jet Fighter, Breakout*, and *Pong*. Mattel's lawyers requested the *Breakout* and *Pong* games be removed, so the final product, called *Triple Action*, shipped with just the *Tank* and *Jet Fighter* games as well as a racing game. The games were named *Battle Tank, Biplanes*, and *Racing Cars*, respectively.[31] APh also ported *Space Invaders* to the console as *Space Armada*. As the Intellivision could only display eight sprites on a line, the programmers used a technique called "sequencing GRAM" that bypassed the exec to directly animate the background graphics to create the invaders.[32]

The new internal team began developing action games as well. For his second project, Minkoff created a *Blockade* clone and an adaptation of an unreleased *Blockade* handheld variant in which the two players control snakes attempting to eat each other's tail. The games were combined on a single cartridge and released as *Snafu*. The most successful action game by the company, and indeed the most successful game ever produced for the

---

[29] Al Backiel, "DP Interviews: Rick Levine," *Digital Press*, 1999, http://www.digitpress.com/library/interviews/interview_rick_levine.html.

[30] Richard Levine, "'PBA Bowling' Among 100 Greatest," Blog: Richard S. Levine, July 7, 2017, https://www.rickslevine.com/blog/pba-bowling-among-100-greatest.

[31] "Intellivision Action Network," Intellivision Lives, accessed February 6, 2018, http://www.intellivisionlives.com/bluesky/games/credits/action.html.

[32] "Intellivision Space Action Network," Intellivision Lives, accessed February 6, 2018, http://www.intellivisionlives.com/bluesky/games/credits/space.html"

Intellivision, was *Astrosmash*, which was created by the first person hired by Mattel specifically to program video games, John Sohl.

A Princeton graduate with a degree in statistics, Sohl moved to California after school to work on a cancer research project at UCLA. After becoming disillusioned by that job and being terminated, Sohl saw an ad in the summer of 1980 for programmers at Mattel Electronics and was hired by Mike Minkoff. Although technically hired to develop handheld product, he was transferred to Intellivision within a matter of weeks. After doing the sounds for Levine and Minkoff's bowling game, Sohl turned to his first project, a clone of the arcade hit *Asteroids*. Rather than copying the game exactly, he programmed a variant called *Avalanche* partially inspired by *Missile Command* in which the player scored points by shooting rocks falling out of the sky and lost points for any that managed to reach the ground. He also included an enemy called a "spinner" that would kill the player if it reached the ground. When head of product development Richard Chang saw the finished game, he ordered Sohl to go back and make a straightforward *Asteroids* clone as he had been instructed.[33]

Sohl developed the *Asteroids* clone under the name *Meteor!* but discovered that he had enough space on the cartridge to include *Avalanche* as well, so he left it in as a second game option. This turned out to be fortunate, because marketing decided that an *Asteroids* clone would never fly legally and asked him to remove it and just ship his falling rocks game. As other Mattel Electronics staff had become incredibly skilled at the game during this period, Sohl added several more enemy types on higher levels to increase the challenge.[34] Mattel released Sohl's game as *Astrosmash* in October 1981, and it quickly became the must-have game for the system. In late 1982, it replaced *Las Vegas Poker & Blackjack* as the game bundled with the system, and by June 1983 it had sold nearly 1 million copies.[35] With *Astrosmash* leading the way, Mattel captured 16% of the software market by dollar volume in 1981.[36] For the fiscal year ending January 1982, Mattel reported record sales and earnings of $1.1 billion and $39.1 million, respectively. Mattel Electronics contributed 25% of the parent company's total sales.[37]

---

[33] "RoundUp 46: Modificability of Doom," *Retrogaming Roundup*, podcast audio, March 2012, http://www.retrogamingroundup.com/shownotes/2012/roundup046_2012.03.php.

[34] Ibid.

[35] "Intellivision Space Action Network."

[36] Frost & Sullivan, 1983, 40.

[37] "Mattel Sales Reach $1.1 Billion," *Playthings*, May 5, 1982, 15.

Magnavox, which in February 1981 ceased to be a subsidiary of Philips and became a brand name for a new entity called North American Philips Consumer Electronics,[38] came in a distant third to the two powerhouses on the market, but it still experienced its best year by far, selling around 500,000 consoles to take 7% of the market by dollar share.[39] External contractor Ed Averett remained the company's most significant development asset. In spring 1981, Philips debuted his *Asteroids* clone *UFO!* and promoted it heavily. In the summer, the company released a hybrid game by Averett called *Quest for the Ring*, a tabletop board game for which the Odyssey cartridge is only used to adjudicate combat between the players and a series of monsters encountered while searching a fantasy realm for ten magic rings. Averett created the game in response to letters from parents wishing for a game that introduced strategy alongside reflex-based gameplay to level the playing field when competing with their children.[40] In late summer, Philips released a game by Averett that could have easily been the company's biggest hit and a system seller, but was instead thwarted by the U.S. court system.

During a layover in an airport in February 1981, Averett and Odyssey product manager Mike Staup beheld *Pac-Man* for the first time. Ed and his wife, Lisa, were busy creating another game at the time, but around May they turned their attention to creating a variant of the coin-op hit. Averett wanted to retain the basic maze chase gameplay but otherwise go in a completely different direction. Staup insisted on something much closer to *Pac-Man*, but different enough to not risk violating copyright or trademark law, which was unsettled in the area of video games at the time.[41] In a compromise, Averett kept the maze, the pursuing enemies, and the dots, but placed only 12 dots in the maze rather than 240. These dots also moved around the playfield over the course of the game. As in *Pac-Man*, certain of these pellets were special and allowed the player to turn the tables on his pursuers. The protagonist and the pursuers strongly resembled the characters in *Pac-Man*, though they were slightly different. Mike Staup initially named the character and the game "Munchkin," but after he joked with Consumer Electronics president Kenneth C. Meinken that they would name the character after him, it ultimately became *K.C. Munchkin*.[42]

[38] Staup, 1981, 225.
[39] Bernstein, 1982, 18 and Frost & Sullivan, 1983, 40.
[40] James Hague, "Ed Averett," Halcyon Days, March 1997, https://dadgum.com/halcyon/BOOK/AVERETT.HTM.
[41] Averett, 1981, 72–73.
[42] Staup, 1981, 244–245.

K.C. Munchkin debuted in August 1981 to brisk sales and favorable comparisons to *Pac-Man*, which was still unavailable in the home. This caught the ire of Atari, which had recently acquired the home rights to *Pac-Man*. Both Atari and coin-op rights holder Midway sued in late 1981 and asked for a preliminary injunction to restrain Philips from selling the game until a verdict was reached. The district court judge denied the injunction, but on appeal, the Seventh Circuit Court of Appeals decided that a finding of infringement was likely under the substantial similarity test and therefore granted the injunction in March 1982. The trial dragged on for at least two more years,[43] by which time Magnavox's window to make any money on the game had passed.[44]

Beyond Atari, Mattel, and Philips, there were essentially no remaining competitors in the North American hardware market. Astrovision, the Columbus, Ohio-based startup that bought the Bally Consumer Division in mid-1980 and continued to market the Bally Arcade, limped along largely by positioning its console as a hobbyist system on which a small, but dedicated group enjoyed using Bally BASIC to create their own games.[45] At the January CES, the company showed off yet another version of the long-promised keyboard add-on, this time sporting a visual language invented at the University of Illinois at Chicago called ZGrass,[46] but it once again failed to enter production. A handful of new games were released near the end of the year, including a *Galaxian* clone called *Galactic Invasion*,[47] as was an improved BASIC marketed as *Astrovision BASIC*,[48] but the system did not attract much interest outside its small niche and captured less than 1% of the total market.[49]

APF fared even worse. At the January 1981 CES, the company debuted an update to its microcomputer hardware called the Imagination System II that integrated the MP-1000 video game system with its computer add-on and incorporated more memory, but it retailed at an unattractive price point of $399 for a system that was limited compared to the competition.

[43] "Final Pretrial Order," Midway Manufacturing Co. v. North American Philips Consumer Electronics Corp., No. 81-6434 (N.D. Ill), December 18, 1984. Note that the case is now Midway v. Philips rather than Atari v. Philips, presumably because Atari, Inc. had ceased to exist by that point and was thus no longer a party to the suit.

[44] The final disposition of the case is uncertain, but it most likely ended in a settlement. There is no evidence in the extant records of the case that a trial ever took place.

[45] Bob Fabris, "An Introduction to the BPA," Bally Alley, April 13, 2001, http://www.ballyalley.com/ballyalley/articles/Robert_Fabris_introduction-edited.html.

[46] "Astrovision Add-On," *The Arcadian*, February 7, 1981, 41.

[47] "New Video Game Schedule," *The Arcadian*, October 5, 1981, 121.

[48] "Astrovision BASIC," *The Arcadian*, December 7, 1981, 14.

[49] Frost & Sullivan, 1983, 40.

An expansion called the System III was also announced that added a disk drive and other peripherals but retailed for an even less attractive $1,195. Lacking faith in this newest offering, the two New York banks that controlled APF's lines of credit demanded that the company exit the video game and computer businesses immediately and return to its core calculator business or they would call in their loans. Owners Sy and Marty Lipper refused and handed over the keys to the company office at a final meeting. APF essentially ceased operations at that point, though it continued to exist on paper for a few years as the banks wound it down.[50]

While the hardware market was coalescing around the leaders, the software market began to expand rapidly once Activision proved the viability of third-party software development. Activision itself continued to lead the way in this uncharted field by releasing four more games before the end of the year: *Freeway* and *Kaboom* in July and *Ice Hockey* and *Stampede* in December. *Ice Hockey* by Alan Miller was another technical tour de force for the VCS that used several tricks to get four players on the screen and have the two teams wear different color uniforms.[51] *Stampede* by Bob Whitehead started with the programmer's desire to do a western-themed game because the genre was underrepresented and featured gameplay inspired by the rows of advancing aliens in *Space Invaders*.[52] The player controls a cowboy pursuing cattle that scroll in from the right side of the screen. The player must lasso the steers before they disappear off the left side of the screen. If too may steers escape, the player loses a life.

The most popular Activision games of the year were *Freeway* by David Crane and *Kaboom* by Larry Kaplan. The idea for *Freeway* was born from two events in Chicago during CES. First, Crane and some friends left the convention center through the wrong exit and had to weave through traffic to reach their destination. The same day, Larry Kaplan observed another pedestrian crossing the street against traffic.[53] Crane decided avoiding traffic made for an interesting play mechanic and developed a game featuring one or two chickens trying to cross the road across multiple lanes of traffic. Crane pulled off an impressive programming feat by cramming 24 moving sprites onto the screen to represent the traffic and discovered that the gray highway

[50] Edwards, 2016.
[51] "Alan Miller on 'Ice Hockey,'" Gamegrid, accessed December 12, 2007, http://www.gamegrid.de/activision.php.
[52] Whitehead, 2018.
[53] "Inside Gaming: Playing 'Chicken' with David Crane," *Electronic Games*, Winter 1981, 12.

background really made the colorful car graphics pop.[54] The fast action and vibrant graphics helped it become a million seller.[55]

The starting point for *Kaboom* was an obscure 1978 Atari coin-op game called *Avalanche* in which several rows of rocks are arrayed at the top of the screen in a similar manner to the bricks in *Breakout*. These rocks begin to fall a few at a time, and the player must catch them using a set of vertically stacked paddles he can move left and right along the bottom of the screen. Kaplan adapted this basic gameplay, but because he could not display as many objects on the screen at once on the VCS, he greatly reduced the number of falling objects while speeding up their rate of descent to make the game more exciting.[56]

Kaplan designed the gameplay himself, but for the graphics he turned to Crane, recognized as the best artist of the group. Crane developed a character called the mad bomber that moves back and forth at the top of the screen hurling bombs at the player. Instead of a generic paddle, the player controls a bucket full of water that he whips back and forth to catch all the bombs. Crane added several impressive graphical touches, including flickering fuses on the bombs and little splashes when the bombs land in the bucket.[57] The combination of Kaplan's perfectly balanced twitch gameplay and Crane's expertly rendered visuals produced yet another million-selling game.[58] In all, Activision shipped 4.5 million cartridges in 1981 on its way to sales in the 1982 fiscal year of $65.9 million and an estimated 20% share of the video game market.[59]

Activision's success in the market caught the attention of Bill Grubb, who resigned from Atari right before CES in January 1981 in large part because he did not like working for Ray Kassar. Grubb thought there would be good money in serving as a manufacturer's rep, so he asked Atari to give him Hawaii, which did not currently have a distributor. The company countered with the Pacific Northwest, which did not interest him. Instead, he approached Jim Levy to become the Bay-Area sales rep for Activision.[60]

Meanwhile, Atari programmer Dennis Koble was becoming unhappy. A UC Berkeley graduate with degrees in electrical engineering and computer

---

[54] "David Crane on 'Freeway,'" Gamegrid, accessed December 12, 2007, http://www.gamegrid.de/activision.php.

[55] Capparell, 1984, 27.

[56] Kaplan, 2006.

[57] Crane, 2018.

[58] Capparell, 1984, 27.

[59] Bernstein, 1982, 33, and Activision Profile, 1982, 6.

[60] Grubb, 2014.

science, Koble spent four years working for defense contractor Applied Technology before a friend at Atari invited him to join. The fourth program-mer hired into the coin-operated games division, Koble programmed the massive hit *Sprint 2*, Atari's *Blockade* clone *Dominoes*, the *Avalanche* game that inspired *Kaboom*, and Atari's first pinball machine, the *Atarians*.[61] In 1978, he was drafted by Steve Bristow into Atari's new handheld game divi-sion and created a handheld adaptation of *Simon* released under the name *Touch Me* in 1979.[62] Once he finished that project, Koble replaced the retiring George Simcock as manager of the VCS programming group at the begin-ning of 1980. Unhappy as a manager and disillusioned with the layers of bureaucracy at the rapidly expanding Atari, Koble asked management to let him set up a small subsidiary so he could focus on making games without the immense pressure of feeding the VCS beast.[63] Koble approached Grubb for advice on how to proceed, and the marketing executive, who missed working for a product development company and was impressed at how much money Activision was making, suggested they acquire some venture funding and become a third-party publisher instead.[64]

Meanwhile, a junior marketing executive at Mattel Electronics named Jim Goldberger was having similar thoughts about entering third-party develop-ment in conjunction with his roommate, Mattel Electronics programmer Brian Dougherty. Grubb had been impressed with Goldberger for some time and had even tried to hire him into Atari, so on April 4, 1981, Grubb, Koble, Goldberger, and Daugherty met at a restaurant and decided to go into business together to provide product for both the VCS and Intellivision.[65] Bill Grubb wrote the business plan and presented it to venture capital firm Kleiner Perkins. The organization agreed to come on board with a $1 mil-lion investment and introduced Grubb to Steve Merrill at the VC firm Merrill Packard, which committed $500,000. Another half million came from an Indian angel investor that Bill Grubb met through an attorney. In total Grubb secured $2 million in financing to establish the company, which incorporated on June 1, 1981 under the name Imagic.[66]

In addition to the four founders, Imagic poached several other Atari and Mattel employees. Grubb brought in his friend Mark Bradlee, who had been

---

[61] Drury, 2012, 88–90

[62] Ibid, 89-90, and "Non-Video Electronic Games Taking Off," *Weekly Television Digest with Consumer Electronics*, February 12, 1979, 8.

[63] Drury, 2012, 88–90.

[64] Drury, 2012, 90, and Grubb, 2014.

[65] Grubb, 2014.

[66] Ibid

with him at Black & Decker and was the national accounts manager at Atari, to run sales. Programmer Rob Fulop knew Koble was leaving and asked to come along after being completely nonplussed that his multi-million-selling *Missile Command* netted him a paltry Christmas bonus of a free turkey from Safeway.[67] Bob Smith also defected from Atari, while a programmer named Dave Durran joined his fellows from Mattel. *Asteroids* programmer Brad Stewart was not there from the start, but he joined in September 1981.[68] While the company did not have any products ready to go for 1981, it promised to be a force to rival Activision in 1982.

***

The defection of so many talented programmers to Activision and Imagic between 1979 and 1981 severely impacted the VCS programming group at Atari. These programmers were not only some of the most proficient at squeezing every last ounce of ability out of the system, but they were also the most experienced game developers. Without Alan Miller or David Crane or Brad Stewart around, the new cohort of programmers expected to lead Atari game development into the future were bereft of mentors to guide them through the most efficient ways to harness the capabilities of a system that was extremely difficult to program well. These experienced programmers were missed all the more as Atari continued to license the latest arcade hits to play on a system intended for nothing more complicated than *Pong* or *Tank*. Porting the big hits of 1981 to the VCS would require every trick in the book, and the less experienced members of the programming team were not necessarily up to the task.

Perhaps no conversion exemplifies these problems better than the big game of 1982, *Pac-Man*, programmed by Tod Frye. Frye wrote his first programs in FORTRAN in 1969 at his junior high school, but the institution did not have access to a computer, so the teacher merely informed the students whether their programs would have worked or not. In high school, Frye programmed on an actual time-shared minicomputer for the first time.[69] A poor student who preferred smoking pot to attending class, Frye dropped out in his junior year, and his father kicked him out of the house. Frye was homeless for a time, but he eventually landed a job on a construction crew and applied himself to become a master carpenter. Through all these hardships, he never

[67] Fulop, 2019.

[68] Stewart, 2001.

[69] Randy Kindig, "ANTIC Interview 174: Tod Frye, Asteroids," *ANTIC*, Podcast audio, May 18, 2016, http://ataripodcast.libsyn.com/antic-interview-174-tod-fry-asteroids.

lost his love of programming, and his high school friend Ian Shepard helped him get a job at Atari in 1979.[70] After porting *Asteroids* to the 400 and 800 and working on some handheld projects, Frye was assigned to bring *Pac-Man* to the 2600.[71]

Porting *Pac-Man* with its 240 pellets and five characters to a machine not intended to support more than five sprites was one of the most challenging tasks a VCS programmer was ever asked to carry out. Because of the limited number of sprite objects, the pellets had to be drawn using playfield graphics, which could only be represented as rectangles. As a result, Atari referred to these as "wafers" rather than "pellets" as in the arcade original. Using backgrounds created its own problems, because the VCS only draws the background on one half of the screen and then doubles or mirrors that image to create the other side. This process requires symmetry in the background, but as *Pac-Man* is eating dots, the background needs to change in an asymmetrical way. Frye used intricate timing techniques to allow both sides of the screen to be updated right before they are drawn, but the cost in limited system resources was immense.[72]

While getting the gameplay of *Pac-Man* to work on the VCS was an extraordinary programming feat, the final product was let down by Frye's inexperience translating coin-operated games to the home. When examining *Pac-Man*, he felt the key attributes of the game were to collect the dots in the maze and the ability for two people to play together by alternating between each lost life. The aesthetics of the game were less important to him. While the original featured a muted blue maze on a black background so that the bright character graphics would shine through, Frye developed a brown maze on a blue background. The main reason for avoiding black was that VCS programmers were discouraged from using black backgrounds outside of space games because it left CRT televisions more susceptible to burn in, but the result was an ugly playfield that did not look much like its inspiration.[73]

The decision to accommodate two players created even worse problems. As in *Asteroids*, showing all the objects on the screen at the same time required the use of a flickering technique to rapidly alternate between two sets of characters. In *Asteroids*, this process works reasonably well due to the way Brad Stewart balanced the use of the system's paltry 128 bytes of RAM. Frye was

[70] "The Story of Pac-Man on the Atari 2600," *Retro Gamer*, no. 179, 2018.

[71] Kindig, 2016.

[72] Montfort and Bogost, 2009, 69–70.

[73] Hans Reutter, "PRGE 2016 – Tod Frye – Portland Retro Gaming Expo," filmed October 22, 2016, YouTube video, posted October 27, 2016, https://www.youtube.com/watch?v=cuTJpZ99P0c.

already memory constrained by the need to update the background graphics asymmetrically, but he placed an additional burden on the memory by requiring the game to store the game state and score of a second player so it could be recalled when his turn on the machine began. This did not leave enough RAM to smooth out the flickering on the graphics.[74] While *Pac-Man* himself remains solid, the ghosts flicker rapidly as they pursue the player. *Asteroids* had noticeable flicker, but because the objects in the game were large rocks moving in set patterns, it was not terribly distracting. When applied to the rapidly moving ghosts of *Pac-Man* the effect became tiresome on the eyes and made the ghosts harder to track.[75] While there was probably no way to avoid some flicker, with more memory Frye could have limited its effects.

Despite its limitations, *Pac-Man* was still *Pac-Man*, the hottest game to ever hit the amusement arcade with a starring character that had become the face of the entire burgeoning video game industry. By the end of 1982, *Pac-Man* had infiltrated all walks of American life. A strategy guide for the game called *Mastering Pac-Man* cracked the *New York Times* bestseller list. A novelty duo called Buckner & Garcia released a goofy song called "Pac-Man Fever" in December 1981 that peaked at #9 on the Billboard Hot 100 in March 1982.[76] Fleer released a *Pac-Man* sticker set and sold 100 million packs in less than a year, General Mills produced *Pac-Man* cereal, and Chef Boyardee added *Pac-Man* shapes to its canned pasta.[77] There were pajamas, lunch boxes, bumper stickers, Hallmark gift cards, and a line of children's clothing from J.C. Penny emblazoned with the characters from the game.[78] In fall 1982, *Pac-Man* even became the star of his own Saturday morning cartoon produced by Hanna-Barbera. In this environment, anticipation for Atari's VCS port ran high.

Atari began counting down the days to the *Pac-Man* release through newspaper ads in late March with slogans like "Soon Pac-Man Will Be Ready for Home Consumption" and "Guess Who's Coming to Dinner?" This campaign culminated in "National Pac-Man Day" on Saturday, April 3, 1982, when the company launched a $1.5 million PR and marketing blitz in 26 U.S. cities.[79] In Chicago, the character appeared on *Bozo's Circus* in the

---

[74] Ibid.

[75] Montfort and Bogost, 2009, 74.

[76] "Pac-Man Fever," *Time*, April 5, 1982, http://www.time.com/time/magazine/article/0,9171,921174,00. html.

[77] Smith, 2016, 432.

[78] "Pac-Man Fever," 1982.

[79] "'Pac-Mania' Celebrated Nationwide," *Playthings*, May 1982, 39, and Victoria Corderi, "Local Video-Game Freaks Gobble Up Home Pac-Man," *The Miami News*, March 30, 1982.

morning and at a Cubs-White Sox charity baseball game in the afternoon. In St. Louis, Atari partnered with a local retail chain to host a ten-kilometer run at the conclusion of which *Pac-Man* was awarded the key to the city. The character showed up at the Dade County Youth Fair in Florida and the Cherry Blossom Parade, in Washington, DC. The day also served as the launching point for a television and radio advertising campaign focused solely on the game.[80]

Anticipating high demand, Atari manufactured over 1 million cartridges in March, more copies than its top-selling *Space Invaders* cartridge sold within its first year. Copies of *Pac-Man* began trickling out to the public in the second half of the month at a suggested retail price of $37.95 and vanished nearly as quickly as they reached store shelves.[81] Thanks largely to *Pac-Man*, Warner Communications reported record first quarter earnings as net income leapt from $49.5 million the year before to $77.9 million. Most of that rise came from a tripling of the profits of the Consumer Electronics Division to $100.6 million. The division, which derived its profits almost entirely from Atari, accounted for two-thirds of Warner's operating earnings.[82] At one of the largest entertainment conglomerates in the world, video games were now a more crucial part of the business than music or movies. The video game appeared to have finally come of age. It would not last.

---

[80] "Pac-Mania,'" 1982.
[81] Corderi, 1982.
[82] "Finance," *Toy & Hobby World*, April-May, 1982.

Epilogue: A Date Which Will Live in Infamy

On December 8, 1982, Warner Communications announced its latest projections for the fourth quarter and 1982 fiscal year. As late as December 7, the company continued to assure analysts that Warner would experience yet another banner year with video game sales driving the firm to 50% growth over 1981. Atari had revised its earnings projections downward significantly on November 17, but Warner executives felt they were still on target.

On the evening of December 7, Atari revised its numbers down again. Warner was forced to issue a press release stating growth was now projected at a mere 10%–15%, the first time its growth rate had slumped year-over-year in 31 quarters.[1] Warner stock fell 17 points by the end of the day.[2] By the next day, it was 45 points lower than before the announcement. On December 13, Manny Gerard stepped before analysts at a meeting in New York City and was savaged by a group that felt deceived by the company's previous rosy projections. The Warner executive could offer no better excuse than to say the company was lulled into a false sense of security by previous successes and that they were "just dumb."[3]

It would take some time for the full ramifications of the Atari announcement to become clear, but by the middle of 1983, everyone realized that the video game industry in the United States was completely collapsing. At the annual shareholders meeting of Warner Communications in May 1983, Steve Ross promised that, despite a $45 million first quarter loss, Atari would return to profitability before the end of the year. Weeks later, Atari reported a staggering second quarter loss of over $310 million.[4] Warner itself lost $283 million in the quarter, the worst showing in the company's history and triple already gloomy Wall Street forecasts.[5]

The damage was not limited to Atari. Just weeks after Warner announced its devastating second quarter loss, Mattel revealed it would lose significantly

---

[1] Andrew Pollack, "The Game Turns Serious at Atari," *The New York Times*, December 19, 1982.
[2] Bruck, 1994, chap. 5.
[3] Pollack, 1982.
[4] Ibid, chap. 6.
[5] Sheff, 1999, chap. 7.

more than $100 million in the first half of the year due to problems with Mattel Electronics.[6] In September, the company announced it would lose over $156 million in the second quarter alone, well more than initial projections.[7] In November, Activision announced a quarterly loss of $4.1 million and laid off 25% of its work force.[8]

By the end of 1984, both Atari and Mattel had pulled out of the home console business entirely. Meanwhile, coin-operated video game sales had already started slowing in 1982, and in 1983 coin drop was cut nearly in half from $4.3 billion to $2.9 billion. In 1984, coin drop dipped below the level achieved in 1980, the first year of the video game boom.[9] After a 10-year period in which consumers went from spending nothing on interactive entertainment to roughly $7 billion per year, video games finally looked to be the flash in the pan skeptics had predicted since the collapse of the first ball-and-paddle market in 1974.

Outside the United States, however, the picture was not nearly so grim. In the United Kingdom, a new home computer market was just starting to take hold, and significant government backing for computer education was poised to nurture a burgeoning population of teenage bedroom coders who would nurture a vibrant video game ecosystem throughout Europe. Meanwhile, in Japan, where video game mania was not diminished by the corporate apocalypse occurring across the Pacific, coin-operated amusement firms that had grown rich licensing their games to U.S. companies were ready to assert complete control over their own destinies and bring a new generation of arcade hardware and video game consoles to both their own domestic population and to the devastated video game market in North America.

---

[6]David E. Sanger, "Mattel Expects to Post Large Loss," *The New York Times*, July 26, 1983.
[7]Eric N. Berg, "Mattel Reports Losing $156.1 Million in Quarter," *The New York Times*, September 9, 1983.
[8]"Activision Sets Layoffs for 90," *The New York Times*, November 12, 1983.
[9]Vending Times Census of the Industry, 1985, 62.

List of Interviewees

The following people were generous with their time and enhanced this book by sharing their recollections:

Richard Ball
Frank Ballouz
Nolan Bushnell
Jim Connelley
David Crane
Joshua Denham
Bob Faught
Jamie Fenton
Manny Gerard
Gerald Gleason
Ron Gordon
Ralph Gorin
Martin Graetz
Arnold Greenberg
Dennis Groth
Bill Grubb
Roger Hector
Howell Ivy
Carol Kantor
Larry Kaplan
Ray Kassar
Michael Katz
Joe Keenan
Don Kingsborough
George Kiss
Ed Krakauer
Malcolm Kuhn
Gene Landrum

Susan Lee-Merrow
Jim Levy
Gene Lipkin
David Marofske, Sr.
Stephen Maine
Steve Mayer
Ed Miller
Ron Milner
Richard Mobilio
Michael Moone
Paul Moriarty
Howard Mullin
Claire Nutting
Craig Nutting
David Nutting
Frank O'Connell
Burt Reiner
Howard Rubin
Jewel Savadelis
Art Schneiderman
Larry Siegel
Jan Soderstrom
Gary Stern
Hugh Tuck
Bob Whitehead
Wayne Wiitanen
Randall Willie

References and Bibliography

"50 Most Memorable Moments." *Digital Press*, May–June 2003.

"Activision Profile 1982." Promotional brochure, 1982.

"The Adventure Begins: Origin of the Text Adventure Game." *Retro Gamer*, no. 31, 2006.

"The American Amusement Machine Charitable Foundation Honors Joe Robbins." Event program, March 10, 1990.

"ANTIC Interview 25: Scott Adams, Adventure International." *ANTIC*. Podcast audio, March 16, 2015. http://ataripodcast.libsyn.com/antic-interview-25-the-atari-8-bit-podcast-scott-adams.

Apple II Reference Manual. Cupertino, CA: Apple Computer, 1978.

"Atari Arcade Production Numbers." Internal document with release dates, prices, and units sold. c. 1999.

The Avalon Hill General Index and Company History. Baltimore, MD: The Avalon Hill Game Company, 1980.

"Bi-Weekly Report, Project 6673, February 2, 1951," Memorandum M-2084, prepared by the Electronic Computer Division of the Servomechanisms Laboratory of the Massachusetts Institute of Technology, February 2, 1951, 5.

"Carmonette Volume I: General Description." CAA-D-74-11. Prepared for General Research Corporation, November 1974.

"Case: The Magnavox Co., et al. V. Chicago Dynamic Industries, et al." Patent Arcade, June 2010. http://patentarcade.com/2010/06/case-magnavox-co-et-al-v-chicago.html.

"Chip Hall of Fame: Zilog Z80 Microprocessor." *IEEE Spectrum*, June 30, 2017. https://spectrum.ieee.org/tech-history/silicon-revolution/chip-hall-of-fame-zilog-z80-microprocessor.

The Coin-Operated and Home Electronic Games Market. New York: Frost & Sullivan, 1976.

"Commodore International Ltd. History." Funding Universe. Accessed June 10, 2019. http://www.fundinguniverse.com/company-histories/commodore-international-ltd-history.

"Current Engineering Assignments." Atari Internal Memo, February 12, 1975. "Design Case History: The Atari Video Computer System." *IEEE Spectrum*, March 1983.

"Design Case History: The Atari Video Computer System." *IEEE Spectrum*, March 1983.

"The Development of Pac-Man." Glitterberri's Game Translations, 2003. https://www.glitterberri.com/developer-interviews/the-development-of-pacman.

"DP Interviews Don Emry." Digital Press, 2004. http://www.digitpress.com/library/interviews/interview_don_emry.html.

Electronic Games & Personal Computers. Cleveland, OH: Predicasts, Inc., 1979.

Electronic Games Market in Europe. New York: Frost & Sullivan, 1981.

The Electronic Games Market in the U.S. New York: Frost & Sullivan, 1983.

"Essential Facts About the Computer and Video Game Industry: 2018 Sales, Demographic, and Usage Data." Entertainment Software Association. Accessed May 27, 2019. http://www.theesa.com/wpcontent/uploads/2018/05/EF2018_FINAL.pdf.

"Executive Games." Pong Story, accessed June 6, 2019. http://www.pong-story.com/executivegames.htm.

"Executive Games Inc." MIT Case Study, 1977.

"Fairchild's Problems: More Than Watches." *BusinessWeek*, August 15, 1977.

Faster Than Thought: The Ferranti Nimrod Digital Computer. Hollinwood: Ferranti, 1951.

"First Dimension." Pong Story. Accessed June 6, 2019. http://www.pong-story.com/firstdim.htm.

"GameSetInterview: Adventure International's Scott Adams." GameSetWatch, July 19, 2006. http://www.gamesetwatch.com/2006/07/gamesetinterview_adventure_int.php.

"Great Achievers: David Rosen." *RePlay*, July 1982.

"Guide to the Records of the Massachusetts Institute of Technology Computation Center." MIT Libraries, accessed June 27, 2019. https://libraries.mit.edu/archives/research/collections/collections-ac/ac62.html.

Home & Coin Operated Electronic Games. New York: Frost & Sullivan, 1979.

"How Agronomy and IT Made the World's First Microcomputer" INRA, April 18, 2016. http://institut.inra.fr/en/Overview/HIstorical-milestones/1970s/Toutes-les-actualites/How-agronomy-and-IT-made-the-world-s-first-microcomputer.

"Imagination Leads to Boom in Amusement Machinery." *Business Japan*, September 1971.

"Inside Gaming: Playing 'Chicken' with David Crane." *Electronic Games*, Winter 1981.

"Intellivison Action Network." Intellivision Lives, accessed February 6, 2018. http://www,intellivisionlives.com/bluesky/games/credits/action.html.

"Intellivision Space Action Network." Intellivision Lives, accessed February 6, 2018. http://www,intellivisionlives.com/bluesky/games/credits/space.html.

"An Interview with Atari 2600 Developer and Imagic Co-Founder Rob Fulop." *Paleotronic*, March 29, 2019. https://paleotronic.com/2019/03/29/an-interview-with-atari-2600-developer-and-imagic-co-founder-rob-fulop.

"Interview with Toru Iwatani, Namco Bandai 'The First Video Game Beginning Part 2.'" Bandai Namco Entertainment, March 6, 2019. https:/www.bandainamcoent.co.jp/asobimotto/page/videogame2.html.

"Joseph A. Weisbecker (1931–1990)." Cosmac Elf. Accessed June 10, 2019. http://www.cosmacelf.com/history/joseph-weisbecker.html.

"Magnavox Odyssey: First Home Video Game Console." Pong Story, accessed June 8, 2019. http://www.pong-story.com/odyssey.htm.

"Magnavox Odyssey: 100-5000 Systems." Pong Story, accessed June 30, 2019. http://www.pong-story.com/odyssey_other.htm.

"The Making of Sprint 2." *Retro Gamer*, no. 89, 2011.

"Management Game: More Difficult than Chess, and More Fun to Watch." Carnegie Mellon University, 2007. http://cmu.edu/corporate/news/2007/features/mgmtgame.shtml.

"Milton Bradley Company History." Funding Universe. Accessed June 10, 2019. http://www.fundinguniverse.com/company-histories/milton-bradley-company-history.

"New Game Machines Cater to Fickle Public." *Business Japan*, August 1977.

"New Markets Being Studied for Amusement Machines." *Business Japan*, September 1975.

"Nicholas F. Talesfore." FND Collectibles. Accessed June 10, 2019. http://www.fndcollectables.com/NINTENDO/NES_C_thru_D/SHIPPING/VIDEO_GAMES/INTELLIVISION/working_interview_notes.html.

"Observations About Crowther's Original Adventure (1975)." Renga in Blue, March 7, 2011. https://bluerenga.blog/2011/03/07/observations-about-crowthers-original-adventure-1975.

"Pac-Man Fever." *Time*, April 5, 1982, http://www.time.com/time/magazine/article/0,9171,921174,00.html.

"The Penny Arcade." *Billboard Magazine*, March 15, 1947.

"Peter L. Jensen and the Magnavox Loudspeaker." Audio Engineering Society. Accessed April 20, 2016. http://www.aes.org/aeshc/docs/recording.technology.history/jensen.html.

"Pong in a Chip." Pong Story, accessed June 8, 2019. http://www.pong-story.com/gi.htm.

"Profile: Chairman and Chief Executive Officer Kenzo Tsujimoto." Capcom Investor Relations. Accessed June 8, 2019. http://www.capcom.co.jp/ir/english/company/views_ceo.html.

"Profile On: William G. Nutting – Heading Up the Computer Generation." *Cash Box*, February 17, 1968.

"Project MAC Progress Report V: July 1967–July 1968." Massachusetts Institute of Technology. c.1968.

"Reminiscing from Richard Maurer." Giant List Archive, January 5, 1999. https://dadgum.com/giantlist/archive/maurer.html.

"RoundUp 24: Oh She's Doing Fine." *Retrogaming Roundup*. Podcast audio, October 2010. http://www.retrogamingroundup.com/shownotes/2010/roundup024_2010.10.php.

"RoundUp 46: Modificability of Doom." *Retrogaming Roundup*. Podcast audio, March 2012. http://www.retrogamingroundup.com/shownotes/2012/roundup046_2012.03.php.

"Sanrio Company, Ltd. History." Funding Universe. Accessed June 10, 2019. http://www.fundinguniverse.com/company-histories/sanrio-company-ltd-history.

"Show 54," *TOPcast*, podcast audio, March 2008. http://www.pinrepair.com/topcast/showget.php?id=54.

Software Strategies: The Home Computer and Videogame Marketplace. Boston, MA: The Yankee Group, 1984.

"Sport in the Nickel Age." *Business Week*, March 29, 1933, 14.

"Star Trek." Games of Fame. Accessed June 9, 2019. https://gamesoffame.wordpress.com/star-trek.

"The Story of Pac-Man on the Atari 2600." *Retro Gamer*, no. 179, 2018.

"The Table Soccer Phenomenon." *RePlay*, February 28, 1976.

"Telstar Arcade." Pong Story, accessed June 8, 2019. http://www.pong-story.com/coleco_arcade.htm.

"Telstar Combat." Pong Story, accessed June 8, 2019. http://www.pong-story.com/coleco_combat.htm.

"Trivia and Stories." Handheld Museum. Accessed June 11, 2019. https://www.handheldmuseum.com/Mattel/Trivia.htm

"Tsujimoto – Capcom's 'Toy Maker' – Talks About Video Business & Video Philosophy." *RePlay*, December 1985.

"The TX-0: Its Past and Present." *The Computer Museum Report*, Spring 1984.

"Varigated Amusement Machines Changing Almost Daily." *Business Japan*, July 1973.

The Video Game Industry: Strategic Analysis. New York: Sanford C. Bernstein & Co., 1982.

"Videomaster Superscore." Pong Story, accessed June 8, 2019. http://www.pongstory.com/vm8.htm.

What to Do After You Hit Return or P.C.C.'s First Book of Computer Games. Menlo Park, CA: People's Computer Company, 1974.

"The Who's Pete Townsend Shares the Story Behind 'Pinball Wizard.'" Guitar World, May 29, 2017. https://www.guitarworld.com/artists/acoustic-nation-whos-pete-townsend-shares-story-behind-pinball-wizard.

"Will Crowther," oral history, March 1994.

"The Year That TV Videogames Took Off." Investors Chronicle, December 23, 1977.

Ahl, David. *More BASIC Computer Games*. New York: Workman Publishing, 1979.

Akagi, Masumi. *It Started from Pong*. Nishinomiya: Amusement Press, 2005.

Akagi, Teppei. *Sega vs. Nintendo: The Future of Multimedia Wars*. Tokyo: Japan Management Association, 1992.

Albaugh, Mike. "Atari Football History." coinop.org, December 30, 2002. https://www.coinop.org/features/football.

Alcorn, Allan (Al). "First-Hand: The Development of Pong: Early Days of Atari and the Video Game Industry." Engineering and Technology History Wiki, November 13, 2009. https://ethw.org/First-Hand:The_Development_of_Pong:_Early_Days_of_Atari_and_the_Video_Game_Industry.

———. Interview by Henry Lowood, April 26 and May 23, 2008. Computer History Museum. https://archive.computerhistory.org/resources/access/text/2012/09/102658257-05-01-acc.pdf.

———. "Story of Pong." Australian Center for the Moving Image, March 6, 2008. http://www.acmi.net.au/talks_gameon_storyofpong.htm.

Allen, Paul. *Idea Man: A Memoir by the Co-Founder of Microsoft*. New York: Portfolio/Penguin, 2011.

Anderson, John J. "Dave Tells Ahl – The History of Creative Computing." *Creative Computing*, November 1984.

Apperley, Thomas H., and Golding, Daniel. "Australia." In *Video Games Around the World*, edited by Mark J.P. Wolf. Cambridge, MA: The MIT Press, 2015. iTunes.

Atari Archive. "Archive Annex Episode 1: RCA, FRED, and the Studio II." YouTube video. posted September 6, 2018. https://www.youtube.com/watch?v=o35y6W9hI-o.

Averett, Ed. Testimony. Atari, Inc. v. North American Philips Consumer Electronics Corp., No. 81-6434 (N.D. Ill), November 30, 1981.

Baba, Hironao. *Nintendo Who Is Frightened by Sega*. Tokyo: Yale Publishing Company, 1993.

Backiel, Al. "DP Interviews Alan Miller." Digital Press, 2003.

———. "DP Interviews Rick Levine." Digital Press, 1999. http://www.digitpress.com/library/interviews/interview_rick_levine.html.

Baer, Ralph. Interview by Gardner Hendrie, October 12 and November 27, 2006. Computer History Museum. https://archive.computerhistory.org/resources/access/text/2013/05/102657972-05-01-acc.pdf.

———. *Videogames: In the Beginning*. Springfield, NJ: Rolenta Press, 2005.

Bagnall, Brian. *Commodore: A Company on the Edge*. Winnipeg: Variant Press, 2010.
————. *Commodore: The Amiga Years*. Winnipeg: Variant Press, 2017.
Ball, Guy. "Texas Instruments Cal-Tech: World's First Prototype Pocket Electronic Calculator." Vintage Calculators Web Museum. Accessed June 6, 2019. http://www.vintagecalculators.com/html/ti_cal-tech.html.
Barnfather, Maurice. "Is Playboy's Luck Running Out?" *Forbes*, May 11, 1981.
Beley, Gene. "Business Preview '77: One Western Opinion." *Play Meter*, January 1977.
Bennett, John M. "Early Computer Days in Britain and Australia: Some Autobiographical Snippets." *Annals of the History of Computing* 12, no. 4 (1990): 281–285.
Berlin, Leslie. *The Man Behind the Microchip: Robert Noyce and the Invention of Silicon Valley*, Oxford: Oxford University Press, 2005.
————. *Troublemakers: Silicon Valley's Coming of Age*. New York: Simon & Schuster, 2017.
Bernstein, Alex, and Michael de V. Roberts. "Computer v. Chess-Player." *Scientific American* 198, no. 6 (1958): 96–107.
Berzerk Interview. Alan McNeil personal website, accessed February 1, 2018. http://a9k.info/qna.html.
Birmingham, Stephen. *The Rest of Us: The Rise of America's Eastern European Jews*. New York: Open Road Media, 2015.
Blanchet, Alexis. "France." In *Video Games Around the World*, edited by Mark J.P. Wolf. Cambridge, MA: The MIT Press, 2015. iTunes.
Blitz, Matt. "Bertie the Brain Still Lives: The Story of the World's First Arcade Game." Popular Mechanics, November 2, 2016. https://www.popularmechanics.com/technology/gadgets/a23660/bertie-the-brain.
Bloom, Steve. "Atari: From Cutoffs to Pinstripes." *Video Games*, December 1982.
————. *Video Invaders*. New York: Arco Publishing, 1982.
Braun, David. Deposition. Magnavox Co. v. Bally Manufacturing Corp., No. 74-1030 (N.D. Ill), June 14, 1974.
Briody, Thomas. Testimony. Magnavox Company v. Activision, Inc., No. 82-5270 (N.D. Cal), 1985.
Bristow, Steve. "Decisions Reached 11–6–74" Atari internal memo, November 7, 1974.
————. Deposition. Bally Manufacturing v. Williams Electronics, No. 78-2246 (N.D. Ill), August 5, 1982.
————. "Grass Valley Conference." 1–11–75. Memo to Nolan Bushnell and Al Alcorn, January 14, 1975.
Britz, John. Deposition. Magnavox Co. v. Bally Manufacturing Corp., No. 74-1030 (N.D. Ill), June 25, 1974.
Bruck, Connie. *Master of the Game: How Steve Ross Rode the Light Fantastic from Undertaker to Creator of the Largest Media Conglomerate in the World*. New York: Simon & Schuster, 1994. Kindle.
Brunsen, Allen. Tony Miller Interview. bb.vg-network.com, accessed December 3, 2008. http://bb.vg-network.com/interviews/tminterview.html.
Bueschel, Richard M. *Encyclopedia of Pinball Volume 1: Whiffle to Rocket 1930–1933*. LaGrangeville, NY: Silverball Amusements, 1996.
————. *Encyclopedia of Pinball Volume 2: Contact to Bumper 1934–1936*. Poughkeepsie, NY: Silverball Amusements, 1997.

————. *Pinball 1: Illustrated Historical Guide to Pinball Machines.* Wheat Ridge, CO: Hoflin Publishing, 1988.

Bueschel, Richard M., and Steve Gronowski. *Arcade 1: Illustrated Historical Guide to Arcade Machines.* Wheat Ridge, CO: Hoflin Publishing, 1993.

Bushnell, Nolan. Deposition. Magnavox Co. v. Bally Manufacturing Corp., No. 74-1030 (N.D. Ill), July 3, 1974.

Bushnell, Nolan. Deposition. Magnavox Co. v. Bally Manufacturing Corp., No. 74-1030 (N.D. Ill). January 13–14, 1976.

Bushnell, Nolan. Deposition. Magnavox Co. v. Bally Manufacturing Corp., No. 74-1030 (N.D. Ill), June 28, 1978.

Butler, Kevin. "Space Wars." *Old School Gamer Magazine,* September 2019.

Campbell-Kelly, Martin. "Christopher Strachey, 1916–1975: A Biographical Note." *Annals of the History of Computing* 7, no. 1 (1985): 19–42.

Campbell-Kelly, Martin, William Aspray, Nathan Ensmenger, and Jeffrey R. Yost. *Computer: A History of the Information Machine,* 3rd ed. Boulder, CO: Westview Press, 2014.

Cantwell, Robert. "The Fun Machines." *Sports Illustrated,* July 4, 1977.

Capparell, James. "Activision's James Levy: A Software Success Story." *ANTIC,* June 1984.

Cassidy, William. "Interview with Odyssey² Artist Ron Bradford." The Odyssey² Homepage. Accessed May 30, 2019. http://www.the-nextlevel.com/odyssey2/articles/bradford.

Ceruzzi, Paul E. *A History of Modern Computing,* 2nd ed. Cambridge, MA: The MIT Press, 2003. Kindle.

Chakravarty, Subrata M. "Albatross." *Forbes,* January 17, 1983.

Chandler, David. "Intellivision History and Philosophy." Internal company memo, c. 1982.

Clardy, Robert. *Cyber Jack: The Adventures of Robert Clardy and Synergistic Software.* Apple Puget Sound Program Library Exchange, 2017.

Clerc-Renaud, Antoine, and Jean-François Dupuis. *Coleco: The Official Book.* Quebec: BOOQC Publishing, 2016.

Cohen, Kalman J., and Eric Rhenman. "The Role of Management Games in Education and Research." *Management Science* 7, no. 2 (1961): 131–166.

Cohen, Scott. *Zap! The Rise and Fall of Atari.* New York: McGraw-Hill, 1984. Ebook.

Copeland, B. Jack. *Turing: Pioneer of the Information Age.* Oxford: Oxford University Press, 2012. Kindle.

————. "What is Artificial Intelligence?" AlanTuring.net, May 2000. http://www.alanturing.net/turing_archive/pages/Reference%20Articles/what_is_AI/What%20is%20AI04.html

Copeland, B. Jack, and Diane Proudfoot. "Alan Turing: Father of the Modern Computer." *Rutherford Journal.* Accessed May 27, 2019. http://www.rutherfordjournal.org/article040101.html.

Costa, Nicholas. *Automatic Pleasures: The History of the Coin Machine.* Cincinnati, OH: Seven Hills Books, 1988.

Craddock, David. *Dungeon Hacks: How NetHack, Angband, and Other Roguelikes Changed the Course of Video Games.* Canton, OH: Press Start Press, 2015. Kindle.

Current, Michael. "A History of Syzygy/Atari." Atari History Timelines. Last modified April 28, 2019. https://mcurrent.name/atarihistory/syzygy.html.

D'Anastasio, Cecilia. "Sex, Pong, and Pioneers: What Atari Was Really Like, According to the Women Who Were There." Kotaku, February 12, 2018. https://kotaku.com/sex-pong-and-pioneers-what-atari-was-really-like-ac–1822930057.

Dabney, Samuel F. (Ted). Interview by Chris Garcia, July 16, 2012. Computer History Museum. https://archive.computerhistory.org/resources/access/text/2012/10/102746459-05-01-acc.pdf.

Davies, D.W. "A Theory of Chess and Nought and Crosses." *Science News* no. 16 (1950): 40–64.

Davies, Jonti. "The Making of Space Invaders." *Retro Gamer*. No. 62, 2009.

DeMaria, Rusel. *High Score Expanded*. New York: CRC Press, 2018.

Derboo, Sam. "Adventure, a game released in the year of wedontknow." Hardcore Gaming 101 Blog, July 17, 2012. http://blog.hardcoregaming101.net/2012/07/adventure-game-released-in-year-of.html.

DeWyze, Jeanette, "San Diego's Gremlin: How Video Games Work." *San Diego Reader*, July 15, 1982.

DillyDylan. "The Blue Box: David Crane on Early Atari Inc." Gaming Alexandria, May 12, 2019. https://www.gamingalexandria.com/wp/2019/05/12/the-blue-box-david-crane-on-early-atari-inc.

Dizikes, Peter. "The Many Careers of Jay Forrester." MIT Technology Review. June 23, 2015. https://www.technologyreview.com/s/538561/the-many-careers-of-jay-forrester.

Donovan, Tristan. *Replay: The History of Video Games*. Lewes, East Sussex: Yellow Ant, 2010. Kindle.

———. "The Replay Interviews: David Crane." Gamasutra, January 3, 2011. https://www.gamasutra.com/view/feature/134618/the_replay_interviews_david_crane.php.

———. "The Replay Interviews: Ray Kassar." Gamasutra, April 29, 2011. https://www.gamasutra.com/view/feature/134733/the_replay_interviews_ray_kassar.php.

Drury, Paul. "In the Chair with Allan Alcorn." *Retro Gamer*. No. 83, 2010.

———. "In the Chair with Howell Ivy." *Retro Gamer*, no. 125, 2014.

———. "Desert Island Discs: Ed Logg." *Retro Gamer*, no. 29, 2006.

———. "Desert Island Disks: Dennis Koble." *Retro Gamer*, no. 107, 2012.

———. "Desert Island Disks: Steve Bristow." *Retro Gamer*, no. 75, 2010.

———. "The Making of Asteroids." *Retro Gamer*, no. 68, 2009.

———. "The Making of Computer Space." *Retro Gamer*, no. 93, 2011.

———. "The Making of Lunar Lander." *Retro Gamer*, no. 79, 2010.

———. "The Making of Pirate Adventure." *Retro Gamer*, no. 89, 2011.

———. "The Making of Simon." *Retro Gamer*, no. 73, 2010.

Edwards, Benj. "Bill Harrison: The First Video Game Hardware Guru." Vintage Computing and Gaming, May 15, 2007. http://www.vintagecomputing.com/index.php/archives/319/vcg-interview-bill-harrison-worlds-first-video-game-hardware-builder.

———. "Computer Space and the Dawn of the Arcade Video Game." Technologizer, December 11, 2011. https://www.technologizer.com/2011/12/11/computer-space-and-the-dawn-of-the-arcade-video-game.

———. "Ed Smith and the Imagination Machine: The Untold Story of a Black Video Game Pioneer." Fast Company, September 2, 2016. https://www.fastcompany.com/3063298/ed-smith-and-the-imagination-machine-the-untold-story-of-a-black-vid.

————. "Forty Years of Lunar Lander." Technologizer, July 19, 2009. https://www.technologizer.com/2009/07/19/lunar-lander.

————. "Jerry Lawson, Black Video Game Pioneer." *Vintage Computing and Gaming*, February 24, 2009. http://www.vintagecomputing.com/index.php/archives/545/vcg-interview-jerry-lawson-black-video-game-pioneer.

————. "Robots, Pizza, and Sensory Overload: The Chuck E. Cheese Origin Story." Fast Company, May 31, 2017. https://www.fastcompany.com/40425172/robots-pizza-and-magic-the-chuck-e-cheese-origin-story.

————. "The Untold Story of the Invention of the Game Cartridge." Fast Company, January 22, 2015. https://www.fastcompany.com/3040889/the-untold-story-of-the-invention-of-the-game-cartridge.

Eickhorst, Eric. "Game Centers: A Historical and Cultural Analysis of Japan's Video Amusement Establishments." Master's thesis, University of Kansas, 2002.

Eimbinder, Jerry. "Home Electronic Game Categories." *Gametronics*, January 1977.

Ellis, David. "Of Mouse Traps and Crossbows: The Exidy Story." GameRoom, August 2006.

Fabris, Bob. "An Introduction to the BPA." Bally Alley, April 13, 2001. http://www.ballyalley.com/ballyalley/articles/Robert_Fabris_introduciton-edited.html.

Faria, A.J., and Ray Nulsen. "Business Simulation Games: Current Usage Levels, A Ten Year Update." *Developments in Business Simulation & Experiential Exercises* 23 (1996): 22–28.

Farman, Irvin. *Tandy's Money Machine: How Charles Tandy Built Radio Shack into the World's Largest Electronics Chain*. Chicago, IL: The Mobium Press, 1992.

Forrester, Jay. Interview by Renee Garrelick, December 6, 1994. Concord Free Public Library. https://concordlibrary.org/special-collections/oral-history/Forrester.

Frederiksen, Jeff. Testimony. Bally Manufacturing v. Williams Electronics, No. 78-2246 (N.D. Ill),

January 3, 1983.

Free, John R. "Microelectronics Shrinks the Calculator." *Popular Science*, June 1971.

Freiberger, Paul, and Michael Swaine. *Fire in the Valley: The Making of the Personal Computer*, 2nd ed. New York: McGraw Hill, 2000. Kindle.

Freimann, Frank M. "Harvard Business School, accessed September 30, 2019, https://www.hbs.edu/leadership/20th-century-leaders/Pages/details.aspx?profile=frank_m_freimann.

Fries, Ed. "Fixing Color Gotcha." Blog, May 25, 2016. https://edfries.wordpress.com/2016/05/25/fixing-color-gotcha.

————. "Fixing Gran Trak 10." Blog, June 14, 2017. https://edfries.wordpress.com/2017/06/14/fixing-gran-trak-10.

Fritsche, Robert. Testimony. Magnavox Co. v. Bally Manufacturing Corp., No. 74-1030 (N.D. Ill), December 28, 1976.

Garin, Manuel, and Victor Manuel Martínez. "Spain." In *Video Games Around the World*, edited by Mark J.P. Wolf. Cambridge, MA: The MIT Press, 2015. iTunes.

Gersh, William. "'Sportlands' Seen as Evolution of the Penny Arcade." Automatic Age, April 1932.

Ghamari-Tabrizi, Sharon. "U.S. Wargaming Grows Up: A Short History of the Diffusion of Wargaming in the Armed Forces and Industry in the Postwar Period up to 1964." StrategyWorld.com. Accessed May 27, 2019. https://www.strategypage.com/articles/default.asp?target=wgappen.htm.

Gividen, Noble J. "High School Education for Rural Youth." A report delivered to the U.S. Department of Health, Education, and Welfare Office of Education, September 1963. 2–21.

Gladwell, Malcolm. "The Terrazzo Jungle." *The New Yorker*, March 15, 2004. https://www.newyorker.com/magazine/2004/03/15/the-terrazzo-jungle.

Goldberg, Marty. "Inside the Atari 2600." *Retro Gamer*, no. 103, 2012.

Goldberg, Marty, and Curt Vendel. *Atari, Inc.: Business is Fun*. Carmel, NY: Syzygy Company Press, 2012. Kindle.

Goldberg, Marty and Curt Vendel. "Back to Our Grass Roots." 2012.

Goldman, Robert P. "Wonderful Willie from Brookhaven." *Parade*, May 18, 1958.

Gorges, Florent. *Space Invaders: Comment Tomohirio Nishikado a Donné Naissance au Jeu Vidéo Japonais!* Chatillôn: Omake Books, 2018.

Grad, Burton. "The Creation and the Demise of VisiCalc." IEEE Annuals of Computing. July–September 2007.

Graetz, J.M. "The Origin of Spacewar." *Creative Computing*, August 1981.

Grannell, Craig. "Making of Battlezone." *Retro Gamer*, no. 59, 2009.

———. "The Making of Berzerk." *Retro Gamer*, no. 47, 2008.

———. "The Making of Defender." *Retro Gamer*, no. 55, 2008.

———. "The Making and Remaking of Pac-Man" *Retro Gamer*, no. 61, 2009.

Gray, Stephen B. "The Early Days of Personal Computers." *Creative Computing*, November 1984.

Greenblatt, Richard. Interview by Gardner Hendrie, January 12, 2005. Computer History Museum. https://archive.computerhistory.org/resources/access/text/2012/12/102657935-05-01-acc.pdf.

Gregg, Alphonse. Testimony, Bally Manufacturing v. Williams Electronics, No. 78-2246 (N.D. Ill), March 19, 1984.

Grinsven, Christelvan, and Joost Raessens. "The Netherlands." In *Video Games Around the World*, edited by Mark J.P. Wolf. Cambridge, MA: The MIT Press, 2015. iTunes.

Hague, James. "Ed Averett." Halcyon Days. Last modified March 1997. https://dadgum.com/halcyon/BOOK/AVERETT.HTM.

———. "Ed Rotberg." Halcyon Days, March 1997. https://dadgum.com/halcyon/BOOK/ROTBERG.HTM.

———. "Jon Freeman & Anne Westfall." Halcyon Days, March 1997. https://dadgum.com/halcyon/BOOK/FREEFALL.HTM.

Handler, Ruth, and Jacqueline Shannon. *Dream Doll: The Ruth Handler Story*. Stamford, CT: Longmeadow Press, 1994.

Harrison, Joseph O. Jr. "Computer-Aided Information Systems for Gaming." RAC-TP-133, September 1964.

Hausrath, Alfred H. *Venture Simulation in War, Business, and Politics*. New York: McGraw-Hill, 1971.

Herzog, G.B. "Fred Systems." Internal progress report on Studio III and Studio IV, c. 1977.

Higinbotham, William A. "The Brookhaven TV-Tennis Game." Unpublished notes, c. 1983.

———. Testimony. Magnavox Co. v. Activision, Inc., No. 82-5270 (N.D. Cal), August 12, 1985.

Hodges, Andrew. *Alan Turing: The Enigma*. London: Vintage, 2014.

Hogan, C. Lester. Interview by Rob Walker, January 24, 1995. Stanford University. https://searchworks.stanford.edu/view/zm237vn0430.

Hu, Arthur. "How I Helped Create Angry Birds." Blogspot, May 9, 2011. http://hu1st.blogspot.com/2011/05/how-i-helped-create-angry-birds.html.

Huhtamo, Erkki. "Slots of Fun, Slots of Trouble: An Archaeology of Arcade Gaming." In *Handbook of Computer Game Studies*, edited by Joost Raessens and Jeffrey Goldstein. Cambridge, MA: The MIT Press, 2005.

Hunter, David. "Exec: Datamost, Inc." *Softalk*, July 1983.

Hurd, Walter W. "A History of Pinball." *Billboard*, May 29, 1943.

Hurst, Jan, Michael Mahoney, Norman Taylor, Douglas Ross, and Robert Fano. "Retrospectives: The Early Years in Computer Graphics at MIT, Lincoln Lab and Harvard." In *ACM SIGGRAPH 89 Panel Proceedings Boston, July 31–August 4, 1989*, 19–38. New York: ACM, 1989.

Inoue, Daisuke, and Robert Scott. "Voice Hero: The Inventor of Karaoke Speaks." The Appendix, December 3, 2013. http://theappendix.net/issues/2013/10/voice-hero-the-inventor-of-karaoke-speaks.

Institute of Electrical and Electronic Engineers. *1977 Electro Conference Record: Presented at Electro 1977, New York, NY, April 19–21, 1977*. New York: Electro, 1977.

Isaacson, Walter. *Steve Jobs*. New York: Simon & Schuster, 2011, ebook.

Jakobson, Cathryn. "The Man Who Never Wanted to Be President." *Inc*, September 1, 1981. https://www.inc.com/magazine/19810901/1015.html.

Jennings, Peter. Interview by Sellam Ismail, February 1, 2005. Computer History Museum. https://archive.computerhistory.org/resources/access/text/2013/05/102657922-05-01-acc.pdf.

———. "Microchess." Peter Jennings personal website. Accessed June 9, 2019. http://www.benlo.com/microchess.

Jensen, Russ E. Pinball Expo '97 (Part 2). Pinball Collectors Resource, accessed June 7, 2019. http://www.pinballcollectorsresource.com/russ_files/expo97-2.html.

———. "A Visit with Harry Williams." Accessed May 28, 2019. http://www.pinballcollectorsresource.com/russ_files/harryvisit.html.

Jerz, Dennis G. "Somewhere Nearby Is Colossal Cave." *Digital Humanities Quarterly* 1, no. 2 (2007). http://digitalhumanities.org/dhq/vol/001/2/000009/000009.html.

Jones, Darran. "Creating Centipede." *Retro Gamer*, no. 141, 2015.

———. "The Making of Missile Command." *Retro Gamer*, no. 88, 2011.

Jones, Jeremy L.C. "Interview with Dave Arneson." *Kobold Press*, April 9, 2009. https://koboldpress.com/interview-with-dave-arneson.

Joss, John. Bob Brown's Odyssey: His Invention Gives TV a '5th Dimension' – Viewer Interaction. *Silicon Valley Engineer Magazine*. June–July 1989.

Kaminski, Michael. *The Secret History of Star Wars*. Self-published, ebook, 2008.

KansasFest. "Bob Bishop's KansasFest 2011 Keynote Speech." YouTube video, posted May 18, 2012. https://www.youtube.com/watch?v=FlsHGmijFP0.

"Kasco and the Electro-Mechanical Golden Age." Shmuplations, accessed May 30, 2019. http://shmuplations.com/kasco.

Kent, Steven L. "Entertainment Empire of the Rising Sun: A Conversation with Sega Founder David Rosen." Sad Sam's Palace, 2006. http://www.sadsamspalace.com/VideoGames/4-Rosen-Sega-story.html.

————. *The Ultimate History of Video Games: From Pong to Pokémon and Beyond – The Story Behind the Craze That Touched Our Lives and Changed the World*. New York: Three Rivers Press, 2001.

Kindig, Randy. "ANTIC Interview 174: Tod Frye, Asteroids." *ANTIC*. Podcast audio, May 18, 2016. http://ataripodcast.libsyn.com/antic-interview-174-tod-fry-asteroids.

Kluska, Bartłomiej, and Mariusz Rozwadowski. *Bajty Polskie*. Łódź: Samizdat Orka, 2011.

Kohler, Chris. "Q&A: Pac-Man Creator Reflects on 30 Years of Dot-Eating." Wired, May 21, 2010. https://www.wired.com/2010/05/pac-man-30-years.

————. "This Game Industry Pioneer Never Gave Up on the Video Arcade." Wired, December 18, 2013. https://www.wired.com/2013/12/eugene-jarvis-pioneer.

Konzack, Lars. "Scandinavia." In *Video Games Around the World*, edited by Mark J.P. Wolf. Cambridge, MA: The MIT Press, 2015. iTunes.

Koon, David. "Centipede Creator Teaches at UALR." *Arkansas Times*, November 19, 2015. https://arktimes.com/entertainment/ae-feature/2015/11/19/centipede-creator-teaches-at-ualr.

Kotok, Alan. Interview by Gardner Hendrie, November 15, 2004. Computer History Museum. https://archive.computerhistory.org/resources/access/text/2013/05/102657916-05-01-acc.pdf.

Kuhfeld, Albert W. "Spacewar." *Analog Science Fiction Science Fact Magazine*, July 1971.

Kurokawa, Fumio. "Narratives of Video Games Part 4: Shigeichi Ishimura." 4Gamer, March 17, 2018. https://www.4gamer.net/games/999/G999905/20180313040.

Kushner, David. "Dungeon Master: The Life and Legacy of Gary Gygax." Wired, March 10, 2008. https://www.wired.com/2008/03/dungeon-master-life-legacy-gary-gygax.

LaFrenz, Dale. Interview by Judy E. O'Neill, April 13, 1995. Charles Babbage Institute. https://conservancy.umn.edu/bitstream/handle/11299/107423/oh315dl.pdf?sequence=1&isAllowed=y.

Lammers, Susan. *Programmers at Work: Interviews with 19 Programmers Who Shaped the Computer Industry*. Redmond, WA: Tempus Press, 1989. Ebook.

Lapetino, Tim. *Art of Atari*. Runnenmede, NJ: Dynamite Entertainment, 2016.

Lécuyer, Christophe. *Making Silicon Valley: Innovation and the Growth of High Tech, 1930–1970*. Cambridge, MA: MIT Press, 2006.

Levering, Robert, Michael Katz, and Milton Moskowitz. *The Computer Entrepreneurs*. New York: NAL Books, 1984.

Levine, Richard. "'PBA Bowling' Among 100 Greatest." Blog: Rchard S. Levine, July 7, 2017. https://www.rickslevine.com/blog/pba-bowling-among-100-greatest.

Levy, David. "Alan Turing on Computer Chess." In *Alan Turing: His Work and Impact*, edited by S. Barry Cooper and J. van Leeuwn, 644–650. Waltham, MA: Elsevier, 2013.

Levy, James. Testimony. Magnavox Company v. Activision, Inc., No. 82-5270 (N.D. Cal), 1985.

Levy, Steven. *Hackers*. Sebastopol, CA: O'Reilly Media, 2010.

Link, David. "Programming ENTER: Christopher Strachey's Draughts Program." *Resurrection* no. 60 (2012–2013): 23–31.

Lockhart, Nate. "Interview with Gilbert Duncan Harrower." The Geekiverse, January 25, 2019. https://thegeekiverse.com/interview-with-gilbert-duncan-harrower-inventor-of-the-pong-on-a-chip.

Lojek, Bo. *History of Semiconductor Engineering*. New York: Springer, 2007.

Loomis, Carol J. "Everything in History Was Against Them." *Fortune*, April 13, 1998. http://archive.fortune.com/magazines/fortune/fortune_archive/1998/04/13/240847/index.htm.

Lowe, Walter Jr. "What Sort of Man Invents Defender?" *Playboy*, March 1982.

Lussenhop, Jessica. "Oregon Trail: How Three Minnesotans Forged Its Path." City Pages, January 19, 2011. http://www.citypages.com/news/oregon-trail-how-three-minnesotans-forged-its-path-6745749.

Lyons, Robert S. Jr. "The Video Game Virtuoso." *LaSalle*, Winter 1983–1984.

MacSween, Cameron A.C., and Derek C. Martin, "Problems & Opportunities for Video Games in the European Market." 1977 *Electro Conference Record*. El Segundo, CA: Electro, 1977.

Maeno, Kazuhisa. "Namco: Maker of the Video Age." *Journal of Japanese Trade & Industry* no. 4 (1985): 38–40.

Maher, Jimmy. "A Few Questions for Lance Micklus." The Digital Antiquarian, July 1, 2011. https://www.filfre.net/2011/07/a-few-questions-for-lance-micklus.

———. "The Trash-80, Part 3." The Digital Antiquarian, June 14, 2011. https://www.filfre.net/2011/06/the-trash-80-part-3.

Maher, Tom. *Silicon Valley Road*. College Station, TX: Virtualbookworm.com Publishing, 2005.

Malone, Billy. *The Early History of the Magnavox Company*. Magnavox Government and Industrial Electronics Company, 1989.

Malone, Michael S. *The Intel Trinity: How Robert Noyce, Gordon Moore, and Andy Grove Built the World's Most Important Company*. New York: Harper Business, 2014.

Manes, Stephen. *Gates: How Microsoft's Mogul Reinvented an Industry – and Made Himself the Richest Man in America*. New York: Touchstone, 1994. Kindle.

Marfels, Christian. *Bally: The World's Game Maker*, 2nd ed. Enterprise, NV: Bally Technologies, 2007.

Markoff, John. *What the Doormouse Said: How the Sixties Counterculture Shaped the Personal Computing Industry*. New York: Viking, 2005.

Marzocco, F.N. "The Story of SDD." SD-1094, October 1, 1956.

McCarthy, John. Interview by Nils Nilsson, September 12, 2007. Computer History Museum. https://archive.computerhistory.org/resources/access/text/2012/10/102658149-05-01-acc.pdf.

———. "Reminiscences on the History of Time Sharing." Stanford University, 1983. http://www-formal.stanford.edu/jmc/history/timesharing/timesharing.html.

McEwan, Charles. Deposition. Bally Manufacturing v. Williams Electronics, No. 78-2246 (N.D. Ill), January 31, 1980.

McHugh, Francis J. *U.S. Navy Fundamentals of War Gaming*. New York: Skyhorse Publishing, 2013. Kindle.

McKenzie, John. Deposition. Magnavox Co. v. Bally Manufacturing Corp., No. 74-1030 (N.D. Ill), October 28, 1975.

Meyers, Richard. "Pinballyhoo: How Pinball Was Hyped into Respectability." *Videogaming Illustrated*, February 1983.

Miller, Tony. "Engineering." Tony Miller personal website, accessed December 3, 2008. http://home.pacbell.net/fmillera/engineering.htm.

————. "Stern/Seeburg." Tony Miller personal website, accessed December 3, 2008. http://home.pacbell.net/fmillera/stern_seeburg.htm.

Mims, Forrest Mims III. "The Altair Story." *Creative Computing*, November 1974.

Mitchell, Ron. "Scott Adams: Adventuring with Atari." *ANTIC*, July 1983.

Monnens, Devin. "'I Beg to Report...' The Sumerian Game 50 Years Later: The Strange and Untold Story of the World's Most Influential Text Simulation Game." Unpublished draft 1.3.2, c. 2017.

Monnens, Devin, and Martin Goldberg. "Space Odyssey: The Long Journey of Spacewar! from MIT to Computer Labs Around the World." *Kinephanos*. Cultural History of Video Games Special Issue, June 2015. https://www.kinephanos.ca/Revue_files/2015_Monnens_Goldberg.pdf.

Montfort, Nick, and Ian Bogost. *Racing the Beam: The Atari Video Computer System*. Cambridge, MA: MIT Press, 2009.

Morph. "Blowing Things Up." Dreamsteep. Accessed November 20, 2008. http://dreamsteep.com/writing/71-interviews/46-blowing-things-up.html.

Nahigian, J. Victor, and William S. Hodges. *Announcing: Computer Games for Business, School, and Home for TRS-80 Level II BASIC*. Cambridge, MA: Winthrop Publishers, 1980.

Nelson, Theodore H. *Computer Lib/Dream Machines*. Chicago, IL: Hugo's Book Service, 1974.

Newell, Allen, J.C. Shaw, and H.A. Simon. "Chess-Playing Programs and the Problem of Complexity." In *Computers and Thought*, edited by Edward A. Feigenbaum and Julian Feldman, 39–70. New York: McGraw-Hill, 1963.

Nicastro, Louis. Deposition. Bally Manufacturing v. Williams Electronics, No. 78-2246 (N.D. Ill), August 1, 1979.

Nicholes, Will. "A Conversation with Carla Meninsky." November 12, 2011. https://willnicholes.com/interviews/CarlaMeninsky.htm.

Nilsson, Nils J. John McCarthy, 1927–2011. National Academy of Arts and Sciences, 2012.

Nutting, David Judd. *Secrets to a Creative Mind: Become the Master of Your Mind*, Denver: Outskirts Press, 2012.

————. Nutting, David. Testimony. Bally Manufacturing v. Williams Electronics, No. 78-2246 (N.D. Ill), January 6, 1983.

Olsen, Ken. Interview by David Allison, September 28–29, 1988. National Museum of American History. https://americanhistory.si.edu/comphist/olsen.html.

Orbanes, Phillip E. *The Game Makers: The Story of Parkers Brothers from Tiddlywinks to Trivial Pursuit*. Boston, MA: Harvard Business School Press, 2004.

Patterson, Patrick Scott. "Icons: Toru Iwatani Gave the World the Gift of Pac-Man." Syfy Games, April 8, 2016. https://syfygames.com/news/article/icons-toru-iwatani-gave-the-world-the-gift-of-pac-man-patrickscottpatterson.

Peterson, Jon. *Playing at the World*. San Diego, CA: Unreason Press, 2012. Kindle.

Petersen, Norm. "Bill and Claire Nutting's Waco SRE." *Vintage Airplane*, March 1992.

Petrakos, Pamela. "Project Local: A Classroom Project with a 13 Year History." *80 Microcomputing*, February 1981.

Piccolo, Stephen. "Gaming in Atlantic City: A History of Legal Gambling in New Jersey, Part 3." Museum of Gaming History. Accessed June 10, 2019. http://museumofgaminghistory.org/mogh.php?p=article&a=55.

Pitts, Bill. "The Galaxy Game." Stanford Infolab, October 29, 1997. http://infolab.stanford.edu/pub/voy/museum/galaxy.html.

Rains, Lyle. "Planet Grab (Invasion) Game Description." Atari pitch document, June 7, 1976.

Ramirez, Anthony and Sarah Smith. "Top Gun in the Toy Business." *Fortune*, March 2, 1987, http://archive.fortune.com/magazines/fortune/fortune_archive/1987/03/02/68727/index.htm.

Ramsay, Morgan. *Gamers at Work: Stories* behind *the Games People Play*. New York: Apress, 2012.

Rankin, Joy. *A People's History of Computing in the United States*. Cambridge, MA: Harvard, 2018. Kindle.

Rauner, R.M. "Laboratory Evaluation of Supply and Procurement Policies: The First Experiment of the Logistics Systems Laboratory." R-323, July 1958.

Recchi, Sal. "Gaming Giant Has Checkered Past, Local Ties." *Boca Raton News*, July 15, 1979.

Reid, T.R. "The Texas Edison." *Texas Monthly*, July 1982.

Reutter, Hans. "PRGE 2016 – Atari Programmers – Portland Retro Gaming Expo." Filmed October 22, 2016. YouTube video. Posted October 29, 2016. https://www.youtube.com/watch?v=P3bA2dnefV0.

———. "PRGE 2016 – Tod Frye – Portland Retro Gaming Expo." Filmed October 22, 2016. YouTube video. Posted October 2, 2016. https://www.youtube.com/watch?=cuTJpZ99P0c.

———. "PRGE 2017 – Ron Milner – Portland Retro Gaming Expo." Filmed October 21, 2017. YouTube video. Posted November 2, 2017. https://www.youtube.com/watch?v=CbaAgAAY77U.

Rice, Robert. "Penny Arcade Philanthropist." *The New Yorker*, October 16, 1948.

Rifkin, Glenn, and George Harrar. *The Ultimate Entrepreneur: The Story of Ken Olsen and Digital Equipment Corporation*. Chicago, IL: Contemporary Books, 1988.

Rignall, Jaz. "'Could they Fire Me? No!' The Warren Robinette Interview." US Gamer, January 2, 2016. https://www.usgamer.net/articles/warren-robinett-interview.

Roberts, Charles S. "Charles S. Roberts in his own Words." CSR Awards. Accessed March 11, 2015. https://www.alanemrich.com/csr_pages/articles/csrspeaks.htm.

Robinett, Warren. *Inventing the Adventure Game: The Design of Adventure and Rocky's Boots*. Unpublished manuscript, 1984. Ebook.

———. *Making the Dragon: How I built the first action-adventure game, planted the first Easter Egg, and helped launch the video-game revolution*. Unpublished draft 1.0.3, 2019.

Ross, Henry. Deposition. Magnavox Co. v. Bally Manufacturing Corp., No. 74-1030 (N.D. Ill), June 25, 1974.

Ross, Kitty. "The Dennisons of Leeds: Pioneers of Penny Slot Machines." Secret Lives of Objects (blog). Leeds Museums and Galleries, August 31, 2016. https://secretlivesofobjects.blog/2016/08/31/the-dennisons-of-leeds-pioneers-of-penny-slot-machines.

Rouse III, Richard. *Game Design Theory & Practice*, 2nd ed. Sudbury, MA: Jones and Bartlett Publishers, 2005. Ebook.

Roy, Gibbons. "Meet Midac and Midsac: Dice, Pool Shooting Fools, Chicago Tribune, June 27, 1954.

RSS Bot. "Important People Who Shaped the TI 99/4A World – Scott Adams." Atari Age Message Board, December 12, 2015. http://atariage.com/forums/topic/246996-important-people-who-shaped-the-ti-994a-world-scott-adams.

RT-55J. "I found an Easter egg from 1977." Select Button, August 7, 2019. https://selectbutton.net/t/i-found-an-easter-egg-from-1977/8828.

Rusch, William. Testimony. Magnavox Co. v. Bally Manufacturing Corp., No. 74-1030 (N.D. Ill), February 19, 1976.

Russell, Steve. Interview by Al Kossow, August 9, 2008. Computer History Museum. https://archive.computerhistory.org/resources/access/text/2012/08/1027 46453-05-01-acc.pdf.

Sacco, Ciro Alessandro. "An Interview with Gary Gygax." OD&DITIES, February 2003.

Sato, Hideki. Interview by Hiroshi Shimizu, part 1-1, February 1, 2018. Hitosubashi University Institute of Innovation Research. http://pubs.iir.hit-u.ac.jp/admin/en/pdfs/show/2165.

———. Interview by Hiroshi Shimizu, part 1-2, February 1, 2018. Hitosubashi University Institute of Innovation Research. http://pubs.iir.hit-u.ac.jp/admin/en/pdfs/show/2166.

———. Interview by Hiroshi Shimizu, part 2-1, February 1, 2018. Hitosubashi University Institute of Innovation Research. http://pubs.iir.hit-u.ac.jp/admin/en/pdfs/show/2167.

Schaeffer, Jonathan. One Jump Ahead: Computer Perfection at Checkers, rev. ed. New York: Springer, 2009.

Schmüdde, D. Jack and the Machine: An Interactive Documentary. Accessed June 7, 2019. http://www.jackandthemachine.com/jack-tramiel.

Schwartz, Evan I. The Last Lone Inventor: A Tale of Genius, Deceit, and the Birth of Television, rep. ed. New York: Harper Perennial, 2003. Kindle.

Scott, Norman R. Computing at the University of Michigan: The Early Years Through the 1960s. University of Michigan, 2008.

Sedensky, Eric. Winning Pachinko: The Game of Japanese Pinball. Tokyo: Charles E. Tuttle Press, 1991.

Seigs, Bill. "Kawaii as Revolution? What's Behind the Famous Japanese Phenomenon." Kawaii Sekai, July 19, 2017. http://kawaiisekai.com/what-is-kawaii.

Shannon Claude E. "A Chess-Playing Machine." Scientific American, February 1950.

———. "Programming a Computer for Playing Chess." Philosophical Magazine 41, no. 314 (1950): 256–275.

Sharpe, Roger C. "Gottlieb Changes Name but Legacy Endures." Play Meter, February 1, 1984.

Sharpe, Roger C., and James Hamilton. Pinball! New York: E.P. Dutton, 1977.

Sheff, David. Game Over, Press Start to Continue: The Maturing of Mario. Wilton, CT: CyberActive Media Group, 1999. Ebook.

Shinozaki, Yoshiki. "Space Invaders Provides Thrills for Game Enthusiasts." Business Japan, July 1979.

Simcoe, Robert J. "The Revolution in Your Pocket." American Heritage Invention and Technology, Fall 2004.

Skow, John. "Games People Play." Time, January 18, 1982.

Slater, Robert. Portraits in Silicon, rev. ed. Cambridge, MA: MIT Press, 1989.

Smith, Keith. All in Color for a Quarter. Unpublished manuscript, 2016.

———. "History of Softape, Part 2." The Golden Age Historian, December 24, 2014. http://allincolorforaquarter.blogspot.com/2014/12/history-of-softape-part-2.html.

————. "Preliminary Report: Was The Devil's Dungeon the First Commercial CRPG and What Was the First Commercial Microcomputer Game?" The Golden Age Arcade Historian, October 22, 2015. http://allincolorforaquarter. blogspot.com/2015/10/preliminary-report-was-devils-dungeon.html.

————. "Softape History, Part I." The Golden Age Historian, November 20, 2014. http://allincolorforaquarter.blogspot.com/2014/11/softape-history-part-i-plus-review-of.html.

Smith, Ryan. "Chicago once waged a 40-year war on pinball." Chicago Reader, May 5, 2018. https://www.chicagoreader.com/Bleader/archives/2018/05/05/chicago-once-waged-a-40-year-war-on-pinball.

Spicer, Dag. "The Data General Nova." Core, March 2001.

Spracklen, Danny, and Kathleen. Interview by Gardner Hendrie, March 2, 2005. Computer History Museum. https://archive.computerhistory.org/resources/access/text/2013/05/102701977-05-01-acc.pdf.

Staup, Mike. Testimony. Atari, Inc. v. North American Philips Consumer Electronics Corp., No. 81-6434 (N.D. Ill), November 30, 1981.

Stern, Arthur P. Interview by William Aspray, July 13, 1993. IEEE History Center. https://ethw.org/Oral-History:Arthur_Stern_(1993).

Stilphen, Scott. "DP Interviews Brad Stewart." Digital Press, 2001. http://www.digitpress.com/library/interviews/interview_brad_stewart.html.

————. "DP Interviews David Rolfe." Digital Press, 2004. http://www.digitpress.com/library/interviews/interview_david_rolfe.html.

————. "DP Interviews Howard Delman." Digital Press, 2011. http://www.digitpress.com/library/interviews/interview_howard_delman.html.

————. "DP Interviews Joe Decuir." Digital Press, 2005. http://www.digitpress.com/library/interviews/interview_joe_decuir.html.

————. "DP Interviews Larry Kaplan." Digital Press, 2006.

————. "DP: Interviews Mark Lesser." Digital Press, 2007. http://www.digitpress.com/library/interviews/interview_mark_lesser.html.

————. "Ed Riddle Interview." Atari Compendium, 2017.

Stuart-Williams, R. "Nimrod: A Small Automatic Computer." Electronic Engineering 23, no. 283 (1951): 344–348.

Sugerman, Myron. The Chronicles of the Last Jewish Gangster: From Meyer to Myron. Amazon Digital Services, 2017. Kindle.

Terdiman, Daniel. "Inside the World's Long-Lost First Microcomputer." CNET, January 8, 2010. https://www.cnet.com/news/inside-the-worlds-long-lost-first-microcomputer.

Thacker, Paul. "Jeff Frederiksen Interview (Part 1)." Bally Alley, September 29, 2011. http://www.ballyalley.com/ballyalley/interviews/Jeff_Frederiksen_Interview.txt.

Thompson, Joe. "Four Revolutions, the Lost Chapter: A Concise History of the LED Watch," Hodinkee, February 26, 2018. https://www.hodinkee.com/articles/four-revolutions-led-watches.

Trionfo, Adam. "Programmers of the Bally Arcade/Astrocade Built-in Programs." Bally Ally. August 17, 2016. http://www.ballyalley.com/faqs/Programmers%20of%20the%20Astrocade%20Built-In%20Programs.txt.

U.S. Congress. Senate. Committee on Government Operations. Fraud and Corruption in Management of Military Club Systems. Report No. 92–418. 92nd Cong., 1st Sess., 1971.

———. Senate. Committee on Government Operations. *Hearings before the Permanent Committee on Investigations of the Committee on Government Operations.* 91st Cong., 1st and 2nd Sess., 1970–1971.

Valentine, Don. Interview by Sally Smith Hughes, October 20 and December 4, 2009. University of California. http://digitalassets.lib.berkeley.edu/roho/ucb/text/valentine_donald.pdf.

Vendel, Curt. "Interview with Joe Decuir." Atari Museum. Accessed June 29, 2019. http://www.atarimuseum.com/articles/joedecuir.html.

Vintage Computer Federation. "VCF East 2019 – Joe Decuir – Atari 800 Series Computers: 40 Years." Filmed May 5, 2019. YouTube video. Posted May 6, 2019. https://www.youtube.com/watch?v=dlVpu_QSHyw.

Visich, Marian Jr., and Ludwig Braun. "The Use of Computer Simulations in High School Curricula." Huntington Computer Project, January 1974.

Walden, David, and Tom Van Vleck. "Compatible Time-Sharing System (1961–1973): Fiftieth Anniversary Commemorative Overview." IEEE Computer Society, 2011.

Ward, John E. "MOUSE Preliminary Instructions." Memorandum, MIT Servomechanisms Laboratory, January 16, 1959.

Ware, Willis. *RAND and the Information Revolution: A History in Essays and Vignettes.* Santa Monica, CA: RAND Corporation, 2008.

Watson, Hugh J. *Computer Simulation in Business.* New York: John Wiley & Sons, 1981.

Watson, Lucinda. *How They Achieved: Stories of Personal Achievement and Business Success.* New York: John Wiley & Sons, 2001.

Webb, Marcus. "Atari Turns 25." *RePlay,* July 1997.

Welsh, David, and Theresa Welsh. *Priming the Pump: How TRS-80 Enthusiasts Helped Spark the PC Revolution.* Ferndale, MI: The Seeker Books, 2013.

Wieder, Robert. "A Fistful of Quarters." *Oui Magazine,* September 1974.

Wile, Raymond. "The North American Phonograph Company: Part 1." *ARSC Journal* 35, no. 1 (2004): 1–36.

Wing, Richard L. "The Production and Evaluation of Three Computer-based Economics Games for the Sixth Grade, Final Report." U.S. Department of Health, Education, and Welfare report, June 1967.

———. "Two-Computer-Based Economics Games for Sixth Graders." *American Behavioral Scientist* 10, no. 3 (1966): 31–35.

Witwer, Michael. *Empire of Imagination: Gary Gygax and the Birth of Dungeons & Dragons.* New York: Bloomsbury, 2015.

Wohlers, Tony, and Eric Schmaltz. "Charles August Fey." In *Immigrant Entrepreneurship: German-American Business Biographies, 1720 to the Present,* vol. 3, edited by Giles R. Hoyt. German Historical Institute. Last modified March 25, 2014. http://www.immigrantentrepreneurship.org/entry.php?rec=51

Wolpman, Jim. "Alive in the 60s: The Midpeninsula Free University." Midpeninsula Free University. Accessed June 10, 2019. http://midpeninsulafreeu.com.

Wong, Kevin. "The Forgotten History of 'The Oregon Trail,' as Told By Its Creators." *Motherboard,* February 15, 2017. https://www.vice.com/en_us/article/qkx8vw/the-forgotten-history-of-the-oregon-trail-as-told-by-its-creators.

Wood, Lamont. *Datapoint: The Lost Story of the Texans Who Invented the Personal Computer Revolution.* Austin: Hugo House Publishers, 2012. Kindle.

Wozniak, Steve, and Gina Smith. *iWoz: Computer Geek to Cult Icon.* New York: W.W. Norton, 2006.

Yasaki, Edward K. "Computing at Stanford." *Datamation*, November 1963.

Yob, Gregory. "Hunt the Wumpus." *Creative Computing.* September–October 1975.

Young, Jeffrey. *Forbes Greatest Technology Stories: Inspiring Tales of the Entrepreneurs and Inventors Who Revolutionized Modern Business.* New York: John Wiley & Sons, 1998.

———. *Steve Jobs: The Journey is the Reward.* Chicago, IL: Scott Foresman, 1988. Kindle.

Zek. *Galaxian Genesis: The History of Kazunori Sawano.* Gee Yume Area 51, 2017.

Zube. "Commodore Nowhere Near the Edge or Commodore Before Commodore." Personal website, March 25, 2007. http://www.cs.colostate.edu/~dzubera/commodore2.txt.

Index

Note: Page numbers followed by "n" denote endnotes.

M

Printed in the United States
by Baker & Taylor Publisher Services